War, Culture and Society, 1750–1850

Series Editors: **Rafe Blaufarb** (Tallahassee, USA), **Alan Forrest** (York, UK), and **Karen Hagemann** (Chapel Hill, USA)

Editorial Board: **Michael Broers** (Oxford, UK), **Christopher Bayly** (Cambridge, UK), **Richard Bessel** (York, UK), **Sarah Chambers** (Minneapolis, USA), **Laurent Dubois** (Durham, USA), **Etienne François** (Berlin, Germany), **Janet Hartley** (London, UK), **Wayne Lee** (Chapel Hill, USA), **Jane Rendall** (York, UK), **Reinhard Stauber** (Klagenfurt, Austria)

Titles include:

Richard Bessel, Nicholas Guyatt and Jane Rendall (*editors*)
WAR, EMPIRE AND SLAVERY, 1770–1830

Eveline G. Bouwers
PUBLIC PANTHEONS IN REVOLUTIONARY EUROPE
Comparing Cultures of Remembrance, c. 1790–1840

Michael Broers, Agustin Guimera and Peter Hick (*editors*)
THE NAPOLEONIC EMPIRE AND THE NEW EUROPEAN POLITICAL CULTURE

Gavin Daly
THE BRITISH SOLDIER IN THE PENINSULAR WAR
Encounters with Spain and Portugal, 1808–1814

Alan Forrest and Peter H. Wilson (*editors*)
THE BEE AND THE EAGLE
Napoleonic France and the End of the Holy Roman Empire, 1806

Alan Forrest, Karen Hagemann and Jane Rendall (*editors*)
SOLDIERS, CITIZENS AND CIVILIANS
Experiences and Perceptions of the Revolutionary and Napoleonic Wars, 1790–1820

Alan Forrest, Etienne François and Karen Hagemann (*editors*)
WAR MEMORIES
The Revolutionary and Napoleonic Wars in Nineteenth
and Twentieth Century Europe

Rasmus Glenthøj and Morten Nordhagen Ottosen
EXPERIENCES OF WAR AND NATIONALITY IN DENMARK AND NORWAY, 1807–1815

Karen Hagemann, Gisela Mettele and Jane Rendall (*editors*)
GENDER, WAR AND POLITICS
Transatlantic Perspectives, 1755–1830

Leighton James
WITNESSING THE REVOLUTIONARY AND NAPOLEONIC WARS IN GERMAN
Central Europe

Catriona Kennedy
NARRATIVES OF THE REVOLUTIONARY AND NAPOLEONIC WARS
Military and Civilian Experience in Britain and Ireland

Catriona Kennedy, and Matthew McCormack (*editors*)
SOLDIERING IN BRITAIN AND IRELAND, 1750–1850
Men of Arms

Ralph Kingston
BUREAUCRATS AND BOURGEOIS SOCIETY
Office Politics and Individual Credit, France 1789–1848

Kevin Linch
BRITAIN AND WELLINGTON'S ARMY
Recruitment, Society and Tradition, 1807–1815

Pierre Serna, Antonino De Francesco and Judith Miller
REPUBLICS AT WAR, 1776–1840
Revolutions, Conflicts and Geopolitics in Europe and the Atlantic World

Marie-Cécile Thoral
FROM VALMY TO WATERLOO
France at War, 1792–1815

Christine Wright
WELLINGTON'S MEN IN AUSTRALIA
Peninsular War Veterans and the Making of Empire c.1820–40

Mark Wishon
GERMAN FORCES AND THE BRITISH ARMY
Interactions and Perceptions, 1742–1815

War, Culture and Society, 1750–1850
Series Standing Order ISBN 978–0–230–54532–8 hardback
978–0–230–54533–5 paperback
(outside North America only)

You can receive future titles in this series as they are published by placing a standing order. Please contact your bookseller or, in case of difficulty, write to us at the address below with your name and address, the title of the series and one of the ISBNs quoted above.

Customer Services Department, Macmillan Distribution Ltd, Houndmills, Basingstoke, Hampshire RG21 6XS, England

Gender, War and Politics
Transatlantic Perspectives, 1775–1830

Edited by

Karen Hagemann
*James G. Kenan Distinguished Professor of History,
University of North Carolina at Chapel Hill*

Gisela Mettele
Professor of History, Friedrich-Schiller-Universität Jena

and

Jane Rendall
Honorary Fellow, Centre for Eighteenth Century Studies, University of York

Editorial matter and selection © Karen Hagemann,
Gisela Mettele and Jane Rendall 2010, 2013
Introduction © Karen Hagemann and Jane Rendall 2010, 2013
Remaining chapters © Respective authors 2010, 2013

All rights reserved. No reproduction, copy or transmission of this
publication may be made without written permission.

No portion of this publication may be reproduced, copied or transmitted
save with written permission or in accordance with the provisions of the
Copyright, Designs and Patents Act 1988, or under the terms of any licence
permitting limited copying issued by the Copyright Licensing Agency,
Saffron House, 6–10 Kirby Street, London EC1N 8TS.

Any person who does any unauthorized act in relation to this publication
may be liable to criminal prosecution and civil claims for damages.

The authors have asserted their right to be identified as the author of this work
in accordance with the Copyright, Designs and Patents Act 1988.

First published 2010 by
PALGRAVE MACMILLAN

First published in paperback 2013 by
PALGRAVE MACMILLAN

Palgrave Macmillan in the UK is an imprint of Macmillan Publishers Limited,
registered in England, company number 785998, of Houndmills, Basingstoke,
Hampshire RG21 6XS.

Palgrave Macmillan in the US is a division of St Martin's Press LLC,
175 Fifth Avenue, New York, NY 10010.

Palgrave Macmillan is the global academic imprint of the above companies
and has companies and representatives throughout the world.

Palgrave® and Macmillan® are registered trademarks in the United States,
the United Kingdom, Europe and other countries

ISBN: 978–0–230–21800–0 hardback
ISBN: 978–1–137–36388–6 paperback

This book is printed on paper suitable for recycling and made from fully
managed and sustained forest sources. Logging, pulping and manufacturing
processes are expected to conform to the environmental regulations of the
country of origin.

A catalogue record for this book is available from the British Library.

A catalog record for this book is available from the Library of Congress.

Contents

Foreword to the Series   vii

Preface   viii

Notes on Contributors   xv

Introduction: Gender, War and Politics: Transatlantic Perspectives on the Wars of Revolution and Liberation, 1775–1830   1
Karen Hagemann and Jane Rendall

Part I   Empire, Colonial War and Slavery

1. Revolution, War, Empire: Gendering the Transatlantic Slave Trade, 1776–1830   41
David Eltis

2. Gendered Freedom: *Citoyennes* and War in the Revolutionary French Caribbean   58
Laurent Dubois

3. Freedwomen's Familial Politics: Marriage, War and Rites of Registry in Post-Emancipation Saint-Domingue   71
Elizabeth Colwill

Part II   Masculinity, Revolution and War

4. Citizenship, Honour and Masculinity: Military Qualities under the French Revolution and Empire   93
Alan Forrest

5. In the Shadow of the Citizen-Soldier: Politics and Gender in the Careers of Two Dutch Officers, 1780–1815   110
Stefan Dudink

6. John Bull into Battle: Military Masculinity and the British Army Officer during the Napoleonic Wars   127
Catriona Kennedy

7. Middle-Class Masculinity in an Immigrant Diaspora: War, Revolution and Russia's Ethnic Germans   147
Alexander M. Martin

Part III Warfare, Civil Society and Women

8   Bearing Arms, Bearing Burdens: Women Warriors, Camp Followers and Home-Front Heroines of the American Revolution   169
    Holly A. Mayer

9   'Habits Appropriate to Her Sex': The Female Military Experience in France during the Age of Revolution   188
    Thomas Cardoza

10 Maintaining the Home Front: Widows, Wives and War in Late Eighteenth-Century Cuba   206
    Sherry Johnson

Part IV Patriotism, Citizenship and Nation-Building

11 Patriotism in Practice: War and Gender Roles in Republican Hamburg, 1750–1815   227
    Katherine B. Aaslestad

12 'Thinking Minds of Both Sexes': Patriotism, British Bluestockings and the Wars against Revolutionary America and France, 1775–1802   247
    Emma V. Macleod

13 Women Writing War and Empire: Gender, Poetry and Politics in Britain during the Napoleonic Wars   265
    Jane Rendall

14 Celebrating War and Nation: Gender, Patriotism and Festival Culture in Prussia during and after the Anti-Napoleonic Wars   284
    Karen Hagemann

Part V Demobilization, Commemoration and Memory

15 Gender, Loyalty and Virtue in a Colonial Context: The War of 1812 and its Aftermath in Upper Canada   307
    Cecilia Morgan

16 Masculinity, Race and Citizenship: Soldiers' Memories of the American Revolution   325
    Gregory T. Knouff

17 'Drying Their Tears': Women's Petitions, National Reconciliation and Commemoration in Post-Independence Chile   343
    Sarah C. Chambers

Index   361

Foreword to the Series

Rafe Blaufarb, *Alan Forrest* and *Karen Hagemann*

The century from 1750 to 1850 was a seminal period of change, not just in Europe but across the globe. The political landscape was transformed by a series of revolutions fought in the name of liberty–most notably in the Americas and France, of course, but elsewhere, too: in Holland and Geneva during the eighteenth century and across much of mainland Europe by 1848. Nor was change confined to the European world. New ideas of freedom, equality and human rights were carried to the furthest outposts of empire, to Egypt, India and the Caribbean, which saw the creation in 1801 of the first black republic in Haiti, the former French colony of Saint-Domingue. And in the early part of the nineteenth century they continued to inspire anti-colonial and liberation movements throughout Central and Latin America.

If political and social institutions were transformed by revolution in these years, so, too, was warfare. During the quarter-century of the French Revolutionary Wars, in particular, Europe was faced with the prospect of 'total' war, on a scale unprecedented before the twentieth century. Military hardware, it is true, evolved only gradually, and battles were not necessarily any bloodier than they had been during the Seven Years War. But in other ways these can legitimately be described as the first modern wars, fought by mass armies mobilized by national and patriotic propaganda, leading to the displacement of millions of people throughout Europe and beyond, as soldiers, prisoners of war, civilians and refugees. For those who lived through the period these wars would be a formative experience that shaped the ambitions and the identities of a generation.

The aims of the series are necessarily ambitious. In its various volumes, whether single-authored monographs or themed collections, it seeks to extend the scope of more traditional historiography. It will study warfare during this formative century not just in Europe, but in the Americas, in colonial societies, and across the world. It will analyse the construction of identities and power relations by integrating the principal categories of difference, most notably class and religion, generation and gender, race and ethnicity. It will adopt a multi-faceted approach to the period, and turn to methods of political, cultural, social, military, and gender history, in order to develop a challenging and multidisciplinary analysis. Finally, it will examine elements of comparison and transfer and so tease out the complexities of regional, national and global history.

Preface

This book addresses from a transatlantic perspective the relationships between war, the shaping of political and national identities and changing gender regimes between 1775 and 1830. The period began with the outbreak of the American War of Independence. By 1830 the Wars of Independence in Latin America were at an end, and the maps of both Europe and the Americas had been redrawn. The French and Haitian revolutions and the Revolutionary, Napoleonic and Ibero-American wars dominated the years in between. Throughout this era of imperial encounters and revolutionary struggles for national liberation, the transatlantic world experienced more or less constant warfare, which touched not only all of Europe but also large parts of Africa, the Americas and the Caribbean archipelago. Essentially, these wars were a contest among the major European powers–Britain, France, Spain and their allies–for global dominance. The slave trade and slavery, both central to the profitable exploitation of Europe's colonies, were therefore inextricably connected to these wars, as was the abolitionist movement.

Inspired by revolutionary or national ideologies, conscripted troops, militias and volunteer units increasingly fought alongside professional forces. As revolutionary and conservative regimes deployed mass armies across Europe and North America, the conduct of warfare was transformed, along with the political, social and gender orders of both old and new worlds. Soldiers and civilians of all classes, races, and ethnicities–men and women alike–were mobilized for war on an unprecedented scale. Revolutionary governments promised men–regardless of their race–personal freedom and political rights in return for military service, while ancien régimes used patriotic rhetoric to recruit men for warfare. When necessary, the armed forces on both sides admitted Native Americans and slaves into their ranks.

While the past decade has produced exciting new scholarship on this period, the lack of collaboration between military, social and gender historians has resulted in widespread scholarly neglect of the gendered dimensions of late eighteenth- and early nineteenth-century warfare. Many military historians continue to overlook the findings of recent feminist scholarship, which identify war as a key site for the negotiation and construction of gender identities. By exploring the significance of gender in relation to war and politics between 1775 and 1830, this volume offers new research and extends the historiographical boundaries of the subject. Our aim is twofold. We seek to advance knowledge of the relations between the military, war, nation and gender in the light of transatlantic connections and comparisons as well as regional and national differences and similarities. We also hope to contribute to the understanding of the relationship between gender and memory by examining not only the legacy of the gender ideals formed between 1775 and 1830 but also the subsequent gendering of the representation and commemoration of these wars. Seventeen authors from six countries, all experts in their fields, ask how empire- and nation-building was related to changes in warfare and in slave economies and what role gender differences played in these contexts. Their chapters are organized into five sections that focus on the following themes: 'Empire, Colonial War and Slavery'; 'Masculinity, Revolution and War'; 'Warfare, Civil Society and Women'; 'Patriotism, Citizenship and Nation-Building'; and 'Demobilization, Commemoration and Memory'.

The idea for this volume originated in the international conference 'Gender, War, and Politics: The Wars of Revolution and Liberation–Transatlantic Comparisons, 1775–1820', which took place from 17 to 19 May 2007 at the University of North Carolina at Chapel Hill. Thirty-eight speakers and commentators from seven countries were invited to address the topics outlined above. Along with the University of North Carolina at Chapel Hill and its Institute for Arts and Humanities, the main sponsors of this event with more than ninety participants were the German Historical Institute in Washington, DC; Duke University; the British-German research group 'Nations, Borders, Identities: The Revolutionary and Napoleonic Wars in European Experience, 1792–1815', funded by the British Arts and Humanities Research Council and the German Research Foundation; and the French Consulate General in Atlanta. A team of organizers directed by Karen Hagemann (UNC–Chapel Hill), which included Katherine Aaslestad (West Virginia University), Dirk Bönker (Duke University), Gisela Mettele (GHI, Washington), Judith Miller (Emory University) and Jane Rendall (York University) developed the concept of the conference. Laurence Hare (now of Emory & Henry College) as conference assistant helped to realize the event. The organizers are greatly indebted to him for the fantastic job he did and thank him warmly. He was also responsible for the organization of the graduate workshop titled 'Gender, Experience, and Memory, 18th–20th Centuries', which took place on 16 May 2007 at the UNC Institute for Arts and Humanities.

The production of the book was, like the conference, a collaborative endeavour. The editors learned much from the conference participants and would like to thank, first and foremost, all those who presented papers, offered comments and engaged in the many stimulating discussions. Selecting the essays for this volume was extremely difficult because of the large number of excellent papers. In the end we chose the papers that best complemented one another and addressed the subject matter in innovative ways. Katherine Aaslestad and Judith Miller helped us not only with this selection but also by commenting on the chosen papers. The editors are deeply grateful for their generous support. We also appreciate our contributors' willingness to revise their conference papers for the book and their patient cooperation during the lengthy editing process. In this Mary Tonkinson of the German Historical Institute played a critical role, and it was a great pleasure for us to work with such a skilled and experienced editor. Finally we also want to acknowledge how much we owe to Friederike Brühöfener (UNC Chapel Hill), our editorial assistant, who, among her many other tasks, produced the index. Our warmest thanks go to the sponsors listed above, who provided funding for the conference. The German Historical Institute also subsidized the publication of this volume. Without their support neither the conference nor the book would have been possible.

Karen Hagemann, Gisela Mettele and Jane Rendall
Chapel Hill, Jena and York

ADDITIONAL NOTE ON THE PAPERBACK EDITION

The editors are very pleased that Palgrave have now produced this new paperback edition, for a wider market. We hope that this will also be possible for other volumes in the series 'War, Culture and Society, 1750–1850', which is now flourishing. For this edition the 'Notes on Contributors' have been brought up to date, but the text is otherwise unchanged.

Karen Hagemann, Gisela Mettele and Jane Rendall
Chapel Hill, Jena and York, May 2013

Notes on Contributors

Katherine B. Aaslestad is Professor of History at West Virginia University. Her main research interests are war and society, gender and political culture in modern German and European history. She is the author of *Place and Politics: Local Identity, Civic Culture, and German Nationalism in North Germany during the Revolutionary Era* (Boston and Leiden, 2005). With Karen Hagemann she has co-edited special issues on war and gender in *Central European History* and *European History Quarterly*. She has published articles on republican political culture in the Hanseatic cities, gender and consumption, and the Napoleonic Wars in northern Europe as book chapters in a variety of edited volumes. She is currently editing the volume *The Napoleonic Continental System: Local, European, and Global Experiences and Consequences*, to appear in 2013 with Palgrave Macmillan.

Thomas Cardoza is Professor of History at Professor at Arizona State University. His main field of teaching and research is early modern and modern French history. His monograph is entitled *Intrepid Women: Cantinières and Vivandières of the French Army* (Bloomington, IN, 2010) He has also contributed articles to *Paedagogica Historica* and *War and Society* as well as a chapter to *Children and War: An Anthology*, edited by James Marten (New York, 2002). His current research project focuses on *enfants de troupe*, children of *cantinières* and soldiers who were officially enrolled as 'children of the regiment'.

Sarah C. Chambers is Professor of History at the University of Minnesota, Minneapolis. Her research explores political culture and citizenship during Spanish America's transition from colonialism to independence. She is currently writing a book on the intersections of family and politics in Chile from about 1780 to 1860. In addition she recently began a new research project on migrations spurred by the Wars of Independence in South America; in it she will trace the paths of internal refugees, political exiles and royalist émigrés, and analyse how these movements affected the formation of new national and gender identities. She is the author of *From Subjects to Citizens: Honor, Gender, and Politics in Arequipa, Peru, 1780–1854* (University Park, PA, 1999) and the co-editor, with Sueann Caulfield and Lara Putnam, of *Honor, Status, and Law in Modern Latin America* (Durham, NC, 2005). She has also published articles in *Hispanic Research Journal*, the *Journal of Women's History*, and the *American Historical Review*.

Elizabeth Colwill is Associate Professor at the Department of American Studies at the University of Hawaii at Manoa. Her fields of teaching and research include gender and the African diaspora; the intersecting histories of gender, slavery and colonialism; the Haitian and French revolutions; the histories of sexuality and the body; and feminist and postcolonial theory. She has long-standing interests in the role of narrative in the shaping of historical memory and in feminist and interdisciplinary pedagogies. Her articles have appeared in the *Journal of Women's History* and *French Historical Studies*. She has also contributed chapters to *Marie-Antoinette: Writings on the Body of a Queen*, edited by Dena Goodman (London, 2003), and *The World of the Haitian Revolution*, edited by David Patrick Geggus and Norman Fiering (Bloomington, IN, 2009). She is currently writing a book on gender, ritual and slave emancipation in revolutionary Saint-Domingue.

Laurent Dubois is Professor of History at Duke University, where he teaches French history, Caribbean history, and Atlantic history. He is the author of *Les esclaves de la République: l'histoire oubliée de la première émancipation, 1789–1794* (Paris, 1998); *Avengers of the New World: The Story of the Haitian Revolution* (Cambridge, MA, 2004); *A Colony of Citizens: Revolution and Slave Emancipation in the French Caribbean, 1787–1804* (Chapel Hill, NC, 2004); *Soccer Empire: France and the World Cup* (Berkeley, CA, 2011); and *Haiti: The Aftershocks of History* (New York, 2012). He is also the co-editor, with John D. Garrigus, of *Slave Revolution in the Caribbean, 1789–1804: A Brief History with Documents* (New York, 2006) and, with Julius S. Scott, of a reader titled *Origins of the Black Atlantic* (New York, 2009). His forthcoming works include a history of the banjo (Cambridge, MA), and a collaborative general history of the Caribbean (Chapel Hill, NC).

Stefan Dudink is Lecturer at the Institute for Gender Studies of Radboud University, Nijmegen. His main field of research is the history of gender and sexuality in modern Western political culture, with a focus on the Netherlands. He has published a study on late nineteenth-century Dutch liberalism, *Deugdzaam liberalisme: sociaal-liberalisme in Nederland, 1870–1901* (Amsterdam, 1997), and various articles and book chapters on masculinity and homosexuality. He is a co-editor, with Karen Hagemann and John Tosh, of *Masculinities in Politics and War: Gendering Modern History* (Manchester, 2004) and, with Karen Hagemann and Anna Clark, of *Representing Masculinity: Male Citizenship in Modern Western Culture* (New York, 2007).

David Eltis is Robert W. Woodruff Professor of History at Emory University, Atlanta. His research interests focus on the early modern Atlantic world, slavery, and migration–both coerced and free. He is the author of *Economic Growth and The Ending of the Transatlantic Slave Trade* (Oxford, 1987) and *The Rise of African Slavery in the Americas* (Cambridge, 2000), and he is the editor of *Routes to Slavery: Direction, Mortality, and Ethnicity in the Transatlantic Slave Trade, 1595–1867* (London, 1997) and *Coerced and Free Migration: Global Perspectives* (Stanford, 2002). He is the co-editor, with Frank Lewis and

Kenneth Sokoloff, of *Slavery in the Development of the Americas* (Cambridge, 2004); with David Richardson, of *Extending the Frontiers: Essays on the New Transatlantic Slave Trade Database* (New Haven, 2008); and, with Philip Morgan, of *New Perspectives on the Transatlantic Slave Trade*, a special issue of *William and Mary Quarterly* (58/1 [2001]). He is a co-creator of *The Transatlantic Slave Trade: A Database on CD-ROM* (New York, 1999). His current projects include a census of the Atlantic slave trade, a book on slave-ship revolts, an analysis of the identity of captive Africans put aboard slave ships and *The Cambridge World History of Slavery*, which he is co-editing.

Alan Forrest is Professor Emeritus of Modern History at the University of York. He works on modern French history, especially the period of the French Revolution and Empire, and on the history of modern warfare. He is the author of *Soldiers of the French Revolution* (Durham, NC, 1990), *Napoleon's Men: The Soldiers of the Revolution and Empire* (London, 2002), *Paris, the Provinces, and the French Revolution* (London, 2004) and, most recently, *The Legacy of the French Revolutionary Wars: The Nation-in-Arms in French Republican Memory* (Cambridge, 2009). He is also the co-author, with Jean-Paul Bertaud and Annie Jourdan, of *Napoléon, le monde et les Anglais: Guerre des mots et des images* (Paris, 2004); co-editor, with Philip Dwyer, of *Napoleon and His Empire: Europe 1804–1814* (Basingstoke, 2007); co-editor, with Peter Wilson, of *The Bee and the Eagle: Napoleonic France and the End of the Holy Roman Empire* (Basingstoke, 2008); and co-editor, with Karen Hagemann and Jane Rendall, of *Soldiers, Citizens and Civilians: Experiences and Perceptions of the Revolutionary and Napoleonic Wars, 1790–1820* (Basingstoke, 2009); co-editor, with Etienne François and Karen Hagemann, of *War Memories: The Revolutionary and Napoleonic Wars in Modern European Culture* (Basingstoke, 2012/2013).

Karen Hagemann is James G. Kenan Distinguished Professor of History at the University of North Carolina at Chapel Hill. She has published widely in German and European history, with a focus on nineteenth and twentieth-century political, military and gender history. Her books include: *"Mannlicher Mut und Teutsche Ehre." Nation, Militär und Geschlecht zur Zeit der Antinapoleonischen Kriege Preußens* (Paderborn, 2002); *Masculinities in Politics and War: Rewritings of Modern History* (ed. with Stefan Dudink and John Tosh, Manchester 2004); *Gendering Modern German History. Rewriting Historiography* (ed. with Jean Quataert, Oxford and New York, 2007, in German: Frankfurt/M., 2008); *Representing Masculinity: Citizenship in Modern Western Culture* (ed. with Stefan Dudink and Anna Clark, New York, 2007/2012); *Civil Society and Gender Justice: Historical and Comparative Perspectives* (ed. with Sonya Michel and Gunilla Budde, Oxford and New York, 2008/2011); *War Memories: The Revolutionary and Napoleonic Wars in Modern European Culture* (ed. with Alan Forrest and Etienne François, 2012/2013). Currently she is writing a monograph titled *Revisiting Prussia's*

Wars Against Napoleon: History, Culture, Memory (Cambridge University Press) and preparing as the general editor the *Oxford Handbook on Gender, War and the Western World since 1650* (Oxford University Press).

Sherry Johnson is Associate Professor of Latin American and Caribbean History at Florida International University, Miami. Her research and teaching interests include Cuba and the Caribbean, environment and climate change, natural disasters, women and gender, the history of medicine and social history. She is the author of *The Social Transformation of Eighteenth Century Cuba* (Gainesville, 2001), *Climate and Catastrophe in the Atlantic World in the Age of Revolution* (Chapel Hill, NC, 2011) and of articles published in *William & Mary Quarterly*, *Hispanic American Historical Review*, *Cuban Studies/Estudios Cubanos*, *Colonial Latin American Historical Review*, and *Florida Historical Quarterly*. Her current projects include an examination of how ordinary summer fevers contributed to the British victory at Havana in 1762 and a study of domestic violence in Cuba from 1766–1800.

Catriona Kennedy is a Lecturer at the University of York. Her research and teaching interests are the Revolutionary and Napoleonic Wars in Britain and Ireland, the history of Irish nationalism, women's and gender history and the history of ideas. Funded by the British Arts and Humanities Research Council, she recently completed a project on the Revolutionary and Napoleonic Wars in Britain and Ireland for the international research project 'Nations, Borders, Identities: The Revolutionary and Napoleonic Wars in European Experience, 1792–1815'. Currently she is revising her dissertation, provisionally titled 'Engendering Ireland: Women, Politics, and Nation, 1789–1848', for publication. She has published *Soldiering in Britain and Ireland, 1750–1850* (ed. with Matthew McCormack) (Basingstoke, 2012). Her book *Narratives of War: Military and Civilian Experience in Britain and Ireland, 1793–1815* will come out in 2013 with Palgrave. She has contributed articles to *Public Men: Political Masculinities in Modern Britain*, edited by Matthew McCormack (Basingstoke, 2007); *Soldiers, Citizens and Civilians: Experiences and Perceptions of the Revolutionary and Napoleonic Wars, 1790–1820*, edited by Alan Forrest et al. (Basingstoke, 2009); and *Women's History Review*.

Gregory T. Knouff is Professor in the Department of History at Keene State College in New Hampshire. His research focuses on early North American history, especially on the history of gender/masculinity and the military and war. His publications include *The Soldiers' Revolution: Pennsylvanians in Arms and the Forging of Early American Identity* (University Park, PA, 2004) as well as chapters in *Friends and Enemies in Penn's Woods: Indians, Colonists, and the Racial Construction of Pennsylvania*, edited by William A. Pencak and Daniel K. Richter (University Park, PA, 2004), and *Representing Masculinity: Male Citizenship in Modern Western Culture*, edited by Stefan Dudink et al.

(Basingstoke, 2008). His current research project is titled 'Seductive Sedition: Loyalists, Language, and Power in Revolutionary New Hampshire'.

Emma V. Macleod is a Lecturer in History at the University of Stirling. Her research focuses on the history of British political ideas in the later eighteenth and early nineteenth centuries in general, with particular reference to the attitudes of the British toward other nations. She is the author of *A War of Ideas: British Attitudes to the Wars Against Revolutionary France, 1792–1802* (Aldershot, 1998); of a chapter in *These Fissured Isles: Ireland, Scotland, and British History, 1798–1848*, edited by Terry Brotherstone et al. (Edinburgh, 2005), and another in *Scotland in the Age of the French Revolution*, edited by Bob Harris (Edinburgh, 2005); and of *British Visions of America, 1775–1820: Republican Realities* (London, 2013).

Alexander M. Martin is Associate Professor of European History at the University of Notre Dame, with a specialization in Imperial Russia. He is the author of *Romantics, Reformers, Reactionaries: Russian Conservative Thought and Politics in the Reign of Alexander I* (DeKalb, 1993). He has also contributed articles to *The Cambridge History of Russia*, edited by Dominic Lieven (Cambridge, 2006); *European History Quarterly*; and *Russian Review*. His current projects include a study of enlightened absolutism and urban modernity in Moscow between 1763 and 1881 and a book on the self-fashioning of J. A. Rosenstrauch in Germany and Russia from 1768 to 1835, which will come out in 2014.

Holly A. Mayer is Associate Professor of History at Duquesne University in Pittsburgh. Her research interests centre on civil-military relations and the social and cultural histories of military forces in late eighteenth-century North America. She has written about women in the British and American forces in the Seven Years War and the American War for Independence, and is currently researching and writing about the Continental Army's 2nd Canadian Regiment. Her publications include *Belonging to the Army: Camp Followers and Community during the American Revolution* (Columbia, SC, 1996); *For the Record: A Documentary History of America*, co-edited with David Shi (5th ed., New York, 2013); a chapter in *War and Society in the American Revolution: Mobilization and Home Fronts*, edited by John Resch and Walter Sargent (DeKalb, 2007); and 'From Forbes to Families: Following the Army into Western Pennsylvania, 1758–1766' in the *Pennsylvania Magazine of History and Biography* 130 (January 2006): 5–43.

Gisela Mettele is Professor of History at the Friedrich-Schiller-Universität Jena. Her focus of interest is social and cultural history from the eighteenth to the mid-twentieth century, with an emphasis on gender, especially the history of urbanization, garden cities, civil society in suburbia, cinematic representations of cities and suburbs, and religion and society in the eighteenth and nineteenth centuries. Her publications include *Bürgertum in Köln*

1775–1870: Gemeinsinn und freie Association (Munich, 1998); *Weltbürgertum oder Gottesreich: Die Herrnhuter Brüdergemeine als globale Gemeinschaft 1760– 1857* (Göttingen, 2009); and chapters in *Historie und Leben: Der Historiker als Wissenschaftler und Zeitgenosse*, edited by Dieter Hein et al. (Munich, 2006) and *Civil Society and Gender Justice: Historical and Comparative Perspectives*, edited by Karen Hagemann et al. (Oxford, 2008).

Cecilia Morgan is a Professor in the Department of Curriculum, Teaching, and Learning at the University of Toronto. She began her career as a historian of British North America from the 1790s to the 1850s, and she has also published studies on late nineteenth- and twentieth-century English Canada. She is currently writing a book on Indigenous and mixed-race travellers from British North America and Canada in Britain and Europe, 1780s-1914. She is the author of *Public Men and Virtuous Women: The Gendered Languages of Religion and Politics in Upper Canada, 1791–1850* (Toronto, 1996); *'A Happy Holiday': English-Canadians and Transatlantic Tourism, 1870–1930* (Toronto, 2008); with Colin M. Coates, *Heroines and History: Madeleine de Verchères and Laura Secord* (Toronto, 2002); and *Creating Colonial Pasts* (forthcoming, Toronto, 2014). She has also contributed essays to *Gender & History* and to *Contact Zones: Aboriginal and Settler Women in Canada's Colonial Past*, edited by Myra Rutherdale and Katharine Pickles (Vancouver, 2005).

Jane Rendall is Honorary Fellow in the History Department at the University of York. Her research focuses on eighteenth- and nineteenth-century British and comparative women's history and, in particular, on Scottish women's history and the Scottish Enlightenment. She is the author of *The Origins of Modern Feminism: Women in Britain, France, and the United States, 1780–1860* (Basingstoke, 1985), editor of *Equal or Different: Women's Politics 1800–1914* (Oxford, 1987) and co-author, with Catherine Hall and Keith McClelland, of *Defining the Victorian Nation: Class, Race, Gender and the British Reform Act of 1867* (Cambridge, 2000). She is also the co-editor, with Karen Offen and Ruth Roach Pierson, of *Writing Women's History: International Perspectives* (Bloomington, 1991); with Mark Hallett, of *Eighteenth-Century York: Culture, Space and Society* (York, 2003); with Alan Forrest and Karen Hagemann, of *Soldiers, Citizens and Civilians: Experiences and Perceptions of the Revolutionary and Napoleonic Wars, 1790– 1820* (Basingstoke, 2009); and, with Richard Bessel and Nicholas Guyatt, of *War, Empire and Slavery, 1770–1830* (Basingstoke, 2010).

Introduction: Gender, War and Politics: Transatlantic Perspectives on the Wars of Revolution and Liberation, 1775–1830

Karen Hagemann and Jane Rendall

In 1801 an unknown Parisian artist produced the engraving on the front cover of this volume, which he entitled *'Rien ne manque plus à sa gloire'* (Nothing more is lacking for his glory). It shows Napoleon Bonaparte as a military leader and sword-bearer standing on top of the globe with the inscription 'General Peace'. He is receiving an olive branch from a young and beautiful female figure representing Peace. Another allegorical female, Abundance, is pouring a cornucopia of goods, a horn of plenty, upon the world below. The engraving represents a moment of hope. In 1801 Bonaparte was still First Consul of the French Republic. Austria had signed the Treaty of Lunéville, Naples had made peace with France, and Britain and the Ottoman Empire had both signed preliminary peace treaties with the French Republic. There was—at least from a French perspective—good reason to expect that the worldwide wars would be over, and peace and prosperity established under Napoleonic rule. Yet the engraving also suggests a divided gender order, one in which the warlike conqueror, successful on the field of battle reserved for men, has secured the world for the calm pursuits of peace, prosperity and private life represented by a woman.

Allegorical representations, however, are always uncertain indicators of gender ideas and practices, and this engraving offers only one illustration of the gender order of a world at war, if a very influential one.[1] The multiplicity, variety and ambiguity of representations of gender between 1775 and 1830 demonstrate its importance in the political and military culture of the time. Simultaneously they also reflect the complexities and paradoxes of this period of accelerated economic, social and cultural change, political upheaval and transatlantic mass warfare, which we have termed the age of the Wars of Revolution and Liberation; we take this to begin with the American War of Independence in 1775, to include the French and Haitian

Figure 1 'Rien ne manque plus à sa gloire' (Nothing more is lacking for his glory), engraving, Paris, 1801, unknown artist. Hoyt Collection, Rare Book Collection, University of North Carolina at Chapel Hill.

Revolutions and the Revolutionary and Napoleonic Wars, and to end in 1830 after the conclusion of the Latin American Wars of Independence. The variety of gender representations to be found in these years suggests the multiple ways in which gender worked. To analyse the relationships between war, politics and changing gender regimes during these wars, we need a dynamic and relational concept of gender. Following Joan W. Scott, we understand 'gender' as both an important subject of investigation and a method of doing research.[2] As Scott recently emphasized, gender as a methodology 'is above all an invitation to think critically about how the meanings of sexed bodies are produced, deployed, and changed'.[3] Recent scholarship on the period from 1775 to 1830 suggests that while a pattern of hierarchy and complementarity shaped gender relationships in most societies to some degree, concepts of masculinity and femininity depended on their historical context, were never constant and were continuously negotiated.[4]

In the eighteenth-century world, ideas about gender order, and gender relations themselves, were in the main shaped by location, class, status, religion and race.[5] From the slaves on American plantations to the urban artisans of European and American cities and the rural lives of peasant and farming communities, from middle-class households to the privileged worlds of European aristocrats, gender regimes were varied and diverse. New approaches emerged, however, during the Enlightenment. Traditional Christian and patriarchal legitimations of gender difference were questioned, though the answers that emerged were divergent. Medical and philosophical writers emphasized the innate physical and psychological differences between men and women, defined as 'natural' and 'universal', and deduced gender-specific and complementary duties for men and women, in the state, including its armies, and in civil society, as in families and households. Other contemporary observers, however, stressed the social convergence between the sexes brought about by historical progress towards a modern 'civilization', evident in patterns of urban sociability and print culture. The Enlightenment provided a new vocabulary for the public discussion of gender issues, though its full impact can only be understood with reference to different national contexts.[6] The dominant gender images that circulated among transatlantic elites in the late eighteenth century, many of which stressed 'separate spheres' for men and women, were not shared by all in the middle and upper classes, nor did they necessarily affect the lives or the culture of the men and women who formed the majority of the urban and rural populations, let alone enslaved and free African-born, creole or indigenous peoples in the Americas. Recent scholarship suggests that there were no universal concepts of masculinity and femininity in the age of the Wars of Revolution and Liberation. In the words of Katherine Aaslestad and Judith Miller, gender relations

> were profoundly shaped by local conflicts and norms, and the models themselves moved rapidly across boundaries only to be reconfigured

in their new contexts.... If gender lines appeared to harden during the war, that development emerged from the instability of a new gender axis where manhood was not a given, and instead had to be performed, repeated and naturalized.[7]

Such an approach makes it necessary to view gender not simply as a concept or ideal order formed by discourse, or produced through legislation or economic and social structures, though prescription, law and material relations all had powerful effects. Gender also needs to be understood through the practices of men and women in daily life, in peace and war, and the individual and collective identities they constructed.

This volume employs such an approach to advance our knowledge of the relations between the military, war, nation and gender, in the light of transatlantic connections and comparisons as well as regional and national differences and similarities. It also seeks to contribute to the understanding of the relationship between gender and the memory of these wars in the nineteenth century. In doing so, we have necessarily had to be selective. In this book we focus on five major themes. In Part I, *War, Empire and Slavery*, we consider the impact of years of revolution and war on slave economies and the slave trade, and on the everyday lives of enslaved and freed black populations, focusing here on female slaves, freedwomen and their families. The relations between *Masculinity, Revolution and War* are the theme of Part II. We ask whether the mobilization of men for mass warfare contributed to more rigid notions of masculinity associated with military service and valour, and what alternative discourses existed. We analyse how masculinities were created through the interplay with categories of difference like class, race, ethnicity and religion and with concepts of citizenship during revolutionary and national struggles. In Part III, *Warfare, Civil Society and Women*, we examine the impact of mass warfare on civil societies and ask how and why women continued to participate in military institutions and found new ways of contributing to the war effort as civilians, despite increasing attempts to construct the military as a solely masculine domain. The links between *Patriotism, Citizenship and Nation-Building* are the subject of Part IV, in which we analyse the gendered political rhetoric and practices associated with patriotism, citizenship and the growth of political and cultural nations in relation to revolution and war. Finally Part V, *Demobilization, Commemoration and Memory*, explores the relationship between gender, social and cultural demobilization and nineteenth-century memories of the wars of 1775 to 1830, including both the legacy of the gender ideals produced during this period and the gendering of the commemoration and collective memory of these wars.

These five themes are also the focus of our introduction, which provides a comparative overview on gender, war and politics during the Wars of Revolution and Liberation. First, however, we briefly discuss the historiography of these wars, reflect on the distinctive character of the period and note the connecting—indeed, irretrievably entangled—histories of transatlantic warfare, empires and nations.

Revisiting historiographies and connecting histories

In the years between 1775 and 1830, the transatlantic world endured a more or less constant state of war, with unprecedented effects across Europe, the Americas and the Caribbean. Some historians go so far as to characterize this as the age of the first modern world wars. These 'revolutionary wars', 'national wars', 'wars of liberation' or 'wars of independence', increasingly fought by volunteers, militia or conscripted troops, were to transform the conduct of warfare and the nature of armies. But they also profoundly affected the nature of civil societies and the lives of the men and women within them.[8]

Nevertheless, the military history of the period has been preoccupied for a long time with what Dennis Showalter called the 'drum and trumpet' history of generals and battles.[9] Military historians have recounted, again and again, the military successes of army leaders such as Washington and Napoleon. In fact, the nineteenth-century emergence of modern military history was closely associated with attempts to understand the lessons of the Wars of Revolution and Liberation for the education of future officers and commanders.[10] In this traditional historiography, the North American and Western European theatres of war were dominant, marginalizing the importance of warfare elsewhere in the transatlantic world, in Eastern Europe, Latin America and the Caribbean. The imperial expansion of the European powers in the New World and the Wars of Independence in the Americas have been studied with little reference to the Revolutionary and Napoleonic Wars in Europe. The history of the plantation economies, the slave trade and the abolition of that trade equally did not form part of the history of those wars, in spite of their impact on the institution of slavery. Since the 1990s, however, this has slowly changed, and an increasing number of transatlantic, or even transoceanic, and comparative studies on empires, wars and slavery have been published.[11]

In the last decade, military historians have begun to stress that mass mobilization, more than revolutionary advances in military operations, tactics, or strategies, determined the 'modernization' of warfare in this period. But they have seldom analysed its civilian side. Unlike current research into North American conflicts, many of the recent studies on the European theatre of war have continued to focus primarily on conventional military themes.[12] We still therefore know relatively little about the economic and social preconditions of these wars, about the often dramatic consequences of the funding of the military for civil society or about the ways in which economic exploitation and the destructive impact of war affected civilian populations.[13] One of the most pressing deficits in research, at least for

Europe, concerns the impact of violence—including the bombardment, sieges and looting of cities, towns and villages, the occasional atrocities and more widespread if unrecorded sexual violence—on civilian lives.[14]

A more comprehensive and comparative examination of the war experiences of civilians will help us to understand both the character of these wars and the causes and nature of popular support for and resistance to warfare.[15] For instance, ample evidence suggests that individuals and groups from different class, race, ethnic and regional backgrounds resisted war participation, military occupation, colonization and slavery, actively and passively. Their resistance took different forms, in escape, desertion, banditry, smuggling, riots and violent protest, and could escalate into local uprisings, if not wars of liberation and independence. An older scholarship often associated resistance and rebellion against colonial rule or military occupation with the rise of revolutionary ideas, patriotism or nationalism. New research indicates that revolutionary and nationalist ideas alone seldom motivated the resistance of ordinary people. Day-to-day problems—slavery, daily exploitation, declining economies, requisitioning, billeting, conscription, plundering and atrocities—often played a more important role, as did the previous wartime experiences of those involved. New ideas, however, helped to voice and legitimate grievances. The motives for resistance and rebellion were, from a transatlantic perspective, as varied as its forms.[16]

We also need more comparative research on postwar societies and the short- and long-term aftermath of different war experiences. The history of the economic, social, and cultural demobilization of armies and societies remains to be written for many areas of Europe and the Americas. Attention must be paid not only to the reintegration of veterans into civilian life, but also to how societies responded to the challenging duties of care for disabled soldiers, war widows and orphans.[17] There are many questions to which we still do not have answers. How were states and nations that had undergone a violent civil war able to transform themselves into peaceful civil societies and to reconcile the enemy parties? What were the conditions for successful demilitarization and reconstruction? What role did the family and female relatives play in the process of integrating former militiamen and volunteers back into the everyday life of peacetime? And it is only in the last decade that the study of the memories of the Wars of Revolution and Liberation has become a thriving field.[18]

Finally, mainstream scholarship on the Wars of Revolution and Liberation has not yet systematically integrated gender issues. Women have generally occupied a marginal position in the military history of the period. The first army women studied by feminist historians were the small and exceptional group of cross-dressing female soldiers.[19] Research on other female roles in armies between 1775 and 1830 has only recently begun.[20] Historians have become more interested in the patriotic activities and writings through which women supported the wars in civil society, and the various ways in which gender functioned in political discourse and culture.[21] A focus on men and masculinity in the history of the military and war is also relatively new; few studies analyse the everyday lives of soldiers and officers, their concepts of masculinity and their perceptions of war. In the last decade, the associations between concepts of masculinity, universal conscription and mobilization, and new forms of political and military culture have been addressed. Recent research underlines the importance of newly constructed relations between military duties and the rights of citizenship, but at the same time highlights the need to historicize and differentiate in respect of class, race, ethnicity and age.[22] However, this scholarship focuses on the army. The gender implications of naval warfare, so crucial for the conflicts of maritime empires, and the production of a distinctive kind of masculinity at war, await further investigation. In this and many other respects, this volume reflects the state of research. We too have no chapter on naval warfare.

Even very recent studies revisiting the wars of the period ignore gender. In his 2007 study of *The First Total War,* David A. Bell offers the concept of 'total war' as an analytical framework for the Napoleonic Empire. Bell argues that it was the 'fusion of politics and war' that distinguished modern 'total war' from earlier incidents of 'unrestrained or even exterminatory' warfare. For him the 'intellectual transformation of the Enlightenment, followed by the political fermentation of 1789–92, produced new understandings of war that made possible the cataclysmic intensification of the fighting over the next twenty-three years'.[23] He criticizes older research that attributed the intensification of war after 1792 mainly to two factors—revolutionary ideology and nationalism—as unsatisfying and suggests a focus rather on the new 'culture of war', characterized by two features: first, a new perception of the armed forces, with the military defined as a largely separate sphere of society from the civilian; second, the phenomenon of militarism, relying on this distinction, and involving the imposition of military values and customs on civilian life.[24]

It is a stimulating approach, one that focuses mainly on the intellectual and cultural dimensions of warfare. But it is unhelpful if we want to explore the gender dimension of war, because it simply ignores it and as a result does not recognize the much more complex and ambiguous processes at work. With the professionalization of the new mass armies from the turn of the nineteenth century, the military was indeed discursively defined as separate from civil society. Yet at the same time as a consequence of the emergence of new forms of mass warfare, civilians were increasingly affected by war. This does not however necessarily mean that military practices were successfully imposed on civil societies in this period. The first studies of demobilization after 1815, for instance, show that most citizens did not appreciate such interventions in their daily lives and that they wanted to return to a peacetime order.[25]

The concept of 'total war' introduced earlier by Roger Chickering and Stig Förster, and developed in a series of five comparative conferences between 1992 and 2005, offers an interesting alternative, because it encourages scholars to conceptualize the period in a global way, and offers a multi-dimensional approach that allows the systematic integration of gender.[26] They argue that 'total war' differed from earlier forms of war mainly because of 'its peculiar intensity and extension' and its tendency to abolish the boundaries that distinguished the battlefront from the homeland. For them the ideal 'total war' would characteristically fulfil most of the following four conditions: first, the theatres of war would extend simultaneously across a large area of the world, involving mass armies made up of 'citizens in uniform ... passionate because ideologically motivated'; second, 'mobilization for war no longer stops at the borders of civilian life', since 'all members of the belligerent states' would need to participate' to conduct a war successfully; third, 'all members of the belligerent states are now the legitimate targets of military action', whether by occupation, blockade, looting and requisitioning or bombing; and fourth, the 'war aims are accordingly directed towards a final victory, if not the extermination of the enemy'.[27] These conditions, or at least some of them, apply not to all but to many conflicts in the period between 1775 and 1830 and characterize them as new, and modern, forms of warfare: national wars, revolutionary wars, mass wars and guerrilla wars.

The concept of 'total war' has been used in different and sometimes unclear ways. It might seem unhistorical and misleading for the study of the Wars of Revolution and Liberation because of its close connection to two twentieth-century world wars. And it is controversial, since a complete mobilization of the resources of any society is impossible, and the absolute destruction of the enemy seldom occurs. Nevertheless, reflection on its applicability requires us to sharpen our awareness of the shared features of the wars between 1775 and 1830. The concept can highlight the transatlantic, even global, dynamic of these wars, in which free and enslaved Africans and Native Americans were involved as well as white Europeans. Moreover, it helps us to recognize that the related political and military goals of these wars, and different forms of mass mobilization, had far-reaching structural consequences. These were significant not only for the military itself and for its conduct of war, but also for the relationships between warfare and politics, and state and nation, as well as for the boundaries between 'front' and 'homeland', soldiers and civilians, and men and women. All these connections remain invisible if we restrict our analysis to the military and warfare in the narrow sense, or include culture without gender. Rather, our investigation must be broadened to include societies as a whole, and to incorporate both culture and gender systematically.

One danger of the application of any concept of 'total war' is that historians project an ideal definition drawn from present-day scholarship onto a historical period that was marked to a considerable degree by ambivalence, frictions, ruptures and contradictions. Between 1775 and 1830, discourses and practices often stood in sharp contrast. The sometimes sudden and dramatic transformations in the economy, politics, the military and society occurred unevenly across the transatlantic world and accompanied stagnation and the persistence of tradition in other areas of work and life, particularly in the culture of everyday life and mentalities. This 'concurrence of non-simultaneity' was one of the chief characteristics of the period.[28] Contemporaries had to cope with the coexistence of accelerated change and cultural continuities, and the contradiction between universalist rhetoric and exclusionary practices. The result was, ultimately, to be a profound and lasting transformation of mentalities—and not only those of the educated strata—through the birth of the autonomous 'modern individual'. Reinhard Koselleck coined the term *'Sattelzeit der Moderne'* to describe this period of transition from the early modern to the modern world, with all its paradoxes.[29]

In this volume we view the conflicts and changes in Europe during the *Sattelzeit* as inseparably connected to the clash of European empires across the Americas, and the dynamism of a transatlantic model of independent nationhood. Throughout the eighteenth century the major dynastic empires of ancien régime Europe, constructed over many centuries through conquest, inheritance and diplomacy—France, Great Britain, the Habsburg and the Russian Empires, Portugal and Spain—were engaged in intermittent but semi-continuous warfare both across and beyond Europe, warfare which also involved the maritime republic of the Netherlands, the monarchy of Prussia, and many smaller powers. The land-based empire of Russia was steadily expanding its frontiers both in Europe and in Asia. And by the end of the Seven Years War in 1763 the transatlantic and imperial dimension of such conflicts, particularly for the leading maritime powers, France and Britain, but also for Spain, Portugal and the Netherlands, had assumed far greater significance.

However, the American War of Independence from 1775 to 1783, between 13 North American colonies of Great Britain and the metropolitan government, marked a decisive change in that it led to the establishment of a new, independent, and self-conscious nation. The American revolutionaries received substantial naval and military help from Britain's major European rivals in the competition for empire, France and Spain, the latter still an important power in North as well as Latin America, governing after 1783 Louisiana and Florida. The new republic of the United States of America had to coexist with the remaining colonies of British North America, including, from 1791, Upper Canada and Lower Canada (formerly Quebec), on its northeastern frontier.

The French Revolution of 1789 initiated 23 years of worldwide wars, from 1792 to 1815. By 1810 French armies had established the dominance of the Napoleonic Empire across Europe, with only Prussia, and the Habsburg and

Russian Empires retaining a precarious independence. The history of these conflicts, and of Napoleon's subsequent defeat, has, of course, been widely studied.[30] These wars, however, were fought not only in Europe but also in the Americas, and especially in the Caribbean. In Saint-Domingue, the declaration of the emancipation of slaves in 1793, in the context of British and Spanish occupation and armed slave rebellion, led to the Haitian Revolution and the foundation of the independent Haitian Republic in 1804.[31] Economic warfare and boundary disputes brought the United States and Great Britain into conflict in the War of 1812, lasting until 1815, amid Canadian fears of American invasion, attempted but never fulfilled. However, overall the United States emerged from this period with very significant gains, through the acquisition of Louisiana and the enormous midwestern territories from the Mississippi to the Rocky Mountains in 1803, and the whole of Florida by 1819.

After Napoleon was finally defeated by the allied powers of Europe in 1815, the boundaries of nations, states and empires, across the Americas as well as Europe, came to be redrawn. In the Caribbean, the French ultimately retained only Guadeloupe and Martinique, the Spanish Cuba and Puerto Rico. British naval and military victories secured her existing colonies in North America and the Caribbean, and brought territorial gains elsewhere, in the former Dutch colonies of Latin America as in the Mediterranean, Asia and Africa. The history of British North America remained troubled, with armed uprisings in Upper and Lower Canada in 1837 and 1838. In 1867, four British North American provinces were united into the internally self-governing dominion of Canada, which became a model for other British colonies of white settlement. Everywhere in North America European settlers continued to displace indigenous populations, often very brutally.

The radical effects of the Revolutionary and Napoleonic Wars continued for much longer in Latin America than in Europe. After Napoleon's invasion of Spain and Portugal in 1807–8, the relationship between the metropolitan powers and their extensive colonies in Latin America was to be broken. Although the elites of the Spanish and Portuguese colonies were nominally loyal to their monarchs, the local power they enjoyed and the spread of nationalist aspirations made it impossible for the restored imperial governments of Portugal and Spain to recreate their empires after 1815. The Wars of Independence, which continued in Latin America for the next 15 years, and were often fought as violent civil wars, saw the establishment of a series of new nations between 1811 and 1830, from Paraguay in 1811 to Mexico in 1830, when for a second time the Spanish crown was forced to accept Mexican independence, which it had challenged in an attempt at reconquest the previous year.[32]

The political landscape in Europe was also transformed after 1815. The Bourbon monarchy was restored in France. The Quadruple Alliance, a coalition of Russia, Austria, Britain and Prussia formed at the behest of Tsar

Alexander I in 1815, became the Quintuple Alliance, including France, in 1818, and imposed a long-lasting if conservative settlement on Europe, its stability briefly threatened by the re-emergence of European revolutionary movements first in 1830, and again, more effectively, in 1848–49. The growth of national identities on the European continent also challenged that settlement and the unity of the Habsburg and Russian Empires. The movements for national independence in Poland, which resulted in the unsuccessful Polish rising against absorption into the Russian Empire in 1831, and the Italian struggle for separation from the Habsburg Empire between 1848 and 1866 are only two of many examples. Such challenges to imperial rule were to continue throughout, and beyond, the nineteenth century in Europe.[33]

Across Europe and the Americas the nineteenth century witnessed the building of nation-states, as the process that began during the last decades of the eighteenth century intensified. Here it is important to differentiate between 'state' and 'nation'.[34] Some nations, including France, the United States, Haiti and the newly founded Spanish-American republics, were in this period already sovereign nation-states, ideally defined by the free political association of adult males and by written constitutions. Others were only cultural nations, constructed through discourse and culture, and rooted in past histories, language, ethnicities and forms of communication.[35] One notable example of the latter is Germany. After the dissolution of the Holy Roman Empire of the German Nation by the Habsburg Emperor Francis II in 1806, 39 German states formed the alliance of the German Confederation in 1815, with Austria and Prussia as the largest members. Most German patriots of the time shared the idea of a German *Kulturnation* (cultural nation), united by language, culture and custom, but did not aim for a centralized nation-state. Their goal was a 'federative nation' with a monarch at its head based on a constitution, which was not realized before German unification in 1871 (and excluded Austria).[36] Similarly, in most areas of Central, Eastern and Southern Europe the spread of the idea of a cultural nation long preceded the appearance of nation-states.[37]

Empire, colonial war and slavery

The challenge of writing the history of the Wars of Revolution and Liberation is, therefore, that it has to encompass both a full recognition of the imperial dimension of these conflicts and a fully gendered understanding of that wide-ranging history. Here we emphasize that the growth of the warring transatlantic empires has to be integrally associated with the development of the slave trade and the establishment of slave-based colonial economies. Following the Portuguese example in Brazil, Spain, France and Britain turned to the African slave trade to provide cheap labour for their plantation colonies in Latin America, the Caribbean and the southern colonies of

North America. By the mid-eighteenth century different models of colonial society had been firmly established in many areas of the Americas, their economies organized around the exploitation of resources for the benefit, first, of the metropolitan power, and, second, of the European settlers. On such plantations African slaves laboured to produce sugar, coffee, tobacco and other foodstuffs for European markets.[38] In the northern colonies, on the other hand, British and other migrants sought to create rural and urban societies not unlike those they had left. In British and French Canada fishing and fur trading attracted small populations. These different colonial societies were coveted, conquered and exchanged in the warfare and diplomacy of European powers, and the institution of slavery was central to the economies of most—and especially to those considered profitable.

The majority of colonies were composed of very disparate free and enslaved populations. David Eltis has traced in this volume the two trading systems which fed the demand for African slaves in the Americas, the northern one dominated by the British, to the Caribbean and the southern United States, the southern led by the Portuguese, with the Dutch also actively participating. Eltis demonstrates that the period between 1775 and 1830 saw the slave trade at its height, with close to 80,000 Africans leaving Africa each year.[39] Slaves were to be found all over North and Latin America and the Caribbean. In the late 1780s, in the French island of Saint-Domingue there were 460,000 slaves working the sugar and coffee plantations, the largest slave population of the West Indies and 88 per cent of all inhabitants. In the same period, in the middle and southern colonies of British North America on average 21 per cent of the population were slaves, mostly exploited on plantations producing tobacco and rice, and from the 1790s cotton; the numbers of free men and women grew very slowly there, in contrast to Latin America.[40] There the Portuguese colony of Brazil had, with almost a million slaves (35 per cent of the population), the largest concentration of African and creole slaves, as well as half a million free coloured people. In the Spanish colonies slaves were, on average, only a comparatively low 2 per cent of the population, though they were a much higher proportion in certain areas such as coastal Peru, Veracruz and Morelos, Mexico, Caribbean Colombia and Buenos Aires. Only Cuba had a significant slave population, 35 per cent of its inhabitants.[41] The populations of the Americas were therefore divided by race and by status, and also by the cultural divisions between the African-born and creole populations, the latter born in the Americas and more likely to synthesize their inherited cultures with those of local European elites.

The slave trade and the institution of slavery were deeply gendered. Fewer women than men were abducted and transported, partly because of the nature of supply from Africa; women slaves were in high demand in the African market. Driven by labour needs, the owners of slaves from an early date accepted the use of African women in field labour as well as domestic work, though they preferred to employ men; over the whole period of the transatlantic slave trade, women formed 36 per cent of those transported. In Saint-Domingue they worked at some of the harshest and most dangerous agricultural and processing tasks.[42] Because of the small proportion of women enslaved, and the harsh work regimes they encountered, African slaves arriving could not reproduce themselves. By the late eighteenth century, the low birthrate among African-born populations was a matter of considerable concern to slave owners, a concern which in Saint-Domingue continued to be expressed after emancipation, as Elizabeth Colwill demonstrates in her chapter. The southern colonies of British North America, where the numbers of native-born slaves were steadily increasing, with a higher rate of reproduction than anywhere else in the Americas, were thus an exception.

Not all white men and women owned slaves. The white populations of the colonial settlements were divided by class, gender and origins, the latter as a result of patterns of voluntary or forced migration. When Florida was ceded to Great Britain in 1763, families with allegiance to Spain were forced to evacuate to Cuba. In late eighteenth-century Grenada, won by Britain from France after 1763, small French- and English-speaking populations coexisted, just under a thousand in all, compared to almost 24,000 slaves. After the American Revolution, Loyalists, including blacks and Native Americans, left the United States to settle in Nova Scotia and in western Quebec, which in 1791 became the English-speaking colony of Upper Canada; English-speakers in British North America were still outnumbered by the French-speaking colonists of Lower Canada.[43] Such migrations continued after the outbreak of war between European powers from 1792 onwards. There was considerable migration of the white and free coloured populations from Saint-Domingue and the former Spanish colony of Santo Domingo in the 1790s to Cuba and other Caribbean destinations.

Increasingly, during the second half of the eighteenth century the institution of slavery came to be questioned in Europe and the Americas. Enlightenment thinkers believed slavery to be both inhumane and a violation of their belief in human liberty and the natural rights of man. In Britain and North America, Quakers and other religious groups, especially evangelical ones, condemned it as un-Christian; the state of Pennsylvania passed the first legislative act against slavery in 1780. In Britain, in the aftermath of the American War of Independence, the opponents of slavery began to organize broader sections of public opinion to campaign for the abolition of the slave trade and of slavery itself, against deeply vested economic interests.[44] The Enlightenment, however, contained a contradictory message in respect of slavery and racial differences, because it also encouraged the study of what were, it was argued, ineradicable physical differences between peoples, based on anatomy, physique and skin colour. Such differences were to be used to justify the hierarchical classification of 'races', and were added to the arsenal of the defenders of slavery.[45]

The British attempts at abolition before the French Revolution were unsuccessful, but they created a climate of expectation, as did the legislation of the Revolution, which appeared to promise civil and political equality to free people of colour. The denial of this by planters in the French colonies brought uprisings by the free coloured population in 1790 and by slaves in 1791. The grant of emancipation in 1793 by the abolitionist French Commissioner in Saint-Domingue preceded the French National Convention's grant of emancipation to slaves in 1794. The hopes this generated for slaves and free coloured populations across the Caribbean were encouraged by the French, who sought to spread rebellion to the British, Spanish and Dutch islands. And though the grant of emancipation was revoked by Napoleon in 1801, Haitian leaders succeeded in establishing the first black republic in Haiti in 1804.[46] That important model remained deeply alarming and ever-present to the other slave-owning territories of the Americas.[47]

One of the many paradoxes of the period was that, as they fought black rebellion, colonial governments recruited large numbers of black slaves to their armed forces, in response to the high mortality rates of white soldiers in tropical climates, and the need to fight slave rebellions in difficult, often mountainous terrain. African military experience proved to be valuable in conflicts with black rebels, in 'guerrilla warfare a decade before the term was coined'. [48] After 1793 the French organized brigades of emancipated slaves, and in 1795 the British established 12 West India Regiments as regular units of the British army.[49] For enslaved men military enrolment was often a path to freedom. Revolutionaries like the Haitian general Toussaint Louverture, and also white and creole army leaders, promised emancipation for dutiful military service.[50]

For most slave women, this was never a formal possibility, although some joined the combat against French troops in both Saint-Domingue and Guadaloupe. But in this volume Laurent Dubois and Elizabeth Colwill show how emancipation in Haiti allowed not only newly freed black men but also women to define themselves as citizens. This might well be in opposition to the policies imposed upon them by both French and black male revolutionary leaders, equally concerned to maintain agricultural labour to ensure the provisioning of armies. If freedwomen remained on the plantation, the payment they were offered as labourers was two-thirds that of men, and they frequently chose to work for fewer days so that they could cultivate their own expanded garden plots for the benefit of their families. If they left, they might well find new war-related forms of employment in urban contexts. In both cases family relations were of extreme importance for their survival and the reconstitution of family life became central to their new freedom.[51]

For the revolutionary governments too the family was of importance. The French commissioners had bound slave emancipation to the structure of the family and to civil rituals of marriage as a means of labour discipline and population growth. This policy was later also endorsed by Louverture. Yet it was at odds with family strategies which had emerged from a combination of African practices and the informal, extended and extra-legal relationships that had developed in the harsh conditions of plantation slavery. Colwill argues that freed black men and women took up civil marriage only in a 'gradual and uneven' way, in response to shifting political and military priorities. Marriage rates peaked at times of effective government enforcement, in response to incentives and when fear of French invasion was high.

Expectations of emancipation were partially met by the abolition of the slave trade by Denmark (1792), France (1794 and 1814), Great Britain (1807), the United States (1807) and the Netherlands (1814). David Eltis has written here of the ways in which this affected the gender balance of slaves in the Caribbean; without the replenishing of the male labour force from Africa, the plantation work force there became predominantly female, though skilled workers remained male. But outside North America there remained considerable pressure from planters to retain the trade in order to renew the numbers of male African slaves. In spite of the temporary difficulties caused by war and by the British policy of suppression, after 1815 the Portuguese and Spanish slave trades recovered and even grew, enabling Brazil and Cuba to expand their sugar production, overtaking that of the British and French Caribbean, until international pressures for abolition prevailed, in Portugal by 1851 and in Spain in 1867. Yet, though the end of slavery itself—abolished by Britain from 1833, and by France for the second time in 1848—was not clearly visible at the end of the period covered by this volume, it could certainly be imagined.[52]

Masculinity, revolution and war

Everywhere in the transatlantic world, the wars of the period from 1775 to 1830 were the first to be conducted with mass armies. The Continental Army under George Washington was the earliest to fight with militia alongside a regular army with conscripted troops and volunteers. John Shy estimates that at least 200,000 soldiers served, or nearly 40 per cent of able-bodied men, from a pool of around half a million.[53] However, as a result of the short span of the average service, no more than 90,000 total men were ever under arms at one time, and because of the extent of the embattled territory, a much lower number, between 3,000 and 10,000, were usually involved in individual campaigns.[54] The size of the Loyalist army, estimated by Jeremy Black as 60,000 men, was much smaller, and spread out from Canada to Florida. The proportion of mercenaries was high; German auxiliaries from Hesse-Cassel alone provided 37 per cent of the British strength in America in 1781. The permanent shortage of soldiers was a major problem for the British army everywhere in the New World.[55] One strategy to solve this, to promise enslaved men freedom when they enlisted for the British army, was already in place during the American Wars of Independence. Some scholars estimate that during these wars between 80,000 and 100,000 slaves escaped, because they hoped to gain freedom on the British side. They emphasize that the issue of such support was critical, both in supporting British war effort and in driving southerners to join the revolution in fear of such defection and its devastating consequences for the slave economy.[56]

The French revolutionaries were greatly impressed by the military powers unleashed by the participation of citizens in the American War of Independence.[57] To be able to confront the armies of the ancien régime, France introduced the *levée en masse* in 1793, followed by a conscription system, permitting substitutes and exemptions, in 1798. The number of soldiers mobilized surpassed anything previously seen in Europe. More than 2 million Frenchmen—7 per cent of the male population—served between 1792 and 1813. Half of them never returned home.[58] Conscripts from annexed and neighbouring regions added another million soldiers.[59] This made it possible to create the huge forces of the *Grande Armée*, which allowed Napoleon to conquer large swathes of Europe.[60]

To meet this massive force, France's enemies in Europe, like Prussia, were compelled to introduce similar forms of mass recruitment. Following the introduction of universal conscription in March 1813, the Prussian field army grew to about a quarter of a million soldiers, of whom 54 per cent were militiamen and volunteers. In 1813 more than 10 per cent of the Prussian male population was mobilized for war, compared to 2 per cent in 1806.[61] Austria, Britain and Russia, too, recruited massive armies but in more traditional ways.[62] One prerequisite for an efficient deployment of armies on the basis of universal conscription or militias was the reform of military systems. Like the Prussian military leaders, other governments sooner or later followed the example of French army reformers, abolishing corporal punishment, professionalizing the military training of soldiers and officers and, most significantly, opening the ranks of officers to non-nobles.[63]

The consequence of these developments was warfare on a previously unknown scale. The *Grande Armée* marched in June 1812 with nearly 650,000 men of very different nationalities—Austrians, Croatians, Poles, Portuguese, German, Italians and Spaniards—and 17 train battalions of 6,000 vehicles through Central Europe to Russia. A similar picture is presented by the 'Battle of the Nations' at Leipzig in October 1813: a total of more than 475,000 men from all over Europe massed in Saxony.[64] The revolutionary and colonial armies in Spanish America and the Caribbean also fought their Wars of Independence with a large and highly diverse soldiery, which as in North America included free and enslaved men of various races and ethnicities.[65] Miguel Hidalgo y Costilla and his supporters started the Mexican War of Independence (1810–21) against Spanish rule in September 1810 with 25,000 combatants, mostly from the rural poor; within a month their army grew to 60,000.[66] In the decisive battle of the Chilean independence struggle at Maipú near Santiago de Chile in April 1818, 5,000 Revolutionaries triumphed over the same number of Spanish Loyalists; one third of them died during and after the battle.[67]

The new forms of mass warfare necessitated the support of large segments of the population. Military mobilization could not have been based on compulsion alone. War mobilization was accompanied by intensely patriotic propaganda, which legitimized the struggle as a 'national war,' 'revolutionary war' or 'war of liberation'. 'Print wars' accompanied military conflicts everywhere in the transatlantic world and were fought on the pages of brochures, leaflets, newspapers and pamphlets.[68] The propaganda reinforced the idea that men were duty-bound as citizens, fathers and brothers to defend their families, homes and nations, and were only 'real men' if they were ready to fight for their personal freedom and the liberty of their nation. Willingness to fight was thus intertwined with masculinity. The 'hero's death on the altar of the fatherland', until then reserved only for noble officers, was now open for the first time to ordinary men and deemed the highest form of patriotic sacrifice. The citizen-soldier willing to fight and die for his nation, and demanding political representation within it, became the new masculine ideal in many, if not most, late eighteenth- and early nineteenth-century societies involved in the wars studied here.[69]

The chapters by Stefan Dudink, Gregory T. Knouff, Alan Forrest and Karen Hagemann demonstrate this development by analysing the Dutch, American, French and Prussian cases. The ideal of the citizen-soldier, its significance and its transfer, is a central theme of this volume. This ideal spread unevenly, alongside continuities with the ancien regime, and needs to be historicized for a clear understanding of the variety of forms it could take, and especially for the association between military duties and political rights at its heart. Dudink shows this most clearly for the turbulent history of the Netherlands, where the Dutch Republic was replaced in 1795 by the Batavian Republic, followed in 1806 by the Kingdom of Holland and in 1815 by the United Kingdom of the Netherlands. By comparing the careers of two Dutch officers in these years, he traces the coexistence of the values of military professionalism with different ideals of the citizen-soldier and their shifting significance in the course of an individual career, depending on specific political circumstances.

Knouff and Forrest emphasize that in America and France, when 'the people' entered the historical stage, war and politics not only became associated with the revolution but the relationship between them changed. Revolutionaries in both nations introduced a new politics that drew on established ideas about republican masculinity, and profoundly changed them. In the United States Constitution of 1787 and the French Declaration of the Rights of Man and Citizen of 1789 ideals of patriotism were connected with the construction of a new nation-state, through the apparently universalizing proclamation of the sovereignty of the people. Thus all free men became citizens, or at least potential citizens, and as such had a duty to volunteer as soldiers. This conflation of the rights of citizenship and military duties compounded the 'virile aspects' of masculinity, 'universalized' them, and thereby distinguished masculinity even further from femininity.[70] Only in France were these citizenship rights extended, if only temporarily, to the colonies with the abolition of slavery in February 1794 and the enfranchisement of freed black men.[71]

The anti-colonial liberation movements in the Caribbean and Latin America learned from the discourses and practices of the American War of Independence and the French Revolutionary Wars, and mobilized for war with militias and volunteer units. The use of these forms of military force, combined with the promise of personal freedom and equal political rights, brought the ideal of the citizen-soldier into play, 'masculinizing' in particular newly freed black soldiers and free coloured men. And such military service did encourage claims to citizenship.[72]

In Central Europe, however, the connection between politics and the military took a different form. Prussia introduced in 1813 the most radical system of universal conscription in Europe, without substitutes. The monarchy promised a constitution and more political rights for all men serving in the army at the end of the war. With this commitment, necessary for war mobilization, the government reluctantly imported early liberal ideas into a conservative political order. After the Wars of Liberation, it reneged on its offer and attempted to suppress all demands for political reform.[73] There were similar developments in many other Central European states. In all these cases the majority of men were in practice simply integrated into the military. Their war service did not make them citizens but reinforced their status as duty-bound subjects.

The British monarchy never introduced universal conscription in this period. Nevertheless the size of the armed forces did increase massively between 1792 and 1815 through voluntary enlistment into the regular army and the proliferation of national defence units. Linda Colley argues that this caused a 'militarization of British political life' and fostered a masculinity of 'heroic endeavour and aggressive maleness', a development that boosted a conception of Britain as an essentially masculine nation.[74] Catriona Kennedy questions this interpretation here, arguing that the ideal of the citizen-soldier was not a dominant one in the British military of the period. Different concepts of masculinity such as the class-specific values of the polite gentleman and the military code of personal honour might be held simultaneously by officers. British private soldiers remained liable to corporal punishment in this period and were subjects, not citizens, throughout the nineteenth century, with most disenfranchised until 1918.[75]

A transatlantic comparison thus suggests that in all the nations and states involved in the Wars of Revolution and Liberation, masculinity had some association with military values, as a means of mobilizing broad strata of men for mass warfare. However, the nature of the connections between the military and political orders varied greatly, as did different notions of masculinity, also shaped by class, race, ethnicity and age. But both conservatives and revolutionaries were united in the view that the citizen was male, for only men could carry out the military duty of protecting home and nation.

Warfare, civil society and women

The deployment of mass armies in warfare changed the interplay between war and politics, fostering new forms of masculinity. And it also had a far-reaching impact on civil society, as troop movements, combined with military engagements, occupations and annexations, encroached upon it more deeply than in earlier eighteenth-century wars.[76] Civilians paid the costs of the new mass warfare. Old systems of supply through state depots were everywhere sooner or later replaced by new systems of requisitioning. Armies had to be fed from the lands they crossed, and here they did not distinguish between friends and enemies. The civilian population had to finance the wars through higher taxes and tariffs and by providing all kinds of goods, including weapons and uniforms along with food, animals and carts. Occupied territories were exploited and compelled to make financial contributions, intensifying economic hardships. This applied across Europe, the Americas and the Caribbean.[77] The Chilean Wars of Independence analysed by Sarah Chambers provide a stark example of this. As in other parts of Spanish America, these struggles were civil wars, prolonged as insurgents and royalists alternated in power. Throughout the country, each side confiscated the properties of suspected enemies, and in the south entire communities were relocated in an effort to prevent the civilian population from providing support to invading troops. Because most wars between 1775 and 1830 were struggles over the very existence of old and new states and nations, legitimated by new and powerful political ideologies, the civilian population became a military target as armies aimed for an annihilating victory over the enemy.

As a result of the dramatically increased number of soldiers, the goal of final victory and the political emotions unleashed, the numbers of the dead rose sharply. The estimated casualty rate in the Continental Army was 25 per cent, and in the campaigns of the Napoleonic Wars 20 per cent on average.[78] The Russian campaign in 1812, from which only 4 per cent of soldiers returned, was the deadliest.[79] At some five million, the number of war-dead in Europe between 1792 and 1815 approached the same percentage of the overall population as in the First World War.[80] The total loss of life resulting from the American Revolutionary War is unknown, but John Shy estimated that its proportions were similar.[81] Only a minority of these victims were men who died in battle. Most perished because of injuries, disease and epidemics that also affected civilians. During the Napoleonic Wars in some Central European regions between 5 and 10 per cent of the population died because of typhus and dysentery, after battles close to their towns and villages.[82] Families lost fathers, brothers and sons, and also female relatives. Thousands of additional soldiers returned home disabled and faced the prospect of survival without adequate state support.[83]

The new forms of mass warfare could therefore only be fought successfully if the civilian population too—men and women alike—was mobilized. The *levée en masse* set out a clear wartime gender order for Revolutionary France: young men of military age were to become soldiers and old men were to support the war effort with material and ideas. Women, by contrast, were to ensure that soldiers were equipped with tents and uniforms, to care for the sick and wounded and to bolster men's fighting resolve.[84] Political differences notwithstanding, similar principles informed the propaganda and policies of most countries involved in the wars. On this issue conservatives and revolutionaries agreed, as several essays in this volume indicate. Both material support for and popular commitment to the wars by civilian populations had become more necessary than ever. Without such backing, many governments would not have been able to wage war. The declared 'national emergency' of war thus opened opportunities for women in public life previously closed to them. They were allowed to expand their 'motherly duties' beyond their families because the 'fatherland was in danger'.[85] In eighteenth-century Cuba, as Sherry Johnson suggests, soldiers' wives functioned as 'deputy husbands'. It was accepted even by the Spanish state authorities that during war they had to replace their spouses at home. And Holly A. Mayer here traces the ways in which women's responsibilities at the home front were widely acknowledged in Revolutionary America.

Because family roles remained entwined with the military and political order, these war-related developments similarly influenced public policy and family relations. Ancien régime monarchies had used family law to regulate the social order, and all newly established republics, including the American, French, Haitian and Chilean, claimed the right to define family structures. Legislation on the family often mirrored political ideologies. In France the Legislative Assembly introduced civil registration for births, marriages and deaths, equality of inheritance and a relatively liberal procedure for divorce, measures later reversed by the Directory, the Consulate and the Napoleonic Empire; in particular the introduction of the Civil Code by the latter made divorce much more difficult for women to obtain.[86] One major interest underlying such policies was the stabilization of the social and political order in times of crisis and war by implementing order in the family, seen as the basis of society and state.[87]

Women who supported the wars at 'home' and fought for the survival of their families were often regarded as 'heroines'. Those who joined the armies as camp followers and cross-dressing soldiers, however, met increasing public resistance. Female camp followers had a long history in early modern armies. They worked as canteen-keepers, laundresses and sutlers and provided the labour necessary to feed, clothe and supply the troops. Many army women were married to a soldier or lived with one in concubinage, bearing them children. Throughout the eighteenth century governments and military leaders had tried to regulate the number of women and children who accompanied the troops during campaigns, but with little success. The partnership of a soldier and a working woman secured the precarious reproduction of both. For lower-class women army life was often the only alternative left, when combat had destroyed their homes and their partner had followed the army.[88] Holly A. Mayer, Thomas Cardoza and Alan Forrest explore the situation of camp followers in the American Continental and French armies, describe the ambivalent perception of these women by the military and society, and illustrate their suppression in national memory.[89] With the rising size of armies, their professionalization and the related changes in the conduct of warfare, military leaders increasingly tried to reduce and regulate the number of camp followers. Because it was difficult enough for them to equip and feed the larger number of soldiers, they now preferred a minimal baggage and a much smaller number of camp following women and children.[90] Cardoza demonstrates the extent of the increased regulation of camp followers in the French army through an analysis of the changes between 1775 and 1820.

Despite their importance camp followers hardly made it to the front page of newspapers during and after these wars. The small number of female soldiers gained much more public attention. As David Hopkin recently emphasized, it is very difficult, if not impossible, to differentiate between fact and fiction when we study the history of women who joined the European and American armies dressed as men.[91] Mayer's examples from the American War of Independence, and the work of other scholars, indicate that in the period between 1775 and 1830 more women than ever before or after tried to join as volunteers the armies that fought for liberation, independence or revolution. We will never know how many women became soldiers, since only cases which came to light, mainly through injuries or illness, can be identified in the sources. Most of these women came from lower-class families. Patriotism was one motive for their engagement, but there were others. They needed to make a living, or wanted to follow their fiancés, husbands or male family members into war or hoped to experience adventure and freedom. When they were discovered, they often had to face fierce criticism, at least from civilian society. The threat to the gender order that fighting women posed on both sides of the Atlantic appears to have been so great that society sought to protect itself by accusing them of being driven by 'dishonourable and unvirtuous' motives.[92] The image of the young woman who follows her lover to war out of passion and 'lasciviousness' was thus a popular topos in literature and poetry.[93]

A transatlantic perspective suggests that the Wars of Revolution and Liberation were a *'gendering* activity—one that ritually marked the gender of all members of a society', as has been observed for other wars.[94] War propaganda appeared to inscribe a more sharply divided gender order, because mass mobilization of soldiers made it necessary to accord all men in principle the duty to defend family, home and country. In such propaganda women of all classes might appear to be assigned primarily domestic roles. And yet such discursively constructed divisions were questioned through everyday practices—as a matter of necessity—as the responsibilities of women in their homes and in the public arena increased. Many women gained a new level of agency and independence during the wars, as did their male relatives. This in turn affected and destabilized the existing gender order and with it the social fabric, given the importance of gender in the cultural ordering of societies. For postwar governments everywhere, it seemed all the more necessary to re-establish the stability of an older gender order, yet the experiences of war made it impossible simply to return to a former world.

Patriotism, citizenship and nation-building

The word 'patriotism' frequently recurs throughout this volume in relation to men and women, civilians as well as soldiers. Yet its meanings were enormously variable in this period.[95] Patriotism could be expressed in relation to republics or monarchies, nations or multinational empires, with reference to a region or even a locality. Patriotic ideas influenced military as well as civilian discourses and practices. The terms 'citizen' and 'citizenship' have also been widely used in this book. They are often employed to indicate the formal relationship of individuals to the state, based on voting rights and rights of representation. A wider perspective conceptualizes 'citizenship' as reflecting both the rights and the duties associated with full political, economic and social membership in the community of the nation, going beyond a purely legal interpretation to include a range of other social relationships. Membership of states and nations was defined through laws and regulations, and social and cultural practices and discourses that excluded both those beyond their boundaries and those within them who failed to qualify.[96] Inclusions in and exclusions from formal citizenship of a state are easily traced in this period. But the ways in which women and men imagined themselves to be members of a national community are more difficult, though not impossible, to recover. That sense of belonging was, like patriotism, shaped—and limited—by factors such as class, gender, race, ethnicity and religion. These collective and subjective identifications were often ambivalent, dependent on historical context and liable to sudden change.[97]

During the Wars of Revolution and Liberation the association between patriotism and citizenship was widespread, and is relevant to many of the essays in this book. Much of the language of eighteenth-century patriotism was rooted in early modern classical republicanism, which identified the virtuous male citizen-soldier with the pursuit of the public good and was associated with the notion of a self-governing community of men under arms.[98] This model, adapted, provided the basis for the male republicanism of the Batavian Republic, analysed here by Stefan Dudink. It was also in another form the basis of the local, commercial and civic patriotism of the city-republic of Hamburg, described by Katherine Aaslestad, where only Lutheran men of substantial means who adhered to a strict moral code could attain the legal status of citizen (*Bürger*). Thus by the end of the eighteenth century around half the male population of Hamburg qualified for citizenship, with each man granted rights according to his financial standing. All unpropertied men, Catholics, Jews and women were excluded.

A more modern, though related, ideal of patriotism and republicanism was embodied in the concept of the citizen-soldier employed by the American, French and Haitian revolutionaries.[99] Their aspirations for more formal rights of universal male citizenship, were, however, also exclusionary, on the grounds both of gender and of race. Here Gregory T. Knouff shows how in 1777 the radical constitution of Pennsylvania appeared to exclude free taxpaying African-Americans from taking that prerequisite of citizenship, the oath of allegiance to the new republic, prefiguring later events. In the United States in the 1780s property qualifications still remained, though by 1830 almost every adult white male possessed the vote but virtually every new state constitution included race and gender exclusions.[100] The revolutionary French constitution of 1793, granting universal male suffrage, was an interesting paper exercise but was never put into practice in France or its colonies in this period.[101]

In Spanish America, uniquely, virtually all new nation-states abolished distinctions of status among free men, and placed no explicit racial limitations on citizenship. The Spanish Constitution of 1812 had already made Indians citizens, but excluded blacks. After independence, slaves were barred but not free blacks and those of mixed ancestry. In practice, however, property and literacy qualifications that limited political citizenship fell disproportionately on non-white populations, but the number of men of colour who fought during the Wars of Independence and subsequently received voting rights is striking compared with other regions.[102]

Yet in the *Sattelzeit* these new ideals of universal male citizenship need to be juxtaposed to continuities with former practices. Most men and women remained the subjects of monarchical and imperial governments, whether of an ancien régime or reforged through war, as in Britain and its colonies, Imperial Russia, Restoration France and the German states. The formal structures of exclusion were in some societies complicated by past legacies, as in widespread and occasionally anomalous property qualifications. Privileged, propertied women could exceptionally exercise a degree of formal as well as informal political influence. Between 1790 and 1807 single propertied women and free blacks were allowed to vote in the state of New Jersey; though both were then excluded together.[103] But throughout the transatlantic world, with the exception of Spanish America, masculinity and whiteness were by the 1820s increasingly identified as essential requirements for formal participation in the government of states and nations. In the language of both modern and traditional republicanism the nation was entrenched firmly in heterosexual difference and the bonds of fraternity among citizens.

The complement of the ideal of the citizen-soldier was in contemporary discourse the 'republican' or 'patriotic' wife and mother, embracing her female 'duties' as educator and housewife. In peacetime this ideal limited female patriotism beyond the home to such actions as a consumer boycott or the support of a 'national fashion'.[104] However, in war women were summoned to support the nation's struggle through charity and the nursing of the ill and wounded. To create a national gender order, contemporary political rhetoric made extensive use of the metaphor of the nation as a family, evoking a seemingly 'natural' social order with clearly defined obligations for both sexes; there are many instances in this volume. Revolutionaries and conservatives alike used the metaphor, because it included women in the nation and at the same time safeguarded their exclusion from the male domain of state politics. Moreover, it legitimated racial, social and generational hierarchies in the political order as 'natural'.[105]

Despite all regional and political differences, most nations and states of the period employed metaphors, myths, symbols, rituals and ceremonies to form emotional bonds. Political culture and propaganda gained increasing importance during the years of the Wars of Revolution and Liberation, for both revolutionary powers and monarchical or imperial states. Governments and the military, in conjunction with political associations and the churches, shaped the political culture of the time. They built on the coronation festivals, the military parades and the religious processions of the ancien régime, but also learnt from the practices of revolutionary republicanism. The symbols of liberty—caps and trees—had been important rallying points in the course of the American Revolution.[106] But it was in France, with the displacement of the Catholic Church and the French monarchy, that new rituals were constructed for a regenerated nation, whether locally in the planting of liberty trees across France or in the more elaborate spectacles planned by the painter Jacques-Louis David for central Paris.[107] Everywhere, even among the enemies of France, political and military leaders followed this example, adapting it to their own circumstances and deploying it in mobilization for war, as analysed for Prussia in this volume by Karen Hagemann. In Colombia during the Spanish-American War of Independence in 1813 the insurgents erected liberty trees adorned with both a cap of liberty and images of Jesus and Mary.[108]

As with republican discourse, this political culture was highly gendered. The symbols, rituals and ceremonies represented the masculinity of the political order. Women often played only ceremonial, sometimes allegorical, roles. During the Wars of Liberation of 1813-15 in Prussia, for instance, the patriots in the government, the military and the Protestant churches introduced induction ceremonies for the newly deployed militia and volunteer units, for which women embroidered flags. Similarly in Britain and in Upper Canada, women presented regiments with their colours.[109] By doing this they claimed their independent place in the nation, complementary to that of fighting men. Formal victory celebrations tended to be carefully choreographed by the state, local authorities and church leaders. Women contributed to these events, but in a less public capacity. They decorated the fairground or the church, prepared the feasts, or collected money for war victims.

Celebrations also drew upon a vision of the nation as a family. In Prussia, during the wars of 1813-15, the monarchy introduced a wide range of patriotic events and festivities that involved the public as a whole in clearly gendered ways; from the paternal monarch downwards, every subject was integrated according to their class, gender and age. In Britain, too, the monarchy and its domestic life became a central focus for the patriotic ceremonies encouraged throughout the country; the same was true for Upper Canada, as Cecilia Morgan suggests here.[110] Through such cultural politics even conservative monarchies such as Prussia tried to exploit patriotic feelings to strengthen identification with the state and foster willingness to fight and sacrifice for the nation. Multinational empires like Britain hoped to promote a sense of common 'British' achievement; the celebration of worldwide military and naval victories was intended to strengthen imperial patriotism. In a very different context Chilean revolutionaries, as Sarah Chambers demonstrates, tried to create the idea of national community in a newly founded state, which was racially highly diverse and politically divided.

Male civilians were able to express their patriotism through participation in militias and volunteer movements, but also through local political institutions and the less formal world of the public sphere described by Jürgen Habermas, in associations and in print culture, though these were limited by class and race.[111] Women, in contrast, rarely participated directly in military activity, and, except for a very few propertied women, had little chance of participation in formal political life. During the American Revolution, women founded local chapters of the Daughters of Liberty, in parallel with the Sons of Liberty, and these continued to exist in the post-revolution era. The brief expansion of women's political clubs in revolutionary France, however, was rapidly ended by decree in 1793, and hostility to 'politicizing women' was widespread across Europe and the Americas.[112] Yet the imperatives of war continued to stimulate the founding of patriotic women's associations in later years. For Germany historians have identified nearly 600 patriotic associations organized by women between 1813 and 1815; a similar growth can be observed during the Napoleonic Wars in Britain and the Wars of 1812-15 in Upper Canada.[113] In Mexico and elsewhere in Spanish America women participated very actively in the struggle for independence.[114] Most of these movements rarely survived the period of war; and their structure was frequently contested as male authority was exerted. Yet in the right local circumstances, philanthropic work started during the war, in parallel with religious and anti-slavery activities, provided a continuing basis for female organization, as the example of republican Hamburg illustrates.

The period between 1775 and 1830 also witnessed the expansion of different forms of print culture—newspapers, periodicals, books and pamphlets—across all the societies discussed here. Jane Rendall argues in this volume that British women of all social classes took advantage of this to make significant contributions to the literary representation of war, here specifically through poetry. Parallels can be found in the publications of female authors of the local elite of Hamburg and in other societies during this period.[115] Nevertheless female authors were constrained as to genre and content by the clearly gendered standards of male critical authorities, and by the competition of the literary marketplace. One most important site for the expression of female patriotism lay in the world of the family and private life. Emma Macleod suggests in her chapter that the correspondence of the British bluestockings in the late eighteenth century, which circulated around friends and acquaintances, engaged directly with politics and warfare while occupying a place somewhere between the public and the strictly personal. Here intelligent and educated women are shown to be as engaged in the events of their time as the average educated, male, civilian observer.

As some of the enlightened British authors discussed by Rendall and Macleod demonstrate, patriotism and an exclusionary nationalism were not always or necessarily the determining factor in shaping a response to national 'others' in this period. Other contemporary forms of identification could include the championing of a religious faith and culture, the values of a common European 'civilization' or a vision of universal peace. Alexander Martin illustrates this by exploring the life-history of the German actor Johann Rosenstrauch, who migrated to Russia, joined the middle-class German minority there, and established himself first as a successful businessman and later as an accredited pietist clergyman. Rosenstrauch distanced himself disdainfully from the backwardness he found around him and adhered to a Western European cosmopolitanism, but was increasingly isolated after Napoleon's troops invaded Russia in 1812. Catriona Kennedy shows how British officers in Spain and Portugal tended to admire the professionalism of their French enemies, and looked down upon the 'backwardness' of their Spanish and Portuguese allies. Such attitudes merged, as Cecilia Morgan indicates, with more explicitly racialized hierarchies, evident in, for example, the response in Upper Canada not only to military deployment of Native peoples by their American enemy, but also to their own Native allies, employed by the British forces.

A small minority in some societies associated itself not with the patriotic call to war, but with a patriotism interpreted in cosmopolitan terms as a universal aspiration for worldwide peace. This had its origins in a strand of enlightened thinking, which rejected war as irrational barbarism, and saw historical progress as progress towards a peaceful and commercial world.[116] These attitudes were influenced by small religious minorities, such as, in Britain and the United States, the Quakers and the Unitarians. The poetry of Anna Barbauld, discussed here by Rendall, is one instance of such an intervention, though Barbauld, like many others, in a republican spirit supported the principle of defensive war. This period also witnessed the first organized associations for peace, in the United States in 1815, and in London in 1816. Such societies were exclusively masculine.[117]

The mobilization of soldiers and civilians—men and women—for war broadened the membership of national communities everywhere in these years. It also expanded the forms through which patriotism was expressed, and the opportunities available to those who wished to claim membership of a nation. The formal model of citizenship in the state, however, stressed that the citizen was male, because only men could protect the home and the 'fatherland', a term used for both existing states and aspirant nations. Through this rhetorical strategy, women were excluded from the centres of political power in state and nation, though they were allowed to support their fatherland when endangered in war. But in peacetime, male conservatives and revolutionaries alike perceived women primarily as the mothers and educators of subjects and citizens. They recognized this work as important for the making of states and nations, but in politics they accepted women only as allegorical representations of their nation, as Columbia, Germania, Liberty or Marianne.[118] Nevertheless, the legacy of participation in a nation at war, whether through patriotic associations, print culture, or simply familial loyalties, allowed some women to maintain their subjective identification with, and sense of membership in, their political communities. This complex process of 'gendering' states and nations continued through postwar demobilization and in later commemoration of the wars.

Demobilization, commemoration and memory

For those who lived through the Wars of Revolution and Independence, whether as children, youths or adults, this was a dramatic time that left lasting impressions. They shared—if from very different perspectives—formative common experiences and memories. Never before had so many people, including, for the first time, educated women and men from the middle classes, been actively involved in war. Many of them tried to come to terms with their experiences of revolution and war by writing letters to family members and friends, keeping a diary, or penning memoirs for themselves, their family or the public. More ego-documents have survived for these events in archives and libraries than for any earlier wars.[119] These documents are highly gendered, because gender images also shaped individual war remembrance and collective memory.

Just as most of the historiography on the wars of the period between 1775 and 1830 has ignored the gendered character of the experiences and memories of these wars, so the extensive theoretical debate on memory has overlooked the importance of gender for the construction of memories. Feminist scholarship, too, has only recently begun to discuss the close interrelationship between the two.[120] This volume emphasizes both that memory is always gendered and that gender is one of the most important interpretive patterns that structures the process of memory production.[121] The case studies presented here confirm Aleida Assmann's observations that women are often the 'subjects of memory' because they transmit more differentiated, complex and often ambiguous 'communicative memories', but at the same time they are also the 'objects of oblivion' for men, who dominate the production of 'cultural memory'.[122] In this context 'communicative memory' is defined as generational and based on collective communication. It spans no more than three generations (a *saeculum*) and is less structured and hierarchical than 'cultural memory', which is sustained by social and cultural institutions in the form of rites and festivities, published texts and monuments. The main function of 'cultural memory' is to create the identities of collectivities (communities, nations, states). Both memories together make up 'collective memory'.[123]

The production of such a memory begins while participants are still at war and continues throughout the process of demobilization, as several authors in this volume stress. As suggested earlier, this is an important, though often ignored, dimension of the history of the period and many questions still remain open. We can only explore two themes: the gendered dimension of cultural and social demobilization and the gendering of commemoration and memory. In particular, we analyse here the ways in which the victorious elites in leadership roles during the Wars of Revolution and Liberation dominated the contested commemoration and memories of these wars afterwards.

As the chapter by Karen Hagemann demonstrates for Prussia, ceremonies and festivities were as important for the cultural demobilization of a society formerly at war as they were for their mobilization. Locally organized homecoming celebrations for militiamen and volunteers clearly signalled the incompatibility of a strictly regulated military order with civilian life.

The main message to the returning Prussian 'citizen-soldiers' was that in peacetime military virtues were not needed. It was more important to be a caring paterfamilias and a patriotic citizen, who willingly performed his collective and individual duties as a man and cultivated an appreciation of both his community and the nation.[124] The parallel message to women was that they should now return to their own domestic and familial duties and assist in the cultural demilitarization of the returning 'warriors' in their 'cosy homes'. They must therefore give up all public activities, and in particular their organizational commitment to the patriotic women's associations.[125]

One important element in social demobilization was the struggle for veterans' and widows' pensions. As the examples of colonial Cuba and Upper Canada, revolutionary Chile, France and Pennsylvania in this volume demonstrate, this was often a fight for the recognition of the patriotism shown through service to and sacrifice for the fatherland, and, equally, for a place in the historical memory of the past wars of community and nation. Sarah Chambers explores women's memories of war as narrated in petitions for pensions to the Chilean state in the early nineteenth century. Because of the fierceness with which the Wars of Independence were fought between 1810 and 1826, the emerging independent republic of Chile was deluged with requests for compensation and pensions from women trying to recover from these hardships. Their petitions narrated both their own personal suffering and the sacrifices of their loved ones, keeping alive memories of past divisions at a time when the country's leaders hoped to forge national unity. In response, the new political elite (the former military leadership) used their discretionary powers to 'wipe the tears' of the unfortunate in an effort to avoid political embarrassment to the new state. As they expanded eligibility for war pensions, widows needed only to provide evidence of their marriages and their husband's military service rather than sorrowful tales.

In other cases memory politics was used more for the construction of a specific national identity and the exclusion of those defined as 'other'. Knouff, for instance, demonstrates how through the memory of the American Revolutionary Wars, former soldiers and officers from Pennsylvania were able to link concepts of white maleness with claims to membership in the new American nation. In so doing they created a foundation for political subjectivity grounded in imagined biological terms for the early United States. The soldiers' war memories bolstered a clear definition of 'whiteness' that united ethnically diverse European-Americans. They constructed an identity as white by implicating other groups, primarily African-Americans and Native Americans, as not white and therefore not entitled to membership in the revolutionary postwar community. The popular concept of a nation of white men further naturalized the exclusion of women from formal politics. Women, African-Americans and Native Americans would increasingly be barred from citizenship of the new republic on the basis of their perceived physical characteristics, not on the grounds of their class, status or culture. Similarly, Cecilia Morgan shows how contested were the memories of the wars in Upper Canada between 1775 and 1830, and the importance, for the conquering side, of sooner or later taking hegemonic control of national memories in order to be able to define national identity.

In this struggle over a dominant national narrative, conventionally featuring male heroism, the active role women played in these wars on both sides of the Atlantic was usually suppressed. The national historiographies of the nineteenth century, almost entirely written by white men, reinforced this elimination of those excluded from formal citizenship in the historical master-narratives of the Wars of Revolution and Liberation.

Notes

We would like to thank Gisela Mettele for her warm support during the writing of this introduction, and Sarah Chambers, Alan Forrest, Wayne Lee and Judith Miller for their helpful comments on earlier versions of the introduction.

1. Marina Warner, *Monuments and Maidens: The Allegory of the Female Form* (London, 1987), 63–87; Silke Wenk, 'Gendered Representations of the Nation's Past and Future', in *Gendered Nations: Nationalisms and Gender Order in the Long Nineteenth Century*, ed. Ida Blom et al. (Oxford, 2000), 63–80.
2. The classical text is Joan W. Scott, 'Gender: A Useful Category of Historical Analysis', *American Historical Review (AHR)* 91/5 (1986): 1053–1075. For the recent debate, see: 'AHR Forum: Revisiting "Gender: A Useful Category of Historical Analysis"', *AHR* 113/5 (2008): 1344–1430; Alexandra Shepard and Garthine Walker (eds), *Gender and Change: Agency, Chronology and Periodization* (Oxford, 2009); Leonore Davidoff et al. (eds), *Gender and History: Retrospect and Prospect* (Oxford, 2000).
3. Joan W. Scott, 'Unanswered Questions', *AHR* 113/5 (2008): 1422–1430, 1423.
4. See, for instance, Pamela Scully and Diana Paton (eds), *Gender and Slave Emancipation in the Transatlantic World* (Durham, NC, 2005); Catherine Davies et al., *South American Independence: Gender, Politics, Text* (Liverpool, 2006); Ulrike Gleixner and Marion W. Gray (eds), *Gender in Transition: Discourse and Practice in German-Speaking Europe, 1750–1830* (Ann Arbor, 2006); Karen Hagemann et al. (eds), *Gender, War and the Nation in the Period of the Revolutionary and Napoleonic Wars—European Perspectives*, special issue *European History Quarterly* 37/4 (2007); Sarah Knott and Barbara Taylor (eds), *Women, Gender and Enlightenment* (Basingstoke, 2005).
5. See for example Merry E. Wiesner-Hanks, *Women and Gender in Early Modern Europe* (2nd edn, Cambridge, UK, 2000), 13–51.
6. Karen O'Brien, 'Introduction', in *Women, Gender and Enlightenment*, ed. Knott and Taylor, 3; idem, *Women and Enlightenment in Eighteenth-Century Britain* (London, 2009), esp. 1–34; Claudia Honegger, *Die Ordnung der Geschlechter: Die Wissenschaft vom Menschen und das Weib, 1750–1850* (Frankfurt/M., 1991), 186–199.
7. Katherine B. Aaslestad and Judith A. Miller, 'Gender, War and Politics: The Wars of Revolution and Liberation—Transatlantic Comparisons, 1775–1820', *Bulletin of the German Historical Institute* 41 (2007): 128–136, 136.
8. Stig Förster, 'Der Weltkrieg, 1792 bis 1815: Bewaffnete Konflikte und Revolutionen in der Weltgeschichte', *Kriegsbereitschaft und Friedensordnung in Deutschland, 1800–1814*, ed. Jost Dülffer (Münster, 1995), 17–38; Paul Fregosi, *Dreams of*

Empire: Napoleon and the First World War, 1792–1815 (London, 1989); Stephen Conway, *The War of American Independence, 1775–1783* (London, 1995).
9. Dennis E. Showalter, 'History, Military', *The Reader's Companion to Military History* (Boston, 1996), 204–207, 205.
10. Jeremy Black, *Rethinking Military History* (London, 2004), 184.
11. For example, Christopher Bayly, *Imperial Meridian: The British Empire and the World, 1780–1830* (London, 1989); Lester D. Langley, *The Americas in the Age of Revolution, 1750–1850* (New Haven, 1996); David Armitage and Michael Braddick (eds), *The British Atlantic World, 1500–1800* (Basingstoke, 2009); Kathleen Wilson (ed.), *A New Imperial History: Culture, Identity and Modernity in Britain and the Empire, 1660–1840* (Cambridge, MA, 2004).
12. For example, Michael V. Leggiere, *The Fall of Napoleon: The Allied Invasion of France, 1813–1814* (Cambridge, UK, 2007).
13. See Wayne Bodle, *The Valley Forge Winter: Civilians and Soldiers in War* (University Park, PA, 2002); Katherine Aaslestad, 'War without Battles: Civilian Experiences of Economic Warfare during the Napoleonic Era in Hamburg', in Alan Forrest et al. (eds), *Soldiers, Citizens and Civilians: Experiences and Perceptions of the French Wars, 1790–1820* (Basingstoke, 2009), 118–136.
14. See for the American War of Independence, Allan Kulikoff, 'Revolutionary Violence and the Origins of American Democracy', *The Journal of the Historical Society* 11/2 (2002): 229–260; Wayne Lee, 'The American Revolution', in *Daily Lives of Civilians in Wartime Early America: From the Colonial Era to the Civil War*, ed. David S. Heidler and Jean T. Heidler (Westport, CT, 2007), 31–69; Jean B. Lee, *The Price of Nationhood: The American Revolution in Charles County, Maryland* (New York, 1994); for Central Europe, Karen Hagemann, ' "Unimaginable Horror and Misery": The Battle of Leipzig in October 1813 in Civilian Experience and Perception', in Forrest, *Soldiers*, 157–178. On sexual violence and its representation, Sharon Block Source, 'Rape without Women: Print Culture and the Politicization of Rape, 1765–1815', *Journal of American History* 89/3 (2002): 849–868.
15. For example, Forrest, *Soldiers*; Ute Planert, *Der Mythos vom Befreiungskrieg: Der deutsche Süden und die französischen Kriege, 1790–1840* (Paderborn, 2007); John Resch and Walter Sargent (eds), *War and Society in the American Revolution: Mobilization and Home Fronts* (DeKalb, 2007).
16. For Europe, see Charles J. Esdaile, 'Patriots, Partisans, and Land Pirates in Retrospect', in *Popular Resistance in the French Wars: Patriots, Partisans, and Land Pirates*, ed. idem (Basingstoke, 2005), 1–24.
17. See Denise Z. Davidson, *France after Revolution: Urban Life, Gender, and the New Social Order* (Cambridge, MA, 2007); Natalie Petiteau, *Lendemains d'Empire: les soldats de Napoléon dans la France du XIXe siècle* (Paris, 2003).
18. Recent examples include: Alan Forrest, *The Legacy of the French Revolutionary Wars: The Nation-in-Arms in French Republican Memory* (Cambridge, UK, 2009); Sam A. Mustafa, *The Long Ride of Major Von Schill: A Journey through German History and Memory* (Lanham, MD, 2008); Sarah J. Purcell, *Sealed with Blood: War, Sacrifice, and Memory in Revolutionary America* (Philadelphia, 2002); Natalie Petiteau, *Napoléon, de la mythologie à l'histoire* (Paris, 1999).
19. See Dianne M. Dugaw, *Warrior Women and Popular Balladry, 1650–1850* (Chicago, 1996); Julie Wheelwright, *Amazons and Military Maids* (London, 1989); Rudolf M. Dekker and Lotte C. Van de Pol, *The Tradition of Female Transvestism in Early Modern Europe* (New York, 1989); Sylvie Steinberg, *La confusion des sexes: le travestissement de la Renaissance à la Révolution* (Paris, 2001).

20. See Holly A. Mayer, *Belonging to the Army: Camp Followers and Community during the American Revolution* (Columbia, 1999); John A. Lynn, *Women, Armies, and Warfare in Early Modern Europe* (Cambridge, MA, 2008).
21. See Linda Colley, *Britons: Forging the Nation, 1707–1837* (New Haven, 1992), 237–283; Cecilia Morgan, *Public Men and Virtuous Women: The Gendered Languages of Religion and Politics in Upper Canada, 1791–1850* (Toronto, 1996); Mary Beth Norton, *Founding Mothers & Fathers: Gendered Power and the Forming of American Society* (New York, 1996); Linda K. Kerber, *Women of the Republic: Intellect and Ideology in Revolutionary America* (Chapel Hill, 1997); Dominique Godineau, *The Women of Paris and Their French Revolution* (Berkeley, 1998); Sarah C. Chambers, *From Subjects to Citizens: Honor, Gender, and Politics in Arequipa, Peru, 1780–1854* (University Park, PA, 1999); Jean Quataert, *Staging Philanthropy: Patriotic Women and the National Imagination in Dynastic Germany, 1813–1916* (Ann Arbor, 2001), 21–52; Joan B. Landes, *Visualizing the Nation: Gender, Representation, and Revolution in Eighteenth-Century France* (Ithaca, 2003); Kathleen Wilson, *Island Race: Englishness, Empire and Gender in the Eighteenth Century* (London, 2003); Harriet Guest, *Small Change: Women, Learning, Patriotism, 1750–1810* (Chicago, 2005); Carole Berkin, *Revolutionary Mothers: Women in the Struggle for America's Independence* (New York, 2006); Davies, *South American Independence*.
22. Robert A. Nye, 'Western Masculinities in War and Peace', *AHR* 112/2 (2007): 417–438; see also Karen Hagemann, '*Mannlicher Muth und Teutsche Ehre*': Nation, Militär und Geschlecht zur Zeit der Antinapoleonischen Kriege Preußens* (Paderborn, 2002); Gregory T. Knouff, *The Soldiers' Revolution: Pennsylvanians in Arms and the Forging of Early American Identity* (University Park, PA, 2004); Matthew Brown, *Adventuring and the Birth of New Nations in Gran Colombia* (Liverpool, 2006).
23. David A. Bell, *The First Total War: Napoleon's Europe and the Birth of Warfare as We Know It* (Boston, 2007), 9.
24. Ibid. 11–12.
25. See Karen Hagemann, 'German Heroes: The Cult of the Death for the Fatherland in Nineteenth-Century Germany', in *Masculinities in Politics and War: Gendering Modern History*, ed. Stefan Dudink et al. (Manchester, 2004), 116–134.
26. Roger Chickering and Stig Förster (eds), *War in an Age of Revolution, 1775–1815* (Cambridge, MA, 2010), is the last of five edited collections from a series of conferences on 'Total War', organized by the German Historical Institute in Washington DC, comparing developments in warfare in the United States and Germany between 1775 and 1945.
27. Roger Chickering, 'Militärgeschichte als Totalgeschichte im Zeitalter des totalen Krieges', in *Was ist Militärgeschichte?*, ed. Thomas Kühne and Benjamin Ziemann (Paderborn, 2000), 301–312, 306; see also Chickering, 'Total War: The Use and Abuse of a Concept', in *Anticipating Total War: The German and American Experiences, 1871–1914*, ed. Manfred F. Boemeke et al. (Cambridge, MA, 1999), 13–28.
28. The phrase 'concurrence of non-simultaneity' (*Gleichzeitigkeit von Ungleichzeitigkeiten*) was coined by Ernst Bloch in *Erbschaft dieser Zeit* (1st edn, Zurich, 1935, Frankfurt/M., 1985).
29. Reinhard Koselleck, 'Einleitung', in *Geschichtliche Grundbegriffe*, ed. Otto Brunner et al. (Stuttgart, 1979), vol. 1, xv.
30. See as overviews, Charles Esdaile, *The Wars of Napoleon* (London, 1995); idem, *The French Wars, 1792–1815* (London, 2001); David Gates, *The Napoleonic Wars, 1803–1815* (London, 1997).

31. Carolyn E. Fick, 'The French Revolution in Saint Domingue: A Triumph or a Failure?', in *A Turbulent Time: The French Revolution and the Greater Caribbean,* ed. David Barry Gaspar and David Patrick Geggus (Bloomington, 1997), 50–75.
32. Langley, *The Americas,* 193.
33. Eric J. Hobsbawm, *Nations and Nationalism since 1780: Programme, Myth, Reality* (Cambridge, MA, 1992).
34. Geoff Eley, 'Culture, Nation and Gender', in Blom, *Gendered Nations,* 27–40.
35. Geoff Eley and Ronald Grigor Suny, 'Introduction: From the Moment of Social History to the Work of Cultural Representation', in *Becoming National: A Reader,* ed. Eley and Suny (New York, 1996), 8. For our understanding of the nation, see Mrinalini Sinha, 'Gender and Nation', in *Women's History in Global Perspective,* ed. Bonnie G. Smith (Urbana, 2004), vol. 1, 229–274; Blom, *Gendered Nations,* 3–80.
36. Jonathan Sperber, *Germany, 1800–1870* (Oxford, 2004).
37. Laurence Cole (ed.), *Different Paths to the Nation: Regional and National Identities in Central Europe and Italy, 1830–1870* (Basingstoke, 2007).
38. David Eltis, *The Rise of African Slavery in the Americas* (Cambridge, UK, 2000); idem and David Richardson (eds), *Extending the Frontiers: Essays on the New Transatlantic Slave Trade Database* (New Haven, 2008).
39. Herbert S. Klein and Ben Vinson III, *African Slavery in Latin America and the Caribbean* (2nd edn, Oxford, 2007), 56.
40. Herbert S. Klein, *The Atlantic Slave Trade* (Cambridge, UK, 1999), 44.
41. Langley, *The Americas,* 89; Laird Bergad, *The Comparative Histories of Slavery in Brazil, Cuba, and the United States* (Cambridge, MA, 2007).
42. On gender and slavery, see for example, David Barry Gaspar and Darlene Clark Hine (eds), *More than Chattel: Black Women and Slavery in the Americas* (Bloomington, 1996); Scully, *Gender and Slave Emancipation*; Barbara Bush, *Slave Women in Caribbean Society, 1650–1838* (Bloomington, 1999); Hilary Beckles, *Centering Women: Gender Discourses in Caribbean Slave Society* (Kingston, 1999).
43. Peter J. Marshall, 'British North America, 1760–1815', in *The Eighteenth Century: The Oxford History of the British Empire,* ed. idem (Oxford, 1998), vol. 2, 386.
44. David Brion Davis, *The Problem of Slavery in the Age of Revolution, 1776–1823* (Ithaca, 1975); Christopher Brown, *Moral Capital: The Foundations of British Abolitionism* (Chapel Hill, 2006).
45. Laurent Dubois, 'An Enslaved Enlightenment: Rethinking the Intellectual History of the French Atlantic', *Social History* 21/1 (2006): 1–14; Pamela Scully, 'Race and Ethnicity in Women's and Gender History', in Smith, *Women's History,* vol. 1, 195–228, 196; Roxann Wheeler, *The Complexion of Race: Categories of Difference in Eighteenth-Century British Culture* (Philadelphia, 2000), 288–302.
46. Fick, 'French Revolution'.
47. David Patrick Geggus, 'Slavery, War and Revolution in the Greater Caribbean', in Gaspar, *A Turbulent Time,* 1–50, 22.
48. Ibid. 23; Geggus, 'Arming Slaves in the Haitian Revolution', in *Arming Slaves: From Classical Times to the Modern Age,* ed. Christopher Leslie Brown and Philip D. Morgan (New Haven, 2006), 209–232; see also Roger N. Buckley, *The British Army in the West Indies: Society and the Military in the Revolutionary Age* (Gainesville, FL, 1998).
49. Langley, *The Americas,* 122.
50. Laurent Dubois, 'Citizen Soldiers: Emancipation and Military Service in the Revolutionary French Caribbean', in Brown, *Arming Slaves,* 233–254.

51. See Bush, *Slave Women*, 83–150; Bridget Brereton, 'Family Strategies, Gender, and the Shift to Wage Labor in the British Caribbean', in Scully, *Gender and Slave Emancipation*, 143–161; Maria Eugenia Chaves, 'Slave Women's Strategies for Freedom and the Late Spanish Colonial State', in *Hidden Histories of Gender and the State in Latin America*, ed. Elizabeth Dore and Maxine Molyneux (Durham, NC, 2000), 108–126.
52. Klein, *Atlantic Slave Trade*, 183–206.
53. John Shy, 'Looking Backward, Looking Forward: War and Society in Revolutionary America', in Resch, *War and Society*, 3–19, 14.
54. Jeremy Black, *War for America: The Fight for Independence, 1775–1783* (1991; new edn, New York, 2001).
55. Ibid. 28–29.
56. Sylvia R. Frey, *Water from the Rock: Black Resistance in a Revolutionary Age* (Princeton, 1991), 211; also Jim Piecuch, *Three Peoples, One King: Loyalists, Indians, and Slaves in the Revolutionary South, 1775–1782* (Columbia, 2008).
57. Geoffrey Best, *War and Society in Revolutionary Europe, 1770–1870* (London, 1982), 54.
58. Alan Forrest, *Conscripts and Deserters: The Army and French Society during the Revolution and Empire* (New York, 1989), 20; Alain Pigeard, *La conscription au temps de Napoléon* (Paris, 2003).
59. Stuart Woolf, *Napoleon's Integration of Europe* (New York, 1991), 172–175; Geoffrey Ellis, *The Napoleonic Empire* (Basingstoke, 2003), 61–63.
60. Frederick C. Schneid (ed.), *Warfare in Europe, 1792–1815* (Aldershot, 2007); Daniel Moran and Arthur Waldron (eds), *The People in Arms: Military Myth and National Mobilization since the French Revolution* (Cambridge, UK, 2003), 8–74.
61. Hagemann, 'Mannlicher Muth', 36–37.
62. Alexander Martin, 'The Russian Empire and the Napoleonic Wars', in *Napoleon and Europe*, ed. Philip G. Dwyer (London, 2001), 243–263, 258; John Cookson, *The British Armed Nation, 1793–1815* (Oxford, 1997).
63. Hagemann, 'Mannlicher Muth', 75–91.
64. Idem, 'Unimaginable Horror'.
65. Langley, *The Americas*, 173.
66. John C. Chasteen, *Americanos: Latin America's Struggle for Independence* (Oxford, 2008), 68; Langley, *The Americas*, 180–183.
67. Robert L. Scheina, *Latin America's Wars, Vol. 1: The Age of the Caudillo, 1791–1899* (Dulles, VA, 2004), 62.
68. See for example, Lynn A. Hunt, *Politics, Culture, and Class in the French Revolution* (Berkeley, 1986); Hagemann, 'Mannlicher Muth', 396–426; Janet Hartley, 'The Patriotism of the Russian Army in the "Patriotic" or "Fatherland" War of 1812', in Esdaile, *Popular Resistance*, 181–200; Emma Vincent Macleod, *A War of Ideas: British Attitudes to the Wars against Revolutionary France, 1792–1802* (Brookfield, 1998); Jack N. Rakove, *Original Meanings: Politics and Ideas in the Making of the Constitution* (New York, 1996).
69. See Stefan Dudink and Karen Hagemann, 'Masculinities in Politics and War in the Age of Democratic Revolutions, 1750–1850', in Dudink, *Masculinities*, 3–21.
70. Ibid.
71. Dubois, 'Citizen Soldiers'.
72. Peter Blanchard, *Under the Flags of Freedom: Slave Soldiers and the Wars of Independence in Spanish South America* (Pittsburgh, 2008).

73. Karen Hagemann, 'Of "Manly Valor" and "German Honor": Nation, War and Masculinity in the Age of the Prussian Uprising against Napoleon', *Central European History* 30/2 (1997): 187–220.
74. Colley, *Britons*, 265 and 303.
75. Sonya O. Rose, 'Fit to Fight but Not to Vote? Masculinity and Citizenship in Britain, 1832–1918', in *Representing Masculinity: Citizenship in Modern Western Culture*, ed. Stefan Dudink et al. (Basingstoke, 2007), 131–150.
76. Clive Emsley, *British Society and the French Wars, 1793–1815* (Totowa, NJ, 1979); Woolf, *Napoleon's Integration*, 156–164; Resch, *War and Society*; Forrest, *Soldiers*.
77. See François Crouzet and Eric Aerts (eds), *Economic Effects of the French Revolutionary and Napoleonic Wars* (Louvain, 1990); Woolf, *Napoleon's Integration*, 133–184; Michael Broers, *Europe under Napoleon* (London, 1996), 144–233.
78. Ibid. 247; Shy, 'Looking Backward', 6; idem, *A People Numerous and Armed: Reflections on the Military Struggle for American Independence* (Michigan, 1991), 249–250. For Napoleonic Europe, Hagemann, 'Unimaginable Horror'.
79. Martin, 'Russian Empire', 260.
80. Gates, *Napoleonic Wars*, 272.
81. Shy, 'Looking Backward', 6–7.
82. Hagemann, 'Unimaginable Horror', 170.
83. Britain began to provide for military families relatively early; see Patricia Y.C.E. Lin, 'Caring for the Nation's Families: British Soldiers' and Sailors' Families and the State, 1792–1815', in Forrest, *Soldiers*, 99–111.
84. See Harriet B. Applewhite and Darline G. Levy, 'Women and Militant Citizenship in Revolutionary Paris', in Sara E. Melzer and Leslie W. Kabine (eds), *Rebel Daughters: Women and the French Revolution* (New York, 1992), 79–101.
85. Emma Vincent Macleod, 'Women at War: British Women and the Debate on the Wars against Revolutionary France in the 1790s', *Enlightenment and Dissent* 15 (1996): 3–32; Godineau, *Women*, 295–346; Colley, *Britons*, 237–282; Karen Hagemann, 'Female Patriots: Women, War and the Nation in the Period of the Prussian-German Anti-Napoleonic Wars', *Gender & History* 16/3 (2004): 396–424; Mary Beth Norton, *Liberty's Daughters: The Revolutionary Experiences of American Women, 1750–1800* (1980; new edn, Ithaca, 1996).
86. Rachel Fuchs, *Contested Paternity: Constructing Families in Modern France* (Baltimore, 2008), 16–58. For the impact of the Civil Code in German states, see Isabel Hull, *Sexuality, State, and Civil Society in Germany, 1700–1815* (Ithaca, 1996), 333–408.
87. Lynn A. Hunt, *The Family Romance of the French Revolution* (London, 1992), 161.
88. Lynn, *Women*, 66–117.
89. See also Mayer, *Belonging*.
90. Karen Hagemann, 'Militär, Krieg und Geschlechterverhältnisse: Untersuchungen, Überlegungen und Fragen zur Militärgeschichte der Frühen Neuzeit', in *Klio in Uniform: Probleme und Perspektiven einer modernen Militärgeschichte der Frühen Neuzeit*, ed. Ralf Pröve (Cologne, 1997), 35–88, 66–77.
91. David Hopkin, 'The World Turned Upside Down: Female Soldiers in the French Armies of the Revolutionary and Napoleonic Wars', in Forrest, *Soldiers*, 77–98.
92. See ibid.; Karen Hagemann, '"Heroic Virgins" and "Bellicose Amazons": Armed Women, the Gender Order, and the German Public during and after the Anti-Napoleonic Wars', *European History Quarterly* 37/4 (2007): 507–527; Rudolf Dekker and Lotte C. Van der Pol, 'Republican Heroines: Cross-Dressing Women in the French Revolution Armies', *History of European Ideas*, 10/3 (1989): 353–363.

93. Dugaw, *Warrior Women*; Wheelwright, *Amazons*.
94. See 'Introduction' and Margaret R. and Patrice L.R. Higonnet, 'The Double Helix', in *Behind the Lines: Gender and the Two World Wars*, ed. Margaret R. Higonnet et al. (New Haven, 1987), 1–18 and 31–50, 4.
95. On concepts of patriotism see Otto Dann et al. (eds), *Patriotismus und Nationsbildung am Ende des Heiligen Römischen Reiches* (Cologne, 2003).
96. Sinha, 'Gender and Nation', 234–235; Anna Clark, 'The Rhetoric of Masculine Citizenship: Concepts and Representations in Modern Western Culture', in Dudink, *Representing Masculinity*, 3–24.
97. Kathleen Canning and Sonya O. Rose (eds), *Gender, Citizenships and Subjectivities* (Oxford, 2002).
98. Dudink, 'Masculinity'; Clark, 'Rhetoric'.
99. For the French Revolution, see Raymonde Monnier, *Républicanisme, patriotisme et Révolution française* (Paris, 2005).
100. Knouff, 'White Men in Arms: Concepts of Citizenship and Masculinity in Revolutionary America', in Dudink, *Representing*, 25–44; idem, *Soldiers*.
101. Dubois, 'Citizen Soldiers'.
102. Chambers, *From Subjects to Citizens*, 189–242; also Brown, *Adventuring*, 133–155.
103. Rosemarie Zagarri, *Revolutionary Backlash: Women and Politics in the Early American Republic* (Philadelphia, 2007), 58–68.
104. Linda K. Kerber, 'A Constitutional Right to Be Treated like American Ladies: Women and the Obligations of Citizenship', in *U.S. History as Women's History: New Feminist Essays*, ed. Linda Kerber et al. (Chapel Hill, 1995), 17–35; Kate Haulman, 'Fashion and the Culture Wars of Revolutionary Philadelphia', *William and Mary Quarterly* 52/4 (2005): 642–661.
105. Hunt, *Family Romance*; Jennifer Heuer, *The Family and the Nation: Gender and Citizenship in Revolutionary France, 1789–1830* (Ithaca, 2005); Rebecca Earle, 'Rape and the Anxious Republic: Revolutionary Colombia, 1810–1830', in Dore, *Hidden Histories*, 127–146.
106. J. David Harden, 'Liberty Caps and Liberty Trees', *Past and Present* 146 (1995): 66–102, 75.
107. Hunt, *Politics*, 1–86; Mona Ozouf, *La Fête révolutionnaire, 1789–1799* (Paris, 1989); Simon P. Newman, *Parades and the Politics of the Street: Festive Culture in the Early American Republic* (Urbana, 1999), 1–43.
108. Rebecca Earle, 'The French Revolutionary Wars in the Spanish American Imagination, 1789–1830', in *War, Empire and Slavery, 1770–1830*, ed. Richard Bessel et al. (Basingstoke, 2010).
109. Colley, *Britons*, 263.
110. Karen Hagemann, ' "A Valorous *Volk* Family": The Nation, the Military, and the Gender Order in Prussia in the Time of the Anti-Napoleonic Wars, 1806–15', in Blom, *Gendered Nations*, 179–205; Colley, *Britons*, 237–282.
111. On the feminist debate around this concept, see Joan Landes (ed.), *Women and the Public Sphere in the Age of the French Revolution* (Ithaca, 1988); Jane Rendall, 'Women and the Public Sphere', *Gender & History* 11/3 (1999): 475–488.
112. Godineau, *Women*, 97–196.
113. For example, Colley, *Britons*, 237–283; Hagemann, 'Female Patriots'; Berkin, *Revolutionary Mothers*, 12–25.
114. For example, Silvia Marina Arrom, *The Women of Mexico City, 1790–1857* (Stanford, 1985), 14–52; Erika Pani, ' "Ciudadana y muy ciudadana"? Women and the State in Independent Mexico, 1810–30', *Gender & History* 18/1 (2006): 5–19; Davies, *South American Independence*, 131–158.

115. Carla Hesse, *The Other Enlightenment: How French Women Became Modern* (Princeton, 2001), 30–78.
116. Bell, *First Total War*, 52–83.
117. Martin Ceadel, *The Origins of War Prevention: The British Peace Movement and International Relations, 1730–1854* (Oxford, 1996); W.H. van der Linden, *The International Peace Movement, 1815–1874* (Amsterdam, 1987).
118. Wenk, 'Gendered Representations'; Landes, *Visualizing*.
119. Alan Forrest et al., 'Nation in Arms–People at War', in Forrest, *Soldiers*, 1–23, 6–12.
120. On the state of research on gender and memory, see Meike Penkwitz, 'Erinnern und Geschlecht', vol. 1, *Freiburger FrauenStudien* 19 (2006): 1–25; idem and Jennifer Moos, 'Erinnern und Geschlecht,' vol. 2, *Freiburger FrauenStudien* 20 (2007): 1–24; Sylvia Paletschek and Sylvia Schraut (eds), *The Gender of Memory: Cultures of Remembrance in Nineteenth- and Twentieth-Century Europe* (Frankfurt/M., 2008), 7–30.
121. Aleida Assmann, 'Geschlecht und kulturelles Gedächtnis', vol 1, *Freiburger FrauenStudien* 19 (2006): 29–46.
122. For instance, Karen Hagemann, 'Reconstructing "Front" and "Home": Gendered Experiences and Memories of the German Wars against Napoleon–A Case Study', *War in History* 16/1 (2009): 25–50.
123. Jan Assmann, 'Collective Memory and Cultural Identity', *New German Critique* 65 (1995): 125–133.
124. See also Hagemann, 'German Heroes'; Karin Breuer, 'Competing Masculinities: Fraternities, Gender and Nationality in the German Confederation, 1815–30', *Gender & History* 20/2 (2008): 270–287.
125. Hagemann, 'Female Patriots'.

Part I
Empire, Colonial War and Slavery

1
Revolution, War, Empire: Gendering the Transatlantic Slave Trade, 1776–1830

David Eltis

The long half century between the American Revolution and the overthrow of the Restoration monarchy in France in 1830 saw the peak of the transatlantic slave trade (as well as the onset of its abolition), the emergence of the first independent nations of the Americas, a dramatic shift in the distribution and degree of specialization in plantation production in the Americas, and 30 years of maritime conflict in the North Atlantic. The same period saw the largely unrecognized feminization of the slave-labour forces of the major European powers. The connections between all these phenomena and the ways in which contemporary military and political events shaped the development of slavery and the transatlantic slave trade have yet to be fully examined. Many historians have nevertheless accorded revolution a central role in determining the great shifts in the Atlantic slave systems.[1] In this chapter I argue, by contrast, that both abolition and changes in constructions of gender evolved gradually in the centuries preceding the Age of Revolution, and that political and military conflict tended to slow down rather than accelerate that evolution.

Understanding the transatlantic slave trade

My argument has implications far beyond slavery and the slave trade. Before discussing these implications, however, we must establish an accurate overview of the slave trade during this tumultuous era and then contextualize the patterns that emerge from that overview within the *longue durée* of human history. The empirical basis of my argument is an online database that contains records of 35,000 slave voyages made between 1514 and 1866. Forty years in the making, this database is now available on an open-access website.[2] The transatlantic slave trade, which conveyed more than ten million Africans to the Americas, represents the most extensive coerced migration in history both in terms of numbers and geographical distance. It also formed the major demographic wellspring for the repopulation of the Americas following the collapse of the Amerindian population. By 1820, for every European who had come to the Americas nearly four Africans had been brought there aboard a slave ship, and women constituted a much larger percentage of the African transplants than of the European immigrants—36 per cent female among the former and about 20 per cent female among the latter. In other words, of the approximately five million women who crossed the Atlantic before 1820, slightly more than four out of five came from Africa.[3] From the late fifteenth century the Atlantic Ocean, until then a formidable barrier that had prevented regular interaction between the inhabitants of the four continents it touched, became a commercial highway that integrated the histories of Africa, Europe and the Americas. As the figures cited above suggest, slavery and the slave trade were the linchpins of this process. With the decline of the Amerindian population, labour from Africa formed the basis of the exploitation of the gold and agricultural resources of the export sectors of the Americas, with sugar plantations absorbing well over two thirds of all slaves transported across the Atlantic by the major European and Euro-American powers. For several centuries slaves were the most important reason for contact between Europeans and Africans, and even after the suppression of the slave trade, it took several decades in most coastal regions of Africa for the value of commodity trade to match and surpass the peak values of the slave trade.

The transatlantic slave trade thus developed in response to a strong demand for labour in the Americas driven initially by European consumers of plantation produce and precious metals. Because Amerindians died in large numbers as a result of exposure to new pathogens carried by Europeans, and because too few Europeans were willing to cross the Atlantic, the form that this demand took was shaped by conceptions of social identity on four continents, which ensured that the labour force would comprise mainly slaves from Africa. But the critical questions of which Africans were transported to a given region of the Americas, which group of Europeans or their descendants organized such a mass relocation, and how that system came to an end cannot be answered without an understanding of the wind and ocean currents of the North and South Atlantic oceans.

Map 1 shows two systems of wind and ocean currents, or gyres, in the Atlantic that resemble giant wheels—one lies north of the equator and turns clockwise, while its southern counterpart turns counter clockwise.[4] The northern gyre largely determined the north European slave trade and was dominated by the English. The southern wheel influenced the huge traffic to Brazil, which for three centuries was the almost exclusive preserve of Europe's largest slave trader, the Portuguese.[5] Despite their use of the Portuguese flag, slave traders who followed the southern gyre ran their businesses from ports in Brazil, not in Portugal. The North and South Atlantic gyres thus enabled two separate slave trades, one supplying the English and Spanish colonies in North America, the other supplying the Portuguese plantations in Brazil. They

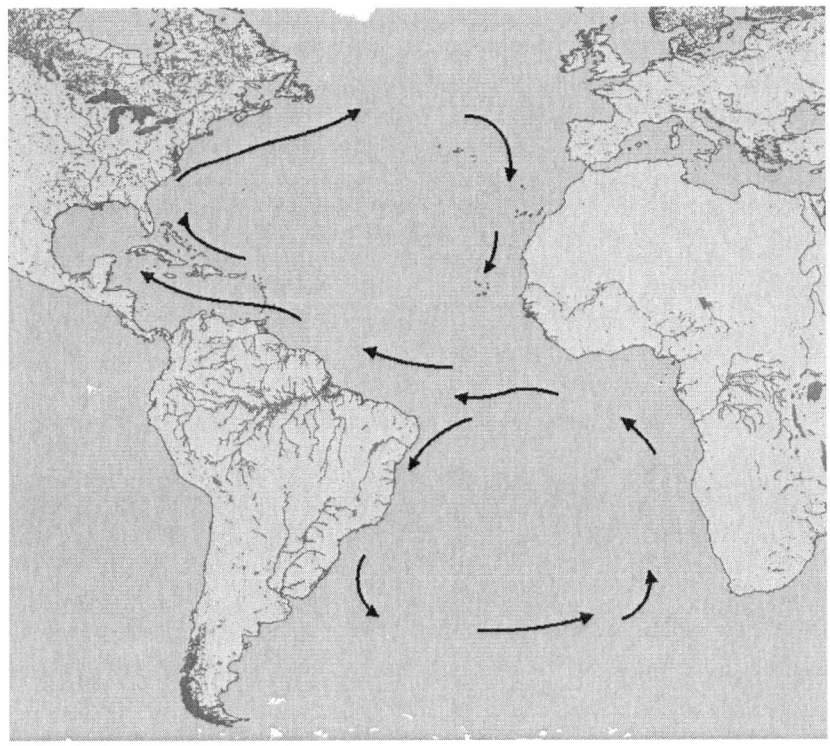

Map 1 Ocean Currents in the Atlantic
Source: Don Larson, Mapping Specialists, Madison, Wisconsin.

ensured that Africans carried to Brazil came overwhelmingly from Angola, with south-east Africa and the Bight of Benin playing smaller roles. They also ensured that Africans carried to North America, including the Caribbean, left from mainly West Africa with the Bights of Biafra and Benin and the Gold Coast predominating. Just as Brazil overlapped on the northern system by drawing on the Bight of Benin, the English, French and Dutch carried some slaves from northern Angola into the Caribbean. But the essential separateness of the two is best illustrated by the fact that when the chief slave traders from the pre-1650 northern system—the Dutch—forcibly entered the southern system through conquest of Pernambuco, they immediately shifted their slaving operations from a triangular trade based in the Netherlands to a bilateral trade rooted in Brazil. Three-quarters of Dutch slavers carrying slaves to Pernambuco began their voyages in Brazil, not the Netherlands. The only southern branch of the Atlantic slave trade in which northern nations participated significantly after 1650 was in the rather marginal Rio de la Plata area.[6] By 1775 only south-east Africa had not yet been fully integrated into one route or the other and was still supplying slaves to both North and South America.

The first African slaves in the New World arrived at the beginning of the sixteenth century and came not from Africa but from Europe. There were few vessels that carried only slaves on this route, so that most would have crossed the Atlantic in smaller groups on vessels carrying many other commodities. Such a trade was possible because an extensive traffic in African slaves from Africa to Europe and the Atlantic islands had existed for half a century before Columbian contact. Ten per cent of the sixteenth-century population of Lisbon was black,[7] and black slaves were common on large estates in the Portuguese Algarve. The first slave voyage direct from Africa to the Americas probably sailed in 1525.[8] Before mid-century, all transatlantic slave ships sold their slaves in the Spanish Caribbean, with the gold mines in Cibao on Hispaniola emerging as a major market. Cartagena, in modern Columbia, appears as the first mainland Spanish-American destination for a slave vessel—in the year 1549.[9] On the African side, the great majority of people entering the early slave trade came from the Upper Guinea coast. Nevertheless, the 1525 voyage set out from the other major Portuguese factory in West Africa—Sao Tome in the Bight of Biafra—though the slaves almost certainly originated in the Congo.

The slave traffic to Brazil, eventually accounting for about 44 per cent of the trade, commenced around 1560 as African slave labour gradually replaced the Amerindian labour force over the period from 1560 to 1620. By the time the Dutch invaded Brazil in 1630, Pernambuco, Bahia and Rio de Janeiro were supplying almost all of the sugar consumed in Europe, and almost all the slaves producing it were African. Thus the two major circuits of the transatlantic slave trade were in operation by 1600; together they accounted for fewer than 7,500 Africans a year carried off from the whole of sub-Saharan Africa, most of them by 1620, from West Central Africa. As sugar consumption steadily increased in Europe, the slave system began two centuries of westward expansion across tropical and subtropical North America. At the end of the seventeenth century the discovery of gold, first in Minas Gerais and later in Goias and other parts of Brazil, triggered further expansion of the slave trade. In Africa the Bights of Benin and Biafra became major sources of supply, in addition to Angola, and were joined later by the more marginal regional sources of Sierra Leone, the Windward Coast and south-east Africa. The volume of Africans carried off reached 30,000 per annum in the 1690s and 85,000 by the end of the eighteenth century. More than eight out of ten Africans pulled into the traffic in the era of the slave trade left their continent in the century and a half after 1700.[10]

Abolition, gender and the slave trade

This introductory narrative and preliminary analysis, derived from recently developed estimates of the slave trade, pose interesting questions for the apotheosis of the slave trade as well as moves to end it. The latest estimate of the overall volume of the slave trade suggests that twelve and a half million captives were transported from Africa between 1501 and 1867.[11] Over one third of this grand total left Africa in the 55 years from 1776 to 1830—or close to 80,000 Africans a year. These years include three of the four highest-volume decades in the history of the trade (the 1780s, 1790s and 1820s), and the fourth occurred immediately *after* 1830. Yet the second half of this 55-year period saw not only the abolition of the US and British slave trades but also numerous treaties designed to end the Portuguese and Spanish trades. The Atlantic slave trade did not die a natural economic death, and it did not gradually lose out to other forms of transatlantic migration. The volume of slaves was at its height (or close to it) when, in 1807, both Britain and the United States passed legislation banning the traffic. Moreover, prices for slaves in both Africa and the Americas were not only at historic highs but also continued to rise, in the Americas, at least, as long as slavery existed.[12] It is thus scarcely surprising that the slave trade persisted even after 1807. Three million Africans were carried off after 1807.[13] Thus, one in four of all those transported from Africa to the Americas arrived after the best-known of the abolition acts became law, although very few of these disembarked in ports belonging to either the United States or Britain. The traffic in slaves was, after all, the most international of business activities, and the US and British acts against it extended only to the citizens and territories of those two nations. In one sense, abolition simply meant that traders of some other nationality took over the traffic and directed it to another part of the Americas.

Nevertheless, a view that reckons with centuries, as opposed to decades, does point to the significance of 1807. First, one should see both the peak and the earliest moves against the slave trade as part of a larger shift in the patterns of transatlantic migration. The shift was discernible not just in migration 'regimes'—the terms under which migrants travelled—but also in the origins of migrant groups and their gender composition. This changing pattern suggests a second, and counterfactual, question about what the consequences of taking no action against the slave trade might have been.

On the first point, a comparison of the slave trade with all other forms of transatlantic migration demonstrates the centrality of coercion to the re-peopling of the Americas. From 1700 until 1820, Africans always outnumbered Europeans on transatlantic vessels by a ratio that now appears to have been four to one. And, as mentioned above, 80 per cent of women crossing the Atlantic before 1820 were from Africa, not Europe. As the overall slave traffic was suppressed, migration from Asia and Europe expanded, with the former going mainly to plantations in the subtropical areas of the Americas as contract labourers and the latter to the temperate Americas as free migrants. Thus contract labourers from Asia and migrants from Europe were in some sense a substitute for the more economically attractive and no longer available African slaves.

Abolition had implications not just for the development of the slave trade but also for the gender composition of labour forces in the Americas. It would be difficult to argue that the status of women in the Atlantic world had significantly improved between 1776 and 1830. Yet this period saw a dramatic shift in the ratio of male to female in the million-strong slave population of the Caribbean. In addition, the slave trade generated, among other great clashes of values, a titanic interaction between African and European constructions of gender. On the African coast, Europeans bought slaves and Africans sold them. While European slave traders sailed to the African littoral in search of men, they frequently brought more women to the Americas as slaves.[14] The result was that Europeans brought more females to the Americas and Africans sold more males into the transatlantic trade than either buyers or sellers would have preferred. A second result was that Europeans in the plantation Americas accommodated themselves to the gender realities of the slave trade. Where Europeans had been reluctant to use European women in field gangs or other forms of intensive agricultural labour, from early in the plantation era they accepted the idea of African women working in the fields. Yet the accommodation was limited. The first gang and most of the second gang on sugar estates comprised males on all plantations prior to the abolition of the slave trade. Planters also reserved for males all the non-domestic skilled occupations in which enslaved blacks were trained. Female skills were always in the domestic sphere.

The gradual ending of the transatlantic slave trade after 1807 forced a change in this pattern. Male slaves had a lower life expectancy than female slaves, and without constant replenishment from Africa the labour forces in the British and Dutch (and, to a lesser extent, French) Americas altered radically in terms of gender composition during the first third of the nineteenth century. First gangs (as the elite part of the plantation labour force was always known), which had once been composed entirely of male slaves, became for the first time predominantly female—a development, it should be noted, that was associated with expanding rather than declining sugar production. There were still no black female carpenters, coopers or blacksmiths in the Caribbean, though black women did effectively take over the retail sector of the Jamaican economy through their ubiquitous huckstering activities.[15] Nevertheless, in a real sense plantation-owners were forced to become the first equal-opportunity employers in the Western world, if we ignore for a moment the racial basis of slavery itself. In one of the strangest ironies of the revolutionary age, this pattern did not survive. When not just the slave trade but slavery itself was finally abolished, beginning with the Haitian Revolution, and then British abolition in 1833, former slaves sought wherever possible to leave the plantations on which they had been exploited. But in a pattern repeated time and again across the slave Americas over the next half century, former female slaves attempted not just to withdraw from plantation work but also to withdraw altogether from the labour market into the domestic sphere (now including smallholding and huckstering), while former male slaves entered the wage-labour market. Polygamy and extended households, common in Africa, largely disappeared, and companionate marriage emerged as the norm in post-emancipation societies. European constructions of gender remained essentially the same, while traditional African notions of gender roles among the millions transported to the Americas were transformed by their experience of slavery. A new construction of gender emerged in this African-American population, one that incorporated both African and European antecedents but which had no contemporary parallel in either Africa or Europe.

The greatest impact of the abolition of the slave trade, however, was probably the restructuring of transatlantic migration in the nineteenth century, as can be seen if we imagine what might have occurred had the traffic remained legal. Without abolition, Britain and especially the United States would have most likely have become even more dominant players in the international slave trade than they were already.[16] A continuing slave trade would have enabled Britain to develop the territories it had acquired in the Napoleonic Wars, such as Trinidad and British Guiana. Open access to African slave markets would have reduced slave prices in the Americas and ensured that voluntary migrants to the Americas went chiefly to regions where there were few plantations. There would have been, as a consequence, somewhat lower levels of unforced transatlantic migration in the nineteenth century and, of course, fewer migrants from Europe. But abolition of the slave trade clearly had an effect not just on voluntary migration but on other forms of coerced migration as well. While not comparable in size to the transatlantic slave trade, these coerced migrations seem to have been chronologically linked with it, since they all began and ended within a century of the start and finish of the slave trade. By the third decade of the twentieth century, not only had the Indian Ocean traffic been brought to an end but also the flow of indentured servants, contract labourers and convicts into the Americas had ceased. As with the slave trade, these migrant streams did not dry up in response to a declining demand for labour. Although still economically viable, all forms of coerced migration were suppressed or suspended because values had shifted sufficiently for these activities to be seen as morally reprehensible for the first time. In terms of its permanent consequences, abolition legislation probably ranks with the eradication of feudal practices, the establishment of the Code Napoleon and the halting steps taken towards representative government as one of the era's major achievements.

The survival of the slave trade

The connection between the final disappearance of feudalism, the adoption of the Code Napoleon, and reformed representative government on the one hand and the Wars of Revolution and Liberation on the other seems self-evident. But what of the supposedly causative links between the abolition of slavery and the slave trade and the cataclysmic events of the era from 1776 to 1830? Revolutions—from the American in 1776 (which laid the groundwork for the US Act of 1807) to the fall of the Bourbon monarchy in 1830 (which triggered the effective suppression of the French slave trade)—were ostensibly bad for the slave-trading business. First the French and then the Haitian Revolution made legislation against the slave trade unnecessary by abolishing slavery itself. Most of the new republics in Latin America followed suit. Yet that the United States normally accounted for less than 3 per cent of the total traffic,[17] and the fact that the French suppressed their slave trade 36 years *after* the first abolition of slavery in France in 1794, underscores Napoleon's decision to reinstate the institution in 1801. The 1794 decision had no permanent practical impact on the slave trade, and while the destruction of the richest slave colony in the world—Saint-Domingue—and the emancipation of its 400,000 slaves did, that impact was temporary. Plantations in the British Caribbean and later in Cuba and Brazil quickly filled the gap by producing more sugar, and expansion of sugar output inevitably meant expansion of the slave trade. As for the Latin American states that abolished slavery, not one had a significant plantation sector. Those that did, Cuba and Puerto Rico, eschewed both independence and abolition. Those that did not bring to mind Adam Smith's famous dictum that the decision of the Quakers in Philadelphia in 1774 to eschew slavery should be recognized as an indication of how small their investment in the system was. Most important of all, neither of the major players in the transatlantic traffic—the British in the north and the Portuguese in the south—had policies shaped by revolution; nor was their withdrawal from the slave trade directly affected by the practices of those countries that did experience revolution.

War was as bad for the slave-trading business as revolution. Over the course of the eighteenth century, the volume of slaves fell by one third to one half between 1744 and 1748, 1756 and 1763, 1776 and 1783, and on several occasions between 1793 and 1815.[18] English naval power easily suppressed the French and Dutch slave trades during most periods of war, as it did for the 22 years between 1792 and 1814, except for the 13-month Peace of Amiens from March 1802 to April 1803, when over 50 French slave vessels once more ventured into the Atlantic and Indian oceans. Yet British slave ships were also captured in large numbers, and war always increased the cost of trade (thus reducing its volume) even in the absence of capture. No fewer than 666 slave vessels were captured in the 29 years of hostilities from 1776 to 1783, from 1793 to 1800, and from 1803 to 1815—or an average of 23 vessels per year. Privateers roamed the seas, and when abolitionist-inspired policies emerged in the early nineteenth century, a right of search was much easier to enforce in an environment of war. Because of their naval supremacy, the British were in effect able to impose their policy of suppressing the slave trade on a large part of the Atlantic world between 1808 and 1815. In these years, the British captured nearly twice as many foreign slave ships (153) in just 8 years as they had during the preceding 32 years. Eventually the British were obliged to pay compensation for many of the

83 Portuguese vessels they captured between 1808 and 1815. In the North Atlantic system, the chances of a slave ship failing to deliver slaves for the original owner went from a normal peacetime rate of one in twenty five to one in six during war. French slave merchants simply reallocated their capital to some other activity and sent out almost no slave ventures until peace was restored. Large plantation areas, such as Martinique and Suriname, and the southern United States were cut off from Africa for years at a time, and others had to make do with greatly reduced supplies of coerced labour. The largest of all, Saint-Domingue, received no slaves at all after 1793. War was always bad for long-distance commerce, but the extent of naval interference with the transatlantic slave trade was considerably greater in these years than it had been in any earlier generalized conflict.

But was the slave trade really under threat? The recovery of the slave trade after 1815 followed a familiar pattern. The decades following the Treaty of Utrecht (1713), the Peace of Paris (1763) and the Treaty of Versailles (1783) saw similar strong recoveries. A series of expensive damage settlements arising from wrongful detentions of Spanish, Portuguese and French slave ships between 1815 and 1818 compelled the British navy to recognize that they could not continue to suppress the slave trades of other countries without the sanction of a treaty. And as we have seen, during the nineteenth century the plantation sectors in Brazil, Cuba and the United States expanded to more than replace sugar output in those regions that no longer had access to slave labour from Africa (or, as in the case of the United States, a slave population experiencing strong natural rates of growth). More important is the fact that war had a much stronger impact on the Atlantic world north of the equator than it had in the southern hemisphere. The Portuguese-dominated South Atlantic system continued to operate with little disruption between 1776 and 1783 and, again, between 1793 and 1815. Indeed, after 1793 the southern system expanded strongly, and from this point to the complete shut-down of the trade in 1867 the transatlantic slave trade's centre of gravity drifted steadily southward, returning to its former location in the mid-seventeenth century, before northern Europeans established colonies in the Caribbean and began importing large numbers of slaves from West Africa.[19] Despite the very different nature of warfare in the aftermath of the French Revolution, the impact of these transatlantic wars for the slave trade was apparently comparable to that of earlier wars—in other words, temporary.

Given that much of the conflict during this period resulted in attenuation of the European imperial structures that had developed since Columbian contact, it is hard to see the end of empires as having greater implications for abolition than had war and revolution. Scholars ranging from neoclassical economists to world-systems theorists have associated the rise of European colonial empires with the rise of coerced labour and migration. But the dismantling of imperial structures between 1776 and 1830 was far from inimical to coerced labour. Newly independent states embraced chattel slavery wherever it proved vital to sustaining exports. The one exception was Haiti, but here, too, the new black governments initially attempted to prevent ex-slaves from leaving the sugar estates. David Brion Davis has recently made an eloquent case for the influence of the Saint-Domingue revolution and Haiti on all nineteenth-century anti-slave-trade and anti-slavery legislation.[20] Yet, as already noted, the British Caribbean and Brazil almost instantly filled the gap that the revolution made in the productive capacity of the plantation Americas. Politically, too, the emergence of Haiti had little impact on anti-slave-trade measures even though the Haitian navy captured several slave ships in the Caribbean in the nineteenth century. Revolution in Europe meant that domestic, or at least European issues, took precedence over colonial matters. The attention of the Constituent Assembly was first caught by the demands of Saint-Domingue's free coloureds for equal rights, and thereafter French and, to a lesser extent, British policy was reactive. France abolished slavery in order to mobilize the slave populations against British invasions and restored slavery when that threat retreated. It might even be argued that British and US abolition of the slave trade was a reform that could be implemented with the least risk to the economic system of slavery and was therefore profoundly conservative.

If we look at the whole of the Atlantic world during the second half of the eighteenth century, it is possible to discern six imperial systems sustained by a slave trade that each system tried to carry on under its own flag. The English, French, Portuguese, Spanish, Dutch and Danish all operated behind major trade barriers and produced a range of plantation commodities—sugar, rice, indigo, coffee, tobacco, alcohol and some precious metals, with sugar usually being the most valuable. It is hardly surprising that Brazil and the British Americas received the most Africans, although, as noted above, both nations became adept at supplying their competitors as well. Throughout the slave trade era, more than seven out of every ten slaves went to Brazil and the British Americas. The French Americas imported about half as many slaves as the British colonies did, with the majority going to Saint-Domingue. The Spanish trade, dominant in the earliest phase before retreating in the face of competition from the north, began to expand again in the late nineteenth century with the growth of the Cuban sugar economy.

Yet, over the next century—between 1750 and 1850—every one of these empires had either disappeared or become severely truncated. A massive shift to freer trade meant that instead of six plantation empires controlled from Europe, there were now only three plantation complexes, two of which—Brazil and the United States—were independent, and the third, Cuba, was far wealthier and more dynamic than its European metropole. Extreme specialization now saw the United States producing most of the world's cotton, Cuba most of the world's sugar and Brazil with a comparable dominance in coffee. While slaves might have disembarked in six separate jurisdictions in the Americas during the eighteenth century, by 1850 they went overwhelmingly to only two areas, Brazil and Cuba. American cotton planters were no longer dependent on imported slaves, having been able for some time to maintain their labour force through natural population growth and a domestic slave trade. Indeed, overall the United States absorbed only 4 per cent of the slaves arriving in the Americas. The elimination of 80 per cent of formal European control of the American continents (measured in land area at least) had led not to the ending of the slave trade but rather to its reorganization. The ideology and rhetoric of liberty associated with the emergence of new nations between 1776 and 1830 had little immediate impact on the size of the transatlantic traffic.

Abolition, sensibility and identity

It would seem, then, that the first abolition initiatives were not just a side effect of war, popular uprisings and imperial defeat in the Age of Revolution. The movement against the slave trade was a combination of actions by both slaves and abolitionists. Neither impulse seems closely connected to political upheavals in Europe. Indeed, it is necessary to disengage the standard connection that historians make between abolition of the slave trade (and eventually slavery) and the Age of Revolution. To put the point differently, abolition of the slave trade becomes more intelligible only when viewed in a much larger historical context than my focus here on the period from 1776 to 1830 permits. Interpretations of the slave trade and abolition have proceeded through an interesting cycle in the past two centuries. Most early abolitionists felt no tension between humanitarianism and economic interest—Africa would take its place in the world once the ravages of the slave trade were ended and slave owners in the Americas would find paid labour just as profitable as slave. When the cotton and sugar plantations did not do well after slavery itself was abolished and thereafter down to the mid-twentieth century, the abolitionists abandoned the economic component of their anti-slavery argument and presented abolition as a humanitarian and often an evangelical moral triumph. But during the half-century that followed publication of Eric Williams's *Capitalism and Slavery* in 1944, it was the economic-interest strand of the original abolitionist position that became the focus of historical scholarship, though with the Industrial Revolution (and the new entrepreneurs it spawned) at centre stage rather than the financial fortunes of the planters themselves. In the past two decades, however, the links between industrialization and abolition have received much less attention. In part this is due to greater interest in how peoples of African descent participated in abolition and also to the difficulty of either identifying abolition's direct economic beneficiaries or establishing ideological links between abolition and industrialization.

The ending of slavery itself, as opposed to the slave trade, is increasingly viewed as the product of interaction between the enslaved and the abolitionists, though the focus is still very much on the last years of slavery, when reports of large-scale slave revolts, triggered in part by rumours of abolition, were integrated into anti-slavery propaganda.[21] But if a much longer time perspective is adopted, such an approach can also offer insights into how the demise of the slave trade came about. In one sense slave resistance was always effective. One of the basic costs of carrying on the slave trade was coping with the rebellions on board slave ships. Extra crew and weapons had the effect of raising those costs and therefore prices of slaves in the Americas. Higher prices of course meant fewer slaves transported.[22] Thus, even unsuccessful slave rebellions had an impact on the volume and direction of slaves carried across the Atlantic. Slave rebellions affected these key parameters in a second way. Shipboard revolts occurred disproportionately on slave voyages leaving the Upper Guinea coast. This pattern not only helped to inhibit slaving in this region of Africa, which in terms of sailing times was closest to Europe and the Americas but it also forced slaving vessels to avoid the Upper Guinea coast and sail further south in order to reduce the incidence of shipboard rebellions. Longer sailing times meant higher costs, and therefore higher slave prices and fewer captives transported.[23] The distribution in the database of the 563 voyages that underwent slave mutinies over the entire slave-trade era indicates that such mutinies peaked in the third quarter of the eighteenth century.[24] Unlike rebellions of slaves in the plantation of Americas, shipboard slave revolts did not increase in tandem with abolitionist activity. (Most of the major slave rebellions in Brazil and the Caribbean came after the French Revolution.) Rather, they preceded and appear to have been independent of European efforts to suppress the traffic.

For three decades after 1750, slave vessels spent more time in the coastal regions where they had traditionally obtained slaves, which included the Gold Coast, the Bights of Benin and Biafra, and Angola broadly defined.[25] It is not clear what was causing this phenomenon, but it is fairly certain that the shift of the largest slave traders—especially the British into the three Upper Guinea regions of Senegambia, Sierra Leone and the Windward Coast—was a direct response to lengthened trading times at the established sites of embarkation. When the trading time to the traditional sites declined once more after 1775, slavers returned to their previous trading locations. Thus the incidence of revolts in the total slave trade increased as Upper Guinea was pulled into the mainstream of the traffic, and then declined after 1775 as the area returned to its former marginal status as a supplier of slaves. But in the nineteenth century an additional factor reduced the number of shipboard revolts. Between 1800 and 1867 the percentage of children carried on slave ships doubled from 18 to 36 per cent.

This pattern of increasing onboard violence in the second half of the eighteenth century intersected with the emergence of abolitionist sentiments in Europe. It is now possible to see abolition as connected to long-term changes in social sensibilities or what might be termed an awareness of others. As the slave trade approached its peak and as both slave resistance and English newspapers paid more attention to reports of such resistance, three strands of opposition to slavery interacted and eventually coalesced—resistance from within (shipboard slave revolts), narrowing conceptions of eligibility for enslavement and an expanding view of what constitutes cruelty. While the historiographical shift in the European elements of this coalescence began with Thomas Haskell, a recent book by Lynn Hunt deals with the same phenomenon from a different perspective.[26]

In previous publications, I have certainly explored possible links between industrialization and abolition, with a focus on the emergence of free-labour ideology. But I now believe that a more productive approach is to see abolition as a shift in conceptions about who was eligible for enslavement.[27] For Europeans the definition of eligibility had certainly included other Europeans prior to the thirteenth century, as a thriving slave trade within the subcontinent saw people from the North captured and carried for sale in the South, many, ultimately, to the prosperous Islamic areas. By the time of Columbian contact, however, eligibility had come to exclude other Europeans. Africa was home to more diverse populations than could be found in any other area of comparable size on the globe. It is therefore unsurprising that Africans did not have a continent-wide conception of insidership—that is, peoples that could not be enslaved. The massive and unprecedented flow of African slaves across the Atlantic may be the result of the difference in pace between the evolution of a cultural pan-Europeanness on the one hand and a pan-Africanism on the other. An interlude of two or three centuries between the former and the latter provided a window of opportunity in which the slave trade rose and fell dramatically. From the mid-fifteenth century to 1867, Europeans were not prepared to enslave each other but were prepared to buy Africans and keep them and their descendants enslaved. Given that 'Africa' scarcely existed as a concept for Africans in any sense before the nineteenth century, most people living south of the Sahara were prepared to enslave others from their identity comfort zone. Throughout history, even the most energetic of slave traders have had definitions of eligibility—and thus ineligibility. 'Ineligibility' implies that some basis for non-slave status has always existed.[28]

After 1492, the oceans that had always divided peoples and cultures from each other turned into highways almost overnight. Before Columbus, migrations took place over time, moving in waves from the more to the less densely populated parts of the globe. But transoceanic contact was sudden, and prevented any gradual adjustment, in terms of values just as in epidemiological terms. A merging of perceptions of right and wrong, group identities and relations between the sexes, to look only at the top of a very long list of social values that came into conflict, could not be expected to occur quickly in a post-Columbian world. In short, cultural accommodation could not keep pace with transportation technology. The result was first the rise and then, as European constructions of the insider-outsider divide slowly changed, the fall of the transatlantic trade in enslaved Africans.

During the centuries of coerced transatlantic migration European and African conceptions of self and community (and eligibility for enslavement) did not remain static. On the African side, one unintended impact of European contact was to force non-elite Africans to think of themselves as belonging not only to a village or a kinship group but also to broader cultural and political entities. This expanded concept of identity was inextricably linked with race through the slave trade, in which the roles of master and slave were determined solely by skin colour. Initially, this group might be Igbo, or Yoruba, and soon, in addition, blacks as opposed to whites. And on board a slave ship with all the slaves always black, and the crew largely white, skin colour defined ethnicity.

Questioning, indeed, awareness of the insider-outsider divide within Europe coincided with the onset of the struggle to suppress first the slave trade and then slavery itself. It can be traced initially through reports of shipboard violence. In the first half of the eighteenth century, court cases might arise from incidents between crew members but never as a result of conflict between crew and slaves.[29] A half century later, however, captains could become infamous for their involvement in the death of slaves aboard their ships. The *Zong* trial of 1781, triggered by the fact that slaves were thrown to their deaths by Captain Luke Collingwood, and the Captain John Kimber case, involving the torture of a slave girl,[30] were unusual only because they became well known, not because it was the first time that such things had happened. These murders would not have attracted attention in the 1680s or the 1730s. In the next decade, as part of the British campaign to suppress the slave trade, Charles James Fox posed to the House of Commons a question that he described as 'the foundation for the whole business'. How would members of Parliament react, he asked, if 'a Bristol ship were to go to any part of France...and the democrats (there) were to sell the aristocrats, or vice versa, to be carried off to Jamaica...to be sold for slaves?'[31] The very posing of this question—and this is the earliest documented example from someone close to power—meant that the issue was not whether the slave trade was to be questioned but rather when it would end.

The shift in humanitarian sensibility—whether presented in terms of altered market forces (Haskell), awareness of others (Hunt) or changing identities (as argued here)—was well under way by 1775 and led to increased public interest in the growing number of slave rebellions, which became the subject of frequent press reports. A greater sensitization towards violence is apparent among seventeenth-century Europeans despite (or perhaps because of) the fact that Europe was probably one of the most violent regions in the world. It appears in relation to religious conflict and in cases where the accepted rules of war were violated. The London press began to publish reports of slave ship rebellions as early as the 1720s. Prior to this, slave revolts had not been considered newsworthy. By the third quarter of the eighteenth century, however, journalistic accounts of such incidents appeared almost every week. Indeed, the upheavals from 1775 to 1830 may all be viewed as a manifestation of this tectonic shift in values. What we are observing here is the emergence of modern values and conceptions of identity, and the implications of these developments, of course, extend far beyond the success of the campaigns to abolish the slave trade and slavery. Unfortunately, historians' attempts to understand how this change occurred have not kept pace with the change itself. Many still pursue a search for motives stemming from economic self-interest and class. While we have begun to track, we have scarcely begun to explain the transformation in European sensibilities during the eighteenth century.

We can now return to the questions posed in the opening paragraph. Rather than interpreting condemnation of the slave trade as a side effect of the American, French, Latin American (often ignored by Europeanists and Americanists alike) and Saint-Domingue revolutions, we should see these as related phenomena, stemming from the same causes. This is not to minimize the role of the millions of victims of the coercive system that Europeans imposed on the Atlantic in getting rid of those systems. On the contrary, the difference between a rebellion and a revolution anywhere is often just a split in the ruling elite, but neither event could occur without action on the part of ordinary people. By the onset of the long half century often termed the Age of Revolution, the shift in humanitarian sensibilities had progressed to the point where divisions in the political and mercantile elites were much more likely than in any earlier age. It is perhaps odd to end an introduction to a book on the Age of Revolution by concluding that European revolutions exerted only a minor influence on abolition. An oddity becomes a presumption when the author of the assessment is known to be a non-Europeanist. Yet the number of pieces that fall into place as a result just may make such an exercise worthwhile.

Notes

1. See, for example, the widely cited study by Robin Blackburn, *The Overthrow of Colonial Slavery, 1776–1848* (London, 1988).
2. Most of my references for this chapter are to the Trans-Atlantic Slave Trade Database at www.slavevoyages.org, developed by Emory University Libraries, the National Endowment for the Humanities W. E. B. Du Bois Institute, and several other institutional partners accessed in July, 2008. The Voyages section of the website contains details of 35,000 slave voyages, three search interfaces to access this information, as well as estimates of the size and direction of the slave trade. For a breakdown of the information and a summary of findings, see David Eltis and David Richardson, 'Introduction', in *Extending the Frontiers: Essays on the New Transatlantic Slave Trade Database*, ed. David Eltis and David Richardson (New Haven, 2008), 3–62.

3. Estimates of the number of migrants from Europe between 1492 and 1820 are from David Eltis, 'Free and Coerced Migrations from the Old World to the New', in *Coerced and Free Migration: Global Perspectives*, ed. idem (Stanford, 2002), 68–74; for the total number of Africans, see the estimates on the Voyages website. Gender ratios of migrants are discussed in David Eltis and Stanley L. Engerman, 'Was the Slave Trade Dominated by Men?', *Journal of Interdisciplinary History* 23 (1992): 237–257. The detailed calculation of the numbers of African females arriving in the Americas to 1820 may be derived from the voyages website.
4. See Daniel Barros Domingues da Silva, 'The Atlantic Slave Trade to Maranhão, 1680–1846: Volume, Roots and Organization', *Slavery & Abolition* 29/4 (2008): 477–501.
5. The Portuguese delivered slaves through two separate trading networks: one operating from the Iberian Peninsula that supplied the early Spanish Americas and Amazonia, and a second, much larger network based in Brazil that brought slaves directly from Africa to northeast Brazil and Rio de Janeiro. Just under half of all African slaves transported to the Americas between 1519 and 1867 were brought there by either Portuguese or Brazilian merchants. Inspect column totals at http://www.slavevoyages.org/tast/assessment/estimates.faces
6. For the Dutch trade to Pernambuco, see http://www.slavevoyages.org/tast/database/search.faces?yearFrom=1630&yearTo=1650&natinimp=8&mjslptimp=50000. Broad departure regions can be derived from the tables linked to this webpage.
7. A. C. de M. Saunders, *A Social History of Black Slaves and Freedmen in Portugal, 1441–1555* (Cambridge, UK, 1982).
8. See http://www.slavevoyages.org/tast/database/search.faces?yearFrom=1514&yearTo=1866&voyageid=46474. The sources for each record of a voyage in the database are readily available on the website. There are, on average, four of these per voyage.
9. See http://www.slavevoyages.org/tast/database/search.faces?yearFrom=1514&yearTo=1866&voyageid=29647.
10. See http://www.slavevoyages.org/tast/assessment/estimates.faces?yearFrom=1501&yearTo=1866. Click on the Timeline tab, then slide left delimiter below timeline to 1700 and right delimiter to 1850.
11. See column totals at http://www.slavevoyages.org/tast/assessment/estimates.faces?yearFrom=1501&yearTo=1866.
12. Laird Bergard, 'American Slave Markets During the 1850s: Slave Price Rises in the United States, Cuba, and Brazil in Comparative Perspective', in *Slavery in the Development of the Americas*, ed. David Eltis et al. (Cambridge, UK, 2004), 219–235.
13. See http://www.slavevoyages.org/tast/assessment/estimates.faces?yearFrom=1808&yearTo=1866.
14. For a full presentation of this argument, see David Eltis, *Rise of African Slavery in the Americas* (Cambridge, UK, 2000), 85–113.
15. B. W. Higman, *Slave Populations of the British Caribbean* (Baltimore, 1984); Gisela Eisner, *Jamaica, 1830–1930: A Study in Economic Growth* (Manchester, 1961), 3–23.
16. David Eltis, 'Was Abolition of the US and British Slave Trade Significant in the Broader Atlantic Context?' *William and Mary Quarterly* 66 (2009): 717–736
17. See http://slavevoyages.org/tast/assessment/estimates.faces?yearFrom=1501&yearTo=1866.

18. See http://www.slavevoyages.org/tast/assessment/estimates.faces?yearFrom=1501&yearTo=1866 for data on specific years. Note the estimates of slaves carried off in roll-over years underneath the X axis at left.
19. Eltis, 'Was Abolition'.
20. David Brion Davis, *Inhuman Bondage: The Rise and Fall of Slavery in the New World* (New York, 2006), 157–174.
21. Gelien Matthews, *Caribbean Slave Revolts and the British Abolitionist Movement* (Baton Rouge, 2006).
22. Stephen D. Behrendt et al., 'The Costs of Coercion: African Agency in the History of the Atlantic World', *Economic History Review* 54 (2001): 454–476.
23. Ibid.
24. For Upper Guinea, see http://www.slavevoyages.org/tast/database/search.faces?yearFrom=1514&yearTo=1866&mjbyptimp=60100.60200.60300. Click on the Timeline tab and in the drop-down box for the Y axis, at top right, and select Rate of Resistance. For all other regions, see http://www.slavevoyages.org/tast/database/search.faces?yearFrom=1514&yearTo=1866&mjbyptimp=60400.60500.60600.60700.60800.60900.80000. Repeat the previous exercise and compare the results with those for Upper Guinea.
25. David Eltis and David Richardson, 'Productivity in the Transatlantic Slave Trade', *Explorations in Economic History* 32 (1995): 465–484.
26. Thomas L. Haskell, 'Capitalism and the Origins of the Humanitarian Sensibility, Part 1' and 'Capitalism and the Origins of the Humanitarian Sensibility, Part 2', in *The Antislavery Debate: Capitalism and Abolitionism as a Problem in Historical Interpretation*, ed. Thomas Bender (Berkeley, 1992). See also Lynn Hunt, *Inventing Human Rights: A History* (New York, 2007). For a broad review of the shifts in the debate and a clear distancing from the older economic interpretations, see Davis, *Inhuman Bondage*, 205–296.
27. A fuller version of the first part of this argument appears in David Eltis, *Rise of African Slavery*. For the earlier ideological approach, see David Eltis, *Economic Growth and the Ending of the Transatlantic Slave Trade* (New York, 1989), 17–28.
28. For a fuller presentation of this argument, see Eltis, *Rise of African Slavery*, 281–292; and David Eltis, 'Abolition and Identity in the Very Long Run', in *Migration, Trade, and Slavery in an Expanding World: Essays in Honor of Pieter Emmer*, ed. Wim Klooster (Leiden, 2009), 227–258.
29. For a journalistic account of the case of John Jane, a Bristol ship's captain convicted of murdering a cabin boy and taunted by a large crowd as he passed through London on his way to be executed at Wapping Dock, see *The Daily Journal*, 26 April 1726 and 3 May 1726. See also the *Whitehall Evening Post*, 26–28 September 1732, for a report on the chief mate of another Bristol ship, the *Mary*, who threw a yam at a member of the crew during a slaving voyage in the Bight of Biafra, causing the sailor's death. The officer immediately absconded from the vessel (not a tempting alternative in the Bight of Biafra) rather than face trial.
30. Emma Christopher, *Slave Ships and Sailors and Their Captive Cargoes, 1730–1807* (Cambridge, UK, 2006), 178–181. At the time of the *Zong* trial, Collingwood was already dead, but neither he nor Kimber was convicted of murder, a fact that is in this context beside the point.
31. Great Britain, *Parliamentary Debates* (1792), vol. 30, 1122.

2
Gendered Freedom: *Citoyennes* and War in the Revolutionary French Caribbean

Laurent Dubois

In the 1790s, slave revolutionaries transformed the societies of Saint-Domingue, Guadeloupe, and Martinique in the French Caribbean, confronting and overcoming slavery and creating a new order based on emancipation and political participation for all colonial citizens. By successfully organizing a resilient insurrectionary force in Saint-Domingue in 1791, these revolutionaries created a crisis and gave themselves a political platform from which they demanded reform first and eventually outright emancipation. The decrees of emancipation issued in 1793 in Saint-Domingue, which were ratified in Paris in 1794, effectively channelled mass slave insurrection into a new national policy, one with enormous political and military consequences. Former slaves became soldiers of the French Republic, fighting simultaneously for the tricolour and for liberty from slavery.

War, of course, powerfully shaped the meaning of citizenship throughout the French Atlantic and in many other areas as well. Its political impact in the Caribbean, however, was particularly radical. Tens of thousands of men went, in a few short years, from being treated as capital stripped of all basic rights to becoming not only free citizens but also prominent bearers of the republican cause. Partisans of emancipation celebrated the figure of the slave turned citizen-soldier in confronting ideas about the incapacity of former slaves to be citizens. They pointed out that these men, once enslaved, were fighting under the colours of France while many of their former masters had betrayed the Republic and joined invading English armies in the Caribbean in the hopes of maintaining slavery. The new militaries of the French Caribbean were, indeed, a striking symbol of the possibility of racial equality. Units brought together metropolitan and locally born whites with former slaves and *hommes de couleur* (men of colour) who had been free before the revolution. The ranks of officers were well populated with men of African descent, many of them ex-slaves, and many whites served under their command.

All of this, however, took place within plantation societies constructed around the production of sugar and coffee for export to metropolitan France. This economic order was not only confronted and deeply challenged by the revolution, but it also of course burdened and shaped the post-emancipation order. The leaders who shaped this order did so with few directions from the metropole, having to improvise and create new discourses and institutions on the ground in the Caribbean. Some were whites from the metropole. These included Léger Félicité Sonthonax, a provincial lawyer with abolitionist sympathies who served as a commissioner in Saint-Domingue from 1792. Such commissioners were appointed by the government in France and given broad powers to govern the colonies they were sent to, though Sonthonax probably went further than those who had chosen him ever expected when, in 1793, he independently declared general emancipation in the colony. Guadeloupe, meanwhile, captured by the British early in 1793, was recaptured by an army led by Victor Hugues, another metropolitan white, who ruled the island from 1794 and became known as the 'Robespierre of the Antilles' for his merciless treatment of royalist whites. In Saint-Domingue, however, it was ultimately a man born into slavery and later freed by his master, Toussaint Louverture, who would come to control and define the course of the Haitian Revolution. These figures had many differences, but they all shared one thing: they were determined to maintain or rebuild the plantation economy on the basis of a system of free labour. What this meant in practice was that the radical possibilities of citizenship were quickly circumscribed, for most of the enslaved, by labour policies that required them—through varying mechanisms of coercion—to continue working on plantations. This new condition was *not* a continuation of slavery, for the formerly enslaved gained the right to payment (usually through a portion of yearly production on the plantation), and in Saint-Domingue were given the right to choose managers in plantation assemblies in which all labourers—including women—were given the right to vote. They also had access to other rights of citizenship that opened up important possibilities in the new society. Nevertheless, the possibilities of freedom were quickly limited, as the former slaves were commanded to continue working, encouraged to do so with the argument that they effectively owed a debt to the Republic that freed them, a debt they should pay back by supporting it through their labour in a time of war and conflict.

For male plantation labourers, there was always another alternative to continuing to cut cane or harvest coffee, that is, joining the army. For women, however, this was never an option. The very terms of the new order excluded them not only, like women in the French metropole, from political participation but also from the major alternative to plantation labour that was available to former slaves in the French Caribbean.

Still, the order of emancipation was never contained by the policies of those who sought to channel and contain it. If the plantation system was smashed by direct armed insurrection in Saint-Domingue and, at times, in Guadeloupe, it was also absorbed and transformed in many other ways. Emancipation opened up a range of legal, social and indeed military opportunities for women, who as *citoyennes* occupied a place marked not only by exclusion but also full of possibilities for contestation.

This chapter, based on my research on Guadeloupe and Saint-Domingue during the revolutionary period, explores how *citoyennes* in the post-emancipation French Caribbean of the 1790s and early 1800s interpreted, exercised and defended their liberty.[1] In doing so, it also reflects on the basic difficulties and limitations inherent in an exploration of enslaved and formerly enslaved women's perspectives and political ideas.

Gendered slavery

The French Caribbean was made up of four colonies: French Guiana, Guadeloupe, Martinique and, the most profitable and important, Saint-Domingue. Martinique and Guadeloupe were first settled by the French in 1635, and during the seventeenth century their economies shifted gradually from the cultivation of tobacco to the cultivation of sugar. In the 1670s, when French settlers began illegally farming the western half of Hispaniola, the island was still a Spanish possession. But while the city of Santo Domingo on the island's southeastern coast had remained an important port city since its founding at the end of the fifteenth century, the western part of the island was essentially unoccupied either by the Spanish or by indigenous groups, which had been largely decimated over the course of the sixteenth century. The French, who were doing their best to gain a foothold in the region, saw an opportunity. Although the western part of the island, renamed Saint-Domingue by the French, was not officially ceded to France until 1697, by then it was already in practice a settler colony. And in the next century it exploded into the most profitable colony in the Americas, outpacing even Jamaica, Britain's most profitable colony, and ultimately producing enough coffee and sugar to account for half of France's imports at the end of the eighteenth century. Martinique and Guadeloupe also expanded enormously over the course of the eighteenth century, while Guiana mostly stagnated because of a harsh environment, though even there plantations multiplied in the second half of the eighteenth century.[2]

The whole system, of course, was based on the exploitation of slave labour brought from Africa. The thriving and brutal plantation societies of the eighteenth-century Caribbean generated complex ideas and practices relating to labour, gender and sexuality. Among enslaved people brought from Africa, men outnumbered women. In Saint-Domingue recent arrivals made up the majority of the slave population, so this imbalance continued on the plantations. But women worked alongside men at the harshest agricultural tasks—planting and harvesting sugar cane—as well as the more dangerous processing tasks, such as feeding cane stalks into the machines used to crush them and release their juice. Women, in fact, were rather more likely to be relegated to the most difficult tasks, since the ranks of the artisans and the labourers who processed the sugar cane, whose working conditions were perhaps slightly better, were essentially closed off to them.[3] Women were, of course, also present among the small minority of slaves who did domestic work on the plantations. There, while they worked in more comfortable circumstances, their proximity to male masters made them more vulnerable to sexual advances and assault, though enslaved women who worked in the field were never safe from these.

As historian Barbara Bush has noted, enslaved women on Caribbean plantations were burdened with both 'productive' and 'reproductive' roles.[4] Central to the agricultural work on the plantation, they were also central to the reproduction of the population of the enslaved. In the plantation colonies of the Caribbean, however, death rates consistently outran birth rates, a fact that generated much discussion and debate about the possible reasons for low birth rates. In the late eighteenth-century French Caribbean, officials became particularly concerned about how to improve birth rates on the plantations. Some proposed providing rewards and releasing mothers from agricultural work under certain conditions. But as with so much else in plantation society, reforms that would have helped the enslaved were effectively dismantled by planter resistance before they could ever be enforced. Repressive tactics aimed at increasing birth rates, notably the establishment of severe penalties for women who were accused of having had or helping to induce abortions, were put into effect, however. In a plantation world defined by brutality, extremely high infant mortality and harsh work regimes, motherhood was both an enormous and often intractable burden and an additional cause for surveillance and intervention on the part of masters and the local government.[5]

Rape was a constant threat for enslaved women. In some cases, masters and slaves developed long-term relationships that combined intimacy, power and coercion. Such relationships were criticized during the seventeenth century, particularly by missionaries, and the 1685 Code Noir required unmarried masters who had children with an enslaved woman to free the woman and marry her, as well as freeing their children. Over time, however, laws increasingly penalized such relationships. These laws, as literary scholar Doris Garraway has convincingly argued in her analysis of what she calls 'the libertine colony' of Saint-Domingue, while 'originally invoked to repress sexual relationships between free persons and slaves, soon functioned to displace responsibility for the taboo act onto slave women and persons of mixed race, thus enabling the continuance of libertinage'.[6]

Meanwhile, by the late eighteenth century highly visible but unofficial relationships between white men and free women of colour played a central role in the social and economic life of towns in the colonies and especially in Saint-Domingue. The hypocrisy of whites who often publicly railed against these sexual relationships and the social danger posed by those children born of them while openly engaging in them was finessed in part through representations of women of colour as 'priestesses of Venus', who through their irresistible sexual charms literally enslaved white men. At the same time, however, some women of colour did have significant power in society, becoming wealthy as merchants and property owners, and often managing the affairs of whites as well.[7]

We can gain a sense of the importance of these relationships in colonial societies of the French Caribbean by exploring the cultural production that took place there in the late eighteenth century. In the most important cultural realm in the colonies, that of theatre, the question of sexual relationships between white men and women of African descent was regularly taken up. As such relationships were represented onstage, they were also cultivated in the theatres themselves, a major site for interactions between white men and women of colour. Unlike residential areas, theatres were segregated, but they nevertheless offered ample opportunities for mixing and meeting. Moreau de Saint-Méry, a Martinican-born man who wrote a three-volume work on the colony of Saint-Domingue published in 1797–98, described how it was nearly impossible to listen to many plays because of the often coarse conversations taking place between white audience members seated in the orchestra and women of colour seated in the balconies above.[8]

Among the plays that directly addressed the question of sexuality was *La Négresse* by Jean-Baptiste Radet, performed in Le Cap in 1788 as *Créoles africaines ou les Effets de l'Amour*.[9] Radet seems to have written his play in metropolitan France; there were, however, also plays written on the topic in Saint-Domingue itself. Indeed, one of the most popular plays on the island in the late eighteenth century focused mainly on race and sexuality. Called *Jeannot et Thérèse* and written in 1758, it was a 'parody' of Jean-Jacques Rousseau's *Le Devin du Village* (1752). The author was Claude Clément, a well-known Haitian performer and director. Although it is not known whether Clément was a Creole, he lived in Saint-Domingue for four decades. He referred to *Jeannot et Thérèse* as a 'Negro-Dramatic-Lyrique opus'. It included dances described as *'pas d'esclaves'* ('slave steps') and *'pas nègres'*, and was advertised as a 'creole opera'. Like several other plays produced by Clément, it was written entirely in the Creole language, representing an extensive incorporation of the new language and expressions being generated in the Caribbean and an important early attempt to create an orthography for the language. Indeed, it is one of the earliest existing literary works in Creole. The action in *Jeannot et Thérèse* is set on a plantation and focuses on the characters' jealous conflict and eventual reconciliation. Throughout the play, sexual liaisons between men and women of different colours are evoked and commented on. A central character of the play is the African-born 'Papa Simon', who is sought out by Thérèse to help her regain the affections of Jeannot. To assist Thérèse, Simon offers an *ouanga* (a ritual object that condenses spiritual power), which he serenades with a song that evokes Dahomey.[10]

Plantation society, then, was both structured and represented—in theatre as well as in contemporary published commentary—through highly gendered categories, but ones that were in many ways unstable and cross-cutting in their implications. This context shaped the terms of revolutionary mobilization and counter mobilization in important ways. As historian John D. Garrigus has shown, the political mobilization of free men of colour often manifested in the assertion of their right to occupy and fulfil masculine roles as property owners, soldiers and citizens.[11] When the slave revolution began, the texts that were produced to narrate and interpret it often described the rape of white women by insurgents alongside other atrocity stories. Here as elsewhere, such stories, simultaneously rooted in actual events and expanded and reified into broad signals that sought to contain and de-legitimize the political meaning of the insurrection, played a powerful role in defining reactions to the events. At the same time, women were active participants in the revolts that transformed the Caribbean during these years. Indeed one commentator, writing of his time as a prisoner in the insurgent camps, claimed that the women there were 'more insolent' and 'harsher' than male insurgents and even more firmly opposed to the idea of returning to the plantations. They had their reasons.[12]

Revolution and emancipation

How did enslaved women act within and view the revolutionary changes of the 1790s? What did revolution and the citizenship it ultimately won for the enslaved mean to them? And what strategies can we use to answer such questions? These three questions will be the focus of this section. The enslaved were excluded from acting as legal subjects and therefore from producing legal documents about themselves. One of the most exciting aspects about the revolutionary period in the French Caribbean is that it created a context in which the enslaved and formerly enslaved transformed themselves into legal subjects and began creating documents as a way of both registering and furthering their struggle for liberty and dignity. Even before emancipation was decreed in Saint-Domingue (in 1793) and in Guadeloupe (in 1794), individual manumissions accelerated and free people of African descent began to assume a major role in reconfiguring the legal and political order in both colonies as well as in Martinique.

Among their concerns, unsurprisingly, were questions of family law and inheritance. The revolt that occurred in Sainte-Anne, Guadeloupe, in August 1793 was partly incited by rumours that the National Convention had granted equal inheritance rights to legitimate and illegitimate children. The rumour was accurate to some extent—the Convention had in fact decreed this—though in practice the law was inconsistently applied, and there were no explicit plans to enforce it in the colony. The implications in the colonial context, of course, would have been particularly revolutionary, since many free people of colour were the illegitimate children of wealthy masters. The revolt was crushed, however, in part because of divisions between free people of colour and enslaved people who joined the revolt but had a very different agenda: that of securing full freedom.[13]

Many individuals, meanwhile, took advantage of the juridical uncertainty and political chaos of the time to register long-standing relationships through marriages. In a few cases, individuals (many of them women) who had gained a de facto freedom by means of a legal ruse—supplying a willing intermediary with the money to purchase them from their masters on the pretext of buying a slave, and then living as free people—stepped forward to explain what they had done in order to be registered officially as free.[14]

In one case, the revolutionary violence of the period actually presented a setback to individual freedom. In Saint-Domingue, one woman who had arranged to purchase her freedom gradually from the manager on the plantation where she lived and was close to making the final payment saw the bargain destroyed when the manager in question was killed by insurgents, and his replacement refused to grant her the freedom she had been promised and for which she had paid.[15]

Such legal documents provide us with evidence of attempts by women in these societies to take advantage of the possibilities for individual freedom created by political transformation. They do not, however, tell us much about how ideas of gender and sexuality animated and were transformed by political debates. New work by historian Elizabeth Colwill, however, powerfully demonstrates how important gender was in shaping the process and performance of emancipation in revolutionary Saint-Domingue. By studying the public events surrounding this transformation, Colwill shows how much can be gained through a gendered reading of the revolution's political dynamics.[16]

One petition produced during the period offers us furtive glimpses of the cultural and philosophical transformations underway in these societies and of how ideas about sexuality, race and virtue were being contested and reformulated. In February 1793, in Saint-Domingue's port town of Saint-Marc, Laurent Jolicoeur presented a petition to the 'citizens' of the local administration requesting that freedom be granted to his slave, Zaïre.[17] Jolicoeur was an African-born man who was free at the time he wrote his petition. He focused his plea for Zaïre's freedom on her capacity for sentiment and suffering and also on what he represented as her sexual loyalty. He noted that she was 'the mother of three children who have her colour, which proves her wisdom and even her virtue'. Confronting the long-standing stereotypes in which the sexual exploitation of enslaved and free women of African descent was blamed on their own powers of seduction and control, Jolicoeur presented Zaïre as a woman who had proven her capacity for freedom by refusing sex with white men. If she became free, he argued, Zaïre would 'be able to claim to be the foremost of all female citizens'.

Jolicoeur emphasized that Zaïre's superior qualities made her suffer slavery in a very acute way. She had been 'particularly grief-stricken since the

Revolution began,' he wrote, suggesting that her awareness of the new possibilities made the limits imposed by her legal condition even more difficult for her to bear. 'Zaïre is not an ordinary individual,' he explained, 'and if she were not enslaved, she would rival any female citizen in terms of the elevation of her sentiments'. Jolicoeur observed how 'her situation makes her suffer constantly' and noted that he had been moved to quote to her 'words from a tragedy that he has seen more than once': 'A quoi! Zaïre, vous pleurez' ('Ah! Zaïre, you are crying'). The line comes from the play *Zaïre* composed in 1732 by the French Enlightenment writer Voltaire, a romantic drama about an enslaved woman and her Muslim master in medieval Jerusalem which became the most successful French play of the eighteenth century and was also a favourite in eighteenth-century Saint-Domingue.

When Jolicoeur married in 1775 in Saint-Marc—under the name Laurent Bochot *dit* Jolicoeur—he described himself as 'of the Fond nation, in Guinea'.[18] His slave Zaïre was also born in Africa. The petition declares that she was of the 'Ibo nation'. Like her owner, she was a survivor of the Middle Passage. Her name was not, however, a reference to her place of origin: although slave ships docking in Saint-Domingue were sometimes noted as having departed from the mouth of the Zaïre River, on the western coast of Central Africa, she came from West Africa.[19] In fact, it is very likely that she received the name either from Jolicoeur, in an allusion to the play of the same name by Voltaire, or from a previous master who was making a similar reference.[20]

In drawing up the petition, Jolicoeur was, then, likely to have been invoking a wide range of ideas about virtue and sexuality linked to Enlightenment discourses, such as those presented in Voltaire's play, as well as ideas about motherhood and republicanism circulating within more recent revolutionary discourses and possibly even West African ideas of sexuality and morality.[21] The petition thus presents us with a rare window on how people of African descent in the colony engaged with and interpreted issues of sexual virtue.

Jolicoeur's petition was rapidly superseded by the events of the 1790s, for within a few years all people in the French colonies of Guadeloupe and Saint-Domingue had gained both their freedom and the right to French citizenship. As this radical change was applied, in ways that were quite contradictory and rapidly offered the possibilities of freedom for most of the former slaves, the question of gender—and particularly of women's roles as plantation labourers—quickly became a preoccupation of officials overseeing the process of emancipation.

Léger Félicité Sonthonax and his co-commissioner, Étienne Polverel, and later Toussaint Louverture in Saint-Domingue and Victor Hugues and other administrators in Guadeloupe all developed policies aimed at maintaining plantation production in the colonies. These policies included paying labourers, generally with a portion of plantation production, for their work. The pay was poor and often deferred, but it was significant nonetheless. So it is hardly surprising that when these policies ensured that women would be paid less than men for doing the same work—as Polverel's policies in Saint-Domingue did—there was immediate resistance on the part of female plantation labourers.

On many plantations in Saint-Domingue, officials sent to oversee and apply the new policies over the course of late 1793 and especially 1794 discovered that the lack of equal pay galled and angered many women. The new plantation regulations allowed for the creation of plantation assemblies at which labourers could make decisions about their managers and work regimes. Polverel gave labourers a choice between working for five days a week and six days a week. If they chose to work for five, however, their pay would be drastically, and disproportionately, reduced. Despite this disincentive, on many plantations the labourers—often led by women—chose the five-day option, preferring to cultivate their own garden plots in order to feed themselves rather than labour for a portion of plantation products. On many plantations, the formerly enslaved focused increasing energy on their own farming and even found ways to claim greater portions of plantation land in order to do so.[22]

If war posed a threat to many women on the plantations, and if the centrality of military service to the definition of citizenship deepened their exclusion, the war economy also opened up some opportunities for them. This was true notably in Guadeloupe, where many corsairs were armed in order to attack British ships and neutral ships going to British islands. The sailors on these corsairs were often former slaves, and they were paid with shares of the loot from the ships they captured. Because they were often only briefly on land between missions, they generally placed their new resources with trusted individuals in the ports out of which they operated, and frequently these individuals were women. More broadly, the corsair trade created booms in port towns, in which women who worked as merchants, inn-keepers and related occupations took part and from which they profited economically. Indeed, despite regulations in Guadeloupe stipulating that women had to stay on the plantations, many did not. Officials complained of seeing groups of women simply packing up and leaving for the towns of the colony, and in at least one case a former slave became the co-owner of a house with a woman who owned a plantation in the same town where she had once been a slave.[23]

The context of war also divided families between Martinique, occupied by the British in 1794, and Guadeloupe. One former slave in Guadeloupe, Geneviève Labothière *dite* Mayoute, struggled to redeem her brother, who was still in Martinique, from slavery. She hired a white man to travel to Martinique—which she could not do, of course, for fear of being re-enslaved—and purchase her brother. She then purchased him herself (using money that her brother had saved up) and brought him to Guadeloupe. Interestingly, when she explained this series of transactions to a notary in

Guadeloupe in order to establish that her brother was in fact a free man, she dwelled on the question of whether she had violated the law of the Republic by participating in the slave trade. She noted that her brother had been 'taken out of slavery by the laws of the Republic', which had abolished slavery in 1794, but lived in 'a colony that had been usurped by the enemies of France'. In arranging for him to purchase his own freedom, then, she had 'carried out an act of fraternity, founded on the laws of nature, without hurting the laws of the republic, since her brother had paid the price of his freedom and was not sold to her'.[24] Through this document, we get a glimpse of how one woman both gained freedom for an enslaved relative and interpreted and justified her legal actions within the context of republican emancipation and the laws of nature. The episode suggests that debates about the meaning of freedom and the foundations of emancipation were an ongoing part of post-emancipation life in the French colonies. This document turned up through research on just one region of Guadeloupe, and it is likely that historians will be able to draw a much fuller picture of the legal strategies and political perspectives of women in Guadeloupe and Saint-Domingue during this period through further sustained research on the topic.

Conclusion

In the early 1800s the French government led by Napoleon Bonaparte decided to reverse the policies of emancipation, setting in motion a series of cataclysmic wars in the French Caribbean that led to the re-enslavement of the population of Guadeloupe in 1803 and the creation of an independent Haiti on the ashes of Saint-Domingue in 1804. Some women, having comprehended the possibility early on that slavery might return, prepared for this eventuality by shoring up their individual freedom through the creation or registration of documents that either declared or reiterated grants of emancipation from owners or former owners.[25]

Many women, however, decided that the use of violence would be both necessary and justified to resist the re-imposition of slavery. Women played important roles in the military conflicts of the early 1800s, often as combatants. In Guadeloupe in 1802, for instance, women in Basse-Terre sang the 'Marseillaise' while distributing ammunition to soldiers behind the lines, and others participated directly in combat against French troops. One officer chastised his men by telling them to 'imitate the women', whom he considered braver in combat. An early nineteenth-century historian, Auguste Lacour, described women animated by a 'superhuman courage', who sang during battle and cried 'Long live death' as cannonballs exploded around them. Among them was the now legendary Solitude—subject of a novel and commemorated in a statue in Guadeloupe—who entered the historical record briefly as a pregnant woman who belonged to an insurgent band and advocated the massacre of white prisoners in the region of

Trois-Rivières.[26] The struggles in Guadeloupe ended in a particularly tragic, and nearly unique, outcome: the re-establishment of slavery, coupled with mass killings and deportations, erased emancipation and began a new period of slavery nearly a half-century long. While many women had escaped the plantations during the period of emancipation and were forced to return, many others had actually continued to work on the plantations. During the period of freedom, however, they had been able to expand their autonomy and control over both their labour and, to some extent, over the space of the plantation, a process sharply reversed by the return of slavery.

The situation was quite different in Saint-Domingue. There, women also played crucial roles as combatants in the war against the French, helping to secure the victory in late 1803 of the army led by Jean-Jacques Dessalines (1758–1806), once a slave on a sugar plantation.[27] The Haitian state was, however, dominated and ruled by men, its discourse heavily saturated with metaphors of the nation as an orderly family led by patriarchal leaders. This discourse was already central to Louverture's 1801 Constitution, which helped to lay the foundation for Haitian independence, and which literally described the plantation order as a kind of family, in which women and dependants had a particular role. This tradition would continue in the laws and political structures of independent Haiti, which maintained a strict political exclusion for women that lasted until the twentieth century.[28]

Throughout the country, however, the autonomous life that was created through small farming sustained a profound transformation for many individuals and families. Fertility rates increased, and women played not only important economic roles in markets but also important religious roles in the evolving religion of Haitian Vodou. Today in Vodou, as well as in some strands of historical writing in Haiti, the role of women within slavery and in making the Haitian Revolution is referenced and sometimes directly recalled. But the full story of the *citoyennes* of the revolutionary French Caribbean, of their daily struggles and their political imagination, has yet to be told.

Notes

1. This chapter draws on material in Laurent Dubois, *A Colony of Citizens: Revolution and Slave Emancipation in the French Caribbean, 1787–1804* (Chapel Hill, 2004); and idem, *Avengers of the New World: The Story of the Haitian Revolution* (Cambridge, MA, 2004).
2. On the early expansion of the French Caribbean, see Philip Boucher, *France and the American Tropics to 1700: Tropics of Discontent?* (Baltimore, 2008).
3. The classic analysis of slave life in the French Caribbean remains Gabriel Debien, *Les esclaves des Antilles françaises (XVIIe–XVIIIe siècles)* (Basse-Terre, 1974); on enslaved women in the French Caribbean, see Arlette Gautier, *Les sœurs de Solitude: la condition féminine dans l'esclavage aux Antilles du XVII au XIX siècles* (Paris, 1985); and Bernard Moitt, *Women and Slavery in the French Antilles, 1635–1848* (Bloomington, 2001).

4. Barbara Bush, 'Hard Labor: Women, Childbirth and Resistance in British Caribbean Slave Societies', in *More than Chattel: Black Women and Slavery in the Americas*, ed. David B. Gaspar and Darlene C. Hine (Bloomington, 1996), 193–217.
5. On this issue, see especially Gautier, *Les soeurs de Solitude*.
6. Doris Garraway, *The Libertine Colony: Creolization in the Early French Caribbean* (Durham, NC, 2005), 197.
7. See Stewart R. King, *Blue Coat or Powdered Wig: Free People of Color in Pre-Revolutionary Saint Domingue* (Athens, 2001); Susan Socolow, 'Economic Roles of Free Women of Color in Cap Français', in Gaspar and Hine, *More than Chattel*, 279–297.
8. Médéric-Louis-Elie Moreau de Saint-Méry, *Description topographique, physique, civile, politique et historique de la partie française de Saint-Domingue*, new ed., rev. Blanche Maurel and Étienne Taillemite, 3 vols ([1797–98] repr. Paris, 2004) vol. 1, 361. Here and in the following paragraphs I draw on a recent article about theatre in Saint-Domingue by Bernard Camier and Laurent Dubois, 'Voltaire, Zaïre, Dessalines: le théâtre des lumières dans l'atlantique français', *Revue d'histoire moderne et contemporaine* 54/4 (2007): 39–69.
9. *Affiches Américaines*, Port-au-Prince, 24 January 1788; on slave characters in French plays, see Léon François Hoffman, *Le nègre romantique* (Paris, 1973), ch. 2; Edward Seeber, *Anti-Slavery Opinion in France during the Second Half of the Eighteenth Century* (Baltimore, 1937). Olympe de Gouges's controversial play about slavery seems not to have been performed in the colony. On this play, see Doris Y. Kadish and Françoise Massardier-Kenny (eds), *Translating Slavery: Gender and Race in French Women's Writing, 1783–1823* (Kent, 1994).
10. On this play and on theatre in Saint-Domingue more broadly, see Camier and Dubois, 'Voltaire, Zaïre, Dessalines'. The history of *Jeannot and Thérèse* was first described in Jean Fouchard, *Le théâtre à Saint-Domingue* (Port-au-Prince, 1955), 281, 297–298. But its content and language were unknown until the recent discovery by Bernard Camier of a complete version of the play in the National Archives, London (HCA 30/381), among a series of papers from French ships captured during the revolutionary period. I have also located another copy of the play in the Du Simitière Papers at the Library Company of Philadelphia. For an annotated transcription of the play in the original Creole, see Bernard Camier and Marie-Christine Hazaël-Massieux, '*Jeannot et Thérèse* un opéra-comique en créole au milieu du XVIIIIème siècle', *Revue de la société haïtienne d'histoire et de géographie* 215 (2003): 135–166. There is a linguistic analysis of the play in Marie-Christine Hazaël-Massieux, 'A propos de *Jeannot et Thérèse*: une traduction du Devin du village en créole du XVIIIe siècle?', *Creolica*, <http://www.creolica.net> (accessed October 2, 2005). Another local playwright, Acquiare, wrote a play with the intriguing title *Arlequin Mulâtresse sauvé par Macandal*, though its only performance was a failure, perhaps because its presentation of a slave character named after Makandal was too incendiary; see *Affiches Américaines*, Port-au-Prince, 4 March 1786.
11. See John D. Garrigus, 'Redrawing the Colour Line: Gender and the Social Construction of Race in Pre-Revolutionary Haiti', *Journal of Caribbean History* 30 (1996): 28–50; and, more generally, John D. Garrigus, *Before Haiti: Race and Citizenship in French Saint-Domingue* (New York, 2006).
12. Dubois, *Avengers of the New World*, 124.
13. Dubois, *A Colony of Citizens*, 137–138.
14. Ibid. 80–84.

15. Dubois, *Avengers of the New World*, 113–114.
16. Elizabeth Colwill, 'Fêtes de l'hymen, fêtes de la liberté: Marriage, Manhood, and Emancipation in Revolutionary Saint-Domingue', in *The World of the Haitian Revolution*, ed. David P. Geggus and Norman Fiering (Indianapolis, 2009), 125–155. See also Chapter 3 by Elizabeth Colwill in this volume.
17. The petition was published in the *Moniteur Général de Saint-Domingue*, 5 February 1793, 322. For more extensive analysis of this petition, see Dubois and Camier, 'Voltaire, Zaïre, Dessalines'.
18. Archives Nationales, Paris, Section Outre-Mer, DPPC, État Civil de Saint-Marc, 4 February 1775.
19. In March of 1793, for instance, one of the last slave ships to arrive in the colony—ironically called *La Nouvelle Société* (The New Society)—was arriving from the 'Zaïre river', according to a newspaper advertisement; see Dubois, *Avengers of the New World*, 151.
20. Naming slaves after classical or literary figures was common in the French Caribbean, and there were slaves in Saint-Domingue with the names Orosmane and Nerestan, clearly references to *Zaïre*; see Jacques de Cauna, *Au temps des isles à sucre: histoire d'une plantation de Saint-Domingue au XVIIIè siècle* (Paris, 2003), 92.
21. Olaudah Equiano, in a passage that drew on Anthony Benezet's *Account of Guinea*, declared that 'in most of the nations of Africa' adultery was often punished with death, 'so sacred among them is the honour of the marriage bed, and so jealous are they of the fidelity of their wives'; see Robert Allison (ed.), *The Interesting Narrative of the Life of Olaudah Equiano* ([1789] repr. New York, 2007), 44. But reconstructing the range of attitudes regarding sexual virtue in eighteenth-century West Africa is a complicated task.
22. For a summary of this process, see my *Avengers of the New World*, 185–186. For detailed explorations of the roles of women on the plantation, see Carolyn Fick, *The Making of Haiti: The Saint-Domingue Revolution from Below* (Knoxville, 1990), esp. 168–173; and Judith Kafka, 'Action, Reaction and Interaction: Slave Women and Resistance in the South of Saint-Domingue, 1793–1794', *Slavery and Abolition* 18 (1997): 48–72.
23. Dubois, *A Colony of Citizens*, 241–248 and 267.
24. The notarial record of the case is translated and presented in Laurent Dubois and John D. Garrigus (eds), *Slave Revolution in the Caribbean: A History in Documents, 1789–1804* (New York, 2006), 136–138.
25. Dubois, *A Colony of Citizens*, 374–378.
26. Ibid. 394–397; and, on Solitude's history as a figure in Guadeloupe, Laurent Dubois, 'Solitude's Statue: Confronting the Past in the French Caribbean', *Outre-Mers* 350–351 (2006): 27–38.
27. Joan (now Colin) Dayan has written eloquently of the interplay of violence and sexuality during the 'last days of Saint-Domingue'; see idem, *Haiti, History, and the Gods* (Berkeley, 1995), esp. ch. 3.
28. For an excellent analysis of politics in post-independence Haiti, see Mimi Sheller, *Democracy after Slavery: Black Publics and Peasant Radicalism in Haiti and Jamaica* (Gainesville, 2000).

3
Freedwomen's Familial Politics: Marriage, War and Rites of Registry in Post-Emancipation Saint-Domingue

Elizabeth Colwill

Scholars, politicians and priests have long noted and often deplored the low rates of formal, state-sanctioned marriage in Haiti. Although the institution of slavery undermined the legal status of marriage between slaves in colonial Saint-Domingue, monarchical agents and the Code Noir nonetheless inveighed against immorality and enjoined marriage.[1] French republicans, Napoleon's generals, Haitian heads of state and revolutionary general Toussaint Louverture himself all invoked the virtues of marriage. Nonetheless, over the centuries social realities have accorded poorly, if at all, with legal codes and moral prescriptions. Church marriage is still typical only of the light-skinned elite. Far more customary in Haiti today are modes of structuring bonds of family and affective life outside the purview of state and church. According to various estimates, extra-legal relationships known as *plasaj* constitute between 60 and 85 per cent of conjugal unions. For most women today, unions are multiple, serial or both; 30 to 60 per cent of all Haitian families are headed by women.[2]

Neither official invocations to marriage, morality and labour nor extra-legal strategies of family construction are recent phenomena in Haitian history. This chapter traces these debates back to the era of slave emancipation in colonial Saint-Domingue, melding tales often told separately—the political history of revolution, the legal history of race, the social history of marriage and family—in an inquiry into the meanings and practices of freedom in an epoch of war. The slave revolution of 1791 that exploded in Saint-Domingue, the rich sugar- and coffee-producing colony known as the 'jewel' of the French Empire, resonated throughout the Atlantic world. A nightmarish vision for defenders of the slave regime, the revolution was a source of inspiration to the enslaved and their allies throughout the western hemisphere. In the decade that followed, war in Saint-Domingue proved persistent and often consuming: revolutionary war in which creole whites' autonomist desires collided with the demands of free men of colour for political equality and the quest of the enslaved majority for freedom; imperial war in which the rise and fall of Girondins, Jacobins, Directory and Napoleonic dictatorship unfolded in uneven tandem with events in the colony; international war between three great rivals—France, Spain and Britain; civil war, reflecting the interests of *nouveaux libres*, *gens de couleur* and poor whites, as well as royalists and secessionists and three distinct provinces.[3] War had many fronts, including revolutionary laws regarding race, rituals of civil registry,[4] and marriage and the construction of family.

If the ability to construct and protect family was inseparable from the experience of freedom, then family and marriage were also preoccupations of the state in the war-torn decade following the general emancipation proclaimed by French commissioners in Saint-Domingue in 1793 and later ratified by the French Convention's abolition of slavery in the French Empire on 16 Pluviôse Year II (4 February 1794).[5] The intimate intersections of labour, military and marital policies of post-emancipation regimes in Saint-Domingue offer unique perspectives on the constraints and possibilities of freedom and the cultural channels through which state power worked. Freedpeople's own economic strategies were intertwined with their distinctive efforts to reconstitute families, although in a manner often contrary to state policy.[6] This essay explores how and why the family in general, and marriage in particular, became a primary field for the operations of power of the post-emancipation state—a space in which the meanings of freedom were delimited, debated and, above all, negotiated with former slaves.

Military service and the marital path to emancipation

The story of emancipation, like that of citizenship, has long been yoked in the Caribbean context to the exemplary figure of the citizen-soldier and to the analysis of race. As a result, we have largely missed the family drama that shaped republican strategies of emancipation.[7] In 1793, against the backdrop of an ongoing war against slave insurgents, a white insurgency and the radicalizing trajectory of revolution in France, Léger Félicité Sonthonax and Étienne Polverel, the French commissioners in Saint-Domingue, constructed a gendered pathway to emancipation: military service for men and marriage for women. On 21 June 1793, in a proclamation that heralded a dramatic shift in French policy in the Caribbean, the commissioners emancipated insurgent slaves willing to fight for the Republic. Through this act, they claimed, the French Republic gave birth to '*hommes nouveaux*' (new men)—an identity as free men and citizens linked directly with military service.[8] In turn, the emancipated 'warriors' demanded freedom for their families, a demand that the commissioners soon harnessed to their own gendered vision of citizenship.[9]

Merely a week after the commissioners' victorious re-entry into Le Cap, now in ashes, they issued the proclamation of 11 July, which authorized free men to emancipate their families through marriage.[10] Free men—white, coloured and black—as well as women, had long invoked Article IX of the Code Noir to free their spouses through marriage.[11] The 11 July decree nonetheless broke strikingly with precedent, for not only did French officials authorize emancipation through marriage, but also they defined it as a republican ritual and agreed to pay an indemnity to the owners of the women thus liberated. Marriage, the commissioners hoped, would exert a civilizing influence upon 'new citizens' to counteract the ravages of war: 'The spirit of family is the first bond of political societies. The free man who has neither wife nor children can be only a savage or a brigand'.[12]

While the number of couples who availed themselves of this pathway to freedom remains opaque, most women, like most men, achieved the legal status of free person not through marriage but through subsequent emancipation proclamations. On 29 August 1793, responding to the exigencies of international war and slave insurgency as well as his own political inclinations, Commissioner Sonthonax abolished slavery in the North Province. The decree—arguably the most radically democratic act of the French revolutionary epoch—also inscribed through the ritual of emancipation marital and nuclear family structures. 'Freedmen, their wives, and their children' were directed to report to the municipality to receive 'certificates of French citizenship'.[13] Swamped with requests for *billets de liberté* (certificates of liberty), the municipal officers of Terrier Rouge reported anxiously that the number of *billets* provided by the government was insufficient. Worse, they complained, marriages were robbing the plantations of female workers. 'The warriors are carrying away their women from the plantations and are bringing them to the camps. Production will suffer from this, and so will the interests of the Republic'. They ended on an almost plaintive note: 'In distributing the certificates to these *citoyennes cultivateurs* (plantation workers), can one require them to return to the fields?'[14]

In fact, the decree had precisely anticipated this need. Sonthonax's emancipation proclamation of the North Province both granted freedom and constrained it, subjecting freedpeople to a new labour regime. Former slaves were bound to remain on their plantation and to work six full days a week in exchange for plantation revenues, a third of which would be divided among the former slaves according to rank, status and sex. Women's work was to be remunerated at two-thirds the value of men's.[15]

The enforcement of work discipline among labourers, male and female, would remain the constant concern of successive regimes, as republican officials scrambled to square legal emancipation with large-scale production of export crops by a subservient labour force.[16] Free labour, in this context, represented not only a revolution in systems of production but also a tool of imperial war. Slave emancipation, ratified by the French Convention on 4 February 1794, had not brought peace to revolutionary Saint-Domingue. Instead, in conflicts that endured for the better part of a decade, large swathes of territory fell under the control of France's imperial rivals, Spain and England, while other areas became enmeshed in internal skirmishes reflecting complex regional allegiances and divisions between colours and classes. Families, like the French republican regime itself, suffered the impact of wars that consumed male labourers while shifting the burden of agricultural labour and the provisioning of armies increasingly onto freedwomen and children. For the French state, although citizenship would remain closely linked to military service, women's agricultural labour was as vital to sustaining the imperial project as was men's military service.

As Carolyn Fick first discovered for the South Province, the new labour regime provoked widespread non-compliance as men and especially women in 1793 and 1794 'actively imposed their own will as legally-free beings upon their situation and in so doing attempted ultimately to transform themselves into free smallholding peasants'. Workers expanded the size of their family plots and cultivated additional sectors of plantation land as their own. When confronted by officials who tried to enforce the work regime, women often took the lead in insisting upon equal pay and an additional free day each week to work the family plot.[17] Each of these economic initiatives followed a logic that elaborated, extended and protected family bonds. They also directly undercut the new labour code, which sought to restore the plantation export economy—and with it, French colonial supremacy.

Confronting this unsettling terrain, French Commissioner Étienne Polverel appealed directly to freedmen in the preamble to his labour code of 7 February 1794 by representing the rebellion of workers against the new labour regime as an insurrection of women against their men. Responding to women's demands for equal pay, he invoked their biological weakness and pathologized their reproductive capacity, citing the natural 'inequality of strength' and their 'habitual and periodic infirmities'. Women should not covet men's portion of the revenues, for men (now invented as indulgent breadwinners) 'work, save, and desire money only to be able to lavish it on their women'.[18]

The commissioners' devotion to the patriarchal family was not simply ideological, for the family was essential to the organization of labour and thus to the prosecution of the war and the preservation of the colony. In a demographic sense, war highlighted the significance of women's productive and reproductive labour in the measure that it consumed men.[19] The defence of family was also an essential ingredient in the identity formation of a new republican regime at once revolutionary and colonial. While the slave system rested upon a process of commodification inimical to family formation, the new regime marked its distance from slavery by abolishing the discursive and legal apparatus of race while sacralizing marriage and family. In revolutionary France and its colonies, the transfer of power from church to state sacralized new material objects and ritual practices. The ritual of Catholic baptism was reinvented as inscription of births in civil registries, Catholic unions reincarnated as republican marriages under the supervision of republican officials. The melding of the language of the sacred and the secular was also evident in labour codes issued throughout the 1790s, which enjoined former slaves to work and to marry, as mutually constitutive undertakings.

Marriage, militarism and labour

During the transitional years between emancipation and Haitian independence, French republican regimes, their colonial emissaries and the pre-eminent black general Toussaint Louverture himself all invoked legal marriage for the *nouveaux libres*, incorporating a tenacious advocacy of matrimony into labour codes and disciplinary regimes. While revolutionary tumult in France granted the colony a *de facto* administrative independence for several years, by 1796 the Directory and its Councils had turned their attention to the project of colonial reclamation, sending a series of agents to restore the plantation economy in Saint-Domingue. Through the twists and turns of French colonial policy in the 1790s, advocacy of marriage remained inseparable from the regulation of labour and economic revitalization.[20] Indeed, the 'Law concerning the constitutional organization of the colonies' of 12 Nivôse Year VI (1 January 1798) authorized the Directory's agents to develop labour policies that would support population growth by 'encouraging marriages and rewarding the fecundity of legitimate unions'.[21]

General Gabriel Hédouville, agent of the Directory, implemented this directive with promptness and exactitude. Even as the decimated British troops embarked grimly from the island's ports, he issued the decree of 6 Thermidor Year VI (24 July 1798), on the policing of the estates and 'the reciprocal obligations' of proprietors and workers. The decree interlaced invocations to paternal obligation, marriage, productivity and morality. Proprietors were to 'conduct themselves as good fathers' by convincing their workers that legal marriage was the best means not only to secure happiness, health and moral purity but also 'to increase the population of each plantation, to extend cultivation and to augment production'. Sonthonax had offered liberty as an incentive to legal marriage; Hédouville offered some combination of material and political rewards. 'Fathers and mothers who produce the most children within legitimate marriages', he promised in terms that mirrored the language of the 12 Nivôse decree, 'will be distinguished by the government, and will obtain encouragement, rewards, and even concessions of land'.[22]

To understand the ways in which the family sanctified the post-emancipation state is also to begin to comprehend the preoccupation with family and marriage displayed not only by French republicans but also by Toussaint Louverture.[23] For Toussaint legal marriage, plantation labour, military service and the Christian faith would etch the boundaries of freedom for thousands of former slaves. Between 1795 and 1798, as France attempted to re-establish its authority in its prized colony, the general rose steadily to power, ejecting from Saint-Domingue first the Spanish, next his French republican allies and finally the British.[24] Having succeeded, Toussaint moved the army onto the plantations to impose a system of conscripted labour—a system that combined a labour and disciplinary regime with a social and matrimonial programme. On 25 Brumaire Year VII (15 November 1798), shortly after his successful dispatch of Hédouville, Toussaint issued a new labour code that outlined his own vision of the intimate relationship between healthy families, public order and economic progress.[25] But it was in the epoch of his greatest power, at the turn of the century, that he delineated most clearly the relationship between marriage and morality, national security and production. After his victory in the bitter two-year civil war that he, along with many *nouveaux libres*, had fought against André Rigaud's free coloured troops, Toussaint issued the decree of 20 Vendémiaire Year IX (12 October 1800).[26]

According to Carolyn Fick, the decree was an attempt to ensure the survival of the economy, to shore up his regime against the tides of political reaction in France and to roll back the expansion of peasant cultivation that had occurred during the relative anarchy of wartime. In so doing, it conscripted the family in the service of the state. All managers, foremen and labourers would be required, like military personnel, 'to fulfil their duties with precision, submission, and obedience'. Parents would serve as mouthpieces for a militarized labour regime. 'The first duty of the model father and mother' was to produce moral and Christian citizens, but, 'above all', the model family was to school children in their duties as workers.[27] In July 1801 the promulgation of an autonomist constitution made Toussaint governor for life, anointed Catholicism as the official state religion and made morality, equated with legal marriage, the guarantor of social welfare. Since marriage purified morals, virtuous spouses would 'always be distinguished and protected by the government'. The constitution also banned divorce while inscribing a clear hierarchy between *enfants naturels et légitimes* (illegitimate and legitimate children).[28]

Toussaint's invocations to marriage apparently had unintended effects. Disorders occasioned by the abuse of the 'sacred institution' prompted another decree devoted exclusively to marriage on 8 Vendémiaire Year X (30 September 1801). The proclamation opened with a retrospective of the events of the Revolution, suggesting that Saint-Domingue would not have offered the world the spectacle of 'such appalling dissolution' had the masses felt the regulatory power of a well-disciplined family. Yet even the best institutions, Toussaint admitted, were not free of abuse. To terminate the scandals produced by 'debauchery or vagabondage' under the 'sacred pretext of marriage', he decreed:

> Art. 1. No member of the military can marry without the approval of the governor of Saint-Domingue. Art. 2. No worker attached to a plantation

can marry a woman attached to another plantation without the express permission of the governor of Saint-Domingue. Art. 3. No soldier can marry without having previously presented his request to his military superior...with a particular concern for the morality of the individual.

The final decision, in murky cases, would rest with the governor himself.[29] A week later Toussaint circulated an order to all parishes and municipal governments of the colony, requiring men and women who were separated but not yet divorced to rejoin their spouses and to live 'in a state of perfect harmony'; those who did not would be 'investigated as bad citizens'.[30]

The increasing urgency of Toussaint's directives may well have reflected his own growing vulnerability. By the fall of 1801, across the Atlantic, Napoleon Bonaparte and his retinue were preparing a historic invasion of Saint-Domingue designed to topple Toussaint from power and restore French colonial pre-eminence. At the same moment, workers in the North Province of Saint-Domingue rose in insurrection, angered by Toussaint's overtures to white planters and labour policies that, while designed to conserve freedom, nonetheless tasted of coercion. Scholars have described the bloody pacification campaign ordered by Toussaint (the War of the Knives) to suppress the workers' uprising, followed by the decree of 4 Frimaire Year X (25 November 1801), which, in the words of historian Claude Moïse, 'organized a veritable police state'.[31] But we have not yet explored the gendering of Toussaint's strategies of military, political and economic repression and how they were intertwined with the militarization of the family itself.

In the decree of 25 November, Toussaint railed against urban parents who had cultivated laziness in their children, producing a flock of 'vagabonds, thieves, and prostitutes'. 'A wise government' would always reward good *ménages* with 'honour, respect, and veneration', but married military officers and public functionaries who sullied their homes with concubines, and unmarried officers who cohabited with 'several women' would be fired. Imposing the death penalty for sedition and requiring passports for all citizens and an inventory of all plantation workers 'of every age and both sexes', he concluded with a gendered vision of labour, virtue and vice: 'laziness is the mother of all vices, work is the father of all virtues'.[32]

Toussaint Louverture's bitterest enemies shared his preoccupation with labour, martial order and marriage. In the summer of 1802, following an invasion of 20,000 French troops under Napoleon's emissary General Victor-Emmanuel Leclerc, Toussaint was betrayed, captured and deported. He would die of cold and hunger in a prison in Fort de Joux in the Jura mountains in April 1803.[33] Leclerc himself would die from yellow fever several months before Toussaint, but not before he had issued a new labour code that mandated workers' 'submission and obedience', bound them to the plantations and restricted marital practice. 'No worker attached to a plantation', Leclerc decreed, 'is permitted to marry a woman attached to another plantation without the express permission of the Captain General'.[34]

The regulation of marriage, whether by black revolutionaries, white republicans or Napoleonic generals, was thus consistently linked to the implementation of labour codes and the imposition of disciplinary regimes. To recognize this connection is neither to conflate the distinct interests of colonizer and colonized nor to minimize the brilliance of the creole general whose militarism was forged in the crucible of resistance to a global economic order bound intimately to slavery. Toussaint's strategies were not mere reflections of French colonial discourse, nor was marriage simply a Catholic gloss on more essential issues of economy, war and international politics. For him, as for French officials in Saint-Domingue, the ritual of marriage consecrated the new labour regime: the family produced, organized and constrained the reproductive and productive labour upon which the plantation system rested and upon which the fate of Saint-Domingue would depend.[35]

Unwed mothers, 'natural children' and the state

With this commitment, agents of the French revolutionary government in Saint-Domingue had long worked to elaborate and regulate the inscription of civil identity in the État Civil (the civil register of births, marriages and deaths). The metropolitan reinvention of marriage as a republican civil ceremony in the law of 20 September 1792, extended to the colonies, symbolically passed authority from the master to the state while sacralizing the nuclear family.[36] Successive revolutionary governments relied on the État Civil not simply to reflect civil status or define individual rights but also to inscribe new familial identities and social relationships. As Laurent Dubois has compellingly argued, the État Civil and notarial records 'became a terrain where previous forms of social silencing and racial identification were contested and negotiated'.[37] The Second Commission's assault on racial prejudice included a ban in 1792 on the use of racial nomenclature in civil registries.[38] The evidence from Saint-Domingue, as from Guadeloupe, suggests that local practices of racial inscription followed the government decree unevenly, its fluctuations reflecting everything from international conquest to the local balance of power and the political idiosyncrasies of particular scribes. These struggles over race in the État Civil were also inextricably struggles over gender and the boundaries of family. Certain practices of inscription—in particular, the demarcation of a child as illegitimate, or *naturel*—served in state registers as a subtle racial marker, a symbol of social status and as a gendered index of virtue.

While officials insisted on the primacy of marriage over free unions among former slaves and specified the formula of inscription in the État Civil, they often lacked the power to enforce their dictates. In both Port-de-Paix and

Fort-Dauphin in the late 1790s, unmarried fathers appeared regularly as *déclarants*, and in the former town the term *'sa femme naturelle'* temporarily displaced that of *'fille'* or *'fils naturelle'*. Nevertheless, in the eyes of the law, most mothers remained unwed, their children branded indelibly in the civil registers as illegitimate.[39] Consider the paradox: in the context of governmental decrees regarding marriage and morality, the foundational act that bestowed civil status upon the child of the unwed mother and inscribed her own identity in the public records would also have marked her moral 'failings'—now officially visited upon the child—in the records of state.[40] Such contradictions suggest that the purported 'unmaking' of race by the post-emancipation state was accomplished, in part, through the elaboration of new gendered hierarchies.[41]

If the État Civil etched racialized and gendered identities, often in new and subtle forms, into the historical record, freedwomen themselves participated in those same rituals with different intentions and to different effect. As Arlette Gautier and Laurent Dubois have demonstrated, freedwomen in the French Caribbean regularly stamped their claims to public identities for themselves and their families in the État Civil during the years that followed emancipation.[42] My research in the North Province of Saint-Domingue suggests that they did so selectively and in strategic negotiation with government dictates.

Marriage and liberty

The historically low marriage and fertility rates of enslaved women in the French Antilles are well known.[43] Given the violence of the slave regime in Saint-Domingue toward affective and familial bonds among the enslaved, one might expect a sharp and immediate increase in marriage among freedpeople after emancipation. But the case is more ambiguous and complex than this formulation would suggest.[44]

The surviving municipal registers of the État Civil of Port-de-Paix and Fort-Dauphin from 1793 to mid-September 1801 do contain records of more than 250 marriages between former slaves.[45] The timing of these unions, like that of birth registrations, reflected the intertwined narratives of war and emancipation. In Fort-Dauphin, in the wake of the burning of Le Cap and the republican decree of 11 July 1793 that permitted men including former black insurgents—who joined the French military forces to free their partners through marriage, the parish records of the priest, Vendemont, ceded suddenly to civil registers overseen by local republican officials. Of the 14 marriages or *promesses de mariage* recorded between August and December 1793, all but two involved brides who had recently been enslaved. Of those unions in which the partners were specifically listed as *cultivateurs* (agricultural labourers, implying former slave status) or named a former master, all but one legitimized children.[46] Marriages that consecrated long-established partnerships no doubt had many motivations, the protection of children being among the most powerful. In claiming children as their legitimate issue in records of state, couples established a legal parental claim while providing their children with inheritance rights and insurance against an uncertain future.

Yet to trace through the 1790s the acts inscribed in the État Civil of Port-de-Paix and Fort-Dauphin is to be struck less by the frequency of marriage than by the high ratio of death and birth registrations to those for marriages.[47] The elimination of racial markers in most of these registers and the effects on record-keeping of war, administrative reorganization and political turmoil make quantitative analysis for this period hazardous at best. Nonetheless, while freedpeople flocked by the hundreds to register young Africans as well as their own children with republican authorities in the heady and uncertain months after emancipation, their embrace of republican marriage appears to have been more gradual and uneven.[48] The evidence suggests that most freedpeople in these two communes in the decade after emancipation—like their enslaved ancestors and their descendants after 1804—defined the bonds of family as distinct from the bonds of legal marriage and in a more complex and multifaceted manner than did the state.

To examine freedpeople's marital strategies in conjunction with state policy leads the historian into the thicket of debate concerning the transformation of African social and cultural practices in diasporic contexts. Here I will simply note that in Saint-Domingue, where new slaves were arriving from African ports at the rate of 30,000 a year in the 1780s and the enslaved population at the time of the Revolution was at least 60 per cent African-born, the question is of central importance.[49] Without a doubt, the familial patterns of freedpeople had deep historical roots, traceable to the Kingdom of Kongo and other regions from which the enslaved had been torn. Marital traditions among the seventeenth-century Kongo permitted a long trial period before a wedding to see if the couple was compatible, and the matrilineal (though flexible) system of kinship surely influenced the development of family structures, particularly in regions where Central West Africans predominated.[50] As Karen McCarthy Brown has noted, the Fon, Yoruba and Kongo societies from which a distinctively Haitian culture emerged 'defined family as including the ancestors and the spirits'. In this sense, 'the need for family was both a social and a spiritual need'.[51]

Yet we would be mistaken to attribute modest rates of republican marriage to 'African retentions', or, for that matter, to follow the binary interpretive framework of 'retention vs. invention'.[52] On the eve of the revolution, some regions of Saint-Domingue were already heavily creolized, with nearly three-fifths of all enslaved adults on the island's northern plain born in Saint-Domingue.[53] The religious cultures conveyed from central Africa included a Kongolese Catholicism that dated back to the seventeenth century.[54] The meanings of family and patterns of family formation in post-emancipation

Saint-Domingue emerged not only from a complex heritage of 'traditional' practices but also in continuous negotiation with enduringly harsh local conditions. It is likely that the responsibilities borne by women for childbearing and rearing, food provision and domestic life, as well as petty commerce and agricultural labour, in the context of political insecurity, war and poverty, supported—then as now—the formation of extended and multiple family relationships and extra-legal definitions of marriage such as *plasaj*.[55]

Rates of marriage, like civil registrations of births, were responsive to shifting political, economic and military realities. Administrative boundaries shifted as parishes were absorbed into communes, and registers swelled with soldiers, refugees, migrants and *cultivateurs* from far-flung plantations. In the wake of the commissioners' decree that granted enslaved women freedom through marriage, the number of marriages in the registers of Fort-Dauphin in 1793 rose then fell again after the Spanish conquest, while the restoration of French military and political power in the region elicited an explosion of birth registrations in Year V but had a less immediate impact on rates of marriage.[56]

In Year IX (23 September 1800–22 September 1801) civil officials recorded an arresting spike in marriages in both Port-de-Paix and Fort-Dauphin, a sharp deviation from the relatively modest rates of marriage of *nouveaux libres* in those two communes.[57] It is difficult to know how to interpret these numbers; the problem requires further research. The increase may reflect the incorporation of adjoining territory into these communes—thus an expansion of the population within the administrative unit—after the French colonial reorganization of 12 Nivôse Year VI (1 January 1798), implemented by agent Philippe-Rose Roume de Saint-Laurent in the following year.[58] It is also possible that the hope of government favour and material rewards promised by republican officials may have prompted some couples to marry.[59] From this perspective, marriage might be read as one among a range of strategies through which freedpeople negotiated with the state to expand their manoeuvring room and to approximate their own ideals of freedom. On the other hand, the sharp increase in Year IX may reveal more about coercion than choice. It is surely significant that this year represented the heyday of Toussaint's power as well as a cessation of conflict following the end of the War of the South. Given the historic conjunction of peace, government centralization and military supremacy, Toussaint was in a position to enforce the policies that he had long supported. Men and women flocked to municipal offices to take their vows in the wake of Roume's forceful directives on compliance with republican laws regulating civil registration and in the months immediately following Toussaint's harsh labour decree of 12 October 1800, which militarized agriculture and explicitly forbade women other than wives to visit the military barracks.[60] One need not assume that freedwomen or men shared Toussaint's vision of marriage, family or morality to understand the strategic significance of a trip to the municipal office that year.

After years of notarizing deeds in Trou, Anne-François Briffault appeared in Fort-Dauphin in the autumn of Year X. In the course of 11 months, his registers filled with scores of marriages absent from the État Civil.[61] In that time, he recorded no fewer than 46 marriages, all but one of which registered the unions of persons of African descent.[62] Most remarkable, 28 of those ceremonies (61 per cent of the total) occurred in the single month of Nivôse (22 December 1801–20 January 1802). This rash of marriages transpired within months of the promulgation of a law that privileged legitimate over illegitimate children—an incentive to marriage reinforced by Toussaint's marriage decree of 8 Vendémiaire Year X (30 September 1801)—and in the immediate aftermath of Toussaint's manifesto of 4 Frimaire Year X (25 November 1801) in response to the failed rebellion of the workers of the North.[63] Most ominously, by then word would have circulated that the long-feared invasion by French forces was imminent. Confronting militarism at home and invasion from abroad, couples flocked to the notary to comply with law, protect their property, legitimize their children and secure their freedom by appearing as contractants—free persons—in official French records. To read the plummeting marriage rates after Nivôse against the historic events of Years X and XI—the invasion of Fort-Dauphin by some 2,000 troops under General Rochambeau, the brutal attempt to restore white rule in Saint-Domingue, and the subsequent genocidal war—is to glimpse the intimate implications of colonial violence.

Conclusion

Throughout the decade following emancipation, freedpeople's familial strategies reveal an awareness of the intersecting politics of reproduction, race, labour and civil status. For women, in particular, inscription of a birth in the État Civil represented political action on behalf of their children and claims on the polity in an increasingly militaristic society that denied women full rights as *citoyennes*, just as their intervention in disputes over labour codes represented an insistence on the value of their labour in a regime that gave most women two thirds of a man's pay. Indeed, these two forms of activism were inextricably interwoven. Recall that women's chief demand when resisting the labour codes of 1794 was an additional free day a week. As women insisted time and again to government representatives sent to enforce the labour regime, free time—that is, time to tend or extend the family's garden plot, time to work a bit of plantation land for their children—was central to the practice of freedom. In this sense, women's labour resistance was fought in the name of family time, at a time when labouring for one's chosen family and shielding it from the depredations of war defined the meanings of freedom. The struggle between two competing economic orders—the peasant proprietorship advocated by most freedpeople and the plantation export economy enforced by the state—was waged not only with military force but also on the terrain of marriage and family.

Indeed, one could argue that the epoch's most radical form of democracy found expression through those very impulses toward the extension, invention and consecration of extended family and community bonds that authorities branded as politically and economically retrogressive. The État Civil provides glimpses, however indistinct, into freedpeople's familial politics: the practices of godparenting, adoption, sponsorship, fictive kinship and enduring relationships of *plasaj*, from which people living in a fragile revolutionary present reconstructed family from shards of an African past. In post-emancipation Saint-Domingue, freedwomen's familial politics entailed a claim to citizenship—not a citizenship derived from voting rights or military service, but rather a citizenship rooted in a dual notion of self-possession and self-determination of the nature of one's own family and community.

I have argued that the importance of marriage to government officials—black, white and coloured, metropolitan and creole—was interwoven with a process of self-invention, as well as a need to secure the martial, reproductive and productive labour of the former slaves. Slaveholders had violated the sanctity of the slave family in the service of profit; post-emancipation regimes in Saint-Domingue conscripted the labouring family for military service and plantation production. In this context, for freedwomen to define their families through extra-legal conjugal unions and relationships of choice, to witness children's registration in the État Civil and to claim an extra day to work the family plot was to extricate bonds of love, labour and kinship from the government's conscription of family in service of war and the export economy.

Those negotiations with power and poverty continued through the next two centuries, the dynamics of kinship and community evolving in dialogue with government policy, ubiquitous poverty and international interventions. As Claude Moïse has noted, 'the provisions on virtuous *citoyennes*, on marriage and on moral purity, are taken up in one form or another, nearly without modification, in the Haitian Constitutions of 1805, 1806, 1807 and 1816...Article 9 on marriage reappears, nearly identically, in the Haitian Constitutions of 1950, 1957, 1964 and 1983'.[64] Yet chosen families, rather than state-sanctioned unions, have persisted in Haiti. In the years after President Jean-Bertrand Aristide's overthrow in 1991, as FRAPH[65] accumulated its human trophies, women stepped in to fill the breach left by disappeared women activists, feeding one another's children and pooling grain—testament that the fluid structuring of kin which extends beyond the bonds of blood or law continues to serve even today as a site of resistance.

Acknowledgements

I am grateful to Aimee Lee Cheek, John D. Garrigus, Peter Arnade, Laurent Dubois, Suzanne Desan and the editors of this volume for their helpful comments on this essay; and to Karen Hagemann, Deborah Nord, Patricia Lorcin and Lynn Hunt for invitations to share earlier versions of this essay with stimulating interlocutors at the University of North Carolina–Chapel Hill, Princeton University, University of Minnesota and UCLA, respectively. A fellowship at the John Carter Brown Library provided the resources and an exceptionally collegial setting in which to complete this essay.

Notes

1. The Code Noir, the royal edict of 1685 designed to regulate the legal status of slaves in the French empire, underwent numerous modifications over the decades. The classic work is by Louis Sala-Molins, *Le code noir, ou le calvaire de Canaan* (Paris, 1987). Sue Peabody explores the transformations of French law regarding race and liberty in *'There Are No Slaves in France': The Political Culture of Race and Slavery in the Ancien Régime* (Oxford, 1996).
2. Stephen J. Williams et al., 'Conjugal Unions among Rural Haitian Women', *Journal of Marriage and the Family* 37/4 (1975): 1022–1031, 1026. Estimates vary, but scholars agree that extra-legal relationships predominate. Carolle Charles notes that 'more than 40 per cent of conjugal relations are not legally sanctioned' ('Gender and Politics in Contemporary Haiti: The Duvalierist State, Transnationalism, and the Emergence of a New Feminism, 1980–1990', *Feminist Studies* 21/1 [1995]: 135–164, 142). Mirlande Manigat places the rate of legal marriage nationally at 15 per cent ; see her *Être femme en Haïti hier et aujourd'hui: Le regard des Constitutions, des Lois et de la société* (Port-au-Prince, 2002), 147.
3. The term *nouveaux libres* was used to distinguish those people freed by the emancipation decrees, while *anciens libres* referred to those who had achieved freedom prior to the Revolution; *gens de couleur* referred to people of mixed African and European descent. See David P. Geggus, 'Slavery, War, and Revolution in the Greater Caribbean, 1789–1815', in *A Turbulent Time: The French Revolution and the Greater Caribbean*, ed. David Barry Gaspar and David P. Geggus (Bloomington, 1997), 1–50; Carolyn Fick, 'The French Revolution in Saint Domingue: A Triumph or Failure?' in ibid. 51–77.
4. This essay is based on a review of extant volumes of the État Civil (hereafter EC) recording births and marriages in Fort-Dauphin (rechristened Bayaha by the Spanish and Fort-Liberté by French republicans) from 1792 to Year IX and in Port-de-Paix from 1793 to Year X, as well as extant birth registrations from Port-au-Prince, rechristened Port Républicain in 1793. I consulted microfilm copies at Family History Centers of the Church of Latter Day Saints in Princeton, NJ, and Poway, CA; Fort-Dauphin, INTL film 1094191; Port-de-Paix, INTL film 1093916; Port-au-Prince, INTL film 1094219.
5. The commissioners were appointed by the French revolutionary regime to govern the colonies, in an attempt to ensure that French law prevailed in the empire.
6. On slavery, marriage and emancipation, see Elizabeth Colwill, 'Fêtes de l'hymen, fêtes de la liberté: Marriage, Manhood and Emancipation in Revolutionary Saint-Domingue, 1793', in *The World of the Haitian Revolution*, ed. David P. Geggus and Norman Fiering (Indianapolis, 2009), 125–155; Myriam Cottias, 'Free but Minor: Slave Women, Respectability, and Social Antagonism in the French Antilles, 1830–90', in *Women and Slavery*, ed. Gwyn Campbell et al., 2 vols (Athens, OH, 2008), vol. 2, 186–206; Arlette Gautier, 'Traite et politiques démographiques esclavagistes',

Population (Fr. edn) 41/6 (1986): 1005–1024; idem, *Les soeurs de Solitude: la condition féminine dans l'esclavage aux Antilles du XVIIe au XIXe siècle* (Paris, 1985); idem, 'Les esclaves femmes du nouveau monde: étude comparative', *Revue haitienne d'histoire et de géographie* 76/210 (2002): 28–47; idem, 'Les familles esclaves aux Antilles françaises, 1635–1848', *Population* (French edn) 55/6 (2000): 975–1001; John D. Garrigus, *Before Haiti: Race and Citizenship in French Saint-Domingue* (New York, 2006); idem, ' "To Establish a Community of Property": Marriage and Race before and during the Haitian Revolution', *Journal of the History of the Family* 12/2 (2007): 142–152.
7. On race and family romance in pre-revolutionary Saint-Domingue, see Doris Garraway, 'Race, Reproduction and Family Romance in Moreau de Saint-Méry's *Description...de la partie française de l'isle Saint-Domingue*', *Eighteenth-Century Studies* 38/2 (2005): 227–246; John D. Garrigus, 'Redrawing the Colour Line: Gender and the Social Construction of Race in Pre-Revolutionary Haiti', *Journal of Caribbean History* 30 (1996): 28–50. On gender and the early Haitian state, see idem, 'Race, Gender, and Virtue in Haiti's Failed Foundational Fiction: *La Mulâtre comme il y a peu de blanches* (1803)', in *The Color of Liberty: Histories of Race in France*, ed. Sue Peabody and Tyler Stoval (Durham, NC, 2003), 73–94. For gendered narratives of slavery, revolution and independence, see Joan Dayan, *Haiti, History, and the Gods* (Berkeley, 1995).
8. Archives Nationales, Paris (hereafter AN), Dxxv/9/90, doc. 12, Polvérel, Sonthonax, Proclamation, Haut-du-Cap, 21 June 1793; David P. Geggus, 'The Arming of Slaves in the Haitian Revolution', and Laurent Dubois, 'Citizen Soldiers: Emancipation and Military Service in the Revolutionary French Caribbean', both in *Arming Slaves: From Classical Times to the Modern Age*, ed. Christopher Leslie Brown and Philip D. Morgan (New Haven, 2006), 209–232 and 233–254, respectively; Laurent Dubois, *Avengers of the New World: The Story of the Haitian Revolution* (Cambridge, MA, 2004), 134–142. On militarism and citizenship, see Mimi Sheller, 'Sword-Bearing Citizens: Militarism and Manhood in Nineteenth-Century Haiti', *Plantation Society in the Americas* 4 (1997): 233–278.
9. On gender and emancipation, see Pamela Scully and Diana Paton (eds), *Gender and Slave Emancipation in the Atlantic World* (Durham, NC, 2005), in particular the chapter by Sue Peabody, 'Négresse, Mulâtresse, Citoyenne: Gender and Emancipation in the French Caribbean, 1650–1848', 56–78.
10. Robert Louis Stein, *Léger Félicité Sonthonax: The Lost Sentinel of the Republic* (Rutherford, NJ, 1985), 86–87; Peabody, 'Négresse', 64.
11. Garrigus, *Before Haiti*, 198–201; Dominique Rogers, 'Les libres de couleur dans les capitales de Saint-Domingue: fortune, mentalités et intégration à la fin de l'Ancien Régime (1776–1789)', doctoral thesis (University of Bordeaux III, 1999), 557–559, 545. On the contradictory marital provisions of the Code Noir, see Lucien Peytraud, *L'esclavage aux Antilles françaises avant 1789: d'après des documents inédits des archives coloniales* (1897; repr. Pointe-à-Pitre, 1973), 197–206; Sala-Molins, *Le code noir,* 106–117.
12. AN, Dxxv/9/91, doc. 8, Étienne Polverel and Léger Félicité Sonthonax, 11 July 1793.
13. AN, Dxxv/10/92, doc. 22, Sonthonax, Cap Français, 29 August 1793.
14. AN, Dxxv/17 /167, doc. 59, letter from the Municipality of Terrier Rouge to the Civil Commissioner of the Republic, 12 September 1793.
15. AN, Dxxv/10/92, doc. 22, Sonthonax, 29 August 1793. For a later period, see regulations cited in AN, Col. CC9b/5 from years IV, V and VI and the *cultivateurs*'

revolt in Fort-Liberté (Fort-Dauphin) in AN, Col. CC9b/8. See on this point Laurent Dubois's essay in this volume.
16. For example, AN, Dxxv/64/648, doc. 22, Extraits des registres de la Commission intermédiaire, Port Républicain, 14 April 1794.
17. Carolyn Fick, *The Making of Haiti* (Knoxville, 1990); idem, 'Emancipation in Haiti: From Plantation Labour to Peasant Proprietorship', in *After Slavery: Emancipation and its Discontents*, ed. Howard Temperley (London, 2000), 11–40, 19–21. See also Judith Kafka, Action, Reaction, and Interaction: Slave Women in Resistance in the South of Saint-Domingue, 1793–94', *Slavery and Abolition* 18/2 (1997): 48–72.
18. Charles, 'Gender and Politics', 137; Fick, *Making of Haiti*, 170.
19. David P. Geggus has shown that despite the greater proportion of men to women on sugar plantations, in the North province in the two decades prior to 1791, two-thirds of the field slaves were women. See his 'Slave Society in the Sugar Plantation Zones of Saint Domingue and the Revolution of 1791–93', *Slavery and Abolition* 20/2 (1999): 31–46, 37.
20. On French colonial policy, see Bernard Gainot, 'The Constitutionalization of General Freedom under the Directory', in *The Abolitions of Slavery: From Léger Félicité Sonthonax to Victor Schoelcher, 1793, 1794, 1848*, ed. Marcel Dorigny (New York, 2003), 180–196.
21. AN, Col. CC9b/9, vol. 6, 24–30, titre 1, art. 9, 'Loi concernant l'organisation constitutionelle des colonies', 12 Nivôse Year VI (1 January 1798).
22. Archives nationales d'outre-mer (hereafter ANOM), Col. F3/202 (Fonds Moreau de Saint-Méry), 95–97, T. Hédouville, 'Arrêté concernant la Police des Habitations et les Obligations réciproques des Propriétaires ou Fermiers et des Cultivateurs', Extrait du Registre des Délibérations de l'Agence du Directoire exécutif à Saint-Domingue, Cap, 6 Thermidor Year VI.
23. For divergent assessments of Toussaint, see Claude Moïse, *Le projet national de Toussaint Louverture et la constitution de 1801* (Montreal, 2001), 131–141; Pierre Pluchon, *Toussaint Louverture: un révolutionnaire noir d'Ancien Régime* (Paris, 1989); Odette Roy Fombrun, *Toussaint Louverture: tacticien de genie, la Constitution indépendantiste de 1801* (Port-au-Prince, 2001); and Madison Smartt Bell, *Toussaint Louverture: A Biography* (New York, 2007). On the legal history and practice of marriage in independent Haiti, see Manigat, *Être femme en Haïti*, 143–208.
24. David P. Geggus, *Slavery, War, and Revolution: The British Occupation of Saint Domingue, 1793–1798* (Oxford, 1982).
25. ANOM, Col. CC9b/9, 95–97, Toussaint Louverture, Général en chef de l'armée de St. Domingue, 25 Brumaire Year VII (15 November 1798).
26. Fick, 'Emancipation in Haiti', 23–25.
27. AN, Col. CC9b/9, vol. 6, repr. in Moïse, *Le projet national*, 131–141.
28. Moïse, *Le projet national*, 105.
29. AN, Col. CC9b/9, vol. 6, 178–179, Toussaint Louverture, Arrêté, Cap, 8 Vendémiaire Year X (30 September 1801).
30. AN, Col. CC9b/9, vol. 7, 139, Toussaint Louverture, 16 Vendémiaire Year X (8 October 1801).
31. Moïse, *Le projet national*, 76.
32. AN, Col. CC9b/9, vol. 6, 179–183, Proclamation, 4 Frimaire Year X (25 November 1801), repr. in Moïse, *Le projet national*, 143–157.
33. Smartt Bell, *Toussaint Louverture*, 266–282.
34. Leclerc, 'Règlement sur la culture', Le Cap, 10 Messidor [Year X], in *Gazette officielle de Saint-Domingue*, 14 Messidor Year X (3 July 1802), 2.

35. Myriam Cottias ('Free but Minor', 188–189) demonstrates that the emphasis on the family's rehabilitative and normative functions and its significance as the foundation of labour and property continued throughout the nineteenth century.
36. The law of 20 September 1792 that prescribed the form to be followed in the laicized État Civil is reprinted in Marcel Garaud and Romuald Szramkiewicz, *La Révolution française et la famille* (Paris, 1978), 203–212.
37. Dubois, *A Colony of Citizens*, 252. See also his essay in this volume.
38. On the opening page of the 1793 registers of Port-au-Prince's État Civil a transcription appears of Polverel's decree, issued on 3 December 1792, abolishing racial distinctions; see EC, Port-au-Prince, vol. 165, 'Naissances, Mariages, Décés, 1791–93', microfilm 1094219.
39. See AN, Dxxv/43/417, 16, 'Au Bureau Municipal du Cap', Cap, 2 August 1793. The rights and status of illegitimate children were the subject of heated legislative debate in revolutionary France, where illegitimacy had historically carried the stain of dishonour and deprived *enfants naturels* of the right to become primary heirs or to inherit from parents who died intestate (Desan, *The Family on Trial*, 178–219, 197). In a radical departure from precedent, explains Desan, the law of 2 Brumaire Year II (2 November 1793) 'accorded inheritance rights to natural children whose parents died after 14 July 1789, provided that their parents had recognized them as their own' (205).
40. It is unlikely that the registrants would have shared officials' view on this point. While the relative infrequency of marriage among all social layers in eighteenth-century Saint-Domingue may have stripped illegitimacy of much of the stigma that it once carried in France, legitimacy held out the promise of access to status, property, and citizenship—all subjects of debate within the new and evolving legal order in the French colony.
41. Dubois suggests that women remained 'bearers of racial difference' under the republican regime (*Colony of Citizens*, 247).
42. Ibid. 249–276; Gautier, 'Les familles esclaves'.
43. David P. Geggus confirms that in colonial Saint-Domingue, 'it is clear that only a small fraction of slave couples were married in church'; see idem, 'Slave and Free Colored Women in Saint Domingue', in *More Than Chattel: Black Women and Slavery in the Americas*, ed. David Barry Gaspar and Darlene Clark Hine (Bloomington, 1996), 259–78, 264; also Bernard Moitt, *Women and Slavery in the French Antilles, 1635–1848* (Bloomington, 2001), 80–89. Arlette Gautier presents evidence of falling rates of marriage in the French Caribbean by the eighteenth century in *Soeurs*, 79–90; idem, 'Les familles esclaves'; idem, 'Les esclaves femmes aux Antilles françaises, 1635–1848', *Historical Reflections/Réflexions historiques* 10/3 (1983): 409–433, 420–421. On resistance to marriage by the enslaved, see idem, 'Les esclaves femmes', 35; idem, 'Les familles esclaves', 988–989. On marital practice among free people of colour, see Garrigus, *Before Haiti*; Rogers, 'Les libres de couleur', esp. 544–589.
44. Myriam Cottias's study of Trois-Îlets in Martinique reveals that 'of women who gave birth to children outside of marriage, 68 per cent remained unmarried'; see Cottias, 'Free but Minor', 198. Jacques Houdaille, in 'La fecondité des anciens esclaves à Saint-Domingue (1794–1801)', *Population* 28/6 (1973): 1208–1210, relies on nearly 1000 marriage acts in the civil registers of Port-au-Prince, Fort-Dauphin, Jacmel, et Cayes du Fond between 1794 and 1801—modest numbers relative to the ex-slave population. Using civil registers from Port-au-Prince, Jacques Cauna discovers low rates of marriage among freedpeople

immediately following Haitian independence; see his 'Les registres d'état civil anciens des Archives Nationales d'Haïti (période colonial et premiers temps de l'Indépendance)', *Revue de la société haitienne d'histoire et de géographie* 46/162 (1989): 1–34.
45. The category of 'freedpeople' is here defined restrictively as couples for whom no surname is listed for both bride and groom, or whose ex-slave status is evident from designations such as *'cultivateur'*. Since former slaves sometimes used surnames, and others married across class and racial lines, these numbers provide only a rough estimate of the actual number of marriages of *nouveaux libres*.
46. Three entries specify that the woman is a *cultivateur*, and four others specify a former master. At least four of the grooms, and perhaps more, were free before the August decree; one or more may be white or of mixed descent. Three grooms are *cultivateurs*; former masters are named in two other cases.
47. The category of *'naissances'* (births) included the registration, or civil baptism, of thousands of African teenagers and adults in Port-de-Paix.
48. We lack reliable census figures for much of the revolutionary period. Census figures from 1783 shared with me by John D. Garrigus put the enslaved population of Fort-Dauphin at 7,327 ('Récapitulation du récensement général des quartiers dépendant du Fort-Dauphin, pour l'année 1783', ANOM, DSC–0180) and of Port-de-Paix at 7,080 (ANOM, DSC–0181). In 1776, Moreau de Saint Méry listed the population of Fort-Dauphin as 700 whites, 600 *affranchis* (free people of African descent), and 6,000 slaves; and that of the town Port-de-Paix as 450 whites, 130 *affranchis*, and 8,972 slaves, with a total of 17,172 slaves in the jurisdiction of Port-de-Paix (including Gros-Morne and Saint-Louis du Nord). Decades later, Marcus Rainsford cited figures of 10,004 for the parish of Fort-Dauphin and 35,467 for the entire quartier, and 29,540 for the quartier of Port-de-Paix; see Appendix, no. XVIII [n.d.], in Rainsford, *A Memoir of Transactions that took place in St. Domingo, in the Spring of 1799*... (London, 1802), 459.
49. Geggus, 'Slave and Free Colored Women'; John K. Thornton, *Africa and Africans in the Making of the Atlantic World, 1400–1800* (Cambridge, UK, 1998), 317; idem, *The Kingdom of Kongo: Civil War and Transition, 1641–1718* (Madison, 1983), 31.
50. Thornton, *Africa and Africans*, 207.
51. Karen McCarthy Brown, 'Afro-Caribbean Healing: A Haitian Case Study', in *Healing Cultures: Art and Religion as Curative Practices in the Caribbean and Its Diaspora*, ed. Margarite Fernández Olmos and Lizabeth Paravisini-Gebert (New York, 2001), 43–68, 45.
52. Paul Christopher Johnson, 'Joining the African Diaspora: Migration and Diasporic Religious Culture among the Garífuna in Honduras and New York', in *Women and Religion in the African Diaspora*, ed. R. Marie Griffith and Barbara Dianne Savage (Baltimore, 2006), 37–59, 38.
53. Geggus, 'Slave Society', 40–41.
54. Terry Rey, 'Kongolese Catholic Influences on Haitian Popular Catholicism', in *Central Africans and Cultural Transformations in the American Diaspora*, ed. Linda M. Heywood (Cambridge, UK, 2002), 265–285.
55. This formulation provides an alternative to understandings that would posit *plasaj* as a direct reflection of women's 'choice' or simply as 'resistance' to state authority.
56. The number of birth registrations in Fort-Dauphin/Fort-Liberté fluctuated sharply.

57. The number of marriages of freedpeople between Year VIII and Year IX recorded in the annual registers jumped from 9 to over 70 in Fort-Liberté (Fort-Dauphin) and from 12 to 82 in Port-de-Paix. See note 45 for the definition of *freedpeople* used in this calculation.
58. AN, Col. CC9b/9, vol. 6, 32, 37.
59. Whether the 'material rewards' promised by Hédouville ever materialized remains a question for future research.
60. AN, Col. CC9b/9, vol. 6, 94–95, Roume, Cap français, 14 Ventôse Year VIII (5 March 1800).
61. This discrepancy offers a reminder of how unreliable quantitative estimates can be and sounds a cautionary note regarding conclusions drawn from the surviving volumes, which in most regions do not permit a systematic comparison of notarial and civil registers. This list of marriages recorded by Briffault is drawn from a Répertoire, or inventory, of marriages recorded in the North Province (ANOM, Dépôt des papiers public des colonies, DPPC NOT SDOM REP 115). The first page of the inventory is missing.
62. In 45 of the 46 marriages, one or both marital partners lacked a surname, appearing by such names as 'Pétronille fille d'Elizabeth' or 'Rose dite Rosette'. Ten of these marriages, including three in the month of Nivôse, duplicate entries in the inventory listed under 'Trou'. It is thus possible, though unlikely, that these marriages were notarized in Trou rather than Dauphin.
63. 'Loi sur les enfans nés hors mariage', 29 Messidor Year IX (18 July 1801) in 'Lois de la colonie française de Saint Domingue', 1801, Bibliothèque Haïtienne des Pères du Saint Esprit, <http://www.ht.refer.org/fonds-colonial/rechercher.php> (19 April 2009); AN, Col. CC9b/9, vol. 6 179, Toussaint Louverture, Arrêté, 8 Vendémiaire Year X (30 September 1801).
64. Moïse, *Le projet national*, 43–44.
65. The acronym FRAPH stands for Front for the Advancement and Progress of Haiti, the anti-Aristide paramilitary organization founded by Emmanuel 'Toto' Constant.

Part II
Masculinity, Revolution and War

4
Citizenship, Honour and Masculinity: Military Qualities under the French Revolution and Empire

Alan Forrest

Just as contemporaries argued about the supposed attributes of the soldiers who fought for revolutionary France during the decade after 1789, so historians have found it impossible to agree about their character or their military qualities. Some regard them as a new creation, the product of a society regenerated by the experience of revolution, an army of militants for whom the notion of honour had a new sense, one born of revolutionary zeal and ideological commitment. For Mona Ozouf, these were 'new men', part of the general regeneration of society.[1] There is certainly enough supporting evidence to make this a plausible proposition: instances of individual soldiers throwing themselves at the enemy with revolutionary slogans on their lips; diaries of Jacobin officers who had sworn hatred of kings and tyrants; letters from infantrymen to their local clubs declaring their love of the republic and their burning patriotism in the face of the enemy. But are we too prone to confuse the words of a few enthusiastic young men, stirred by republican speeches and heroic images on the eve of battle, with the spirit of the army as a whole? Or were they, as Tim Blanning would claim, just soldiers like any other, ordered and disciplined in the language and demagogy of revolution but otherwise little different from the generations of French soldiers who had gone before them, and fighting not for ideology but for the conventional foreign-policy objectives of eighteenth-century states?[2] Is there something unique, in other words, about the role played by soldiers at the time of the French Revolution, something symbiotic in the relationship between revolution and war that changes the character and motivation of the individual and leads him to question traditional views of honour and masculinity in wartime?[3] Or are they soldiers first and foremost, the significance of their citizenship relegated by the circumstances of war to a secondary and supportive role?

Citizens as soldiers

Contemporary discourse and state propaganda would certainly imply that for the citizen-soldiers of the Revolution their citizenship had a more critical importance. It was what distinguished them as free men, different in kind and in rights from the mercenary troops who routinely served in the armies of monarchs, and united by these rights with the civil society they represented and defended. They were, after all, full members of French society; their freedoms encapsulated in the Declaration of the Rights of Man and guaranteed by the constitution. Citizens, as the revolutionaries insisted, were a new breed of men, part of the political community and thus the focal point of political activity in the new France.[4] And if some citizens were now soldiers, it was because they had offered themselves, had voluntarily agreed to forgo some of the privileges of citizenship in the interests of the common good. Their recruitment had not been forced, or bullied, or purchased, as was habitual in monarchies, where serving soldiers were often the weakest and poorest members of society, roughly press-ganged into reluctant service by poverty, hunger or market forces. Nor were they bands of foreign mercenaries from Sweden or Switzerland, Hesse or Ireland, the customary makeweights of every European army in the eighteenth century. They were Frenchmen, and as a consequence they deserved to be treated with respect, honoured by their fellow-citizens for their sacrifice, a sacrifice made for the good of others and one to which they had freely consented; in this sense honour was given a new meaning, one that emanated from the regard of their fellows. It was this regard, this *considération*, which soldiers were urged to compete for, and it was presented to them as the kind of honour that mattered far more than any gifts or titles, medals or ribbons.[5] They were the defenders of society, the young men on whom the rest of society depended for their liberty, playing out the role of the heroes of antiquity on a modern stage; and recognition by that society, and its pride and gratitude, constituted the most prized form of republican honour. Or such, at least, was the theory, a theory repeatedly propounded in government proclamations, in speeches on the eve of battle and in the military press.

The insistence on the identity of the citizen-soldier was not unique to the French Revolution, nor was it invented during the revolutionary years. Citizen militias had fought in the American War of Independence, citizen-soldiers fighting against the British colonial power in the name of the American people. Indeed, the idealized image of the American militiaman fighting for the common good rather than for material inducements was a common trope of American pamphlets and patriotic imagery from the first months of the revolution in 1776.[6] And in Prussia, Spain and other states across continental Europe the experience of French rule during the Revolution and Empire would drive other nations to turn to partisans, guerrillas or some other form of nation-in-arms. This was not merely a military device to help resist the onslaught of the revolutionary armies. It was more than that—it represented the adoption of a new kind of military paradigm, in which a political definition of citizenship replaced an older, corporatist model.[7] Meyer Kestnbaum defines this change crisply, presenting it as the merging of two closely linked processes. One is derived from political change in a system based on the rights and duties of citizenship, where 'the citizen has a formally egalitarian, political relation to the state', and where 'only the individual owes a military service, solely due to his membership in a territorial political community'. National citizenship, in other words, becomes the only recognized basis for extracting military service. The second process was economic, part of the move from a corporate to a liberal economy. 'Military service' becomes 'decommodified, that is, political ties are substituted for earlier market ties'.[8] Under this system soldiers are seldom in the army for life, or as a professional career. Every soldier also has a role to play in civil society; one to which he can hope to return once the period of his military engagement is over. The basic character of the army inevitably changes—its composition, the relationship of the men with their officers and above all the relations between soldiers and civilians.

A citizen-army cannot be wholly divorced from society or become a fourth estate of the realm. It is answerable to society precisely because it is integrally part of society, the sons and brothers of civilians temporarily performing a military function before being reintegrated into the life of their towns and villages. This close interrelationship with civil society is what is so innovative about the revolutionary period: the citizen, even when he is in uniform, is identified by his rights and obligations as a member of a national society, his relations with other citizens defined and controlled by the remit of the revolutionary state.[9] Each would serve according to his or her capacities: women, like men, had to contribute to the war effort, though the roles each played were defined in a gendered way. The law of August 1793 which instituted the *levée en masse* was unequivocal in its insistence that the army was the concern of all. 'Until the enemies have been driven from the territory of the republic', it declared, 'the French people are in permanent requisition for army service'. The law went on to define the form that service would take:

> The young men shall go to battle; the married men shall forge arms and transport provisions; the women shall make tents and clothes, and shall serve in the hospitals; the children shall turn old linen into lint; the old men shall repair to the public places to stimulate the courage of the warriors and preach the unity of the republic and hatred of kings.[10]

Under the Consulate and Empire any vestige of spontaneous enthusiasm risked being extinguished as the army, levied by means of annual conscription, became both more international in composition and more professional in spirit. Yet according to the French republican myth that would achieve such popularity in the course of the nineteenth century—and most especially during the years of the radical Third Republic after 1879—these soldiers were victorious in battle precisely because of their status as citizens, free and equal in rights with civil society. Valmy was not won by classical military formations or the drill-sergeants of the eighteenth century: it was won because of flair and élan, generosity and a spirit of self-sacrifice that were born of the Revolution itself.

When, after the humiliating defeat at Sedan in 1870, republicans came to analyse the shortcomings of their own military and to compare them with the strengths of their German conquerors, it is surprising how often they turned to civic values and broad social qualities rather than to more technical issues such as weaponry or training. They took very literally Robespierre's claims that the army of the Year II was distinguished by its passion and devotion to the public good, and that it was these qualities of patriotism and morality that had been critical in forging fighting spirit and military morale.[11] Albert Sorel, for instance, the distinguished historian appointed in 1898 as a specialist lecturer on the French Revolutionary armies to the officer-cadets at the French military academy at Saint-Cyr, exuded passion for the civic qualities of the revolutionary soldiers. He did not try to discuss tactics or battlefield manoeuvres; rather he concentrated on questions of morale and fighting spirit, produced from within the people of France and inspired by an idealism that was 'the very soul of France'. He waxed lyrical about the *volonté* (commitment) of the young soldiers—especially the volunteers of 1791 and 1792, whom he designated 'the pure military generation of the Republic'. His theme was the importance of patriotism, at the end of the nineteenth century as at the end of the eighteenth; and his paeans of praise for the volunteers of the Year II underscored their dedication and their sense of civil responsibility. They were not interested in medals and the traditional honours of war, and they brought, he said, a new sense of selflessness and a devotion to the common cause that ran like a thread through French history. 'It is the Gaul of Vercengetorix, the France of the Crusades, the France of Joan of Arc. The voices that they heard were the same voices that Joan heard: they came from above—from the skies of France—as they had done throughout our history'.[12]

Military service and masculinity

But if soldiering was now linked to citizenship, it was also, quite specifically, about male citizenship. As in ancient Greece, it was the young men on whom the duty—and, in that sense, the honour—of bearing arms fell. The revolutionaries might try to undermine traditional notions of military honour, refusing to reward bravery with medals and epaulettes, but they still identified soldiering with masculinity, going further than ancien régime governments in defining the armies as specifically masculine spaces within the republic. The soldier was depicted as a warrior, the role that from antiquity had fallen naturally on the young men of the community and which now fell, in the manner of ancient Sparta, on those citizens who were young, able-bodied and male.[13] Their preferred image of the French republican soldier, popularized in speeches and eulogies and burnished for posterity, was one of comradeship and patriotic commitment, of a young man who served a cause in which he believed, and who accepted the separation from his family and the spirit of sacrifice which service entailed.[14] The decision to leave his village, the sublimation of sentiment which marked the moment of departure, these were favoured themes of painters and illustrators, themes chosen to represent not only the youthful spirit of patriotism but also the conscious separation of society into male and female, young and old. It was at this moment that the young recruit was shown to choose the defence of the republic over the comforts of family life, recognizing that it was only by abandoning his loved ones for the masculine world of the regiment that he could do his duty to the republic and his duty as a man.[15] Etchings on the theme of *Le départ du volontaire*, often executed in the sentimental tradition of Jean-Baptiste Greuze, celebrated those who accepted that duty and manfully abandoned everything for the cause of the nation. The caption on an engraving by Laurent Guyard sums up the thoughts of a generation. The picture shows a young soldier stealing a last kiss from his fiancée before leaving for the front, and the caption reads unambiguously, 'At the first sound of the drum he sacrifices his property, his life and his love for his country'.[16] By way of contrast, those left behind were predominantly female, tearful girlfriends and weeping mothers. The young man was symbolically leaving the world of women behind him as he set out for the front to do his duty as a man.

The degree of his sacrifice did not pass unnoticed. It gave him a newfound status and guaranteed a degree of public esteem, reflected in military parades, public ceremonial and civic masses to commemorate the dead, essential elements in the propagation of a new military masculinity.[17] It also brought him tangible political rights. In the first years of the Revolution, when the distinction between 'active' and 'passive' citizens was maintained on the basis of wealth and tax payments, 16 years of army service could substitute for economic substance and gain a man the privilege of being a *citoyen actif*.[18] Under the Jacobin republic the state sought to ensure that his patriotism did not entail any threat of material loss when national lands were being sold. The law specifically allowed serving soldiers to apply for lands in their home villages through the proxy of a friend, brother or father, and there are many cases in which village mayors intervened on behalf of young villagers who were absent through service in the army.[19] The message to all was clear. Soldiers were now perceived as volunteers—a term that would continue to be applied long after levies and military quotas came into use—men who were doing their duty to their fellow-citizens, who were acting in the time-honoured way as the protectors of the weak, of the old, of women and children, and who should expect to be lauded and respected for it. By performing military service they were demonstrating masculinity—the new, fraternal masculinity of revolutionary society—and applying their bodily strength for the defence of others.[20] For this they would be rewarded with membership in the explicitly masculine political world of the French republic, a world deliberately constructed to exclude female participation and mobilize the newly forged equality of men.[21]

This role was emphasized, throughout the 1790s, in paintings, in festivals and in theatre, a medium especially well suited to reinforcing cultural ideals, in this case the relationship between the man in arms and the women he was there to protect. Plays often depicted soldiers as their principal characters—appropriately in a country so continuously engaged in war—though they generally used the war as a backdrop rather than a major theme. There was good commercial reason for this, since the eighteenth-century theatregoer showed a marked preference for plays about human relationships, dramas about human frailties, about love and jealousy and retribution. The Revolution did little to change that, and plays about the triumph of virtue over temptation or the agonies of unrequited love proved the most consistently popular with audiences, far outselling dramas of a more directly political or propagandist character. Plays emphasized the heroism of the soldier, his sense of sacrifice and the ever-present threat of death. But these were scarcely ever articulated as elements of the main plot line. Their concern was with the soldier as a private individual—his gallant demeanour, his humour in the face of war, his companionable nature, his love of wine and song, his affairs with the girls he met along his route and the heartbreak he caused for wives and sweethearts left behind in France. The action of the play was seldom set on the battlefield or close to the front line; rather it dealt with the soldier's domestic concerns, his personal world, and the relations he sustained with others, especially women. This helped to create the human drama on which the success of the play depended.[22] In this way it emphasized the soldier's masculinity not only through references to honour and duty but also, more tellingly, by a portrayal of the emotional and psychological ordeals that his presence in the army and his absence from civil society entailed.

Defining masculine values

The world of the soldier was, of course, an archetypically masculine one where comradeship was highly valued, orders were obeyed without question, a strict military discipline was observed and morale depended on the close bonding of young men with others engaged in a common cause. In many ways theirs was the culture of all armies, of men who lived through danger and sought escape in one another's company, in the telling of stories and in the conviviality offered by drink. As the correspondence of revolutionary soldiers makes clear, the company of others—particularly of the young men from the towns and villages of their home province with whom they shared a common patois and a familiarity with the local terrain that built bonds between them—provided reassurance through communal knowledge and experience.[23] Their sense of being soldiers, of having a life together in the armies that was strangely cut-off from the norms of civil society, helped to strengthen these bonds, and goes far to explain why they later found it so difficult to talk about their years in uniform with those who had no first-hand experience of soldiering. In the revolutionary years they were intensely aware of their status as citizens, yet their way of life, their discipline, their itinerant lifestyle and opportunities for travel all served to distinguish them from the young men they had been. The vast majority took pride in the job they had been given to do and talked enthusiastically of the victories they had won and the battle honours bestowed on their units. Under the Empire that sense of a military culture spread further, with new opportunities for promotion, for personal reward, even a chance of the *Légion d'Honneur*. The speeches they heard, the songs they sang on the march or around the campfire, all helped to equate soldiering with masculinity. And, as Michael Hughes recently noted, their culture was imbued with images of sexual prowess as much as with military glory. Napoleon's *braves* did not just fight bravely and win honour on the battlefield. They also took pride in other manly activities; if songs like 'Aux braves de la Grande Armée' are any guide to their priorities when off duty, then they had few peers in drinking, dancing and capturing the hearts of local women. Manliness was about aggressive heterosexuality as well as physical courage; and it could be demonstrated as well in the bedroom as on the field of honour.[24]

Of course, not all young Frenchmen lived up to this stereotype or concealed the distress they felt in the army. Their sense of homesickness, of *nostalgie* or *mal du pays*, even of alienation, could be overwhelming;[25] and although this was recognized as a form of illness, it was only shallowly understood by the medical profession, and well into the nineteenth century it continued to be decried as a sign of provincial backwardness, of immaturity, even of effeminacy.[26] The desire of young soldiers for familiar sights and sounds showed through in so many ways. In letters home, they make frequent references to others from their own region of France whom they encountered in the army, whether fighting at their sides or belonging to other regiments which they met on the road or in the towns where armies converged. They want to talk with them, to exchange news of home or share the gleanings of a letter from their village: so chance meetings of this kind would often provide a conduit for news between the soldiers and their families and friends back in France. In contrast, in their writings as in many of their lives, it is noticeable how seldom they mention women, either girls they may have encountered on their travels or girlfriends left back home. In part this may be because of the context—their limited literacy, their inability to express emotion, the conventions of eighteenth-century letter-writing or the fact that they were usually writing to their mothers about things they supposed mothers wanted to hear. But it also reflects an absence of female company in what was an intensely masculine world.[27]

The place of women in the French armies

This does not mean, however, that women were entirely absent from soldiers' lives, or that military camps, garrisons and, indeed, the battalions themselves should be seen as totally masculine spaces. That had never been true of the French army, any more than it was true of most European armies in the eighteenth century. Camp followers were an established part of eighteenth-century life, criss-crossing Europe with their respective armies. French women are known to have travelled with the military in large numbers, especially when the armies were on French soil or in regions close to the front, serving the soldiers in a non-combatant capacity, often as seamstresses, laundresses or purveyors of food and drink, the *cantinières* and *vivandières* beloved of nineteenth-century folklore and popular culture.[28] Many wives and *compagnes* accompanied men in the regiments, drawn by love or driven by loneliness to accompany their partners to the very brink of battle. Officers had long been accustomed to take their wives with them on campaign, and there was not a great deal they could do to prevent other ranks from imitating their example. Besides, the law of March 1793 that allowed soldiers to marry without the permission of their superiors undoubtedly had the effect of swelling the numbers of wives who upped sticks to join their husbands, often with young children in tow.[29] What the law did seek to eradicate was any form of sexual permissiveness that would encourage prostitution in the army, a reform that had its roots not so much in moral attitudes—though the pervasive desire under Robespierre to create a republic of virtue may have favoured this dimension—as from fear of the spread of sexually transmitted disease that would drain the energy of the troops and destroy their effectiveness in battle. There was much talk of the 'hordes' of prostitutes—variously described as *femmes de mauvaise vie*, *filles de joie* and *filles débauchées*— who were attracted by the presence of the army and who milled around the columns as they marched across the countryside. The problem for the authorities lay in distinguishing them from the wives, girlfriends and stallholders who might so easily become regimental prostitutes, whether through financial necessity or sexual temptation.[30]

If these women went to war, it was always in a secondary capacity; they did not challenge the monopoly of arms which was the recognized prerogative of young males. But others did, responding to the call of the nation and wishing to defend their country alongside their male counterparts. For some it was a matter of family tradition; others followed husbands and loved ones into their units; while for a few it was a question of equality, a feminism born of the Revolution itself. Théroigne de Méricourt, for instance, haranguing the women of the Faubourg Saint-Antoine, urged them to arm themselves, since 'we are entitled to do so by nature and even by the law'.[31] How many women served in the armies we can never know, since not all signed on as women, preferring to conceal their gender and to dress as men; but from the troop records at Vincennes we can know of some eighty to a hundred women, some cross-dressing but others openly flaunting their true identity, who served in the battalions at some time during the revolutionary years.[32] There may have been more. Most of those who are known to us were in the armies during 1792 and the early part of 1793, a period of relative tolerance towards the idea that service in the military might be other than a male preserve. In these months some women served without any attempt at disguise or imposture; where they displayed courage and fortitude, they generally won the admiration and respect of their fellows, and in a few cases they were even promoted to higher ranks. Thus when Catherine Pochelat, serving with the former Régiment du Vivarais, helped her unit defeat Cobourg at Jemappes, she was rewarded for her efforts—and for the wounds she had received in combat—by being promoted to second lieutenant. Like a high proportion of the women who volunteered, she came from a strongly military family, with a father and brother already serving, and was drawn from an early age to admire military exploits.[33] It was this, she explained, that had led her to seek her fortune with the military.

On 30 April 1793, however, a decree ordered the immediate expulsion of all women from the armies, even the wives of generals and other high-ranking officers. It was doubtless intended as a measure to clean up the camps and end the lives of libertinage which, it was claimed, some officers openly led. 'You must know', Legendre told the Paris Jacobins on 9 June, 'that our generals are turning their camps into places of pleasure. They have women as aides-de-camp. Any man on whom the Republic bestows the honour of commanding its armies must renounce women, he must not allow himself the pleasures of love till he has won great victories'. Dumouriez's army seemed especially degenerate: it was believed to be awash with mistresses, singers, actresses, girlfriends and prostitutes, to the extent that his military headquarters 'had much in common with the harem of a vizier'.[34] Legendre then turned his guns on Custine, who 'has in his army women who dress as soldiers. A general may not know any other passion than a passion for victory'.[35] In his eyes women had no more place in the military than they had in clubs, sections and other parts of the public sphere. For the citizen-soldiers they were a distraction and a dangerous source of temptation, undermining the health of virile young troops by spreading syphilis and other venereal diseases in the ranks.

102 *Alan Forrest*

Custine defended himself, and his judgement, but to no avail. From the summer of 1793 women were systematically driven out of the army, compelled to lay down their weapons and to serve the republic in a way more suited to their gender. Even those who had fought bravely and won battle honours now found themselves relegated to the rear of the armies or returned to civilian life, and the role of warrior was once again identified as the monopoly of men. But the *femmes soldats* did not retreat silently to their towns and villages. They had served the republic and now considered themselves entitled to receive pensions from the state. So they wrote to their deputies or appeared before the Convention to recount their exploits under fire and plead for some recompense. Often they came with letters of support from their officers, who testified to their bravery and resolve. Their displays of valour were discussed in the Convention. And the response of the deputies showed how deeply they were impressed by the tales they heard—the same deputies who had made the service of women illegal and had decreed that all those currently serving in the regiments should be cashiered and removed from the war zone. In the majority of cases, they voted pensions for service they had now branded as illegal, an attitude that may strike us as curiously ambivalent in men who were so unwavering in their support for the rule of law.[36] Some of the women, such as Rose Barreau, who was still serving in the army when she was six months pregnant, became national celebrities: she was referred to by her immediate superiors as a 'republican heroine' and was fêted and applauded by the administrators of her department, the Gers.[37] Far from rebuking the women for overstepping their proper area of activity, politicians heaped praise on them for their courage and devotion to the motherland, even as they confirmed that in future they must stay away from the front line.

Republican ambivalence and sexual transgression

This ambivalence shows, too, in the terms in which politicians praised the women's contribution to the war, terms that frequently emphasized their masculine qualities, and the success with which they had filled an essentially male role, in a manner that any soldier would find inspiring. Rather, like Joseph Bara and Agricol Viala, the boy soldiers who had sacrificed their lives rather than betray the republic, they were presented as masculine heroes, their masculinity concealed, yet somehow enhanced, by its presence in a woman's or a child's body. David's painting of *La Mort de Bara* makes the point well, the boy's body curiously feminine, the whole image deliberately androgynous, the boy martyr who had performed the role of a man without having a man's physique or his strength.[38] His courage was underlined, and his heroic stature exaggerated, by the fact of his extreme youth, and the fragility, physical and emotional, which that youth conveyed. And so it was with those women warriors who were portrayed as having acted with all the courage and brute force of men even though endowed with none of their physical attributes. It was the male virtues that were most praised, like heroism and calmness under fire. They were warriors in their own right, devoted to the cause of the nation, and endowed with the skills and the temperament of soldiers. Or, like the Fertig sisters, the daughters of a public official in the Nord, they had been brought up from childhood to exercise, ride and fight; soldiering was in their education and their nature. They were, in the words of the Convention, 'accustomed from childhood, in spite of their delicate constitution, to mount a horse, aim with a bow, and fire a gun'; and once they had cast aside their women's clothing, 'they had joined peasant partisans in pushing the Austrian invaders back from French soil'.[39]

'In spite of their delicate constitution': there is a sense in which the praise is for women who had overcome the disadvantages of their sex to fight like lions among men. Femininity, in other words, is something to be erased, concealed, even apologized for in the context of the battlefield, which is still presented as a masculine sphere. But it was not always so. Among the praises heaped on those female warriors who appeared before the Convention were appreciations of specifically feminine virtues that were presented as the key to explaining the acts of bravery these women performed. Rose Bouillon, for instance, who served from March until August 1793 in the Army of the Moselle, had left her two young children—one aged only seven months— with relatives in the village when she joined up, and she continued to fight even after her husband was killed at her side. Only then did she ask for leave. 'I ask for it only so that I can provide the care for my children that I owe them as a mother, having fulfilled those duties that I owed to my husband and my country'.[40] Her maternal instincts, love and affection—such archetypically female virtues in this masculine world—are subtly blended with a stoical courage.

So, too, it was often fidelity that led soldiers' wives to accompany their husbands into the military, while, once there, they continued to care for and minister to them. Rose Barreau, as extolled in Léonard Bourdon's *Recueil des actions héroïques et civiques des républicains français*—published in five issues during 1793 and 1794—combined the roles of soldier and wife and is shown conquering her feelings and family loyalties in the service of the republic. She remained at her post even after seeing her brother mowed down in battle; then her husband fell beside her, a cannonball searing through his body. 'At that moment', says the report, 'republican virtue triumphed over love just as she had triumphed over nature'. The wording here is interesting, and the sense quite explicit: she was a woman doing a man's job. She continued to advance, helped to capture the fortress and fought on until the battle was won. Then and only then did she allow her feminine emotions to emerge. 'Liberté Barrau returned to where her husband lay, she bandaged his wound, caressed him in her arms, and carried him, along with her comrades in arms, to the military hospital'. And there, finally, unashamedly, she acted as a woman, and again helped save the day. 'Lavishing him with the care that comes from a wife's tenderness, she proved that she had not renounced the virtues of her sex, even though she had earlier deployed all those that seemed to be the preserve of the other'. Courage and tenderness were presented by Bourdon as complementary qualities, each with a place on the battlefield.[41] But the tender, feminine attributes, it was clear, were not those of the fighting man; they belonged in the caring professions, the auxiliary services, to the wife and mother, the nurse in the hospital ward, the *vivandière* or *cantinière* proffering comfort to the troops in the form of food or alcohol.[42]

But we should not be deceived. This paean to one of the few heroines of the revolutionary armies was not intended to expand the role of women in the military—the decree banning them from active service was not withdrawn—but rather to praise the qualities of the ideal soldier and to offer inspiration to the men in arms. The military under the Revolution would remain as uncompromisingly a gendered space as at any previous time in French history, and if the defence of the republic was reserved for citizens, there was no doubting that it was a duty assigned to males. Women played a vital role, as they had always done, in supporting the soldiers, accompanying the armies on campaign and feeding, supplying, tending and sexually satisfying the young warriors. As soldiers, their main contribution remained an iconic one, encouraging patriotism and sacrifice in others rather than making that sacrifice themselves. The supposed legions of amazons so beloved of nineteenth-century imagists and novelists were figments of the romantic imagination, since, despite the urgings of early feminists like Olympe de Gouges, there is little to suggest that more than a few score of women ever volunteered for the battalions. The image, however, remained a powerful one. The *fille-soldat* in her various manifestations became a standard trope of popular culture from songs and chapbooks to vaudeville and boulevard theatre. On the Parisian stage she would remain during the Revolution and Empire, just as she had been in the last years of the ancien régime, one of the stock figures of sexual comedy and popular drama. Yet the recurrence of such characters as *La fille hussard* or *La belle Milanaise* should not lead us into thinking of them as real soldiers any more than contemporary audiences did.[43] For the republic the notion of women in uniform, fighting and killing, bleeding and dying on the *champ d'honneur* (field of honour) was steeped in ambivalence, and the battlefield, just like the political stage, remained a consciously masculine sphere, where the involvement of women created considerable unease. Their heroism was never in doubt, but it was tainted by the suspicion of cross-dressing and subterfuge, by a pervasive sense that their presence in the regiments was an act of sexual transgression. The men of the First Republic were too classically correct, too steeped in puritanical morality, to find such ambivalence acceptable.

Conclusion

Over a quarter-century of war, during which the revolutionary and Napoleonic regimes sent levy after levy of young Frenchmen to the front, the practice of conscription and, with it, strong elements of the tradition of the citizen-soldier became embedded in French national identity. In the nineteenth century the political question was not whether young men should be balloted and forcibly enrolled in the army but what proportion of them and for what period of time; and in periods of national crisis when the territory of France was invaded—most notably in 1870—the country turned almost instinctively to the traditions of the Revolution and Empire, the new republic calling unashamedly upon the people to rise spontaneously against the invader as their ancestors had done in 1793. Military service would again become an obligation for young Frenchmen, the ballot and the cursory medical examination that would decide if they were *bons pour le service* (fit for service) a rite of passage that signalled the end of adolescence and the arrival of adult responsibility. And though there were few large-scale European wars in the nineteenth century after peace was signed at Vienna, the Crimea and the Franco-Prussian War were sufficient to remind successive generations of the reality of warfare; while others gained a first taste of soldiering in the uncompromising conditions of colonial Algeria. Here, too, the army provided a sharp, often brutal test of their masculinity. For raw recruits this could be a most daunting assignment, with the perils of heat and disease adding to the military dangers that they faced. A test of physical endurance as much as of courage or tactical skill, it was also one of the principal reasons why so many army officers, even in the republic, were reluctant to endorse the revolutionary view of the nation-in-arms or to advocate a short period of military service for all. Colonial service filled the fever wards and took a heavy toll in young lives. It was yet another reminder to young Frenchmen, if any were needed, that drawing a low number so soon after their twentieth birthday could determine the shape of their lives, the possibility of learning a trade or taking up a profession, their hopes of marriage and starting a family. They might laugh, drink, dance and enjoy the warmth of peer-group support in the hours after the ballot, but for those condemned to serve, this was a rite of passage like no other, one that remained critically important.

Throughout the nineteenth century the moment of the *tirage* (ballot) weighed heavily on every town and village in France. It would establish whether a young man could continue his civil existence and devote himself to his career and his family, or whether he had to leave the community behind and spend long years in the military. The time of the ballot was commonly turned into a popular festivity that united local people behind their young men and gave them the opportunity to celebrate their newly acquired manhood together.[44] Among the young, the looming threat of military service was also a shared bond, a common identity as a *classe*, providing a natural friendship group, a category of belonging defined by their age, their gender and the standing that gave them in their local community. On the eve of the ballot, they were given the freedom of their town or village, celebrating together their virility, their lifelong friendships and the threshold of their adult lives. It was a moment when they were expected to dress up, to drink copiously and to celebrate their youth, and the public space—the streets, the market square, the bars—was given over to them for two or three noisy, bibulous days of festivities. A high level of licence was afforded to the *conscrits*: the boys of the *classe* would shout and sing, sound horns, get wildly drunk and take part in the dances and banquets that marked the *fête*, and in the evening there was considerable sexual licence, too. Older men, those of previous *classes*, had their place in the ceremonies, as did the families of the young. As for the conscripts themselves, it was a ceremony to mark their transition into manhood, a moment that marked their departure from the protection of their families to play their own part in the nation and the wider community. During the Third Republic it became the principal rite of passage between first communion and marriage.[45]

The ceremony left an indelible mark on all those who took part. It was, as one conscript from Saint-Victor in the Ardèche recalled many years later, a moment that he and his friends had been waiting for ever since leaving school. They had watched their elder brothers process through the streets of the village, carrying their flag and shouting out their identity as conscripts. They had admired them as they strode past with their numbers attached to their hats—just as they would be shown in songs and lithographs, etchings and woodcuts.[46] And when they in turn reached the age of eighteen, they, too, followed the village tradition, pooling their savings and going together to the *bureau de tabac* in the nearest town—for them it was in the next *département*, at Tain l'Hermitage—where they would buy their own flag, choosing the design and ordering it, along with the statutory cane and ribbons and a little barrel for transporting liquor, from a firm that specialized in making goods for *fêtes*. The ritual did not change from one *classe* to the next as the day of the ballot approached. Tentatively, they proceeded to the first public showing of their flag: 'we agreed on the day, always a Sunday, and the time, always at the end of mass, and the route, which had been unchanged for generations', and 'timidly' walked through the village, no-one willing to carry the flag or blow the trumpet. But the diffidence did not last. During their first practice run, villagers feigned disbelief, exclaiming, not without reason, 'They are still kids!' But the second time no-one faltered. They were boys who had come of age, young men whose maturity won the respect of their community.[47] They were ready to take their place as citizens and to play their part as men in the life of the nation.

Notes

1. Mona Ozouf, 'La Révolution Française et la formation de l'homme nouveau', in *L'homme régénéré: Essais sur la Révolution Française* (Paris, 1989), 116–157.
2. T. C. W. Blanning, *The French Revolutionary Wars, 1787–1802* (London, 1996).
3. Jonathan R. Adelman, *Revolution, Armies, and War: A Political History* (Boulder, CO, 1985), 2.
4. Renée Waldinger, 'Preface', in *The French Revolution and the Meaning of Citizenship*, ed. Renée Waldinger et al. (Westport, CT, 1993), x.
5. For a discussion of the various resonances of the idea of *considération*, see Claudine Haroche and Jean-Claude Vatin (eds), *La considération* (Paris, 1998), 9–12.
6. This theme is developed in a comparative context by Olivia Zoë Kahr, 'The Image of the Patriot Soldier in the American and French Revolutions', Ph.D. thesis (University College London, 2007).
7. For a comparative perspective, see Stefan Dudink and Karen Hagemann, 'Masculinity in Politics and War in the Age of Democratic Revolutions, 1750–1850', in *Masculinities in Politics and War: Gendering Modern History*, ed. Stefan Dudink et al. (Manchester, 2004), 3–21; on male citizenship and military service in this period, see *Representing Masculinity: Male Citizenship in Modern Western Culture*, ed. Stefan Dudink et al. (Basingstoke, 2007), 25–130.
8. Meyer Kestnbaum, 'Citizen-soldiers, National Service, and the Mass Army: The Birth of Conscription in Revolutionary Europe and North America', in *The Comparative Study of Conscription in the Armed Forces*, ed. Lars Mjøset and Stephen van Holde, special issue of *Comparative Social Research* 20 (2002): 117–144. The quotations are taken from the editors' introduction, 30–31.
9. Bertrand Taithe, *Citizenship and Wars: France in Turmoil, 1870–1871* (London, 2001), 4.
10. John Hall Stewart, *A Documentary Survey of the French Revolution* (New York, 1951), 472–474.
11. Norman Hampson, 'The French Revolution and the Nationalisation of Honour', in *War and Society: Historical Essays in Honour and Memory of J. R. Western, 1928–1971*, ed. M. R. D. Foot (London, 1973), 199–212, 209.
12. Albert Sorel, 'Programme du cours', repr. in *L'armée à travers les âges: conférences faites en 1898 à l'Ecole Militaire de Saint-Cyr*, ed. Ernest Lavisse (Paris, 1899), 184–200, 192.
13. Claude Mossé, *L'antiquité dans la Révolution Française* (Paris, 1989), 82–86.
14. John A. Lynn, *The Bayonets of the Republic: Motivation and Tactics in the Army of Revolutionary France, 1791–94* (Urbana, 1984), 139.
15. For a comparative perspective on this common motif in images, see Karen Hagemann, 'The Military and Masculinity: Gendering the History of the French Wars, 1792–1815', in *War in an Age of Revolution, 1775–1815*, ed. Roger Chickering and Stig Förster (Cambridge, UK, 2009), 331–352.
16. 'Le départ d'un volontaire' (1792), reproduced in *La Révolution Française: Images et récit*, ed. Michel Vovelle, 5 vols (Paris, 1986), vol. 3, 52.
17. See George L. Mosse, *The Image of Man: The Creation of Modern Masculinity* (New York, 1996).
18. Jean-Paul Bertaud, *La révolution armée: Les soldats-citoyens et la Révolution Française* (Paris, 1979), 63.
19. Peter Jones, *The Peasantry in the French Revolution* (New York, 1991), 161–164.
20. Sean M. Quinlan, 'Men without Women? Ideal Masculinity and Male Sociability in the French Revolution, 1789–99', in *French Masculinities: History,*

Culture and Politics, ed. Christopher E. Forth and Bertrand Taithe (Basingstoke, 2007), 31–50, 38.
21. Joan B. Landes, 'Republican Citizenship and Heterosocial Desire: Concepts of Masculinity in Revolutionary France', in Dudink, *Masculinities*, 96–115, 112.
22. Erica Joy Mannucci, 'Le militaire dans le théâtre de la Révolution Française', in *Les arts de la scène et la Révolution Française*, ed. Philippe Bourdin and Gérard Loubinoux (Clermont-Ferrand, 2004), 379–380.
23. André Palluel-Guillard, 'Correspondance et mentalité des soldats savoyards de l'armée napoléonienne', in *Soldats et armées en Savoie: Actes du Congrès des Sociétés Savantes de Savoie, Saint-Jean-de-Maurienne, 6 et 7 septembre 1980* (Chambéry, 1981).
24. Michael J. Hughes, 'Making Frenchmen into Warriors: Martial Masculinity in Napoleonic France', in Forth and Taithe, *French Masculinities*, 51–66, 51–52.
25. Marcel Reinhard, 'Nostalgie et service militaire pendant la Révolution', *Annales historiques de la Révolution Française* 30 (1958): 1–15.
26. Bertrand Taithe, 'Neighbourhood Boys and Men: The Changing Spaces of Masculine Identity in France, 1848–71', in Forth and Taithe, *French Masculinities*, 67–84, 71–72.
27. For a discussion of letter-writing among soldiers in the Revolutionary Wars, see Alan Forrest, *Napoleon's Men: The Soldiers of Revolution and Empire* (London, 2002), 21–52.
28. For a more detailed discussion of the role played by these women, see Chapter 9 by Thomas Cardoza in this volume.
29. Joan B. Landes, *Visualizing the Nation: Gender, Representation, and Revolution in Eighteenth-Century France* (Ithaca, NY, 2001), 160.
30. Patrick Bouhet, 'Les femmes et les armées de la Révolution à l'Empire: un aperçu', *Guerres mondiales et conflits contemporains* 198 (2000): 11–29, 14.
31. Sylvie Steinberg, *La confusion des sexes: Le travestissement de la Renaissance à la Révolution* (Paris, 2001), 249.
32. Jean-Clément Martin, 'Travestissements, impostures, et la communauté historienne : A propos des femmes soldats de la Révolution et de l'Empire', *Politix* 74 (2006): 31–48.
33. Fernand Gerbaux, 'Les femmes soldats pendant la Révolution', *Révolution Française* 47 (1904): 47–61, 52.
34. Steinberg, *La confusion*, 258.
35. Léon Hennet, 'Une femme-soldat: Anne-Françoise-Pélagie Dulierre', *Annales Révolutionnaires* 1 (1908): 610–621.
36. Steinberg, *La confusion*, 260–261.
37. Rudolf M. Dekker and Lotte C. van de Pol, 'Republican Heroines: Cross-Dressing Women in the French Revolutionary Armies', *History of European Ideas* 10 (1989): 353–364, 353.
38. Marie-Pierre Foissy-Aufrère et al. (eds), *La Mort de Bara* (Avignon: Fondation du Muséum, 1989).
39. Gerbaux, 'Les femmes soldats', 52.
40. Ibid. 54.
41. Quoted in Steinberg, *La confusion*, 255.
42. Cardoza develops the question of sexual division in the French army and on the battlefield in Chapter 9 of this volume.
43. This theme is treated at greater length in David Hopkin, 'Female Soldiers in the French Armies of the Revolutionary and Napoleonic Epoch', in *Soldiers, Citizens and Civilians: Experiences and Perceptions of the French Wars, 1790–1820*, ed. Alan

Forrest et al. (Basingstoke, 2008), 77–95. A more general treatment of the question appears in John A. Lynn II, *Women, Armies, and Warfare in Early Modern Europe* (Cambridge, UK, 2008).
44. These celebrations lingered longest in rural areas of France; from the nineteenth century we have particularly good descriptions of village *fêtes* in regions like Burgundy and the Beaujolais.
45. Michel Bozon, 'Conscrits et fêtes de conscrits à Villefranche-sur-Saône', *Ethnologie française* 1 (1979): 29–46.
46. Henri George, *Conscription, tirage au sort et imagerie populaire* (Paris, 1981), 7–11.
47. *Les conscrits de Saint-Victor (Ardèche): Exposition organisée par Chatelermuze, Saint-Victor, 1995.* The catalogue, typed and cheaply reproduced, is in the collection of the Musée des Arts et Traditions Populaires in Paris. For similar ceremonies in Prussia, which were introduced with universal conscription in 1813, see Chapter 14 by Karen Hagemann in this volume.

5
In the Shadow of the Citizen-Soldier: Politics and Gender in Dutch Officers' Careers, 1780–1815

Stefan Dudink

Military officers' experiences of the Revolutionary and Napoleonic Wars differed dramatically for reasons that are obvious in some cases and in others merit further consideration. If not cut short by injury or death, an ambitious officer's career was largely shaped during this period by his ability to adapt both to the changing nature of war and politics and to the evolving relationship between them. Historian David A. Bell has recently characterized these changes in terms of an increasing differentiation of the military from the civilian sphere. By the late eighteenth century, Bell argues, a 'culture of war' that was dominated by aristocrats who did not sharply distinguish their professional roles as military officers from their social identity as noblemen gave way to a new culture organized around a separation of the military from civil society. This new culture came with an 'infrastructure of difference' that segregated the military institutionally by housing soldiers in barracks, educating them in military academies and regulating their conduct by means of a separate legal system. Officers were required to wear uniforms that visually displayed their military status, to spend more and more time soldiering and to espouse a political cause rather than a code of honour to which they were unconditionally bound. Instead of belonging to a warrior class that adhered to a concept of honour that pre-dated the nation-state, they were becoming professionals in the service of a state government, regardless of whether they fought for their native country.[1]

Bell's account is part of his wider study of modern total war, which he sees emerging for the first time over the course of the French Revolution and the Napoleonic Wars. The separation of the military from civil society, he argues, was a prerequisite for the imposition of the former's values and practices on the latter. The emergence of modern militarism—which entailed the subordination of civil to military—rested on the prior construction of these two spheres as opposites.[2]

In Bell's history of the creation and subsequent transgression of modern boundaries between military and civil spheres, the citizen-soldier of classical antiquity occupies a contradictory position. Locating the origins of modern total war in the intellectual transformations of the Enlightenment and the dynamics of revolutionary politics, Bell shows how important to Enlightenment thinkers and revolutionaries alike was the idea of an ancient civic virtue that found its worthiest expression in male citizens taking up arms. In a way, however, Bell also refuses the citizen-soldier his due. He calls it 'a great irony' that notions of war and politics derived from classical antiquity—notions he consistently refers to as 'fantasy' and 'dreams'—should contribute to the rise of a quintessentially modern regime of warfare.[3]

This chapter interprets the careers of two Dutch officers during the Revolutionary and Napoleonic Wars as expressions of the citizen-soldier ideal and the political masculinity it represented. While not primarily concerned with the emergence of total war, my interpretation does build on Bell's analysis of the changing nature of war and politics in this period. The ideal of the citizen-soldier holds a central place in the following discussion, less in terms of fantasy than in relation to its shaping influence on early modern and modern European and Atlantic political cultures. Well preserved in the 'republican tradition', the legacy of the citizen-soldier of antiquity helped to define important aspects of (early) modern politics.[4] Given this influence, and given the assumptions about the fundamental unity of the elements of public life that the citizen-soldier embodied, it is, perhaps, less ironic than Bell suggests that this ideal contributed to a modern culture of war in which the distinction between military and civil spheres ultimately collapsed.

The differing fortunes of the two officers discussed here can be explained: first, as effects of the varying degrees to which they were willing and able to emulate the classical citizen-soldier; and, second, as a reflection of the contemporary fortunes of the citizen-soldier ideal, which rose to prominence in the early years of the Dutch Age of Democratic Revolutions but thereafter fell from grace. To embody the citizen-soldier implied the ideological and practical performance of a specific kind of masculinity. The ideal of the citizen-soldier was highly gendered, centring on notions of male virtue, valour and self-sacrifice. Imagined as precarious, these qualities and masculinity itself were never assumed or conferred but always had to be actively pursued, while effeminacy—that peculiarly pre- and early modern category of gender—had to be avoided.[5] To attain such a virtuous masculinity was also to forge a connection between aspects of society. Politics and war, in particular, were linked, or at least prevented from becoming separate domains, in the process of achieving the masculinity that was specific to the citizen-soldier. Becoming a truly virtuous male citizen entailed rejection of a life devoted to private interests and pleasures without any attention to public duties. Admittedly, this pre- and early modern topography of the societal spheres differs from the modern separation and subsequent fusion of the military and civil society that is crucial to Bell's story. Nevertheless, the set of gendered political and military ideas and practices that rested on this earlier topography provided the context for changes that occurred in both the nature of and the relations between war and politics during the revolutionary and Napoleonic periods. The lives and careers of the two men that are the subject of this chapter were substantially shaped by it.

Becoming citizen-soldiers

David Hendrikus Chassé (1765–1849) and Herman Willem Daendels (1762–1818) began their professional lives with the ancien régime expectation that they would follow in their fathers' footsteps.[6] For David Chassé this expectation proved to be well founded. At ten years of age he joined the regiment of the Dutch Republic's army in which his father served as an officer, and six years later he entered the ranks of subaltern officers as a lieutenant—an event he would celebrate yearly for the rest of his life. Herman Daendels was bitterly disappointed when, after completing his study of law at the age of 21, it became clear that he would not succeed his father, the owner of a brickyard, as alderman of Hattem, a small town in an eastern province of the Dutch Republic, where he had been born.

Chassé's success and Daendels's misfortune formed the opening movements of their individual biographies, but they were also linked to wider, long-term political processes and struggles in the Dutch Republic that would gain dramatic momentum in the early 1780s.[7] By that time, contradictions in the Republic's political structure that had haunted it since its creation had become too stark to contain and set it off on a course leading to revolution and civil war. In some respects an anomaly among early modern European states, the Republic was (in)famous for the political and civic liberties enjoyed by its citizens and for its high degree of decentralization. At the heart of its constitutional system, however, it harboured monarchical tendencies that were manifested in the status accorded to the princes of the House of Orange, who occupied the post of 'Stadholder'. Officially the servant of the provincial estates and the Estates General, the Stadholder possessed authority that, when asserted, could make him the most powerful person in the Republic. Stadholders commanded both the army and the navy, and had the right to appoint numerous local and state officials. These entitlements gave them, depending on individual skill and political circumstances, considerable influence. As a result, the political history of the Republic was largely a record of continuous struggle between the Stadholder and the provincial estates and Estates General over power and privileges. Promotions such as that of Chassé were the prerogative of the Stadholder, who, like his immediate predecessor, had exercised this right generously in order to increase his power by creating clients in the military. Daendels was not considered for a modest administrative position in the local government of his hometown because the Stadholder claimed the right to make this particular appointment. The protracted legal contest that followed was only one of many such skirmishes throughout the Republic, skirmishes that over the course of the 1780s escalated into a national conflict ending in a revolution.

From 1780 onwards, attempts on the part of the estates and local bodies to maintain or restore traditional privileges became entwined with political arguments of a more radical, democratic kind. The so-called Patriot movement connected complaints about economic and moral decline that had been voiced in enlightened Dutch public opinion for over 50 years with the struggle over the proper locus of power in the Republic. Accusing the Stadholder of usurping power that belonged to 'the people' and its representatives, the Patriots viewed the Stadholder and his clients as obstacles on the road to national recovery. They called for democratization as part of a broader programme to regain economic prosperity and international power. A crucial aspect of Patriot politics was the revival of militias, which symbolized a culture of 'urban republicanism'. Patriots called on male citizens to arm themselves in order to defend, maintain or, if necessary, regain the rights and liberty that were theirs. Throughout the country existing militias were taken over by Patriots, and new militias—the so-called free corps—were formed. Both would sustain the Patriot movement's bid for power.[8]

Herman Daendels was not slow in linking his own situation with the country's broader political struggles. In 1783 he established a militia in Hattem that drilled, under his command, after Sunday morning church service and played an increasingly vital role in his attempts to regain the political rights that the Stadholder had supposedly usurped. When in 1786 this struggle led to a unilateral decision on the part of the town government to re-appropriate these rights, the Stadholder sent his troops to restore order and re-establish his authority. Daendels and his militia did not stand a chance and were forced to flee the town. Nevertheless, these events provided the Patriot movement with a striking narrative of arbitrary rule and despotic abuse of power, and offered Daendels the pedestal on which he could begin to raise himself as military hero of the revolution.

For reasons that are harder to fathom, the fervour of Patriot politics had also touched David Chassé. In 1786 he had resigned from the army and joined a Patriot free corps. By this time the Patriot revolution was bordering on civil war. Assisted by Prussian troops, the Stadholder managed in 1787 to crush the Patriot movement and its army, in which Chassé and Daendels then served as captain and major, respectively. The subsequent restoration of the Stadholder's regime forced them into exile in France.

Like many of their compatriots, Daendels and Chassé had heeded the Patriots' call to take up arms and join the newly established free corps or the militias that had been roused from their slumber by Patriot zeal. Patriot political language of the early 1780s consisted to a large extent of calls for collective self-transformation. In 1783, the same year in which Daendels had his fellow-citizens perform military drills after Sunday church services, one of the main Patriot weeklies published series of articles devoted to the militia. The authors of these articles directly addressed their male readers, urging them to take the duties of citizenship seriously. As one contributor put it: 'You are a Citizen of the Netherlands—and this means you are also a defender of the Netherlands. Liberty is the greatest civil sanctuary of the Netherlands, and who shall protect her better than he who is a true Patriot?—You must be a warrior!'[9] In a poem that appeared in a later issue of this weekly, the same writer made it clear that this process of citizens becoming warriors involved shaking off a debilitating effeminacy and replacing it with a masculinity worthy of the true citizen. 'Dolled up noblemen,' he wrote, paraded in front of 'women's mirrors', but the citizen-soldier caught his own reflection in the shining blade of his sabre:

> Does not your noble heart beat stronger
> Does not your manly countenance shine
> Do you not feel your Liberty
> When you see yourself in arms?[10]

Bridging the gap that separated citizen from warrior also required bridging the gap between a shameful, cowardly present and a glorious, valorous past. Another contributor to this Patriot weekly urged Dutch citizens to mirror the virtuous example set by their mytho-historical ancestors, the Batavians, a Germanic tribe that had successfully revolted against the Romans in 69–70 AD. If belonging to an 'enlightened people' implied 'effeminate baseness' and indifference to safeguarding one's rights and liberties, then the author preferred the barbaric condition of the Batavian. His proud posture, the toughness in his glance and the power of his muscles—all were the result of the Batavians' devotion to training in the use of arms. 'Yes! Dutchmen! This is what your ancestors did! They were Barbarians!'[11]

Citizens were to become soldiers, but, conversely, soldiers also had to become citizens. In response to articles about the militia and free corps, several authors argued for the need to develop a republican *esprit militaire* in the Dutch armed forces. Because the Stadholder was the commander of army and navy, and because the former included large numbers of soldiers from European monarchies, the Dutch military was, according to one writer, dominated by a military ethos that emphasized the honour and glory of the prince and instilled a passion for recognition and rewards from the prince in his soldiers. A republican military spirit, in contrast, was guided by the will to serve 'the independence, liberty, and wellbeing of the entire Dutch people'. Anyone who doubted the value in battle of such a lofty spirit was advised to consult the military histories of the Greek and Roman republics.[12]

This republican military spirit could emerge only under specific institutional conditions. One way to 'unite the citizen with the soldier' was to stop the annual transfer of all garrisons. Moving from city to city prevented officers and soldiers from developing permanent ties and from considering the interests of the place where they were briefly stationed as their own: 'This is the sword that cuts through all the links that naturally exist between the Citizen and Soldier as members of the same body'.[13] Here, too, reconnecting the soldier and the citizen involved reshaping his masculinity. Soldiers and officers who knew that their posting was only temporary were prone to seducing citizens' wives and daughters; were they to reside in a city permanently, their ties to that place would be simultaneously formed and expressed in their marriage to local women.

The unification of citizen and soldier under the aegis of a redeemed masculinity was a crucial aspect of Patriot ideology, but it was not free from contradictions. For instance, the fact that the militias and free corps were military organizations was not always easily reconciled with their main purpose: the defence of liberties, or liberty, against tyrannical rule. The militias and free corps were the clearest manifestation of the Patriot ambition to restore sovereignty to the citizens. As the Patriot weekly advised a militia officer to tell one of his soldiers: 'Listen, your *Liberty* consists in you being *master* of yourself; would you not be in possession of your *Liberty*, somebody else will be your master.'[14] But apart from being an expression of, and means to, political self-determination, the militias were also military organizations that imposed hierarchy and a duty to obey orders on their members. One Patriot claimed that military subordination forced soldiers in the regular army to obey any order without question, whereas citizen-soldiers were free to refuse—implying that the first were potential instruments of tyranny while the latter would always protect liberty.[15] In response, a 'German Staff Officer' sympathetic to the Patriots and the militias argued that strict discipline was just as necessary to the regular army as to the militia. At moments when soldiers were gripped by fear, it served the purpose of preventing the military machine from falling apart or not moving when told to do so. 'If an able and courageous Citizen colonel...gives the order "March!", his men should not begin to deliberate the dangers, etc., but should...blindly follow [his] orders'.[16]

This contradiction in its politics made the militia vulnerable to attacks from the Patriots' opponents. Such politics could easily be depicted as a Patriot brand of despotism and arbitrary rule, in part because militias were used to exert political pressure and often played a decisive role in Patriot attempts to take over and reform local governments. Herman Daendels certainly seems to have been drawn to the model of the citizen-soldier and to the militia because of the authority and hierarchy that defined them—even if these qualities sat uneasily with Patriot claims to protect liberty. When Daendels established a militia in Hattem, When Daendels established a militia in Hattem, he found a gratifying compensation for the slight he had received when the Stadholder had reserved the right to make the appointment Daendels had sought. Commanding the militia immediately placed him in a position of authority over his soldiers and in time paved the way to obtaining the post that he had been denied. Backed by the force of his 'troops', Daendels built up a local powerbase and persuaded the town government to re-appropriate the right formerly claimed by the Stadholder.

Although the reasons why David Chassé felt attracted to the militia and the citizen-soldier are less clear-cut, in his case, too, a vulnerability in Patriot politics seems to have formed a point of entry for subjective identification. The citizen-soldier embodied a heroic effort to confront the decay that threatened republics as prosperity and luxury ate away at the virtues on which they had been built. This ideal figure could make republican time stand still and even lead his political community back to that earlier and more virtuous state in which they had previously lived. The militia's valour was bolstered by references to heroic examples from ancient Roman, Greek and, above all, local history.[17] Endorsements of the 'barbaric' virtues of the Batavians made it easy, however, for opponents to point to a dangerously primitive streak in Patriot politics. They argued that the militias represented a variety of republicanism that was archaic and primitive, incompatible with the level of civilization and progress achieved in the commercial, urbanized world of the Dutch Republic.[18] From this perspective, the masculinity patriotism advocated was equally archaic and primitive and could lead only to chaos and discord.[19]

For those of a somewhat unruly nature, the militias' defiance of authority and the opportunities they offered for untoward kinds of self-assertion and illicit violence may well have been the point in joining them. Chassé seems to fit this description. His nineteenth-century biographer writes that the young Chassé sympathized with Patriot ideas about liberty, but he also suggests that it was an irascible temperament that led the junior officer to actually embrace them.[20] Critics of the Patriot movement who feared that chaos must ensue from politics driven by dangerous passions would have found their worst suspicions confirmed by the course of events that followed Chassé's enlistment in a Patriot militia in 1786. Apparently, he soon regretted his decision and was appalled at the civil war that broke out in 1787. Although he fought energetically on the side of the Patriots against the Prussian troops that assisted the Stadholder in suppressing the revolution, his courage seems to have been partly the product of inner turmoil and a desire to find death on the battlefield. In the end, his conflicting political loyalties resulted in another's death. Outraged by what he considered an overly offensive remark made by a fellow Patriot about the Stadholder, Chassé challenged the man to a duel and killed him.[21]

The Stadholder's victory and the vengeful restoration that followed drove Daendels and Chassé into exile in France, together with thousands of other

Patriots. The two men took with them a shared experience of participation in the Patriot movement and of their service as citizen-soldiers. In remarkably different ways this experience shaped their outlook on the nature of, and relations between, war and politics, and helped to define their strategies for future professional advancement. His years as a Patriot citizen-soldier taught Daendels two valuable lessons that guided his behaviour in the years to come. He would not forget that the kind of soldiering that derived its legitimacy from a political struggle against despotic powers created unprecedented possibilities for upward mobility. And, judging by his future actions, he also remembered that military force could remarkably accelerate the tardy pace of politics. For Chassé, transgressing the line that separated politics from war seems to have had less to do with realizing professional ambitions and political self-assertion than with the emergence of irresolvable conflict between citizens—a conflict reflected so painfully in his own divided loyalties and the violence they had produced.

Parting ways

Revolution had driven Chassé to France. Once there, it was the ancien régime practice of recruiting soldiers on an international market for military personnel that allowed him to sign up with France's royal army in 1788. The political upheaval he had left behind overtook him with a vengeance. He witnessed the fall of the Bastille and, four years later, the execution of Louis XVI. Perhaps these events reinforced his dislike of radical politics and politics in general. What seems clear, however, is that, unlike Daendels, he did not regard the dramatic political transformations of these years as political opportunities, much less as events that he might actively help to shape.

When revolutionary France went to war in 1792, the Patriots in exile saw a chance to resume their own armed struggle. Daendels played a leading role in convincing French revolutionary leaders to allow the formation of a *Légion Franche Étrangère* (Free Foreign Legion). One battalion of this legion was composed of former members of the Patriot militias and recruited its officers from among the more than 200 Patriot officers dismissed from the Dutch army in 1787.[22] With the establishment of the Foreign Legion, a military career in French service began for Daendels, who was appointed lieutenant-colonel of its Dutch battalion.

Although the demand for troops and officers in the French revolutionary army rose sharply after 1792, Daendels was not an immediate candidate for an important position in this army. His military experience was negligible compared to that of professional soldiers, and during the Reign of Terror the suspicion of treason easily fell on foreigners. Nevertheless, Daendels quickly rose to the rank of brigadier-general, and his ability to embody the ideal of the citizen-soldier helps to account for his swift ascent.[23] Deeply motivated by radical-revolutionary ideals, apparently fearless in battle and displaying a bravado that bordered on the reckless, Daendels became the model citizen-soldier. He also made sure that people in high places heard of his exploits. While in the field, he wrote to one of the National Convention's deputies on mission with the army about his preference for hand-to-hand combat using the bayonet, a form of combat that was considered peculiarly French, manly and revolutionary, and in which, according to Daendels, 'the French…have always and at all times been victorious'.[24] Also, he appointed as adjutant a journalist who made sure that Daendels was mentioned—and invariably described as 'brave'—in the relevant papers. During the dangerous years of the Terror he, along with 60 other 'Batavians', signed a letter congratulating the National Convention on the discovery of yet another conspiracy.[25]

In 1792, Chassé joined the *Légion Franche Étrangère*. He, too, was promoted, though less spectacularly than Daendels, becoming a captain. His career not only advanced more slowly than that of Daendels but it also started to be built more on soldierly accomplishments than on political agility. After a confrontation in which a large number of Frenchmen had been killed, Chassé threatened to shoot a deputy attached to his battalion if he dared to criticize either Chassé or his troops.[26]

Between 1792 and 1795, Daendels and Chassé both fought in the Austrian Netherlands and the Dutch Republic, to which they returned as glorious 'liberators' in the first months of 1795. Daendels had already announced his impending arrival in October 1794 in a proclamation distributed in the eastern provinces where he had grown up. In it he called on his compatriots to arm themselves in order to assist in their liberation and advised them 'to elect as captains not the richest or the most beautifully dressed,…but those who are best at leading you in and out of battle.' Aided by himself and his men, he predicted, the locals would see 'haughty and beautifully powdered little officers and their soldiers run from farmers' boys in their linen overalls.'[27] He presented himself, once again, as the exemplary and manly citizen-soldier but also overestimated the room for political manoeuvre that this political self-fashioning afforded him. The French authorities were not amused by Daendels's attempt to position himself at the head of a local revolutionary movement, and he barely escaped demotion and transfer.

The French invasion brought a 'Velvet Revolution' to the Republic that ended the Dutch ancien régime and established a new 'Batavian Republic'. The Stadholder and his family fled to England, a unitary constitution replaced the Republic's federative political structure, and male citizens over 20 years of age elected a National Assembly. Chassé and Daendels were given permission to join the army of the Batavian Republic. Daendels was commissioned a lieutenant-general and charged with the reorganization of the army. He transformed it from a decentralized organization into a centrally managed national force, removing as many foreign troops and officers who had served under the Stadholder as he could spare and modelling the new army on the French example.[28]

Both men subsequently fought in the Batavian Army that supported French troops, for instance in Germany in 1796. In the decade that followed, Chassé's career continued to develop much as it had in the French army since 1788. Based solely on his merits as a soldier, he made relatively unremarkable but steady upward progress through the ranks and never sought greater glory or power through involvement in politics. He attained the rank of colonel in 1803 and that of major-general in 1806, but he also experienced periods of inactivity and undertook missions with no opportunity for distinction.

Daendels, on the other hand, went as far as one could go in these years as a citizen-soldier. He typified what David Bell has called the new figure of the 'political general', who 'actively manoeuvred and schemed within the treacherous world of...politics.'[29] When the revolution in the new Batavian Republic appeared on one occasion to have come to a standstill and, on another, to be straying from the radical track, Daendels intervened with an armed coup, arresting and imprisoning representatives to the National Convention who stood in the way of true revolutionary politics.

His ability to embody the citizen-soldier paved the way for Daendels's career success, but he also paid dearly for the moments when he was unable to perform this part. At the height of his power, Daendels painfully experienced the fragile nature of success under a revolutionary government when, in 1799, an Anglo-Russian invasion force landed at the northwestern shore of the Batavian Republic. Although the invasion was successfully repulsed, Daendels made some strategic errors that led to an accusation of treason against him. Here the intersection of politics and war that the citizen-soldier represented revealed a darker side: military failure inevitably implied political subversion. Although officially cleared of these charges, Daendels suffered a severe blow to his reputation and resigned his commission. By 1801 his role in the Batavian Republic was over. He withdrew to a country estate, hoping to make a fortune with agricultural innovations.

Spain and Java

At its establishment the Batavian Republic had been placed under French supervision that expanded with the years. In 1806, Napoleon appointed his brother Louis as king of this satellite state in order to control and exploit it more effectively. For both Chassé and Daendels the new political constellation—in particular the fact that their country's fate increasingly depended on ever-widening international military dynamics—reversed their fortunes.

In 1808, Chassé was finally given an assignment that offered him the opportunity to shine and to leave his mark as a commander. Napoleon had ordered his brother to make Dutch troops available for his war in Spain. Chassé was given command of a Dutch brigade that was to join the French army in Spain. He led 3,000 men into a war from which only a handful of

Dutch soldiers and officers would return. Chronic shortages of supplies and equipment, a harsh climate and guerrilla warfare took their toll, as did the tendency of the French command to sacrifice foreign troops.[30] For Chassé the Spanish campaign also brought rewards: a knighthood in the *Légion d'Honneur*, a barony and promotion to brigadier-general. Perhaps these distinctions satisfied his ambition, but they were obtained at a high cost. Twenty years after his deeply frustrating participation in a civil war that had erased the boundaries between politics and war, Chassé found himself in the middle of a conflict that effaced another set of boundaries, with even more appalling results. Chassé was sharply aware that the war he fought in was of a new kind and that its novelty lay in the dissolution of the distinctions between soldier and civilian. He recognized that what made this war distinctive was not the fact that civilians participated in it but the dynamics of total destruction that resulted from an inability to distinguish between official combatants and the general population:

> This campaign is surely the most singular I have ever experienced. One day one pursues the regular enemy and believes one need not worry about the inhabitants of the country; the next day a troop of 4 to 500 brigands and armed farmers appears: this seems to be a second Vendée that will not end except in total destruction. ... the king of Spain will rule this country only after the majority of its cities have been destroyed and the soil has been drenched in the blood of his ... citizens and allies.[31]

This was a war, as Chassé's biographer remarks, that required 'great vigilance and effort' but offered no corresponding opportunity to win glory.[32] The French considered the Dutch troops to be particularly suited for counter-guerrilla warfare, and, as a result, Chassé and his men were often occupied with hunting 'brigands'—a task that the officers disdained for its lack of military prestige.[33] Ultimately, however, Chassé's only ideological justification for fighting in this war was honour, in its limited meaning of a determination to do one's duty regardless of the moral value of the cause.[34] A bare pride in dutiful soldiering was the only way left to confer meaning on a war he resented. After Napoleon's 1810 annexation of the Netherlands this resentment grew even stronger. Chassé then found himself once again in French service, but this time not of his own accord and deprived of the sense of honour which came from the belief that, until that moment, he had at least been serving his country.

Since the failure of the Patriot revolution, Chassé had operated professionally on the basis of minimal ideological commitment. His service in Spain reduced this even further to an entirely abstract code of honour. In later years, Chassé's biographer and nineteenth-century military historians, all in the business of creating nationalist historiography, would attempt to compensate for the limited nature of the honour that was left to him. In these works, Chassé and his men received lavish praise for the dutiful performance of their part in the war in Spain, despite the many less elevating aspects of this episode.[35] What this valorization of duty masked in Chassé's case was the enormous distance that separated the competent soldiering of the commander of the Dutch brigade in Spain from the ideologically charged participation in the Patriots' army of citizen-captain Chassé. Where the latter had identified with a political programme built around a principled link between politics and war, the former was motivated by a military code that had been reduced to its purest essence. Chassé had been attracted to the citizen-soldier because of a wild streak in his own nature, to which the potentially unruly masculinity of this ideal had appealed. Subsequently, he had built a career on military rather than political grounds. The radical dissolution of boundaries between soldiers and civilians in the Spanish war forced him to withdraw even further to what could be called a minimal military masculinity: duty and duty alone.

The 1806 appointment of Louis Bonaparte as king of the Netherlands ended Daendels's retirement from public life. Known for his revolutionary ardour, military experience, loyalty to France and hatred of Britain, Daendels landed one of the most coveted jobs in the country. In 1807 he was appointed governor-general of Java and given explicit instructions to save the island from British annexation. Ordered to clean up a corrupt administration and to reform the colonial economic system as well, Daendels set sail to Java. He had been granted near dictatorial powers and was in proud possession of the title Field Marshal of Holland. After his arrival, he began to dismantle a colonial administration untouched by the revolutionary changes that had swept over Europe. He made plenty of enemies by a heavy-handed reform of an administration in which appointments were considered private property to be exploited for individual profit. He centralized government, reorganized the army and had fortifications built. Energetic and at times violent in pursuing his military plans and in his fight against what he considered the feudal administrative practices of the Dutch and of the Javanese nobility, he was less inclined to change the colony's economic structure. He maintained the system of forced production of lucrative crops, and, apart from some minor changes in the system of statute labour, the Javanese peasants gained nothing from Daendels's Napoleonic fight against the colonial ancien régime.[36]

His biographers have tended to interpret Daendels's 1801 resignation from the army of the Batavian Republic as a major break in his life and career. After that moment they see Daendels casting off revolutionary ambitions in the service of his country and embarking on a course of action designed solely to serve his personal desire for wealth and status.[37] And although Daendels's years as governor-general of Java certainly show him pursuing fortune and fame, at times ruthlessly, certain aspects of this period also testify to a persistence of the habits of the citizen-soldier. He looked upon Dutch colonial and Javanese administrative and political practices as constituting a corrupt ancien régime that needed to be rooted out, and in order to achieve this goal, he resorted to force—the justice of the semi-revolutionary cause apparently legitimizing the means. When he decided to use military troops to install new and more obedient leaders in Javanese kingdoms that had still possessed relative autonomy under Dutch rule, he almost re-enacted the change of local government that the Patriots had enforced in the Netherlands with the help of their militias during the revolutionary 1780s.[38]

In a colonial context the impatient citizen-soldier, risen to the highest rank but still burning with the desire to destroy the ancien régime, could be reborn and aspire to great achievements because of the powers he wielded and the assumption of superiority on which colonial domination rested. In Java, too, however, Daendels's zeal soon reached its limits. By 1810 his enemies managed to convince Louis Bonaparte that Daendels could no longer be trusted with final authority over the island, and the king dismissed him from his post.

After he was forced to leave Java, Daendels started work on what became a four-volume justification of his tenure as governor-general, a work that he hoped would rehabilitate him politically and perhaps even persuade William I, the new king of the Netherlands, to reappoint him. But despite his intention to present himself as a loyal subject, capable administrator and well qualified to serve under the new regime, Daendels could not help echoing the language of the revolutionary citizen-soldier. Upon his arrival in Java, he wrote, he had found the government so rife with corruption that only its 'total transformation' could save the colony. That was what he had set about to achieve, acting according to a set of 'fixed principles' and making sure everyone understood that 'no opposition would be tolerated'.[39] Even when it was clearly advisable to do so, Daendels found it hard to abandon a self-representation in which revolutionary politics necessitated, and blended into, the use of force. His was still the masculinity of the citizen-soldier: a male self-assertion bolstered by the twin attributes of political zeal and military force.

Upon his return to the Netherlands in 1812—by that time part of the First French Empire—Daendels found Napoleon unwilling to appoint him to a position commensurate with his experience. He once more joined the French army, as brigadier-general—the rank at which he had left it 17 years earlier. He fought in northeastern Germany, was sent to Russia, was lucky enough to return and ended his French military career as a prisoner of war in Warsaw. Chassé, who had been ordered to leave Spain in early 1814, spent the last months of Napoleon's empire fighting in northeastern France, sustained a number of serious injuries and resigned from French service as a lieutenant-general in the same year.

Waterloo and St George d'Elmina

After Napoleon's fall, William I, son of the last Stadholder, had returned to the Netherlands, where, without noticeable protest, a monarchy was established in 1813. Eager to prove his usefulness to the great powers to which he owed his position and hoping to extend the borders of his new state beyond those of the old Republic, King William needed all the soldiers he could get. Experienced officers were particularly in demand, a situation from which Chassé benefited. He was accepted into the new Dutch army and had to pay for his past revolutionary enthusiasm and French service with only a slight demotion: he entered service as a major-general. Waterloo was his chance to rehabilitate himself once and for all and to secure a future in the Dutch military. He succeeded: his contribution was considered important enough to merit the highest military decoration the new kingdom had to offer.

Daendels fared less well, despite the new king's intention to incorporate members of all political and administrative circles of the old Republic and its successors into his state, including his erstwhile opponents. Daendels was unable to dissociate himself from the role of revolutionary citizen-soldier that he was so suited to by temperament and with which he had identified so energetically. King William I profoundly mistrusted him, and Daendels was initially excluded from the policy of forgiving and forgetting that guided the king's appointments. In 1814, Daendels offered his services to the king and, in 1815, even offered to fight against Napoleon as a volunteer, but both offers were refused. Daendels soon had to give up any hope of reappointment as governor-general of Java. In 1815 he was finally offered the governorship of the Netherlands' smallest colony: St George d'Elmina, on the African West Coast. In fact not much more than a cluster of Dutch fortresses amid a larger chain of European citadels and trading posts, St George d'Elmina had lost its importance after the Dutch, under British pressure, had abolished the slave trade in 1814. In a way Daendels's appointment to the governorship of a number of nearly deserted fortresses thousands of miles from the Netherlands can be considered a form of banishment. Daendels developed one grandiose scheme after another to revitalize the colony and saw them all fail. He died of yellow fever in 1818.

A biographical article published ten years after his death shows the extent to which the contradictions surrounding liberty and the use of military force in the politics of the Patriot militias determined public perception of Daendels 45 years after he had become a citizen-soldier. According to the author, Daendels's life and especially his time in Java revealed just how much the advocate of popular sovereignty and the despot resemble one another. The arbitrary nature of many of the measures Daendels took and his lack of respect for intermediary powers, tradition and custom and human life were, the author concluded, characteristic of both the sovereign national assembly with unlimited powers and the capricious absolute ruler.[40]

Chassé's biography, published in 1848, the year of his death, demonstrates that it was considerably easier to draw Chassé out from the shadow of the citizen-soldier. Like Daendels, Chassé acquired a reputation for his preference for the bayonet and the close-quarters style of combat it required. In his biography, Chassé's successful reliance on the bayonet is mentioned several times as proof of his courage. But instead of linking the bayonet to the military style of the French revolutionary armies, Chassé's biographer, by emphasizing Chassé's decisive contribution at the Battle of Waterloo, locates the weapon ideologically as emblematic of general soldierly characteristics rather than adherence to revolutionary methods of warfare.[41] With the bravado and tactics of a French revolutionary soldier, Chassé defeats Napoleon and rehabilitates himself as a Dutch soldier at the same time.[42] In a career built on duty, the meaning of the bayonet was as malleable as the soldier who handled it.

Conclusion

The republican citizen-soldier, and the mutual permeation of politics and war that this figure represented, initially appeared to two ambitious young soldiers in the Dutch Republic as an ideal that promised to advance their careers and to satisfy their desires for power and prestige. By 1815, an association with this republican ideal was enough to condemn one of its adherents to political and military marginality. The other had already abandoned political soldiering for pure duty that, eventually, became linked with the concept of service to the nation. With this disciplining of the citizen-soldier, a specific form of masculinity was also subdued: a masculinity defined by an ability to transgress the boundary between politics and war. Considered proof of virtue by its proponents, its critics viewed this ability as dangerous, expecting it to lead to chaos and, ultimately, despotism. To them, bringing the citizen-soldier under control was crucial to ending the long years of revolution, tyranny and war. In the post-Napoleonic world ambitious young men would have to model themselves after political and military masculinities that had been uncoupled and assigned their appropriate places.

Notes

1. David A. Bell, *The First Total War: Napoleon's Europe and the Birth of Modern Warfare* (London, 2007), 11–12, 24–37.
2. Ibid. 12.
3. Ibid. 137–138.
4. On the republican tradition, see J. G. A. Pocock, *The Machiavellian Moment: Florentine Political Thought and the Atlantic Tradition* (Princeton, 1975); Martin van Gelderen and Quentin Skinner (eds), *Republicanism: A Shared European Heritage*, 2 vols (Cambridge, UK, 2002).
5. On effeminacy in eighteenth-century (political) culture, see Michèle Cohen, *Fashioning Masculinity: National Identity and Language in the Eighteenth Century*

(London, 1996); Linda C. Dowling, *Hellenism and Homosexuality in Victorian Oxford* (Ithaca, NY, 1994), 5–12; Vincent Quinn and Mary Peace (eds), *Luxurious Sexualities: Effeminacy, Consumption, and the Body Politic in Eighteenth-Century Representation*, special issue of *Textual Practice* 11 (1997): 405–415.
6. My description of Chassé's life and career relies on the following works: W. J. Del Campo, *Het leven en de krijgsbedrijven van David Hendrikus baron Chassé* (Hertogenbosch, 1849); A. Haak, *Chassé* (Rijswijk, 1938); Leo Turksma, *Wisselend lot in een woelige tijd: Van Hogendorp, Krayenhoff, Chassé en Janssens, generaals in Bataafs-Franse dienst* (Westervoort, 2005). Biographical information on Daendels in this essay is drawn from F. van Anrooy et al., *Herman Willem Daendels, 1762–1818: Geldersman, patriot, Jacobijn, generaal, hereboer, maarschalk, gouverneur van Hattem naar St. George del Mina* (Utrecht, 1991); Isidore Mendels, *Herman Willem Daendels, vóór zijne benoeming tot gouverneur-generaal van Oost-Indië (1762–1807)* (The Hague, 1890); Paul van 't Veer, *Daendels: Maarschalk van Holland* (Bussum, 1983).
7. For overviews of this period, see Remieg Aerts, 'Een staat in verbouwing: Van republiek naar constitutioneel koninkrijk 1780–1848', in *Land van kleine gebaren: Een politieke geschiedenis van Nederland 1780–1990*, ed. Remieg Aerts et al. (Nijmegen, 1999), 11–95; Jonathan I. Israel, *The Dutch Republic: Its Rise, Greatness, and Fall, 1477–1806* (Oxford, 1995); Margaret C. Jacob and Wijnand W. Mijnhardt (eds), *The Dutch Republic in the Eighteenth Century* (Ithaca, 1992).
8. Israel, *Dutch Republic*, 1101–1107; S. R. E. Klein, *Patriots Republikanisme: Politieke cultuur in Nederland 1766–1787* (Amsterdam, 1995), ch. 5; H. L. Zwitzer, 'De militaire dimensie van de patriottenbeweging', in *Voor vaderland en vrijheid. De revolutie van de patriotten*, ed. F. Grijzenhout et al. (Amsterdam, 1987), 27–51.
9. *De Post van den Neder-Rhijn*, Vol. 3, no. 126 (1783), 1115.
10. Ibid. no. 134, 1188.
11. Ibid. no. 129, 1138.
12. Ibid. no. 137, 1205–1216.
13. Ibid. no. 148, 1315–1319.
14. Ibid. no. 248, 819.
15. Ibid. no. 142, 1260–1261.
16. Ibid. no. 147, 1307, 1309.
17. Stefan Dudink, 'Masculinity, Effeminacy, Time: Conceptual Change in the Dutch Age of Democratic Revolutions', in *Masculinities in Politics and War: Gendering Modern History*, ed. Stefan Dudink et al. (Manchester, 2004), 77–95.
18. Ibid. 87; W. R. E. Velema, 'Contemporaine reacties op het patriotse politieke vocabulaire', in *De droom van de revolutie: Nieuwe benaderingen van het Patriottisme*, ed. H. Bots and W. W. Mijnhardt (Amsterdam, 1988), 32–48, 39–43; W. R. E. Velema, *Enlightenment and Conservatism in the Dutch Republic: The Political Thought of Elie Luzac* (Assen, 1993), 161–169.
19. Dudink, 'Masculinity, Effeminacy, Time', 87.
20. Del Campo, *Het leven*, 8.
21. Ibid. 9.
22. Jos Gabriels, 'Tussen Groot-Brittannië en Frankrijk: De landstrijdkrachten van een onmachtige mogendheid', in *Met man en macht: De militaire geschiedenis van Nederland, 1550–2000*, ed. J. R. Bruijn and C. B. Wels (Amsterdam, 2003), 143–178, 158.
23. I draw here on the analysis of Daendels's French career in J. G. M. M. Rosendaal, 'Daendels' stormachtige loopbaan tot burger-generaal', in van Anrooy, *Herman Willem Daendels*, 35–45.

24. Mendels, *Daendels*, 40.
25. Rosendaal, 'Daendels' stormachtige loopbaan', in van Anrooy, *Herman Willem Daendels*, 42–45.
26. Del Campo, *Het leven*, 12.
27. 'Daendels, Generaal Major (de Brigade) bij de Franse Armee aan zijne Geldersche en Overijselsche Landgenoten', quoted in Veer, *Daendels*, 48.
28. For these reforms, see Gabriels, 'Tussen Groot-Brittannië en Frankrijk', in *Met man en macht*, 159–165.
29. Bell, *First Total War*, 132.
30. For the Dutch Brigade and the Peninsular War, see J. A. de Moor and H. Ph. Vogel, *Duizend miljoen maal vervloekt land: De Hollandse Brigade in Spanje 1808–1813* (Amsterdam, 1991).
31. Chassé to the Dutch minister of war, 29 March 1809, quoted in ibid. 100.
32. Del Campo, *Het leven*, 38.
33. Moor and Vogel, *Duizend miljoen*, 101, 159.
34. For this originally aristocratic notion of honour and its relation to emerging nationalism and its demands for loyalty, see Bell, *First Total War*, 35–36; Christopher Duffy, *The Military Experience in the Age of Reason* (Ware, 1998), 74–80.
35. Del Campo, *Het leven*, 39–43; J. Bosscha, *Neerlands heldendaden te land: Van de vroegste tijden af tot op onze dagen*, 4 vols (Leeuwarden, 1873), vol. 3, 212, 229, 232–234, 254, 263, 267.
36. On Daendels's years in Java, see Veer, *Daendels*, chs 6–9. For an overview of his reforms, see H. W. van der Doel, *Het Rijk van Insulinde: Opkomst en ondergang van een Nederlandse kolonie* (Amsterdam, 1996), 14–17.
37. On the end of ideologically motivated revolutionary ambitions, see N. C. F. van Sas, 'Caesar, Brutus, Cincinnatus: Daendels als redder van Nederland, 1797–1799', in van Anrooy, *Herman Willem Daendels*, 61–70; for a stress on the turn to private interests, see Veer, *Daendels*, 97–100.
38. Ibid. 148–150.
39. Herman Willem Daendels, *Staat der Nederlandsche Oostindische Bezittingen, onder het bestuur van den gouverneur-generaal Herman Willem Daendels, ridder, luitenant-generaal, enz. in de jaren 1808 tot 1811*, 4 vols (Amsterdam, 1814), Vol. 1, 4–5, 19, 20.
40. N. G. van Kampen, *Vaderlandsche karakterkunde, of karakterschetsen van tijdperken en personen, uit de Nederlandsche geschiedenis, van de vroegste tijden af tot op de omwenteling van 1795*, 2 vols (Haarlem, 1828), Vol. 2, 743–744.
41. Del Campo, *Het leven*, 25, 45.
42. Ibid. 61.

6
John Bull into Battle: Military Masculinity and the British Army Officer during the Napoleonic Wars

Catriona Kennedy

>...Oh plenteous England, comfort's dwelling place
>Blest be thy well-fed, glossy John Bull face!...
>Inoculated by wild Martial ardour
>Why did I ever leave thy well-stored larder?
>Why fired with scarlet-fever in ill time
>Come here to fight & starve in this cursed clime!...
>Turn here your eyes & give a pitying stare
>Behold how Britain's gallant warriors fare
>Think not of ballroom strut or lounging gait
>In public walks our military [b]ait
>To catch your daughters, of[t] ten thousand prize,
>Our gold and scarlet sparkling like their eyes;
>But see the crimson coat seamed o'er with stitches
>The torn, degenerate regimental breeches....[1]

A dominant theme in recent scholarship on gender and war has been the tendency of societies to value military masculinity and its associated attributes more highly than the forms of masculinity associated with civic virtue.[2] In this narrative the Revolutionary and Napoleonic Wars are accorded a pivotal role, the mass mobilization required by the war effort contributing, it is argued, to the production of a newly virilized and martial model of gendered national identity.[3] In France, the conflation of citizen and soldier following the revolution led to an identification of military service with political rights and an emphasis on the horizontal and fraternal bonds that united men as 'brothers-in-arms' within the republican army.[4] Similarly, the reform of the Prussian army that followed its catastrophic defeat at the hands of Napoleon in 1806 constructed Prussia as a 'manly' nation and introduced a new cult of valorous and sacrificial heroism.[5] Unlike France and Prussia, Britain during this period saw neither the introduction of mass conscription nor the expansion of political rights, but the size of the armed forces did increase massively through voluntary enlistment into the regular army and the proliferation of national defence units. This militarization of British national life, Linda Colley argues, encouraged an ethos of 'heroic endeavour and aggressive maleness' and fed into a conception of Britain as an 'essentially "masculine" culture...caught up in an eternal rivalry with an essentially "effeminate" France'.[6]

Though British national masculinity may have been shaped by war, it is by no means clear that the national character was understood as martial or militaristic. The lines quoted above, written by a British officer during the Peninsular campaign, give some sense of the tensions between military masculinity and prevailing constructions of British national character.[7] The stout, round-faced figure of John Bull invoked in these verses embodies what were considered to be key characteristics of British manliness: he was bluff, forthright and down-to-earth.[8] In contrast, the soldier dressed in 'gold and scarlet' and distinguished by his particular gait is a flashy and sexually dangerous figure. By differentiating between the manly qualities of the men fighting for Britain and those for whom they fight, the soldier-author suggests a fundamental disparity between civilian and military modes of masculinity, though he does not necessarily privilege the latter. To a certain extent, this gulf can be understood as representative of the differences between class-specific forms of masculinity: the stolid figure of John Bull was traditionally represented as a put-upon shopkeeper or country yeoman and is here juxtaposed with the aristocratic ostentation of the British officer class. The combination of admiration and suspicion in John Bull's view of the soldier also points to a more fundamental ambivalence in British attitudes towards the professional army, which was simultaneously esteemed as a source of national pride and feared as a potential instrument of tyranny and repression.[9]

The image of the starving soldier in his tattered uniform, yearning for home comforts, indicates a further gulf between the rhetoric of military heroism and the realities of life in the army. Though fantasies of masculine adventure and heroism may have fired him with martial ardour, the diminished figure of the war-weary subaltern officer suggests that it was not necessarily in the theatre of war that British manhood found its fullest expression. While historians of eighteenth-century Britain have increasingly pointed to the importance of war in public debates on national masculinity, gender historians rarely explore the military context in which many men's masculinity was formed and performed.[10] Drawing on soldiers' letters and diaries written during the Napoleonic Wars, this chapter explores how masculinity was practised and understood by members of the British army. It focuses in particular on the experiences of subaltern officers—commissioned officers below the rank of captain—in the years of the Peninsular campaign, from 1808 to 1814. Arguably, this group's relatively subordinate position within the army made the attainment of a secure and stable masculine identity a matter of pressing concern. Moreover, life in the army both problematized the achievement of certain masculine ideals and required a negotiation between different and sometimes competing modes of masculine conduct.

The British army, 1793–1815

As already noted, the British army did not undergo any substantial reform between 1793 and 1815.[11] It did, however, expand rapidly: on the eve of the war its troop strength was at 50,000, and by 1811 it had reached 219,000.[12] This massive augmentation of the armed forces was largely dependent on manpower drawn from Britain and Ireland. Whereas Britain had relied heavily on foreign auxiliaries in previous conflicts, less than 20 per cent of the expanded army was of foreign extraction.[13] The rest constituted a genuinely pan-British force: in 1813 there was roughly one-half English or Welsh, one-sixth Scottish, and one-third Irish. Within the officer corps Scots and Irish were even more strongly represented: one estimate is that 24 per cent were of Scottish origin while 35 per cent came from Ireland.[14] In addition to the augmentation of the professional army, the national defence corps—the militia, volunteers and yeomanry (volunteer cavalry units)—also underwent a dramatic expansion. These bodies drew on a long-standing 'amateur military tradition' in Britain, and at the peak of the invasion scare in 1804 roughly 400,000 civilians, an estimated 18 per cent of all men of military age, were in arms. While the militia depended on a ballot system to fill its ranks, the volunteers, as the title suggests, were recruited voluntarily and often operated in a democratic fashion that was far removed from the more authoritarian and hierarchical structure of the regular army.

A key military difference between Britain and other leading European powers was that the latter were predominantly land powers whose armed expansion relied on the army, while Britain was primarily a naval power. As a result, much of the nation's psychological investment in the armed forces was focused on the navy, which provided exemplars of masculine patriotism in the form of the plain-speaking ordinary seaman, 'Jack Tar', and through the figure of the admiral-hero, most notably Horatio Nelson. The Royal Navy, with its long history of engagement in expansionist overseas wars, was perceived as a crucial agent of British commercial power and a bulwark of the nation's constitutional liberties.[15] During the first phase of the Revolutionary and Napoleonic Wars, it was the navy, rather than the army, that achieved the most emphatic victories. It was not until the future Duke of Wellington, Arthur Wellesley, took command of the British forces in the Iberian Peninsula in 1808 that the army began to rise in the national estimation. Although its reputation would suffer in the wake of the

Convention of Cintra (1808) and the retreat to Corunna (1809), the army's prestige would eventually be consolidated by victory over the French in 1814 and in the climactic contest against the Napoleonic forces at Waterloo in 1815. These victories, particularly Waterloo, bolstered the army's image as a crucible of patriotic manliness, contributing to what Colley describes as a 'cult of élite heroism'.[16]

The elite nature of this culture of military heroism points to another key feature of the British army: the dominance of the officer ranks by the younger sons of the aristocracy and gentry. Admittance into the British officer ranks did not, as in some other eighteenth-century European armies, require proof of noble birth, but the purchase system acted as a relatively effective social filter nonetheless. Under this system, men entered the army by buying a commission as an ensign (second lieutenant) or cornet (the cavalry equivalent) and would ascend the ranks by purchasing vacancies that appeared above them as officers retired, sold out or transferred into another regiment.[17] According to the Victorian military historian Charles Clode, the Duke of Wellington favoured the purchase system because it helped bring into the army 'men of fortune and character—men who have some connection with the interests and fortunes of the country'.[18] The British army made some moves towards professionalization during this period. While serving as Commander-in-Chief of the British Army from 1798 to 1809, Prince Frederick, Duke of York, instituted reforms that eliminated the worst excesses of the purchase system; and in 1799 a Royal Military College was established.[19] Yet the army was far from being a 'career open to talents' or one that expected its officers to have a scientific schooling in the arts of war.[20] A stress on personal comportment and gentility appears to have been maintained into the wars; a gentleman and an officer 'assumed his rightful position because of who he was, not what he had learned or achieved'.[21] The officer corps therefore continued to act as a repository for codes of masculinity suited to the gentry, 'based on sport and codes of honour derived from military prowess'.[22] In this respect, the culture of the military was set in tension with evolving modes of middle-class professionalism in which masculine identity was linked with freedom from patronage and intellectual expertise, 'the manipulation of the pen and ruler rather than the sword and the gun'.[23]

The expansion of the officer corps, however, meant the entrance into the army of many men who were not by birth 'gentlemen'. While the army may have attracted men with wealthy connections, part of its appeal rested on the paid employment that it offered to the younger sons of the gentry, who would not expect to inherit land or titles.[24] However, members of the lesser gentry, who formed the largest group within the British officer class, often lacked sufficient money or interest to advance through the ranks. Their opportunities greatly increased with the outbreak of war. Rapid augmentation of the army led to an expansion of the officer corps, while the loss of officers in battle enabled advancement through the ranks without purchase. By 1810 as many as four-fifths of all army commissions had been acquired by methods other than that of purchase.[25] The large number of Scots and Irish who obtained commissions during the wars provides further evidence of the social dilution of the officer corps. Members of elite corps often looked with disdain upon the provincial officers of limited means who filled the ranks of less exalted regiments. Lieutenant John Mills of the aristocratic Coldstream Guards wrote sarcastically of the 'Irish Gentlemen with great landed property in the north' who officered the 58th Regiment.[26] Though the king's commission remained a powerful indicator of status, the 'gentlemanly' identity of the officer could be precarious. For junior officers, nonetheless, war offered the possibility of social mobility and the achievement of that most vaunted of British masculine attributes: independence.

Manly independence and the subaltern officer

The idealized figure of the independent man, as Matthew McCormack has shown in a recent study, was held out as the epitome of manliness, citizenship and national character in Georgian Britain. In addition to its significance in a social and political context, during the wars this concept of independence also assumed a military character as 'the unthinking, impoverished automatons of the French army were contrasted with free virile Britons'.[27] Defined in contrast to feminine 'dependency', masculine independence connoted self-mastery and financial autonomy. The purchase of an army commission, in itself a form of personal property, supposedly provided the conditions in which this autonomy could be exercised. As one officer observed to his mother, who was anxious for him to leave the service, 'My profession alone renders me independent'.[28]

At the same time, the idea of manly independence was deeply rooted within a discourse of classical republicanism that was traditionally suspicious of professional armies. Consequently it was often the non-regular civilian forces—the militia and volunteers—that were understood as the true repositories of Britain's masculine and martial independence. As radical commentators pointed out, it was difficult to reconcile the ideal of national independence with the realities of military life. Mary Wollstonecraft notably compared professional soldiers with women insofar as both were 'fond of dancing, crowded rooms, adventures, and ridicule', and she denounced the enervating effects of military subordination on the 'needy *gentleman*' who, anxious to advance, 'becomes a servile parasite or vile pander'.[29]

Entry into the 'profession of arms', then, constituted an avenue through which young officers could achieve social advancement and independence, but it also required submission to a potentially oppressive regime of military control. From the 1790s, British soldiers were increasingly housed in barracks rather than billeted among local communities, a development that foreshadowed an eventual segregation of the military from the civil sphere. For new recruits entrance into the military barracks often marked a painful transition from civilian freedom to military subordination. Having joined the 87th Regiment of Foot at the Colchester barracks, Ensign Wright Knox deplored the enclosed and isolated world that he had entered. 'I am afraid', he informed his brother,

> it will require a length of time and pleasant quarters to reconcile me to a Military life, at present I am in no great aspirations about it: coming from a healthy situation, a numerous and pleasant acquaintance, a house where you were your own Master: to a nasty bog, a set of strangers, and a Miserable wooden hut.[30]

In subsequent letters he expanded on the feeling of isolation that barrack life engendered, 'we are 12 miles from any town [with] no amusement whatever; I have not seen 5 men in coloured clothes since I came here'.[31] As Knox's reference to the absence of men in 'coloured' or civilian clothes suggests, soldiers were not only physically separated from civilian life but their uniforms also served as a powerful visual marker of this separation. Of course, the opportunity to don 'gold and scarlet' was often cited as one of the army's chief attractions. Regimental dress flattered and enhanced the male physique and instantly signalled the manliness and 'respectability' of the wearer. Yet, as with other aspects of army life, the uniform could also constitute a site of conflict, bringing individual autonomy and military conformity into tension. Indeed, the ostentatious regimental wear was not dissimilar to the traditional livery worn by servants of the nobility. 'The uniform's connotation of servility', as Scott Hughes Myerley notes, could therefore reinforce 'the ideal of soldiers' total subservience to the will of those in command'.[32] The authority to dictate the design and pattern of military uniforms was one of the legal prerogatives of the British monarchy, but colonels often asserted regimental independence by introducing deviations in the standard design. For an officer of straitened means these frequent alterations in dress could be both a financial burden and a trivial imposition. As one disillusioned officer pointed out, a subaltern's pay was not sufficient to cover 'the costly vain frippery [of] ornamental dresses which our Lt. Col. was always loading us with'.[33]

Among subaltern officers, however, the most common complaint was their subjection to a strict system of military hierarchy and, as one lieutenant put it, 'the Power that a commanding Officer has to annoy and if he pleases to act unlike a Gentleman'.[34] The subaltern's 'want of independence' and 'slavish subordination' are a recurring theme in soldiers' letters from this period. This tension between the ideal of masculine independence and the realities of service in the British army is well illustrated by the letters of W. C. Coles. A member of the lesser gentry, who purchased an ensigncy in 1805, Coles was a fairly typical example of a younger son from a respectable family background who aspired, through the army, to achieve some independence of fortune. The prospect of promotion and personal gain offered by wartime service was at the forefront in Coles's account of his participation in the British capture of Montevideo (now in Uruguay) in 1807. As he informed his father, the deaths in his regiment following the assault led to several promotions, including his own to the rank of lieutenant. In addition, he looked forward to receiving a share of the prize money, imagining that the campaign would 'prove of advantage to our pockets'.[35]

An increasingly fractious relationship with his commanding officer, Colonel Kemmis, however, soon dampened Coles's optimism regarding life in the army. Believing that Kemmis had singled him out for persecution, Coles denounced his commander's 'arbitrary conduct'. In his complaints against the colonel, he deployed the highly gendered vocabulary of 'virtue', 'corruption', 'luxury' and 'effeminacy' which was so central to eighteenth-century classical republican political discourse.[36] Coles declared that Kemmis had 'become effeminate from comfort and indulgence' and was 'as much capable of commanding a Regt. in the Field as a Serjeant of Militia'.[37] Chief among his accusations was his claim that the colonel had become involved with the wife of a common soldier. The figure of the immoral and despotic ruler unduly governed by female influence was a common trope of classical republicanism, and, likening the regiment to a political state, Coles interpreted the officers' subjection to the 'caprice of a woman who has neither education, modesty or virtue' as having a similarly corrupting and degrading influence.[38] In such a situation it was impossible to practise the self-mastery and individual autonomy necessary to independent masculinity, and Coles lamented that the 'pleasure of being one's own master' was a concept unknown in the army, 'as a more slave-like profession cannot exist'. Though the army might offer the means to establish the subaltern officer as an 'independent man', it did not necessarily provide the context in which that masculinity could be most fully expressed. As Coles wrote to his brother: 'I wish professional profits would allow me to secure an Independence in some way and the De'll [Devil] take me if I would not pitch the Red Coat to the Bottom of the Sea.'[39]

Personal, regimental and national honour

While Coles's letters devoted a great deal of attention to his hopes of personal advancement within the army, he claimed that his decision to remain in the service was motivated by more than self-interest. The indignities suffered by the subaltern officer would be unbearable, he wrote, were it not for 'one leading principle, the Amor patrie [love of country]'.[40] This display of patriotic sentiment would seem to support Colley's claim that a 'cult of elite heroism' and an associated ethos of self-sacrifice in the service of the nation not only came to dominate British public discourse during this period but also shaped individual conduct.[41] It also appears to fit in with a broader development in modern military masculinity noted by Robert Nye, whereby the personal honour that resided in the individual soldier came to be shared with the nation in a kind of reciprocal embodiment.[42] Yet an examination of British officers' personal writings from this period suggests that their individual sense of masculine honour was not, in general, calibrated through reference to a nationally constituted ideal of the manly hero. Certainly, there were some notable displays of patriotic self-sacrifice by members of the British army: following his fatal wounding during the retreat to Corunna, General Sir John Moore reputedly declared, 'I have always wanted to die this way', adding 'I hope the people of England will be satisfied'.[43] For the majority of junior officers, however, the mirror that reflected their honourable self-image was the one held up not by the nation but by their fellow officers. Ensign Samuel Lumsden, a relatively new recruit, noted with a degree of unease the strict enforcement of codes of masculine honour and courage among members of his regiment, who had a reputation as 'hard fighters' and a history of 'cutting' or shunning officers who did not 'do their duty':

> there is at present a Brevet [temporary] Lt. Col. & Captain of the 1st Battn. with us here and tho' he is fifty years of age & has a wife & two daughters yet do the officers treat him with the utmost contempt for his avoiding active Service, he has been extremely particular to me but I could not meet with an intimacy as it would be against the general sense of the Officers....[44]

The system of ostracizing officers was a powerful means of enforcing adherence to a shared code of military duty. In wartime, the 'stay at home' soldier was an object of derision, and Lumsden was at pains to stress his eagerness to leave behind the world of the barracks and enter the theatre of war, 'for *here* I look upon myself with contempt. I am neither of service to society, or my Country, all the energies of the mind and body are dormant.'[45] Upon entering the profession of arms, officers agreed to serve abroad willingly, to share the rigours of campaigning and to face the dangers of combat. Those who shirked these duties were dismissed as effeminate, lured by the glamour and spectacle of the military but unwilling to endure its hardships. 'I am sorry the army is disgraced by such beings', observed one lieutenant, 'who study nothing but dress, foppery & debauchery'.[46] There is little evidence, however, that soldiers questioned the masculinity of civilians who remained in Britain or that they expressed any marked hostility towards the homefront. Although Britons' inability to comprehend fully the horrors of war was a common theme in officers' letters from the Peninsula, the letters also expressed their authors' personal investment in the continuation of a war that they hoped would advance their careers and keep them from the penury of peacetime half-pay. Those with relatives involved in trade acknowledged that peace would benefit British commerce, but many shared the sentiment that 'if the general sense of the army were taken[,] it would be for perpetual war'.[47]

Personal and professional self-interest, then, rather than national honour, played a leading role in officers' assessments of appropriate masculine conduct. Nowhere was this emphasis on personal reputation and honour more evident than in the continued culture of duelling within the army. The armed forces had long been considered a bastion of the duel, as officers carried an aristocratic code of honour with them into service, but the army's attitudes towards such affairs remained ambivalent.[48] The duel could challenge the state's legal monopoly on violence and disrupt the internal unity of the officer corps and was officially forbidden under the Articles of War. Yet it also demonstrated the qualities of physical courage, martial skill and honour that were central to constructions of military masculinity. Officers therefore had to negotiate between a powerful informal code of honour and official military law. The etiquette of the duel prescribed a specifically elite form of interpersonal violence. When two Irish officers came to blows over a woman at the Plymouth garrison in 1812, they were court-martialled, their offence compounded by the fact that the brawl had taken place in full view of the private soldiers and without weapons. As one officer remarked: 'Had they fought with pistols or swords they would have been regarded as Gentlemen and caressed, but fighting with their hands has completely ruined their character.'[49] The quarrelsome and amorous Irish soldier was a stock figure in Georgian drama, and the spectacle of brawling Irish officers may have confirmed a perception of Irish manhood as bereft of the civilized restraint that regulated the performance of gentlemanly masculinity, even in its most violent incarnations.

For soldiers from more modest backgrounds duelling could be a means of affirming their claims to gentility, but it was also at odds with the British middling classes' growing distaste for violent and excessive displays of aristocratic status.[50] Those used to this more moderate mode of manly conduct could find the army's honour code oppressive. William Thornton Keep, whose family was 'respectable' but not wealthy, described how such 'ridiculous punctilios' had brought two of his comrades, formerly the best of friends, to the brink of duelling. Keep managed to orchestrate a reconciliation but recognized that, 'had it been found out…[,] my conduct would have been considered highly dishonourable'.[51]

To a certain extent, the regiment provided a link between this punctilious sense of individual honour and the honour of the nation. Officers did not yet have that intense attachment and loyalty to their regiment that would characterize the British army from the late nineteenth century, and they often moved rapidly through different regiments as commissions became available for purchase. Ordinary soldiers were much more closely tied to their regiments: an estimated 80 per cent spent their military careers in a single unit.[52] Nonetheless, it was as part of a regimental unit that junior officers' conduct in battle was judged by the public. Particular instances of collective gallantry were noted in the battle dispatches and marked through the distribution of battle honours, which recognized a unit's battlefield accomplishments by incorporating the title of the campaign or battle into the regimental colours. In the weeks following a battle, subalterns would anxiously scan the military gazettes to see if their regiment's participation had been mentioned with approbation. A lieutenant in the 53rd Regiment of Foot recalled that his father had declared it 'the happiest day of his life' when he read an account of the Battle of Talavera which praised the gallantry and discipline of his son's regiment.[53]

Equally, if a regiment was judged to have behaved badly, it could be considered a source of deep personal shame for its officers. This is well illustrated by the case of Lieutenant George Woodberry of the 18th Hussars, a regiment whose reputation rapidly declined towards the end of the Peninsular campaign. When he embarked for active service in Spain at the beginning of 1813, Woodberry was eager to go into action and confident that the regiment would not 'disgrace themselves' but would 'return home ... with Laurels'. This optimism soon turned out to be misplaced. The Battle of Vittoria in June 1813, though a significant victory for Wellington, was followed by excessive looting by British troops, and both the men and officers of the 18th Hussars were heavily implicated. The Duke of Wellington singled out the officers for his particular disapprobation, banning all promotion within the regiment. This was a source of intense anguish for Woodberry. 'I want language to express the grief I feel on the Occasion', he confided in his journal, 'to think I should have come out with a Regiment who have contrary to all expectation acted so differently'. The situation was made even worse when he realized that reports of the regiment's disgrace had reached England. By September 1813, Woodberry writes, 'Every subaltern officer of the Regiment that is out here seems anxious to leave the service, all disappointed—I may say disgusted—having entered the Service in a Regiment that all Ireland [the 18th were nominally an Irish regiment] & England look'd to for something great.'[54] For Prussia, Karen Hagemann has suggested that after the introduction of universal conscription in 1813, the 'willingness to die for the nation' became, in public discourse, 'the extreme heroic form for the suturing of the male individual and the nation'.[55] In the case of the British army, however, it appears that the stitches that bound together the soldier and the nation still remained loosely threaded, dynamically interwoven between personal reputation, regimental honour and national glory.

Homosociality and 'polite' masculinity

While Woodberry's experiences point to the often uneasy relationship between personal, regimental and national honour, the regimental system continued to play an important role in promoting group solidarity and was a way of containing and sometimes masking differences between multiple and unequal masculinities. The absence of women, as several recent analyses of the military have noted, was considered crucial to the development of male camaraderie.[56] Women were often viewed as a source of conflict within the officer corps, variously cited as a corrupting influence on the regiment, as was the case in William Coles's complaints against his colonel, and as the cause of duels between 'brother officers'.[57] In the largely homosocial environment of the barracks and the regimental mess, these antagonisms could be defused through the development of alternative fraternal bonds. For William Keep this was one of the most congenial aspects of military service, where 'the intimacies formed...keep one in heart and cement an attachment to it'.[58] An ethos of masculine conviviality was sustained through recreational pursuits such as hare coursing, fox hunting and gaming, in which officers eagerly participated even when on active service. While in cantonments in Portugal in 1813, the officers of the 88th Regiment of Foot established an evening club where, after dispensing their duties, they ate supper together and played cards. According to William Grattan, the main object of this gathering was 'the keeping up of a gentlemanly and social feeling amongst the corps'.[59] These recreational activities reproduced a mode of eighteenth-century masculinity traditionally associated with the British upper classes and which found expression in hunting, riding and drinking.[60]

Yet this was not the only version of gentlemanly masculinity that existed in the long eighteenth century, or even the dominant one. Michèle Cohen argues that during this period it was the polite, cultured gentleman who represented hegemonic masculinity.[61] Politeness encompassed a range of interlinked modes of behaviour variously denoting elegance in manners and comportment, sophisticated taste in art and literature and an ease and sociability in mixed company.[62] Women were central to the practice of polite masculinity and were understood to play a key role in shaping and refining the male character. As Carroll Smith-Rosenberg summarizes:

> The eighteenth-century gentleman sought always to please and charm—especially the ladies. To accompany ladies at balls, the gentleman became an accomplished dancer and knowledgeable about music. To entertain them at tea parties, he played an instrument, composed a bit, made himself familiar with the latest play, the newest novel.[63]

Although the concept of polite masculinity has been identified as breaking down in this period because of its negative associations with the French, its residual influence can still be discerned in the conduct of British officers during the wars.[64] The absence of women may be understood as presenting a significant stumbling block to the performance of polite masculinity within the army. At the same time, the British army was not an exclusively homosocial institution. Many women accompanied regiments on expeditions abroad: it has been estimated that in 1813, when the army was at its greatest strength, as many as 33,000 women were also on campaign.[65] But nearly all these women were attached to the rank and file and would have been deemed insufficiently 'respectable' to participate in the polite model of genteel heterosociality. As one officer wrote from winter quarters in Portugal: 'Two things are yet wanting to make us completely comfortable: books and the society of pleasant women.'[66] During the Peninsular campaign, the British army made up for this lack of female company by hosting balls for members of the local Spanish and Portuguese elite, often displaying a great deal of resourcefulness in their organization. In 1811 the officers of the Coldstream Guards celebrated George III's birthday in Puebla by holding a ball in two makeshift huts constructed of oak branches, illuminated with lamps and adorned with transparencies of the British and Spanish kings. There they entertained the local ladies and dignitaries with a lavish supper consisting of all their rations and punch served from camp kettles, dancing late into the night to music provided by the regimental band.[67]

The need to cut an impressive figure at such assemblies meant that the acquisition of polite accomplishments was considered of some importance to an officer. Before embarking for the Peninsula, Lieutenant James Gardiner devoted himself to studying drawing and dancing, 'for it will never do for an officer not to be able to dance'.[68] While on campaign, certain officers made an effort to stay abreast of developments in arts and literature: in Portugal, John Rous asked his mother to send him the latest fashionable books and also to arrange for two literary periodicals, the *Quarterly Review* and the *Edinburgh Review*, to be posted to him.[69] Both at home and abroad, British officers produced and acted in amateur theatricals and, 'as in Shakespeare's days', happily performed the female roles.[70] Furthermore, many officers used the opportunities afforded by Continental expeditions to develop the cultural refinement traditionally associated with politeness. Following the British bombardment of Copenhagen in 1807, one officer picked his way through the rubble to view some of the city's monuments and recorded his visits to a museum with 'many valuable curiosities' and a gallery 'with a fine collection of paintings, principally, I believe, of the Dutch school'.[71] Similarly, Major Alexander Jackson travelled to Paris during the brief cessation of hostilities that followed the Peace of Amiens in 1802, propelled by his curiosity to see 'the vast Treasures it contained of the first Works of Art'. While there, he took lessons in French and was greatly impressed by the superior politeness displayed by the Parisians: 'I feel no scruples in saying that my worthy Countrymen are much behind in those external Marks of attention, civility and politeness which is nearly an invariable characteristic of a Frenchman.'[72] Over a decade later, these comments were echoed by an officer serving with the British army of occupation in Paris. He observed with admiration the mingling of the sexes in French society and its beneficial influence on French men, who, 'endeavouring to please...[,] are always attentive to propriety and acquire a portion of that polish and elegance which are the particular attributes of the sex'.[73] As these examples suggest, far from rejecting politeness because of its association with the French, British army officers continued to value and even emulate this model of masculine behaviour. Moreover, this form of masculinity provided an element of continuity between military codes of conduct and the civilian world of polite society.

Gender identity and national 'others'

So far this chapter has considered some of the various tensions that threatened the coherence of British military masculinity. While the British officer class may have been unable to elaborate a single unified model of masculinity, contact with and differentiation from foreign 'others' held out the possibility of achieving a more stable and homogenous sense of gendered national identity. As Carroll Smith-Rosenberg has observed in the context of ante-bellum America: 'Internally fragmented and contradictory subjects assume the appearance of coherence when juxtaposed to multiple others, who through their difference serve to consolidate and bestow an appearance of cohesion upon the fragmented subject.'[74] It was not, however, the French who were the dominant 'other' in soldiers' constructions of national masculinity. Popular xenophobic discourse may have represented the Gallic foe as cringing, effeminate, undernourished fops, but under Napoleon they had proved themselves a formidable military power; and the attitude of British officers towards their opponents was often more emulative than contemptuous. Their most extended reflections on national difference tended to focus on the Spanish and Portuguese, alongside whom they lived and fought for nearly six years.

British officers in the Peninsula had a complicated relationship with their Portuguese and Spanish allies. Styling themselves as the liberators and protectors of the Iberian Peninsula, they tended to adopt a patronizing attitude towards its inhabitants. The Portuguese were usually deemed backward and superstitious; and while greater respect was accorded to the Spanish on account of their historical influence and power, that nation was perceived as having degenerated from its former proud position as the 'bulwark of Christendom'. Both peoples were used as a foil for British virtues, which were often defined in gendered terms. It was impossible to esteem these foreigners, one officer explained, because 'they are deficient in manly principles which particularly elevate Englishmen above the Inhabitants of any other Country'.[75] At its most basic, the contrast between the virile, masculine British forces and their effeminized allies was articulated through a comparison of their respective physical attributes. Describing the entrance of the Royal Horse Guards into Salamanca in 1812, an observer emphasized the effect of this imposing spectacle of British manhood upon the Spanish: 'so different did they appear to the astonished Inhabitants from their own diminutive Horses and their degenerate Soldiers that they seemed to look upon these noble Troops as more than mortal'.[76]

As this example suggests, British officers had little regard for the military abilities of either the Portuguese or the Spanish. They were scornful of the 'cowardly timidity of the Portuguese character'[77] and viewed the Spanish elite as 'vain cowards'.[78] The Spanish guerrillas' efforts to expel the French from their country inspired the British to adopt a more admiring view of the nation's peasantry, in whom they discerned traces of a 'manly independence' not dissimilar to their own countrymen's. In contrast to 'freeborn Britons', however, this national manliness had become enervated and effeminized under a corrupt and despotic regime, and consequently, as one officer commented, 'the Spanish character so individually independent, is nationally dependent'.[79] Members of the British army were particularly critical of the Spanish officers, whom they blamed for the wretched state of the national army. 'A certain education is necessary to make an officer', George Bingham concluded, 'and I fear there are no traces of that through the country[;] there seems an equality of cultivated intellect, between the possessor of the soil, and the labourer that tills it'.[80] As this remark indicates, officers' aspersions on the Spanish elite centred upon their failure to uphold a class-specific model of masculinity and to display the qualities of command and authority that distinguished their British counterparts.

One significant aspect of the construction of national difference during this period involved the observation and comparison of the relationship between the sexes that prevailed in different countries. Enlightenment of sociological and ethnographic discourses stressed the multiplicity of gender relations exhibited by different societies and judged nations' claims to civilization according to the relative status and treatment of women.[81] Britain prided itself on the elevated condition of its countrywomen, and this perceptual frame was clearly employed by British soldiers, who wrote critically of the seclusion and segregation of women in Turkish, Egyptian and Portuguese societies and of the despotic behaviour of their male relatives. As Lieutenant William Coles observed of the Portuguese:

> by custom great restrictions are placed on the women, in fact you never see a Female who has any pretensions to respectability on the outside of the Door of the house. ... Altho' the men have little courage or conduct to

boast of in the field, where real courage is requir'd, they are the greatest Tyrants in the World over the female part of their family.[82]

Through these various observations on national difference a more unified image of British military masculinity could emerge, obscuring the tensions that threatened the individual officer's male identity and bolstering his own sense of masculine superiority. In comparison to the diminutive and cowardly Spanish and Portuguese, the British soldier was physically impressive and courageous. As a 'freeborn Briton' whose liberties were ensured under the British constitution, he exemplified a manly independence that contrasted with the enervated and dependent state of the Iberian Peninsula. As a member of the British officer class, he provided the intelligent military leadership that the Spanish army sorely lacked. And finally, unlike men in less civilized nations, he did not abuse his superior position by tyrannizing over women but treated them with humanity.

Conclusion

Given the long duration of the Revolutionary and Napoleonic Wars, the expansion and rising prestige of the British army and the social dilution of the officer corps, it is perhaps surprising that a more authoritative and inclusive model of military masculinity did not emerge in this period, one based on the rugged fraternity and enhanced professionalism of Wellington's battle-hardened troops. Rather than producing a hegemonic model of masculinity, in which national character, martial values and manly identity were seamlessly blended, the 'gentleman-amateur' ethos of the British officer corps incorporated various modes of masculine behaviour, some of which were drawn from the civilian sphere with others relating more specifically to the culture of the army. Personal reputation remained as important as patriotic sacrifice in the service of the nation, while the officer's performance in the ballroom could be as highly valued as his skill on the battlefield. The subaltern of non-aristocratic origins had to steer a course through these complex and sometimes competing codes of manly behaviour in order to assert his status as both a gentleman and an officer.

Though war may be understood as contributing to the construction of a more militarized model of national masculinity in this period, it is important to remember that it was not necessarily those professional soldiers in the front line of the British war effort who most fully embodied this manly ideal. While their civilian brothers, banded together in volunteer regiments, would both defend and exemplify British manly independence, officers in the regular army, as we have seen, often felt that their personal autonomy was undermined by the strict regime of military subordination within the army. The identification between the soldier and the nation was further attenuated by the codes of personal honour and regimental loyalty that continued to prevail within the officer corps. The frustrations expressed by subaltern officers and their anxiety to prove themselves polite and genteel even when on campaign suggest the pressures generated by the effort to be at once a gentleman, a soldier and an exemplar of British independence. It was in part through contact and comparison with national 'others' that the tensions between these conflicting modes of masculinity and the lived experience of subaltern officers could be resolved.

Acknowledgments

I would like to thank Matthew McCormack and the editors and readers of this volume for their very helpful comments on earlier drafts of this chapter.

Notes

1. National Army Museum, London (hereafter NAM), 7101–20, excerpts from a poem found among the personal papers of Lieutenant James Penman Gairdner, who served in Portugal during the Peninsular War. The verses were apparently transcribed by his grandson and labelled 'Parody on Pope's "Eloisa" by a Subaltern Officer in Cantonment in Portugal, March 1813.' Another version of this poem, entitled 'An Elegy, By a Subaltern Officer in Cantonments on the Banks of the Coa in 1811', was published in 1854 in an anonymous collection that has since been attributed to John Stepney Cowell. According to Cowell, copies of the poem were printed on a 'perambulating press' based at the cantonments of the Light Division in Gallegos and circulated among the author's friends and fellow officers, with whom it achieved a degree of popularity. See [John Stepney Cowell], *Leaves from the Diary of an Officer of the Guards* (London, 1854), 191–195. For a modern text of Alexander Pope's heroic epistle 'Eloisa to Abelard' (1717), see *Alexander Pope: A Critical Edition of the Major Works*, ed. Pat Rogers (Oxford, 1993), 137–146.
2. Robert A. Nye, 'Western Masculinities in War and Peace', *American Historical Review* 112 (2007): 417–438, 417.
3. Stefan Dudink and Karen Hagemann, 'Masculinity in Politics and War in the Age of Democratic Revolutions, 1750–1850', in *Masculinities in Politics and War: Gendering Modern History*, ed. Stefan Dudink et al. (Manchester, 2004), 3–21. For a comparative perspective, see also Stefan Dudink et al. (eds), *Representing Masculinity: Male Citizenship in Modern Western Culture* (Basingstoke, 2007).
4. Lynn Hunt, *The Family Romance of the French Revolution* (Berkeley, 1992); Joan B. Landes, 'Republican Citizenship and Heterosocial Desire: Concepts of Masculinity in Revolutionary France', in Dudink, *Masculinities*, 96–115.
5. See Karen Hagemann, 'German Heroes: The Cult of Death for the Fatherland in Nineteenth-Century Germany', in Dudink, *Masculinities*, 116–134; and idem, 'Of "Manly Valor" and "German Honor": Nation, War, and Masculinity in the Age of the Prussian Uprising against Napoleon', *Central European History* 30/2 (1997): 187–220, where Hagemann emphasizes social and generational differences in her discussion of Prussian images of masculinity.
6. Linda Colley, *Britons: Forging the Nation, 1707–1837* (London, 1996), 265, 303.

7. Pope's poem 'Eloisa to Abelard' was inspired by the tragic twelfth-century lovers Héloïse and Abelard. In it, Eloisa, sequestered in the gothic gloom of a convent, writes of her passionate yearning for her lover, famously castrated as a punishment for their illicit romance. This intriguing choice of literary template further suggests some of the complexities of the campaigning soldier's gendered subjectivity, as he adopts the persona of the desiring woman addressing her emasculated lover.
8. Colley, *Britons*, 265. Though often identified as the personification of Englishness, the figure of John Bull was also sometimes invoked to represent a broader British national character. See Tamara L. Hunt, *Defining John Bull: Political Caricature and National Identity in Late Georgian England* (Aldershot, 2003), 121–169.
9. Scott Hughes Myerly, *British Military Spectacle from the Napoleonic Wars through the Crimea* (Cambridge, MA, 1996), 10.
10. Karen Harvey, 'The History of Masculinity, circa 1650–1800', *Journal of British Studies* 44 (2005): 296–311, 308.
11. Geoffrey Best, *War and Society in Revolutionary Europe, 1770–1870* (London, 1982).
12. G. A. Steppler, 'The British Army on the Eve of War', in *The Road to Waterloo: The British Army and the Struggle against Revolutionary and Napoleonic France, 1793–1815*, ed. Alan J. Guy (London, 1990), 4–15, 4.
13. Clive Emsley, *The Longman Companion to Napoleonic Europe* (London, 1993), 138.
14. John E. Cookson, *The British Armed Nation, 1793–1815* (Oxford, 1997), 126–127.
15. On the navy in British culture and society during this period, see Margarette Lincoln, *Representing the Royal Navy: British Sea Power, 1750–1815* (Aldershot, 2002); Kathleen Wilson, 'Nelson and the People: Manliness, Patriotism and Body Politics', in *Admiral Lord Nelson: Context and Legacy*, ed. David Cannadine (Basingstoke, 2005), 49–66.
16. Colley, *Britons*, 195.
17. J. A. Houlding, *Fit for Service: The Training of the British Army 1715–1795* (1981; repr. Oxford, 2000), 100, 104.
18. Charles M. Clode, *The Military Forces of the Crown*, 2 vols (London, 1869), vol. 2, 608, quoted in Richard Holmes, *Redcoat: The British Soldier in the Age of Horse and Musket* (London, 2002), 159.
19. Penelope Corfield, *Power and the Professions in Britain, 1700–1850* (London, 1995), 192; John E. Cookson, 'Regimental Worlds: Interpreting the Experience of British Soldiers during the Napoleonic Wars', in *Soldiers, Citizens and Civilians: Experiences and Perceptions of the Revolutionary and Napoleonic Wars, 1790–1820*, ed. Alan Forrest et al. (Basingstoke, 2008), 23–42, 28.
20. Here, the British army stands in contrast to the French, which, as David Bell argues, became increasingly professionalized during this period; see David A. Bell, *The First Total War: Napoleon's Europe and the Birth of Warfare as We Know It* (Boston, 2007).
21. N. A. M. Rodger, 'Honour and Duty at Sea, 1660–1815', *Historical Research* 75/190 (2002): 425–447, 427.
22. Leonore Davidoff and Catherine Hall, *Family Fortunes: Men and Women of the English Middle Class, 1780–1850* (London, 1987), 110.
23. Ibid. 205.
24. See Stana Nenadic, 'The Impact of the Military Profession on Highland Gentry Families, c. 1730–1830', *Scottish Historical Review* 85/1 (2006): 75–99, 93.
25. Houlding, *Fit for Service*, 100.

26. Letter from Lieutenant John Mills to William Mills, 20 May 1810, in *For King and Country: The Letters and Diaries of John Mills, Coldstream Guards, 1811–1814*, ed. Ian Fletcher (Staplehurst, 1995), 144.
27. Matthew McCormack, *The Independent Man: Citizenship and Gender Politics in Georgian England* (Manchester, 2005), 1, 151.
28. NAM, 6807–163, 'Typescript letters from George Ridout Bingham to his mother', 3 vols, vol. 2, 98, letter of 3 October 1812.
29. Mary Wollstonecraft, *A Vindication of the Rights of Men and A Vindication of the Rights of Woman*, ed. Sylvana Tomaselli (Cambridge, UK, 1995), 84, 92.
30. Public Record Office, Northern Ireland, Belfast (hereafter PRONI), 'Some letters from Spain written by an officer', TS 1125/3, letter from Wright Knox to William Knox, 18 November 1808, 4.
31. Ibid. 5.
32. Myerly, *British Military Spectacle*, 42.
33. National Library of Ireland, Dublin (hereafter NLI), MS 1577, Lieutenant David Powell, 'Some Account of a Campagne in 1794', 195.
34. NAM, 6902–5, diary of Lieutenant James Penman Gairdner, entry dated 26 November 1811.
35. NAM, 6807/419, letter from W. C. Coles to Charles Coles, 7 February 1807.
36. J. G. A. Pocock, *Virtue, Commerce, and History: Essays on Political Thought and History, Chiefly in the Eighteenth Century* (Cambridge, UK, 1985).
37. NAM, 6807/419-2, letter from W. C. Coles to John Coles, 19 December 1808.
38. NAM, 6807/419, letter from W. C. Coles to Charles Coles, 21 November 1808. On the equation of female influence with sexual and political corruption in French republican discourse, see Joan B. Landes, *Women and the Public Sphere in the Age of the French Revolution* (Ithaca, NY, 1988), 39–65.
39. NAM, 6987/419-2, letters from W. C. Coles to John Coles, 14 January 1810 and 21 April 1808.
40. NAM, 6807/419, letter from W. C. Coles to Charles Coles, 27 July 1807.
41. Colley, *Britons*, 195.
42. Nye, 'Western Masculinities', 421.
43. Quoted in Robert Harvey, *The War of Wars: The Epic Struggle between Britain and France, 1793–1815* (London, 2006), 529.
44. PRONI, D/649/2, letter from Samuel Lumsden to William Lumsden, 23 April 1813.
45. Ibid., letter from Samuel Lumsden to William Lumsden, 10 September 1813.
46. NAM, 6807/267, George Woodberry, 'The Idle Companion of a Young Hussar during the year 1813', 8 August 1813, 204.
47. Letter from George Hennell, 25 November 1813, in *A Gentleman Volunteer: The Letters of George Hennell from the Peninsular War, 1812–1813*, ed. Michael Glover (London, 1979), 148; PRONI, D/649/8, letter from Samuel Lumsden to William Lumsden, 10 May 1814.
48. Rodger, 'Honour and Duty', 436–437; Arthur N. Gilbert, 'Law and Honour among Eighteenth-Century British Army Officers', *Historical Journal* 19 (1976): 75–87.
49. Letter from William Thornton Keep to his mother, 10 September 1812, in *In the Service of the King: The Letters of William Thornton Keep, at Home, Walcheren, and in the Peninsula, 1808–1814*, ed. Ian Fletcher (Staplehurst, 1995), 92–93.
50. Donna T. Andrew, 'The Code of Honour and its Critics: The Opposition to Duelling in England, 1700–1850', *Social History* 5/3 (1980): 409–434.
51. Letter from William Thornton Keep to his mother, 10 September 1812, in Fletcher, *In the Service*, 94.

52. Cookson, 'Regimental Worlds', 33.
53. NAM, 6807–163, 'Typescript letters from George Ridout Bingham to his mother', vol. 2, 80, letter of 7 August 1812.
54. NAM, 6807/26, George Woodberry, 'The Idle Companion of a Young Hussar', 16, 156, 230.
55. Hagemann, 'German Heroes', 117.
56. Joanna Bourke, *Dismembering the Male: Men's Bodies, Britain, and the Great War* (London, 1996), 133; Marcia Kovitz, 'The Roots of Military Masculinity', in *Military Masculinities: Identity and the State*, ed. Paul R. Higate (Westport, CT, 2003), 9.
57. Gilbert, 'Law and Honour', 78.
58. Letter from William Thornton Keep to his brother, 12 August 1812, in Fletcher, *In the Service*, 84.
59. William Grattan, *Adventures with the Connaught Rangers, 1809–1814*, ed. Charles Oman (London, 2003), 317.
60. Davidoff and Hall, *Family Fortunes*, 110.
61. Michèle Cohen, '"Manners" Make the Man: Politeness, Chivalry, and the Construction of Masculinity, 1750–1830', *Journal of British Studies* 44/2 (2005): 312–329, 312.
62. Lawrence Klein, 'Politeness and the Interpretation of the British Eighteenth Century', *Historical Journal* 45 (2002): 869–898.
63. Carroll Smith-Rosenberg, 'The Republican Gentleman: The Race to Rhetorical Stability in the New United States', in Dudink, *Masculinities*, 61–76, 64.
64. Cohen, '"Manners" Make the Man', 315.
65. Louise Carter, 'British Women during the Revolutionary and Napoleonic Wars: Responses, Roles, and Representations', Ph.D. thesis (University of Cambridge, 2005), 175.
66. NAM, 6807–163, 'Typescript letters from George Ridout Bingham to his mother', vol. 1, 80, letter of 14 November 1809.
67. Letter from John Mills to his mother, 11 June 1811, in Fletcher, *For King and Country*, 40; NAM, 8208–8, letter from Captain G. H. Percival to his aunt Mrs Charles Drummond, 2 June 1811.
68. NAM, 7011–21–1, letter from Lieutenant James Penman Gairdner to his father, 10 September 1810.
69. Letter from John Rous to his mother, 15 March 1813, in *A Guards Officer in the Peninsula: The Peninsular War Letters of John Rous, Coldstream Guards, 1812–1814*, ed. Ian Fletcher (Staplehurst, 1992), 50.
70. Letter from William Thornton Keep to his brother, 23 April 1813, in Fletcher, *In the Service*, 142.
71. Captain Thomas Henry Browne, 'Journal of the Expedition to Copenhagen, 1807', in *The Napoleonic War Journal of Captain Thomas Henry Browne, 1807–1816*, ed. Roger N. Buckley (London, 1987), 61.
72. NAM, 7010/13, journal of Major Alexander Crosby Jackson, Paris, 13 January 1803.
73. NAM, 6902–5, diary of Lieutenant James Penman Gairdner, July 1815.
74. Smith-Rosenberg, 'The Republican Gentleman', 69.
75. NAM, 6807–419–2, letter from W. C. Coles to John Coles, 1 April 1810.
76. NAM, 8211–162, diary of William Paterson, 149.
77. Ibid. 83.
78. Letter from John Rous to his mother, 28 May 1813, in Fletcher, *A Guards Officer*, 59.

79. Letter from John Mills to his sister Charlotte, 25 March 1812, in Fletcher, *For King and Country*, 126.
80. NAM, 6807–163, 'Typescript letters from George Ridout Bingham to his mother', vol. 3, 37, letter from Bingham to Mr Grundy, 12 June 1813.
81. Kathleen Wilson, *The Island Race: Englishness, Empire and Gender in the Eighteenth Century* (London, 2003), 24–25.
82. NAM, 6807/419–1, letter from W. C. Coles to Charles Coles, 21 November 1808.

7
Middle-Class Masculinity in an Immigrant Diaspora: War, Revolution and Russia's Ethnic Germans

Alexander M. Martin

In the lands of northwestern Europe subject to prolonged French rule, the Napoleonic Wars encouraged nationalist, civically engaged, often democratic and militarized conceptions of masculinity. By contrast, in the more tradition-bound societies of southern Europe, French rule was simultaneously more tenuous and more destructive and tended to stimulate conservative responses.[1] The dynamic factors at work were different again in multi-ethnic empires, where prosperous but unpopular and politically vulnerable minorities could experience fear, not exhilaration, when faced with revolutionary ferment and xenophobic belligerence among the dominant nationality. These last two phenomena—the violence of Napoleon's encounter with Europe's periphery and the conservative instincts of a middle-class diaspora—came together in the case of the German minority in the Russian Empire, which this chapter will explore by examining the life of Johannes Ambrosius Rosenstrauch (1768–1835).

Rosenstrauch's eventful biography illustrates wider forces shaping masculine identities in the revolutionary era. Before emigrating to Russia in 1804, he had been a wandering actor in Germany, which exposed him not only to Enlightenment culture but also to economic insecurity, humiliating dependence on aristocratic patronage and probably the disdain of genteel society. After 1804, he achieved in Russia what had earlier eluded him in Germany: through repeated career changes and by migrating ever deeper into Russia, he was able to leave his past behind and reinvent himself as a respectable bourgeois. He discovered, however, during Napoleon's invasion of 1812 that as an ethnic outsider he had much to fear from any mass nationalist mobilization of Russian society. As a result of all these experiences, he developed an ethos that was recognizably bourgeois yet devoid of the militarized nationalism or heightened political awareness that the Napoleonic Wars inspired both in the Russian nobility and in the Prussian middle classes among whom Rosenstrauch had been born and raised.[2]

An immigrant on Europe's periphery

Rosenstrauch's biography must be seen in the context of Russia's semi-colonial relationship with Europe. Although a leading political power governed by a native nobility, Russia was treated by its own rulers as a backward country that they proposed to raise by force to the standards of the European Enlightenment. Its power structures were therefore both harsh and brittle, and it developed pathologies associated elsewhere with colonialism. Powdered wigs, Palladian mansions and other symbols of foreignness served as markers of social power, while privileged status—including ownership of the enserfed peasantry—was restricted to the Westernized nobility. As if they were a colonial elite, men of the nobility were torn between rigid subordination to the regime and unbridled power over their serfs, between defiant national pride and admiration for an imagined West; Russian writers, scorned by their Western European role models yet alienated from the mass of their compatriots, faced similar dilemmas.[3]

The Russian Empire resembled a colonial regime (or even Napoleon's Empire) not only in the exploitative authoritarianism and cultural schizophrenia induced by its domestic 'civilizing mission' but also in its openness to foreigners with the right cultural capital. Although the proliferation of Italianate palazzi and French governesses suggested a Latin orientation, in fact the inspiration for Russia's 'well-ordered police state' was mainly German and Protestant, as were many of the engineers, physicians, scientists and other specialists who made up a distinct—though clearly subordinate—stratum within the Westernized Russian elite.[4] Along with respect for their skills, these Germans encountered ethnic chauvinism and class resentment among Russia's snobbish aristocracy, its insular and xenophobic middle classes and the oppressed masses of the poor. For their part, like other Western Europeans, the Germans stereotyped Russian peasants as childlike primitives, mocked the shallowness of the nobility's veneer of Westernization, criticized the venality and despotism of Russia's power structures and depicted Moscow—the historic capital—as a city more Asian than European. By the same token, however, habits and expectations formed in the highly segmented society of ancien régime Germany made it easier for these immigrants to assimilate into a Russian society that assigned them to a particular social niche under the wider aegis of an enlightened absolutist regime. Besides, they generally regarded Russians as youthful people, as yet uncorrupted by civilization, whom Germans were guiding towards enlightenment, and they saw a partly German-run Russia as a conservative counterweight to the forces of revolution and social disintegration in Europe after 1789.[5]

Rosenstrauch's story illustrates what Germans faced when they sought to start life anew by emigrating to Russia, as well as the relationship they imagined to exist between Russia and Europe and the effects of the experience of the Napoleonic Wars on their worldview. His surviving writings, which have received virtually no scholarly attention, date from the last decade of his life, when he was a pastor in the town of Kharkov (today the Ukrainian city of Kharkiv). They include: the letters he wrote between 1826 and 1835 to a German pastor named Kylius in the Crimea; his 1833 account of his work ministering to the terminally ill;[6] and his unpublished narrative of the Napoleonic occupation of Moscow, written sometime in 1835.[7] He was deliberately stingy with biographical detail: amid a diaspora teeming with migrants and transients, Rosenstrauch chose to be a man without a past. It is only by reading him against the grain and drawing on a range of other sources that we can sketch the outlines of his story.

Rosenstrauch was apparently born in 1768 to merchant parents in the Prussian city of Breslau[8] and seems to have been a Catholic.[9] As a youth he became an actor.[10] The little evidence we have suggests that he was often on the move and saw at first hand the diversity of Germany in the eighteenth century as well as the crisis that was overtaking it: in 1788 we find him in Brilon, Westphalia, one of those tight-knit, insular German 'home towns' described by Mack Walker; in 1792 and 1793 he was in war-torn Holland; in 1794 in Kassel, a minor princely capital; in 1795 in Mainz, seat of a Rhenish prince-archbishop and recently a Jacobin republic; and from 1801 to 1804 in the Junker-dominated Baltic duchy of Mecklenburg-Schwerin. In none of these very different milieux was there much respect for rootless, travelling entertainers, and there is no evidence that Rosenstrauch enjoyed more than average professional success. Finally, like many socially frustrated Germans before and after, in 1804 he emigrated to Russia to seek his fortune.[11] He never moved back to Germany, or even to the long-established German communities in Russia's Baltic provinces. Instead, he tied his fate more and more closely to the German diaspora in the Russian interior and its role in the tsarist project of Westernization, and he sought to create for himself a social identity that would free him from the humiliation and precariousness of aristocratic patronage. Initially, he joined the German theatre in St Petersburg, the city that was Russia's 'window to Europe', where as an actor he helped to bring German Enlightenment culture to the diaspora and the Russian court. He left the theatre in 1809 to open a luxury-goods business that disseminated European material culture among Russians, and in 1811 he pursued new opportunities by expanding his business to the cultural and commercial hub of Russia's 'Asiatic' heartland, Moscow, where he arrived in time to be swept up in the Napoleonic invasion but where he prospered after the war.

By then he had assimilated into the diaspora—but *not* into mainstream Russian society—by adopting its Protestant faith, sending his son to study at Russia's only German-language university (Dorpat, in Estonia), marrying two of his children into Moscow-based foreign merchant families and joining Masonic lodges that had many foreign members.[12] In 1820 he sought a third career as a Lutheran clergyman, so he struck out for Odessa, the booming port city on the recently annexed Black Sea steppe. Determined to turn this sparsely settled region—grandly renamed 'New Russia'—into a showcase of its civilizing mission, the government in the 1780s had trumpeted its natural abundance, peppered it with classical Greek toponyms and built the famous Potemkin villages as a preview of future greatness.[13] By the 1820s, Russian and foreign settlers, including many Germans, were streaming into the region, giving rise to an urgent need for new churches and clergy. Among the newcomers was Rosenstrauch, who—thanks to the assistance of one of his Masonic 'brothers' from Moscow—received a crash course in divinity in Odessa, was ordained there in 1821 and in the following year was assigned to the position in Kharkov that he held until his death in 1835.[14]

Russia thus offered Rosenstrauch multiple opportunities to reinvent himself. The price he paid, however, was a deepening insularity as he joined communities that were increasingly small and remote. The police registered the presence of a mere 1,349 Germans in Moscow (about 0.5 per cent of the city's population) when Rosenstrauch arrived in 1811, and they were said to be far less affluent, cosmopolitan and culturally refined than their compatriots in St Petersburg.[15] This must have been even more the case in Kharkov, where the entire province recorded only a few hundred Lutheran communicants annually during his pastorate.[16] He had correspondingly less access to educated society and printed literature—by 1835 he had seen no published accounts of the occupation of Moscow in 1812.[17] These factors and the nature of his pastoral preoccupations may explain why his written reflections on the human condition begin and mostly end with the souls of individuals. As a cosmopolitan former theatre professional who had seen plenty of history in the making, he had once no doubt been conversant with the ideas of his time about politics and the social order. However, in his writings he never articulates a broader theory of society that might undergird a bourgeois civic consciousness to match the bourgeois values—warmth and sincerity in personal relationships, service to the community, respect for social and gender hierarchy, an austere work ethic and keeping a tight rein on one's passions—that he advocated in the domestic and personal sphere.

Rosenstrauch's moral critique of society

In his published writings, Rosenstrauch presented himself as a wise, pious old man who had been tempered by unspecified trials of life and now offered his moral and spiritual reflections on society. Of greatest interest to him, judging by the sheer number of pages, were the men of the middle class and lower nobility; he had far less to say about the common people or the aristocratic elite, still less about women of any class. The focus on the lack of religious faith specifically among men may have been related to the widening gender imbalance in religious practice, or 'feminization of religion', that was observed in much of the Christian world.[18] With the men of the educated classes he shared bonds of sociability and intellectual culture, and he may have recognized in them his own past faults. Yet by the 1820s at the latest, he felt estranged from their values and strained against the dependency and subordination that suffused his relationship with them.

Their crippling character flaws, Rosenstrauch wrote, stemmed from an unwillingness to acknowledge the inevitability of death and the importance of a humble faith in God's mercy. These were his central themes as he recounted his observations at the deathbeds of men from the upper levels of Kharkov's German community: a professor, an army officer, a medical student, a merchant, an artist and several officials.[19] The wealthy were too distracted by worldly matters to give thought to eternity, he found, and they believed in any case that good works could buy them salvation; 'but even if a rich or noble patient were to become convinced of this necessity, it is in his very station or fortune that he would find the greatest obstacles to his heart's desire for a complete reconciliation with God'. The patient, his family and his physician were afraid to tell each other hard truths, and even a short-lived physical recovery was enough to undo whatever spiritual progress a patient had achieved. This was an important point to which Rosenstrauch returned often, as when he wrote to Pastor Kylius in 1829: 'God permits it that *rich* people live every day in splendour and joy; but how soon does even the longest life come to an end, and who would then not prefer to have been *Lazarus* instead of the richest man. Both things—happiness *here* and bliss *there*—seem nearly impossible to unite.' And again, in 1833: '*Already in this life*, the happiness that God offers goes hand in hand with our eternal bliss. It consists not in owning and obtaining, but in *doing without* that which one must in any case some day leave behind.'[20]

The other source of fatal spiritual distraction was 'philosophy', evidently the religious scepticism of the Enlightenment. Rosenstrauch told of an officer who had grown up a devout Christian, only to lose his faith during his university studies when two professors 'gave him entirely persuasive proof that the Christian religion was unfounded'. Nor were only the upper classes susceptible: a dying German tailor said that he had been raised in a pious family, but that 'during his journeyman travels, seduced by conversations, examples and books, he had learned first to despise and then to mock the Christian religion'. During the cholera epidemic of 1830, Rosenstrauch noted that the disease seemed to choose its victims at random, reducing the irreligious to mortal terror: 'Let philosophy boast', he wrote grimly, 'let it call man *good* by his nature, *still* the Holy Scripture is right, and the depiction of the human heart as it was given by *Jesus Christ* still remains the truest portrayal.' Not even the clergy were immune from his criticisms: 'the scribes and Pharisees of our *own* church', he thundered in one of his few recorded sermons, were taking liberties in interpreting the Holy Scripture—'*they* are the wolves in borrowed sheep's clothing whom every pious soul should fear and flee'.[21]

An austere ethic of service, compassion for the suffering of others, determination not to let worldly illusions obscure cosmic truths—this is the outlook that Rosenstrauch reveals in his writings. How had this former actor and merchant of luxury goods arrived at this way of thinking? The only clue he has given us is in his account—which apparently remained unknown to his contemporaries—of his war experiences in 1812. Chance events, which he later interpreted as a sign from Providence, had prevented him from leaving Moscow in time to avoid the Napoleonic occupation. It was the horrors he witnessed there and the terrors he experienced, he wrote, that made him a true Christian.

Gender and social upheaval

Rosenstrauch's narrative prominently foregrounds the class tensions and xenophobia simmering beneath pre-war Moscow's surface. As the Grande Armée approached, the authorities and upper classes fled the city, leaving behind a disoriented populace that was further radicalized by the government's anti-French propaganda. As a result, the city rapidly descended into a chaos that Rosenstrauch interpreted through a particular national and gendered lens.

Looking back in 1835, Rosenstrauch shared the German diaspora's prevailing view that common Russians formed a turbulent rabble but not a denatured revolutionary mob or *classe dangereuse* of the sort that increasingly haunted the Western imagination. His portrayals of the crowds in 1812 eschew animalistic imagery and references to participation by women, two standard tropes of European anti-revolutionary propaganda. The crowds he described mostly pursued the immediate gratification of the coarsest impulses—to murder him, loot his possessions, rape his daughter—but were sometimes easily cowed, while lower-class women appeared on the scene not as revolutionary viragos but in the familiar guise of prostitutes.[22]

Rosenstrauch's sense of isolation was a matter not only of class but also of nationality. He personally knew some of the Russian rioters and was fluent in their language—the narrative is full of untranslated Russianisms—but his sympathies and solidarity lay with a cosmopolitan European diaspora. Nowhere did he refer to any Russian friends, nor did he appear to share in the Russian sense of wartime patriotic commitment. Later, when he was ordained as minister in 1821, he made a point of inviting Catholic, Lutheran and Reformed clergy to participate in the ceremony, but apparently not their Orthodox counterparts.[23] As for the Russian leaders in 1812, he mentioned them at all only to condemn General Kutuzov for holding out deceptive hopes of victory and Moscow Governor-General Rostopchin for encouraging popular xenophobia.

As Moscow descended into anarchy, he hoped that the French would restore order and conduct themselves with restraint, as they had elsewhere in Europe, and was therefore shocked when instead their discipline collapsed and they sacked the city.[24] As we know from other sources, Napoleon's troops viewed Russia and its people with a mix of disdain and terror and engaged in a callous destructiveness that they rarely displayed towards Europeans except in Spain. One might expect Rosenstrauch to express dismay at their habit of mistreating poor Russians or desecrating Orthodox churches.[25] Instead he stressed how the Russian lower classes—male looters and female prostitutes alike—fraternized with the enemy in a concerted assault on order, morals and property.

Amid this violence and anarchy, women of somewhat higher status sought safety through alliances with enemy officers, who replaced the Russian upper class as defenders of order. Rosenstrauch's shop and apartment were located on Kuznetskii Most, a downtown street famous for elegant shops staffed by attractive, supposedly loose young saleswomen; when soldiers came to loot these shops, Rosenstrauch noted, 'regular skirmishes' broke out as French officers rushed to the ladies' defence. Relationships with French officers could also be a source of power and patronage for local women. One day, for instance, a French officer came to Rosenstrauch's shop to obtain ink for Napoleon's chancery. When the Frenchman wanted to take the ink without paying, a beautiful woman of dubious reputation who lived nearby came to Rosenstrauch's defence; she was the mistress of a certain French general, she announced 'with heroic dignity', and would not tolerate an officer's besmirching the great Napoleon's name by taking goods without paying for them. Whereupon 'the courteous Frenchman' paid for the ink, offered her 'a courteous compliment' and left. 'With the grace of a queen', Rosenstrauch added, 'the lady promised me her future protection and bade me seek her assistance in similar situations, for which thank God I had no need.'[26] Women thus entered Rosenstrauch's narrative not as participants in revolutionary violence but through the loose sexuality that was widely imputed to Russian women as well as aristocratic elites in general.

Rosenstrauch's relationship with women and with the very notion of femininity was not without ambivalence. In theory, at least in his later years, he unequivocally endorsed the Christian nuclear family with the chaste, pious wife and mother at its core, but in real life he was not a classic paterfamilias.[27] While bourgeois men in Germany typically waited until around the age of 30 to marry and then chose brides about 10 years their junior, Rosenstrauch was a mere 20 when he married in the small Westphalian town of Brilon.[28] What caused him to marry so young—romantic passion perhaps, or an unplanned pregnancy, or some other consideration— remains unknown because he and those who knew him never mention his wife; there is no sign of her after their (apparently) last child was born in 1796. Even though he was a charming, outgoing and well-connected man—and, by middle age, also a rich one—he did not remarry, and a newspaper account from 1821 described him as a widower.[29] It may have been a factor that in Moscow there were two German males for every female, but it also appears that he thrived in all-male milieux such as the Masonic lodges and the clergy.[30]

His own preferences thus seem to have been homosocial, yet the way he made his living hardly qualified him as a paragon of virtuous masculinity in the eyes of society. Whether as an actor or a seller of 'cosmetic goods' (evidently, fashion accessories and elegant house wares), Rosenstrauch traded in deceptive appearances and operated in a bohemian, heavily female environment where success required cultivating a refined epicureanism among rich women who were his social superiors. This was not only emasculating but, by 1812, downright dangerous. When he arrived in Moscow in 1811, Francophobic chauvinism—whose embodiment was Moscow's wartime Governor-General Rostopchin—had already caused many Russian nobles to deride Kuznetskii Most as the bridgehead of a French culture that was effete, unpatriotic and ideologically subversive. Though personally a French-speaking cosmopolitan, Rostopchin aggressively promoted the propaganda stereotypes associated with Kuznetskii Most, and as the Napoleonic army approached, he ostentatiously deported foreign residents from the city and harassed the Masonic lodges.[31] Rosenstrauch also recalled the brutality of Cossack troops towards French women.[32] Though he himself spoke almost no French, selling 'cosmetic goods' on Kuznetskii Most implicated him in cultural images of an effeminate and aristocratic Frenchness. This made him a target for Russian hostility, but it also created opportunities for accommodation with the French occupiers in 1812.

Contrasting masculinities

Rosenstrauch may have been disdainful of his neighbour's willingness to be a French general's mistress, but in fact he and she were in the same boat. Afraid for himself and his shop, he similarly found himself a group of officers whom he offered room and board along with diligent service and ingratiating conversation, just as his neighbour most likely did with 'her' general, although she perhaps offered sex in lieu of victuals. In turn, Rosenstrauch was treated with the same condescending bonhomie and accorded the same *noblesse oblige* protection that a general's mistress could expect. We do not know what these officers thought of him—the stories they told after the war seem to have dwelt on their battlefield adventures, the savage fanaticism of the Russians and the horrific retreat from Moscow[33]—but on Rosenstrauch the encounter left an indelible impression.

Uncertain about the correct French spelling of their names, Rosenstrauch identified his lodgers as 'Marshal Bertier's adjutants colonels Flahau, Noail, Bongard, [and] Couteil'.[34] All but Bongard spoke good German, and soon they were all on excellent terms, the French regaling him with gossip from Napoleon's headquarters while he used supplies from his shop to wine and dine them. The officers, we know from other sources, were classic examples of nobles of the ancien régime who adapted successfully to the Napoleonic Empire and its successor regimes.

Only one of them, Vicomte Joseph-Barthélémy de Bongard (or Bongars) de Roquigny (1762–1833), belonged to Rosenstrauch's generation: he had been Louis XVI's equerry (*écuyer cavalcadour*), and after meritorious service in the cavalry of Napoleon—who rewarded him by creating him a baron—he resumed his former status as royal equerry for the coronation of Charles X in 1825.[35]

The other three were children of the revolution who reached manhood under Napoleon. Baron Charles de Flahaut (or Flahault) de la Billarderie (1785–1870) was an illegitimate son of Talleyrand, and his mother was herself the illegitimate offspring of Louis XV.[36] While his mother's much older husband, a retired general, was guillotined during the Terror, she fled with young Charles to England. After their return to France, Charles joined Napoleon's army and made a name for himself as an officer, enthusiastic Bonapartist and ladies' man. Among his conquests was Hortense de Beauharnais, the daughter of Napoleon's first wife, Joséphine, and wife of his brother Louis, queen of the Netherlands and mother of the future Napoleon III. Recalling Flahaut's charm but also his roving eye, Hortense later described him as having 'an air that was distinguished, a spirit that was lively, agreeable, even scintillating, but also thoughtless, more animated by the desire to please than imbued with a need to be loved'.[37] A portrait by Napoleon's court painter Gérard shows him in uniform around 1810: finely chiselled aristocratic features, confident gaze, stiff upturned collar, magnificent epaulettes—a young god of 25.[38] He later married a British admiral's daughter and held prestigious ambassadorships under the July Monarchy and the Second Empire. Flahaut's remaining two comrades were men of similar background. Baron Alfred de Noailles (1786–1812) had lost much of his family to the guillotine but fought zealously for Napoleon until his death on the Berezina.[39] As for Baron Charles Emmanuel Le Couteulx de Canteleu (1789–1844), he came from an ennobled merchant, shipping and banking family with extensive transatlantic connections. His father had served in the Estates General, been imprisoned during the Terror, supported Napoleon's coup of the Eighteenth Brumaire and helped found the Bank of France. After Napoleon's fall, the father was named as a member of the new Chamber of Peers, while the son became aide-de-camp to the Dauphin.[40]

Rosenstrauch liked and respected 'these four brave warriors' for their stoic self-discipline, tolerant cosmopolitanism and good-natured gentility.[41] They cheerfully bantered in German with Rosenstrauch, whom they benevolently called 'monsieur le maître' and who in turn bonded with Flahaut's elderly Dutch valet over memories of Holland and a shared antipathy to

Napoleon that Flahaut tolerated out of gratitude to the valet for helping his family during the Terror. Le Couteulx, meanwhile, risked his own safety to shield Rosenstrauch against marauding soldiers, insisted on paying him for the red wine that he took along when the French left Moscow and praised the bravery of the Russian peasants who had ambushed his unit and nearly killed him.[42] A further bond uniting them was that they were trapped in the smoking ruins of Moscow, each facing an uncertain future and grumbling about their respective side's leadership.

Yet a vast chasm divided them. The officers were young (save Bongard), blue-blooded, up-and-coming members of what seemed the world's leading nation and greatest war machine, and this gave them a sense of privilege, idealism, martial bravado and noblesse oblige. Rosenstrauch had none of their youthful élan or sense of entitlement. Middle-aged, a disillusioned ex-actor who had finally achieved a prosperity and respectability that the war threatened to destroy, he was immune to the romance of war and revolution.[43] Instead, he was appalled at the war's irrational destructiveness and the breakdown of respect for property. He recorded proudly that he had never appropriated stolen goods, instead zealously safeguarding his landlord's property; by contrast, the officers willingly took looted goods and even offered to share them with him.[44]

Nor did he share their ethos of blind physical courage. Rosenstrauch offers three models of behaviour in the face of danger. At one extreme were cowards: in the chaos preceding the arrival of the French, a German manufacturer named Knauf had selfishly refused to offer Rosenstrauch shelter in his heavily fortified house, and Rosenstrauch later took a grim satisfaction when Knauf was robbed and evicted from his house by his own workers. At the opposite end of the spectrum were the suicidal risks to which the French officers were driven by their sense of honour, and the lower classes by their greed and destructiveness. Rosenstrauch saw himself as occupying a middle ground of courage and prudence: he boldly stood up to serfs bent on looting his landlord's property and to soldiers who were about to execute innocent peasants, but he avoided unnecessary risks and even refused to leave the safety of his home without pressing cause. For this reason, even though Napoleon rode daily past his house, Rosenstrauch never saw him.[45]

His evident lack of desire to gaze upon their emperor annoyed the French officers, which prompted Rosenstrauch to respond by inventing various lame excuses. For all his bitterness at Russian xenophobia, he felt no sympathy for either Napoleon or his cause. Far from acknowledging the Napoleonic Empire as a civilizing or liberating project led by a man of destiny, he saw it as a destructive drive for *gloire* by an egotistical charlatan. With the trained eye of a jaundiced theatre professional, he viewed the entire enterprise as a grand but hollow spectacle, devoid of substance, and Napoleon himself as a shallow, vulgar, small-minded man with a hankering for grandiose, tasteless stage effects.[46]

Rosenstrauch was the only one of their company (save Bongard) who had been an adult witness to the beginnings of the expansion of revolutionary France. This allowed him to exchange his usual role of ingratiating host for that of an older man of superior experience and wisdom; it also provided the occasion for his sole written reminiscence about his life before coming to Russia. As he later recalled, he had offered his young lodgers this historical perspective on their current predicament: in 1792 and 1793, 'I saw the French army in Holland as *children* under Dumorieux [General Dumouriez]—at the time, there were only decrepit old men, many insolent women who fought in the ranks, and beardless boys who had barely outgrown children's shoes and essentially went barefoot and without proper trousers [*ganze Hosen*].' France's anarchy—complete with the bellicose women who symbolized the revolutionary threat to social order—eventually ended but only through the substitution of a theatrical, aestheticized, warlike masculinity whose dangerous homoerotic appeal Rosenstrauch felt but whose fateful dynamism would prove self-destructive: 'On the Rhine in 1795, [I saw them] as *youths*. In *Moscow*, as *men*—for one could not see a more handsome army than the 80,000 men of the Guards who marched into Moscow, among whom every *Old* Guardsman could have served as model for a Jupiter or Hercules, and every *Young* Guardsman, for a Ganymede. Now', he concluded ominously, 'I can only wait to see these men in their *senescence*.' He seemed to feel that the French themselves, both his chivalrous lodgers and the contemptible Napoleon, sensed that they were prisoners of the forces they had unleashed. Reflecting on his prediction about their impending doom, he added: 'Napoleon surely would not have forgiven me this prophecy, had it reached his ears. Our colonels laughed and made a joke of it; only Flahau gave me a friendly warning to refrain from such observations.'[47]

Rosenstrauch's writings are silent about whether he ever believed in the emancipatory mission proclaimed by the French Revolution and the Napoleonic Empire, or—conversely—the civilizing project of the Romanovs. As an actor, freemason and purveyor of luxury consumer goods, he had promoted the same kind of elitist civilizing process, but in 1812 it had come crashing down around him. That experience left him with a growing distaste for the morals and aesthetics of an imperial elite—its bohemian mores and 'enlightened' religious scepticism, its snobbery, theatricality and martial ethos, and the autonomous role it sometimes allowed women. Instead, he laid increasing stress on an opposing complex of values that had deep roots in his own eighteenth-century German middle-class heritage and which could help him redefine his identity as a man, a bourgeois and a citizen.

Merchant, humanist, Christian

As a businessman, Rosenstrauch cultivated an ethic of work and service—one of his friends in 1822 praised his 'rectitude, conscientiousness, [and] love of order'[48]—and these habits continued when he became a minister. As he later recalled:

> I was certainly very busy. The community in town was large and additionally included several [outlying] colonies that needed to be visited from time to time, besides which I gave daily religious instruction in the school, and there was no shortage of paperwork. However, I gained much time by withdrawing from all social amusements—which are as time-consuming as they are spiritually draining—and lived entirely for my official duties.[49]

In both the self-imposed austerity of his lifestyle and the social authority he wielded as minister, Rosenstrauch modelled a masculinity very different from that which prevailed on the stage or on Kuznetskii Most. In addition, his business success had left him wealthy enough to be able to serve as pastor without pay, and he could act as a stern moralist even towards affluent members of his congregation—he was free at last from the humiliating, emasculating dependence on aristocratic favour.

Aside from embracing bourgeois ideals of work, order and independence, Rosenstrauch also shared German humanism's belief—strongly present in the Enlightenment theatre—in the importance of inner moral maturity as a prerequisite for external freedom and in education (*Bildung*) as the path towards achieving that maturity. He evidently subscribed to the German Enlightenment ideal of the balanced 'whole man' (*ganze Mann*), who was rational yet in touch with his emotions, successful professionally but also a family man.[50] His critique of society accordingly focused on the failure of both lower- and upper-class men to free themselves of their collective passions and prejudices, be they class hatreds, the illusions of rationalism or martial honour, or the allure of worldly pleasures. We also see the humanist influence in his embrace of Freemasonry, with its belief in elitist, cosmopolitan, masculine brotherhood and individual self-perfection, and in his efforts to educate and uplift elites and masses alike—as an actor, supporter and founder of church schools in Moscow and Kharkov, preacher, minister to the sick and writer.

The humanist and mercantile influences in his life were tempered, however, by the religious preoccupations that predominated in the last fifteen years of his life. Rosenstrauch underwent, as an adult, a profound religious conversion. While apparently of Catholic origin, by 1803 he had become a Freemason; and by 1807 at the latest he was so committed to Protestantism that the Russian thespian Stepan Zhikharev reported: 'they say he is a very good, religious man and is supposedly preparing to become a pastor, but while he waits for a good pastorate, he performs in the theatre'.[51] By the last decade of his life, he had evolved into an orthodox Lutheran who quoted few sources other than Luther and the Bible, inveighed against non-literal readings of Scripture and insisted that faith and grace were the only path to salvation. Like many of his contemporaries in Russia, his spiritual journey had taken him from the Enlightenment to Freemasonry and thence ultimately back to denominational orthodoxy.

Rosenstrauch's turn to religion was intensified by the war, which many in Russia experienced as the proverbial bolt out of the blue—a senseless calamity that brought only horrific destruction and ended as inexplicably as it had begun. Yet he was also grateful to Providence for allowing him to save his business, thereby making possible his postwar prosperity, and he marvelled at the sheer scale of the drama that unfolded in 1812. Pride in his own accomplishments mixed with a heightened sense of man's cosmic smallness—such a response to the war was widely shared in Russia, most conspicuously by Tsar Alexander I himself, whom it inspired to found the Holy Alliance. The tsar's family and entourage included numerous Germans, Freemasons and Pietist-influenced mystics, and Rosenstrauch appears to have had some connection—most likely through the Masonic lodges or the St Petersburg German theatre—with these circles and with the tsar himself. Tantalizing evidence of such a connection is contained in an enigmatic passage from a letter of 1821 in which the tsar confided to Prince Aleksandr N. Golitsyn, one of his chief advisers: 'I have marked in pencil and with a dog-ear one of Rosenstrauch's letters that deserves your attention. I agree completely with what he says.'[52]

Becoming an austere man of the cloth was more than the culmination of a spiritual pilgrimage, however, for it also reflected something fundamental about Rosenstrauch's attitude towards his own past. The German- and British-inspired religiosity that spread among the Russian upper classes after 1812 was strongly influenced by Pietism. Rosenstrauch shared Pietism's central beliefs that formal theology and church structures were of little importance next to a warm, communal piety that required believers to speak publicly about their own autobiographical journey from sin to spiritual 'awakening'. In this spirit, he had expounded to Pastor Kylius on the need to write letters to each other that 'are faithful to the truth in describing the conditions of our lives such as they really are'. And he added, in a rare instance where his language hinted at his earlier years as an urbane society man: 'It is in her deepest *négligé* that beauty is loveliest. With make-up and a careful *toilette*, even ugliness can conceal her repulsiveness.'[53] Surely his own story would have made for a compelling tale of sin and redemption, yet he carefully avoided telling almost anything at all about his past. His best friend in Kharkov later wrote a glowing account of Rosenstrauch's character but averred that he could not reconstruct his biography because Rosenstrauch had 'always told me only individual fragments [of his personal story], while the linkages between even these episodes remained unknown to me'.[54]

What could have moved Rosenstrauch to be so tight-lipped about his past? The most likely explanation, in my view, is the sense of social marginality and rejection that he must have suffered, and which emigration had eased but not erased. As an actor in eighteenth-century Germany, he was an outsider in a tight-knit corporatist society and consigned to a status well below his own merchant background. In Russia, where few knew his history and Europeans were in high demand, he could reinvent himself as a respectable man of commerce, especially once he had moved to faraway Moscow. Yet his success at fashioning a new identity had both limitations and pitfalls. Whether as an actor or a merchant, his function was to feed a lifestyle that many Russians envied even as they despised it for humiliating their masculinity and national dignity. The vulnerability of his position in 1812 demonstrated in addition that a man with few roots could find himself alone in times of crisis.

By becoming a pastor, Rosenstrauch could pursue his deepening spiritual calling and escape his social frustrations, but the attempt to join the Lutheran clergy would place him once more at the mercy of an insular corporation that might look askance at his chequered history. This is probably the reason why he apparently pursued neither a conventional clerical education—say, at Dorpat, where he had sent his son Wilhelm to study pharmacy—nor a clerical appointment in the clannish, small-town society of Russia's Baltic Lutheran heartland. Instead, the empire's semi-colonial character came to his rescue by opening opportunities in the recently annexed steppe.

Not surprisingly, the unorthodox career path of the ex-entertainer and *nouveau riche* seller of 'cosmetics' did not endear him to all his new colleagues, one of whom dismissed him as an 'actor turned shopkeeper'.[55] As Rosenstrauch wrote to Pastor Kylius in a rare moment of bitter autobiographic candour:

> Because I was ordained only in my fifty-third year, I extended my hands in all directions to seek instruction and counsel from experienced Christians. But everywhere—especially among my brother ministers—I was rejected with disdain and often with mockery, for I was misunderstood, and people took for hypocrisy what was my heart's most ardent longing.

When he sought appointment as minister to his former church in Moscow in 1822, he lost the election despite widespread community support for his candidacy; one of the criticisms raised against him was that he had once been an actor. Perhaps this disappointment lay behind the lines he wrote to Kylius in 1829: 'In the nine years that I have been away from *Moscow*, from my children, grandchildren, and friends, I have not once felt the desire to go there, even though that would have been very easy for me to arrange.'[56]

Conclusion

While rooted in eighteenth-century German Protestant culture, Rosenstrauch's notion of manhood was also moulded by the context of war and the Russian Empire. The role of these factors emerges more sharply when we compare him with two German contemporaries: the religious writer Johann Heinrich Jung-Stilling (1740–1817) and the Jewish merchant from Königsberg, David Markus (1787–1846), whom we meet in the autobiography of his daughter Fanny Lewald.[57]

Rosenstrauch lived a peripatetic life, considered himself a plain-spoken moralist, found his faith when he was already an adult, cared deeply about the suffering of humanity and wrote to bring his spiritual experience and simple wisdom to a wide audience. In all these respects he resembled Jung-Stilling, whose widely read fictionalized autobiography chronicled his struggles as a self-made man seeking to live his 'awakened' faith and help the needy while resisting his own religious doubts and the temptations of scepticism.[58] Also like the celebrated 'patriarch of the Awakening', Rosenstrauch acquired—indeed, cultivated—the aura of a wise old man tempered by the trials of a hard life, and he further resembled Jung-Stilling in his embrace of a bourgeois ethos of self-discipline, work, economic success and the patriarchal family. The latter were attitudes he also shared with Markus, who, although nineteen years his junior, resembled Rosenstrauch in being a merchant's son from a Prussian provincial capital who grew up to be an affluent social outsider and who similarly felt alienated, as a Jew and religious sceptic, from the religious mainstream of his society.

This, however, is where the similarities end. The narratives of Jung-Stilling and Markus place the two men in geographically circumscribed, socially segmented milieux that embedded a man in a deep sense of history and a dense web of relationships even while constraining his social mobility. The worlds of both men constitute a solid matrix of genealogy, family lore, folk traditions, subtle status gradations and a physical environment saturated with collective memories. Moreover, in keeping with late eighteenth-century middle-class values, the narratives of Jung-Stilling and Markus foreground the comforts of family and married bliss based on romantic love.[59] Rosenstrauch, by contrast, appears as though in a vacuum. For decades he kept a diary, suggesting that he constructed his own persona with some deliberation; so it is no doubt intentional that we hear nothing at all from him about his ancestors, parentage, family, childhood, education, marriage or acting experience.[60] He conveys no sense of 'rootedness' in the traditions of either his native or his adoptive country. Surrounded by German transients and isolated from the Russians, he apparently neither told the stories nor was asked the questions that would have been customary in the more sedentary world of the 'old country'. Markus, like other assimilated European Jews, sought to remove the stigma of his roots by gaining admittance to the ruling nationality, but Rosenstrauch had assimilated into an immigrant diaspora that deemed itself culturally superior and had no desire to blend into the native majority. His portrayal of the social order in Russia is therefore built on stark polarities: Russian versus foreign, elite versus common. Like an emigrant overseas, he left behind his past and the complex hierarchies of his homeland and entered instead an order built on simpler—but therefore also more harsh and brittle—distinctions of ethnicity, wealth and privilege.

A final important point of comparison among the three men is their conception of historical change. Jung-Stilling's account of his early years, written well before the French Revolution, conveys no real sense of a social order in flux. However, his later writings on religious themes, which were widely disseminated in Pietist circles in Russia and elsewhere and which deeply influenced Tsar Alexander I, interpreted the French Revolution and its aftermath from a distinctly eschatological perspective.[61] This reading of current events resonates with Rosenstrauch's own understanding of the primarily spiritual significance of his experience in the war of 1812. Rosenstrauch shared with Markus the experience of change brought on by the Napoleonic armies, but how they interpreted it reflects their disparate social and geographic vantage points. David Markus found that the French troops in Königsberg were bearable neighbours who brought a whiff of cosmopolitanism and excitement to his staid provincial world, while Rosenstrauch regarded them as agents of senseless destruction.[62] The long French occupation of Prussia encouraged Markus's hopes for a humanistic German nationalism that might embrace even the previously despised Jews as fellow-citizens. Rosenstrauch, on the other hand, associated the short-lived French invasion of Russia with an upsurge of Russian xenophobia that left a restored cosmopolitan old regime as his only hope. Markus's business took him all over a Germany that remained politically unsettled after 1815; his heightened political awareness remained intact, and between 1830 and 1832 he cheered the revolution in France, watched with rapt attention the uprising in Poland and made a detour from a business trip to watch nationalist students rally for a unified German republic at the Hambach Festival.[63] By contrast, Russia returned to its earlier stability, and Rosenstrauch himself moved steadily away from its metropolitan centres and into an increasingly provincial world. His writings contain no references at all to social change or political developments; although he titled his narrative of the war 'Historical Events in Moscow in the Year 1812', he structured it entirely around his own experience, without placing the war into any wider context. Markus ultimately attributed the upheavals of his time to purposive historical forces that would one day lead to a liberal society. Rosenstrauch, closer in this regard to Jung-Stilling, discerned only a horrific but temporary turmoil driven by an inscrutable divine will.

Markus and Rosenstrauch shared many elements of the mercantile, patriarchal, humanistic culture of the North German bourgeoisie, but their differences also exemplify the differences between Europe's core and its periphery. Markus, who never moved away from his ancestral hometown at the heart of Europe, saw liberal changes in society and politics as a plausible hope—indeed the only hope—for removing the burden he carried as an ethnic and religious outsider. As for Rosenstrauch, emigration to the periphery allowed him to bury his past, reinvent himself and parlay his own outsider status into a privileged social position, but it would also have left him isolated and vulnerable if the hierarchical order of Russia's multinational empire had ever weakened. A liberal-nationalist civic consciousness was thus a natural dimension of bourgeois manhood for David Markus, while it could never be that for Johannes Ambrosius Rosenstrauch.

Acknowledgements

Research for this chapter was made possible by funding from the American Councils for International Education (ACTR/ACCELS), the National Council for Eurasian and East European Research and the Nanovic Institute for European Studies at the University of Notre Dame. I would like to thank Karen Hagemann, Gisela Mettele and the two anonymous readers for their helpful advice and kind assistance.

Notes

1. Michael Broers, *Europe under Napoleon, 1799–1815* (London, 1996), 266.
2. Karen Hagemann, *'Mannlicher Muth und Teutsche Ehre': Nation, Militär und Geschlecht zur Zeit der Antinapoleonischen Kriege Preußens* (Paderborn, 2002), 53–65, 304–350; see also the essays in *Representing Masculinity: Male Citizenship in Modern Western Culture*, ed. Stefan Dudink et al. (Basingstoke, 2007).
3. For an introduction to these themes, see, for example: Esther Kingston-Mann, *In Search of the True West: Culture, Economics, and Problems of Russian Development* (Princeton, NJ, 1999); Dale E. Peterson, *Up From Bondage: The Literatures of Russian and African American Soul* (Durham, NC, 2000); Richard S. Wortman, *Scenarios of Power: Myth and Ceremony in Russian Monarchy*, 2 vols (Princeton, NJ, 1995–2000).
4. Marc Raeff, 'Les Slaves, les Allemands et les "Lumières"', *Canadian Slavic Studies* 1 (1967): 521–551; idem, *The Well-Ordered Police State: Social and Institutional Change through Law in the Germanies and Russia, 1600–1800* (New Haven, 1983).
5. I discuss some of the evidence for these attitudes in 'Sewage and the City: Filth, Smell, and Representations of Urban Life in Moscow', *Russian Review* 67 (2008): 243–273, 249–254; see also Kingston-Mann, *In Search of the True West*, 40–41, 62–64.
6. Both Rosenstrauch's 1833 account and his letters to Kylius were originally published in Dorpat in the journal *Evangelische Blätter* (1833, 1836–38); reissued in *Mittheilungen aus dem Nachlasse von Johannes Ambrosius Rosenstrauch, früherem Consistorialrath und Prediger in Charkow* (Leipzig, 1845).
7. Division of Written Sources, State Historical Museum, Moscow, fond [collection] 402, delo [file] 239, 'Geschichtliche Ereignisse in Moskau *im Jahre 1812*, zur Zeit, der Anwesenheit des Feindes in dieser Stadt'. I am grateful to Andrei Dmitrievich Ianovskii of the State Historical Museum for allowing me to photocopy the entire manuscript, and to my father, Dr Donald W. Martin, for transcribing the text. Rosenstrauch's authorship of the unsigned manuscript is apparent from internal evidence, and key details of the narrative are confirmed in a letter signed

by Rosenstrauch: Central Historical Archive of Moscow, fond 20, opis' [inventory] 2, delo 2219, fo. 171^{r-v}. The only text to make reference to the narrative (though without identifying its author)—indeed, the only scholarly study of any of his writings—appears to be M. Korelin, 'Novyia dannyia o sostoianii Moskvy v 1812 godu', *Russkaia mysl'* 10 (1896): 57–73.
8. F. Bienemann, *Werden und Wachsen einer deutschen Kolonie in Süd-Rußland: Geschichte der evangelisch-lutherischen Gemeinde zu Odessa* (Odessa, 1893), 108.
9. Documentary evidence indicates that both Rosenstrauch's marriage and his son's baptism took place in Catholic churches: Katholische Kirche Sts Petrus und Andreas, Brilon (Westphalia), Kirchenbuch 1633–1874, <http://www.familysearch.org> (5 March 2007); baptismal record for Carl Wilhelm Rosenstrauch, Zaltbommel (The Netherlands), 22 September 1792 (Streekarchief Bommelerwaard, DTB 1901, 191; I thank the archivist drs. Sil van Doornmalen for his kind assistance).
10. F. O. Reingardt, 'Rozenshtraukh, Ioann-Ambrozii, pastor g. Khar'kova', *Khar'kovskii sbornik: literaturno-nauchnoe prilozhenie k 'Khar'kovskomu kalendariu' za 1887 god* 1 (1887): 153.
11. Mack Walker, *German Home Towns: Community, State, and General Estate, 1648–1871* (Ithaca, 1971); 'Geschichtliche Ereignisse', fo. 43^v; H. W. Bärensprung, *Versuch einer Geschichte des Theaters in Meklenburg-Schwerin* (Schwerin, 1837), 183–202; the *Kasselsche Polizei- und Kommerzienzeitung* records that he was an actor in the employ of the court of Kassel as of August 1794 (I thank Frank-Roland Klaube of the Stadtarchiv Kassel for this information). On Rosenstrauch's acting career in St Petersburg, see N. V. Gubkina, *Nemetskii muzykal'nyi teatr v Peterburge v pervoi treti XIX veka* (St Petersburg, 2003).
12. A. Hasselblatt and G. Otto (eds), *Album academicum der kaiserlichen Universität Dorpat* (Munich, 1889), 35; E. Amburger, 'Die Konsulate der Freien Stadt Frankfurt, Kurhessens, Hessen-Darmstadts und Nassaus im Russischen Reich', in *Festschrift für Heinz F. Friedrichs*, ed. G. Geßner (Neustadt/Aisch, 1980), 17 n. 7; A. I. Serkov, *Russkoe masonstvo 1731–2000: Entsiklopedicheskii slovar'* (Moscow, 2001), 1135.
13. Willard Sunderland, *Taming the Wild Field: Colonization and Empire on the Russian Steppe* (Ithaca, 2004), esp. chs 2–3.
14. Bienemann, *Werden*, 77, 110; A. W. Fechner, *Chronik der Evangelischen Gemeinden in Moskau*, 2 vols (Moscow, 1876), vol. 2, 118.
15. G. Reinbeck, *Flüchtige Bemerkungen auf einer Reise von St. Petersburg über Moskwa, Grodno, Warschau, Breslau nach Deutschland im Jahre 1805*, 2 vols (Leipzig, 1806), vol. 1, 214–216, 278–283.
16. P. I. Shchukin (ed.), *Bumagi, otnosiashchiiasia do Otechestvennoi voiny 1812 goda*, 10 vols (Moscow, 1897–1905), vol. 4, 225–228; A. Döllen, *Kurze Geschichte der evangelisch-lutherischen Kirche und Gemeinde zu Charkow* (Kharkov, 1880), 148.
17. 'Geschichtliche Ereignisse', fo. 3.
18. See, for example, Hugh McLeod, 'Weibliche Frömmigkeit—männlicher Unglaube? Religion und Kirchen im bürgerlichen 19. Jahrhundert', in *Bürgerinnen und Bürger: Geschlechterverhältnisse im 19. Jahrhundert*, ed. Ute Frevert (Göttingen, 1988), 134–156.
19. On the Germans in Kharkov, see Diana Zypina et al., *Deutsche in Charkiv: Ihr Leben und Wirken (19. Jahrhundert—Anfang des 20. Jahrhunderts)* (Kiev, 2004), 4 and passim.
20. *Mittheilungen*, 27–28, 81, 111. In this and subsequent quotations from this source, italicized passages follow the original.
21. Ibid. 30, 39, 88, 177.

22. 'Geschichtliche Ereignisse', fos 5ᵛ–6, 9ᵛ–10. A German eyewitness account that shares Rosenstrauch's interpretation is Anton Wilhelm Nordhof, *Die Geschichte der Zerstörung Moskaus im Jahre 1812*, ed. Claus Scharf and Jürgen Kessel (Munich, 2000).
23. Bienemann, *Werden*, 77, 110; Fechner, *Chronik*, vol. 2, 118.
24. 'Geschichtliche Ereignisse', fos 9–9ᵛ.
25. I discuss some of the relevant sources in Alexander Martin, 'The Response of the Population of Moscow to the Napoleonic Occupation of 1812', in *The Military and Society in Russia, 1450–1917*, ed. Marshall Poe et al. (Leiden, 2002), 469–489.
26. 'Geschichtliche Ereignisse', fos 24, 28ᵛ, 29.
27. Ibid.
28. On age at marriage, see Anne-Charlott Trepp, *Sanfte Männlichkeit und selbständige Weiblichkeit: Frauen und Männer im Hamburger Bürgertum zwischen 1770 und 1840* (Göttingen, 1996), 31, 49, 145.
29. *Staats- und Gelehrte Zeitung des Hamburgischen unpartheyischen Correspondenten*, 19 September 1821, no pagination.
30. On Moscow's demographic makeup, see Shchukin, *Bumagi*, vol. 4, 225–228. The role of Masonic lodges in promoting a highly emotional male sociability is discussed in Stefan-Ludwig Hoffmann, 'Unter Männern: Freundschaft und Logengesellschaft im 19. Jahrhundert', in *Der bürgerliche Wertehimmel: Innenansichten des 19. Jahrhunderts*, ed. Manfred Hettling and Stefan-Ludwig Hoffmann (Göttingen, 2000), 193–216. On male sociability more generally, see Jürgen Martschukat and Olaf Stieglitz, *'Es ist ein Junge!' Einführung in die Geschichte der Männlichkeiten in der Neuzeit* (Tübingen, 2005), esp. ch. 7.
31. I discuss some of the relevant sources in Alexander Martin, *Romantics, Reformers, Reactionaries: Russian Conservative Thought and Politics in the Reign of Alexander I* (DeKalb, 1997).
32. 'Geschichtliche Ereignisse', fo. 29ᵛ.
33. In a letter to his mother, Flahaut mentions lodging with the three officers in the house of Mr Demidov (Rosenstrauch's landlord) but not Rosenstrauch himself: Archives Nationales (Paris), 565 AP 5, dossier 5, fo. 109, letter of 27 September 1812. See also Geneviève Daridan, *MM. Le Couteulx et Cie, banquiers à Paris: Un clan familial dans la crise du XVIIIe siècle* (Paris, 1994), 321; Françoise de Bernardy, *Son of Talleyrand: The Life of Count Charles de Flahaut, 1785–1870*, trans. Lucy Norton (London, 1956), 92–97; Hortense de Beauharnais, *Mémoires de la reine Hortense, publiés par le prince Napoléon*, 3 vols (Paris, 1927), vol. 2, 159; Gaëlle Thiébaut, 'Charles de Flahaut, un diplomate de l'Europe impériale vers une Europe des nations' (Université Paris Sorbonne—Paris IV, mémoire de maîtrise, 2004), 29–31, <http://www.charles-de-flahaut.fr/Ressources/Flahaut.pdf> (22 January 2008); Lord Frederic Hamilton, *The Days Before Yesterday* (New York, 1920), 51–52.
34. 'Geschichtliche Ereignisse', fo. 16.
35. Louis de la Roque and Edouard de Barthélemy, *Catalogue de la noblesse des colonies et des familles anoblies ou titrées sous l'Empire, la Restauration, et le gouvernement de juillet* (Paris, 1865), 42; M. Darmaing, *Relation complète du sacre de Charles X* (Paris, 1825), 170.
36. A. Marcade, *Talleyrand: Prêtre et évêque* (Paris, 1883), 134.
37. *Mémoires de la reine Hortense*, vol. 2, 110.
38. The painting is reproduced in Bernardy, *Son of Talleyrand*, facing 32.
39. *Biographie universelle, ancienne et moderne, Supplément Mu-Ny*, vol. 75 (Paris, 1844), 413–417.

40. Daridan, MM. Le Couteulx et Cie; Michel Zylberberg, Capitalisme et catholicisme dans la France moderne: La dynastie Le Couteulx (Paris, 2001), chs 8–9.
41. 'Geschichtliche Ereignisse', fo. 27.
42. Ibid. fo. 38.
43. On the increasing 'militarization' of Western masculinity from the late eighteenth century onward, see Wolfgang Schmale, Geschichte der Männlichkeit in Europa (1450–2000) (Vienna, 2003), 195–203.
44. 'Geschichtliche Ereignisse', fos 24–25.
45. Ibid. fos 7^v, 11^v–12, 13^v–14, 21.
46. Ibid. fos 35^v–36^v.
47. Ibid. fos 43^v–44.
48. Fechner, Chronik, vol. 2, 117.
49. Mittheilungen, 4–5.
50. This concept is discussed in Martina Kessel, 'The "Whole Man": The Longing for a Masculine World in Nineteenth-Century Germany', Gender & History 15/1 (2003): 1–31.
51. S. P. Zhikharev, Zapiski sovremennika, 2 vols (Leningrad, 1989), vol. 2, 84.
52. Nikolai Mikhailovich, Imperator Aleksandr I. Opyt istoricheskago izsledovaniia, 2 vols (St Petersburg, 1912), vol. 1, 557.
53. Mittheilungen, 72–73.
54. H. Blumenthal, 'Johannes Ambrosius Rosenstrauch', Evangelische Blätter, 19 July 1836, col. 253.
55. K. Limmer, Meine Verfolgung in Rußland: Eine aktenmäßige Darstellung der Jesuitischen Umtriebe des D. Ignatius Feßler und seiner Verbündeten in jenen Gegenden (Leipzig, 1823), 176.
56. Mittheilungen, 79, 142; Fechner, Chronik, vol. 2, 116–121.
57. Fanny Lewald, The Education of Fanny Lewald: An Autobiography, trans. and ed. Hanna Ballin Lewis (Albany, 1992); Gabriele Schneider, Fanny Lewald (Reinbek, 1996).
58. The Autobiography of Heinrich Stilling, Late Aulic Counsellor of the Grand Duke of Baden, &c., &c., trans. S. Jackson (New York, 1844); the sections on Jung-Stilling's childhood and youth were first published in 1777–78. On Jung-Stilling's autobiography, see also Martin Hirzel, Lebensgeschichte als Verkündigung: Johann Heinrich Jung-Stilling—Ami Bost—Johann Arnold Kanne (Göttingen, 1998).
59. On romantic love and the centrality of family in the late eighteenth century, see Trepp, Sanfte Männlichkeit, 39–45, 212–213.
60. 'Geschichtliche Ereignisse', fo. 22^{r-v}.
61. On Jung-Stilling's apocalyptic writings, see Gerhard Schwinge, Jung-Stilling als Erbauungsschriftsteller der Erweckung: Eine literatur- und frömmigkeitsgeschichtliche Untersuchung seiner periodischen Schriften 1795–1816 und ihres Umfelds (Göttingen, 1994).
62. The Education of Fanny Lewald, 12–20.
63. Ibid. 120, 126–128, 144–145.

Part III
Warfare, Civil Society and Women

8
Bearing Arms, Bearing Burdens: Women Warriors, Camp Followers and Home-Front Heroines of the American Revolution

Holly A. Mayer

Was the American War for Independence a revolutionary war? In addressing this question, historians have examined the conflict from many angles, including that of women's positions in the Revolution. Some say that the War for Independence does not qualify as revolutionary simply because women participated in it, for women have always been a part of warfare, if not as soldiers then as military retainers, home-front supporters, resisters or victims. Others argue, however, that their participation had revolutionary effects, given the crucial influence women's actions during the rebellion and the later representations of their varied wartime services had on American perceptions of women and their place in society.

Societies have proclaimed—and historians in the past often analysed—the military and the home as distinct, intrinsically masculine or feminine physical and social spaces. Institutionally the contrast has validity. Yet individuals have also recognized that war and women do not exist in entirely separate spheres. America's War for Independence and recent scholarship on it confirm that observation. While their presence and actions with the Continental Army did not revolutionize the military by 'feminizing' it, women did contribute to its revolutionary function and image as a people's army. Women's activities at the home front, in turn, helped to make the War for Independence a 'people's war' as they dealt with the impact of military events on domestic domains.[1]

Rulers and rebels alike have used the phrase *people's war* to enlist soldiers in fights against outside invaders or internal oppressors.[2] As defined here, however, the term signifies a combination of civil and revolutionary war, in which political, military and domestic aspects of the conflict intertwine with and reinforce each other.³ That was the case in eighteenth-century America when various peoples contending over a new political order produced a new nation. Women's extensive participation in the conflict was a direct result of its being a people's war; more importantly, women's agency legitimized it as such. Furthermore, this people's war challenged the conceptions of women's roles and divisions between private and public spheres that Americans then and later sought to buttress.

Over the course of the War for Independence between 1775 and 1783, women on the British, or Loyalist, as well as American sides assumed additional responsibilities in domestic production and family defence—duties that became politically charged. Such labours could not be avoided as both Continental and British forces pressured women not only to choose a side but also to support it. In making a choice, women, though civilians, became not just targets but also essentially combatants. Neither civilian status nor their female gender preserved them from the burdens of war.⁴ Domestic life was too interwoven with the public conflict to be sacrosanct. That was particularly apparent on the American side, where women mobilized for the Revolution by bearing arms and burdens both in army encampments and on the home front.

Such mobilization presented the Revolutionaries with a dilemma, since they tended to see their cause as one of resistance and reform rather than rebellion. The British deemed them rebels, but the colonial dissenters believed themselves to be acting within the English Whig tradition as they tried first to preserve and protect their rights within the British system and then to implement their ideal forms of government outside it. The rebels engaged women in the political and economic defiance that marked the beginning of the Revolution. When political tensions erupted into war, women colonists also participated in military resistance. As long as they combined their efforts with those of their male counterparts, these women were generally welcome; but when they acted in ways judged unfeminine and thus implicitly or explicitly challenged the social order, men—and even other women—constrained their rebellion. That combination of mobilization and restriction, which has shaped interpretations of women's roles in the Revolution and the effects of the Revolution on women's status in America ever since, will be the focus of the following analysis.

'Remembering' the revolution's women

Contradictory and equivocal attitudes towards women in war, and especially women with the military, appear throughout American history. They hold particular interest, however, in terms of the War for Independence because the Revolutionaries were beginning to define not only the American man but also the American woman. Succeeding generations used the Revolution as a touchstone in the ongoing development of these definitions. What was condemned, accepted or celebrated during the rebellion and thereafter helped to construct and define women's cultural personas and places in the republic. Later popular and academic writers then illustrated women's activism in the Revolution so as to prove women's historical agency in general as well as their importance to the founding of the nation in particular.

The problem for many early commentators was that women's participation in the American Revolutionary War appeared to be socially and politically subversive, as women's actions challenged gender roles that the young republic regarded as indicative of its virtue and essential to its success. Thomas Jefferson, the author of the Declaration of Independence and champion of equality among white men, believed that women were as important to the republic as free men, and in this sense had equality. Yet he defined that equality differently when he argued for natural *rights* for men and natural *roles* for women. Those roles—marriage, motherhood and housewifery—determined the 'pursuit of happiness' for women and sustained the nation's life and liberty.[5]

Many Americans who celebrated women's historical agency shared Jefferson's opinions and were thus unable to applaud actions that other women might emulate to the detriment of gender order and public welfare. Their solution, echoed in Elizabeth Ellet's mid-nineteenth-century *The Women of the American Revolution*, was to approve extraordinary actions for extraordinary circumstances, to judge strength of character as a commendable trait, and to praise those who performed heroically within designated female bounds or, especially in the case of young women, those who quickly returned to that 'private' place after their 'public' service.[6]

Such an approach to women's contributions in the American Revolution reflected what was at stake for the nation. The Revolutionaries sought not just independence but a virtuous, well-ordered society. When women stepped out of their assigned roles to support independence (their own or the republic's), they threatened that goal of a properly constituted society.[7] Indeed, even when women stayed within their roles but stepped outside their homes to perform them, as the army's followers did, they disturbed the image if not the reality of what the Revolutionaries were trying to create.

Women were supposed to send their men off to war, not follow them into camp and battle. A woman's place was the home that people idealized over the course of the war as a place removed from public strife, one representing peace and prosperity. Yet, as literary scholar Nina Baym has pointed out, 'when most manly business had been conducted in or around the home space...[,] it was obvious that public and private spheres were metaphorical rather than actual places, that public and private were different ways of behaving in the same space'.[8] Similarly, when women conducted domestic business in military camps, the separation of public and private spheres was also more metaphorical than literal. War gave substance to the metaphor by making the separation real when men marched off holding an image of woman and home as *apart from* the martial sphere. Other soldiers, however, took not the image but the family, who then made 'home' *a part of* the martial community. Female followers still represented part of what the men were fighting to protect—family—but not the idealized domestic scene. Thus, except for a few singular cases, women were honoured for holding down the fort at home but not for being at home in the forts.

American society's conflicted attitudes about women in war is evident when looking at how later generations, to paraphrase Abigail Adams, 'remembered' the Revolution's 'ladies'. First, such remembering was gendered, in that women were more likely than men to write about women's contributions. Second, some writers—women and men—as they used history to establish and secure the nation's identity, defined that identity as predicated upon 'masculine' ideals rather than 'feminine' materiality.[9] Women, who were certainly a material part of warfare, were then ignored as authors focused on ideas, leaders and strategies. The third factor was the professionalization of history. As a result of this, with few exceptions, women's actions in the Revolution were remembered more in popular rather than academic venues.[10] And such remembering tended to celebrate domestic virtues over martial adventures.

The Daughters of the American Revolution (DAR), organized in 1890, certainly commemorated domestic valour. As women were required to prove descent from a Revolutionary patriot to join, the association's preservation and education efforts were heavily genealogical. Members, however, also interpreted the past to promote patriotism in the present. The past, as they saw it, prescribed the proper civic duties for women just as it did for men. In 1895 member Martha Jennings Small poetically summarized the virtues that distinguished women of the Revolution:

> Our grandmothers plied the spinning wheel,
> And with deft fingers, the yarn did reel;
> Then wove the cloth, and made the clothes,
> In which our grandsires met their foes.
> And sent them forth with anxious heart,
> In freedom's battle to bear their part;
> While *she*, in homespun gown arrayed,
> At home, a noble record made.

Small concluded that surely their granddaughters, after reading in 'history's page' of these 'heroic deeds', would be 'inspired to emulate | Each valiant act and noble trait.'[11]

By the turn of the twentieth century, professional historians tended to dismiss 'amateur' and 'romantic' chronicles and, with them, much of women's work in history. Historical societies, writers of popular history and a few conscientious scholars, however, prevented women's contributions to

Revolutionary America from being lost.[12] Then, in the 1960s and 1970s, the rise of the new social history and women's studies, along with the interest engendered by the bicentennial celebrations of the United States, led to the republication of older works and the introduction of new ones that re-evaluated women's contributions inside and outside the home and included considerations of race and class.[13]

Such scholarship escalated substantially in 1980 with Mary Beth Norton's *Liberty's Daughters* and Linda Kerber's *Women of the Republic*. Both historians addressed the war's impact on women but focused more on the intellectual and social ramifications of the political conflict. Other historians did the same, but a few, such as Paul Kopperman and Linda Grant De Pauw, looked specifically at women's roles with the military.[14] Exploration has continued through the turn of the century as historians have dug deeper into the gender issues intrinsic to this revolution and war. Joan Gundersen and Carol Berkin, for example, provided closer looks at women's agency during the conflict. Alfred F. Young concentrated on one Revolutionary woman, the soldier Deborah Sampson, while I analysed the complex relationships between the Continental Army and its camp followers.[15] This recent scholarship not only incorporates more examination of the ethnic, dispossessed and working women that Revolutionaries and later generations of Americans tended to dismiss but also emerges from and poses questions about the concept of separate spheres.[16] These interpretations may also reflect how the incorporation of women in modern military forces challenges that concept today.

Women warriors in truth and tale

The term *heroine* frequently, though not invariably, refers to a woman who has exhibited valour within—or at least straddling the bounds of—what society defines as properly feminine. Historically, Americans have commended women who endured much in order to defend their homes and sustain their families, but they have shown ambivalence about female courage in battle. The desire to extol spirit and sacrifice in the name of cause and country has come up against the desire to enforce social order. Yet the Revolutionary era in America and Europe provided many opportunities for women to take on the warrior role and for other people to recount their feats in print and performance.

The female warrior figured in literature as authors explored the nature of women's roles and character. In the 1790s, for instance, Charles Brockden Brown championed women's abilities in his novel *Ormond; or the Secret Witness* (1799). Of particular note in that work, according to Paul Lewis, is the character of Martinette de Beauvais, 'a trans-Atlantic, cross-dressing Revolutionary who provides a model of the woman warrior'. This 'manly' woman teaches the protagonist, Constantia Dudley, and by extension Brown's readers about the propriety of defending themselves.[17]

But while Constantia Dudley learns self-defence from the cross-dressing de Beauvais, she does not change her gender identity by donning male clothing. She exercises her power within acceptable boundaries. Other stories about female warriors of the Revolutionary era acknowledge female daring but also ultimately reinforce gendered norms. Many tales show what societies at the time imagined to be the right, corrective ending: after the young woman leaves her father's house and dresses as a man in order to follow her love into battle, the female hero becomes a heroine by resuming feminine garb, marrying her sweetheart and settling in his home.[18] Deborah Sampson neither left her father's house nor pursued a lover to war, but her story essentially followed that script.

Sampson, single and in her early twenties, served in the Continental Army under the name of Robert Shurtliff for over a year. She engaged in battle, was wounded, and was discovered in 1783 only when she became so ill that a doctor had to treat her. After resuming her female identity, she married Benjamin Gannett, bore children and raised crops. In 1792 she successfully petitioned the Massachusetts legislature for back pay, and in 1797, after others had written about her 'Female Heroism', she collaborated on her own memoir with Herman Mann, who also helped her to prepare for a lecture tour in 1802–3. In her public addresses Mrs. Gannett was careful to show herself a feminine patriot, one who slipped from her sphere when young and hot for the Revolutionary cause but who now championed, in the masculine public sphere, the importance of women acting within their own circle to support America. Although Congress finally gave her an invalid's pension in 1805 and a veteran's pension in 1821, it did not particularly commend her for having been a woman warrior. By then neither did society, and Deborah Sampson Gannett became quieter about her exploits so as to retain respectability.[19]

Deborah Sampson escaped being driven through town to the tune of the 'Whore's March', unlike another woman whose masquerade was discovered when she attempted to enlist. And while Sampson's fine soldiering did not lead to a promotion, as did that of 'Samuel Gay' (whose real name was apparently Ann or Nancy Bailey) in 1777, nor did she suffer the disgrace of arrest, trial and summary discharge that Bailey endured for having dressed in 'Man's Apparel' to enlist and then absconding with bounty money. Nor was Sampson jailed, as was the disguised Anne Smith when she tried to enlist in Springfield, Massachusetts, in 1782. In Smith's case there were additional transgressions, since, as one account put it, 'our heroine began this rout with stealing a horse'. Adding insult to injury, 'She acted the man so perfectly well through the whole, that she might probably have passed, had not the want of a beard and the redundance of some other matters led to a detection'.[20] Bailey and Smith represented what the Revolutionaries and their descendants definitely did not want to see developing in their new America: women lacking feminine decorum.

Attire and attitude, along with age, rank and marital status, appeared to be key to the celebration of heroines rather than female heroes. A few women dressed up as men in order to perform the deeds for which America commemorated them, but most did so while appropriately garbed for their gender. That suggests that although the masquerading female warrior was a favourite character in some ballads and romances that crossed the Atlantic in the eighteenth century, popularity did not translate into widespread emulation or commendation.[21]

Ultimately Americans preferred to create a romantic icon rather than celebrate such cross-dressing women as Deborah Sampson or Anna Maria Lane. Lane received a pension from the Virginia General Assembly for more than double the amount awarded to other new pensioners in 1808, but her story as a combatant at the Battle of Germantown in September 1777, where 'in the garb, and with the courage of a soldier, [she] performed extraordinary military services, and received a severe wound', appeared to have died with her in 1810. Even less is known of other women who donned the uniform, including Sally St Clare, who was killed in the war.[22] Their stories faded as the tale of a female cannoneer, 'Molly Pitcher', began to circulate.

The only women with the army whom others truly commemorated, besides the generals' ladies, were those who stepped out of line—but not out of their skirts—to become warriors. These 'Girls Behind the Guns', American versions of St Barbara, patron saint of the artillery, were the 'Mollies': Margaret Corbin, the 'Captain Molly' of Fort Washington fame, who should be remembered not just for her valour but also for representing the wounds women endured; and Mary Ludwig Hays (later McCauley), supposedly the 'Molly Pitcher' of Monmouth.[23]

Margaret Cochran Corbin followed John Corbin when he enlisted in the Pennsylvania Artillery. An author writing in 1926 excused that act by saying that Corbin was without children or other family and then, ennobling her, announced how 'Margaret Corbin endeared herself to her husband's comrades by the exercise of various womanly virtues, tending the sick and wounded, carrying water to them during an engagement, or cooking and mending during periods of ease'.[24] Yet it was not such womanly virtues that made her memorable but her actions during the battle at Fort Washington, New York, on 16 November 1776. When the gunners, including her husband, fell wounded or dead, she stepped in and continued firing one of the guns until she, too, was severely wounded and taken prisoner. In 1779 the Executive Council of Pennsylvania awarded her thirty dollars and recommended her case to the Board of War. The board, in turn, commended her 'fortitude and virtue' to the Continental Congress, arguing that she was 'as entitled to the same grateful return which would be made to a soldier in circumstances equally unfortunate'. Congress put her on the payroll of the Corps of Invalids and then awarded her a pension. After the war the Commissary of Military Supplies maintained Corbin at West Point, where she was known as Captain Molly and for being dirty and offensive. After she died, around 1800, people remembered her more as an eccentric than as a heroine until the early twentieth century, when a Margaret Corbin Chapter of the DAR was established and some writers decided to engender patriotic spirit by honouring this Molly.[25]

The other Molly was Mary Hays, whose story has served as the basis for one of America's national legends. In 1911 John B. Landis argued that Molly Pitcher was not imaginary 'but a real buxom lass, a strong, sturdy, courageous woman. ... [whose] conduct at Monmouth certainly contributed to the favourable results of that battle'. Landis attributed the title to Mary Ludwig Hays, following the lead of the citizens of Carlisle, Pennsylvania, who celebrated a local woman they said trailed John Casper Hays into the Battle of Monmouth, New Jersey, on 28 June 1778. More recent writers postulate that this Molly was married to a William Hays. That debate aside, an artilleryman fell wounded at his cannon that day and a woman took his place and kept the gun in action. It appears to have been a Mary Hays who, when her husband died after the war, married another veteran named McCauly. The Pennsylvania legislature awarded her not a widow's pension but one for her own unspecified services in the war; an honour that, along with the brief testimonies from Monmouth veterans, may have inspired the Molly Pitcher story.[26] The woman's name is disputed, and the title was a nineteenth-century creation, but the heroism appears to have been real.

The factual and fictional accounts of women bearing arms reveal generational and cultural issues with women acting as soldiers. Americans accepted that their people's war included women's service, but they questioned women's service in and with their people's army.

Women followers of the American army

Like the two 'Mollies', most of the women with the Continental Army were part of a couple or family. These women, who bore children in camp and baggage on the march, provided services that contributed to the stability and strength of the Continental Army. They cooked meals over camp and cabin fires, washed clothes in nearby creeks and rivers, and packed provisions and gear when the troops were on the move. They were also nurses and purveyors of goods. Thus while most, especially officers' wives, were domestic helpmates, many soldiers' wives were also working women. As those labouring followers supported their families, they helped to maintain military cohesion both socially and logistically; yet neither the military nor society recognized that service as heroic.[27] This refusal to acknowledge followers' military value reflected the prevailing opinion that these women did both what they had to do and what they were not supposed to do. Following a husband or other family member was accepted but not celebrated, for it was a legitimate response to necessity. Following for money or adventure was less acceptable and thus had to be explained, condemned or ignored. Recognition, or lack thereof, thus also related to social rank.

The majority of enlisted soldiers came from American society's lower classes. Many were young and single, but some had family responsibilities. The married soldier had to worry about his wife's ability to sustain the family and perhaps a farm or business. If she or other relatives could not do that, the soldier could ask for a furlough or discharge, desert the army or family, or bring his family to camp. Private Ezekiel Mott faced that dilemma when he visited his home after an expedition and found that his wife had died during his absence. Returning to duty, he took his five children, or at least the two sons who testified later, with him as his unit moved into New Jersey.[28] Society expected men to care for their families, and the army could not gainsay that. That expectation, along with the fact that absence—whether due to furlough, discharge or desertion—wrecked military readiness, forced commanders, including General George Washington, to accept such followers.[29] Accommodation did not, however, translate into commendation.

Honouring the women who followed the army was problematic because, although they performed the proper womanly duties of bearing up their households, many of them appeared not to do so 'virtuously'. Unlike the women who remained at home, they did not surrender their husbands to war. Such criticism, however, ignored the women at home who urged their soldiers, as the 'disconsolate and Solitary' Elizabeth Morrison did, not to let 'pecuniary influence, or any other encouragement' sway them 'to stay beyond the limited time'.[30] The criticism also disregarded the fact that many of these women were refugees and had nowhere else to go.

Contemporaries did have some pity for the refugees who streamed after the Continental Army when British army occupation forced people out of their homes. In general, however, observers condemned the followers' ragged appearance and rough behaviour, calling them 'ugly' and 'wild beasts', and thus, with a few notable exceptions, failed to view them as worthy republican women.[31]

The wives of officers, especially those of senior officers, served as more appealing models of American womanhood. These women usually came from the upper or middling ranks of society. Their class status, the fact that most of the officers' ladies only visited camp rather than residing in it throughout a campaign, and their feminine manners made their actions socially acceptable. On the other hand, they were not seen as particularly heroic, the much lauded Martha Washington notwithstanding.

Yet Theotist Paulin, the wife of Captain Antoine Paulin of Moses Hazen's 2nd Canadian Regiment, did sacrifice heroically to support her husband's dedication to the American cause. This French Canadian woman gathered up her four children, left her home, and followed her husband when he decided to remain with the Continental Army as it retreated from Canada in the spring of 1776. She and her children stayed with him throughout the war, living with him in the barracks in winter, and waiting in garrison during the summers when he was on campaign.[32]

Madam Paulin's children and those of numerous other refugee followers spent most of their young lives with the army. Paulin's children and others who had been with the French Canadian contingent remembered decades later how, as they reached their mid-to-late teens, many of the boys enlisted and the girls married soldiers.[33] Not all of the French Canadians in camp wed within that ethnic and religious group; nor were most of the soldiers in the 2nd Canadian Regiment from Canada. The Canadian soldiers as refugees, however, were more likely to have family followers, and, as it turned out, they and their followers tended to provide copious depositions when they applied for pensions. Their applications and those of other veterans and widows show that while war and military service made forming and supporting a family difficult, they obviously did not prevent it.

Susannah Lambert Myers provides another example of how soldiers created or maintained families within the military community. Myers was the sister of a soldier and possibly the daughter of one, for she was living 'with her Fathers family in said Fort at Fort Plain' when she married John Myers, a private or sergeant with Colonel Marinus Willett's New York Levies, in May 1783. She then lived with her spouse at the fort for about one month before his discharge.[34] While she was not a soldier's wife for long, thousands of other women followed for years, and they found that marriage to a soldier meant 'marrying' the army.

The numbers of followers varied over time and according to the unit involved—militia, state or Continental regiments. More appear to have been with the long-serving Continental regiments. A Valley Forge return of December 1777 shows approximately one woman for every forty-four enlisted men with the main army, whereas a return of January 1783 at New Windsor reveals a ratio of 1 woman to every 26 enlisted men. In between those times the ratios may have ranged from 1 to 30 to 35. While early in the war it may have been unremarkable for an individual company to have no female followers, that was not the case in 1783 'when the average was two women for each company with the main army'.[35]

The Continental Army demanded that followers accept its authority, especially if it was provisioning them. The relationship between them was defined by the Articles of War, which stated that followers were retainers to a camp and thus 'subject to orders, according to the rules and discipline of war'.[36] This directive, found in the British Articles of War, provides evidence of how this people's army was modelled on the European militaries of the age. It also shows that military law recognized women as a part of the army community though still distinct from the army itself.

While most followers apparently obeyed officers' commands and regulations, it seems they also tested them. Evidence for that deduction includes the recurring orders directing them to stay with the baggage and off the wagons when the army was on the move. Other orders threatened severe punishments for plundering homes, stealing from the army or cheating their fellow Continentals. Colonel Hazen in 1780, for instance, warned the soldiers and women of the 2nd Canadian Regiment that those found with property that was neither part of their public allocation nor officially sanctioned would have to forfeit such goods and face a court-martial for 'Disobedience of Orders' and 'suspicion of theft'. Hazen knew that his troops were trying to support themselves, but profiteering was unacceptable.[37]

Fighting each other was not acceptable either—not to the officers or to the writers intent on promoting American virtues. Such virtue was notably absent in the women and other members of Hazen's regiment who brawled one summer's day in 1780. What started as a women's quarrel led to a sergeant striking a soldier and then a captain hitting some of the combatants, including a woman. That woman may have been the sergeant's wife, for the sergeant then snarled at the officer. This affront to discipline led to courts-martial in which one of the followers was banished from the regiment and most of the other charges were dismissed.[38] This episode provides a clue as to why Revolutionaries and later generations rarely honoured camp followers. They remembered some of them decades later when the government finally issued surviving spouses with pensions, but they preferred to celebrate those who performed nobler actions.

Yet, if not always illustrious, the services of those women who 'married' the army were essential to the troops' welfare. Many of these followers acted as nurses in the camps and hospitals. And if not enough followers volunteered for hospital duty, the army impressed them. Commanders compelled the women by promising full rations and allowances for volunteers and threatening to withhold rations from shirkers. Reluctance to volunteer was understandable given the possibility of contracting diseases from patients. In addition, those who volunteered, whether they were followers to start with or became followers as nurses, probably had to hound officials for their pay during the war or after, as the Irish Mary Cawfield, who had served at Easton, Valley Forge, and elsewhere, did in 1786.[39]

Some followers cooked and scrubbed as servants for officers (and their visiting wives), but the frequent mention of washerwomen in orderly books and returns indicates that laundry was a primary task for these working women. In 1776 a captain recorded three washerwomen along with his seventy-two soldiers and two officers. In 1780 Captain George Fleming asked Colonel John Lamb to register four laundresses for his company in accordance with an apparently standard complement of one woman washing for ten men. Registered washerwomen received extra provisions along with what they earned. Other followers could also charge for laundering, but they, too, had to comply with regulations.[40]

Female followers also peddled, both legally and illegally, inside and outside camp boundaries. Licensed sutlers had authorization to sell provisions, liquors and articles of personal and military equipment in camp. Most sutlers were men, but some wives partnered with their husbands in this enterprise; and a few women were accepted as petty sutlers of minor items—whether independently or as wives of soldiers. On a related note, selling supplies could be associated with gathering information. A woman peddling thread and other sundries in the American camp in the summer of 1778 used her access to spy for the British.[41]

Although the American army made a mistake in admitting that sutler-spy, its acceptance of female followers was not open-ended. For example, while it allowed women to sell goods, it tried to repel and expel those who peddled their bodies. The problem was particularly acute when troops encamped in or near such urban areas as New York City and Philadelphia, but it also appeared elsewhere, as when a group of officers created a brothel outside camp lines at Newburgh in 1783.[42] While a number of followers may have traded sexual favours for goods, most were not working as prostitutes. Yet the behaviour of some of these women left the impression of lewdness rather than virtue, at least among the Revolutionaries and their descendants who defined virtue in Jeffersonian-republican or middle-class terms. That was another reason why women with the army became mere footnotes in the history books.

Heroines on the home front

Americans did commend a few women, or, more accurately, iconic images of virtuous women who served in or with the Continental Army as soldiers and followers. This praise, however, was limited compared to how Revolutionaries and later generations commemorated the women who displayed fortitude when the Revolution disrupted the domestic economy and courage when the war brought enemy soldiers marching through their doors. The founders praised such women as heroines, and subsequent generations told their stories to honour and encourage womanly civic activism.

In 1897, DAR member Jennie Goodwin presented a roster of women who, even when threatened with violence, defended families and property, cause and country during the War for Independence. She noted how they used their wits and courage. And yet, after recounting the heroism of the pistol-packing wife of a Colonel Johnston of Vermont, Goodwin devalued the other women who bore arms so as to make a point about bearing burdens at home. She proclaimed that 'in the great struggle of our country for freedom, woman proved herself man's helpmate, as God intended her to be. Not hers to bear the musket, wield the sword, or charge with bayonet upon the field of battle'. Goodwin's heroines embodied the qualities admired by Jefferson and the domestic ideals implicit in what was then the DAR's motto: 'Home and Country'.[43]

Assuming male clothing and a male identity in the military sphere was one thing, performing female domestic roles in camp another, and taking on male duties within the domestic sphere yet another. The latter had already been justified before and during the Revolution when society accepted women as 'deputy husbands' during their spouses' absence and as matriarchs after they were widowed.[44] The women who acted in those home-front roles appeared the least disturbing to those who desired to maintain a traditional gender order in and after the Revolutionary era. And yet, by fulfilling their expanded responsibilities, such women contributed much not only to the Revolution's success in the short term but also to revolutionary change in the long term. As succeeding generations of women celebrated these founding mothers as heroines and followed their lead in later wars, they increased the power and status of women privately and publicly. Thus the women who maintained the home front, while behaving most conventionally, may ultimately have been the most revolutionary.

Contemporary accounts and later histories laud women who supported the Revolution by displaying a feminine form of the public virtue of patriotism. Heroines served the commonweal by taking on greater household duties and binding them to the aims of the new republic that was their larger 'home'.[45] Some Pennsylvania women in 1774, for example, assured their Virginia sisters that by assisting their men 'in their honest endeavours to extricate America from the evils that threaten her', they themselves were demonstrating civic virtue, and would in time be venerated for it.[46] Before 1775 such virtue included boycotting British wares, but once war broke out, it meant relinquishing their husbands and sons for public service. It was not enough to do without goods; women had to do without their men and their men's labour.

Apart from death, the most fundamental disruption to family life came when a man enlisted or accepted a commission in the Continental Army (or other forces). Elizabeth Morey, for example, married Silas in 1768 and then had ten children, bearing and caring for five of them during the war while her husband was in service. Other women married soldiers when the men were home between stints with militia units or on furlough from the regular forces, as did Huldah Moor, who may have been pregnant at the time of her marriage in December 1779, a ceremony hastened by her parents. Others included Anna Myers, who said she married John in 1781 because he was anxious to have her take care of his aged parents while he was away. In 1777 Elizabeth Shafer married Henry, a militia sergeant who had served in 1775 and 1776, only to see him head back to duty every year from 1778 to 1782. And the African-American Flora Taggart married Pomp Sherburne (who may have used his bounty money to buy her freedom) sometime around 1780, before he returned to serve Colonel George Reid of the New Hampshire line.[47]

These were the women who 'held down the fort' at home. Decades later, when applying for spousal pensions, the widows said little about what they did during the war, for the government had no interest in that. Pensions were granted in recognition of their husbands' service, not their own sacrifices and work. Yet sacrifice and work defined their service to the nation. Whether their men served continuously, as Silas Morey did, or repeatedly, as Henry Shafer did, women like Elizabeth Morey and Elizabeth Shafer had to handle the men's domestic responsibilities along with their own. They conducted 'manly' business as well as womanly business in and around the home space. Like the camp followers, then, the women at home were 'a reserve labour force', mobilized when there was not enough manpower to sustain both military operations and the civilian economy.[48]

Women waged war by working. Many managed family farms and businesses, just as Mary Fish Silliman did, first when her husband and stepson galloped off to defend Connecticut and again when Loyalist raiders kidnapped them and turned them over to the British in 1779. Other women found domestic work outside their own homes, or combined conventional roles with business activities, becoming tavern keepers, for example. And some found jobs doing piecework in the military's 'laboratories' from Philadelphia to Springfield making cartridges or the like. Others responded to advertisements for nurses in military hospitals. The absence of men due to wartime service and deaths thus increased the need for women to work and expanded their opportunities to do so.[49]

In addition to defending their children, their homes and themselves when armies invaded their supposedly separate sphere, women had to contend with the crimes and diseases that marched through their communities in the troops' wake. The forces of both sides plundered in this war, but, as one might expect, contemporary American accounts charged the British troops and their German auxiliaries of doing the most and worst of it. Drunkenness and deprivation sharpened anger, which in turn sometimes escalated the robbery of plunder into the destruction of pillaging. Rapine also led to rape.

Being civilian and being at home did not protect women from attack, and when soldiers deemed them enemies, not just targets of opportunity, they may have been especially vulnerable. In 1776, as British forces and Loyalist raiders threatened Connecticut, Gold Selleck Silliman warned his wife to prepare for possible attack and to be especially careful to avoid Hessians, whom he believed to be savage rapists. Yet it appears to have been primarily British soldiers who perpetrated the many rapes that occurred in New Jersey that autumn. On Long Island, New York, Privates John Dunn and John Lusty raped Elizabeth Johnstone, the widow of an American soldier, in her own home in the presence of her four-year-old daughter and elderly lodger. According to the records of their court martial, Dunn and Lusty at first denied committing the rape and described Johnstone to the soldiers who arrested them as 'a Yankee whore or a Yankee bitch'. The adjective is telling and was undoubtedly meant to undermine the credibility of Johnstone's accusation and perhaps even to justify the assault. Although the court ultimately sentenced her assailants to death, Elizabeth Johnstone was left as a victim in history's footnotes rather than a heroine because she did not successfully fend off the assault on private and, by extension, public virtue.[50]

Women as well as men also had to combat disease, the deadliest follower of armies. Although Americans accused the British army of deliberately exposing soldiers and civilians alike to smallpox, Continental forces were equally guilty of spreading it and other diseases. American troops were less disciplined in hygiene and less likely to be inoculated, at least initially. As a result, they and the civilians in and near military camps suffered from various fevers, dysentery, venereal disease and other disorders besides smallpox; especially when an army commandeered private homes as well as public houses for use as hospitals.[51]

Even when the war ended, its plagues receded, and soldiers returned home, women still had wounds to bind and family lives to rebuild. Women who had been with the army faced the same tasks, with the added challenges of moving to new communities or re-establishing themselves in former ones. As they did so, many must have thought as Mary Silliman had back in 1776, that she had 'acted the *heroine* as well as my dear Husband the Hero'.[52]

Conclusion

The American War for Independence both undermined and reinforced the notion of separate spheres. The war contributed to the idealization of the home and of women's position in that domestic domain, especially in later constructions of a public memory of the Revolution, but it also initiated changes in the reality of both. While the image of the woman warrior has had the greatest romantic appeal and has served as an icon of revolutionary change in gender roles, cumulatively the female followers and women at home performed the most service in the War for Independence. They did so within the traditional, socially prescribed realm but also by acting in untraditional ways. Furthermore, the need for both material and ideological support increased public recognition of women's roles and influence. Whether as combatants or non-combatants, whether participants by choice or chance, as women mobilized, they made this people's war a revolutionary one.

Notes

1. Recent works on this people's war include: Wayne E. Lee, 'The American Revolution', in *Daily Lives of Civilians in Wartime Early America: From the Colonial Era to the Civil War*, ed. David S. Heidler and Jeanne T. Heidler (Westport, CT, 2007), 31–67, 34–40; Gregory T. Knouff, *The Soldiers' Revolution: Pennsylvanians in Arms and the Forging of Early American Identity* (University Park, PA, 2004); Wayne Bodle, *The Valley Forge Winter: Civilians and Soldiers in War* (University Park,

PA, 2002); John Resch, 'The Revolution as a People's War', in *War and Society in the American Revolution: Mobilization and Home Fronts*, ed. John Resch and Walter Sargent (DeKalb, 2007), 70–102.
2. Karen Hagemann, '"Heroic Virgins" and "Bellicose Amazons": Armed Women, the Gender Order and the German Public during and after the Anti-Napoleonic Wars', *European History Quarterly* 37/4 (2007): 507–527, 508. See also Chapter 9 by Thomas Cardoza in this volume.
3. John Shy delineates a 'triangularity of the struggle' in 'The American Revolution: The Military Conflict Considered as a Revolutionary War', in *Essays on the American Revolution*, ed. Stephen G. Kurtz and James H. Hutson (Chapel Hill, 1973), 121–156.
4. Joan R. Gundersen, *To Be Useful to the World: Women in Revolutionary America, 1740–1790* (New York, 1996), 149–154. For discussions about limits on defining civilians as noncombatants, see Armstrong Starkey, 'Wartime Colonial America', in Heidler and Heidler, *Daily Lives of Civilians*, 1–30, 1–2; John Grenier, *The First Way of War: American War-Making on the Frontier* (New York, 2005), 146–169.
5. Brian Steele, 'Thomas Jefferson's Gender Frontier', *The Journal of American History* 95 (2008): 17–42, 18, 26, 28, 40.
6. Elizabeth F. Ellet, *The Women of the American Revolution*, 2 vols (1848–49; repr. Williamstown, MA, 1980). Also see Nina Baym's *American Women Writers and the Work of History, 1790–1860* (New Brunswick, NJ, 1995), 217–236.
7. Ruth H. Bloch, 'The Gendered Meanings of Virtue in Revolutionary America', and Joan R. Gundersen, 'Independence, Citizenship, and the American Revolution', *Signs* 13 (1987): 37–58 and 59–77, respectively.
8. Baym, *American Women*, 11.
9. Bonnie G. Smith, *The Gender of History: Men, Women, and Historical Practice* (Cambridge, UK, 1998), 150.
10. Besides the works of Baym and Smith, see Julie Des Jardins, *Women and the Historical Enterprise in America: Gender, Race, and the Politics of Memory, 1880–1945* (Chapel Hill, 2003), 1–2, 4, 15–17, 19.
11. Martha Jennings Small, 'Ode to the Daughters of the American Revolution', *The American Monthly Magazine* 7 (July 1895): 19.
12. Des Jardins, *Women*, 25–26, 30, 72–73, 81.
13. Among the many records and studies of Revolutionary women that were either reissued or first published during the mid-1970s, see Ellet, *The Women*; Walter Hart Blumenthal, *Women Camp Followers of the American Revolution* (New York, 1974); Elizabeth Evans, *Weathering the Storm: Women of the American Revolution* (New York, 1975); Sally Booth Smith, *Women of '76* (New York, 1973); Debra L. Newman, 'Black Women in the Era of the American Revolution in Pennsylvania', *Journal of Negro History* 61 (1976): 276–289; Mary Beth Norton, 'Eighteenth-Century American Women in Peace and War: The Case of the Loyalists', *William and Mary Quarterly* 33 (1976): 386–409; Joan Hoff Wilson, 'The Illusion of Change: Women and the American Revolution', in *The American Revolution*, ed. Alfred E. Young (DeKalb, 1976), 383–431.
14. Mary Beth Norton, *Liberty's Daughters: The Revolutionary Experience of American Women, 1750–1800* (Boston, 1980); Linda K. Kerber, *Women of the Republic: Intellect and Ideology in Revolutionary America* (Chapel Hill, 1980). Other works, besides those noted elsewhere, include Barbara E. Lacey, 'Women in the Era of the American Revolution: The Case of Norwich, Connecticut', *The New England Quarterly* 53 (1980): 527–543; Betsy Erkkila, 'Revolutionary Women', *Tulsa Studies in Women's Literature* 6 (1987): 189–223. On the military, see Paul E. Kopperman,

'Medical Services in the British Army, 1742–1783', *Journal of the History of Medicine* 34 (1979): 428–455; idem, 'The British High Command and Soldiers' Wives in America, 1755–1783', *Journal of the Society for Army Historical Research* 60 (1982): 14–34; Linda Grant De Pauw, 'Women in Combat: The Revolutionary War Experience', *Armed Forces and Society* 7 (1981): 209–226; idem, *Battle Cries and Lullabies: Women in War from Prehistory to the Present* (Norman, 1998); Janice E. McKenney, '"Women in Combat": Comment', *Armed Forces and Society* 8 (1982): 686–692.

15. See Gundersen, *To Be Useful*; idem, '"We Bear the Yoke with a Reluctant Impatience": The War for Independence and Virginia's Displaced Women', in Resch and Sargent, *War and Society*, 263–288; Carol Berkin, *Revolutionary Mothers: Women in the Struggle for America's Independence* (New York, 2005); Alfred F. Young, *Masquerade: The Life and Times of Deborah Sampson, Continental Soldier* (New York, 2004); Holly A. Mayer, *Belonging to the Army: Camp Followers and Community during the American Revolution* (Columbia, SC, 1996); idem, 'Wives, Concubines, and Community: Following the Army', in Resch and Sargent, *War and Society*, 235–262.

16. On the spheres trope in American history, see Linda K. Kerber, 'Separate Spheres, Female Worlds, Woman's Place: The Rhetoric of Women's History', *Journal of American History* 75 (1998): 9–39; idem et al., 'Beyond Roles, Beyond Spheres: Thinking About Gender in the Early Republic', *The William and Mary Quarterly* 46 (1989): 565–585; Cathy N. Davidson, 'Preface: No More Separate Spheres!', *American Literature* 70 (1998): 443–463.

17. Paul Lewis, 'Attaining Masculinity: Charles Brockden Brown and Woman Warriors of the 1790s', *Early American Literature* 40 (2005): 37–55, 37–39.

18. Dianne Dugaw, *Warrior Women and Popular Balladry, 1650–1850* (Cambridge, UK, 1989), 4, 157; David Hopkin, 'The World Turned Upside Down: Female Soldiers in the French Armies of the Revolutionary and Napoleonic Wars', in *Soldiers, Citizens and Civilians: Experiences and Perceptions of the Revolutionary and Napoleonic Wars, 1790–1820*, ed. Alan Forrest et al. (Basingstoke, 2008).

19. Young, *Masquerade*, 185–186, 223–224, 258–260.

20. William Barton to unknown addressee, 17 November 1778, Sol Feinstone Manuscripts #82, David Library of the American Revolution (hereafter DLAR), Washington Crossing, Pennsylvania; Robert Fridlington, 'A "Diversion" in Newark: A Letter from the New Jersey Continental Line, 1778', *New Jersey History* 105 (1987): 75–78; De Pauw, *Battle Cries*, 124; *The Pennsylvania Packet*, 25 June 1782.

21. Dugaw, *Warrior Women*, 1–2, 84, 143–144.

22. Sandra Gioia Treadway, 'Anna Maria Lane: An Uncommon Common Soldier of the American Revolution', *Virginia Cavalcade* 37 (1988): 134–143.

23. Fairfax Downey, 'The Girls behind the Guns', *American Heritage Magazine* 8 (1956): 46–48.

24. Vincent Fleming O'Reilly, 'Irish Margaret Corbin of Revolution', *The Irish World and American Industrial Liberator*, 7 August 1926, 3.

25. Ibid. 10; William Davison Perrine, *Molly Pitcher of Monmouth County, New Jersey, and Captain Molly of Fort Washington, New York, 1778–1937* (Princeton [n.p.], 1937), pamphlet. For more information on Margaret Corbin, see the file of letters in the Revolutionary War Pension and Bounty-Land-Warrant Application Files (hereafter RWPF) in the Records of the Veterans Administration at the National Archives and Records Administration of the United States, Washington, DC, Record Group 15, Microfilm 27, Reel 653.

26. John B. Landis, 'Investigation into the American Tradition of a Woman Known as "Molly Pitcher"', *Journal of American History* 5/1 (1911): 83–95, 86; J. A. Murray, 'Molly McCauley', repr. from *American Volunteer*, Carlisle, PA, 12 September 1883; Elizabeth Cometti, 'McCauley, Mary Ludwig Hays', in *Notable American Women, 1607–1950: A Biographical Dictionary*, ed. Edward T. James, 3 vols (Cambridge, MA, 1971), vol. 2, 448–449; 'DAR Lineage on "Molly Pitcher"', signed by Lois W. Davidson, Cumberland County Chapter of the DAR, 1 June 1985; Constance M. McDonald, 'About Molly Pitcher', *Field Artillery Magazine*, August 1990, <http://www.usfaa.com/usfaa_awards/about_molly.html> (23 April 2007); Emily J. Teipe 'Will the Real Molly Pitcher Please Stand Up?' *Prologue* 31 (1999): 119–126.
27. Mary Wechsler Segal has offered a labour framework within which to analyse the nature of women's participation in the armed forces; see her essay 'Women's Military Roles Cross-Nationally, Past, Present, and Future', *Gender & Society* 9/6 (1995): 757–775, 761.
28. RWPF, Microfilm 27, Reel 1782, Ezekiel and Jane Mott pension file, depositions of Ezekiel Mott, junior, dated November 1819, and Elijah Mott, dated 13 August 1819.
29. G[eorge] Washington to Robert Morris, 29 January 1783, in *The Writings of George Washington from the Original Manuscript Sources, 1745–1799*, ed. John C. Fitzpatrick, 39 vols (Washington, DC, 1931–44), vol. 26, 78–80.
30. Elizabeth Morrison, Bedford [MA], to John Morrison in Captain Samuel McConnel's Company, Bennington [VT], 13 September 1777 (original on deposit at the American Philosophical Society), Sol Feinstone Collection #2401, DLAR.
31. Joseph Plumb Martin, *Ordinary Courage: The Revolutionary War Adventures of Joseph Plumb Martin*, ed. James Kirby Martin (1830; St James, NY, 1993), 117; unidentified author, Diary for 21 April–25 September 1780, Virginia Historical Society, Richmond, Virginia, entry dated 20 September 1780.
32. RWPF, Microfilm 27, Reel 1891, Theotist Paulin's pension application, 17 January 1837, in Antoine Paulin pension file. For more on French Canadian families with the army, see Mayer, 'Wives, Concubines, and Community', 235–262.
33. For examples, see RWPF, Microfilm 27, Reel 524, Sally Chartier's pension application, in John Mary Chartier pension file, and Polly Chartier's declarations, in Peter Chartier pension file.
34. RWPF, Microfilm 27, Reel 1799, John and Susannah Myers pension file, declarations of 1818, 1820, 1842, 1843 and 1844.
35. John Rees, '"The Multitude of Women": An Examination of the Numbers of Female Camp Followers with the Continental Army', Parts 1 and 3, *The Brigade Dispatch* 23 (Autumn 1992): 5–17, 5; and 24 (Spring 1993): 2–6, 3. See also Mayer, 'Wives, Concubines, and Community', 241.
36. Article 23, Section XIII, 1776 American Articles of War.
37. Mayer, *Belonging*, 135–142; Historical Society of Pennsylvania (hereafter HSP), Philadelphia, John H. Hawkins Orderly Book No. 1 (1 January–23 April 1780), 2nd Canadian Regiment, Regimental Orders, Headquarters, 25 March 1780. See also the Peter Force Collection, Series 8D, vol. 68, Manuscript Division, Library of Congress, Washington, DC, The Papers of Moses Hazen, Orderly Book (1 January–27 April 1780), HQ, 28 January 1780.
38. HSP, John H. Hawkins Orderly Book No. 2 (23 April–26 July 1780), 2nd Canadian Regiment, Headquarters, 7 and 8 (9) July 1780.
39. Mayer, *Belonging*, 134, 142, 222–223; Charles Pettit to John Nicholson, 5 September 1786, *Letters of Delegates to Congress, 1774–1789*, ed. Paul H. Smith (Washington, DC, 1995), vol. 23, 551.

40. Mayer, *Belonging*, 140–141.
41. Ibid. 86, 37–38.
42. Mayer, *Belonging*, 110–112; Blumenthal, *Women Camp Followers*, 59. For examples of orders, see Isaac Bangs, New York, 25 April 1776, *Journal of Lieutenant Isaac Bangs, April 1 to July 29, 1776* (1890; repr. New York, 1968), 29–31; and Orderly Book of Col. Alexander McDougall's 1st New York Regiment (25 March–15 June 1776), Headquarters New York City, 7 May 1776, Early American Orderly Books Collection, The New York Historical Society. The brothel is noted in *Winding Down: The Revolutionary War Letters of Lieutenant Benjamin Gilbert of Massachusetts, 1780–1783*, ed. John Shy (Ann Arbor, 1989), 86–87.
43. Jennie J. B. Goodwin, 'The Women of the Revolution', *The American Monthly Magazine* 11 (1897): 350–356. I am indebted to Rebecca Baird, Archivist, Office of the Historian General, National Society Daughters of the American Revolution, for information on the DAR's motto, which in 1972 was changed to 'God, Home, and Country'.
44. Laurel Thatcher Ulrich, *Good Wives: Images and Reality in the Lives of Women in Northern New England, 1650–1750* (New York, 1983), 35–50.
45. Katherine Aaslestad notes a similar connection in 'Republican Traditions: Patriotism, Gender, and War in Hamburg, 1770–1815', *European History Quarterly* 37 (2007): 582–602, 585. See also Chapter 11 in this volume.
46. Clementina Rind (ed.), *Virginia Gazette*, 15 September 1774.
47. RWPF, Microfilm 27, Reel 1763: Elizabeth (and Silas) Morey pension file, declarations of 1837; Reel 1752, Huldah (and Elias) Moor pension file, declarations of 1837 and 1841; Reel 1799, Anna (and John) Myers pension file, declarations of 1837 and 1838; Reel 2156, Henry and Elizabeth Shafer pension file, declarations of 1839; Reel 2171, Flora (Sherburne) Bell (and Pomp Sherburne) pension file, declarations of 1844 and 1845.
48. Segal, 'Women's Military Roles', 764.
49. Joy Day Buel and Richard Buel Jr., *The Way of Duty: A Woman and Her Family in Revolutionary America* (New York, 1984), 98, 145–147; Martin Schultz, 'Occupational Pursuits of Free Women in Early America: An Examination of Eighteenth-Century Newspapers', *Sociological Forum* 3 (1988): 97–102; Mayer, *Belonging*, 218, 221, 233n.
50. Buel and Buel, *Way of Duty*, 125; David Hackett Fischer, *Washington's Crossing* (New York, 2004), 174–179; Great Britain, War Office, Judge Advocate General Office, Court Martial Proceedings and Board of General Officers' Minutes, Microfilm 675, WO 71/82, Reel 2, 405–425: New Town, Long Island, Tuesday, 3 September 1776; Sharon Block, *Rape and Sexual Power in Early America* (Chapel Hill, 2006), 126.
51. Ann M. Becker, 'Smallpox in Washington's Army: Strategic Implications of the Disease during the American Revolutionary War', *Journal of Military History* 68 (2004): 399–400, 408, 423–424; Mayer, *Belonging*, 64–65.
52. Quoted in Buel and Buel, *Way of Duty*, 129.

9
'Habits Appropriate to Her Sex': The Female Military Experience in France during the Age of Revolution
Thomas Cardoza

Thousands of women served with French military units between 1775 and 1820, yet the subject of French women's military participation in the Age of Revolution has never been covered comprehensively. Between 1792 and 1815, France was almost constantly at war and, as the centre of revolution, underwent numerous regime changes, each with potential ramifications for both gender relations and military institutions. The French army included far more women than did the armies of other European powers.[1] Each of the French army's female roles had unique characteristics, but all involved women working in a largely male world and engaging in combat at least occasionally. Therefore, by definition, these roles implicitly challenged ideas of women as unsuited to military service, particularly combat. Yet despite numerous variations and exceptions, a remarkable continuity prevailed across four and a half decades and numerous regime changes. While women participated in the male activity of war far more extensively than they did in other European armies of the time, the French government and military officials carefully regulated and circumscribed their activities, confining them as much as possible to the roles of mother, nurse and housekeeper. When it became impossible to do so in reality, powerful men still did so in perception, by determining which women received recognition for heroism, and by controlling rewards, pensions and the narrative of women's actions. While some women managed to subvert or avoid this paradigm, most military women were boxed into 'female' roles as they struggled to reconcile two sets of conflicting values. On one hand, the everyday reality of working-class women required them to work to support their families; on the other hand, emerging ideas of middle- and upper-class femininity—ideas that increasingly influenced government and military leaders—asserted that women should not be employed outside the home and strongly condemned those 'amazons' who engaged in combat. Despite this conflict, thousands of women still made great contributions to the French military effort, and a few even achieved relative independence. In this chapter I analyse female experiences in the French army between 1775 and 1820.

Women in the army of the ancien régime

Whether they were British 'wives on the strength', Prussian '*Marketenderinnen*' or French '*vivandières*', women made vital contributions as support personnel in European armies of the eighteenth and nineteenth centuries. A few women also served as soldiers, though the illegal and therefore covert nature of this service makes an exact count impossible. Nevertheless, most recent studies on military women focus on this interesting but decidedly limited topic, while ignoring the far more numerous women providing support behind the front lines.[2]

Women served in three capacities in the French army: as *femmes soldats* (female soldiers), as *blanchisseuses* (laundresses) and as *vivandières* (sutlers). Republicans viewed women soldiers as oxymoronic, and attempts by French women to serve their nation openly in arms met with complete official rejection by 1793. After that, women could serve legally only in roles regarded as traditionally feminine: laundresses and *vivandières*. Nevertheless, a number of *femmes soldats* continued to serve even after 1793, and many *blanchisseuses* and *vivandières* also took part in battle, suggesting that women and combat were not as mutually exclusive as some men claimed. While the ratio of female to male soldiers was very low, thousands of women bore arms or supported army units at the front lines; and many were a crucial part of the French military effort.

One way to assess the impact of women's military participation in France is to study continuities and discontinuities. The period 1775–1820 covers at least four distinct French governments: the ancien régime, the First Republic, the First Empire and the Restoration monarchy. These governments had different agendas and backgrounds, yet all of them employed thousands of *blanchisseuses* and *vivandières*, as well as varying numbers of *femmes soldats*. Nevertheless, while a number of continuities existed, and indeed dominated, certain discontinuities also prevailed, most notably in the treatment of *femmes soldats*. The Law of 30 April 1793, in particular, stands out as a watershed in terms of women's military participation. Passed by the National Convention as a way to rid the army of 'useless women', this law has often been cited, and rightly so, as an example of the republican backlash against female agency in the public sphere. Like most important historical events, however, the 30 April law had more than one facet. A deliberate attempt to prevent women from acting outside their 'proper' sphere, it also granted wide and sweeping independence to *vivandières*, whose role at the front was feminine in theory but in practice often blurred the line between helpmate and combatant.

Vivandières were the most important women in the French military system. Known in English as sutlers, they sold food, drink and sundries to the troops. The linguistic comparison, however, is misleading, since in the Anglo-Saxon military tradition sutlers were usually men whose connections to the units they served were very tenuous. *Vivandières*, in contrast, were tied permanently to their regiments by marriage. Before 1789 a regiment's colonel would authorize women to serve as *vivandières* only if they were married to one of the eight enlisted soldiers designated as *'vivandiers'*, and who were issued a license known as a *patente de vivandier*. These men held the right to sell food, drink and sundries to the soldiers of their regiment, but the *vivandier*'s military duties prevented him from actually engaging in this trade; so a wife, or *vivandière*, was necessary. The *vivandière* was entitled to travel with the army and to sell to the troops solely on the basis of her husband's position as *vivandier*. In 1789, there were 240 regiments or regimental equivalents in the French army, making the authorized number of *vivandières* approximately 1,920. Although they did not wear uniforms, *vivandières* were recognizable by the small brandy barrel they carried known as a *tonnelet*.

Vivandières fulfilled a vital and necessary function in the larger French military system. In the armies of pre-revolutionary France, logistics were primitive and desertion rates high. The most effective way for commanders to prevent desertion was to keep their troops in camp, where they could be constantly supervised. It therefore became desirable to provide soldiers with both daily necessities and occasional luxuries on site. Even under ideal conditions, the army's own supply system was frequently inadequate; and when tested by more challenging circumstances, such as bad weather during a campaign, the system often broke down entirely.[3] The *vivandière* was an entrepreneur who could offer troops food, alcohol, tobacco, sundries and a sheltered place to socialize, as well as a modicum of female companionship. Because she was not a soldier, she could leave the garrison or camp to forage and otherwise acquire goods, which she could then sell to the captive soldiers. Her marriage to a soldier meant that the army had a means of influencing and controlling her behaviour by punishing her husband.

The relationship of the government and the military to *vivandières* during the ancien régime was problematic. The War Ministry profoundly mistrusted *vivandières* but found it impossible to do without their services. It therefore did its best to regulate their behaviour and to punish wrongdoing. Many *vivandières* were willing to supplement their earnings by illegal means, and smuggling was widely practised, as indicated by this entry in the index to a 1724 compilation of army regulations: *'Vivandière*, see contraband'.[4] *Vivandières* also ran gaming tables, but despite vague and often implicit assertions by some historians that any 'camp follower' was by definition a prostitute, no evidence exists that *vivandières* engaged in prostitution.[5] The absence of evidence is in itself indicative, but so was the reality of the *vivandières'* situation; prostitutes plying their trade in the vicinity of an army were subject to severe punishment, while *vivandières* had a variety of lucrative (and legal) business options open to them. While one cannot say with certainty that no *vivandière* ever engaged in prostitution, there was little incentive for them to do so, and the silence of official records on this subject is telling.

Vivandières were a source of strength and not weakness for the army. Aside from feeding the troops, *vivandières* raised children who were perfectly suited to army life. The children of most *vivandières* grew up in the barracks and camps of the French army and spent much of their lives on campaign.[6] Because of this, daughters of *vivandières* often became *vivandières* themselves, and records show that several assumed a masculine disguise and enrolled as common soldiers.[7] In addition, starting in 1766, sons of *vivandières* were officially recognized as *enfants de troupe*, or children of the regiment. These boys started drawing pay and rations at age two, and at eighteen they were permitted to enlist as privates with sixteen years of seniority already accumulated.[8] Sources suggest that *vivandières* of the ancien régime did not fight but stayed behind the battle lines until the fighting was over, though at times a retreat might result in the battle sweeping over them.[9]

Blanchisseuses, or laundresses, represented another category of officially sanctioned military women, and they generally were the wives of soldiers who were not *vivandiers*. Since doing laundry was far less lucrative than selling food and drink, the job of *blanchisseuse* was not highly prized. However, it represented an opportunity for a family to stay together and at the same time earn a meagre living. Seven to ten *blanchisseuses* accompanied each regiment, meaning that approximately 1,700 to 2,400 served at any given time.

Since neither *vivandières* nor *blanchisseuses* were *militaires*, neither were entitled to military pensions. However, the monarchy did grant one-time payments, or '*gratifications*', to these women, and the circumstances under which it did so are enlightening. A woman who had served as a *vivandière* or *blanchisseuse* was eligible for a *gratification* based on her own service; and while records for the period before 1789 are scarce, it seems clear that the monarchy recognized these women as having *served* their country, as opposed to merely having 'followed the army'. For example, Mme Andierne, a retired *vivandière*, wrote to the Minister of War in 1776 asking for a pension. Her letter included no reference to her husband at all but stated that she 'had participated in all the campaigns in Flanders following the King'.[10] From the War Ministry, the Count de Saint-Germain asked the controller general to support her application 'in consideration of the frequent services that she rendered to the army during the last war and notably her bravery'. He also noted that her actions deserved 'recompense not common among persons of her sex'.[11] The count's arguments were based not on the husband's service but on Mme Andierne's own service. Neither her letter nor the internal War Ministry memos mention her husband's service at all. But the count also suggested that this woman was somehow 'male' in her actions and in her merit. She received a *gratification* of 150 livres.

Ironically, while thousands of women served the Bourbons as *vivandières* and *blanchisseuses*, the few dozen women who served as *femmes soldats* are far better documented and have consequently received a great deal more attention. Their stories are varied, but if we can generalize, then it is fair to say that women who served as soldiers, while they were ejected from the ranks if discovered, did receive a degree of respect and toleration for their bravery and sacrifice. Because they never engaged in 'feminine' work, they received more praise and more money as recompense for their service. However, no matter how excellent a soldier's record, once she was 'recognized as a girl', she was immediately ejected from the military and encouraged to adopt 'habits appropriate to her sex'.[12]

Thus the army of the ancien régime, while it purported to be a male institution, included at any given time approximately 4,000 women who performed a number of vital tasks. *Femmes soldats* were certainly the most visible of these women, but they represented only a tiny proportion of the women who served. While the ancien régime marginalized women and devalued the feminine, it made financial payments to women who served and, perhaps more important, recognized their actions as service. At the same time, the monarchy insisted on an official version of reality in which gender roles were strictly separated, gender norms strictly enforced and women subordinated to men. In short, women could perform non-combatant duties revolving around food and laundry, while men could perform combat duties that brought glory and recognition. *Femmes soldats* might receive a cash payment, but once found out, there was no question of their staying in uniform. Likewise, *vivandières* might come and go from camp far more easily than their husbands, but in the end it was the husband who held the *patente de vivandier*, and the wife owed her position as *vivandière* entirely to him. Therefore, while the ancien régime offered women a number of military opportunities, those opportunities were limited by the norm of masculine dominance.

The French Revolution: change and continuity

The French Revolution of 1789 brought a number of sweeping changes in the condition of military women, but ultimately the continuities prevailed. Perhaps most striking was the general change to the structure of the army itself: after two-thirds of the largely aristocratic officer corps fled the country between 1789 and 1792, commoners were able, for the first time, to rise above the rank of sergeant in large numbers. Moreover, the loss of over 70,000 enlisted men on the battlefield during those same years meant that the royal army was indeed broken. In 1791–92, and in the subsequent period of *la patrie en danger*, the army reorganized itself along much more democratic and egalitarian lines, and once the war began, the French army grew dramatically, filled out in part by patriotic volunteers and later by reluctant draftees. One consequence of this increase was a change in battlefield formations. While historians have disputed whether French units attacked in 'hordes' or 'swarms', there is no denying that the strictly enforced rigidity of royal-army battle tactics gave way to something looser and more flexible.[13] The reduced social distance between officers and soldiers, in combination with the less rigidly enforced battle discipline, opened the way for *vivandières* to move onto the battlefield during combat and to provide soldiers with food and drink even under fire. Increasingly, *vivandières* became active participants in battle, and their casualties increased as well.

Key changes also took place in 1793 when the National Convention voted to allow soldiers to marry without the permission of their officers. The subsequent flood of women into the army camps outraged the Convention's Representatives on Mission, who bombarded Paris with letters demanding the elimination of this 'scourge' and equating women with weakness, disease and impotence.[14] The Convention voted on 30 April 1793 to eliminate all 'useless women' from the army. While the law was ostensibly aimed at the thousands of spouses, girlfriends and prostitutes crowding the bivouacs, Article XI specifically stated that 'the women who are now serving in the armies will be excluded from military service'; it also offered them the same severance that any soldier's wife would receive: a passport and five sous per league of travel to their homes.[15]

The Convention, then, not only saw *femmes soldats* as 'useless' but also put them in the same category with spouses, girlfriends and prostitutes. It did recognize two groups of women who were, by implication, 'not useless'. Not surprisingly, these were the same women that the royal army had traditionally authorized: *vivandières* and *blanchisseuses*. Article III allowed four *blanchisseuses* per battalion. Each demi-brigade would thus have 12 *blanchisseuses*, and with 198 demi-brigades, this would amount to a total strength of 2,376 *blanchisseuses* in the infantry alone. However, the actual number of women was undoubtedly far higher, as evidenced by a steady stream of regulations over the next decade reminding commanders of the limits on women and demanding that they respect those limits.[16] Obviously, many commanders were more interested in assuring the comfort, hygiene and morale of their troops than in obeying the law. Moreover, many *femmes soldats* continued to serve even after they were banned, often with the collusion of their commanders and comrades.[17] Finally, Article VII left a major loophole, one that many officers exploited. It stated: 'Generals of Divisions will deliver a distinctive mark to *vivandières* whom they believe are absolutely necessary to the needs of their divisions'. Given that ancien régime practice demanded eight *vivandières* per regiment, and given that the logistical demands of the new mass army were even greater, it is likely that most units retained more women than this. Since the law left this decision up to commanders, and since it used the verb *croire* (to believe) rather than *démontrer* (to demonstrate) or *prouver* (to prove), large numbers of women could remain with the army as long as the divisional commander was willing to certify them as 'necessary'. The Army of Italy even printed up blank 'Certificates of Usefulness to the Army', to be filled in by soldiers' wives.[18] The relatively small number of wives who could legitimately accompany their soldier-husbands would hardly have justified printing such a form. Only a widespread 'creative interpretation' of the regulations would have made such an undertaking worthwhile. Furthermore, while Article X effectively charged the *gendarmerie* with enforcing the law, the *gendarmes* were hardly immune to the problem of excessive female companions: one representative noted an instance where 'eighty gendarmes were followed by 50 to 60 women'.[19] Ultimately, the law, while it did force some women to leave the army, proved largely ineffective. Not only did they continue to serve as soldiers but also far more women than those authorized by the Convention served as *vivandières* and *blanchisseuses*.

A certain vagueness soon crept into the *patentes* women received from their units. Many *patentes* listed the holder's position as '*vivandière or blanchisseuse*', '*blanchisseuse-vivandière*' or even 'attached to the battalion'.[20] Increasingly between 1793 and 1800, the distinction between the two groups broke down, and by the dawn of the nineteenth century a general-purpose *vivandière*, often referred to as a '*cantinière*' (canteen-keeper), largely replaced the two pre-revolutionary categories of *blanchisseuses* and *vivandières*.[21]

The law had one other effect, and given the Convention's general attitude towards women, it was most likely an unintended effect. During the ancien régime, male soldiers held *patentes de vivandier* that entitled their wives to work as *vivandières*. The new law, drafted in some haste, removed the husband entirely from the process of applying for a *patente*. While the law implied (but did not explicitly state) that being the legitimate spouse of a soldier in the regiment was a prerequisite for employment, Article VII ordered women to apply directly to the commanding officer for a *patente de vivandière*. Under the old system, the wife was effectively a subcontractor employed by her husband, who owned the license. After 1793, *vivandières* owned their licenses and became independent business owners. This change of status had far-reaching implications. One captain wrote that a former *vivandier* of his regiment married a new *vivandière* in 1793 'so as not to sink below his station' by losing his former position.[22]

The *vivandières*' new battlefield role was immediately reflected in higher casualties, and the manner in which the First Republic dealt with them is illuminating. *Vivandière* Angélique Brévilier of the 7th Hussars was a 'Volunteer of '92'. She was in combat near Celestat on 7 Ventôse Year II, when an Austrian howitzer shell removed her left leg at the thigh and filled her right leg with shrapnel, which four months later still caused her 'horrible suffering', according to an army medical report.[23] The War Ministry rejected Brévilier's requests for a pension on the grounds that she was not a soldier and was therefore ineligible for an invalid's pension; and her husband was not dead, so she was ineligible for a widow's pension. She was caught in a nebulous middle ground solely because she was a woman. The ministry's formal response stated that 'the law of 28 Fructidor is not applicable to Citoyenne [Brévilier]', and that her sole benefit was a socket for a wooden leg, to be obtained from the Hôtel des Invalides. The leg itself and any other associated expenses were her responsibility.[24]

Two women who did receive public acclaim are worth noting, for their stories tell us a great deal about what sorts of behaviours were considered appropriate for women. Attached to the 45th Demi-brigade, Jeanne Girard was a passenger on the warship *Cazira* in 1795 when it engaged a British squadron off Corsica. Her husband was killed in the cannonade, but Jeanne resolutely tended the wounded for eight hours, bandaging, watering, and comforting the injured and the dying. The captain of the *Cazira* requested that the War Ministry give prompt attention to her pension request, and the Representative of the People in Toulon organized public festivals in her honour as well as luxury travel for her return home, where she received a generous widow's pension.[25]

Likewise, Marie Dauranne, *vivandière* of the 51st Demi-brigade, was lauded in 1797 for her extraordinary courage. At the crossing of the Piave River, two soldiers fell into the water. While others hesitated, Dauranne swam out and pulled both men to safety. One witness wrote in his diary, 'the courage that this woman showed for these brave grenadiers on this day merited her a gold medal...with these words engraved "first quantinière [*sic*] of the army"'.[26] General Bonaparte personally decorated her, the Directory acclaimed her, and she featured in several printed bulletins. Like Jeanne Girard, she showed a willingness to risk her life but only in the context of saving men's lives, not by replacing men in combat. Both were safe models for female participation in war. It appears doubtful that either would have been recognized had they fought and killed the enemy. Instead, the government picked female role models whose actions were deemed appropriate to their sex.

Pension procedures reinforced this distinction. There were various pension laws between 1790 and 1800, but all of them shared two factors: they all demanded rigorous documentation that often took two or more years to assemble and submit, and they all insisted that a woman had a right only to a widow's pension, earned by her husband's service.[27] Women's service as a *blanchisseuse* or *vivandière* did not justify a claim for recompense. Some women submitted claims on the basis of their own service. For example, Marianne Boyer of the 48th Demi-brigade applied for a pension in Year III. She argued that she deserved a pension because she had 'made six campaigns as *blanchisseuse*, and so been useful to my country'.[28] Boyer received her reply on the standard printed form: 'The Citoyenne_____, born the_____, department of_____, widow of Citizen_____, has the right to a pension of_____, in recompense for the services of her husband'.[29]

This form, by excluding any mention of women's service, created its own reality in which men alone could earn the right of a military widow to feed herself.

Overall, the French Revolution left a mixed legacy but one marked more by continuity than by change. While the law of 30 April 1793 opened up new opportunities for *vivandières* and granted them a hitherto unheard of independence, this was an unintended side effect; and it was certainly not the primary purpose of the law, which was designed to reduce the number of women attached to the army. Moreover, the law very explicitly outlawed *femmes soldats*. By defining them as 'useless women', the law implied that armed woman could not make a meaningful contribution to France's military defence. While some *femmes soldats* continued to serve, the number of women fighting in the ranks declined steeply in the years after 1793. A regularized system of widows' pensions was in some ways an advance over the *gratifications* of the ancien régime, but the caveat that only men could earn pensions by their service marked a step backward from the monarchy, which sometimes granted *gratifications* to women for their service alone. Thus the paradox of the Republic was that it advanced the rights of women in the military in some respects, and curtailed them in others, ending ultimately with women being confined as much as possible to the 'traditional' female roles of nurse, cook and laundress.

The Napoleonic Empire: a mixed legacy

The reign of Napoleon produced further changes but tended toward continuity. The expanded military and the more sweeping scale of strategy and operations meant that more women served in the years from 1800 to 1815 than ever before. Napoleon insisted that soldiers should 'travel light' to be able to march fast. As a result *vivandières* (increasingly called *cantinières*) became more important and more numerous. As the Grande Armée grew and increasingly included conscripts from occupied foreign territories and forced allies, and as campaigns lasted longer and occurred farther from France, the army began to incorporate foreign women on a scale unequalled even during the ancien régime. Spaniards, Swiss, Germans, Italians, Hungarians, Dutch and Poles all became *vivandières* as the French armies swept across Europe.[30] The exact fate of these women remains unknown, as most never applied for pensions. They were either killed, captured or abandoned as the French armies retreated in defeat from 1812 to 1814. A new law that closed the loopholes in the 1793 legislation drastically reduced the number of *blanchisseuses* on the official rosters of the French army. Likewise, *femmes soldats* became even more rare. Both of these trends were counterbalanced by the expanding roles of *cantinières*.

The consular decree of 7 Thermidor Year VIII (26 July 1800) established a limit of four women per battalion and two per cavalry squadron, regardless of function. This change created a disincentive to license laundresses because each *blanchisseuse* meant one less *vivandière*. The number of ambiguously worded *patentes* shot up immediately, resulting in a decline in the number of *blanchisseuses*, at least officially. Apparently units on the march often employed local laundresses and kept them off the books.[31] Increasingly, *vivandières* did laundry as part of their duties.[32]

Under the First Empire, *vivandières* campaigned even more extensively and aggressively than they had during the Republic. Though *femmes soldats* all but disappeared, more *vivandières* fought with musket and sabre alongside their men. As Captain Montigny wrote of one of his *vivandières*, 'Her place on a day of battle was at the most perilous point. ... Marie knew how to fire her musket and follow up with a bayonet thrust.'[33] Evidence suggests that while many *vivandières* fought, most did so only to defend themselves and their children. However, their defence could be fierce and determined. A dramatic example is the following episode, which occurred in 1805 when a detachment of the 7th Hussars was overrun by a superior Russian force. During the battle *vivandière* Madeleine Kintelburger's husband was killed, four of her six children were blinded by an exploding artillery caisson, and her own right arm was nearly severed by a cannon ball. Despite her injury and armed only with a sword, Kintelburger fought fiercely to protect her children, sustaining ten further wounds from enemy lances and sabres. The Cossacks finally shot her once in each leg, then carried her and her children away. She was six months pregnant with twins.[34] Another example is the story of a *cantinière* of the Neuchâtel Battalion who fell behind the column after the defeat of the French army in the Battle of Leipzig in October 1813. Her column hastily retreated to the French border. A pursuing Cossack, believing her an easy victim, approached the lone woman, who was out of musket range of her unit. The *cantinière* 'produced her pistol and shot him out of the saddle. She rejoined the battalion mounted on the Cossack's horse, to the applause of all the column.'[35]

The Empire honoured women who participated in combat, as long as they fought in self-defence. This equates neatly with Dominique Godineau's argument that a fundamental dichotomy had to be observed: 'the traditional division between interior/exterior', in which men dealt with 'weapons and combats' while women's heroism would consist of 'carrying the weight of the household and domestic cares'.[36] In the case of the French army, 'interior' work meant cooking, sewing, serving and especially laundering—all tasks that the men avoided whenever possible. 'Exterior' work referred to combat on the battlefield. While it is true that some women (such as Captain Montigny's exemplary *vivandière* Marie) transgressed this boundary, it appears from surviving evidence that most did not, and those who did received neither penalty nor praise. Marie's final reward was death at Waterloo. Madeleine Kintelburger, who showed 'masculine' bravery in defence of the 'feminine' interior (her family), received an emergency *gratification* as well as a generous pension, even though she was unable to provide any of the required documents. Supporting letters from General Rapp and Marshall Kellerman trumped an otherwise total lack of documentation.[37] In this case at least, a woman's heroism, largely because it demonstrated her maternal feelings, won out over bureaucracy.

While women who fought were sometimes rewarded, sometimes tolerated, the most common (and most lauded) battlefield roles for women during the Empire remained traditionally feminine: nourishing the troops and nursing the wounded. Both fit neatly into the 'interior' category as activities that supported but did not replace or threaten men. For example, at the Battle of Chiclana in Spain in March 1811, Catherine Baland of the 95th Infantry Regiment stayed at the firing line and distributed drinks to the soldiers, saying to them 'in a bright encouraging tone, "Drink, drink, my brave fellow; you can pay me tomorrow." She must have known when she saw so many men falling around her that most of her debtors would not answer the roll-call the next day.'[38] The traits that caused Baron Lejeune to immortalize her in a painting were a willingness to nourish the men and a selfless compassion, exactly the characteristics that Frenchmen associated with the feminine ideal in this period.[39]

Likewise, nursing the wounded became *vivandières*' unofficial but customary role during the First Empire. A recurring theme in the genre of Napoleonic memoirs, the 'angel of the battlefield' was willing to risk her life but only in the pursuit of what were then considered exclusively feminine vocations: nursing and nurturing. For example, Jacques-Louis Romand of the 81st Infantry Regiment wrote of a *cantinière* at Waterloo in June 1815: 'During the heat of the action, which didn't frighten her in the least, she did not content herself with thinking of her personal safety.... She stayed on the battlefield until nightfall, always keeping the same *sang-froid*, the same attention for the wounded.'[40] Again we see the courage and selflessness of a mother, rather than the fierce aggression of a warrior; ultimately, it was such traditional stereotypes that earned men's praise.

Women's pensions under Napoleon were small, but he could and did augment pensions personally or grant pensions where no documentation existed. For the most part, however, *vivandières* and *blanchisseuses* received little or nothing from the Emperor. This was particularly true since widows' pensions were granted only to women whose husbands died in combat or later of wounds; husbands who died of disease, accidents or other causes did not qualify.[41] Women who did receive pensions usually waited from two to seven years and then received amounts much smaller than those granted under the Republic.[42]

While the numbers of *vivandières* expanded under the Empire, those of *femmes soldats* shrank further. Documentation of *femmes soldats* in the period from 1800 to 1815 is scanty, yet men had a strong curiosity about women serving in disguise, and mentions occur in various primary accounts, precisely because they were so unusual. Only about five have turned up for Napoleon's reign, suggesting that this practice, if not totally extinct, had become even more rare than before.[43]

Overall, the Napoleonic Empire presented military women with expanded opportunities to serve, yet the nature of these opportunities was limited. Fewer women served as *femmes soldats*; and while *vivandières* effectively functioned as soldiers, their numbers remained small and their actions unappreciated. Though Napoleon occasionally rewarded a woman for bravery, it was for bravery in defence, not audacity in the attack. With widows' pensions smaller and more difficult to obtain, fewer chances to serve in the ranks, and a focus on nourishing and nursing, French women found a military arena that was paradoxically larger and more limited than in previous eras.

The Bourbon Restoration

While the Bourbon Restoration was also characterized by continuities that overshadowed some significant changes, a few key discontinuities are worth mentioning. One was the near-total eclipse of the *femme soldat*. Only one case of a woman masquerading as a male soldier was recorded during the period of the restored monarchies, and the woman's rapid discovery merely highlights how difficult this practice had become.[44] Still, the years 1815 through 1820 saw several milestones in the development of the female military experience. Perhaps most importantly, the returning Bourbon monarchy wanted to purge those loyal to the Republic or the Empire from the army, regardless of rank or station. While *cantinières* were certainly not the deciding factor in Napoleon's ability to return to power in 1815, they did on the whole exhibit remarkable loyalty to the Emperor.[45] None of this was missed by the royalists. As one officer later wrote, 'to be authorized, a *cantinière* had to demonstrate her loyalty by painting her tonnelet white'. Since few of the surviving women were willing to do this, their jobs were turned over to women with royalist sympathies.[46]

Archival evidence supports this argument. In December 1815, the commander of the Fort de Goux at Besançon reacted to rumours that the fort's *cantinière*, Mme Maire, was a Bonapartist. He revoked her license and replaced her with the wife of a royalist officer, Mme Charlet. In a series of letters, Mme Maire and her benefactor, Colonel Marion, brought the dispute all the way to the Minister of War, who sided with Mme Maire. Her defence hinged not on her abilities or her past service but on strong protestations of loyalty to the Bourbons, despite her long service to Napoleon.[47] Her case, which was brought as early as six months after Waterloo, signalled that political loyalty was the primary factor in selecting or retaining women with the army.

Mme Daubigny was less fortunate. She had served as a *vivandière* to a cavalry regiment from 1794 to 1804, when age and infirmities forced her to retire. Napoleon granted her a post as a sedentary *cantinière* at the Rue de Grenelle barracks in Paris, but in 1817 a new unit of the Royal Guard took over the barracks and unceremoniously tossed the sixty-year-old woman into the street. Her appeals went unheeded.[48]

A similarly harsh reaction set in regarding pensions issued under the previous two regimes. Many widows saw their pensions revoked by the Bourbons, and getting them reinstated was difficult or impossible. Pointing out one's devoted service to the Republic or the Empire merely highlighted one's treasonous activities, and women who did so invariably failed to regain their pensions.[49] Catherine Sabatier, who took a more careful rhetorical approach to her pension request, could do so because she was applying in 1815 for the first time. Sabatier's life could have been a dime-store romance novel. Born in 1767 to a *vivandière* and a sergeant, she became a *vivandière* in 1783 and participated in every major campaign of the next thirty-two years. Her father and two husbands were killed in the wars, and her three sons became *enfants de troupe* and then soldiers. Even after becoming a widow, she was granted extraordinary permission to continue serving, and in 1815 she wrote a letter that studiously avoided politics, implying instead that her service to France transcended the politics of any single regime. Her commanding officer wrote a supporting letter, but the War Minister, acutely aware of the events of the recent past, denied her application. Her commander gave her 50 francs out of his own pocket, but she was now yet another old woman on her own in the new France.[50]

The vindictiveness that characterized the early days of the new regime did not last, and by 1818, women who had served previous governments were again able to find some sympathy for their requests. This was partly due to the appointment of Gouvion Saint-Cyr as Minister of War. Saint-Cyr saw several of his close friends rescued by *vivandières* during the retreat from Russia, and he had a broad and deep network of acquaintances in the ranks of former Napoleonic officers. He took a personal interest in the cases of several women, especially those seeking a return to the army, often writing to the relevant unit commanders.[51] In one case he wrote: 'I can only invite you to have regard for the demands of this *militaire*, if nothing is opposed to it.'[52] Saint-Cyr quite specifically used the word *militaire* to describe the woman, suggesting that he saw *vivandières* as members of the army, not merely as civilian *employées*, though his successors were less sympathetic.

Despite ongoing attempts to control, limit or vet women, the restored monarchy continued to employ both *vivandières* and *blanchisseuses*, again creating a strong continuity. The need for female labour in the army continued, the only limiting factor being political loyalty. Individual women came and went, but the Bourbons retained *vivandières* and *blanchisseuses* because they remained as essential as they had always been. Successful petitioners of all types found that the most effective way to achieve their ends was, as before, to frame their requests in terms designed to appeal to men's ideas of women's proper place. Whether women presented themselves as destitute mothers trying to feed their children or devoted wives trying to support their husbands, the same general rules applied in 1820 as had applied in earlier eras. One woman whose appeal included explicit maternal imagery was Mme Decker, a daughter of the regiment and former *vivandière*. In 1818 she wrote to the Minister of War and begged for a position as a *blanchisseuse* in her son's unit, so she could 'support the existence of her numerous family with her work'.[53] Françoise Verier argued that she needed a *cantinière* position not to escape poverty but to support her husband; 'I don't pretend at all, Monseigneur, to be a burden to my husband.... On the contrary, my intentions in making myself close to him are to do the most possible to soften his lot by my work.'[54] When Geneviève Bouquet's husband was drafted, she applied for a position as '*blanchisseuse* or *vivandière*' in the 4th Regiment of the Royal Guard. She had a three-month old son and felt the need 'to put myself to work to provide for his nourishment'.[55] All of these women depicted themselves as mother, wife, nurturer and caregiver. Whether they were old veterans like Mme Decker or newcomers like Mmes Bouquet and Verier, their successful appeals portrayed them as serving the 'interior' in support of the 'exterior'.

Overall, the restored monarchy tried to move women's military service back to its pre-1789 footing. Though there was no general revision of regulations until 1832, the new legions authorized far more *blanchisseuses* than was the case in the years from 1793 to 1814, thus restoring the ancien régime division of female labour into laundresses and *vivandières*. Beyond restoring larger numbers of *blanchisseuses* and trying to guarantee Royalist political sympathies, the restored Bourbons' treatment of female auxiliaries was remarkably consistent with past practice, suggesting that no substantive changes had occurred. This supports Jennifer Heuer's argument that 'neither the experiences of the Terror nor the Napoleonic Code—nor even the establishment of the Napoleonic Empire or the Bourbon Restoration—completely consolidated or broke with previous developments' in respect of the gender order.[56] Rather, each regime attempted to alter previous practices with which it disagreed but maintained stability and, in this case, military efficiency. It also buttresses Suzanne Desan's statement that 'while powerful beliefs in female inferiority and dependency remained, they were nonetheless sharply undercut in law, discourse, and social practice during the Revolution'.[57] This was also true through the Napoleonic and Restoration eras, suggesting that women's experience in these supposedly repressive periods was far more rich, varied and dynamic than previously believed.

The story of the army's *vivandières* did not end in 1820. Through a series of evolutions, *vivandières* grew in numbers and in prestige in the years from 1830 to 1870, but *blanchisseuses* eventually disappeared with the adoption of the steam laundry in 1854. During their heyday in the years between 1854 and 1870, *vivandières* saw their numbers per unit double, their uniforms become increasingly ornate, and their respectability and popularity skyrocket. It was only after the defeat of 1870–71 that their fortunes declined, and only in 1906 that they were finally abolished. It took that long to overcome the strong traditions that military women had established in the wars from 1792 to 1815.

Conclusion

The Age of Revolution, and in particular the period between 1775 and 1820, was the formative era for what became the largest and longest-lasting female military institution in French history, and it showed a strong and consistent demand in the French army for traditional 'interior' labour by women, regardless of regime. France's use of female labour in its military effort was far more extensive, systematic and organized than that of its enemies, even as women in most of those armies provided essentially the same basic types of services.[58] While the French Revolution may have opened new possibilities for many citizens, the Republic reinstated the prohibition on women soldiers even as it granted sweeping independence to *vivandières*; and although women continued to serve as soldiers after 1793, their relative numbers declined steadily, especially considering the much larger size of the army and the greater frequency of wars and decisive battles. However, the number and importance of women filling more traditional roles with the army grew and continued to do so well into the nineteenth century. Thus the outcome of French women's military experience during the Revolutionary and Napoleonic Wars between 1792 and 1815 was mixed. In theory, French military women remained confined to 'habits appropriate to their sex', yet they also established a precedent for a strong female presence in the French army, one that lasted for a century and earned *vivandières* a privileged position of independence.

Notes

1. Holly A. Mayer, *Belonging to the Army: Camp Followers and Community During the American Revolution* (Columbia, SC, 1996); Karen Hagemann, '"Heroic Virgins" and "Bellicose Amazons": Armed Women, the Gender Order, and the German Public during and after the Anti-Napoleonic Wars', *European History Quarterly* 37/4 (2007): 507–527; Gunther Rothenberg, *The Art of Warfare in the Age of Napoleon* (Bloomington, 1978), 14, 87–88; Barton Hacker, 'Women and Military Institutions in Early Modern Europe: A Reconnaissance', *Signs* 6 (1981): 643–671; John Tone, 'Spanish Women in the Resistance to Napoleon, 1808–1814', in *Constructing Spanish Womanhood: Female Identity in Modern Spain*, ed. Victoria Enders and Pamela Radcliff (Albany, 1998), 259–282; Peter Wilson, 'German Women and War, 1500–1800', *War in History* 3 (1996): 127–160. See also Chapter 4 by Alan Forrest and Chapter 8 by Holly A. Mayer in this volume.

'Habits Appropriate to Her Sex' 203

2. Susan P. Conner, 'Les Femmes Militaires: Women in the French Army 1792–1815', *The Consortium on Revolutionary Europe, 1750–1850: Proceedings 1982*, ed. Warren F. Spencer (Athens, GA, 1983), 291–302; Sylvie Steinberg, *La confusion des sexes: le travestissement de la Renaissance à la Révolution* (Paris, 2001); Dominique Godineau, 'De la guerrière à la citoyenne: Porter les armes pendant l'Ancien Régime et la Révolution française', *Clio* 20 (2004): 1–20. A recent exception is for the early modern armies, John A. Lynn II, *Women, Armies and Warfare in Early Modern Europe* (Cambridge, MA, 2008).
3. See Léon Mention, *L'Armée de l'ancien régime de Louis XIV à la Révolution* (Paris, 1900), 57; Antoine-Rigobert Mopinot de la Chapotte, *Sous Louis le bien-aimé: Correspondance amoureuse et militaire d'un officier pendant la Guerre de Sept-Ans* (Paris, n.d.), 25–55.
4. Archives de la Guerre, Service Historique de l'Armée de Terre (hereafter AG), Vincennes, France, de Bonnelles, *Ordonnances militaires* (1724) [uncatalogued ms], index.
5. Martin Van Creveld offers typical (and erroneous) dismissals of all camp followers as 'whores' in his *Men, Women, & War: Do Women Belong in the Front Line?* (London, 2001).
6. Musée de l'Armée, Paris, Charles Cozette, *Vue du Camp du havre en 1756*, oil on canvas; anonymous, *Un camp de cavalerie*, lithograph [n.d.]; Pierre l'Enfant, *Vue du Camp de Calais en 1756*, oil on canvas.
7. Godineau, 'De la guerrière', 4.
8. Baron de Saugeon, *Collection des ordonnances militaires* (Paris, n.d.), 53, 66–67.
9. Mopinot, *Sous Louis le bien-aimé*, 79.
10. AG, Vincennes, Xs11 (Andierne), letter from Mme Andierne to the Minister of War, 1776.
11. Ibid. letter from the Count de St Germain to M. de Clugny, Controller General, 20 September 1776.
12. AG, Vincennes, Ya507 (Kellerin, Madeleine), copy of the discharge and disposition of Antoine Lehr and Madeleine Kellerin, 8 March 1745.
13. Rothenberg, *Art of Warfare*, 67, 114–115.
14. Letter from Carnot and Duquesnoy to the Convention Nationale, 16 April 1793, transcribed in Étienne Charavay (ed.), *Correspondance générale de Carnot*, 4 vols (Paris, 1892–1907), vol. 2, 116–117.
15. AG, Vincennes, Xs11, 'Decree of the National Convention No. 804', Article XI: 'To dismiss all useless women from the armies'.
16. Charavay, *Correspondance*, vol. 3, 62–63; August Philippe Herlaut, *Le Colonel Bouchotte, ministre de guerre en l'an II*, 2 vols (Paris, 1946), vol. 1, 245–246; Xavier de Pétigny, *Un bataillon de volontaires (3ème bataillon de Maine-et-Loire 1792–1796)* (Angers, 1908), 87–88; *Correspondance de Napoléon I* (Paris, 1858–1870), Items 38, 49, 161.
17. AG, Vincennes, Xr48 and Xr49.
18. Ibid. Xs11 (Bertaux, dit Chopard), Army of Italy, Certificate of Usefulness to the Army, 12 Vendémiaire Year III (3 October 1794).
19. 'Letter from Pierre Gadolle to Ministre LeBrun, 27 April 1793', *Correspondance de Carnot*, vol. 2, 117.
20. For examples, see: AG, Vincennes, Xs12 (Daunay, née Braque), 7e Bataillon de Paris, Certificate of Service of Charlotte Daunay, 12 July Year II [sic] (30 June 1794); ibid. (George, née Rost), Compagnie des Cannoniers du 4e Bataillon des Ardennes, Certificate of service as blanchisseuse-vivandière, 6 August 1793; ibid.

(Sicard, née Gourau), extract from the register of deliberations of the district of Fougères: public session of 29 Floréal Year III (18 May 1795).
21. The new title may have also reflected an even higher importance placed on the sale of alcohol, though both titles were used interchangeably until at least 1870.
22. Elzéar Blaze, *Souvenirs d'un officier de la grande armée* (Paris, n.d.), 112.
23. AG, Vincennes, Xs12 (Brévilier, née Pélletier), letter from Meurisse, chief medical officer of the military hospital at Lorient, 9 Messidor Year II (27 June 1794).
24. Ibid. (Brévilier, née Pélletier), certificate of visitation by the General Inspector of the Army Health Service, 18 Brumaire Year VI (8 November 1797).
25. Ibid. (Girard, née Deluille), various documents.
26. Jacques Kryn, *Le petit tambour d'arcole, 1777–1837* (Cadonet, 1987), 267.
27. Isser Woloch, 'War-Widows' Pensions: Social Policy in Revolutionary and Napoleonic France, *Societas* 6/4 (1976): 235–254.
28. AG, Vincennes, Xs11 (Boyer, née Ressouce), letter from Mme Ressouce to the Minister of War, 3 Vendémiaire Year III (24 September 1794).
29. Ibid. (Boyer, née Ressouce), Office of Widows, Report, 16 Messidor Year III (4 July 1795).
30. Robert Guillemard, *Mémoires de Robert Guillemard, sergent en retraite de 1805 à 1823*, 2 vols (Paris, 1826), vol. 1, 185; John Elting, *Swords Around A Throne: Napoleon's Grande Armée* (New York, 1988), 611; J. J. Pelet, *The French Campaign in Portugal, 1810–1811* (Minneapolis, 1973), 313. See also Adrien Jean-Baptiste François Bourgogne, *The Memoirs of Sergeant Bourgogne 1812–1813* (New York, 1979), 4, 5, 62, 118–119, 217.
31. AG, Vincennes, Xs11 (Angot), letter from Colonel Petri to the Duc de Feltre, 19 November 1810; Bourgogne, *Memoirs*, 62; Guillemard, *Mémoires de Robert Guillemard*, vol. 1, 185; Elting, *Swords Around a Throne*, 611; Pelet, *French Campaign*, 313; Bourgogne, *Memoirs*, 52.
32. Silvain Larreguy de Civrieux, *Souvenirs d'un cadet, 1812–1823* (Paris, 1912), 100.
33. Louis de Montigny, *Souvenirs anecdotiques d'un officier de la grande armée* (Paris, 1833), 327–328.
34. AG, Vincennes, Xs12 (Muller, née Kintelberger), letter from General Rapp to the Minister of War, 26 July 1806; extract from the minutes of the Secretary of State of the Tuileries Palace, 3 March 1809; letter from Madeleine Kintelberger to Minister of War Berthier, 6 February 1806.
35. Alfred Guye, *Le Bataillon de Neuchâtel au service de Napoléon 1807–1814* (Neuchâtel, 1964), 199.
36. Godineau, 'De la guerrière', 4, 13.
37. AG, Vincennes, Xs12 (Muller, née Kintelberger), Fifth Division, Section C, report made to the Minister [of War].
38. Louis-François Lejeune, *Memoirs of Baron Lejeune, Aide-de-camp to Marshals Berthier, Davout, and Oudinot*, trans. Mrs. Arthur Bell, 2 vols (London, 1897), vol. 2, 69.
39. Musée de Versailles, *La Bataille de Chiclana*. See also: Blaze, *Souvenirs d'un officier*, 49–50; Jean-Claude Quennevat (ed.), *Les vrais soldats de Napoléon* (Paris, 1968), 158; Louis Maurer, 'Une *cantinière* du terrible 57e', *Feuilles d'histoire* (1911): 414.
40. Louis-Jacques Romand, *Mémoires de ma vie militaire: 1809–1815* (Besançon, 1981), 72.
41. Woloch, 'War-widows' Pensions', 244.
42. AG, Vincennes, Xs12 (Hoccard, née Pierrette), extract of the minutes of the Secretary of State, 25 March 1811; Ibid. (Huin, née Toulouse), pension report, imperial decree of 29 November 1809.

'Habits Appropriate to Her Sex' 205

43. For one rare exception, see Antoine Dedem van de Gelder, *Un général hollandais sous le premier empire: Mémoirs du général de Dedem de Gelder* (Paris, 1900), 280–281.
44. Douglas Porch, *The French Foreign Legion: A Complete History of the Legendary Fighting Force* (New York, 1991), 8.
45. Guillaume de Peyrusse, *Mémorial et archives de M. le Baron Peyrusse, trésorier général de la Couronne pendant les Cent-Jours* (Carcassonne, 1869), 291; Sylvain Larreguy de Civrieux, *Souvenirs d'un cadet, 1812–1823* (Paris, 1912), 151.
46. Capitaine Richard, *Cantinières et vivandières françaises* (Paris, 1886), 158.
47. AG, Vincennes, Xs11 (Charlet, née —), letter from the 6th Army Division to the Minister of War, 24 September 1815; letter from Colonel Marion to the Minister of War, 28 December 1815.
48. Ibid. (Daubigny, née —), various documents.
49. Ibid. (Meynier, née Dieulevant), letters from Mme Meynier to the Minister of War, 6 July 1816, 27 February 1819; ibid. (Bory, née Peter), various documents.
50. AG, Vincennes, Xs12 (Sabatier, née Campagne), various documents.
51. AG, Vincennes, Xs11 (Dossier 13), letter from Marie Françoise Verier to Gouvion Saint-Cyr, 1 April 1819; letter from Gouvion Saint-Cyr to the Colonel of the Légion de la Loiret, 9 August 1819; letter from Gouvion Saint-Cyr to the Colonel of the Légion de la Seine Inférieure, 2 September 1819.
52. Ibid. (Unmarked Dossier), letter from Gouvion Saint-Cyr to the Colonel of the Légion du Tarn et Garonne, 1 July 1818.
53. Ibid. (Unmarked Dossier), letter from Mme Decker to the Minister of War [n.d.].
54. Ibid. (Unmarked Dossier), letter from Femme Petier to the Minister of War, 1 April 1819.
55. Ibid. (Unmarked Dossier), letter from Mme Bouquet to the Minister of War, 21 March 1820.
56. Jennifer Heuer, *The Family and the Nation: Gender and Citizenship in Revolutionary France, 1789–1830* (Ithaca, NY, 2005), 10.
57. Suzanne Desan, *The Family on Trial in Revolutionary France* (Berkeley, 2004), 313.
58. Kathleen Wilson, *The Island Race: Englishness, Empire and Gender in the Eighteenth Century* (London, 2003), 103; Hagemann, '"Heroic Virgins"'; Wilson, 'German Women', 129; Tone, 'Spanish Women', 272, 276; Myna Trustram, *Women of the Regiment: Marriage and the Victorian Army* (Cambridge, UK, 1984), 12.

10
Maintaining the Home Front: Widows, Wives and War in Late Eighteenth-Century Cuba

Sherry Johnson

In Havana in July 1794, Doña María Rosario Molina received the news that no military wife wants to hear: her husband, adjutant major Tomás García, had died on campaign on the neighbouring island of Santo Domingo.[1] Case studies such as that of Rosario Molina offer rare glimpses into the personal life of military families in Cuba during a period punctuated by international conflicts with consequences throughout the Caribbean. This chapter examines the wartime experiences of Cuban women compared to and contrasted with those of women elsewhere in the Atlantic world. As a result of the demands that war—indeed, even the threat of war—placed on Cuba as a whole, women routinely took on roles traditionally assigned to men. Over time, these reversed roles became second nature to many military wives, widows and daughters, giving Cuban women a degree of agency that was unique in the Hispanic Caribbean.[2]

The historiographical and theoretical framework for this study draws upon nearly forty years of research on women in the Caribbean and Latin America and includes recent works on the relationships among gender, power and honour.[3] Most historians accept implicitly that gendered relations of power were rooted in patriarchy and that 'social circumstances distributed virtue'.[4] Honour and virtue accrued to women of the higher ranks, while plebeian women, because of their status and ethnicity, were susceptible to temptations that led to dishonour, disloyalty and even treachery. Under normal circumstances, a woman's greatest contributions were to support her husband, to manage her home, and to bear and raise children.[5] Widowhood conferred a certain freedom. Widows were venerated as models of exemplary feminine behaviour, and they were charged with the instruction and care of younger women.[6]

Cuba's situation both within the Spanish empire and within the context of the Atlantic world in the Age of Revolutions was unique. Its culture combined canons of Latin American gender relations with Iberian cultural traditions derived from Spain's seven-century military struggle against Moslem domination (711–1492), the *Reconquista* or Reconquest. Cultural cornerstones were the glorification of military exploits and the prestige that went along with heroic conduct. Social relations in Cuba were predicated on the warrior mentality of the Reconquest because of its singular function within the empire: military defence. Throughout its 300-year domination of the Americas, Spain never maintained a large military presence. Spanish imperial administration was thus similar to both British and French colonial policy in that regular troops were usually not a factor in determining the makeup of society. Indeed, in most populated areas of the New World, civilians far outnumbered soldiers. The fortified cities of the Hispanic Caribbean were the exception. Cuba's defensive function in the Spanish empire required a considerable army. Havana, in particular, was characterized by a military force that was many times greater than that in other areas of the Spanish New World, making it the most militarized society of all.[7] The number of regular army troops and naval personnel in Cuba was equal to or greater than the number of adult civilian men in the city. Civilian men, both white and free men of colour, did their part by serving in the militia.[8] In the rarefied society of the island, honour and loyalty in a family context thus had the same intrinsic meaning as they had for women elsewhere in the empire; but in the face of war and foreign invasion, the concepts of dishonour and betrayal broadened to encompass society as a whole. For all Cubans, the consequences of dishonour were (quite literally) death.

Militarization came with distinctive criteria of responsibility and honour, one of which was that every citizen was liable for the defence of the island. If every citizen, regardless of race or status, was potentially capable of heroic behaviour, then non-Europeans, members of the free community of colour and slaves were also worthy of honour. The extension of privileges to persons of colour in Cuba contradicted the ideology that governed relations between racial groups and between masters and slaves in the non-Hispanic Caribbean. It also infuriated and disturbed the elites in enemy nations (most notably Great Britain) who were responsible for launching attacks against Spanish territory. Racial barriers so enshrined elsewhere were often breached in Cuba in order to ensure the island's defence, and the same responsibility, autonomy and agency that were intrinsic to white military families were extended to free coloured and slave women.

The following analysis of military life in Cuba complements recent research in women's studies that examines life on the 'home front'. Studies that analyse how military families experienced war are important, but usually the autonomy granted to women during wartime was finite. While men were away at war, women performed extraordinary tasks; but once men were restored to their families, women returned to their traditional roles. In Cuba, however, militarization was universal, permanent and unparalleled in its contemporary context in the eighteenth-century Atlantic world. Forty-one per cent of white males served on active duty or in the militia, and 66 per cent of free coloured men on the island were also members of the militia. An undetermined number of slaves were affiliated with the garrison and/or the militia.[9] Everyone in Cuba lived under the constant threat of war.

Responsibility and sacrifice

After 1763, women and their families raised in Cuba's militarized society accepted the circumstances of their lives without question, even more so than in the past. During the Seven Years' War (1756–63), Havana had been conquered and occupied by the British army from August 1762 to July 1763. Men on active duty were evacuated as prisoners of war, leaving the women of the city behind to fend for themselves.[10] The British occupation taught Spanish crown officials a valuable lesson and became the catalyst for reform once the war ended.[11] In the wake of that reform, which led to the total militarization of the island, family life came to be predicated on the phrase, *'Debo seguir mis banderas'* (I must follow my flag), a principle that was instilled in even the youngest members of society.[12] Hundreds of comrades-in-arms and their families recognized that family responsibilities were subordinate to their obligations to the Spanish state.

In the face of their impending deployment, married men drafted appropriate documents, such as wills and powers of attorney, so that their wives could act as 'deputy husbands' while they were gone.[13] One such deputy husband was Victorina Guillén, who assumed this role even before her husband, Colonel Antonio Fernández of the mounted dragoons, left with an expeditionary force in 1780 to attack British-held Pensacola. He needed a manservant to accompany him; the task of finding such a companion was left to his wife, who contracted with Agustín Pérez for the services of his slave, José Manuel Gato. Gato was hired out to Fernández, but it was Victorina who accepted the financial burden of reimbursing Pérez for Gato's daily wage of approximately 25 cents.[14] At the same time, newly wed María Mercedes Rodríguez del Junco suddenly found herself in charge of the affairs of her husband, Lieutenant Vicente Folch, who had orders to join the planned expedition against Jamaica in 1782.[15] A decade later, in 1792, deputy husbands Josepha de Azze and María Leonora Mungrey became the heads of their households when their men were deployed as a part of the expeditionary force sent to invade French Saint-Domingue.[16] Unmarried men relied on other female relatives, such as mothers and sisters, to care for their estates. Antonio Alonzo, a bachelor and sergeant in the artillery corps, placed his trust in his sister, María Alonzo; while lieutenant Tomas de Cotilla named his mother, Teresa Llanes, as his executor in case of his death.[17]

The extraordinary deathbed testament of Rosario Molina's husband, Tomás García, provides rare insight into one military couple's marital life.

In 1794, García was dying of fever in a cramped and filthy barracks in the military encampment of San Rafael on the contested frontier between Saint-Domingue and Spanish Santo Domingo. He knew that his death was imminent and that under military regulations, he was allowed to make a verbal last will and testament in front of witnesses. His friend Jaime Garciny and his commander Domingo de Ugarte agreed to act as his witnesses, and a sergeant in the battalion was chosen to act as a notary. Surrounded by his comrades, García mechanically listed his assets and his creditors; then he began to speak of his family. 'I am married to Doña María Rosario Molina', he testified. He acknowledged that 'time was short', but his mind was clear, and he insisted that the notary record on paper 'the profound love he had for her'. The dying man named his wife as the executor of his will and the caretaker of their three children. Garcia wanted his estate to be divided among his heirs, with the exception of a special bequest to Rosario of 2,000 pesos, equivalent to a year's salary, 'for the good union that she has maintained during [our] marriage'.[18]

Garcia's testament was unique in many respects, not the least of which is that it survived the rigours of battle, the confusion of a Spanish retreat back across the border into Santo Domingo and the transfer to Havana, where it was probated in late 1794. These urgent words of a dying man were a rare expression of affection. Such emotions were often intimated but seldom set down in so tangible a manner. Most military testaments were formulaic documents, crafted prior to leaving for a campaign. Yet the confidence that military men had in their wives' honour and competence was emphasized again and again in the wills they prepared in the event that they did not return. One such testament was created by Captain Julián de Parreño, who expressed complete trust in his wife, María Rodríguez del Toro. Daughter of a cavalry officer, niece of another and the wife of a third, she was the mother of three children in 1794, when her uncle by marriage, Bernardo de Parreño, the sergeant major of the Infantry Company of Havana, brought her the news that young Parreño had also succumbed to his wounds at San Rafael.[19] Soldiers from the lower ranks rarely recorded their last wishes on paper, probably because they had no property to be disposed of upon their deaths. Their widows were left to fend for themselves. As a result of the Pensacola campaign in 1781, women such as Ana Bermúdez, widowed with six children, all minors, and her sister-in-law, Petrona Labatc, with four young children, were left to survive on half of their husbands' enlisted military pay.[20]

The dangers inherent in military service were constant even after open hostilities had ceased. Following the implementation of reforms designed in 1763 to fortify the island, every town, village and hamlet had military outposts established in their midst and military detachments quartered there to protect the royal interests. These units doubled as a police force, and at any sign of trouble, they were called into action. Ironically, it was during one such peacetime deployment that Isabel Mancebo y Garvey lost her husband, Francisco Mancebo. After surviving three years on campaign in the early 1780s in the disease-infested tropical jungle in Central America, Mancebo returned to eastern Cuba, where he was assigned to local duty. In 1785, several slaves from the mines of El Cobre escaped into the mountains, and Mancebo was among the men sent to capture the runaways. The military column was ambushed as they passed through a narrow, densely forested valley, and Mancebo was killed. Left alone with four young children, the oldest of whom was only ten years old, his widow petitioned the crown for a pension and for appointments for her two young sons as cadets in the Regiment of Havana. Royal officials commented on the 'truly pitiful' circumstances of the widow and her family, and how her husband had 'sacrificed his life for his country'. Yet because the soldier had not attained sufficient rank, Isabel's petition was denied; the crown did, however, agree to accept her two sons into the Noble Corps of Cadets, despite their youth.[21]

The usual compensation for losing a husband, father or son in combat was a pension system that awarded survivors half the soldier's pay.[22] In other cases the crown would accept a fallen soldier's sons into the cadet corps.[23] Yet pensions and other forms of compensation were not automatic, and Cuban women routinely forsook the home for the public sphere, where they actively confronted royal officials on behalf of their family. Women who lost the primary source of family income sought to hold royal officials accountable for the compensation implicitly promised for military service. In doing so, they emulated the indomitable women evacuees from Florida in 1763 who waged a successful campaign to have their sacrifices recognized and rewarded.[24]

For much of the eighteenth century the Spanish province of Florida was the front line of battle in the territorial contest between Spain and Great Britain. Families assigned to the frontier outposts of St Augustine, Apalachee and Pensacola were constantly under threat of attack from southeastern Indian groups aligned with the British. In 1731 the Spanish crown set up a pension system for the surviving female relatives of men who had served in this dangerous region. When Florida was ceded to Great Britain in 1763, families forced to evacuate to Cuba lost everything.[25] The pension system for widows and children became the model for an expanded system on the island, and being a *floridana* was synonymous with duty, loyalty to Spain and, above all, sacrifice.[26] The *floridana* women also set an example of persistence in demanding that tight-fisted treasury officials in Cuba comply with the provisions of the law. From 1764 they waged an incessant battle for compensation that by 1772 had royal officials complaining of the 'continuous clamour' of military women.[27] Success was theirs in 1773, when Charles III acknowledged that these were 'extraordinary women' and ordered that their pensions be paid without delay.[28]

Among the *floridana* women whose life was intimately tied to military service was Ursula de Avero, widow of Raymundo de Arrivas, a captain in the infantry. A descendant of seventeenth-century Florida governor, Juan de Peñaloza, Avero's military pedigree was impeccable, as she reminded royal officials when she demanded recognition of her family's sacrifices for the crown. She founded her claims for a pension on the service of her current husband, her late first husband, her father, her grandfather, her great-grandfather, her sons and her sons-in-law, all of whom were or had been in military service.[29] Even women of the highest status were obliged to petition for compensation. Josepha Eligio de la Puente, whose military heritage also stretched back for generations, was widowed in 1780 when her husband Juan de Miralles died suddenly while serving on a diplomatic mission as the Spanish representative to the Continental Congress in Philadelphia. After the war was over, she had to petition for reimbursement of 1,578 pesos for her husband's expenses and for the cost of his funeral and burial during a visit to Commander-in-Chief of the Continental Army George Washington at his encampment in Morristown.[30]

The strategies employed by Cuba's women extended well beyond simple pension requests, since these wives often interfered in their husbands' careers in ways that would be considered unthinkable in the modern military. In 1789, for example, long after the war with Britain had ended, María González grew weary of struggling to survive in Havana while her husband, adjutant major Josef Bekens served in a regiment in Spain. Her life was one constant battle, she complained, nursing her widowed mother, who was 'prostrate in bed', and taking care of her orphaned sisters. Calling on the 'caring and pious heart of Your Excellency', María assured royal officials that 'she did not want anything for herself'. She was requesting only that her husband be transferred back to Havana to be incorporated into one of the new regiments that had just been created. Compassionate officials in Spain recommended to Havana's governor that her request be approved.[31] In 1793, Spain opened war against republican France on two fronts in the Caribbean: one was in Saint-Domingue and the other in Florida, where military officials faced an aggressive government in the young United States, whose political officials openly supported the ideals of the French Revolution. María Luisa de Herrera's husband and son were in the vanguard on the second front, standing ready on the Florida frontier to repel an invasion from Georgia. Back at home in Havana, Luisa approached military officials time and again on behalf of her husband, Blas du Bouchet, hoping to gain him a promotion or to have his salary increased.[32]

When treasury officials seemed to be dragging their heels, some women became aggressive, as did Rosa Conde, widow of Lieutenant-Colonel Matias Sastre, whose son, José Sastre, was on active duty as a member of a local patrol. Among his duties was to ferret out contraband activity, for which the patrol members would receive a portion of the confiscated goods when sold at auction. In 1788, after young Sastre had participated in three such raids, Rosa complained that local officials had not compensated her son, and she demanded that he be rewarded for his bravery.[33] Often the uncertainties of war allowed the re-emergence of old grievances based on generations of enmity within a community. In 1781 in the eastern town of Bayamo, Ysolda Núñez Villavicencio refused to become a double victim, of war and of the vindictiveness of the local parish priest, an enemy of her absent militiaman husband. When the rogue priest spread 'scandalous rumours' about her and her husband, Núñez Villavicencio, although barely literate, was sophisticated enough to dictate a long letter to the captain general, in which she established her innocence and protested the defamation of herself and her family.[34]

Militarization and the community of colour

Both necessity and the warrior tradition demanded that all citizens be ready to defend their homes; so from the earliest days of colonization, the Spanish crown deliberately integrated the free coloured and slave communities into its local defence policy. To this end, in the late sixteenth century, the crown created militia battalions of free *pardos* and free *morenos*, and by the end of the eighteenth century approximately two-thirds of the free coloured men on the island served in their respective militias.[35] The crown reinforced the importance of free coloured men and their families again and again in decrees such as that promulgated in 1714 demanding that the volunteers in the *pardo* and *moreno* battalions 'be attended with the good treatment that they deserve'.[36]

As a part of the reform initiative that followed the return of Havana to Spanish control, military reformers took an extraordinary step to incorporate the free community of colour into military service. In December 1763 two members of the battalion of *morenos*, mason Antonio Soledad and carpenter Ignacio Alvarado, boarded a transport ship bound for Spain. There they were taken to the court of Charles III, where they were given the honour of displaying their prowess at arms and kissing his majesty's hand. In turn, the king awarded each man a medal of merit, a decoration reserved for the most esteemed and valiant soldiers in the militia.[37]

Iberian law also established that slaves could earn their freedom in several ways. In the military context, if a slave performed with exceptional valour in times of war, then he could be freed upon the recommendation of his commanding officers.[38] Former slave and shoemaker Andrés Gutiérrez earned his freedom by this means when he exhibited extraordinary bravery against the British in 1762.[39]

The militarization of men of colour conferred an uncommon degree of status and autonomy on Cuba's free women of colour, who made up approximately half of the island's free female population, or one quarter of the total female population.⁴⁰ Their husbands, fathers and sons serving in the militia were ordinary men—Havana artisans, tradesmen and labourers, including carpenters, tailors, shoemakers, masons and silversmiths—just as were the men in the white militia battalions.⁴¹ In this, their status was similar to communities of colour everywhere in the Americas. Yet the privileges these families enjoyed had no counterparts either in the other Caribbean colonies, on the North American mainland, or in Europe. All members of the Cuban military community—men on active duty, militiamen and their household dependents—were entitled to protection under the well-studied *'fuero militar'* (the military privilege of immunity), a benefit that, when extended to all those in the military in 1771, was also unique to the island.⁴² As mentioned above, meritorious service could earn men in the militia special recognition, such as the medal of merit or a gold or silver medallion stamped with the monarch's likeness and, significantly, permission to wear the medal in public.⁴³ In addition, the Bishop of Havana deliberately integrated the families of the officer corps into the religious hierarchy of the church when, in 1765, he named their members as leaders of the religious brotherhood (*cofradía*) in the Iglesia Espíritu Santo, the largest congregation in Havana.⁴⁴

A reconstruction of the daily lives of Cuba's free women of colour illustrates well the tangible rewards that made their existence infinitely more comfortable than that of free coloureds in other Caribbean colonies. Militia service provided a degree of financial security that the average *jornalero* (day worker) could not ordinarily achieve.⁴⁵ Uniforms were indispensable for promoting military discipline and set the militiaman apart from the ordinary urban dweller. Affluent families in the free coloured community often owned several houses and garden plots, slaves and such personal property as gold crucifixes, earrings and brooches set with precious stones.⁴⁶ Although most militiamen lived in private households, on occasion, the poorest retired military families were provided with housing free of charge.⁴⁷ Members of the militia and royal slaves received medical treatment and medicines courtesy of the crown.⁴⁸ Military families had their own commissary close to the Castillo de la Fuerza where their women could buy meat at the same prices charged to the regular troops.⁴⁹ Free women of colour purchased their daily bread at the royal bakery for government employees, where they rubbed elbows with white women of similar status who enjoyed the same privilege because of their husbands' militia service.⁵⁰

Complicated kinship and friendship linkages bound the families in both battalions to each other in enduring personal relationships such as the one revolving around Gabriela Pérez, the matriarch of a large family network in the *pardo* community. Gabriela's husband, shoemaker Francisco Xavier Carques, entered militia service in 1726, eventually attaining the rank of captain. Their son, Cristóval, a tailor, joined the militia in 1748, and both father and son fought valiantly against the British in 1762.

Their brother-in-arms was carpenter Juan Joseph de Flores, who joined the militia in 1739, and who similarly participated in the numerous military campaigns. A junior member of their corps was second lieutenant and shoemaker Antonio Álvarez.[51] But these men were not just comrades; they also became relatives when Cristóval married María Josepha de Flores in the 1760s. After María Josepha died, the kinship network brought the Álvarez family into its sphere of influence when Cristóval subsequently married María Rosa Álvarez, and after her death, her sister, María Isabel Álvarez.[52] Thirty years later, in 1790, the continuity of kinship persisted in the military command structure. By then, Juan Joseph de Flores commanded the battalion of *pardos*; captains of the individual companies included Cristóval Carques and his brother-in-law, Antonio Álvarez. Josef Joaquín Carques, Cristóval's son and Antonio's nephew, was a young second lieutenant, who, along with his cousin, Bruno de Flores, was being groomed for command in the tradition of their grandfathers.[53]

Campaigns were as hard on Cuba's military families of colour as on their white counterparts, and although men could retire after 20 years, military service entailed so many economic advantages and social benefits that it became a lifetime commitment. It was not uncommon for men like Carques and Flores to celebrate 50 years of service.[54] Soldiers who served in the battalions of free *pardos* and free *morenos* retired with full military privileges, and the status of their widows and orphans was in some respects comparable to that of white women.[55] María Loreto Escovedo evacuated to Cuba from Florida in 1764 with her husband, free *moreno* militiaman José Ricardo Escovedo, and settled in Regla, across the bay from Havana.[56] Forty years later José Ricardo was long deceased, but María Loreto was still on the list of pensioners receiving a monthly stipend.[57] Among the recipients of bad news after the Pensacola campaign were widows of men in the battalions of free *pardos* or free *morenos* such as Agustina Bayona, wife of Basilio Pérez; María Pastora de León, wife of Pedro Arriasola; María Soledad Marrero, wife of Vicente Marrero and Josefa Joaquina Sanabría, wife of Antonio Castellanos. Like all military widows, they received half of their lost husband's monthly salary for the remainder of their lives as long as they did not remarry. In the euphoria that followed the Spanish victory at Pensacola, the crown was especially generous to the victims' families and awarded pensions to María Quiros, mother of Juan Machado; María Josefa del Espíritu Santo, mother of Jacinto Navarro; Gregoria Martínez, mother of Francisco del Castillo; Manuel de Prados's mother, Gabriela Josefa Oquendo and Eliseo Pedroso's elderly widowed mother, María Dionisia Rosario. All of the women also received half of their son's military salary.[58]

Militia service provided status for free families of colour, but more important, it offered a chance for slaves to gain their freedom. While male slaves could earn their liberty by serving with uncommon valour, women had a unique opportunity to escape from bondage legally by purchasing their freedom in a process known as *coartación*.⁵⁹ This process is detailed in notarial records of hundreds of transactions in which slaves purchased their freedom. Once free themselves, the men took steps to free their wives and families. A notable example within the battalion of free *morenos* was the family network revolving around the matriarch María Antonia Díaz, who arrived in Cuba in the 1730s on a slave ship from Guinea. While still a slave, she legally married the enslaved Juan Bautista Arenciba. By the 1750s the couple had earned their freedom and purchased a wattle-and-daub house on the street leading to the church of Santo Christo. Their lives were made more comfortable by their two female slaves, Ana María and María Francisca, and Ana María's two young boys probably played in the courtyard with their own son, Antonio, born in the 1740s. On feast and festival days the family wore their precious possessions, a gold rosary set with emeralds hung from a gold chain, silver earrings and gold buttons for Juan Bautista's coat.⁶⁰ Their son, Antonio, continued his parents' resourcefulness. He joined the *moreno* militia at an early age, attaining the rank of captain, and like so many of his comrades, he served for over forty years. By the time of his death in 1795, the family network created by his once-enslaved parents had endured and prospered. Antonio's wife, Catalina Serafina, assumed the role of matriarch when María Antonia died. The couple lived in a substantial house that he bought 'with his own money', while their daughter, María Soledad Díaz purchased her own house for 247 pesos in 1767. Not surprisingly, their three sons, Tomás, Joseph and José María, followed in their father's footsteps and served in the *moreno* militia.⁶¹

To earn the money to purchase their freedom, enslaved women routinely hired out their services, giving up a portion of their wages to their masters but keeping the remainder for themselves. The military garrison, in particular, employed slave women to make uniforms or to wash laundry for the hospitals. From 1767 through 1772, treasury officials paid the slave wives over 3,370 pesos for the uniforms they sewed in their homes on a piecework basis.⁶² Legally the property of the king, the wives of royal slaves in a specially created artillery battalion were allowed to work outside their homes if they secured the permission of their husbands.⁶³ Perhaps this was the way that María Dolores Castillo purchased her freedom for 257 pesos from her owner, militia soldier Roque Castillo in December 1779.⁶⁴

An enduring myth about Cuban slavery is that the process of gaining one's freedom was primarily an urban phenomenon that occurred when war and invasion threatened. In reality, the processes by which female slaves acquired their freedom spanned time and place. As early as 1752, well before the wars that chronologically bracket this study, María Gertrudis Montero earned her freedom in Havana in a most unusual fashion. Her owner, Manuel Montero had pledged 300 pesos to purchase her freedom, but there was no notary in the small town of Güines where they lived. When Montero died suddenly, his son, José Montero, inherited his father's estate and his obligations.

Shortly thereafter, the younger Montero travelled to Havana with María Gertrudis, where in December 1752 he went before the government notary, Miguel de Ayala, declaring the woman 'free of all subjugation, captivity and servitude'.[65] In the far western province of the island, Pinar del Río, in 1775, Nicolás Hernández freed Rosa, his native-born (*criolla*) slave, as a reward for her good service to him.[66] Ten years later, lieutenant José María de la Torre, from a career military family, crafted similar documentation in favour of his slave Magdalena, whom he had purchased just two years previously.[67]

Danger and protection

One of the unique features of Cuba's military society was the overwhelming government presence throughout the island, even outside Havana. Ironically, although soldiers enjoyed a degree of immunity from prosecution by civil courts under the *fuero militar*, they were exponentially more vulnerable to arrest in Cuba where their superior officers were omnipresent.[68]

The combined codes of military conduct, the privileges and responsibilities of the *fuero militar* and the provisions of the decree of 1714 all came together in striking fashion in an incident that occurred in one of Havana's market squares in 1791. Many women from marginalized social groups sold fruits, vegetables and other food products in the public markets of the island's towns and villages. One such woman, an unnamed free black woman, was assaulted by a cadet in the light cavalry regiment, Juan Manuel du Bouchet, the son of Luisa Herrera, mentioned above. While seriously inebriated, the young du Bouchet tried to steal a corn tortilla from the woman's food stand. When she caught him in the act and tried to recover the tortilla, he took out his small sword and stabbed her. She was rushed to the hospital, where she was treated and recovered, and du Bouchet was dismissed from military service as a consequence.[69] In another case, another free black woman street vendor was injured and her basket of eggs knocked over when she got in the way of a fight between two military men in front of a popular tavern on one of the main plazas in Havana. Both men were reprimanded for their unbecoming and dishonourable behaviour.[70]

Scandalous behaviour on a personal level violated the military code of conduct as well as challenging concepts of honour. Close to Havana, the hamlet of Prensa housed a detachment of the Light Cavalry that was assigned there to patrol the coast and sound the alarm at any sign of the enemy. Corporal Joseph Antonio Quiñones was a member of the corps when he began an affair with widow Maria Manuela. The furious constable (*capitán del partido*) of Prensa confronted Quiñones and Manuela about their behaviour, which was scandalizing the village, but the enamoured couple was unrepentant. Quiñones invoked his immunity under the *fuero militar*, challenging the constable's authority over him since the constable was a civilian and Quiñones was a member of the regular military forces.

The matter was passed on to Havana, where it came to the attention of the captain general, Diego José Navarro, who asserted his supreme authority on the island to resolve the issue. A contingent of soldiers was sent out from the capital, Quiñones was placed under military arrest and transported to prison, and Manuela wound up in the women's jail in Havana for living in open concubinage.[71]

Unmarried and widowed women were vulnerable, but for most women, violence came in the form of domestic abuse from male relatives. Violence against women was not influenced by either status or ethnicity. Nor was the justice dispensed by local constables, by military officers stationed within local communities and by the royal authorities in Havana, all of whom worked together. In the barrio of Guadalupe, free *pardo* Joseph Ramos was 'continually drunk', and in four years of matrimony, he had never provided for his wife. He had withheld food and clothing and had repeatedly beaten her. The beating he administered in June 1766 was so severe that she fled from their house and sought asylum in the church. At that point the local military constable, Juan de Dios Castro Palomino, intervened on the side of the abused wife.[72] The military constable of the village of Managua, Félix Cantón, sent free black Joseph Antonio Caravali to Havana for punishment for repeatedly abusing his wife, and the captain general sentenced the man to labour on the fortifications.[73] Even in the remote countryside, well away from the prying eyes of royal officials, abusive husbands could face punishment for mistreating their wives. In 1796, in the hamlet of Rio Blanco del Sur, far to the east of Havana, Catalina de Arcias complained about the violence inflicted by her husband, Antonio Hernández. He, too, was sent to Havana, facing months of hard labour intended to remedy his abusive behaviour.[74]

One of the most notable differences in gender relations between Cuba and other areas of Latin America was the way in which domestic disturbances were resolved. Elsewhere, community censure or the intervention of village elders (*viejos*) mediated personal disputes. Because of the patriarchal nature of Hispanic society, such mediation often skewed the outcome in favour of the husband. In other instances, this powerful male local influence was mitigated by female solidarity among older women, usually widows, who were the guardians of community norms of behaviour as well as the guardians against the excesses of power within the male community.[75] Both factors were relevant to one domestic disturbance in the Regla neighborhood south of the city of Havana, but like the previous examples the outcome was not mediated by the community but was determined rather by military justice. There, in the late 1770s, the public tranquillity of the main street, Calle de Regla, was violated time and again when the household of retired infantry soldier Josef Baquero erupted in violence. Finally, Baquero's wife Juana Delgado brought charges against her drunkard husband. The constable of Regla, militiaman Francisco Blandino, sought the counsel of Baquero's neighbours, who confirmed his chronic abuse of his wife. Had the dispute occurred elsewhere, Baquero might have avoided prosecution, but in Regla, an enclave of militiamen, retired military and evacuees from Florida, the circumstances were different. Baquero's house at number 39 Calle de Regla was surrounded by households headed by military widows—Eulalina del Pino at number 36, María Margarita da Silva at number 39 and Manuela Cancloro at number 40. Next door to Baquero, at number 37, lived *floridana* evacuee Maria Dolores Navarro and her mother, military widow María Montes de Oca, and in number 44, *floridano* militiaman Fernando Xavier de Salas headed the household that included his *floridana* wife María Dolores del Pozo.[76] Four of these neighbours testified to Baquero's 'vituperative' verbal abuse, and instead of being protected by his military immunity, he received six months' hard labour on the new government house in Havana.[77]

Although being a member of the militia conferred a certain protection on men accused of criminal acts while they were on active duty, the pervasive military influence meant that if one stepped outside the law, pursuit was relentless. Such was the case in a sensational and heinous murder in Bayamo in 1777. A member of the light cavalry, Fernando de la Cruz, flew into a rage when he discovered that his unmarried sister, María Catalina de la Cruz, was pregnant.[78] After he murdered the girl in their own house, he fled to the woods and remained at large for nearly three years. Even though de la Cruz qualified for immunity from civil prosecution under military law, the constable of Bayamo, José Tejada, was so appalled by the violence of an attack that had 'made the walls of the family home run red with the victim's blood' that he pursued criminal charges against the militiaman and secured an indictment and conviction in absentia.[79] For two years, de la Cruz was a fugitive, pursued by Tejada and military units throughout the island. The captain general in Havana closely followed the progress of the case, and when Tejada captured the fugitive in 1780, he wrote a commendation letter praising the local efforts to bring the murderer to justice.[80]

Conclusion

One of the difficulties in the practice of gender history is complying with the fundamental goal of historiography to establish change over time. Such a goal is even more challenging when scholars set out to investigate personal relationships, since emotions—love, pride, anger and jealousy—are rarely preserved in sterile government documents. Despite these obstacles, the evidence of personal behaviour, in conjunction with the outcomes of innumerable court cases and petitions, demonstrate that women in Cuba in the late eighteenth century enjoyed both personal agency and the freedom to act on behalf of their families. These rights resulted from the combination of two powerful cultural traditions. The first united the principal tenets of patriarchy and honour. The second reflected the warrior mentality of the Reconquest. On the surface, at least, these concepts should have contradicted each other; instead they became mutually supportive and reinforcing. The need for an adequate military defence allowed concepts of honour and sacrifice to permeate Cuban society well beyond the European population, and over time persons of colour who served in the island's military or militias came to enjoy the same privileges and perquisites accorded to other members of their military community.

By the mid-nineteenth century, however, women's roles had undergone a sharp reversal. White women were infantilized, free women of colour were victimized and slave women were brutalized. How did this happen? The debate over which events contributed to the proscription of women's activities continues and involves many factors, some of which are examined in other essays in this volume. The changing political conditions of the Atlantic world as a consequence of the Age of Revolutions, along with the expansion of plantation slavery in the nineteenth century, cannot be discounted. For Cuban women the freedoms that they enjoyed even while coping with danger were curtailed just a few generations later. The very agency that enabled them to step outside traditional gender roles also meant that their independence would become a threat rather than an asset. Ironically, the Age of Revolutions, which championed individual rights, would work against at least one sector of society that had, by linking them to militarization, made such rights possible.

Notes

1. Archivo Nacional de Cuba, Havana, Cuba (hereafter ANC), Escribania de Guerra, Tomás García, testament, San Rafael, 3 July 1794. In addition, documents have been consulted in the following archives: Library of Congress, Washington, DC, East Florida Papers (hereafter EFP), microfilm copies in P. K. Yonge Library of Florida History, George A. Smathers Libraries, University of Florida, Gainesville, FL; Archivo General de Indias (hereafter AGI), Seville, Spain; Archivo General de Simancas (hereafter AGS), Simancas, Spain; Houghton Library (hereafter HL), Harvard University, Cambridge, MA; Biblioteca Nacional José Martí, Havana, Colección Cubana (hereafter BNJM); Archivo Histórico Provincial de Pinar del Rio (hereafter AHPR), Pinar del Río, Cuba. Archival documents will be cited using the abbreviation of the archival repository followed by the document group consulted, which may also be abbreviated, as in: AGS, Secretaría de Guerra Moderna (hereafter AGS, Guerra); AGI, Audiencia de Santo Domingo (hereafter AGI, SD); AGI, Indiferente General (hereafter AGI, IG); AGI, Papeles de Cuba (hereafter AGI, PC). Citations may also contain references to the microfilm reel, the bundle or *legajo* (hereafter 'leg.') and the folder or *expediente* (hereafter 'exp.').
2. See Sherry Johnson, *The Social Transformation of Eighteenth-Century Cuba* (Gainesville, 2001); idem and K. Lynn Stoner (eds), *Trespassing Historic Gender Boundaries in Cuba*, special issue *Cuban Studies/Estudios Cubanos* 33 (2003); and Sarah L. Franklin, 'Suitable to Her Sex: Race, Slavery, and Patriarchy in Nineteenth-Century Colonial Cuba', Ph.D. diss. (Florida State University, 2006).
3. Steve J. Stern, *The Secret History of Gender: Women, Men and Power in Late Colonial Mexico* (Chapel Hill, NC, 1995), 11–20; Ann Twinam, *Public Lives, Private*

Secrets: Gender, Honor, Sexuality, and Illegitimacy in Colonial Spanish America (Stanford, 1999); Susan Midgen Socolow, *The Women of Colonial Latin America* (Cambridge, UK, 2000); Sueanne Caulfield, 'The History of Gender in the Historiography of Latin America', *Hispanic American Historical Review* 81 (2001): 477–481; Verena Martinez-Alier, *Marriage, Class, and Colour in Nineteenth-Century Cuba: Attitudes and Sexual Values in a Slave Society* (1974; repr. Ann Arbor, 1992).
4. Stern, *Secret History*, 15.
5. Silvia Marina Arrom, *Women of Mexico City, 1790–1857* (Stanford, 1985), 26.
6. Asunción Lavrin, 'In Search of the Colonial Woman in Mexico: The Seventeenth and Eighteenth Centuries', in *Latin American Women: Historical Perspectives*, ed. Asunción Lavrin (Westport, CT, 1978), 24–34.
7. Johnson, *Social Transformation*, 64–96; Allan J. Kuethe, *Cuba, 1753–1815: Crown, Military and Society* (Knoxville, 1986), 46–48; Lyle N. McAlister, *The 'Fuero Militar' in New Spain, 1764–1800* (Gainesville, 1957), 6–11 and 45–51; Juan Marchena Fernández, *Oficiales y soldados en el ejército de América* (Seville, 1983).
8. In the city of Havana and her immediate suburbs among eligible civilian adult males aged 15 to 50, approximately 30 per cent of whites and 66 per cent of free coloured males were militiamen. Similar numbers are calculated for the population centres throughout the island. These calculations are based upon the number of troops in 1776. ANC, Revista de la Tropa, 9 May 1776, leg. 2, exp. 11, Asuntos Políticos. Troop numbers are compared to the population figures for the census of 1778 in AGI, IG, leg. 1527, Diego José de Navarro, 'Padrón General de la Isla de Cuba formado a consequencia de Real Orden de 1º de noviembre de 1776', 1778, repr. in *Revista de la Biblioteca Nacional José Martí* 29 (1987): 25. Comparable studies of militarized societies argue that if 20 to 25 per cent of the population is under arms the society is fully mobilized. Stanislav Andreski, *Military Organization and Society* (Berkeley, 1968), 33–74.
9. Johnson, *Social Transformation*, 58–64. In 1778, there were approximately 5,300 regular troops and 11,000 civilian men in the city. Two years later, the numbers were roughly equal at 11,000 each. Of 2,600 free coloured men, nearly 1,600 served in the militia.
10. Sherry Johnson, '*"Señoras en sus clases no ordinarias"*: Enemy Collaborators or Courageous Defenders of the Family?' in Johnson and Stoner, *Trespassing*, 11–37, 22–23.
11. Johnson, *Social Transformation*. The standard works are McAlister, *'Fuero Militar'*; Mark A. Burkholder and David S. Chandler, *From Impotence to Authority: The Spanish Crown and the American Audiencias, 1687–1810* (Columbia, SC, 1977); Nancy M. Farriss, *Crown and Clergy in Colonial Mexico, 1759–1821* (London, 1968); John Lynch, *The Spanish American Revolutions, 1808–1826* (New York, 1973), 8. Works particular to Cuba include Kuethe, *Cuba, 1753–1815*; Jorge I. Domínguez, *Insurrection or Loyalty: The Breakdown of the Spanish Empire* (Cambridge, MA, 1980); and John Robert McNeill, *Atlantic Empires of France and Spain: Louisbourg and Havana, 1700–1763* (Chapel Hill, NC, 1985).
12. ANC, Escribanía de Guerra, Cadet José López de Soto to Nicolás de Villa, proxy power of attorney, 27 March 1782, as he prepared for his departure with Bernardo de Gálvez's army in 1782.
13. Ibid. Pedro de Moncada, Marqués de Villaforte to María de Berrio Camp y Coz, power of attorney, 30 December 1779; EFP, Escrituras, reel 170, leg. 369, Bernadino Segui to Agueda Villalonga, power of attorney, 7 October 1786. The term 'deputy husband' was introduced by Laurel Thatcher Ulrich in *Good Wives: Image*

and Reality in the Lives of Women in Northern New England, 1650–1750 (New York, 1982), 35–50.
14. ANC, Escribanía de Guerra, Antonio Fernández to Victorian Guillén, power of attorney, 9 October 1780. Over a decade later, she made arrangements for her daughter's dowry in her husband's absence. The property she pledged as collateral came from properties she had inherited from her mother's family. EFP, Escrituras, reel 170, leg. 369, Victorian Guillén, dowry bond, 6 July 1794.
15. ANC, Escribanía de Guerra, Vicente Folch to María Mercedes Rodríguez del Junco, 1 March 1783, revoked on 30 June 1794. See also Pedro José Rodríguez del Junco to María Mercedes Rodríguez del Junco, marriage license, ibid. 9 July 1782.
16. Ibid. Gines de Oliva to Josepha de Azze, power of attorney, 17 February 1792 and Sebastián Piñero to María Leonora Mungrey, power of attorney, 9 March 1795.
17. Ibid. Antonio Alonzo to María Alonzo, power of attorney, (day illegible) January 1793.
18. Ibid. Tomás García, testament, San Rafael, 3 July 1794.
19. Ibid. Julián de Parreño, testament, probated 5 November 1795 (originally written 1788).
20. AGS, Guerra, leg. 6913, exp. 9, 'Relación de los Individuos que fallecieron en la conquista de Panzacola, a cuias viudas, padres, y madres respectivamente…', 6 February 1782.
21. Ibid. leg. 6876, exp. 38, Isabel Mancebo y Garvey, petition, Santiago de Cuba, 22 July 1797.
22. D. S. Chandler, *Social Assistance and Bureaucratic Politics: The Montepíos of Colonial Mexico, 1767–1821* (Albuquerque, 1991).
23. BNJM, *Reglamento del pie, servicio, gobierno y disciplina de la noble compañía de cadetes de la Havana, aprobado por S.M. y mandada su observancia por R.O., expedida en Sn Ildefonso a 24 de octubre de 1764* (Havana, 1765). See also Fernández, *Oficiales*, 75.
24. Sherry Johnson, 'Casualties of Peace: Tracing the Historic Roots of the Florida-Cuba Diaspora, 1763–1804', *Colonial Latin American Historical Review* 10 (2002): 91–125.
25. AGI, SD, leg. 2585, 'Report of Juan Eligio de la Puente', 8 May 1770. Several additional lists detail the amounts of money provided to *floridanas*: ANC, Fondo de las Floridas, leg. 14, exp. 93, 'Relación de las floridanas', 30 October 1789, and AGI, PC, leg. 412-A, 'Certificación de las Familias de Florida', 1 September 1795. These lists do not include the innumerable individual requests from widows, orphans and mothers for royal assistance scattered throughout Cuban, Spanish and Florida archives. See also Johnson, 'Casualties of Peace'; Duvon C. Corbitt, 'Spanish Relief Policy and the East Florida Refugees of 1763', *Florida Historical Quarterly* 27 (July 1948): 67–82, 70, 75–76. In six months, the Florida evacuation increased Havana's population by roughly 10 per cent. By the 1790s, 331 *floridanas* were still on the pension rolls, representing the largest single bloc of women pensioners on the island.
26. Serving in Florida had always entailed sacrifice. The Spanish Crown specifically recognized how dangerous Florida duty was for men and, by extension, granted special privileges to Florida women. ANC, Fondo de las Floridas, leg. 14, exp. 93, 'Relación de las floridanas', 30 October 1789, reiterates the concessions granted to Florida women since 1731. A collection of all the petitions is AGI, PC, leg. 1228, 'Familias de la Florida, 1772–1800'.
27. Ibid. 29 November 1773.
28. Johnson, '*Senoras…no ordinarias*', 22–23.

29. AGS, Guerra, leg. 6850, exp. 45, 'Petitión de Da. Ursula de Avero', Havana, 11 April 1793; ANC, Escribanía de Guerra, Ursula de Avero, testament, 15 September 1791. She was also the widow of peninsular captain Diego de Repilado; Charles W. Arnade, 'The Avero Story: An Early St. Augustine Family with Many Daughters and Many Houses', *Florida Historical Quarterly* 40 (1961): 3–33.
30. AGI, PC, leg. 1368-A, Josepha Eligio de la Puente to Bernardo de Gálvez, Havana, 22 March 1785.
31. AGS, Guerra, leg. 6880, exp.73, María Gonzáles, petition, Havana, 28 February 1789.
32. Ibid. leg. 7222, exp.15, María Luisa de Herrera, petition, Havana, 27 November 1792.
33. Ibid. leg. 6842, exp.76, Rosa Conde to the Council of the Indies, Madrid, 24 May 1788.
34. AGI, PC, leg. 1254, Ysolda Núñez Villavicencio to the captain general, Bayamo, 16 January 1781.
35. The seminal study is Herbert S. Klein, *Slavery in the Americas: A Comparative Study of Virginia and Cuba* (1967; repr. Chicago, 1989), 193–227; see also Johnson, *Social Transformation*, 31–70; Matt D. Childs, *The 1812 Aponte Rebellion in Cuba and the Struggle Against Atlantic Slavery* (Chapel Hill, 2006); Jane Landers, *Black Society in Spanish Florida* (Bloomington, 1999). The terms *pardo, moreno* and *negro* refer to phenotypical characteristics. A *Pardo* (Spanish/Portuguese for 'brown') is a person of mixed blood, African and European, visible in a light brown skin colour. *Moreno* (Spanish/Portuguese for 'dark') refers to a person of predominantly African blood with darker brown colouring. *Negro* (Spanish/Portuguese for 'black') refers to a person whose skin is a very dark brown or black colour.
36. AGI, SD, leg. 337, 20 May 1714, quoted in Klein, *Slavery in the Americas*, 213.
37. AGI, PC, leg. 1136A, 'Libros de servicio de los oficiales y sargentos de las batalliones de pardos y morenos de la Havana', 1774.
38. HL, José Escoto Archive, Part II, Box 1, Folder 20, *Reglamento para el govierno militar político y económico de la compañía de artillería compuesta de negros de SM y sus familias* (Havana, 1768). See also Evelyn Powell Jennings, 'State Enslavement in Colonial Havana, 1763–1790', in *Slavery Without Sugar: Diversity in Caribbean Economy and Society Since the Seventeenth Century*, ed. Verene A. Shepherd (Gainesville, 2002), 152–182; Evelyn Powell Jennings, 'War as the "Forcing House of Change": State Slavery in Late-Eighteenth-Century Cuba', *William and Mary Quarterly* 62 (2005): 411–440.
39. AGI, PC, leg. 1136-A, 'Libros de servicio', 1774.
40. AGI, IG, leg. 1527, Diego José Navarro, 'Padrón General', 1778. In 1778, there were 4,728 free women of colour, 8,579 white women and 5,008 female slaves. For a complete breakdown of population numbers see Johnson, *Social Transformation*, 191.
41. AGI, PC, leg. 1071, 'Noticia de los hombres (de 15 a 45 anos) que sean hallado abiles para las armas en el quartel que corresponde al alcalde de barrio Don Francisco de Toledo cuios corresponden a la 7ª compania', 14 December 1770; 'Compania 1o de batallion de voluntarios blancos de la Havana', 16 December 1770; '3ª compania de la battallion de voluntarios blancos de la Havana', 18 December 1770.
42. Johnson, *Social Transformation*, 39–70.
43. BNJM, *Papel Periódico de la Havana*, 15 November 1792.
44. Manuel, 'The King's Loyal Vassals', ch. 2.
45. Fernández, *Oficiales*, 33, 81–82; Kuethe, *Cuba*, 142.
46. ANC, Escribanía de Guerra, Antonio Abad del Rey, testament, written 15 July 1788, probated late October 1796.

47. ANC, Realengos, Extramuros, leg. 73, exp. 33, 1793. See also Fernández, *Oficiales*, 335–336.
48. AGI, PC, leg. 1472, Río Blanco del Norte reported on its status as the site of a hospital for king's slaves and prisoners, 15 October 1791. See also HL, José Escoto Archive, *Reglamento...de la compañía de artillería*...; Manuel Pérez Beato, *Habana antigua; apuntes historicos*, 2 vols (Havana, 1936), vol. 1, 229; Levi Marrero, *Cuba, economia y sociedad*, 15 vols (Rio Piedras, 1972–1992), vol. 8, 81; Torres Ramírez, 'Alejandro O'Reilly', 1379.
49. AGI, PC, leg. 1136-A, 'Petición de Tomasa María Castilla Cabesa de Vaca', 15 May 1766; Antonio José Valdés, *História de la isla de Cuba: y en especial de La Habana* (1813: repr. Havana, 1964), 208.
50. AGI, PC, leg. 1071, 'Noticia de los hombres', 14 December 1770; 'Compania 1o', 16 December 1770; '3ª compania', 18 December 1770; Johnson, *Social Transformation*, pp. 39–70.
51. AGI, PC, leg. 1136-A, 'Libros de servicio', 1774.
52. ANC, Escribanía de Guerra, Cristóval Carques, power of attorney, 6 March 1780, and Cristóval Carques, testament, 29 November 1794.
53. AGS, Guerra, leg. 6846, exp. 14, Revista de Inspección, Batallon de Pardos de la Havana, Havana, 27 December 1790. See also AGI, PC, leg. 1357, Inspector of the Troops to the captain general, 26 September 1783.
54. BNJM, *Papel Periódico de la Havana*, 15 November 1792.
55. See, for example, ANC, Escribanía de Guerra, María Teresa de Silva, testament, 2 October 1793, in which the widow of a retired militiaman has access to free government notarial services.
56. AGI, PC, leg. 548, 'Familias de la Florida', Havana, 1764.
57. Ibid. leg. 412-A, 'Certificación de las Familias de Florida', correspondence of the captain general, 1 September 1795.
58. AGS, Guerra, leg. 6913, exp. 9, 'Relación que manifiesta los individuos de los cuerpos que se hallan de Guarnición en esta Plaza, y fallecieron en la conquista de Panzacola, con expreción de las Familias que dexan', 2 November 1781; 'Relación de los Individuos que fallecieron en la conquista de Panzacola, a cuias viudas, padres, y madres respectivamente...', 6 February 1782. Marcos Martínez's elderly father, Juan Antonio Martínez, was also awarded his son's benefits. Ironically, since militia members received a salary only when they were activated, the pension privileges granted to survivors may have been greater than their regular civilian wages.
59. Klein, *Slavery in the Americas*, 196–200.
60. AGS, Guerra, leg. 6846, exp. 14, Revista de Inspección, Batallion de Morenos de la Havana, Havana, 27 December 1790; ANC, Escribanía de Gobierno, Juan Bautista de Arenciba and Maria Antonia Díaz, testament, 18 August 1756.
61. ANC, Escribanía de Guerra, Antonio José Díaz, testament, 11 December 1795; ANC, Escribanía de Gobierno, María Rosario Oquendo to María Soledad Díaz, land sale, 30 March 1767.
62. AGI, PC, leg. 1153, Intendant of Havana to the captain general, 18 May 1773.
63. HL, José Escoto Archive, *Reglamento...de la compañía de artillería*....
64. ANC, Escribanía de Guerra, Roque Castillo to María Dolores Castillo, manumission, Havana, 16 December 1779.
65. ANC, Escribania de Castro (Gobierno), leg. 1752–1757, Joseph Montero to María Gertrudis Montero, manumission, 7 December 1752.
66. AHPR, Escribanía de Gobierno, leg. 1775–1789, Nicolás Hernández to Rosa, manumission, [no day or month] 1775.

67. AHPR, Escribanía de Gobierno, leg. 1775–1789, José María de la Torre to Magdalena, *conga* (a woman born in Africa), manumission, 16 September 1785.
68. Johnson, *Social Transformation*, 39–70.
69. AGS, Guerra, leg. 6866, exp. 15, proceso contra Juan Manuel du Bouchet (1791–1800), 27 September 1800.
70. AGS, Guerra, leg. 6848, exp. 59, 'Informe...Máximo du Bouchet', 21 April 1792.
71. AGI, PC, leg. 1269, Juan del Castillo to the captain general, Prensa, 12 May, 14 May 1780.
72. Ibid. leg. 1095, Constable of Guadalupe to the captain general, 11 June 1766.
73. Ibid. leg. 1269, Constable of Managua to the captain general, 16 August 1780.
74. Ibid. leg. 1472, Constable of Rio Blanco del Sur to the captain general, 14 March 1796.
75. The most comprehensive examination of interpersonal and community relations in the late eighteenth century is Stern, *Secret History*.
76. AGI. PC, leg. 1687, Francisco Blandino, 'Padrón general que manifesta los becinos e habitantes que ay en el Partido de Nuestra Senñora de Regla...', February 1786.
77. AGI, PC, leg. 1269, Francisco Blandino to the captain general, 2 October 1779.
78. Ibid. leg. 1254, José de Tejada to the captain general, 21 October 1777.
79. Ibid. leg. 1254, 18 February, 30 March 1780.
80. Ibid. leg. 1269, the captain general to José de Tejada, Havana, 22 May 1781.

Part IV
Patriotism, Citizenship and Nation-Building

11
Patriotism in Practice: War and Gender Roles in Republican Hamburg, 1750–1815

Katherine B. Aaslestad

Shortly following the March 1813 liberation of Hamburg by Cossack troops and a call to arms to defend the city from the French, the press published an appeal to Hamburg's women. Drawing on emotional, religious and patriotic language similar to that used in militia recruitment, an anonymous daughter of Hamburg pressed her sisters to support the 'holy and honourable enterprise' that would ensure Hamburg's independence from French control, by volunteering to outfit the city's defenders with uniforms and other necessities. By sacrificing fashion and pleasure, women could 'contribute to the liberation of their beloved home town (*Vaterstadt*)'.[1] Evidence in diaries, letters and literature indicates that women, like their fathers, brothers, husbands and sons, shared the experience of wartime mobilization and militarization of society during the Napoleonic Wars. In December 1814, for example, Wilhelmine Amsinck, who belonged to one of the leading families in the Hanseatic city-state Hamburg, chastised her brother Wilhelm for refusing to fight with the Hanseatic Legion, the local volunteers corps organized to defend the city. She admonished him, 'if you neglect to devote yourself with love and allegiance to your Fatherland and gladly make use of all your abilities and strength for the benefit of the same, you are not a true patriot.'[2]

Throughout northern Germany, Prussia and elsewhere in Central Europe, women mobilized to support the Wars of Liberation of 1813–15 in a variety of ways, illustrating that patriotism was not for men alone. Through their participation in wartime projects, women gained opportunities to integrate into civil society and develop new political identities.[3] Yet in republican Hamburg, one of the many small states in the Holy Roman Empire until 1806, women's patriotic sentiments and practice had a long history associated with the city's political culture. Although there were no 'generally accepted mandatory codes indicating how patriotic women should act' in Prussia or other parts of German Central Europe, a strong sense of civic identity provided common points of patriotic reference, meaning and action to women in the Hanseatic city state.[4] The absence of women from formal political life did not mean that they were absent from republican political culture. In Hamburg, women practised civic patriotism prior to the Revolutionary and Napoleonic era and drew on those traditions to expand their patriotic activism when their city endured military occupation and war. Indeed, in wartime Hamburg, the words and actions of women and men gave new meaning to patriotic practices.

The following overview of women's place in the civic culture of Hamburg during the late eighteenth and early nineteenth centuries, especially among the city's educated elite, follows recent scholarship in broadly defining the term *politics* and analysing public activities and civic identity rather than specific political rights.[5] This approach moves beyond emphasizing women's obvious exclusion from formal politics and focuses instead on the sites and spaces where women engaged in public life and civic activism. A study of Hamburg's patriotic women also calls attention to the dynamic relationship between urban life and the civic identity of the disenfranchised. Most studies that explore the crucial role of cities as the incubator of citizenship and civic identities focus scant attention on gender differentiation. Jacobin revolutionaries understood that cities provided residents with a 'silent course in civic ethics,' and this educational process extended beyond France and included both women and men.[6]

Within German Central Europe local patriotism (*Lokalpatriotismus*), regional patriotism (*Landespatriotismus*) and imperial patriotism (*Reichspatriotismus*) coexisted alongside dynastic and religious loyalties; patriotism could call for reforms as well as venerate the past.[7] The patriotism of the north German Hanseatic cities was unique and integrally tied to their republican political culture. Neither inspired by Rousseau and the French revolutionaries nor awakened by Napoleonic occupation, patriotism in Hamburg was fiercely local, and the Revolutionary and Napoleonic Wars heightened popular allegiance to the republic, as Hamburgers sought to regain their independence and autonomy. An analysis of contemporary public discourse, however, elucidates a clear transformation in patriotic sentiment between 1780 and 1815. In eighteenth-century Hamburg, the traditional notion of patriotism found expression in the performance of civic duties for the benefit of the community. Patriotic rhetoric in Hamburg's public sphere conveyed a republican worldview that regarded public and private as fluid and overlapping and in which self-interest was linked to community interests. Gender-neutral republican values meant that women, like men, framed their work and activities as contributions to the common good. In 1813, after years of military occupation and war, the citizens of Hamburg developed a 'valorous patriotism' in which collective responsibility for the common good meant defending the city from foreign conquest.[8] Although women helped to articulate this new patriotic rhetoric, their activism rarely took a martial form. Instead, Hamburg's women expanded their earlier patriotic service by supporting soldiers, the wounded refugees, war widows and orphans, thus underscoring gender distinctions in the practice of wartime patriotism.

Patriotic practice in eighteenth-century republican Hamburg

Economically independent and politically self-governing burghers managed all spheres of public life in Hamburg. Preservation of the city's autonomy and prosperity, rather than political theories, formed the basis of Hamburg's republicanism.[9] The city's constitution and political practices emphasized the reciprocity between rights and duties among members of the body politic and stressed communal participation in determining and administering public welfare. The constitution governing the city since 1712 invested legislative and executive power in two civic bodies, the senate (*Rath*) and the citizens' council (the *Bürgerschaft*), which were composed primarily of the propertied citizenry (*Erbgesessene Bürgerschaft*). Only Lutheran men of substantial means who adhered to a strict moral code could attain the legal status of citizen (*Bürger*). By the end of the eighteenth century approximately half of the male population of Hamburg qualified for citizenship, with each man granted rights according to his financial standing, which was designated as 'large', 'small' or 'propertied'.[10] Denied citizenship themselves, women could still serve as a vehicle to citizenship through marriage. For example, Lutheran foreigners who desired to open a public business, join a corporate body, or marry a native's daughter or widow, were obliged to become citizens and forsake extraterritorial obligations. If Hamburg's constitution provided only limited direct political enfranchisement, its very existence stimulated a specific political culture described by visitors to the city as a 'republican spirit' that expressed a proud and 'clear consciousness of being part of an independent constitutional republic'.[11] This 'appreciation of liberty' (*Freiheitssinn*) created a political and social identity that transcended social rank and gender. In this light, the statement by Johann Carl Daniel Curio, a contemporary writer and pedagogue, that Hamburg recognized only one class, that of the *Bürger*, reflects not the legal category of citizenship but the provocative communitarian image that characterized the city's republican political culture.[12]

Along with the constitution, commerce shaped Hamburg's republican ethos. Commercial and republican rhetoric celebrated diligence, thrift, moderation and public service, virtues that fuelled the economy and served the common good (*Gemeinwohl*). In fact, such virtues reconciled individual with community interests to ensure political stability and civic order in an expanding commercial society.[13] In a city-state without legally defined social estates, a table of ranks, or an aristocracy, the commercial and educated middle classes consciously forged a republican civic identity that manifested itself in a strong moral code. Celebrated as a distinctive 'Hanseatic virtue,' Hamburgers viewed industriousness—more than just the means to pursue wealth—as an inherent value. The republic's eighteenth-century poor relief reforms, evident in constructive educational programmes and schools of industry, inculcated the values of frugality, restraint and, above all, hard work.[14] Furthermore, the emphasis on republican virtues and civic ethos politicized a wide range of social activities from the proper limits of personal consumption to the education of future citizens and residents. Thus, the primacy of virtue in Hamburg's political culture generated a 'politics of the personal' that exceeded categories of legal citizenship.[15] Within this broad conception of citizenship, women practising republican virtues interpreted and helped shape civic culture.

Participation in civic life, not dynastic allegiances or martial values, embodied patriotism in Hamburg. Patriotism, the most important civic virtue, emphasized one's duty to serve the community and support activities that benefitted the entire society.[16] Serving the common good, however, was neither altruistic nor self-abrogating; rather it acknowledged the community's goals as one's own. A self-governing republic required patriotic engagement to safeguard its liberty and affluence. In fact, contemporaries believed that the viability of the republic depended on the transmission of patriotic values across socioeconomic, gender and generational boundaries. Successful merchants and professionals were expected to devote their time, effort and fortune to public causes and to serve in civic offices or perform voluntary administrative duties (*Ehrenämter*). Evidence suggests that they did so in growing numbers. After 1750, enlightened sensibilities combined with republican virtues to motivate numerous volunteers to serve their city; many turned to poor relief as the spectre of poverty threatened traditional civic order and prosperity.[17] Participation in communal affairs provided fundamental education for those who would eventually assume leadership in Hamburg's senate, citizens' council and political administration. City burghers also found opportunities to affirm their patriotism through societies, clubs and associations. The most important organization geared for public service was the Society for the Promotion of the Arts and Useful Crafts, popularly known as the Patriotic Society (*Patriotische Gesellschaft*). Its membership grew steadily until 1810, and its activities were manifold, including improvements in street illumination and paving, installation of lighting rods as fire prevention, formation of rescue societies, construction of a grain warehouse, installation of a water-purification system for the new city and the establishment of the General Poor Relief Institute.

The virtues of industriousness and prudence imparted in the masculine world of the counting house and citizens' council also underpinned the household, the basic social unit of the republican community. Eighteenth-century Hamburgers understood the household as part of a functional community rather than an autonomous intimate domestic space.[18] In Hamburg, republicanism framed eighteenth-century views of the household as the 'domestic republic' (*häusliche Republik*).[19] The site of both family business and family life, the household depended on women's competence as managers and mothers for its economic viability. Women's domestic proficiency could advance or damage the family's social and commercial interests. Saving money was as important as making money in the 1700s, and running a household economically was a valuable skill handed down from mother to daughter through practical education.[20] It required industriousness, moderation and frugality—the very virtues upheld in merchant handbooks and moral weeklies such as *Der Patriot*. Regardless of their sphere of action, both women and men adhered to the values associated with a republican ethos.[21]

Within the household—the most basic economic unit of the commercial republic—the responsibilities and labours of wives and mothers served the common good and civic order.[22] Paralleling her husband's management of customers, clerks and apprentices in the counting house, the household mistress oversaw family accounts, shopped for provisions and supervised domestic servants.[23] In fact, the ideal mistress rewarded her female servants not with wages alone but with the education (*Erziehung*) that would enable them to become competent housewives, prepared to manage their own small households. Raising and educating children was the most crucial function of the family, as children would ultimately be expected to assume their parents' duties and social roles. Women were responsible for modelling proper conduct and transmitting republican virtues to all members of the household, family as well as servants; and the education and socialization they provided in the home reinforced the values of the wider community.[24] The republican home, therefore, emerged as a political space for nurturing civic-mindedness and patriotism.[25]

In Hamburg, the prosperous household was also a key site of urban culture. Women enhanced the family business or promoted enlightened sociability when they hosted or attended teas and dinner parties.[26] The Enlightenment in Hamburg offered women and men increased if unequal opportunities to participate in public life. Although excluded from formal politics and most civic associations, women developed their own social networks that featured enlightened social exchange, philanthropic activities and intimate circles of friends.[27] Informal groups assembled at private homes to enjoy evenings devoted to music, lectures, readings or open conversation. Wives of scholars, professionals and merchants hosted semi-public gatherings that by the end of the century had grown in size and reputation, evidence of a vibrant mixed-gender sociability in the city-state. Within Hamburg, the homes of Margaretha Augusta Büsch, Elise Reimarus, Sophie Hennings Reimarus and Magdalena Pauli were well known for stimulating sociability. Between the late 1770s and 1783, a group known as the Reimarus 'tea table' met in the same place where early meetings of the Patriotic Society had been held—the Reimarus home. More a literary salon than a social event, this meeting of writers, reformers and pedagogues was renowned in northern Europe for its exchange of enlightened ideas.[28] Outside the city, natives and foreigners alike congregated in the houses of Fredericke Poel and Meta Klopstock in Altona, Rebekka Claudius and Ernestine Voß in Wandsbek, Engel Christine Westphalen in Billwärder and Johanna Margaretha Sieveking in Neumühlen. More than sociability for its own sake, discussions by men and women at these gatherings advanced the Enlightenment's reform agenda.

Women clearly shared opinions and contributed to public debates on political, social and local issues as evidenced in their correspondence, diaries and literary works.[29] The course of the French Revolution and the international struggle between France and England, which generated a fierce commercial contest over Hamburg's economy, emerged as serious themes addressed in both men's and women's correspondence. Like their male counterparts, women of the city elite acclaimed the Revolution by participating in Bastille Day parties in 1791 and bemoaned the trial of Louis XVI and the fall of the Girondins in 1793.[30] Engel Christine Westphalen, wife of the wealthy merchant and senator Johann Ernst Friedrich Westphalen, anonymously published a drama about Charlotte Corday that popularized the tragedy of Marat's murderess and generated a Corday cult in Hamburg.[31] The radicalism of the French Revolution prompted public disputes over the meaning of republicanism in Hamburg.

Elise Reimarus engaged in these discussions and political debates by anonymously publishing essays in which she described her understanding of republican citizenship. As a well-educated member of a leading Hamburg family, she exemplifies the ambiguous position that women of her social rank occupied in Hamburg's civic life. In her essays she addressed the issue of women's role in the republic without explicitly challenging women's formal political exclusion. She argued that women's abilities qualify them to participate in public life, but she also declared women's domestic responsibilities equal to men's civic work in contributing to public welfare.[32] Elise Reimarus taught outside the city at an educational institute for girls, founded by her friend, the writer and educator Caroline Rudolphi, and she contributed a significant number of her writings to periodicals such as the *Pädagogische Unterhandlungen* and *Kleine Kinderbibliothek* published by the well-known pedagogue, writer and publisher Joachim Heinrich Campe. Along with essays on the virtues of industry and thrift, Reimarus penned dialogues on education for girls which emphasized social responsibility and practical skills that would prepare them to manage a self-reliant and well-regulated household.[33] She advocated educating children of both sexes to become citizens (*Bürger* and *Bürgerinnen*). Reimarus's writings illustrate her deep understanding of the republic's civic culture. In 1780, for example, she published an article in the journal *Deutsches Museum,* addressing the pursuit of personal pleasure in a republic.[34] In 1791, in her anonymous pamphlet *Freiheit* (*Freedom*), written in the form of a dialogue, she presented an overview of the merits of citizenship (*Bürgerschaft*) in a republican city-state Hamburg. This piece and a later treatise entitled *Versuch eine Läuterung und Vereinfachung der Begriffe von natürlichem Staatsrecht* (Attempt to Explain and Simplify the Concepts Contained in Natural Civil Law) discussed liberty, duty, rights and state authority in a simple and instructive manner. The anonymity of these essays indicated her understanding of the limits of women's scope of public action but diminished neither her acute perception of her city's political culture nor her identification with it.[35]

Through household and community duties, women and men expressed a civic identity that underscored specific republican mores. Despite obvious inequalities between the sexes, Hamburgers expected both women and men to embody the republican virtues and recognized both as contributing to the economic and social well-being of the city through their work in the home, markets, counting houses and city administration. This perception of both sexes as responsible for patriotic values and conduct became apparent at the turn of the century, when the republic experienced a period of economic growth that generated vigorous public discussion of excessive consumption and social frivolity. Indeed, criticism of extravagant lifestyles expanded the discourse on the meaning and practice of patriotism.[36] Social critics lambasted both men and women for abandoning traditional republican values, asserting that conspicuous consumption not only led to bankruptcy, neglect of children and families and mismanagement of households and businesses but would also inevitably damage the prosperity and viability of the republic.[37]

Social critiques charged both sexes with the same vices—frivolity, ostentation and ultimately selfishness—and held both accountable for disregarding the virtues of moderation and diligence along with their civic obligations. Instead of employing essentialist notions of femininity and masculinity, commentators at the end of the eighteenth century assigned men and women separate but complementary responsibilities and obligations according to their social and familial status. These responsibilities and tasks had not yet become linked to physiological differences between the sexes but were legitimized by their distinct social functions. In the republican worldview of this period, men and women were both capable of patriotic conduct and equally responsible for its decline.[38]

War and the militarization of patriotic practice

Between 1792 and 1815 international warfare disrupted daily life and civil society throughout Europe. In Hamburg, the 'French Wars' threatened Hamburg's autonomy and economic prosperity. From 1792 to 1806 Hamburg's leaders sought to negotiate the republic's neutrality rather than defend it with ineffectual fortifications and the civic guard (*Bürgerwache*).

Martial skills and sentiment were scarce in a republic where public service defined virtue. Intent on demonstrating goodwill to all nations, Hamburg destroyed its inconsequential fortifications in 1804. By melting their cannons and transforming the city walls into promenade parks and potato fields, city authorities hoped to portray Hamburg as a haven of free trade and peace. After the decisive defeat of the Prusso-Saxon army in November 1806, however, Imperial troops occupied the Hanseatic cities along with vast territories in northern Germany and Prussia. Following the 1806 Berlin Decrees, Napoleon's Continental System and trade embargo on Britain disrupted commerce and industry; and Hamburg, like other occupied regions, experienced widespread poverty and economic dislocation. Ongoing requisitions, billeting obligations, conscription and exploitative administrative structures, combined with the loss of livelihoods, destroyed an earlier willingness to accommodate French rule. Residents of the city experienced years of severe hardship, as economic warfare and military occupation brought the war into homes, marketplaces, counting houses and seaports. The situation worsened when France annexed the coastal stretch between the Ems and Elbe rivers in December 1810. Hamburg became the seat of the Department of *Elbmündung* under the governance of French Marshal Louis Nicolas Davout.[39]

By March 1813 public hostility and the approaching Russians caused the French to retreat from Hamburg temporarily. Liberated by Russian Cossacks under the leadership of General Friedrich von Tettenborn, Hanseatics in Hamburg and Lübeck formed a volunteer corps, the Hanseatic Legion (*Hanseatische Legion*), and created the Citizens Guard (*Bürgergarde*) to defend their cities from another French conquest. Male inhabitants between 18 and 45 were called upon to serve in the Citizens Guard. Years of economic decline and military occupation combined with the rousing infusion of patriotism associated with the city's March liberation to generate enormous support for the war against the French in North Germany. Fourteen hundred infantry volunteers and 200 cavalry volunteers signed up to form the Hanseatic Legion within days of Hamburg's and Lübeck's liberation. By April, the Legion comprised 3,800 men divided into three battalions of infantry, cavalry and artillery. Up to this point, most Hanseatics had been content to let other Europeans do the fighting while they themselves simply awaited liberation from French rule. But on 30 May 1813, French soldiers retook Hamburg. The poorly equipped Hanseatic Legion and the Citizens Guard could not defend the city from reoccupation. As they abandoned Hamburg to fight another day, leading patriots and their families sought refuge outside the city.[40] The Hanseatic Legion continued the fight with financial support from the British, and men in the Citizens Guard who had fled the city organized the Corps of the Hanseatic Citizens Guard (*Corps der Hanseatischen Bürgergarde*).

The formation of the Hanseatic Legion and the Citizens Guard in March 1813 and their continuation of the struggle after the defeat of 30 May thus represented a rupture in Hamburg's traditional political culture. This break is also visible in Hamburg's vibrant press, at least in the short period of liberation from French rule between 18 March and 30 May 1813 and after the final liberation of the town on 31 May 1814. Freed from imperial censorship, old as well as new publications generated a new patriotic rhetoric in spring 1813, as the recently liberated press actively sought to mobilize the city's population against the French. Political writers provided new forms of patriotic discourse that addressed men and women alike. As in Prussia, sentiment in Hamburg became increasingly militaristic as public discourse explicitly linked patriotic action with defending Hamburg against the French.[41] Jurist and essayist Ferdinand Beneke observed that war had changed Hamburgers and awakened within his compatriots an 'old militaristic yearning for freedom'.[42] Indeed, Beneke reflected on the militarization of public life in his diary when he noted, 'before everything political meant [affairs] associated with Hamburg, now it's military business.'[43] Likewise, Danish envoy Johann Rist observed: 'Tension reigned everywhere in Hamburg...an unusual mixture of military elements and civic bustle, which the city had never experienced before. It was the focal point of all political-mercantile-military relations in the north'.[44]

Described as 'the enthusiasm for arms' to liberate the city, local notions of patriotism were transformed in wartime Hamburg.[45] In the *Liederbuch der Hanseatischen Legion* (Songbook of the Hanseatic Legion), published in April 1813 to support the voluntary corps, the song 'Der Patriot' demonstrated this shift when it asserted that, along with promoting the well-being and prosperity of his city, the patriot now must be willing to fight and die for his home.[46] One contemporary poem entitled 'Bürgersinn und Patriotismus' (Public Spirit and Patriotism) praised a group of young Hamburgers who had left comfortable positions in England to fight under the flag of the Hanseatic Legion.[47] This militarization of patriotic sentiment was also evident in private correspondence. Before joining the Citizens Guard in May, Karl Sieveking, son of enlightened philanthropist and merchant Georg Heinrich Sieveking, who had sought to preserve Hamburg's independence through diplomatic negotiations and bribes, communicated in letters to his mother his conviction that patriotic action required an armed defence of his city. He claimed that only the 'right war' and 'right peace' would secure his hometown.[48] Wealthy merchant Johann Joachim Hanfft exemplified the patriotic ideal by 'abandoning comfort and peace and sacrificing a substantial part of his fortune' to establish, provision and lead his own cavalry squadron under the flag of the Hanseatic Legion.[49]

The patriotic press, as in Prussia, encouraged and celebrated civilian participation in the war effort. Appealing to inhabitants of Hamburg to help equip the Hanseatic Legion, the senate urged Hamburgers to donate 'as much as one's patriotism compels one'.[50] The press played a central role in organizing the state's campaign to collect money and matériel in spring 1813 to equip the volunteer corps and the militia. In fact, all donations to the Hanseatic Legion were recorded in the local press as 'Patriotic Contributions'. Journals listed each benefactor of the Hanseatic Legion, noting in particular the children who emptied small savings accounts, wives who donated wedding rings and old women who knitted stockings and sewed flags as exemplars of patriotic commitment. Female domestic servants in Hamburg collected and donated over 10,300 *Mark Banco* to the cause. Hamburgers from every level of society rallied to support the Legion. Without such contributions from the civilian population, the Legion could not have been outfitted and equipped.[51]

Patriotic action was clearly not for men alone. In fact, as men were called on to take up arms to defend their freedom and independence, women were summoned to support the war in a variety of other ways. Women were urged to sacrifice their material belongings and pleasures in order to outfit the soldiers protecting their beloved hometown.[52] Spouses of patriotic activists, Karoline Beneke and Karoline Perthes volunteered to nurse wounded soldiers and sew flags and standards.[53] Voluntary recruitment relied heavily on patriotic appeals, and women reinforced these appeals by encouraging their men to fight. Especially following the fall of Hamburg to the French in May 1813, the Hanseatic Legion relied on women's patriotism to persuade them to release their sons and husbands for the defence of the city and to think of their 'ancestors, bridegrooms and husbands' as they donated their jewellery and treasured possessions to supply the Legion.[54] Women recognized their role in supporting the war, as this proclamation of March 1813 by the Lübeck Women's Association clearly illustrates:

> In all times, whenever a beloved Fatherland liberates itself from ignominious chains and is rescued from a powerful and urgent danger, it has been the spirit of women who awakened patriotism, valour, courage and endurance in the souls of men and decided the direction of these virtues.... then each of you, women, be you mother or daughter, wife or sister, relation or bride, arouse with fiery passion in the circle of your family life love for God and Fatherland.'[55]

The welfare of the republic required women to sacrifice their husbands, sons, fathers and material goods at a time of increasing distress during Hamburg's second occupation. Many women were compelled to flee the city with their families after the return of French troops in May. Scattered as war refugees, many were left alone to provide for their families in crowded quarters in the neighbouring cities of Altona, Kiel, Bremen and Lübeck and nearby small towns, such as Bergedorf and Buxtehude. Kiel was overrun with 7,000 refugees from Hamburg, and chronic shortages of potatoes, bread, coffee and wood made daily life a hardship.[56] Women and families, who remained within the city, had an even harder time due to siege conditions, limited food and epidemic disease. In late December 1813, Marshal Davout expelled between 22,000 and 25,000 unprovisioned residents from Hamburg, many of whom became utterly dependent on charity. Hamburg's women and their families did not have to face combat on the battlefields to experience the consequences of war. Even women of means confronted the hardships of the war as they welcomed refugees into summer homes along the Elbe and raised money for their maintenance.[57] All of these women worried about the fate of husbands, fathers, brothers, sons and lovers who had volunteered to fight the French. Pregnant Karoline Perthes, for example, cared for her seven children, two sisters and parents while sharing tight quarters with another family in refugee-crowded Kiel. She wrote to her husband, who had joined the Hanseatic Legion and was also a member of the government in exile, the Hanseatic Directory, that she faced 'every hour with anxiety and worry'.[58] For these women and their families, the combat front and home front remained closely entwined.[59]

Women's public writings and private correspondence alike demonstrate the militarization of patriotism. In neighbouring Bremen, renowned pedagogue Betty Gleim anonymously published a pamphlet in 1814, *Was hat das wiedergeborne Deutschland von seinen Frauen zu fordern*? (What does Reborn Germany Demand of its Women?) in which she called on women to encourage their men to fight, 'Stir their courage and strengthen their hearts'.[60] In Hamburg, Engel Christine Westphalen published a collection of poetry and songs, dedicated to all Hanseatic soldiers, that glorified the battle against the French. Much of her work articulated the difficulties Hamburg endured during French occupation and the city's struggle for liberation. Her poems and songs celebrated the soldier willing to die for freedom and fatherland. In 'Lied der jungen Hanseaten' (Song of the Young Hanseatic) she assumed the first-person voice of the youthful warriors: 'We gladly choose a hero's death, rather than live the shame of slavery anew; to battle rings out the call, until the last shackle breaks'.[61] She also commemorated those fallen during the war as worthy heroes who gave their all for freedom.[62] In fact, Westphalen's celebration of these citizen-soldiers suggested that only those who bore arms to fight for their homes, freedom and honour could truly call themselves men.[63] Such enthusiastic support for battle against the French, expressed in the press and other printed ephemera, reflected a new martial patriotism. In letters to her brother, Wilhelmine Amsinck described her eagerness for the defeat of Napoleon, but she assured him that she would not follow the example of Anna Lühring, a seventeen-year-old dressmaker from Bremen who had disguised herself as a man and joined the Lützow Corps in 1813. Wilhelmine Amsinck could not reconcile herself to denouncing her femininity and considered other ways in which her sex could 'devote itself to our fatherland'.[64]

Though women openly expressed their passionate support of the armed struggle, few of them experienced combat firsthand. Like Wilhelmine Amsinck, most women recognized their ability to contribute tangibly to the war effort through practical means. On 21 March 1813, Elisabeth von Struve and Philippine Kleudgen established the Hamburg Women's Association (*Hamburger Frauenvereins*) at the Church of St Katharine to sew shirts and knit socks for the Hanseatic Legion, and the organization expanded its service dramatically over the course of the war.[65] Women's wartime activities to supply the volunteer corps and local militia with uniforms, sew flags and standards, donate and collect money for the Legion, nurse the wounded and find shelter for war victims and refugees demonstrated women's solidarity with the armed militia and its mission to defend the city. In these many practical functions, women claimed a role for themselves during the Anti-Napoleonic Wars.[66]

Reflecting the cooperative efforts of the Hanseatic Legion and the Citizens Guard, women's associations from Hamburg, Lübeck and Bremen worked together to provision the men of these military units and later to care for Hanseatic refugees and wounded soldiers.[67] In Bremen, women formed an association to collect coin, medals, silver and gold to equip the Legion; they also established another patriotic association to collect and send medical supplies to the Legion in the field. Henriette Klugkist attempted to establish a field hospital in Bremen.[68] In Lübeck, women worked with the Provisioning Commission (*Unterstützungs-Commission*) to feed, clothe and nurse the 5,495 refugees that arrived there between December 1813 and June 1814.[69] Women, like their male counterparts, celebrated German cultural nationalism and experienced intense religious sentiments associated with wartime mobilization, but their work and allegiance remained local and regional. Hamburg's tradition of republican patriotism precluded a shift of patriotic sentiments from the city-state to an abstract German nation.[70] Indeed, cooperation among the women's associations in Hamburg, Bremen and Lübeck in provisioning the Legion and caring for war refugees underscored a growing Hanseatic solidarity, reflected in the regional militias.[71]

Women's patriotic activities were not controversial in Hamburg. In fact, the press recognized and celebrated women's patriotic activism. One journal recounted the dedication at St Michaelis Church of five flags for the Hanseatic Legion in mid-April, observing that the women who had produced them had distinguished themselves by their 'true patriotic enthusiasm'.[72] Engel Christine Westphalen opened her collection of wartime poetry with a tribute to the noble work of the Women's Associations.[73] Journalists documented and celebrated such heroines as Anna Lühring and the anonymous maid who, during a battle near Lüneburg, retrieved weapons and ammunition from fallen French soldiers for Russian and Prussian troops.[74] These women were the exception, however, to the broader female experience of supporting the war by ministering to the needs of soldiers' families, the wounded and refugees. Women professed and on occasion participated in the passions of battle, but their own patriotic activities clearly fit within a longstanding tradition of service for the common good.

After the first defeat of the French in May 1814, women warmly welcomed their soldiers home. In May the Corps of the Hanseatic Citizens Guard and in June the Hanseatic Legion paraded through the streets of Hamburg, where young girls clad in white greeted them with garlands and flowers. Attired like brides, these young women symbolized the city's honour defended and preserved by the returning heroic warriors, illustrating how women allegorically embodied the city.[75] Patriotic speeches, toasts, songs, poetry and sermons filled the air and marketplace stalls, and city residents voluntarily illuminated their homes to honor the return of allied and local soldiers alike. Without any assistance or funding from the reinstated city authorities, the men and women of Hamburg organized a huge feast for the Legion and its officers, described by one contemporary as a 'community party' (*Volksfest*).[76] In addition to demonstrating women's patriotic sentiments and their symbolic association with the city, these popular celebrations represented a transition in women's patriotic activism as they shifted their attention from provisioning soldiers to caring for veterans, their families, the wounded, returning refugees and other victims of war.

Women used the welcome celebration for the Hanseatic Legion in June 1814 to seek charity for war victims. During the thanksgiving service at St Michaelis Church, sisters and other female relatives of the soldiers collected donations at the church doors and later went house to house soliciting contributions for the families of soldiers who did not return.[77] The women of Hamburg petitioned the senate to take up a collection for war widows, orphans and disabled veterans on the anniversary of the Hanseatic Legion's return, and in 1817 this collection became an annual state practice that continued until 1863.[78]

Within months of the city-state's liberation in 1814, the senate abruptly disbanded the Hanseatic Legion and the Citizens Guard with minimal compensation. Many female patriotic activities initiated during the war, however, continued in the Hanseatic city. Hamburg's Women's Association proceeded to raise money and develop programmes for the benefit of disabled veterans, widows and orphans.[79] Throughout the summer of 1815 the Women's Association in Bremen collected not just money for distribution to veterans and their dependents but also medical supplies for delivery to field hospitals in Aachen.[80] By 1816, Hamburg's Women's Association had been subdivided into six battalions, mirroring the organization of the new Hamburg Civic Militia (*Bürgerwehr*), and had begun to document its activities to raise money and collect material goods for veterans, their dependents and the deserving poor.[81] In 1865 the statutes of the Hamburg Women's Association proudly asserted that the organization founded in 1813 had accomplished its mission to support soldiers and their families during and after the war. They highlighted their postwar service to veterans and the worthy poor, in particular the founding of a school for the daughters of veterans.[82] The ongoing work of the Women's Association in Hamburg is noteworthy since most of the wartime women's associations in other parts of German Central Europe failed to survive the postwar period. In Prussia, for example, only 10 per cent of the nearly 600 patriotic women's associations formed during the wars between 1813 and 1815 continued after the war.[83] Moreover, the Women's Association also set the precedent in establishing material support for veterans and their families. Four years after the war, veterans founded the Hanseatic Association (*Hanseatische Verein*), and in 1827 they inaugurated the Friendship Club of Hanseatic Comrades from 1813 and 1814 (*Freundschafts-Club der hanseatischen Kampfgenossen von 1813 und 1814*). Originally social in nature, both associations eventually developed programmes to benefit disabled veterans and their dependants.[84] These organizations were, however, simply following the model and practices established in 1813 by the Women's Association.

Conclusion

Patriotism, manifested as voluntary service in the public interest, had a long tradition in the Hanseatic city-state. Although their spheres of action were often very different, women as well as men engaged in the rhetoric and practice of patriotism founded on republican virtue. This pre-war conception of patriotic practice emphasized the shared goals and separate but complementary obligations of women and men in the republican community.

The crisis of occupation and war, however, associated particular expressions of patriotism with specific gender roles. The Wars of Liberation redefined and gendered patriotic activism more sharply than before,[85] thus creating a rupture in traditional notions of communal patriotism in Hamburg. Both men and women voiced the new martial patriotism, but women rarely engaged in combat; rather, they demonstrated their patriotism in philanthropic activities that drew on the established republican tradition of serving the common good. War demanded from Hamburg's men new forms of patriotic activism, such as joining the local and regional militias to defend the city from the French. While only men expressed their patriotic vigour in the armed defence of their homes and city, women applied their energies to provisioning soldiers and caring for the victims of war—the wounded, disabled, widowed, orphaned and displaced.

When the war ended, women's patriotic activism moved quickly into the realm of poor relief and other public charity work. Republican traditions and virtues in the Hanseatic city provided women with clearly defined public duties that expanded during the war. Women's mobilization and the growth of their wartime roles set new precedents for their patriotic service later in the nineteenth century. In 1831, for example, Amelia Sieveking established the Female Association for the Care of the Poor and Sick in response to the cholera epidemic.[86] Unlike women in other regions of German Central Europe, the women of Hamburg remained active in the public sphere long after the Wars of Liberation had been won, reflecting both their patriotism and the republican political tradition of their city-state.

Acknowledgements

This chapter is a revised version of my article 'Republican Traditions: Patriotism, Gender, and War in Hamburg, 1750–1815', *European History Quarterly* 37/4 (2007): 582–602. My thanks to editor Lucy Riall at *EHQ* for her kind permission to reprint the article; to John Lambertson, Karen Hagemann and Jane Rendall for their helpful comments on the revision; and to 'Hamburger Stiftung zur Förderung von Wissenschaft und Kultur—Beneke Edition' for giving me access to the Beneke diaries and correspondence.

Notes

1. *Wöchentliche gemeinnützige Nachrichten von und für Hamburg* (hereafter *GNH*) no. 54, 24, March 1813.
2. Letters from Wilhelmine Amsinck to Wilhelm Amsinck, 6 December 1814. Staatsarchiv Hamburg (hereafter Sta Hbg), 622–1 Familie Amsinck, I. 11 f.
3. Karen Hagemann, '*Mannlicher Muth und Teutsche Ehre': Nation, Militär und Geschlecht in der Zeit der Antinapoleonischen Kriege Preußens* (Paderborn, 2002); idem, 'Female Patriots: Women, War and the Nation in the Period of the Prussian-German Anti-Napoleonic Wars', *Gender & History* 16/2 (2004): 397–424; Jean H. Quataert, *Staging Philanthropy: Patriotic Women and the National Imagination in Dynastic Germany, 1813–1916* (Ann Arbor, 2001); Dirk Alexander Reder, *Frauenbewegung und Nation: Patriotische Frauenvereine in Deutschland im frühen 19. Jahrhundert* (Cologne, 1998).
4. Ute Frevert, *A Nation in Barracks: Modern Germany, Military Conscription and Civil Society*, trans. Andrew Boreham with Daniel Brückenhaus (Oxford, 2004), 32.
5. See Sarah Knott and Barbara Taylor (eds), *Women, Gender, and Enlightenment* (Basingstoke, 2005); and Karen Hagemann and Jean H. Quataert (eds), *Gendering Modern German History: Rewriting Historiography* (New York, 2007), 39–62 and 107–128.
6. Lynn Hunt, *Politics, Culture, and Class in the French Revolution* (Berkeley, 1984), 20–21.
7. Heinrich Buse, 'Patriotismus und Offentlichkeit', in *Volk—Nation—Vaterland*, ed. Ulrich Hermann (Hamburg, 1996), 67–88; Otto Dann et al. (eds), *Patriotismus und Nationsbildung am Ende des Heiligen Römischen Reiches* (Cologne, 2003).
8. For more on this concept in the German discourse of the time, see Hagemann, '*Mannlicher Muth*', 271–350; and idem, 'Of "Manly Valor" and "German Honor": Nation, War, and Masculinity in the Age of the Prussian Uprising against Napoleon', *Central European History* 30/2 (1997): 187–220.
9. Heinz Schilling, *Religion, Political Culture, and the Emergence of Early Modern Society: Essays in German and Dutch History* (Leiden, 1992), 4–13.
10. Categories of citizenship (*Bürgerschaft*) in Hamburg were based on the size and nature of one's business and the amount of dues one paid. For more on this

topic, see Katherine Aaslestad, *Place and Politics: Local Identity, Civic Culture, and German Nationalism in North Germany during the Revolutionary Era* (Leiden, 2005), 35–45; and Franklin Kopitzsch, 'Zwischen Hauptrezeß und Franzosenzeit, 1712 und 1806', in *Hamburg: Geschichte der Stadt und ihrer Bewohner*, ed. Werner Jochmann and Hans-Dieter Loose, 2 vols (Hamburg, 1982), vol. 1, 351–414, 366. For a useful discussion of the contemporary discourse on *Bürgerschaft* and *Staatsbürgerschaft* in Prussia, see Karen Hagemann, 'The First Citizen of the State: Paternal Masculinity, Patriotism, and Citizenship in Early Nineteenth-Century Prussia', in *Representing Masculinity: Male Citizenship in Modern Western Culture*, ed. Stefan Dudink et al. (Basingstoke, 2008), 67–88.

11. Thomas Nugent, *Travels Through Germany: Containing Observations on Customs, Manners, Religion, Government, Commerce, Arts, and Antiquities...*, 2 vols (London, 1768), vol. 1, 58; J. P. Willebrand, *Hamburgs Annehmlichkeiten von einem Ausländer beschrieben* (Hamburg, 1772), 63.
12. Johann Carl Daniel Curio, *Hamburg und Altona* 2 (1803): 78; see also Aaslestad, *Place and Politics*, 38–39.
13. Mary Lindemann, 'Fundamental Values: Political Culture in Eighteenth-Century Germany', in *Patriotism, Cosmopolitanism, and National Culture: Public Culture in Hamburg, 1700–1933*, ed. Peter Uwe Hohendahl (Amsterdam, 2003), 17–32.
14. Mary Lindemann, *Patriots and Paupers: Hamburg, 1712–1830* (Oxford, 1990), 102, 154–163; Frank Hatje, 'Das Armenwesen in Hamburg und die Ausbreitung der Aufklärung in Bürgertum und Unterschichten zwischen Integration und Abgrenzung', in *Das Volk im Visier der Aufklärung: Studien zur Popularisierung der Aufklärung im späten 18. Jahrhundert*, ed. Anne Conrad et al. (Hamburg, 1998), 179–197.
15. Judith A. Vega, 'Feminist Republicanism and the Political Perception of Gender', in *Republicanism: A Shared European Heritage*, ed. Martin van Gelderen and Quentin Skinner, 2 vols (Cambridge, UK, 2002), vol. 2, 157–174, 160.
16. Lindemann, *Patriots and Paupers*, 79; Rudolf Vierhaus, 'Patriotismus: Begriff und Realität einer moralisch-politischen Haltung', in *Deutsche patriotische und gemeinnützige Gesellschaften,* ed idem (Munich, 1980), 9–29.
17. Ibid.; Frank Hatje, ' "Ehrenamt und Gemeinnützigkeit": Zwischen Familientradition und Geselligkeit, Hamburg, 1740–1840', in *Eliten um 1800: Erfahrungshorizonte—Verhaltensweisen—Handlungsmöglichkeiten*, ed. Anja V. Hartmann et al. (Mainz, 2000), 201–229; idem, 'Zwischen Republik und Karitas: karitative Ehrneamtlichkeit in Hamburg des 18. und 19. Jahrhunderts', *Westfälische Forschungen* 55 (2005): 239–266; Franklin Kopitzsch, 'Die Hamburgische Gesellschaft zur Beförderung der Künst und nützlichen Gewerbe im Zeitalter der Aufklärung: Ein Überblick', in Vierhaus, *Deutsche patriotische*, 71–118.
18. Heide Wunder, *He is the Sun, She is the Moon: Women in Early Modern Germany*, trans. Thomas Dunlap (Cambridge, MA, 1998), 203–207; Marion W. Gray, *Productive Men, Reproductive Women: The Agrarian Household and the Emergence of Separate Spheres during the German Enlightenment* (New York, 2000), 123–126; Karen Hagemann, 'Familie—Staat—Nation: Das aufklärerische Projekt der "Bürgergesellschaft" in geschlechtergeschichtlicher Perspektive', in *Europäische Zivilgesellschaft in Ost und West: Begriff, Geschichte, Chancen*, ed. Manfred Hildermeier et al. (Frankfurt, 2000), 57–84.
19. Karin Sträter, *Frauenbriefe als Medium bürgerlicher Öffentlichkeit: Eine Untersuchung anhand von Quellen aus dem Hamburger Raum in der zweiten Hälfte des 18. Jahrhunderts* (Frankfurt, 1991), 90–96.

20. August Ferdinand Cranz, *Ueber Sitten, Gebräuche und Gewohnheiten als drittes Schreiben an einen Freund in Berlin* (Hamburg, 1785), 23–24; Sträter, *Frauenbriefe*, 107–112; Andrea van Dülmen ed., *Frauenleben im 18. Jahrhundert* (Munich, 1992), 108–109, 160–161; Anne-Charlott Trepp, *Sanfte Männlichkeit und selbständige Weiblichkeit: Frauen und Männer im Hamburger Bürgertum zwischen 1770 und 1840* (Göttingen, 1996), 240–255.
21. Vega, 'Feminist Republicanism', 164.
22. Wunder, *He is the Sun*, 203; Ulrike Gleixner and Marion W. Gray, 'Introduction: Gender in Transition', in *Gender in Transition: Discourse and Practice in German Speaking Europe*, ed. Ulrike Gleixner and Marion W. Gray (Ann Arbor, 2006), 1–24, 6.
23. Trepp, *Sanfte Männlichkeit*, 250.
24. Ute Planert, 'Vater Staat und Mutter Germania: Zur Politisierung des weiblichen Geschlechts im 19. und 20 Jahrhundert', in *Nation, Politik und Geschlecht: Frauenbewegungen und Nationalismus in der Moderne*, ed. Ute Planert (Frankfurt, 2000), 15–65, 25–26.
25. See Suzanne Desan, 'The Politics of Intimacy: Marriage and Citizenship in the French Revolution', in Knott and Taylor, *Women, Gender, and Enlightenment*, 230–648.
26. Brigitte Tolkemitt, 'Knotenpunkte im Beziehungsnetz der Gebildeten: Die gemischte Geselligkeit in den offenen Häusern der Hamburger Familien Reimarus und Sieveking', in *Ordnung, Politik und Gesellikeit der Geschlechter im 18. Jahrhundert*, ed. Ulrike Weckel et al. (Göttingen, 1998), 175–202; Trepp, *Sanfte Männlichkeit*, 388–390, 392–396.
27. Franklin Kopitzsch, *Grundzüge einer Sozialgeschichte der Aufklärung in Hamburg und Altona* (Hamburg, 1982), 573–574 and 705–707; Trepp, *Sanfte Männlichkeit*, 265–283; Sträter, *Frauenbriefe*, 4–8 and 55–80; Tolkemitt, 'Knotenpunkte', 167–202.
28. Almut Spalding, *Elise Reimarus (1735–1805), The Muse of Hamburg: A Woman of the German Enlightenment* (Würzburg, 2005), 182–196.
29. Trepp, *Sanfte Männlichkeit*, 269–280; Kopitzsch, *Grundzüge*, 596–597 and 705–709; Sträter, *Frauenbriefe*, 71–84; *Caspar Voght und sein Hamburger Freundeskreis: Briefe aus den Jahren 1785 bis 1812 an Johanna Margaretha Sieveking, geb. Reimarus*, ed. Annelise Tecke (Hamburg, 1964).
30. Horst Gronemeyer and Harald Weigel, *Paris an der Alster: die Französische Revolution in Hamburg—Vertretung der Freien- und Hansestadt Hamburg* (Herzberg, 1989), 25; Adolf Freiherr von Knigge, *Aus einer alten Kiste: Originalbriefe, Handschriften und Dokumente aus dem Nachlasse eines bekannten Mannes* (Leipzig, 1853), 220; Sträter, *Frauenbriefe*, 83–84.
31. [Engel Christine Westphalen], *Charlotte Corday: Tragödie in fünf Akten mit Chören* (Hamburg, 1804). See Inge Stephan, 'Die erhabene Männin Corday: Christine Westphalens Drama "Charlotte Corday" (1804) und der Corday-Kult am Ende des 18. Jahrhunderts', in *Sie, und nicht Wir: Die Französische Revolution und ihre Wirkung auf Norddeutschland und das Reich*, ed. Arno Herzig (Hamburg, 1989), 177–206.
32. Spalding, *Elise Reimarus*, 130–134.
33. Ibid. 248, 251–253. See also Michael Nagel, '"... Darum, Oh ihr Jungfrauen, weidet Eure Seele nur auf classischem Boden ...": Die Bremer Pädagogin Betty Gleim (1781–1827) in ihren Gedanken zur Jugendlektüre', in *Klassizismus in Bremen: Formen bürgerlicher Kultur*, ed. Martina Rudloff (Bremen, 1994), 213–222.

34. 'Philolaus und Kriton: Ein Gespräch aus dem Griechischen', *Deutsches Museum* (6 June 1780): 547–551.
35. Spalding, *Elise Reimarus*, 280–291.
36. Katherine B. Aaslestad, '*Sitten und Mode*: Fashion, Gender, and Public Identities in Hamburg at the Turn of the Nineteenth Century', in Gleixner and Grey, *Gender in Transition*, 282–318.
37. 'Hamburgischer Gemeingeist, kann man in unsern Zeiten noch annehmen?', *Hamburg und Altona* 2 (1802): 209–217; 'Hamburgs alte und neue Zeit: Eine Parallele', *Hamburg und Altona* 2 (1803): 292–293; 'Ueber Luxus, besonders in Beziehung auf Hamburg', *Hamburg und Altona* 5 (1806): 313–324.
38. For a useful discussion of the contemporary discourse on the gender order and its change in the German-speaking lands, see Claudia Honegger, *Die Ordnung der Geschlechter: Die Wissenschaften vom Menschen und das Weib, 1750–1850* (Frankfurt, 1991); Karin Hausen, 'Family and Role-Division: The Polarisation of Sexual Stereotypes in the Nineteenth Century—An Aspect of the Dissociation of Work and Family Life', in *The German Family: Essays on the Social History of the Family in Nineteenth- and Twentieth-Century Germany*, ed. Richard J. Evans and W. R. Lee (London, 1981), 51–83.
39. See Katherine Aaslestad, 'War without Battles: Civilian Experience of French Economic Warfare in the Hanseatic Cities, 1806–1812', in *Soldiers, Citizens and Civilians: Experiences and Perceptions of the Revolutionary and Napoleonic Wars, 1790–1820*, ed. Alan Forrest et al. (Basingstoke, 2009), 118–136.
40. See Karen Hagemann, 'Die Perthes im Krieg: Kriegserfahrungen und –erinnerungen einer Hamburger Bürgerfamilie in der "Franzosenzeit"', in *Eliten im Wandel: Gesellschaftliche Führungsschichten im 19. und 20. Jahrhundert*, ed. Karl-Christian Führer et al. (Munster, 2004), 72–101, 79–86; idem, 'Reconstructing "Front" and "Home": Gendered Experiences and Memories of the German Wars against Napoleon—A Case Study', *War in History* 16/1 (2009): 25–50, 32–39.
41. Hagemann, '*Mannlicher Muth*', 271–350; idem, 'Francophobia and Patriotism: Anti-French Images and Sentiments in Prussia and Northern Germany during the Anti-Napoleonic Wars', *French History* 18/4 (2004): 404–425.
42. Ferdinand Beneke, *Briefe eines Hamburgischen Ausgewanderten im Anfang des Jahres 1814: Zweytes Stück* (Hamburg, 1814), 3.
43. Sta Hbg, Familienarchiv Beneke C 2, Tage Buch von 1813, 20 April 1813.
44. *Johann Georg Rist in Hamburg: Aus seinen Lebenserinnerungen*, ed. G. Poel (Hamburg, 1913), 248.
45. Beneke refers to the 'Eifer der Bewaffnung' in his manuscript, Sta Hbg, 622–1 Familie Beneke C-15.
46. *Liederbuch der Hanseatischen Legion gewidmet* (Hamburg, 1813), 145–147.
47. 'Bürgersinn und Patriotismus', *Die neue Biene*, 27 March 1813.
48. Sta Hbg, 622–1 Karl Sieveking E-6, Briefwechsel mit seiner Mutter: Karl Sieveking to Johanna Sieveking, 1 March and 14 May 1813.
49. 'Johann Joachim Hanfft', *Die neue Biene*, 31 March 1813.
50. *GNH*, 9 April 1813.
51. 'Patriotische Beyträge für die Hanseatische Legion', *GNH*, 8 May 1813. Karen Hagemann describes very similar practices in Prussia during this period; see '*Mannlicher Muth*', 396–426.
52. *GNH*, 24 March 1813.
53. Sta Hbg, Familienarchiv Beneke C 2, Tage Buch von 1813, entry for 21 April 1813, Rudolf Kayser (ed.), *Karoline Perthes im Briefwechsel mit ihrer Familie und ihren Freunden* (Hamburg, 1926); for more, see Hagemann, 'Reconstructing'. On the

importance of the female flag consecrations, see Chapter 14 by Karen Hagemann in this volume.
54. 'Ueber die Hanseatische Legion', Bremen, 22 November 1813, in Sta Hbg, 622–1 Lorenz-Meyer, CVll e.
55. 'Eine Wort an deutsche Frauen und Mädchen, Im März 1813', in *Der Frauenverein von 1813 während der ersten 100 Jahre seines Bestehens*, ed. Dora Eschenburg ([Hamburg] 1913).
56. Dieter Kienitz, *Der Kosakenwinter in Schleswig-Holstein 1813/14* (Heide, 2000), 68; Otto Mathies (ed.), *Aus der Franzosenzeit in Hamburg von Wilhelm Perthes und Agnes Perthes* (Hamburg, 1910), 54–85.
57. See Renate Hauschild-Thiessen, 'In der belagerten Stadt; Tagebuchaufzeichnungen von Henriette Brock aus dem Jahre 1814', *Hamburgische Geschichts- und Heimatblätter* 10 (1977): 45–68; Marianne Prell, *Erinnerungen aus der Franzosenzeit in Hamburg von 1806 bis 1814* (Hamburg, 1913); Hans Nirrnheim (ed.), 'Briefe von Peter Godeffroy und George Parish aus den Jahren 1813 und 1814', *Zeitschrift des Vereins für Hamburgische Geschichte* 18 (1914): 115–169; Carl Amsinck (ed.), 'Elizabeth Dorothea Mollers Tagebuch aus der Belagerung Hamburgs in den Jahren 1813 und 1814', *Zeitschrift des Vereins für Hamburgische Geschichte* 11 (1903): 184–226.
58. Kayser, *Karoline Perthes*, 69.
59. Ibid. 27.
60. Dieter Buse, 'Finding the Nation in Bremen: The Lower Class and Women after Napoleonic Occupation', *Canadian Journal of History* (April 2005): 1–23, 12–13; see also Hagemann, 'Female Patriots'.
61. Engel Christine Westphalen, *Gesänge der Zeit* (Hamburg, 1815), 58.
62. Ibid. 71.
63. Ibid. 119–120. See also Karin Baumgarten, 'Valorous Masculinities and Patriotism in the Texts of Early Nineteenth-Century German Women Writers', *German Studies Review* 31/2 (2008): 325–344.
64. Sta Hbg, 622–1 Familie Amsinck, I. 11 fo.: Letter from Wilhelmine Amsinck to Wilhelm Amsinck, 30 March 1815. For more on Anna Lühring and other female 'amazones' in the Prussian and German armies of the time, see Karen Hagemann, '"Heroic Virgins" and "Bellicose Amazons": Armed Women, the Gender Order, and the German Public during and after the Anti-Napoleonic Wars', *European History Quarterly* 37/4 (2007): 507–527.
65. Prell, *Erinnerungen*, 60; Elise Campe, *Hamburgs außerordentliche Begebenheiten und Schicksale in den Jahren 1813–1815* (Hamburg, 1908), 19; Herbert Freudenthal, *Vereine in Hamburg* (Hamburg 1968), 98–99.
66. See also Reder, *Frauenbewegung*; Quataert, *Staging*, 21–52; Hagemann, 'Female Patriots'.
67. Eschenburg, *Der Frauenverein*, 9–37.
68. See Elisabeth Meyer-Renschhausen, *Weibliche Kultur und soziale Arbeit: Eine Geschichte der Frauenbewegung am Beispiel Bremens, 1810–1927* (Cologne, 1989), 46–49.
69. *Allgemeiner Bericht über die Wirklichkeit der Unterstützungs-Commission zu Lübeck für die vertriebenen Hamburger von 1sten Januar bis Ende July 1814* (Roemhild, 1815).
70. Helga Schutte Watt, 'Sophie La Roche as a German Patriot', in *Gender and Germanness: Cultural Productions of Nation*, ed. Patricia Herminghouse and Magda Mueller (Providence, 1997), 36–50.
71. See Hagemann, 'Female Patriots'.
72. *Der Deutsche Beobachter*, 22 April 1813.
73. Westphalen, *Gesänge*, i–ii.

74. 'Patriotismus eines deutschen Dienstmädchens', *Die neue Biene*, 8 May 1813. This article probably refers to Johanna Stegen, who collected cartridges from the field of battle to aid in defending Lüneburg. See Karen Hagemann, 'Das Heldenmädchen von Lüneburg', in *Geschichte in Geschichten; Ein historisches Lesebuch*, ed. Barbara Duden et al. (Frankfurt, 2003), 253–260.
75. For more on the welcome ceremonies, see Chapter 14 by Karen Hagemann in this volume; idem, 'Of "Manly Valor"'; and Frevert, *Nation*, 34.
76. Karl Gries to Deiderich Gries, July 1814, in Heinrich Reincke (ed.), 'Aus dem Briefwechsel von Karl und Diederich Gries 1796 bis 1819', *Zeitschrift des Vereins für Hamburgische Geschichte* 25 (1924): 226–277, 266.
77. Ibid.; Sta Hbg, 111–1 Senat Cl VIII Lit Ha Vol I 6b, No 4.
78. Sta Hbg, 111–1 Senat Cl VII Lit Gb No 9. Vol O, Fasc 1 and Fasc 2.
79. 'Der Hamburgische Frauen-Verein, zum Besten verwundeter und hülfsbedürftiger Krieger', *GNH*, 4 May 1815; 'Hamburg Frauenverein', *GNH*, 29 July 1815; 'Lotterie des Frauen-Vereins weibliche Hand-und Kunst Arbeit', *GNH*, 28 September 1815; and Freudenthal, *Vereine*, 99.
80. See *Bremer Wöchenlichen Nachrichten*, 10 July–10 August 1815.
81. *Bericht des Hamburgischen Frauen-Vereins über seine bisherige Wirksamkeit und Plan zur Fortsetzung derselben: 1816 September* (Hamburg, 1816), 3–6.
82. *Statuten des Hamburger Frauen-Vereins von 1813* (Hamburg, 1865), Sta Hbg, 111–1 Senat Cl VII Lit Qa Nr 3 Vol 14.
83. Karen Hagemann argues in 'Female Patriots' that Prussian women's associations were accepted by the public only in the extraordinary times of a 'War of Liberation'; see also Reder, *Frauenbewegung*.
84. Freudenthal, *Vereine*, 96–97.
85. Karen Hagemann, 'A Valorous *Volk* Family: The Nation, the Military, and the Gender Order in Prussia in the Time of the Anti-Napoleonic Wars, 1806–15', in *Gendered Nations: Nationalism and Gender Order in the Long Nineteenth Century*, ed. Ida Blom et al. (Oxford, 2000), 179–206; Dirk Alexander Reder, '"Natur und Sitte verbieten uns die Waffen der Zerstörung zu führen..."': Patriotische Frauen zwischen Friede und Krieg', in *Kriegsbereitschaft und Friedensordnung in Deutschland, 1800–1814*, ed. Jost Düffler (Munster, 1995), 170–182.
86. Catherine M. Prelinger, *Charity, Challenge, and Change: Religious Dimensions of the Mid-Nineteenth-Century Women's Movement in Germany* (New York, 1987).

12
'Thinking Minds of Both Sexes': Patriotism, British Bluestockings and the Wars against Revolutionary America and France, 1775–1802

Emma V. Macleod

'Without intending it, I have slid into politics', wrote the poet Anna Seward at the end of a long letter to a regular correspondent, Colonel Dowdeswell of Shrewsbury, in November 1797. 'In a period so momentous,' she explained, 'their attraction, to thinking minds of both sexes, is resistless.'[1] This quotation might suggest that Seward had forgotten herself temporarily to make a brief aside that touched on some political question. In fact, her whole letter had been devoted to discussing the war against revolutionary France—her enjoyment of a concert in Birmingham given to celebrate Admiral Duncan's victory at Camperdown the previous month; the civility of the eighty French prisoners of war exiled in her home town of Lichfield in Staffordshire for the past ten months; the prisoners' inhospitable reception by most of the other residents of Lichfield and their recent removal to Liverpool jail; her musing on the sufferings of British prisoners of war in France; the miseries and evils of war in general; and the prejudice and corruption of the Pitt administration in its refusal to seek peace with France sooner. The 'slide' into politics that she mentions therefore represents no momentary lapse but rather a natural shift from describing her experience, as a genteel woman, of the British home front during the war against revolutionary France—through appropriately feminine expressions of anxiety about British prisoners and the horrors of war—to clearly political judgement regarding the errors of government policy. The statement that she had found herself writing about politics 'without intending it' may imply, however, that such political comment was not necessarily regarded as suitable from women.

Harriet Guest, among others, has pointed out the difficulty of defining 'the nature of patriotism, and the form in which it might be appropriate to women' in Britain in this period, in which national politics were increasingly factionalized, and in which an increasing emphasis was placed on the domestic roles of middle-class women.[2] This chapter considers some of the forms of patriotism which have previously been identified as open to British women during the wars of the late eighteenth century and suggests another, which may be described as 'independent patriotism': a non-gendered, non-partisan engagement with the political affairs of one's country. It does so by focusing mainly on the correspondence of two English bluestockings (members of a network of literary salons and correspondence),[3] Anna Seward and Elizabeth Carter, each with clearly different political proclivities, and examining the ways in which they discussed these conflicts.

The Revolutionary Wars took place during a period of crystallizing political connections in Britain. The war against revolutionary America was fought by the administration of Lord North, and opposed in Parliament by groups of Whigs following the leadership of the Marquis of Rockingham and the Earl of Chatham (the elder Pitt), respectively. Both groups believed initially that the British government ought to conciliate rather than coerce the American colonists and, later (in the Chathamites' case, after the death of their leader), that independence was inevitable and that amicable relations should be restored as soon as possible. By the time the Revolution in France broke out, William Pitt, the younger son of the Earl of Chatham, was prime minister. The Foxite Whigs, successors to the Rockinghamites, split into those who crossed the floor of both Houses of Parliament to support the government on the issue of the war, and those who, under Charles James Fox, opposed the military struggle fought by Pitt's administration and its successors against France for almost all of its 22 years. Anna Seward (1747–1809) held opinions that generally aligned her with the Foxite Whigs in opposition to the Pitt administration. Her published correspondence begins after the end of the American war, so this chapter refers only to her views on the French war. Elizabeth Carter (1717–1806), the renowned Greek scholar, tended towards opinions similar to those of Edmund Burke on both conflicts. Burke, the chief spokesman for the Rockingham Whigs, opposed the government's policy on America. Famously, however, he was the first to break with the Foxite Whigs and support the war against the French Revolution.

Female patriotism

Louise Carter has recently discussed many of the ways in which British women were not merely permitted but positively encouraged to engage actively in support of the war against revolutionary France, describing them collectively as 'female patriotism'. These were patriotic activities that were deemed fitting for women to perform but which were not superfluous, merely decorative additions to the national war effort, suggested simply to allow women to feel involved and keep them out of the way of more important work. Rather, these tasks emerged from the needs and challenges created by the scale of this conflict, and a range of discourses characterizing women as patriots as well as moral and religious exemplars justified their participation in these ways. They included sacrificing the presence and support of male relatives to active armed service away from home, contributing financially to the cost of the wars, writing loyalist publications, dispensing military patronage, performing charity work and travelling on campaign with the British armed forces.[4] Just as the need to mobilize broad public support during the war forced the British authorities to accept the politicization of many non-elite men, and, as Karen Hagemann has shown, just as the Prusso-German elite had to promote patriotic activity by women in their struggle against Napoleonic France, so, too, the British governing classes needed not only to countenance but also even to solicit the active loyal support of women.[5] In the Voluntary Contribution of 1798 towards the prosecution of the war, for instance, donations from women accounted for 20 per cent of the total funds collected.[6]

Harriet Guest suggests that this kind of 'female patriotism' may be seen as a form of eighteenth-century sensibility, an emotionally driven response to national need, in which both men and women extended physical affection for their own families 'to embrace the public good'.[7] Anna Seward's nationally acclaimed poetry discussed war, for instance, through the lens of her distress over the death of her friend Major John André.[8] Elizabeth Carter's entry into political engagement in her letters in the 1770s can be explained by her use of the common characterization of the American war as a conflict between parent and child. Carter's view, widespread among those who opposed the war, was that the normal trajectory of colonies was to mature over time and, eventually, become independent. It was painful for parents to let go but wrong for them to continue to demand submission. This domestic vocabulary, Guest proposes, allowed women such as Carter admission into the discussion by forming a bridge from the private into the public.[9] The languages of morality, compassion and religion, and an attention to the details of daily life, provided acceptable and often distinctively feminine ways of writing about war, whether from a loyalist or an anti-war standpoint; not only did they draw on traditionally feminine concerns and domains, but they also offered to women a legitimate sense of obligation to act.[10] Patriotism construed as a local and domestic matter was suited and open to women. Emma Major has argued that public events took on private importance in this period, notably in the bluestocking correspondence.[11] Contemporary writers would have agreed. Charlotte Smith, for example, wrote in her 1792 novel, *Desmond*: 'Women it is said have no business with politics.... Why not?—Have they no interest in the scenes that are acting around them in which they have fathers, brothers, husbands, sons or friends engaged?'[12]

In many ways, the correspondence of the bluestockings conformed to this understanding of 'female patriotism'. They frequently expressed pain on behalf of the families of soldiers and sailors, concern for the poor, fear of invasion and desire for peace, however worthwhile the objects of the war. 'It made me melancholy to reflect how many would probably never return to their families, and their country', Elizabeth Carter wrote after watching troops embark for Holland from her home town of Deal in September 1799. She discussed the anxiety of local fishermen not to be pressed into naval service in 1776; she was pleased that her friend was due to take a journey north in 1778, further from any likely French landing point than was her home in London; and she rested her hopes in the good Providence of a powerful God.[13] In a similar way, Anna Seward could not see that the balance of power in Europe should be a priority for Britain in 1791, when war with Russia threatened: 'Why should we augment the ruinous weight of our immense national debt, and grind the faces of the poor with taxes in endless accumulation, beneath a visionary dread lest the balance of power should be lost in Europe?'[14] Peace, she reflected in 1797, 'is worth any price to England, short of the reduction of her navy'. The value of Britain's foreign conquests, which might be conceded to secure peace, 'is as dust in the balance against the miseries of protracted war'.[15]

But how far did these women also engage with the political and ideological aspects of the Revolutionary Wars, or were they restricted only to commenting on the more practical issues? Contemporary discussion of women and war did not suggest that women might take an intelligent interest in armed conflict. The assumption was often that women were weak, passive objects of defence. The conservative writer Laetitia Matilda Hawkins claimed in her *Letters on the Female Mind* (1793) that most British women knew very little about the French Revolution or the war.[16] At best, they might be moral supporters of the wars and guardians of the home front; at worst, they were potential sexual traitors, waiting eagerly for invading French troops.[17] Even those writers who encouraged a positive, active patriotic role for women during the wars, encompassing charity, propaganda and other forms of moral support, distinguished this type of effort from politics. 'In directing the attention of our female readers to these transactions,' warned J. A. Stewart, the author of *The Young Woman's Companion or Female Instructor*, 'our object is not to make them *politicians* but *patriots*'—that is, moral supporters of the war, not analysts of its causes or conduct.[18] Anna Seward's *Monody on Major André* (1781) was praised for its poetry by the anonymous author of the *Dialogues Concerning the Ladies* (1785) but criticized for its attack on George Washington for the manner of André's death. The author of the *Dialogues* chose to excuse this, however, because 'the laws of war are not a very natural or ordinary subject of female inquiry'.[19]

Louise Carter argues that the majority of women's published views on the war against revolutionary France were therefore 'framed in terms of the human consequences of the conflict rather than the loss or advantage to the state or military and were cloaked in the language of morality rather than political analysis'. While the personal papers of many women show that they did take an interest in high politics and military strategy privately, they did not usually express this interest publicly.[20] Anne K. Mellor has shown that women skilfully used different genres of literature to take part in public debate about war and other political subjects, but this was necessarily a subtle form of political discussion.[21] However, the bluestocking letters engage directly with some of the political issues raised by the wars, while inhabiting a space between the public and the strictly personal, being passed around among a number of friends and acquaintances and, in Seward's case, being deliberately prepared by her for posthumous publication.[22] Kathleen Wilson has recently suggested that they 'mimicked and supplemented' public reportage, circulating news and intelligence and exchanging opinions on political affairs discussed in newspapers and pamphlets.[23] Since drawing-room salons were the other major element of bluestocking sociability, it is not surprising that the bluestocking correspondence often has the air of salon contributions.[24] While Carter articulated her reluctance to having her letters read by anybody other than the named recipient, it is clear that her letters were regularly shared with others in the bluestocking circle, and it is possible that she also contemplated posthumous publication.[25] Lord Bath, returning one of her letters in 1761 to her chief correspondent, Elizabeth Montagu, expressed pleasure for Carter and Montagu themselves that they were to spend much of the coming winter together, but he also admitted: 'I wish you very often separated, & apart from each other, that mankind hereafter may be benefited by such a Correspondence'.[26]

These writers were, then, self-consciously observers of (rather than participants in) political action, but this should not be seen as necessarily a female role. English women were obvious bystanders during wars, with the exceptions of camp followers, nurses and navy wives, but it does not inevitably follow that intelligent and highly literate women were any less engaged in the political events of their era than the average educated, male, civilian observer of the times. Jonathan Clark has recently argued, for instance, that relatively few people in Britain, presumably of either sex, Edmund Burke included, really grasped the significance of American revolutionary events at the time.[27]

It is true that both Carter and Seward made occasional remarks to the effect that politics were not an appropriate subject for women. Yet, rather than reinforcing the view that war consolidated gender difference, their letters tend to demonstrate, if anything, a narrowing of the gap between men and women. War was a subject which, as the opening quotation from Seward suggests, attracted the notice of women as much as men; and the bluestocking letters show that they paid close attention to the political and military situation and assumed the same interest in their readers.

Eighteenth-century patriotism and the independent country gentlemen

A broader form of patriotism open to women may be suggested, therefore: the 'independent patriotism' proposed above. As Anna Clark has noted, before the conservative patriotic resistance to the revolutionary French appeared in the 1790s, for most of the eighteenth century the primary British understanding of patriotism was of opposition to the government— defending one's country by holding its administration to account. From the 1770s, however, a further, cosmopolitan patriotism promoted the rights of humanity and not just those of the freeborn Englishman.[28] While the loyalist patriotism of the 1790s made room for women in the various forms of female patriotic activity described above, Clark has suggested that the oppositional patriotic model, centred on Parliament, was 'highly masculine and xenophobic'; and only relatively few women, such as the historian and political writer Catharine Macaulay, aligned themselves with the radicalism of the cosmopolitan patriots.[29] A fifth, less vociferous genre of eighteenth-century patriotism may also be considered, however. It is possible to draw a parallel between the kind of patriotism displayed by some of the bluestockings and that adopted by independent country gentlemen sitting in the House of Commons in the eighteenth century, and so to suggest a further form of patriotism open to women in the later eighteenth century. For this it is necessary to consider briefly these men and their notion of patriotism.

The independent country gentlemen constituted a non-partisan sector of MPs first formally identified and analysed by Lewis Namier in *The Structure of Politics at the Accession of George III* (1928). He divided those he described as 'the inevitable parliament men'—those who were more or less predestined for parliamentary service from birth—into two groups. These were the 'politicians' and the 'country gentlemen'. The 'politicians', or those who sought careers in politics, were active within either the 'Court' or the 'Country' connections and generally saw patriotism as a matter of supporting government or opposing government respectively. The independent country gentlemen, however, stood in Parliament because this proved their standing and influence in their own counties and in order to defend their local and class interests. Their distinguishing political characteristics, Namier argued, were 'as a rule neither political acumen and experience nor Parliamentary eloquence, but an independent character and station in life, and indifference to office'.[30]

There were only around 60 to 80 of these MPs in the mid-eighteenth century, out of a total House of Commons membership of 558; but they were enough to allow the loose Parliamentary opposition usually termed 'Country' to defeat the Court if they threw their collective weight against the government on any particular issue.[31] They rarely troubled to do this. They believed that government was the responsibility of the Crown and its ministers, and that Parliament was there only to hold the administration to public accountability, not to hinder or prescribe government policy. Therefore, while they enjoyed visiting London and Westminster during 'the Season', and they did attend the House periodically, they did not feel obliged to attend every session nor to inspect and dissect every government action. They did not accept the 'Country' argument that it was a patriot's duty to oppose the Court party on most matters because the Court was attempting to subvert the constitution in favour of the Crown; rather, their default position was one of support for the Court, but with the freedom to oppose and defeat it when they were convinced that the policies and tactics of the government were corrupt or catastrophically incompetent. Regular, organized opposition was certainly factious and possibly treasonable. In their eyes, 'patriotism' meant defence of the national interest, which was unlikely to mean permanent opposition to the government of the Crown. Permanent opposition, they believed, was more likely to be motivated by personal ambition than by pursuit of national welfare. Specific measures might be resisted with discrimination, but not the government as such.[32]

The bluestockings as independent patriots

Matthew McCormack is, of course, right to emphasize the masculinity inherent in the concept of independence in seventeenth- and eighteenth-century England, from the emergence of a neoclassical political creed based on the independent citizen during the English Civil War, to the definition of 'the independent man' by 1832, which allowed the electorate to be substantially enlarged.[33] His discussion, however, is largely concerned with the campaign for the acquisition of active political rights, which Elizabeth Carter and Anna Seward did not consider, so far as is known. And it is arguable that the patriotism observed by the independent country gentlemen was, in some telling respects, analogous to that practised by Carter, Seward and other bluestockings quite as much as it was open to male observers of British politics outside the Houses of Parliament. The independent country gentlemen, while distinguished from such observers primarily by their membership in the House of Commons and their potential to effect change when they chose, were most frequently characterized by an attitude of detached observation rather than any desire for active interference. They had the right to express their own opinions on political matters because they were dependent on no-one, whether patrons or political parties, for their seats in Parliament, and those opinions could swing between political connections according to the issue under discussion. On the other hand, they had no independent power to change government policy.

Similarly, the bluestocking letters, 'mimic[king] and supplement[ing]' public reportage, were written by women free from partisan obligations. Both Carter and Seward emphasized the detachment that characterized their individual states of life. Carter retired from publishing in the mid-1770s, and Seward frequently drew attention to her provincial life and distance from the metropolis. They also underlined their independence from political groups and stances. After the outbreak of the war with America, Carter berated both sides in Parliament:

> What wretched accounts of the state of things in America, and what folly in the measures on all sides, which have involved the nation in such a difficulty! The government by urging an unprofitable right, if a right it be, and the opposition by heightening the refractory spirits of the colonists![34]

Reginald Blunt, the editor of a selection of Elizabeth Montagu's correspondence in 1923, dismissed such a political attitude. Mrs Montagu, he wrote, was 'very little of a politician. Her interests were largely personal, and she numbered among her friends prominent people on both sides in Parliament.'[35] However, such an independent patriotism—a non-partisan, intelligent engagement with political events, unrestricted by the approved forms of 'female patriotism'—was open to women of independent means and intellectual ability, such as the bluestockings. Their correspondence about the wars demonstrates a broad knowledge of events and a keen desire for informed analysis; their observations were frequently acute and expressive. Most interestingly, perhaps, they demonstrated a willingness to think independently and to change their minds, unshackled as they were by party ties.

Carter was always hungry for political and military information, and she often voiced scepticism regarding the quality of public information and complained about its paucity. 'We have here the same strange want of intelligence as ever,' she grumbled in April 1780, 'and nobody can tell if the French fleet has, or has not, been in the Channel.'[36] However, because she lived just north of Dover in the coastal town of Deal, a safe anchorage not far from the mouth of the River Thames, she in fact often obtained news carried by ships from America very quickly, though she treated it with caution. In December 1776, impatient for news, she seized on a story 'received from the masters of several transports just arrived in the Downs', all agreeing on the same events; yet, she commented, 'Common ship-news is so very suspicious, that I know not how far this intelligence may be credited'.[37] 'What strange contradictory accounts of American transactions!' she exclaimed in 1777. 'I have long since forborn [sic] giving credit to any but such as are transmitted by the Generals themselves. Most of the private accounts, I suppose are forgeries for stock-jobbers, who win or lose a battle just as it suits their own particular interests.'[38] Such trust reposed in 'the Generals' was not so indirect as it may appear: in 1778 she told Mrs Montagu, 'I just saw a gentleman who is secretary to our Admiral, and I find by him that there is not likely to be any formal declaration of war [against France], till it is known what is the success of our commissioners in America'.[39] Living in Deal also allowed her to verify stories for herself. 'I am never much dejected by patriotic wailings', she wrote later in 1778, using the word 'patriotic' in its older, oppositional sense:

> Some time ago I had a letter, in which my correspondent told me, she had met a patriot in her visits, who just before he left the room let off, by way of news, that the French had taken the [British] Jamaica fleet. On the very day I received this letter, the said Jamaica fleet, in great safety and quietness, sailed through the Downs.[40]

In Bath in December 1781, she had much less opportunity to secure news: 'I suppose the present important crisis of public affairs engages the mind of all who think, and the conversation of all who talk, in London. At Bath nobody thinks or talks of any such matter.'[41]

Both Carter and Seward read and discussed such essential publications as Edmund Burke's *Reflections on the Revolution in France* (1790) and Thomas Paine's *Rights of Man* (1791–92). While Carter had not seen Fanny Burney's new novel, *Cecilia* (published on 12 June 1782), by September because it had not yet reached her local circulating library, she did manage to read Burke's *Reflections* within six weeks of its publication on 1 November 1790 and thought it 'a very noble performance', though she expressed misgivings about the notorious passages on Marie-Antoinette.[42] On the other hand, she found Paine's *Rights of Man* an 'execrable performance'.[43] Seward made do with extracts from Burke's pamphlet in the newspapers for several weeks and preferred the radical *Letters from France* by her friend Helen Maria Williams (published in the same month as Burke's *Reflections*) for showing her 'the sunny-side of the French Revolution', as opposed to the 'darkness, clouds, and shadows' thrust upon it by Burke.[44] By 19 December 1790, however, she felt obliged to read his *Reflections* properly for herself: 'You will wonder', she wrote to a friend,

> when I tell you that as yet I have read only in extracts, that publication upon which the eye of all Europe is bent. Accident, and not want of inclination, has occasioned this abstinence. I shall have it next week, and I mean to read and consider it with the most impartial eye.[45]

By the time she finished the letter, she had read the book and was, she confessed, 'reluctantly convinced that the boasted liberty of France is degenerating into coercive anarchy, not likely to end well', though she did not like Burke's 'Quixotism about the Queen of France' nor his vindication of hereditary honours.[46] Seward also read various replies to Burke, such as those by Sir Brooke Boothby, Tom Paine and David Williams. She admired all these works for their criticisms of the *Reflections*, but none of them convinced her that Burke was wrong about the disastrous nature of the revolution in France.[47]

Although Seward was the more politically liberal of the two, neither sympathized with radicals nor with the republican model. Gary Kelly is correct to point out that the bluestockings were so rooted in the established order that they had an interest in upholding it and that most of them resisted radical change to it.[48] 'I have ever loved and venerated the cause of liberty', Seward claimed in August 1792,

> ...but I every day grow more and more sick of that mischievous oratory which ferments and diffuses the spirit of sedition...Paine's pernicious and impossible system of equal rights, is calculated to captivate and dazzle the vulgar; to make them spurn the restraints of legislation, and to spread anarchy, murder, and ruin over the earth.[49]

She praised the government's success, by January 1793, in deflating the radical movement and stirring up national loyalty; and her message in April 1793 to those who were still dissatisfied with the British constitution even in the light of the vortex of violence in France was blunt: 'America is accessible'. She had little sympathy for the campaign of the Dissenters for equal political rights with Anglicans, conflating this with the republicanism of 'their leader, [Joseph] Priestley'.[50] Seward's opinions often naturally aligned her with the Foxite Whigs in opposition to the government, but her views on their attitude towards the radicals clearly demonstrate her independent patriotism, and, indeed, she used the word 'patriotism' in this sense. After the failure of the government's treason trials in 1794, she criticized the leading opposition MPs, Charles James Fox, Richard Brinsley Sheridan and Thomas Erskine, for supporting the radicals during the trials and for demanding the repeal of the government's legislation to repress radical activities. 'Serjeant Adair and Mr Wilberforce are the only men, one on the H[abeas] Corpus Act, the other on the war, who appear to have spoken, independent of selfish short-sighted ambition and party connections, the dictates of true patriotism, suited to the ominous complexion of the times.'[51]

As early as 1782, after hearing about Richard Price's *Letter to the Volunteers* on the subject of parliamentary reform, Elizabeth Carter had made the suggestion that radicals should consider emigrating to America.[52] The French Revolution only increased her revulsion. Denying that she had felt any anxiety about public disorder on 14 July 1791, the anniversary of the storming of the Bastille, because she had believed government measures to have been adequate to deal with any such attempts, she nonetheless admitted: 'I felt a very great horror of the general spirit that gave rise to that absurd celebration....It is astonishing that some people, even of sense and virtue, should give an encouragement to the wretches who would contrive our ruin'.[53]

Carter, whose views tended to chime with those of Edmund Burke, was uneasy about the war with America, thinking it an impossible task for

Britain: 'all but peace is ruin'. 'I am no American', she protested in 1777, but, where colonies demand independence, 'the truest policy is at once to give up the point'.[54] She also criticized the management of the war by the North administration. She hoped, for instance, that the Irish Parliament would receive the trade concessions it sought in 1779, which might have been granted to it with better grace the previous year. 'But this is a procrastinating age. Our armies march too late, our fleets sail too late, and our concessions are made so late that some will not receive, and others not thank us for them.'[55] Like Burke, however, she had fewer qualms about the conflict against France, though she continued to regret warfare in itself and to wish it over as soon as possible.

Anna Seward, on the other hand, was highly critical of the Pitt administration during the French wars, at least from mid-1794 onwards. She offers a fascinating example of independence of mind, which might uncharitably be dismissed as a 'feminine' inability to make up her mind, but which is more accurately described as the ability to follow events and to admit with great candour when she changed her thinking as the issues changed. Like an independent country gentleman in the House of Commons, she was under no obligation to adhere to her party leadership through thick and thin but could follow events and revise her opinions as she saw fit.

Seward began the French Revolutionary era, as we have seen, by admiring Helen Maria Williams's perspective on the Revolution.[56] But she realized that these letters 'do not attempt to reason, they only paint, and shew the illumined side of the prospect'; and when, reluctantly, she finally read Burke's *Reflections*, she was persuaded by his pessimism regarding France and his fear of the consequences for Britain (if not by his view of the Glorious Revolution in Britain). While the early radical replies to Burke pleased her in terms of their general political philosophies, none of them convinced her of a more optimistic view of the French Revolution. Even while, as a liberal Whig, she hoped that, eventually, 'the French may prove a pattern...of public virtue and public happiness, to the whole world', she agreed with Burke that, currently, the revolutionaries were engaged in a 'hazardous experiment; in which all the links were broken in that great chain of subordination which binds to each other the various orders of existence'.[57] This did not mean that she adopted all of Burke's political principles, however, since she continued to wish for a more liberal constitution in Britain; but she recognized, with Burke, that, '[t]he frailty of human nature considered, we have no more right to expect perfection in governments than from individuals'.[58]

Further criticisms of Burke's stance, however, published later in 1791 caused her to wobble in her assessment of his accuracy:

> Mr Burke's book has greatly fallen in my estimation, since the replies have proved upon it much misrepresentation and suppressed evidence—have hunted its arguments into all their artful recesses and demonstrated their sophistry....I looked through the darkened telescope of Burke, and

believed [the ruin of France] inevitable; but, at present, the prophecy wears no likelihood of completion.⁵⁹

She began to doubt her own judgement: 'As to politics, I do not think myself at all qualified to talk about them; to speak with any degree of certainty upon the event of that great, but hazardous experiment, which France is making...'.⁶⁰

A year later, in autumn 1792, as the Revolution became more sweeping and more violent, and as radical societies flourished in Britain, she had regained certainty of her opposition to the Revolution. This did not mean, however, that she was glad to see the German invasion of France: they merely added to the 'rivers of blood' already running high in France, and she could not see that they would be either victorious or successful in restoring the monarchy.⁶¹ She hoped that the Pitt administration would 'keep us out of the bloody Quixotism, in which so considerable a part of Europe has engaged', and she did not consider the defence of Britain's ally, the Dutch Republic, to be a sufficient cause of Britain declaring war on France—the Dutch, after all, had proved themselves to be a faithless ally by joining America's war against Britain in 1780.⁶²

Yet by January 1793, Seward found herself applauding those opposition Whigs who were forming the so-called 'Third Party' to support the Pitt administration in its move towards war with revolutionary France and repression of radicalism at home, while still opposing it on most other grounds. This, she said, was 'to see true patriotism breaking out, like the sun, from beneath the clouds of party and prejudice'.⁶³ In April 1793, she defended the war against France. After the public threats made in the French National Convention 'to assassinate our ministers, bring our monarch to the block', and after French revolutionary ideas were promulgated all over Britain, abetted by 'those unhappy distempered people, who were endeavouring to communicate their plague-spots to our yet healthy region', it was surely time to repel the French by force. 'If ever it was right to petition Heaven for a blessing on the unsheathed sword, it is now that it has been drawn against the lawless, the murderous, the impious, seeking to infect and to subjugate every happier country.'⁶⁴ Moreover, where once she had hoped for parliamentary reform in Britain, now, she admitted, this had been a 'romantic folly', since

> the mischiefs of individual representation are fully demonstrated by the guilty, the ruinous anarchy into which it has plunged our unfortunate neighbours. We are now, however unwillingly, taught by experience, that, through the natural depravity of human nature, people of property, who have a considerable stake in their country, are, in general, the only real patriots—that they alone can be safely entrusted with the management of its interests.⁶⁵

By mid-1794, however, Anna Seward had returned to her usual stance of opposing Pitt, the war having proved both unsuccessful and enormously expensive: 'From the moment Mr Pitt declared in the senate, that the war must be pursued at every hazard, even of national ruin here, he fell in my confidence, from the highest elevation of wisdom and virtue that ever minister attained.' Moreover, she wondered, what sense did it make to squander British resources of armed forces and money abroad which could be used to defeat radicalism at home more effectively?[66] Having earlier attacked Fox for his opposition to the war and his support of the radicals in 1794, by 1797 she admitted that 'his struggles against the commencement and continuance of this disastrous war, ... clearly prove his right to be entitled the People's Friend'.[67] She was highly critical of Burke's four *Letters on a Regicide Peace* (1796), which argued vehemently against attempting to negotiate peace with the French Republic; and she remained opposed to the Pitt administration, the war and the government's 'despotic' policies at home for the rest of the conflict, remarking of Pitt after his passing in 1806, 'He has died too late'.[68] In the same letter, she argued that Bonaparte was no worse than any other European monarch and certainly not a reason for Britain to remain at war with France.[69] Discussing her change of mind over the war, Seward had told a correspondent in November 1796, 'You will perhaps think I am wading beyond my depth, when I thus write to you of politics...but I am not too proud to confess myself mistaken, beneath the force of such disastrous proofs of it exhibited by this ruinous war. Time is a broad mirror, which often shows us the fallacy of our own judgment.'[70]

While Elizabeth Carter and Anna Seward made frequent references to individual military and naval events in their correspondence, they tended not to discuss them in any detail, concentrating on the human losses that resulted from them, on the political significance of such actions or on the broader politics of war and peace. Their interest generally was political rather than strictly military, but their correspondence certainly shows their awareness of military and naval events as they unfolded. 'I had an account from London which calls the late skirmish between the two fleets, on our side, a victory', wrote Carter on 7 August 1778 of Admiral Keppel's engagement with the French off Ushant. 'But the express sent to our Admiral, is not very encouraging', she accurately continued. 'We have three or four hundred men killed and wounded, and we have taken nothing from the enemy.'[71]

Conclusion

The bluestockings discussed the wars of the late eighteenth century vigorously. It is true that they often cherished their insulation from the problems and trials of involvement in public political life, and it may be, as Harriet Guest has suggested, that this was a factor in their freedom from partisan ties.[72] It did not, however, prevent them from engaging passionately with political issues as independent patriots, at least by the period of the Revolutionary Wars. This was neither the patriotism of militant conservatism, nor that of opposition for opposition's sake, nor that of cosmopolitan radicals but rather a 'love of country' that demanded a citizen's attention to political events and an intelligent, independent judgement of the issues as they arose. Nor was this the socially acceptable and publicly sanctioned female patriotism of charitable donations and moral support—it was political engagement despite the restrictions on women's politicking in the late eighteenth century. These were not typical women—neither did all men observe politics so acutely, so far as can be known—but this was another form of patriotism open to them. They operated within their context: in some ways, their responses to the conflicts were typically gendered, distinctively preoccupied with the human consequences of war and reinforced the developing notions of domestic ideology.[73] Yet the bluestocking letters also provide evidence of women breaking this domesticated mould in a quiet, semi-public way and choosing to follow a path of independent patriotism alongside the one of female patriotism that they were encouraged to tread.

The independent country gentlemen declined in numbers steadily during the Napoleonic Wars as the Pittite and Foxite groups of MPs developed into the Tory and Whig parties and the British Parliament moved towards a bilateral party system; and there are many instances of nineteenth-century women's political writing that took clear party political stances, including the war poetry discussed by Jane Rendall in this book. It would, however, be surprising—given their lack of political rights, their frequent freedom from party ties and yet their access to increasing volumes of political information—if both women and men of independent means did not often continue to opt for the route of independent patriotism during the nineteenth century; and, indeed, independent patriotism retained a place in nineteenth-century political discourse as part of the self-definition of the parliamentary Liberal Party.[74]

Notes

1. Anna Seward to Colonel Dowdeswell, 30 November 1797, in *Letters of Anna Seward: Written between the Years 1784 and 1807*, 6 vols, ed. Archibald Constable (Edinburgh, 1811), vol. 5, 20.
2. Harriet Guest, *Small Change: Women, Learning, Patriotism, 1750–1810* (Chicago, 2000), 175.
3. The 'bluestocking circle' originated in the 1750s in the form of intellectual tea parties, hosted by society women in London, especially Elizabeth Montagu, Frances Boscawen and Elizabeth Vesey. They were attended by both men and women of the upper and professional classes and maintained by a network of correspondence, visits and philanthropic projects, both in London and in the country. The term bluestocking probably came from the blue worsted stockings worn as a

sign of serious intellectual priorities by a leading member of the group, the scientist Bishop Benjamin Stillingfleet, and perhaps others in opposition to the white or black silk stockings worn by upper-class men and courtiers; but it came to be used satirically of the female members. See Gary Kelly, 'General Introduction', in *Elizabeth Montagu*, ed. Elizabeth Eger, vol. 1 of Gary Kelly (gen. ed.), *Bluestocking Feminism: Writings of the Bluestocking Circle, 1738–1785*, 6 vols (London, 1999), ix–xi.
4. Louise P. Carter, 'British Women during the Revolutionary and Napoleonic Wars, 1793–1815: Responses, Roles and Representations', Ph.D. thesis (University of Cambridge, 2005), 208–209.
5. Robert R. Dozier, *For King, Constitution and Country: The English Loyalists and the French Revolution* (Lexington, KY, 1983), 54–55; David Eastwood, 'Patriotism and the English State in the 1790s', in *The French Revolution and British Popular Politics*, ed. Mark Philp (Cambridge, 1991), 146–168, 150; Karen Hagemann, 'Female Patriots: Women, War and the Nation in the Period of the Prussian-German Anti-Napoleonic Wars', *Gender & History* 16/2 (2004): 397–424, 402–405.
6. Carter, 'British Women', 105–106.
7. Guest, *Small Change*, 203.
8. Anna Seward, Monody on Major André (Lichfield, 1781); see Guest, *Small Change*, 178, 254.
9. Elizabeth Carter to Elizabeth Montagu, 20 July 1777, in *Letters from Mrs Elizabeth Carter to Mrs Montagu, between the Years 1755 and 1800: Chiefly upon Literary and Moral Subjects*, ed. Montagu Pennington, 3 vols (London, 1817), vol. 3, 30–31; Guest, *Small Change*, 178.
10. Emma Vincent Macleod, *A War of Ideas: British Attitudes to the Wars Against Revolutionary France, 1792–1802* (Aldershot, UK, 1998), 165–169; Carter, 'British Women', 69–78, 86; Guest, *Small Change*, 146; Claire Brant, 'Varieties of Women's Writing', in *Women and Literature in Britain, 1700–1800*, ed. Vivien Jones (Cambridge, 2000), 285–305, 288.
11. Emma Major, 'The Politics of Sociability', in *Reconsidering the Bluestockings*, ed. Nicole Pohl and Betty A. Schellenberg (San Marino, CA, 2003), 175–192, 182–185.
12. Charlotte Smith, *Desmond*, ed. Janet Todd and Antje Blank (London, 1997), 6, cited in Carter, 'British Women', 64.
13. Carter to Montagu, 2 September 1799, in Pennington, *Letters*, vol. 3, 355; idem, 23 November 1776, in ibid. vol. 3, 18–19; idem, 21 June 1778, in ibid. vol. 3, 75; idem, 3 September 1799, in ibid. vol. 3, 353–354.
14. Seward to David Samwell, 15 May 1791, in Constable, *Letters*, vol. 3, 61.
15. Seward to Colonel Dowdeswell, 30 November 1797, in ibid. vol. 5, 19.
16. Laetitia Matilda Hawkins, *Letters on the Female Mind*, 2 vols (London, 1793), vol. 2, 194.
17. John Bowles, *Remarks on Modern Female Manners, as Distinguished by Indifference to Character, and Indecency of Dress; extracted from 'Reflections Political and Moral at the Conclusion of the War'* (London, 1802), 12; Macleod, *War of Ideas*, 173–177.
18. J. A. Stewart, *The Young Woman's Companion or Female Instructor* (3rd edn, Oxford, 1815), 435, cited in Carter, 'British Women', 16. See also *Lady's Magazine* 30 (1799): 450–451.
19. *Dialogues Concerning the Ladies* (London, 1785), quoted in Guest, *Small Change*, 170.

20. Carter, 'British Women', 68.
21. Anne K. Mellor, *Mothers of the Nation: Women's Political Writing in England, 1780–1830* (Bloomington, 2000).
22. Guest, *Small Change*, 13–14. For similar comments on the correspondence between Catharine Macaulay and Mercy Otis Warren, see Kate Davies, *Catharine Macaulay and Mercy Otis Warren: The Revolutionary Atlantic and the Politics of Gender* (Oxford, 2005), 7–9.
23. Kathleen Wilson, *The Island Race: Englishness, Empire and Gender in the Eighteenth Century* (London, 2003), 110.
24. *Elizabeth Carter*, ed. Judith Hawley, vol. 2 of Kelly, *Bluestocking Feminism*, 376; Susan Staves, 'Church of England Clergy and Women Writers', in Pohl and Schellenberg, *Reconsidering*, 81–104, 82.
25. Hawley, *Elizabeth Carter*, vol. 2 of Kelly, *Bluestocking Feminism*, 375–376.
26. Huntington Library, San Marino, CA, Montagu Correspondence 4238, William Pulteney, Earl of Bath, to *Elizabeth Montagu*, 21 September 1761, quoted in Eger, Elizabeth Montagu, vol. 1 of Kelly, *Bluestocking Feminism*, 142.
27. Jonathan C. D. Clark, 'Edmund Burke's Reflections on the Revolution in America (1777), or, how did the American Revolution relate to the French?', in *An Imaginative Whig: Reassessing the Life and Thought of Edmund Burke*, ed. Ian Crowe (Columbia, SC, 2005), 71–92, 76.
28. Anna Clark, '1798 as the Defeat of Feminism: Women, Patriotism and Politics', in *These Fissured Isles: Ireland, Scotland and British History, 1798–1848*, ed. Terry Brotherstone et al. (Edinburgh, 2005), 85–104, 85–86.
29. Ibid. 86. Macaulay, as Kate Davies has suggested, was identified with the bluestocking network but went beyond the more feminine bluestocking style with her vocal and republican politics. Davies has further argued that the patriotism embodied by Macaulay gained its 'masculine' self-determination paradoxically in part because of her status as a learned woman, which earned her respect and a certain license to comment politically. This license was largely withdrawn during the American War of Independence as loyalist anxieties overtook national pride in her intellectual achievements, and as her private life caused public scandal, so that her femininity became associated with political betrayal. See Davies, *Catharine Macaulay*, chs 1–3.
30. Sir Lewis Namier, *The Structure of Politics at the Accession of George III* (2nd edn, London, 1957), 6.
31. Ibid.
32. H. T. Dickinson, *Liberty and Property: Political Ideology in Eighteenth-Century Britain* (1977; repr. London, 1979), 176, 178–179.
33. Matthew McCormack, *The Independent Man: Citizenship and Gender Politics in Georgian England* (Manchester, 2005).
34. Carter to Montagu, 3 June 1775, in Pennington, *Letters*, vol. 2, 310.
35. Reginald Blunt (ed.), *Mrs Montagu. 'Queen of the Blues': Her Letters and Friendships from 1762 to 1800*, 2 vols (London, 1923), vol. 2, 116–117.
36. Carter to Montagu, 18 April 1780, in Pennington, *Letters*, vol. 3, 125.
37. Idem, 21 December 1776, in ibid. 21, 23.
38. Idem, 23 November 1777, in ibid. 49.
39. Idem, 27 July 1778, in ibid. 82.
40. Idem, 7 August, 1778, in ibid. 85.
41. Idem, 17 December 1781, in ibid. 162.
42. Idem, 21 September 1782, in ibid. 176; idem, 15 December 1790, in ibid. 322.

43. Idem, 18 July 1791, in ibid. 328.
44. Seward to Helen Maria Williams, 12 December 1790, in Constable, *Letters*, vol. 3, 44.
45. Seward to the Rev. T. S. Whalley, 19 December 1790, in ibid. 46, 48.
46. Seward to Mrs Taylor, 10 January 1791, in ibid. 52.
47. Seward to Mrs Knowles, 19 May 1791, in ibid. 75–78.
48. Gary Kelly, 'General Introduction', in Kelly, *Bluestocking Feminism*, vol. 1, xiii.
49. Seward to Lady Gresley, 29 August 1792, in Constable, *Letters*, vol. 3, 159–160.
50. Seward to Helen Maria Williams, 17 January 1793, in ibid. 208–209; Seward to Mrs Stokes, 25 April 1793, in ibid. 218.
51. Seward to Mrs Jackson, 21 January 1794 [1795], in ibid. vol. 4, 34. William Wilberforce, the slave trade abolitionist, was a close friend of Pitt and generally supported his government in the House of Commons. Between December 1794 and December 1795, however, he opposed the war, on the grounds that Britain had achieved what it had originally set out to do in 1793 and no longer needed to maintain the waste of men and money involved in conflict. He returned to support the war at the close of 1795 after the government's efforts to negotiate peace were rejected by France. Similarly, Serjeant James Adair might have been expected, from his previous Foxite convictions, to have opposed the suspension of habeas corpus (the right to have a court determine whether or not a prisoner's detention is lawful), but, as a Portland Whig, preferred to support the government on this issue, though he was inconsistent in his stance on reform throughout the 1790s.
52. Carter to Montagu, 26 November 1782, in Pennington, *Letters*, vol. 3, 187–188.
53. Idem, 18 July 1791, in ibid. 327.
54. Idem, 6 October 1776, in ibid. 10; idem, 20 July 1777, in ibid. 30–31.
55. Idem, 16 November 1779, in ibid. 117.
56. See also Seward's sonnet in the *Gentleman's Magazine*, 59 (August 1789): 743, which publicly expressed her approval of the early events of the French Revolution.
57. Seward to Mrs Knowles, 19 May 1791, in Constable, *Letters*, vol. 3, 75–76, 78;
58. Ibid. 76; Seward to Helen Williams, 17 January 1793, in ibid. 209. See also Seward to Edward Jerningham, 5 March 1796, in ibid. vol. 4, 182–183.
59. Seward to Miss Weston, 7 July 1791, in ibid. vol. 3, 87–88.
60. Seward to Rev. William Fitzthomas, 5 June 1791, in ibid. 80.
61. Seward to Lady Gresley, 29 August 1792, in ibid. 160; Seward to the Rev. T. S. Whalley, 4 September 1792, in ibid. 163–164.
62. Seward to the Rev. T. S. Whalley, 4 September 1792, in ibid. 164.
63. Seward to Colonel Dowdeswell, 3 January 1793, in ibid. 200. See also Seward to Mrs Adey, 14 June 1793, in ibid. 259.
64. Seward to Mrs Stokes, 25 April 1793, in ibid. 218–220.
65. Ibid. 216.
66. Seward to the Rev. T. S. Whalley, 25 July 1794, in ibid. 377–378. See also Seward to Sir Brooke Boothby, 7 May 1797, in ibid. vol. 4, 339.
67. Ibid. 340.
68. Seward to Mrs H. Thornton, 11 December 1796, in ibid. 281–283; Seward to the Rev. R. Fellowes, 10 March 1800, in ibid. vol. 5, 281; Seward to Miss Catherine Mallet, 14 April 1806, in ibid. vol. 6, 255.
69. Seward to Miss Catherine Mallet, 14 April 1806, in ibid. 251–253.
70. Seward to Edmund Wigley, 19 November 1796, in ibid. vol. 4, 279–280.

71. Carter to Montagu, 7 August 1781, in Pennington, *Letters*, vol. 3, 85–86. See also her account of Admiral Cornwallis's skilful manoeuvre against the French to save the *Mars*, also off Ushant, in June 1795: Carter to Montagu, 7 July 1795, in ibid. 344–345.
72. Guest, 'Bluestocking Feminism', in Pohl and Schellenberg, *Reconsidering*, 67.
73. Kelly, 'General Introduction', in Kelly, *Bluestocking Feminism*, vol. 1, ix–li.
74. See Jonathan Parry, *The Rise and Fall of Liberal Government in Victorian Britain* (New Haven, 1993); idem, *The Politics of Patriotism: English Liberalism, National Identity and Europe, 1830–1886* (Cambridge, 2006), chs 1 and 2.

13
Women Writing War and Empire: Gender, Poetry and Politics in Britain during the Napoleonic Wars
Jane Rendall

> Still the loud death drum, thundering from afar,
> O'er the vext nations pours the storm of war:
> To the stern call still Britain bends her ear,
> Feeds the fierce strife, the alternate hope and fear.[1]

In her poem *Eighteen Hundred and Eleven* (1812), Anna Barbauld, then aged sixty-eight, a dissenter in religion, a pacifist and a much-published poet and educationalist, wrote of Britain's military engagement in the global 'storm of war' as part of the expansion of its empire and commerce. She did so in no triumphalist spirit but in meditation on the destructive effects of a war that brought with it famine, death and economic ruin to a once free and powerful nation. Published at the height of the Peninsular War, the poem evoked a hostility from critics that has become legendary. Most reviewers denounced it as unpatriotic and subversive, its criminality exacerbated by the sex of the writer and her technical accomplishment. The most notorious attack appeared in the conservative *Quarterly Review*, where John Wilson Croker spluttered:

> We had hoped, indeed, that the empire might have been saved without the intervention of a lady-author: we even flattered ourselves that the interests of Europe and of humanity would in some degree have swayed our public councils, without the descent of (dea ex machina) Mrs. Anna Letitia Barbauld in a quarto, upon the theatre where the great European tragedy is now performing. Not such, however, is her opinion; an irresistible impulse of public duty—a confident sense of commanding talents—have induced her to dash down her shagreen spectacles and her knitting needles, and to sally forth...in the magnanimous resolution of saving a sinking state....[2]

On the same page Croker termed Barbauld, who had been widowed three years earlier, a 'fatidical [prophetic] spinster' who had abandoned the superintendence of the nursery to wage war on statesmen and warriors. The *Anti-Jacobin Review*, the *British Critic*, the *Eclectic Review* and other periodicals all responded in similar if marginally less savage ways and even some of Barbauld's own liberal friends were unsympathetic.[3] Critics focused on Barbauld's aberrant femininity, her assumption of knowledge of public affairs and policy and her direct intervention, in calling upon the conscience of the reader to acknowledge complicity in the crimes and militarism of the empire. In emphasizing what James Chandler has called the 'mismatch between gender and genre' in this poem, Croker indicated a boundary beyond which women writers should not venture.[4] According to her niece Lucy Aikin, Barbauld was so disheartened by 'the scorns of the unmanly, the malignant, and the base' that she never published again.[5]

Yet the hostility was not quite universal. The reviewer for the *Monthly Review* (a liberal journal to which Barbauld herself contributed), though not in total agreement with her, wrote sympathetically of her true patriotism and regretted the brevity of the poem. The *Monthly Repository*, representing rational religious dissenting opinion, called the poem 'deeply interesting' for its description of war's 'miseries and crimes', admired its cosmopolitanism and lamented that the author had not extended its lessons for a nation 'drunken with blood'. And in 1815 the *British Lady's Magazine* suggested that 'too much excitement to the slaughter of our species, by flattering views of false glory', had made it impossible to apprehend the 'counter-spirit of peace, reason and religion' which the 'genuine patriotism' of Barbauld's poem had tried to raise.[6]

These varied responses may help us to understand the gendered boundaries of such writing on public affairs as well as the shifting discourses of gender in the later years of the war. The silencing of Barbauld coincided with what a number of literary scholars have identified as a remasculinization of culture in an age of Romanticism and increasingly professional criticism.[7] Yet a comparison of *Eighteen Hundred and Eleven* with Anne Grant's epic poem *Eighteen Hundred and Thirteen*, written in response to Barbauld's and published in 1814, allows us to contextualize both works more fully. A comparative reading indicates that women poets' imaginative representations of war were both diverse and complex, shaped by differences of class and political perspective as well as by gender.

This chapter first considers the poems of Anna Barbauld and Anne Grant, before exploring some common themes relevant to the poetry written by women during the later years of the Napoleonic Wars. The close attention that literary scholars have paid to gender politics in this period may help historians to understand how individual women found their own public voices, even against a background of shifting discourses of gender. Mary Favret, for instance, has stressed the correspondence of war and domesticity in poetic representations of women and children at war. She focuses less on the patriotic mother than on the war widow, an ambivalent 'image of ideological instability', signalling both the possibility of domestic security and the vulnerability of the soldier's body.[8] In a survey of war poems by women, Stephen Behrendt describes their mobilization of sentiment and appeal to the shared experience of loss in poems of death and anguish, extending even to the battlefield, as in 'The Victims of War' (1808) by Christian Gray, the blind farmer's daughter from Perth, or 'The Soldier's Widow, at the Grave of her Only Child' (1811) by Dorothea Primrose Campbell from the Shetland Islands.[9] But he notes, too, that the implications of such poems and the ambivalence of many women poets went far beyond engagement with individual loss, arguing that their work 'discloses an important thread of oppositional poetic discourse'.[10] Writers indicated their desire for peace, universalized their compassion for the victims of war beyond national boundaries and criticized the indifference of the wealthy to such suffering. A few expressed their hostility to war directly.

The bourgeois public sphere defined by Jürgen Habermas mediated between society and the state, as it came to be the bearer of public opinion through the press and associational life. His model was Britain, where such a sphere was in existence by the beginning of the eighteenth century.[11] From the late 1980s, feminist political scientists and historians criticized this concept for its failure to reflect gender differences.[12] It has been suggested that for a full understanding of politics and public opinion we need to theorize alternative and counter public spheres, including a feminist one, which make possible critical responses to the masculine bourgeois model. However, here it is argued that in interpreting the public interventions of women poets, it is more helpful to consider the classical bourgeois public sphere described by Habermas as fundamentally hierarchical and divided, structured by gender and genre, by social class and in this period by increasingly clear political differences.[13] These divisions are discussed with reference to the strength and the limits of British print culture in this period, the changing poetic discourses of war and the politicization of war.

From Barbauld to Grant: *Eighteen Hundred and Eleven* and *Eighteen Hundred and Thirteen*

Barbauld's *Eighteen Hundred and Eleven* is an exciting poem that has attracted much critical attention over the past two decades, and it is impossible to do justice to its 334 lines in this article.[14] It is an eclectic jeremiad, a prophetic lamentation, which in conservative form and subject follows Samuel Johnson's Juvenalian satire on London of 1738 yet is also indebted to the Comte de Volney's visionary *Ruins...of Empires*, first translated from the French in 1792, and to many other treatments of the same theme.[15] Barbauld forecasts the ultimate downfall of the great imperial city of London, once at the very heart of international commerce, where the peoples of the world had mingled. In the future, she writes, the ingenuous young from North America would come to a decaying Britain to visit sources of political and cultural inspiration such as Magna Carta and to remember Shakespeare and Newton, the abolitionist Thomas Clarkson, the orientalist Sir William Jones and the landscapes praised by the poets William Cowper, William Wordsworth and Walter Scott. Above all, they would come to the ruins—the crumbling squares and antique tombs—of a 'fallen London' (211). Barbauld's vision was of a progressive Spirit moving 'o'er the peopled earth' (215) from the great commercial cities and empires of the past, from Egypt, Carthage, Babylon and Troy to the far Scandinavian north, to Venice and the Netherlands and then to London. There, for a time, Britons enjoyed the plenty of the world's goods, as their power and influence extended across the globe. But 'arts, arms and wealth destroy the fruits they bring' (315), and the corruptions, crimes and ambitions of the British Empire saw that progressive Spirit shift westward, to the new nations just appearing in South America, where, as Barbauld wrote in her final line, 'Thy World, Columbus, shall be free' (330).

The Scotswoman Anne Grant, the daughter of an officer in the British army who served in the American War of Independence, was already an established author when, at the age of 59, she wrote *Eighteen Hundred and Thirteen: A Poem, in two parts*.[16] Her poetry was characterized by patriotism and a significantly more conservative outlook than that of Barbauld. Her previous publications, based on her knowledge of the Scottish Highlands, had enjoyed some literary success.[17] Composed as a response to Barbauld, Grant's poem of nearly 3000 lines openly celebrated Britain's recent military victories in the Iberian Peninsula and its growing imperial power across the globe. The first part of *Eighteen Hundred and Thirteen* relates the history of conflict in Europe from the first appearance of British troops in Portugal in 1808 to Napoleon's march to Moscow in 1812 and subsequent Russian advances; to the battles of Lützen, Bautzen and Leipzig; then to Wellington's final victories in the Peninsular War, the military recovery of the Netherlands and the first stages of the occupation of France in late 1813. Grant concludes this narrative with a look forward to the future reign of a female monarch in Britain, the Prince Regent's daughter, Princess Charlotte.

The second part of the poem turns from war to review the present condition of Britain. Though threatened, Britain had resisted political infection from France, partly through the strength of its religious faith, becoming a refuge for 'exiled princes, peers, and kings' as its own monarchy, while flawed and ailing, survived (II:125–129). So, too, did London, which Grant described in terms reminiscent of Barbauld's portrait of the city at its most powerful, though even here it was shown to be not without its corruptions and its vices. Grant's poem recounts the achievement of the unity of Great Britain. Eight pages are devoted to the history of Scotland, from William Wallace and the memories of older wars to James Macpherson's Ossianic lays. Two old and warlike enemies—Scotland and England—had come together to form an expanding imperial power, and Scotsmen were now known, she writes, throughout the empire, across Asia and the Americas, 'on Ganges' banks', 'by Hudson's stream' and 'on Oroonoko's shore' (II:539–541). Ireland, while suffering deprivation and the ravages of a greedy nobility, had great natural resources in people and land, and for this part of the kingdom Grant recalled the intention of the Irish-born politician, Edmund Burke, 'from servile bonds thy sons to free' and the hopes of the novelist Maria Edgeworth that education and industry would redeem the country (II:789–806). She looked to 'a constellation of high-gifted bards'—Lord Byron, Walter Scott, Joanna Baillie and Thomas Campbell—to inspire a new British zeal for freedom and to counter the modern spirit of utilitarianism and self-interest (II:881). Finally, she wrote of the moral as well as the military power of Britain, which would soon bring peace, the restoration of the balance of power in Europe and Britain's children 'spread[ing] o'er Earth's remote extremes' the values of 'truth and freedom' (II:1925). While in many passages complacently nationalistic, a hymn to the growth of empire, the poem is not entirely uncritical. Grant recognized British moral failures in the vice and corruption of London and the many casualties of economic expansion. She wrote with sorrow of the emigration of former soldiers from the Highlands of Scotland who, 'by Poverty's gaunt form at length pursued', were compelled to seek 'a new Glengarrie in the wild' (II:1368–1389). As Pam Perkins has suggested, it is 'as much an exhortation as a celebration': the British must be chastened by their past experience if they are to realize her vision of the future.[18]

It is hardly surprising that Grant's poem met with a reception very different from the one critics gave to Barbauld's. Again, reviewers were divided, but ostensibly more over the quality of the poetry than over the politics of the poem. The conservative *British Critic* recommended its easy and graceful flow and trusted it would find the attention it deserved. The reviewer for the more liberal *Eclectic Review* did not object to the subject, which it deemed 'good for an ode', but found the poem far too long and wished the author would return to writing prose. The conventional *Gentleman's Magazine* found it a 'spirited and polished work' and commented on its 'very energetic and poetical' representations of Bonapartist power as well as British excellence in government and encouragement of liberty.[19] The diversity of responses to Barbauld and to Grant illustrated here, along with the disparity in their treatment, need to be placed in the context of the growing yet increasingly structured market for women's writing.

The poetry of war: women, publishing and politics

The British book trade steadily expanded in the last quarter of the eighteenth century, a development that accelerated during the years of war. The number of master printers doubled between 1785 and 1808. The number of bookbinders grew by around 80 per cent between 1794 and 1808.[20] Of all the novels published in the decade from 1800 to 1810, 47 per cent bore the names of women authors on the title page, while 37 per cent could be attributed to male authors.[21] Such detailed statistics do not yet exist on other genres. Women's exclusion from a classical education made it difficult for them to approach the most ambitious forms of poetry: epic, tragedy, satire. Nevertheless, even though they faced restricted notions of the subjects and genres thought appropriate for them, from the 1730s onwards women of every social class took advantage of the enlarged print culture, contributing poetry to periodicals and newspapers and producing broadsides, ballads and single poems published separately, as well as more conventional volumes. We have at present no way to quantify the growth of women's writing during this period. One survey suggests that the ratio of male to female poets between 1770 and 1835 was five or six to one, but this figure relates only to published volumes where authors are identifiable.[22] By the 1780s, women poets such as Anna Seward, Helen Maria Williams and Charlotte Smith were attaining prominence in the world of fashionable poetry, though some recent scholarship suggests that Wordsworth's *Lyrical Ballads* in 1798 and the broad appeal of Romantic subjectivity succeeded in reclaiming the heights of poetic genius as masculine.[23]

Poetry was at this time a part of everyday life for the reading nation, but that nation was of course limited to the literate. Perhaps just over half of all Britons could read, with a significantly higher proportion able to do so in London and lowland Scotland. Their access to different kinds of literature was structured by many factors: gender; wealth, which enabled access to the latest publications; and the availability of circulating libraries, reading societies and other collective literary resources.[24]

Some women poets found publishers for their work, as did Barbauld and Grant, who in earlier works had both contributed to the genre of war poetry.[25] Some, like the middle-class Mary Russell Mitford, paid for publication.[26] Poorer women authors were more likely to have their work privately printed, financed by subscriptions from wealthy patrons; Christian Milne, the wife of a ship's carpenter of Aberdeen, dedicated her volume to the Duchess of Gordon and had a long list of subscribers, as did Elizabeth Bentley of Norwich, a self-taught shoemaker's daughter who kept a small school.[27] Many women contributed poems to periodicals and newspapers, both national and local, though only a few, like Barbauld, wrote reviews and essays, as she did for the *Monthly Review* and *Monthly Repository*. The *Lady's Magazine* published poems by unknown authors like Eliza Baxter of

Newington, Joanna Squire and the pseudonymous 'Marina' on such subjects as 'The Farewell [of a Soldier]', 'The Russian Maid's Farewell to her Lover' and an 'Ode to Pity', which called on the Russian armies to show mercy towards the French columns retreating from Moscow.[28] Elizabeth Bentley contributed to the *Norfolk Advertiser,* and the schoolmaster's daughter, Isabella Lickbarrow of Kendal, to the *Westmorland Advertiser.*[29]

But the conditions of publication were shifting in other ways as well. Cultural historians and literary critics are generally in agreement with Marilyn Butler's view that in 1802 the foundation of the *Edinburgh Review*—in Edinburgh—'set out to break the mould of existing journal culture'.[30] For the first time, professional, well-paid reviewers evaluated the latest works in articles that were often sharply critical, in the hope of making the republic of letters a space for gentlemen; the *Quarterly Review,* founded in London in 1809 as a conservative rival to the Whig *Edinburgh Review,* was a part of this movement. The pages of both journals commented on new works of poetry, fiction, political economy, history, military affairs, travel and more. The reviewers were members of a young intellectual elite, clever, sarcastic and much feared; and both journals set clear boundaries for the subjects thought appropriate for women. No women were invited to contribute to either the *Edinburgh Review* or the *Quarterly Review* until 1835, although a small but growing number wrote for less critically ambitious publications.[31] Barbauld had no personal acquaintance with the reviewers of these elite periodicals. Grant, on the other hand, was well integrated into Edinburgh's literary society and enjoyed the company of the *Edinburgh Review*'s founding editor, Francis Jeffrey. His review of her *Essays on the Superstitions of the Highlanders* noted her 'active, ambitious, and somewhat ill-regulated fancy' and 'decidedly bad taste in jocularity', though Jeffrey also recognized that she 'ha[d] talents to command a very high place among the female writers of her day'. Grant's response to this review is recorded in a letter to her son, in which she says: 'such is the general severity of this critic that I consider myself as gently dealt with & others consider me as briefly prais'd.'[32] Her letter demonstrates the anxieties of reception engendered by such severe professional criticism and gendered standards.[33]

Older models of writing about war coexisted with appealing new forms of chivalric and Romantic poetry. Poetic representations of the victims of conflict typically drew on familiar models: simple sentimental odes or sonnets, elegiac verse and ballads. William St Clair has argued that such writing was encouraged by the publication of many inexpensive anthologies of verse immediately after the copyright decision of 1774—anthologies that included work by such poets as Oliver Goldsmith, Thomas Gray and William Cowper, who wrote on topics considered especially suitable for poetry: man's love of God, nature, familial love and affection and elegies for the dead.[34] Many women poets who wrote of war acknowledged their debt to such collections.[35] As Betty Bennett has observed, 'it was the poetry written in response to the war which was the chief means of popularizing the ballad and its variants'.[36] The ballad form encouraged simple diction and vernacular speech, and it appealed to patriots and radical critics of government alike. Both Grant and Barbauld were familiar with the form. Grant wrote many songs for publication, including the comic 'Nilecrankie', a parody of Robert Burns's 'Killiecrankie', on Napoleon's expedition to Egypt.[37] In 1803 Barbauld composed her 'Song for the London Volunteers', when, in response to rumours of a French invasion, all her nephews joined the Loyal London Volunteers. While sceptical about any real danger, she wrote to a friend that 'it becomes every man, as a man, to learn the use of arms', and she approved in principle of a self-defending citizen-militia whose members remained 'sons of peace'.[38]

However, the best-selling poet of the Napoleonic Wars—and the writer who transformed the imagining of war in Britain—was undoubtedly Walter Scott.[39] Scott began his writing career in the ballad tradition with the collection *Minstrelsy of the Scottish Border* (1802–3). But the lengthy metrical romances that he published between 1805 and 1810—*The Lay of the Last Minstrel* (1805), *Marmion* (1808) and the *Lady of the Lake* (1810)—portrayed war as heroic, picturesque and waged according to chivalric codes. It is hard today to understand the impact of these narrative romances, which relate stories of the rivalry between England and Scotland in the fifteenth and sixteenth centuries. Tales of war and chivalry, they unite a martial subject matter for male readers—assumed to be warriors or, at the very least, volunteers, as was Scott himself in the Royal Edinburgh Light Dragoons—with a romantic element for female readers. At the height of the Peninsular Wars, between 1809 and 1811, Scott's four works together sold over 50,000 copies, far outselling all competitors in spite of their exceptionally high price.[40] Scott wrote less of war's horrors than of its glories and in particular of heroic individual actions, and he framed his poetry with references to contemporary military and political events. *Marmion*, with its detailed depiction of the Battle of Flodden in 1516, a disastrous defeat for Scotland, was to prove a significant model for representations of the battles of the Napoleonic Wars.

The man who most immediately and successfully adapted the form of Scott's romances, his dramatic settings and his descriptions of combat was his friend John Wilson Croker, Barbauld's reviewer, also a poet. His *Battles of Talavera*, a poem on Wellington's victory over the French army, was published in July 1809 and went through eight editions in its first year.[41] Scott himself reviewed it, anonymously and very favourably, in the *Quarterly Review*, commenting that he was 'involuntarily reminded...of the sixth book of Marmion'.[42] Many poets followed Croker in writing of Talavera and later battles in the same spirit, and in 1811 Scott also turned to Spain in his long poem *The Vision of Don Roderick*, encouraged by the example of Lord Byron, Robert Southey and other leading poets of the day.[43]

Anna Barbauld understood something of Scott's popularity, analysing it in her review of *The Lay of the Last Minstrel* for the *Annual Review* in 1805. '[W]ar', she wrote, 'is always most picturesque where it is least formed into a science', and she remarked on the variety and interest of heroic adventures set in 'half-civilized times', when no effective civil authority existed, in contrast to the drudgery of modern professional warfare, which depended on 'a park of artillery and battalions of drilled soldiers'.[44] In *Eighteen Hundred and Eleven* Barbauld predicted that Scott's lines on the ruins of Melrose Abbey would be remembered long after the downfall of the empire (156). Yet as a committed pacifist in a commercial society, she could support only a defensive citizen army.

Anne Grant knew Scott personally, and his influence pervades *Eighteen Hundred and Thirteen*. In it she writes of Anglo-Scottish battles, of William Wallace and Robert Bruce, Bannockburn and Flodden; and she devotes three full pages to Scott, making specific references to individual poems. The *Gentleman's Magazine* noticed that 'Mr Scott receives the strongest praise the Poetess can bestow' when he is presented as Shakespeare's heir in the representation of history.[45] In her earlier *Poems* and *Essays*, Grant had emphasized the significance of social bonds within the rapidly declining clan system of the Scottish Highlands and the importance of a military career for Highlanders in regiments whose collective spirit, she argued, closely mirrored the loyalty and sense of common purpose of the clan.[46] Like Scott, Grant used the past history of conflict between England and Scotland to celebrate British unity during wartime.[47]

The differences in these two women's reactions to Scott also had a political dimension. The politicization of war during the years in which Barbauld and Grant wrote needs to be stressed. Between September 1808, when the controversy over the Convention of Cintra was still fresh, and the victories of Sir Arthur Wellesley (the future Duke of Wellington) on the Iberian Peninsula in 1813, the conduct of the war and British participation in it were continuously debated both inside and outside the House of Commons. There were differences within the government, with its boldest members—including George Canning, in alliance with the Wellesley brothers—advocating a more aggressive military policy. The more liberal Whig opposition was initially hostile to the Peninsular campaign, and it remained critical of Wellington, even after his later successes. A few radicals and dissenters, such as William Roscoe, Member of Parliament for Liverpool, whose 'patriot breast' (147) Barbauld remembers in *Eighteen Hundred and Eleven*, continued to urge peace.[48] Most leading periodicals and newspapers had a clearly defined political perspective, understood by their readers and by each other, which helped to shape their attitudes to the conduct of war. Their political inclinations determined the critical reception of poems by the radical Barbauld and the conservative Grant. So the infamous Croker was not only a poet and critic but also Member of Parliament for Downpatrick, thanks to the patronage of Wellington himself, and, as Secretary to the Admiralty, a junior government minister and a friend and supporter of George Canning.[49] Given all these associations, Croker's reaction to Barbauld was entirely predictable.

Another conservative periodical, the *Anti-Jacobin Review*, mentioned Barbauld's poem only in a review of other journals, in which it criticized the liberal *Monthly Review* for its favourable remarks on *Eighteen Hundred and Eleven*, which were interpreted as evidence of the 'alarming progress of disaffection' among Jacobins and dissenters. The author of this review also noted Barbauld's failure even to mention Wellington or 'the triumphs of the British arms in the Peninsula'; and he mocked her lines on Sir John Moore, who had died at Corunna in what he called 'a memorably disastrous campaign' which 'left a stain upon the British character'.[50] The heroic status given to Moore after the event has obscured the contemporary debate surrounding him. Moore, an energetic and idiosyncratic general and committed army reformer, was distrusted by leading government ministers, including Canning; and his conduct of the campaign was deeply controversial. The many verses published in his memory could contain political overtones. Barbauld, reviewing Mary Cockle's *Lines on the Lamented Death of Sir John Moore* (1810), reprimanded the conservative Walter Scott for failing to pay tribute to Moore, as did Francis Jeffrey in the *Edinburgh Review*.[51] Anne Grant remembered Moore in *Eighteen Hundred and Thirteen*, along with what she called the 'ineffectual' nature of the 'fatal strife' until the 'cool experience' of Wellington took command (II:212–221). In these exchanges between Barbauld, Grant and the reviewers, gender, genre and political disagreements were negotiated in complex ways.

Gender, genre and the writing of war

By publishing their poems, Barbauld and Grant had claimed the right to comment on the moral, political and military state of the British nation; and gender issues were inextricably woven into their public and political voices. Barbauld wrote of 'loved Joanna' (101), the Scottish playwright Joanna Baillie, one of the best-known woman writers of the period, and saluted the moral purpose of Baillie's historical *Plays on the Passions* (1798–1812), in twelve lines on British drama, which focus on her works and only briefly mention Shakespeare (101–112). Grant placed Baillie second only to Scott on her list of British bards to be acclaimed by an 'exulting Caledonia' (II:1070–1078). These tributes to Baillie are paid to a morally committed woman playwright, ambitious to write a philosophically rooted historical drama. Yet neither Barbauld nor Grant sought to advance the situation of women or women writers collectively in any direct way. Barbauld, responding to Mary Wollstonecraft's *Vindication of the Rights of Woman* (1792) in her poem 'The Rights of Woman', called on her readers to 'abandon each ambitious thought' and to learn from 'Nature's school' that 'separate rights are lost in mutual love', though critics have doubted whether this should be seen as her final judgement on women's rights.[52] In 1804 Barbauld replied to Maria Edgeworth's suggestion that they join forces to publish a women's periodical by saying that 'there is no bond of union among literary women, any more than among literary men; different sentiments and different connections separate them much more than the joint interest of their sex would unite them'.[53] Grant, reacting in a letter to Wollstonecraft's work, asserts 'that this intellectual equality that the Misses make such a rout about, has no real existence'. Instead, she suggests, 'the great advantage that women, taken upon the whole, have over men, is that they are more gentle, benevolent, and virtuous'. Women of talent, she adds, would not feel so heavily burdened if their abilities were not so unusual.[54]

Barbauld's constitution of her own independent public voice is deliberately confusing, in a poem that constantly shifts perspectives, from the observer of war to the patriot, from the personification of Fancy to the spirit of Progress moving across the earth. In *Eighteen Hundred and Eleven* she chooses to use an apparently anachronistic Augustan form and demonstrates her familiarity with a broader masculine canon. But she was also accustomed to write on more orthodox feminine topics. As a poet of sensibility, she mobilized the figures of the grieving mother and widow in representing the victims of war:

> Fruitful in vain, the matron counts with pride
> The blooming youths that grace her honoured side;
> No son returns to press her widow'd hand,
> Her fallen blossoms strew a foreign strand.
>
> (23–26)

Where eighteenth-century civic humanism had identified feminized luxury as the source of national corruption, Barbauld saw the masculine pursuit, simultaneously, of 'arts, arms and wealth' (315) as the corrupting force. For Barbauld, 'war's least horror is the ensanguined field' (22), and it was rather the effects of famine, disease and rape, along with the loss of sons, husbands and fathers, that represented a far greater horror. As she prophesied national decline, she also demanded, authoritatively, of the nation, 'And thinkst thou Britain, still to sit at ease...?' (39) as war raged overseas. Her answer was clear: 'Britain, know, | Thou who has shared the guilt must share the woe' (46). Although she represented the consequences of war emotively, she also appealed to the civic virtue and moral responsibility of individual citizens, male and female. But it was a fatalistic call, for 'Commerce, like beauty, knows no second spring' (316), and there was to be no regeneration, no rebirth, for the once-great nation. Barbauld's independence of mind could, however, be appropriated to a feminist purpose. Her appeal was to be heard again in a late review in the newly launched *British Lady's Magazine* of 1815, a periodical inspired by the conviction that women had begun to partake 'to an unprecedented degree' in the intellectual pursuits of civilized life.[55]

While Croker misrepresented Barbauld as an elderly spinster, the literary world was very well aware of, and sympathetic to, Anne Grant's personal situation. She had begun to write only after her husband's death in 1803, in order to support her eleven children. Familial imagery pervades *Eighteen Hundred and Thirteen*. Josephine McDonagh suggests that Grant identifies the British imperial nation with the maternal body: 'Her children spread o'er Earth's remote extremes, | Or by Columbia's lakes or Ganges' streams' (II:1925–1926).[56] North American offspring, temporarily deceived by 'alien foes', would again 'with rekindled filial love' return (II:1931–1934). The union of England and Scotland is shown as a marriage, in which the proud and martial nation of Scotland did not yield to slavery but became 'a willing bride' (II:572). Grant, however, wrote not only of the family but also of the broader social sympathies generated by the life of the clan in the Highlands, in 'modest Nature's last retreat' where she had been privileged to live and which had preserved the values of an earlier age (II:1411). Throughout her work the Highlands represent the bonds of community and simple, even feminized, manners. She idealized that earlier time in the Highlands when 'the finest emotions of the heart, and the most vigorous and vivid paintings of the fancy were felt and understood' with an innocence now threatened by the advance of 'high civilization'.[57] Anne Grant's work was tolerated by the critics for its acceptable mediation of the domestic, the political and the military; for its patriotic hymning of British unity; and for its admiring echoes of Scott.

It is clear from the major periodicals of the era that women responded to contemporary military events through poetry, whether in representations of loss and bereavement, expressions of patriotism, elegies for dead heroes, or depictions of battle. Their literary opportunities and their critical reception were shaped by the kinds of concerns illustrated above. Their poetry was not limited to the domestic or sentimental, though familial concerns were often a central theme. Mary Russell Mitford's 'On the Victory of Barrosa' (1811) is dedicated to the mother of a hero of that battle.[58] Towards the end of the war, celebratory poems included Mary Cockle's *National Triumphs* (1814), Elizabeth Cobbold's *Ode on the Victory of Waterloo* (1815), Charlotte Caroline Richardson's *Waterloo: A Poem on the Late Victory* (1815), Elizabeth Bentley's 'Lines on the Thanksgiving Day, January 18 1816' and many others.[59] Cobbold's *Ode*, in particular, was well reviewed and her gory scenes of battle extensively quoted, though the *British Critic* suggested that 'perhaps too little of the battle is described. But it is not wonderful that a female should shrink from the task of describing the horrors of a field of blood'.[60] Even within this patriotic verse, political differences were evident. To the conservative Cobbold, the restoration of religion, law and monarchy brought 'Order, Peace, and Liberty'—in that order—to France and an expanding commerce to Britain's United Empire.[61] To the Quaker Isabella Lickbarrow, whose poem 'The Vision' (1814) was clearly indebted to Barbauld's *Eighteen Hundred and Eleven*, victory and the restoration of freedom were to be celebrated—'Rejoice ye nations, now the world is freed'—but the final stanzas point to the next task as the freeing of the slave.[62]

Younger women writers were especially ambitious to follow Walter Scott's example and to use the language of heroic and chivalric romance in relation to war, although the high cost of Scott's works meant that readers, and poets, on low incomes could not enjoy them as they came from the press. The shoemaker's daughter Elizabeth Bentley recognized the limitations of her own self-education in an older canon, compared to this 'bolder style of poetry'.[63] But those who could afford to read Scott's newly published works took up the challenge. Margaret Holford's long metrical romance, *Wallace; or, the Fight of Falkirk* (1809), published in a 250-page quarto and now almost entirely forgotten, was widely reviewed and much praised when it first appeared. The *Critical Review* declared it the work of 'a poetical genius', the *European Magazine* thought it abounding with 'just and glowing sentiments', the *Eclectic Review* saw in it 'a strength and greatness of conception', and the *Scots Magazine* found it particularly successful 'in those departments which seem most beyond the reach of a female pen'.[64] It includes a substantial section on the battle of Falkirk in 1298, in which Holford draws attention to the similarity between the gallantry of Sir John Stewart in the thirteenth century and that of a Colonel Vassall at the storming in 1807 of Montevideo, now in Uruguay.[65] Both Mary Russell Mitford and Felicia Hemans (née Browne), influenced by Scott and the attractions of chivalry, incorporated themes from Spanish romances and ballads into their narrative poems.[66] Some reviewers expressed scepticism as to the suitability of Scott's style for young women writers, with the *Monthly Review* counselling Mitford to restrain her 'petty larcenies from the property of Sir Walter Scott'.[67]

The very young Felicia Hemans, who had two brothers serving in the Peninsular War, responded directly to changing representations of war. Four years before she married Captain Alfred Hemans in 1812, Felicia Browne published a substantial poem, *England and Spain; or, Valour and Patriotism*, in which she presents both British and Spanish forces as champions of freedom in chivalric terms; it was ignored by reviewers.[68] Her next volume, *Domestic Affections* (1812), was misleadingly titled in that it also contained a range of war poems. The longest of these, 'War and Peace', predicted British victories leading to peace across Europe, though even as it resounded with confidence in the national cause, it lamented the losses suffered by the widowed and the orphaned. This collection also included several poems addressed to her brothers, presenting patriotic sentiments through familial identity.[69] More recent evaluations of Hemans, who was to become the best-selling woman poet of the nineteenth century, have emphasized not her appeal to bourgeois domesticity but the degree of ambivalence in her verse and a patriotism that consistently betrayed a sense of vulnerability and of the closeness of death.[70]

Broader issues of gender politics emerged during this period which require much more detailed discussion than can be given here. How, for example, did the popular revival of chivalry as a means of imagining war—one that consciously echoed Edmund Burke's lament for the 'age of chivalry'—affect contemporary constructions of masculinity and femininity?[71] Increasingly in his poetry Scott emphasized the heroic rather than romantic elements, although he consciously appealed to his substantial female readership. His female characters are vulnerable and to be protected. They are also conventionally supportive of their heroes, recognizing masculine codes of honour, rewarding courage and caring for the wounded. Occasionally, and especially in times of national crisis, these characters actively participate in battle, uniting with the nation in its time of need, as does Edith, disguised as a page, in *The Lord of the Isles* (1815). Scott's heroines, though conventional, imaginatively identify with the sentiments of the warrior and the nation.[72] Nevertheless, such a valorization of chivalry, which distances the representation of battle from the immediate realities of modern warfare, could entrench images of female weakness and vulnerability, and of male heroism, honour and protectiveness. Even if, in Scott's version, women are admitted into the imagining of the nation at war, in ways allowing chivalry to be feminized as a means towards a more peaceful and domesticated future, the ideal of chivalry still incorporates a recharged and conservative version of femininity.

Conclusion

The silencing of Barbauld illustrated the zeal of a new generation of professional critics to impose limits on women writers and readers, notably in relation to war and politics, although it was equally provoked by Barbauld's remarkable radicalism and pacifism. Political hostility was fanned by her disregard for masculine standards. But the range of women's imaginative responses to war and the growth of empire, here considered through two major poems, suggests that women made significant contributions to the literary representation of war in the public sphere. They took advantage of an expanding yet highly gendered print culture in ways that reflected their own social and political positions. Working-class women poets, such as Elizabeth Bentley, a shoemaker's daughter and keeper of a small school, and Christian Milne, a carpenter's wife, continued to depend on patronage and on support from their local communities throughout the war years. Middle-class writers, however ambitious, were aware of the need to conciliate the gendered standards of the critics. Radical and dissenting periodicals were—though there were many exceptions—more receptive to women's writing that challenged conventions; they were also more likely to question the values of chivalry. In the postwar period, feminist and anti-feminist arguments were to engage more directly with the gendered legacies of the chivalric and heroic literature that characterized the later years of the Napoleonic Wars.

Acknowledgement

I would like to thank Kathryn Gleadle and Gisela Mettele for their helpful suggestions for the revision of this chapter.

Notes

1. Anna Barbauld, *Eighteen Hundred and Eleven: A Poem* (London, 1812), ll. 1–4. All quotations from this work follow the text in *The Poems of Anna Letitia Barbauld*, ed. William McCarthy and Elizabeth Kraft (Athens, 1994); subsequent line references are given parenthetically after each citation.
2. John Wilson Croker, 'Mrs Barbauld's 1811', *Quarterly Review* (hereafter *QR*) 7 (1812): 309–313, 309.
3. *Anti-Jacobin Review* 42 (1811): 203–209; *British Critic* (hereafter *BC*) 40 (1812): 408–409; *Eclectic Review* (hereafter *EcR*) 8 (1812): 474–478; *New Annual Register* 33 (1812): 377; William Keach, 'A Regency Prophecy and the End of Anna Barbauld's Career', *Studies in Romanticism* 33 (1994): 569–577.
4. James Chandler, *England in 1819: The Politics of Literary Culture and the Case of Romantic Historicism* (Chicago, 1998), 114–120, 114.
5. Lucy Aikin, 'Memoir' prefixed to *The Works of Anna Laetitia Barbauld* (1825; repr. London, 1996), lii; for other biographical information on Anna Barbauld, see Betsy Rodgers, *Georgian Chronicle: Mrs Barbauld and her Family* (London, 1958); Anne Janowitz, *Women Romantic Poets: Anna Barbauld and Mary Robinson* (Tavistock, 2004).
6. *Monthly Review* (*MR*) 67 (1812): 428–432; *Monthly Repository* 7 (1812): 108; *British Lady's Magazine* 2 (1815): 318–321.
7. Gary Kelly, *Women, Writing, and Revolution, 1790–1827* (Oxford, 1993), 165–191; Simon Bainbridge, *British Poetry and the Revolutionary and Napoleonic Wars: Visions of Conflict* (Oxford, 2003), 31–38; Clifford Siskin, *The Work of Writing: Literature and Social Change in Britain, 1700–1830* (Baltimore, 1998), 224.
8. Mary Favret, 'Coming Home: The Public Spaces of Romantic War', *Studies in Romanticism* 33 (1994): 539–548.
9. Stephen C. Behrendt, '"A few harmless Numbers": British Women Poets and the Climate of War, 1793–1815', in *Romantic Wars: Studies in Culture and Conflict, 1793–1822*, ed. Philip Shaw (Aldershot, 2000), 13–36; Christian Gray, *Tales, Letters and Other Pieces in Verse* (Edinburgh, 1808), 34–35; Dorothea Primrose Campbell, *Poems* (Inverness, 1811), 25–28.
10. Behrendt, '"A few harmless Numbers"', 32; see also Stephen C. Behrendt, 'The Gap That Is Not a Gap: British Poetry by Women, 1802–1812', in *Romanticism and Women Poets: Opening the Doors of Reception*, ed. Harriet Kramer Linkin and Stephen C. Behrendt (Lexington, 1999), 25–45.

11. Jürgen Habermas, *The Structural Transformation of the Public Sphere: An Inquiry into a Category of Bourgeois Society* (Cambridge, MA, 1989).
12. See particularly Joan Landes, *Women and the Public Sphere in the Age of the French Revolution* (Ithaca, 1988); Joanna Meehan (ed.), *Feminists Read Habermas: Gendering the Subject of Discourse* (New York, 1995); Jane Rendall, 'Women and the Public Sphere', *Gender & History* 11/3 (1999): 475–488.
13. See Orrin N. C. Wang, 'Romancing the Counter-Public Sphere: A Response to Romanticism and its Publics', *Studies in Romanticism* 33 (1994): 579–588; see also the other contributions to this special issue on 'Romanticism and its Publics: A Forum'.
14. Recent critical discussions, besides those mentioned below, include Anne Janowitz, *Women Romantic Poets: Anna Barbauld and Mary Robinson* (Tavistock, 2004); William Keach, 'Barbauld, Romanticism, and the Survival of Dissent', *Essays and Studies* 51 (1998): 62–77; Penny Mahon, 'In Sermon and Story: Contrasting Anti-War Rhetoric in the Work of Anna Barbauld and Amelia Opie', *Women's Writing* 7 (2000): 23–38; Marlon Ross, 'Configurations of Feminine Reform: The Woman Writer and the Tradition of Dissent', in *Re-Visioning British Romanticism: British Women Writers 1776–1837*, ed. Carol Shiner Wilson and Joel Haefner (Philadelphia, 1994), 91–110.
15. Samuel Johnson, 'London: A Poem in Imitation of Juvenal's Third Satire', in *The Oxford Authors: Samuel Johnson*, ed. Donald Greene (Oxford, 1984), 2–8, cited in William Levine, 'The Eighteenth-Century Jeremiad and Progress-Piece Traditions in Anna Barbauld's "Eighteen Hundred and Eleven" ', *Women's Writing* 12 (2005): 177–186; Constantin-François de Volney, *The Ruins, or, A Survey of the Revolutions of Empires... Translated from the French* (London, 1792).
16. Anne Grant, *Eighteen Hundred and Thirteen: A Poem* (Edinburgh, 1814). Part and line numbers are given parenthetically in the text and follow those of the electronic text in *The English Poetry Full-Text Database*, Version 4.0 (Cambridge, UK, 1995). For biographical information on Anne Grant, see J. P. Grant, 'Memoir of the Life of Mrs Grant', in *Memoir and Correspondence of Mrs Grant of Laggan*, ed. J. P. Grant, 3 vols (2nd edn, London, 1845), 1–32.
17. Anne Grant, *Poems on Various Subjects* (Edinburgh, 1803); *Letters from the Mountains; being the Real Correspondence of a Lady, between the Years 1773 and 1803*, 3 vols (London, 1806); *Essays on the Superstitions of the Highlanders of Scotland*, 2 vols (London, 1811). For useful readings of Anne Grant's work, see Peter Womack, *Improvement and Romance: Constructing the Myth of the Highlands* (Basingstoke, 1989); Pam Perkins, 'Anne MacVicar Grant 1755–1838: Critical Essay' in Scottish Women Poets of the Romantic Period, <http://www.alexanderstreet2.com/swrplive/bios/S7024-D001.html> (18 January 2007); Kenneth McNeil, '"Not Absolutely a Native nor Entirely a Stranger": Anne Grant and the Highland Travelogue', in *Scotland, Ireland and the Romantic Aesthetic,* ed. David Duff and Catherine Jones (Lewisburg, PA, 2007).
18. Perkins, 'Anne MacVicar Grant', 10.
19. *BC*, ns 2 (1814): 324–326; *EcR*, 2nd ser., 2 (1814): 101–103; *Gentleman's Magazine* 84 (1814): 458–459.
20. See William St Clair, *The Reading Nation in the Romantic Period* (Cambridge, UK, 2004), 456–457.
21. Peter Garside et al. (eds), *The English Novel 1770–1829: A Bibliographical Survey of Prose Fiction Published in the British Isles*, 2 vols (Oxford, 2000), vol. 1, 46–47, vol. 2, 73.

22. St Clair, *Reading Nation*, 172n. 73; J. R. de J. Jackson, *Romantic Poetry by Women: A Bibliography 1770–1835* (Oxford, 1993).
23. Roger Lonsdale, 'Introduction', *Eighteenth-Century British Women Poets: An Oxford Anthology* (Oxford, 1989); Betty T. Bennett, *British War Poetry in the Age of Romanticism* (New York, 1976).
24. For a full recent discussion of these issues see St Clair, *Reading Nation*, esp. chs 6, 11, 13 and 17.
25. Anne Grant, 'To the Right Honourable Henry Dundas, with a poem on the death of Sir Ralph Abercromby', 'To His Royal Highness the Duke of York, with an invalid soldier's petition', 'On the Marquis of Huntly's Departure for the Continent with his Regiment in 1799', 'To The Blue Bell of Scotland', in *Poems*, 219–235, 286–289, 407–409; 'To a Great Nation. Written by a Lady', 'Peace and Shepherd', 'Song for the London Volunteers', in *Poems of Anna Letitia Barbauld*, 124–125, 137–138, 141–142.
26. Mary Russell Mitford, *The Life of Mary Russell Mitford: Related in a Selection from Her Letters to Her Friends*, ed. Alfred G. K. L'Estrange, 3 vols (London, 1870), vol. 1, 91.
27. Christian Milne, *Simple Poems on Simple Subjects* (Aberdeen, 1805); Elizabeth Bentley, *Poems* (Norwich, 1821). On working-class women's poetry, see: Donna Landry, *The Muses of Resistance. Laboring-Class Women's Poetry in Britain, 1739–1796* (Cambridge, UK, 1990); Lonsdale, 'Introduction', xxxvii.
28. Eliza Baxter, 'The Farewell', *Lady's Magazine* (*LM*) 42 (November 1811): 526; Joanna Squire, 'Stanzas...on reading an extract from Mr Scott's "Vision of Don Roderick"', Supplement to *LM* 42 (1811): 618; Joanna Squire, 'Ode to Pity', *LM* 44 (March 1813): 145–146; Marina [pseud.], 'The Russian Maid's Farewell to Her Lover', *LM* 43 (November 1812): 522; and Marina [pseud.], 'Alleyne and Francis', *LM* 44 (April and May 1813): 191–192 and 241–242.
29. Bentley, *Poems*, xix; Isabella Lickbarrow, *Collected Poems*, ed. with a biographical study by Constance Parrish (Grasmere, 2004), 7–8.
30. Marilyn Butler, 'Culture's Medium: The Role of the Review', in *The Cambridge Companion to British Romanticism*, ed. Stuart Curran (Cambridge, UK, 1993), 120–147, 131. See also Jon Klancher, The *Making of English Reading Audiences 1790–1832* (Madison, 1987), 47–75; Ina Ferris, *The Achievement of Literary Authority: Gender, History and the Waverley Novels* (Ithaca, NY, 1991), 19–78.
31. Jane Rendall, 'Bluestockings and Reviewers: Gender, Power and Culture in Britain c. 1800–1830', *Nineteenth-Century Contexts* 26 (2004): 355–374, 370.
32. Anne Grant to John Hatsell, 27 November 1806, and Anne Grant to Mrs Hook, 5 June 1810, in J. P. Grant, *Memoir and Correspondence of Mrs Grant*, vol. 1, 77–79, 245–246; Francis Jeffrey, 'Mrs Grant on Highlanders', *Edinburgh Review* (hereafter *ER*) 18 (August 1811): 480–510, 482; Edinburgh University Library (hereafter EUL), MS La II. 357, fos 205–210, Anne Grant to her son Duncan Grant, 25 October 1811.
33. See Lucy Newlyn, *Reading, Writing and Romanticism: The Anxiety of Reception* (Oxford, 2000), 3–48.
34. St Clair, *Reading Nation*, 122–139, 539–545.
35. Bentley, *Poems*, xxi; Milne, *Simple Poems on Simple Subjects*, 7–8 and 11–20.
36. Bennett, *British War Poetry*, 51.
37. 'Nilecrankie: or, the French Expedition to Egypt. Air – Kilicrankie[sic]', in Anne Grant, *Poems*, 410–413; EUL, MS La II. 357, fo. 35^v, Anne Grant to George Thomson, n.d. See also 'Come to Battle', fo. 39^r.

38. 'Song for the London Volunteers', *Poems of Anna Letitia Barbauld*, 141–142; Barbauld to Susannah Taylor, in Mary B. Whiting, 'A Century-Old Friendship: Unpublished Letters from Mrs Barbauld', *London Mercury* 26 (1932): 434–445, quoted in Barbauld, *Poems*, 302.
39. Here I am much indebted to Bainbridge, *British Poetry*, 1–2, 17–18, 120–147, 159–170.
40. Peter Murphy, *Poetry as an Occupation and an Art in Britain, 1760–1830* (Cambridge, UK, 1993), 139; St Clair, *Reading Nation*, 180, 216–218, 632–36.
41. [John Wilson Croker], *The Battles of Talavera, a Poem* (London, 1809).
42. Walter Scott, 'The Battles of Talavera', *QR* 2 (November 1809): 427–433, 428.
43. Bainbridge, *British Poetry*, 159–170.
44. *Annual Review* 3 (1805): 600–604, quoted in ibid. 121–125.
45. *Gentleman's Magazine* 84 (1814): 458–459.
46. Anne Grant, 'The Highlanders: or Sketches of Highland Scenery & Manners: with Some Reflections on Emigration', in Anne Grant, *Poems*, 19–138; Anne Grant, *Essays on the Superstitions of the Highlanders*, vol. 2, 122–145.
47. Anne Grant, *Eighteen Hundred and Thirteen*, 75–93; Richard Cronin, *The Politics of Romantic Poetry: In Search of the Perfect Commonwealth* (Basingstoke, 2000), 103–109.
48. J. E. Cookson, *The Friends of Peace: Anti-War Liberalism in England, 1793–1815* (Cambridge, MA, 1982), 132, 220–223.
49. Rory Muir, *Britain and the Defeat of Napoleon, 1807–15* (New Haven, 1996), 59; Bennett, *British War Poetry*, 10–23.
50. *Anti-Jacobin Review* 42 (1811): 203–209.
51. *MR* 66 (1811): 431; Jeffrey, 'Scott's *Vision of Don Roderick*', *ER* 18 (1811): 390.
52. 'The Rights of Woman', in McCarthy and Kraft, *Poems of Anna Letitia Barbauld*, 121–122, 289; see also Keach, 'Barbauld, Romanticism', 56; Janowitz, *Women Romantic Poets*, 69; Adelaide Morris, 'Woman Speaking to Women: Retracing the Feminine in Anna Letitia Barbauld', *Women's Writing* 10 (2003): 47–72.
53. Barbauld to Maria Edgeworth, 30 August 1804, in Anna Letitia Le Breton, *Memoir of Mrs Barbauld including Letters and Notices of Her Family and Friends* (London, 1874), 86–87.
54. Anne Grant to Miss Ourry, 2 January 1794, in J. P. Grant, *Memoirs and Correspondence of Mrs Grant*, vol. 2, 267–277.
55. 'Introductory Address', *British Lady's Magazine* 1 (1815): 1–4; 'Introductory Address', ibid. 2 (1815): 318–321; Alvin Sullivan (ed.), *British Literary Magazines: The Romantic Age, 1789–1836* (Westport, CT, 1983), 62–66.
56. Josephine McDonagh, 'Barbauld's Domestic Economy', *Essays and Studies* 51 (1998): 63–77.
57. Anne Grant, *Essays on the Superstitions of the Highlanders of Scotland*, vol. 2, 60.
58. 'On the Victory of Barrosa. To Mrs Taylor of Hartley Court, near Reading, mother of Colonel Norcott', in Mary Russell Mitford, *Poems* (2nd edn [with considerable additions], London, 1811), 255–257.
59. Mary Cockle, *National Triumphs* (London, 1814); Elizabeth Cobbold, *Ode on the Victory of Waterloo* (Ipswich, 1815); Charlotte Caroline Richardson, *Waterloo, A Poem on the Late Victory* (London [1815]); 'Lines on the Thanksgiving Day, January 18 1816', in Bentley, *Poems*, 122–123.
60. *BC* 5 (1816): 217–218; see also *MR* 78 (1815): 92–94; *Augustan Review* 1 (1815): 785–794; *EcR* 4 (1815): 570–578.
61. Cobbold, *Ode on the Victory of Waterloo*, 17–18.

62. Lickbarrow, *Collected Poems*, 194–201, 201.
63. Bentley, *Poems*, xxi.
64. Margaret Holford, *Wallace; or, the Fight of Falkirk: A Metrical Romance* (London, 1809); *Critical Review* 19 (1810): 130–149; *European Magazine* 57 (1810): 44–50; *EcR* 6 (1810): 1103–1112; *Scots Magazine* 72 (1810): 925–929. See also *MR* 62 (1810): 26–39; *BC* 37 (1811): 37–43; *QR* 3 (1810): 63–69; *Literary Panorama* 8 (1810): 413–423.
65. Holford, *Wallace*, 246.
66. In Mitford's work, see, for instance, 'Sybille: A Northumbrian Tale', in Mitford, *Poems*, 5–22; Mitford, 'Blanch', in *Narrative Poems on the Female Character in the Various Relations of Life* (London, 1813), 3–259.
67. *MR* 65 (1811): 249–256, 253; see also *MR* 68 (1812): 318–319; *BC* 42 (1813): 230–237; *Critical Review* 3 (1813): 638–646.
68. Felicia Browne [Hemans], *England and Spain, or, Valour and Patriotism* (London, 1808); Bainbridge, *British Poetry*, 156–159.
69. Ibid. 150–155; Felicia Browne [Hemans], 'War and Peace', and 'To my eldest brother with the British Army in Portugal', *The Domestic Affections, and Other Poems* (London, 1812), 89–121 and 145–147.
70. For instance, Susan Wolfson, ' "Domestic Affections" and "the Spear of Minerva": Felicia Hemans and the Dilemmas of Gender', in *Re-Visioning Romanticism*, 128–166; Tricia Lootens, 'Hemans and Home: Victorianism, Feminine "Internal Enemies", and the Domestication of National Identity', *PMLA* 109 (1994): 238–253.
71. Susan Manning, 'Walter Scott, Antiquarianism and the Political Discourse of the *Edinburgh Review*' in *British Romanticism and the Edinburgh Review: Bicentenary Essays*, ed. Massimiliano Demata and Duncan Wu (Basingstoke, 2002), 102–123, 111–115.
72. Bainbridge, *British Poetry*, 139–147.

14
Celebrating War and Nation: Gender, Patriotism and Festival Culture during and after the Prussian Wars of Liberation

Karen Hagemann

In Berlin the Prussian wars of Liberation began as a celebration. When Russian troops under General Peter von Wittgenstein marched into the city on 11 March 1813, men, women and children of all ages and classes thronged the streets, cheering as they went to welcome the approaching army. Church bells rang out everywhere, and in the evening the entire city was illuminated, even without the usual orders from the municipal government. Berliners remained outdoors far into the night, generously distributing food and drink to their Russian liberators and enjoying the festive atmosphere.[1]

Wars hardly seem to be times for festivities. They usually evoke associations of blood, violence, death, aggression, fear and terror. Yet the Wars of Liberation of 1813-15 in Prussia demonstrate the importance of spontaneous and organized public celebrations for (post)war culture. The well-known 'National Festival of the Germans', held for the first time on 18 and 19 October 1814 to commemorate the decisive victory over Napoleon in the Battle of Nations at Leipzig, is recognized as the largest festival of the period and is even considered the 'matrix of German national festivals in the nineteenth century'.[2] Many smaller patriotic celebrations, however, have gone unnoticed until now: induction ceremonies for volunteers and militiamen, flag consecrations, thanksgiving and victory celebrations, festivities to welcome homecoming soldiers, homage ceremonies (*Huldigungsfeiern*) for the new government, peace festivals and commemorations of the dead as well as of specific battles and heroes. In the Prussian monarchy the government mandated many of these festivals, but several others were initiated independently on a local level by municipalities, the clergy and the citizenry or spontaneously celebrated by the population. The 'patriotic-national'[3] festival culture was particularly well developed in Prussia, but similar ceremonies and festivities were organized in other German territorial states, too, especially in the north and west.[4]

After the crushing defeat of 1806–7, the Prussian government had tried in every possible way to mobilize broad segments of the population for war. In particular the self-styled 'patriots'—educated officers and state officials, schoolteachers, professors and pastors—called for 'revenge' and stipulated reforms of the Prussian state and military that should enable the monarchy to start a victorious war against France. For them one of the most important reforms was the introduction of universal conscription. Its implementation became possible, however, only after the government resolved the fierce resistance from the middle class by reforming the army and gaining broad support for a new war. Because the terms of the Treaty of Tilsit signed on 9 July 1807 restricted the size of the Prussian army, the monarchy had to wait until the day after declaring war against France on 16 March 1813 to introduce universal conscription for the duration. All able-bodied men between the ages of 17 and 40 years who did not belong to the standing army or a volunteer corps were required to serve in the newly created militia (*Landwehr*). Proxies were not permitted, and only a few men deemed 'indispensable' or 'frail' were exempted from conscription. The militia had to be raised, clothed and equipped by the provincial districts, which depended to a large extent on the financial and practical aid of the civilian population. Only with the broad support of its subjects could the Prussian monarchy wage war in 1813. A high level of military mobilization was achieved in just a few months; by August of that year volunteers represented 8 per cent and militiamen 46 per cent of all soldiers in the Prussian Army.[5] The provincial districts were also responsible for assisting the families of soldiers, war widows and orphans as well as disabled veterans, largely through donations. In addition, the civilian population paid the war-related duties and taxes that enabled the nearly bankrupt Prussian state to make war. For all these reasons it was necessary to mobilize the entire population, not just soldiers and recruits. Rituals, ceremonies and festivities became an important form of patriotic-national war mobilization.[6]

Early modern European monarchies had traditionally used public ceremonies and festivals to display and stabilize their political power and prestige. The king's coronation, his birthday or important battlefield victories were typically celebrated with grand festivals. Military parades in radiant dress uniforms became a part of these ceremonies when early modern states introduced standing armies and the drilling of soldiers became commonplace. Churches were often used for state-ordered intercession and thanksgiving services during and after wars, and eighteenth-century Prussia was no exception in this regard.[7]

In the 1770s and 1780s, however, a novel discourse emerged in Central Europe and elsewhere. Enlightened reformers proposed a refashioning of the public festival culture, which they now understood as part of 'national culture'. They believed that such celebrations could be used to develop patriotism and a feeling of national belonging among the population.[8]

Revolutionary France was the first state to demonstrate vividly the potential of a state-organized festival culture for national mobilization in the early 1790s, and it became a model for others.[9] In Prussia, an intensive discussion about a patriotic festival culture began after the monarchy's defeat in the war of 1806–7, in the context of the debate on the best forms of war mobilization. The patriots pointed to the example of the French enemy and argued that patriotic rituals, ceremonies and festivities would reach even illiterate strata of the population and be far more effective than newspapers and leaflets, because they would touch the emotions and the senses.[10]

New research conclusively demonstrates that rituals, ceremonies and festivities can help to form collective identities by combining textual, visual and material languages with cultural practices and allowing for the active participation of individuals and groups.[11] The importance of gender differences in the form and content of festival culture is often overlooked, however. Here the term *gender* refers to both the subject itself and the research methodology used to investigate it, which can illuminate a whole range of social cleavages and cultural practices.[12] The extensive scholarship on nation and gender has shown that gender images proved crucial in the discursive construction of the new patriotic-national ideologies and national identities; the creation of national movements; mobilization for war; and the subsequent emergence of a collective memory of war.[13] In interaction with other factors—such as the ensemble of participating social groups (their class, sex, age and so on), their place in the events of the celebration, the chosen location and the symbols used—gendered images and symbols also formed the message of patriotic ceremonies and festivities as well as the notions of a society and its gender order that they conveyed. I therefore analyse the festival culture in its specific historical contexts, using the methodology of 'thick description' and a gender perspective.[14]

In what follows, I shall show how public ceremonies and festivities were used during and after the wars between 1813 and 1815 to promote a highly gendered form of patriotism.[15] My analysis will focus on induction ceremonies and flag consecrations, thanksgiving and victory celebrations and festivities marking the homecoming of soldiers that had been held throughout the old and new Prussian territories and other regions of western and northern Germany. I will ask which notions of political and social order and gender images these ceremonies and festivities embodied, and how the symbolic orchestration was used to create affective ties to state and nation and to mobilize for war.

Induction ceremonies for volunteers and militiamen

Already in the years before the introduction of universal conscription, Prussian patriots had discussed how an induction ritual for conscripts could be used to encourage the idea of arming the people.[16] Most influential for the form of this ritual became the proposal by the well-known political author and patriot Ernst Moritz Arndt. In order to mobilize for the coming war against France and promote universal conscription, he wrote the pamphlet *Was bedeutet Landsturm und Landwehr?* (What Do Territorial Reserve and Militia Mean?), which was produced by the Prussian army in February 1813 and disseminated in a print run of close to 100,000 copies. In this text Arndt recommends that an induction ceremony be organized for the militia in each of Prussia's provincial districts:

> Once the young men of a district are assembled, a solemn worship service will be held and it will be explained to the youths what war more generally and what war for the fatherland and against the French means, and that they are a far better and nobler people than the French, and thus must not suffer the latter to remain their masters; they will be told and admonished that their own land was once fortunate and glorious, and that it will become so again by their virtue and honesty; they will be reminded that dying for the fatherland is high praise in Heaven and on earth, and speeches, prayers and sacred and military songs will ignite loyalty, glory and virtue in their hearts.[17]

At the end of the ceremony the young men would swear a 'precious and stalwart oath'. To intensify the community-creating emotions, Arndt advised that this oath be taken 'in a large company', so 'that several hundred or thousand swear at the same time'. On this occasion the militia's flags would also be consecrated 'with Christian prayer and earnest devotion'.[18] Arndt's argument for the necessity of war against France was typical of its time. He, like many of his contemporaries, consistently characterized the struggle as a 'holy war', a 'war for the fatherland', which must be fought unto 'victory or death'. The Christian symbolism was therefore very pronounced in his proposed model for the induction ceremony.[19]

Contemporary press reports suggest that the organizers of most induction ceremonies—the local authorities, the military and the protestant churches—followed Arndt's recommendations.[20] One of the first and best-documented ceremonies is the induction of the Lützow *Freikorps*, the first volunteer corps approved by the Prussian king, which took place near Breslau on 28 March 1813. The *Preussische Correspondent* gave a vivid description:

> At twilight, the assembled corps arrived at the church in Rogau, which was brightly illuminated by candles and torchlight. Martial music welcomed them. The choir struck up a heart-lifting chorale penned especially for the occasion by Körner, and Luther's powerful hymn 'A Mighty Fortress is our God!'
>
> With concise words spoken from the steps of the altar, the pastor reminded the assembled company of the duties of the warrior, the dangers of war, admonishing each to fulfil the former loyally and face the

latter with courage. The soldiers then shouted as in one voice: 'We swear it!' and the pastor knelt down before God, loudly calling upon Him to 'Save the fatherland' and 'Lead the warriors to victory or death!' The warriors then raised their hands to Heaven and swore steadfast loyalty unto death to God, king and fatherland. The quiet, devout emotion of all those assembled poured forth in rivers of tears.[21]

The account portrays the ceremony, which involved a thousand volunteers, as a regional-patriotic (*landespatriotisch*) event, in which the soldiers vowed to fight for 'God, king and fatherland'. Only the reference to Theodor Körner, a well-known Saxon poet and member of the *Freikorps*, explicitly indicates the ceremony's German-national orientation, reflecting the composition of the unit, which accepted volunteers from all German territories. In his 'Lied zur feyerlichen Einsegung des Königlich Preußischen Freicorps' (Song for the Solemn Consecration of the Royal Prussian Freikorps), Körner describes the war against Napoleon as the 'German people's sanctified struggle for freedom'.[22]

Autobiographical recollections of the ceremony more strongly emphasize their German-national character. At the same time, these texts document the gender dimension of a ceremony that constituted an initiation ritual in which young men were transformed into soldiers. The oath was correspondingly taken not just at the altar and thus before God but also on the swords of the officers, the symbol par excellence of martial masculinity. Battle-tested sword bearers and experienced soldiers administered the oath to the fledgling warriors and introduced them to their new role.[23] The degree to which sacred, patriotic-national, military and gender elements mingled and mutually reinforced each other in the ceremony by arousing or heightening powerful emotions among the participants is evident in a letter written by Körner on 30 March 1813 to his friend Henriette von Pereira in Vienna:

> After the singing of a song of my own composition, the local pastor gave a powerful and moving sermon, leaving not a dry eye. At last he had us swear the oath.... We swore. Thereupon he fell to his knees and begged God's blessing for his warriors. By the Almighty, it was a moment when the consecration of the dead trembled aflame in every breast, when every heart beat heroically.[24]

The induction of the Lützow volunteers was not the only ceremony to have such an emotional effect. Other accounts also describe the company as so moved that they were 'overcome' by their feelings and wept copiously. In this period men were still permitted and indeed expected to develop strong feelings for their country and could display them publicly without embarrassment. The patriots understood male empathy as an important precondition for patriotism and heroism. It was only later during the nineteenth century that emotions came to be regarded as weak and therefore feminine.[25] Christian rhetoric and symbolism played an important role in fuelling the emotions of the ceremony. Patriotic-national thoughts and feelings were couched in a religiously coloured language familiar to broad segments of the population. Religion, too, was not yet viewed as primarily 'feminine'.[26]

Most of the induction ceremonies, which became common for volunteers and militias, first in the old Prussian territories and shortly thereafter in the liberated northern and western regions of Germany, proceeded along similar lines. Organized by the provincial district administration and the military, in cooperation with local church parishes, the ceremonies typically began with the militia inductees marching up to the church. The ringing of the church bells announced the ceremony itself, which took place either on the square in front of the church or inside, before the altar. Framed by patriotic-religious songs, the sermon and the communal oath were the main focus. The ceremonies were public and seem to have generated great interest everywhere. When the induction took place in the unit's home district, which was the rule for the militia, it was attended not just by the immediate family but also by an extensive network of kin and friends. The local authorities and clergy were always represented, and the programme invariably featured a parade by the town's citizen guard (*städtische Bürgergarde*).

The ceremonies for volunteers and militias differed mainly in three respects: first, the militia ceremonies were far more rooted in the regional community; second, their political orientation was regional-patriotic, not German-national like most volunteer ceremonies; and third, the recruits frequently lacked the enthusiasm of the volunteers.[27] Accounts of the militia induction ceremonies rarely mention enthusiasm for war. Instead they frequently stress the 'quiet and earnest' mood of the militiamen who were taking the oath.[28] This may well have reflected the fact that many of them served only reluctantly.[29] The military leadership, local authorities and clergy thus used the induction ceremonies to remind militia recruits in no uncertain terms of 'men's sacred duty to defend the fatherland'.[30]

At the induction ceremonies, volunteers and militiamen alike were called on to make a 'voluntary self-sacrifice for the fatherland', which was now deemed the highest form of patriotism, but the emphasis differed. For the mainly young volunteers this self-sacrifice was represented as a ritual of initiation into male adulthood, while the war was depicted as a national 'struggle for liberation against Napoleon'. In the case of the militia recruits, who were of varying ages, the stress was on the necessity to sacrifice as 'defenders' of family, home and fatherland, which referred to both the individual territorial state and to the 'German nation' as a whole. This direct linking of the personal, the local, the regional and the national was intended to mobilize the masculine willingness to fight.[31]

Flag consecrations

Actors in the induction ceremonies were exclusively male. As a rule, women attended the events as mere spectators. Even in the symbolic repertoire of these ceremonies they had no place. The only exceptions were those associated with flag consecrations. In these rituals women played a central role as flag embroiderers.[32] This is evident from a report in the *Deutsche Blätter* that describes an induction ceremony for 950 volunteers held on 25 January 1814 in Düsseldorf. The town was the capital of the 'Governorate between Weser and Rhine', created after the battle of Leipzig by the Central Administration of the allies and became Prussian in 1815. Under the direction of the governor-general, the event, with 'many thousands' of participants, took place before and inside the largest church in the city. After the swearing of the oath at the end of the usual ritual, 'young female citizens of Elberfeld', a nearby town, presented the flag and banner they had made for the volunteers. The governor-general 'introduced the standard- and flag-bearers to the noble donors from whose hands they received this symbol of public spirit'; then a Catholic priest and two Protestant ministers jointly consecrated the flag.[33] During the war cooperative efforts by Protestant and Catholic clergy were typical in regions with a large Catholic population, such as the Rhineland or Silesia. Propaganda stressed the common ground among German Christians to create unity.[34]

In 1813–14 flag presentations by girls and women took place not just in Prussia but also throughout central, northern and western Germany whenever induction ceremonies of the militia or volunteers were celebrated. Usually members of the local patriotic women's organization initiated the embroidering of a flag. Following the declaration of war in March 1813, nearly 600 of these associations were founded in the German states, 414 in Prussia alone. These associations supported the war by collecting money and goods for the militiamen and volunteers, by caring for wounded and sick soldiers and by providing for soldiers' needy families, widows and orphans. The younger members of these associations particularly wanted to support their volunteering brothers, fiancés and friends with an embroidered flag.[35] A song written by a Dresden association of 'skilled embroideresses from the upper ranks of the citizenry' illuminates their motives. This patriotic women's association 'embroidered flags for the militia as well as the banner of the volunteers' and presented them in solemn flag-consecration ceremonies in various Saxon towns.[36] The song, dedicated to the 'Banner of the Saxon Volunteers,' begins

> What you have kept so long enclosed in silent hearts,
> Is now fulfilled!—The laurels have sprouted!
> The free banner of the Saxons waves!
> Receive it from your sisters, all you dear ones,
> With utmost ardour, as it passes
> From our hands to yours![37]

The flag embroiderers here portray themselves as 'sisters' alongside their fighting 'brothers'. In so doing, they remain within the highly gendered image of the nation as a *Volk* family, in which rich and poor, young and old, men and women, led by kings and princes, each had specific patriotic duties in accordance with their social status, age and gender. This image was the centrepiece of the national gender order, which—in the words of one contemporary writer—assigned to 'man the public and woman the domestic sphere, man the universal and woman the particular, man the business of the world and woman the affairs of the family.'[38] Already in the second half of the eighteenth century this middle-class model of the gender order was widely accepted in educated circles, but in the context of continuing warfare since the 1790s it was universalized, as compulsory military service now conferred on all men in principle the duty to defend family, home and country. In a complementary way, during the 'exceptional time' of a war all adult women were expected to perform their female patriotic duties, such as the nursing of sick and wounded soldiers and participating in war charities. Both tasks were socially acceptable because they did not challenge the prevailing idea of separate spheres.[39]

In this national gender order of war times, girls and young women were assigned the role of the 'hero's sister' and 'warrior's bride'.[40] When they handed over the flag, they demonstrated publicly their willing acceptance of this role, but they expected their 'brothers' and 'sweethearts' to do their complementary patriotic-national duty as volunteers. The flag was meant to 'fire' them on and 'guide' their 'youthful steps | To great and daring manly deeds'[41] that would prove them capable protectors and thus good future husbands. With the flag, the young women symbolically accompanied the 'heroic lads', remained united with them in spirit, spurred them on to battle and inspired them to defend the flag to their last drop of blood.

It was above all women and girls from the middle classes who embroidered flags for the newly formed volunteer and militia units and presented them in the context of consecration ceremonies.[42] Through this activity they could express their solidarity with the war's patriotic-national aims. At the same time, by claiming a place at the centre of the induction ceremonies, they also symbolically claimed a central place in the 'valorous fatherland'. The work of embroidery and the public presentation of the flag were unmistakably associated with the message that women considered themselves part of the 'nation at arms', attentively observed national affairs and the progress of the war and contributed their part to victory.

The significance of the embroidering, presentation and consecration of the flags and banners derived from their function as political and military symbols. Into the nineteenth century, flags, along with signal instruments, were the most important means of leading the infantry and cavalry during combat. They served as rallying points for the troops and were deployed as identifiers and directional signs. On the battlefield they communicated orders and enabled soldiers to organize their lines in the heat of a skirmish. In addition to their purely utilitarian value, flags possessed a symbolic power that reflected their importance in crisis situations as emblems that could encourage wavering troops to attack. A flag thus represented not simply a unit's identity but above all its 'spirit' and glory.

Regimental flags, which usually incorporated the state insignia, were granted only by the monarch as sovereign and supreme commander of the military. The act of bestowing a flag was at once an expression of his military and political sovereignty and an acknowledgement of extraordinary military achievements, above all courage and unbending loyalty. Every regiment of the Prussian standing army possessed at least one traditional flag, which in peacetime was kept in the quarters of the regimental commander. All members of the regiment took an oath to follow this flag during battle no matter what happened. The honour of a troop unit was tightly linked with the fate of its flag. To be chosen as flag-bearer was thus considered a special distinction and entailed serious responsibility, for the loss of the regimental flag was deemed a disgrace to the entire regiment.[43]

Only when viewed against this background does the political nature of the act of presenting a flag to newly formed volunteer and militia units by women and girls become clear. In so doing, they not only assumed a role reserved for the monarch but, by handing over a flag to the volunteers and militiamen before they had proven themselves in battle, also placed untried units on the same footing with the experienced and trusted troops of the standing army. From the viewpoint of the government and the military, this act represented a double sacrilege. The Prussian king thus sought as early as April 1813 to squelch the quickly spreading custom of dedicating flags to militia and volunteer units by prohibiting it.[44] When this measure failed, he reinforced the prohibition on 11 May 1813 with a royal Cabinet Order:

> I cannot grant the petition to provide the militia with flags. ... In days to come I shall award flags to such militia brigades as cover themselves with glory through courage and determination in the face of the foe; I deem the subject to be too sacred, however, to permit ladies to give flags to the militia. This privilege must be reserved solely for the government, and you are thus instructed to reject all relevant requests in accordance with this view of the matter.[45]

In order, however, to recognize and honour the 'loyal disposition' women expressed in the flags they embroidered, the king simultaneously authorized the preservation of all military flags in the churches 'as mementoes of the universal enthusiasm for the good cause'.[46]

The ban on presenting flags to individual troop units did not prevent patriotic-minded women and girls from continuing to dedicate embroidered flags. It apparently seemed to them no less honourable to have their flags preserved in the local church as a memorial to the attainment of 'national independence and autonomy'. When the presentation and consecration of a flag occurred separately from an induction ceremony, the female flag donors even became the centre of attention. Walking with the town's citizen guard and local notables in the parade of honour, they carried the flag to the church and held it during the act of consecration at the altar.[47]

Since the middle-class public clearly could not imagine a military formation without a flag, and since volunteers and militiamen felt that a newly established unit without its own flag would be inferior to the standing army, the king announced in the same royal Cabinet Order of 11 May 1813 that when the war ended, he would recognize those militia brigades that had distinguished themselves by granting them a flag. Because he nevertheless received repeated petitions to grant a flag, he reiterated this pledge in his 'Army Order for the Four Army Corps' of 1 October 1813.[48]

The pressure to recognize the militias' 'bravery' with a flag during the war was so powerful that only one month after the first French surrender on 30 May 1814, when the war of 1813–14 officially ended, the king issued an order to grant flags to all new militia units, 'with the exception of those that either have not faced the enemy or only participated in blockades or have not taken part in decisive battles'.[49] The manufacture of flags and their accoutrements proved so time-intensive, however, that it was not until months after the second war, which had begun in March 1815 and ended with the final capitulation of French troops on 3 July 1815, that militia regiments officially received their flags.

Typical for the postwar flag-consecration ceremonies was the programme of the Second Silesian Militia infantry regiment in Glewitz, described in the 27 March 1816 issue of the *Schlesische Privilegierte Zeitung*. First, the flag was nailed to a flagpole in the market square before a large audience that included 'the most respected inhabitants of the town'. This task was performed 'by the officer corps and the troops chosen for this duty from each rank and company'. Afterwards the military and civil authorities dined together at a local inn, 'while breakfast was also distributed among the remaining troops on the market square'. The regiment's 'unforgettable day'—as the article stresses—ended with a ball 'in which the notables of the town cheerfully participated.'[50]

The official awarding of a flag was an outstanding event for a militia unit. With it, the king acknowledged the bravery and loyalty of the regiment. Since after the Wars of Liberation the patriotic-minded elites of urban and rural Prussia continued to regard the militia as a form of 'arming the people', the act of consecrating the flag was, less a military celebration than a patriotic-national event, in which the men of a specific region demonstrated not only their devotion to king and fatherland but also their fighting capacity and valour.

Thanksgiving and victory celebrations

The rousing welcome that met the Russian troops under General von Wittgenstein when they marched into Berlin in March 1813 was the prelude to a whole series of spontaneous celebrations during the Anti-Napoleonic Wars between 1813 and 1815. Above all the great victories at Leipzig in October 1813 and at Waterloo in June 1815 as well as the first and second capitulations of the French in May 1814 and July 1815 drove people in town and countryside out into the streets and squares to share first their hopes and later their relief, gratitude and joy.[51] Usually they celebrated not just the victory of their own army but also that of the whole coalition, because they were aware that only by fighting together had the allies been able to defeat Napoleon's army.

The thanksgiving and victory celebrations ordered by the Prussian government after great victories and after the peace treaties of 1814 and 1815, which were announced in the newspapers, thus met a public need. At all of the thanksgiving services, which were modelled on the traditional ceremony developed during the eighteenth century, a long ringing of church bells was followed by a sermon of thanks; then the *Te Deum* was sung and a collection taken up for the 'wounded defenders of the fatherland'. The state-sanctioned religious service was usually embedded in a civilian ceremony and, on many occasions, a military celebration as well. These events were often preceded by a parade of the town's citizen guards or the marksmen's guild and culminated in an evening banquet and dress ball for the local elite and neighbourhood dances for the rest of the community. Contemporary press reports from cities and towns in Prussia and other parts of northern and western Germany confirm this unvarying programme of thanksgiving and victory celebrations. Even the tiniest villages did their best to mount suitable festivities.[52]

In Prussian ceremonies, with their strongly regional-patriotic orientation, the religious aspect was foregrounded. They were to offer God proper thanks for his aid while strengthening the faithful's piety, trust in God and spirit of self-sacrifice. Collections to benefit the victims of the war were ordered to demonstrate that war relief was a communal task. The military parades by local garrison troops and citizen guards represented manly valour far from the front. Even in his absence, the Prussian king, as the 'heroic general and beloved father of his country', was always honoured with hurrahs, songs and poems.[53]

Everywhere the same people—local authorities and church leaders—thanksgiving and victory celebrations. Their prominent role in these events demonstrated their position of power in the social hierarchy. In the garrison towns the local military leadership was also involved. Thus the visible actors were always men. Women were present mainly as spectators in the streets, as members of the church choirs and congregations or as participants at the evening balls or community dances. The patriotic women's associations were frequently active in preparing the festivities, however. They arranged the decoration of streets, squares and halls, and they supervised the preparation of the festival banquets. In addition, they were often responsible for collecting donations for sick, wounded and disabled soldiers or for war widows and orphans. Yet in the official programme of such ceremonies these important contributions by women were never mentioned.

The homecoming of volunteers and militiamen

The festivities organized to welcome the homecoming volunteer detachments and militia regiments presented a different picture. They had more the character of a *Volksfest*, a celebration of the people.[54] The mothers and fathers, wives and sweethearts, children and neighbours of the returning soldiers welcomed home their 'liberators and heroes' from the front. In these events women and men played equally significant roles, which indicate the complementary importance of the home front during the wars.[55] The welcome festivities were not ordered by the state but initiated by the municipalities. There was no model of earlier celebrations for the organizers to use; the programme of these homecomings was consequently far less ritualized.[56]

Newspapers everywhere reported on the festivities held in and around the Prussian capital of Berlin to mark the return of the first volunteer corps on 5 July 1814. The events began with several squadrons of the municipal militia riding out to meet the returning units at the village of Schöneberg, half an hour's ride from the city, where they formed an honour guard. Berliners followed their example and left the city to stand along the road where their sons, brothers, husbands and friends would soon be marching.[57] The 'motley throng' took the homecoming soldiers into their midst and joined the columns.[58] 'Nearly all of the fair sex, without distinction of estate', bore flowers and wreaths 'with which they strewed the path and adorned the volunteer troops'. Groups of white-clad young girls had 'set themselves up in a semi-circle' in the road to throw wreathes of oak and laurel leaves over the troops as they marched by.[59] In the village of Schöneberg, where garlands were suspended over the streets, as on the entire way to and in Berlin, the princes, generals and majors as well as the commander of the city militia awaited the volunteers and placed themselves at the head of the procession. A company of the marksmen's guild had taken up position at the festively decorated Potsdam Gate, which marked the entrance to Berlin. A deputation from the municipal government (*Magistrat*) welcomed the detachment there. One member gave a solemn speech and thanked the returning soldiers 'in the name of the city and the fatherland'. More than one hundred 'daughters of Berlin' from every social stratum, all 'dressed in white garments with roses in their streaming hair', completed the delegation and 'presented the young warriors with flowers, wreathes and poems'. A choir sang 'Heil Dir im Siegerkranz!' (Hail to Thee in Victor's Crown), and 'the dense throng of spectators' joined in and shouted one "Hail to the King" after another.'[60] Then began the solemn entry into the capital, in the 'strictest military order', which the relatives of the members of the volunteer unit soon disrupted. Everyone was jumbled together, 'overcome with joy and happiness'.[61] The streets were full of people who waved scarves from their windows and tossed flowers down onto the passing troops. In the evening the 'young heroes' were invited to a performance at the *Schauspielhaus*, followed by a 'peace banquet' sponsored by the municipal government and town councillors and attended by the 'city's highest military and civilian authorities'. Berliners illuminated their windows without any royal orders.[62]

Press accounts suggest that everywhere in Prussia and other regions of northern and western Germany the reception of the volunteers and militiamen who began returning home in July 1814 turned into joyful celebrations. Such rejoicing was, however, largely reserved for volunteers and militiamen, the ordinary male citizens who had fought 'to defend their fatherland'. One finds scarcely any press reports of similarly enthusiastic homecomings for regular army units. The most notable exception was the celebration marking the 'Solemn Entry of His Majesty the King and the Berlin Royal Guards' on 7 August 1814. The centrepiece of this official event, in which the royal guards were welcomed as representatives of the entire army of the line, was a large and brilliant military parade, which demonstrated the might of the army and the king as its commander-in-chief.[63]

After the second war in 1815, the newspapers reported only sporadically on larger ceremonies to welcome the volunteers and militiamen who returned in the autumn and winter of that year. They simply noted that the approaching troops were warmly received everywhere.[64] This striking difference between 1814 and 1815 may be attributed above all to the fact that the second, shorter, military campaign was largely conducted with troops of the line. In addition, the general restorative political development had caused patriotic enthusiasm to wane significantly since autumn 1814.

Wherever homecoming celebrations were held, a central component was a large group of young girls dressed in the white 'national costume' and crowned with flowers who presented the returning soldiers with bouquets and oak or laurel wreaths as well as poems. To dress in the white, 'modestly' tailored 'German gown' was one of the few ways in which girls and young women could actively participate in patriotic-national festivities. By wearing their 'national costume', they could publicly demonstrate their patriotism and support for the 'War of Liberation'.[65] The ritual surrender of wreathes by girls dressed in white dramatized the image, widely propagated in the poetry of the time, of the 'German maiden' who wove a wreath of German oak leaves for the victorious returning 'heroic lad' and bestowed it on him publicly as a symbol of his valour. The message associated with this ritual was that the fiancée, as an 'honourable German girl', had 'kept herself chaste and modest' and would now fulfil her promise, made at the beginning of the war, to give her hand in marriage only to a man who had proved himself a 'protector and defender of home and fatherland' and thus a suitable husband.[66]

The young women who participated in these festivities were well aware of the symbolism of their public appearance. At the same time, it had a very personal significance for many of them, such as Agnes Perthes, the eldest daughter of the well-known Hamburg publisher and bookseller Friedrich Perthes. In her 1864 memoirs she describes her emotions at the entry of the 'Hanseatic Legion', the volunteer corps of the Hanse cities, on 30 June 1814 in Hamburg.[67] Then sixteen years old, she was among the white-clad maidens who welcomed the homecoming volunteers, eagerly anticipating the return of her fiancé, cousin Wilhelm Perthes:

> Many young girls gathered at our house and made no secret of their plans to hand a laurel wreath to this one or that one. ... All at once—hark, hark—the sounds of the Hanseatic march rang in our ears. This had an electrifying effect on all of the girls. Beet-red [they ran] into the streets, struggled through the ranks, handed over the wreath, pressed hands and saw dear, kindly eyes and ran away again! The officers could scarcely keep order to prevent the entire procession from disintegrating; it had to hold until the town hall.[68]

Agnes Perthes was overjoyed to find her beloved safe and sound. The symbolic presentation of a laurel wreath to 'her' returning hero gave her a public opportunity to express her feelings in a seemly manner. The rejoicing of mothers, wives and sweethearts at the happy reunion with their men did not always correspond to the mood of the men themselves, whose joy was mixed with the pain of separation from their fellow soldiers and fears for the future. Wilhelm Perthes wrote about the same event in his 1844 memoirs, which were based on diaries he had kept during the wars:

> The occasion for taking up arms was achieved and nothing further could bind me to the soldier's trade, although it was painful to part from friends and comrades who had honestly shared good days and bad. The battalion and company had been my home for the duration of my service in the field. The separation would have been more difficult still, by the way, had it occurred when all of us still stood together, but when we marched into Hamburg we began at once to dissolve and disperse in all directions.[69]

The civilian chaos of the joyful welcome, created mainly by the women and girls, thus helped to disperse the male community of the military.

The celebrations to welcome volunteers and militiamen were accompanied by the clear message from authorities and loved ones that those returning home should integrate as quickly as possible into civilian society. This message was expressed with particular clarity in the 'Lied für die heimkehrenden Verteidiger des Vaterlandes' (Song for the Returning Defenders of the Fatherland) written by the popular poet Matthias Claudius to mark the homecoming of the Hanseatic Legion. The song was soon reprinted in newspapers and disseminated all over Germany.[70] What made it so popular, apart from the theme, was the fact that it could be sung to the melody of the extremely popular horseman's song 'Wohlauf, Kameraden, aufs Pferd, aufs Pferd' (Up, Comrades, Up, to Horse, to Horse) by Friedrich Schiller, one of the best-known German poets of his era. Claudius's song begins:

> Come, comrades, and dismount your horse!
> Lay down your armour now!
> In your own home, at your own hearth
> There's no need for arrow and bow.
>
> War is good only in times of need,
> Only good for the sake of peace.
> Truly blessed will those be
> Who earn their bread through industry.
>
> Something else then comes to the fore:
> Happiness as in days of yore.
> Only domestic bliss is true,
> And so again we return to you.
>
> ...We all return, hand in hand,
> Light-hearted and content to our land;
> Each man into the rank and trade
> That destiny his life has made.[71]

These verses remind the homecoming volunteers and militiamen of their civic duties and call on them to return to the rules and standards of peacetime society, represented by Claudius as an extended family in which every man performs the work assigned to him by destiny. From the perspective of civilian society, an important postwar task was the 'demilitarization' and 'civilization' of the hegemonic image of masculinity. The volunteers and militiamen had to become peaceful citizens once again, appreciate domesticity and accept their generational and social rank. As citizens, however, they must remain willing to take up arms again if necessary, but their foremost duties now were to devote themselves to their obligations as (future) paterfamilias and family breadwinner and to demonstrate their patriotism through active dedication to the common good. The often-presumptuous mores and attitudes associated with military service had to be set aside and modest civilian behaviour again practised.

Claudius's poem concisely summarizes the message conveyed by the homecoming celebrations for volunteers and militiamen. The festivities expressed symbolically the inevitable social and cultural demobilization. The homeland integrated its returning 'warriors' into peacetime society. Any particular political conceptualization of the state and the nation was irrelevant to this transformation. What mattered most was to remind the 'defenders of the fatherland' through the symbolic order of the festivities that it was time to bid farewell to the military's exclusively male 'band of brothers' and reintegrate into the gender-mixed *Volk* family. The course of the homecoming celebrations signalled the incompatibility of a strictly regulated military order with civilian life. The undisciplined behaviour of the civilians, especially female relatives, prevented the troops from entering the city in marching order, the symbol par excellence of military discipline. This does not mean that the citizens lacked respect for the military achievements of the returning men. Many may also have shared the view that every man would be expected to display combat-readiness and, if necessary, defend home and country. In peacetime, however, it was more important for him to be a caring paterfamilias, a patriotic citizen and a good Prussian or German, who willingly performed his collective and individual manly duties and cultivated an appreciation of both his home region and the nation.[72] The parallel message to women was that they should now return to their own domestic and familial duties and assist in the cultural demilitarization of the returning 'warriors' in their 'cosy homes'. They must therefore give up all public activities, in particular their organizational commitment to the patriotic women's associations.[73]

Conclusion

During the Wars of Liberation public ceremonies and festivities became an important means of promoting combat-readiness and patriotism in Prussia and in large areas of northern and western Germany. They facilitated a collective emotional experience that incorporated broad segments of the population and became a central part of political culture. The patriotic-national ceremonies and festivities and their symbolic elements expressed perceptions and interpretations that were also always shaped by gender. Most importantly the celebrations lent concrete form to gendered visions of the state and the nation and to the roles assigned to various social groups, generations and both sexes within those visions. The state was seen either as an absolutist paternalistic monarchy with the splendid sovereign at its helm, a military 'community' with the monarch as the 'father' and supreme commander of the male fraternity of the army; or as a 'band of brothers' composed of citizen-soldiers with the king as *primus inter pares*. These different dramatizations vividly reflected and transmitted the competing absolutist, enlightened-conservative or early-liberal ideas of the day and the political orders they advocated. The nation was generally envisioned, however, as a *Volk* family with the king and queen as loving, caring parents of their people. This representation created national unity and, at the same time, a seemingly 'natural' hierarchical social order, which integrated every subject in a class-, gender- and age-specific way and assigned to each group distinct patriotic duties that differed in war- and peacetime.[74] As the thanksgiving and homecoming ceremonies demonstrate, rituals and festivals were necessary not only to mobilize for war but also to promote cultural demobilization after the war and to foster a demilitarization of the 'citizens in uniform'—the volunteers and militiamen who had to be reintegrated in civil society. For these purposes the public festival culture was immensely important because it reached broad segments of the population well beyond the readership of the daily papers. By deploying symbols and rituals, it affected the emotions, which were much more crucial for the moulding of patriotic-national bonds than intellectual arguments.[75]

The symbolic order of the festival culture and the roles played in the ceremonies and celebrations by individual social groups also reflect their position in society, even if the representations naturally did not accord with social reality.[76] Thus rituals, ceremonies and festivities simultaneously generated and mirrored the national gender order of Prussia's wartime and postwar society. These cultural practices, images and ideas not only formed collective identities and individual perception but also shaped collective memory in a process that had already begun during the wars between 1813 and 1815.[77]

Acknowledgements

I would like to thank Pamela Selwyn for her translation, Mary Tonkinson for her careful editing and Gisela Mettele and Jane Rendall for their helpful comments.

Notes

1. 'Der Triumpf-Einzug des Grafen von Wittgenstein in Berlin: Anders erzählt als in den Berliner Zeitungen', *Russlands Triumpf* 1/4 (1813): 79–84.
2. See Dieter Düding, 'Das deutsche Nationalfest von 1814: Matrix der deutschen Nationalfeste im 19. Jahrhundert', in *Öffentliche Festkultur: Politische Feste in Deutschland von der Aufklärung bis zum Ersten Weltkrieg*, ed. idem et al. (Reinbek, 1988), 67–88.
3. Following Miroslav Hroch, I use 'patriotic-national' in this chapter as a collective term to express the ambivalence, simultaneity and diversity of the nationalized rhetoric in the period under discussion; see his 'From National Movement to the Fully-Formed Nation: The Nation-Building Process in Europe', in *Becoming National: A Reader*, ed. Geoff Eley and Ronald Grigor Suny (New York, 1996), 60–77, 62.

4. See Karen Hagemann, '*Mannlicher Muth und Teutsche Ehre*': *Nation, Militär und Geschlecht zur Zeit der Antinapoleonischen Kriege Preußens* (Paderborn, 2002), 457–508.
5. Ibid. 397–416.
6. Ibid. 75–91; and Karen Hagemann, 'Occupation, Mobilization, and Politics: The Anti-Napoleonic Wars in Prussian Experience, Memory, and Historiography', *Central European History* 39/4 (2006): 580–610. On the state of research, see Katherine Aaslestad and Karen Hagemann, '1806 and Its Aftermath: Revisiting the Period of the Napoleonic Wars in German Central European Historiography', ibid. 547–579.
7. See Uwe Schultz, *Das Fest: Kulturgeschichte von der Antike bis zur Gegenwart* (Munich, 1988), 140–243; R. Mulryne et al. (eds), *Europa Triumphans: Court and Civic Festivals in Early Modern Europe* (Aldershot, 2004); Karin Friedrich (ed.), *Festive Culture in Germany and Europe from the Sixteenth to the Twentieth Century* (Lewiston, NY, 2000).
8. See Paul Münch, 'Fetes pour le peuple, rien par le peuple: Öffentliche Feste im Programm der Aufklärung', in Düding, *Öffentliche Festkultur*, 25–45.
9. See Mona Ozouf, *La Fête révolutionnaire, 1789–1799* (Paris, 1976).
10. See, for example, Friedrich Ludwig Jahn, *Deutsches Volksthum* (Lübeck, 1810), 337–360. Jahn was well aware of the debates and the French example.
11. For an overview of the research and current theoretical and methodological debates, see Michael Maurer (ed.), *Das Fest: Beiträge zu seiner Theorie und Systematik* (Cologne, 2004).
12. For a classic definition of the term as I use it here, see Joan Wallach Scott, 'Gender: A Useful Category of Historical Analysis', *The American Historical Review* (AHR) 91/5 (1986): 1053–1075. For a more recent debate, see '*AHR* Forum: Revisiting "Gender": A Useful Category of Historical Analysis', *AHR* 113/5 (2008): 1344–1430; and *Gender and Change: Agency, Chronology and Periodisation*, ed. Alexandra Shepard and Garthine Walker (Chichester, 2009). On the history of masculinity, war and politics, see Stefan Dudink et al. (eds), *Representing Masculinity: Male Citizenship in Modern Western Culture* (Basingstoke, 2007); idem et al. (eds), *Masculinities in Politics and War: Gendering Modern History* (Manchester, 2004).
13. For a useful summary of the state of research and the current theoretical and methodological debates, see Mrinalini Sinha, 'Gender and Nation', in *Women's History in Global Perspective*, ed. Bonnie G. Smith (Urbana, 2004), 229–274; Ida Blom et al. (eds), *Gendered Nations: Nationalisms and Gender Order in the Long Nineteenth Century* (Oxford, 2000), 3–80.
14. See Clifford Geertz, *Thick Description: Toward an Interpretive Theory of Culture* (New York, 1973); Maurer, *Das Fest*, 19–54.
15. See Manfred Hettling and Paul Nolte (eds), *Bürgerliche Feste: Symbolische Formen politischen Handelns im 19. Jahrhundert* (Göttingen, 1993), 8–36.
16. On the induction ceremonies of the French army, which had introduced *levée en masse* in 1792 and universal conscription in 1798 and practised similar rituals since the 1790s, see Chapter 4 by Alan Forrest in this volume.
17. Ernst Moritz Arndt, *Was bedeutet Landsturm und Landwehr?* ([Königsberg] 1813), 13.
18. Ibid. 13–14.
19. See Karen Hagemann, 'Francophobia and Patriotism: Anti-French Images and Sentiments in Prussia and Northern Germany during the Anti-Napoleonic Wars', *French History* 18/4 (2004): 404–425.

20. See, for example, 'Preußisches National-Kavallerieregiments: Königsberg, den 29ten März', *Preußischer Correspondent* (hereafter *PC*), no. 6, 10 April 1813.
21. 'Schreiben aus Breslau v. 29ten März 1813', *PC*, no. 2, 3 April 1813.
22. Theodor Körner, 'Lied zur feierlichen Einsegnung des Königl. Preußischen Freicorps', in *Zwölf freie deutsche Gedichte. Nebst einem Anhang* ([Leipzig] 1813), 5–6.
23. See 'Körner an Henriette v. Pereira in Wien, 30 March 1813', in *Theodor Körners Briefwechsel mit den Seinen*, ed. Augusta Weldler-Steinberg (Leipzig, 1910), 231–232.
24. Ibid. 232.
25. See Karen Hagemann, 'Of "Manly Valor" and "German Honor": Nation, War, and Masculinity in the Age of the Prussian Uprising against Napoleon', *Central European History* 30/2 (1997): 187–220; idem, 'German Heroes: The Cult of the Death for the Fatherland in Nineteenth-Century Germany', in Dudink, *Masculinities*, 116–34, 127–130; Martina Kessel, 'The "Whole Man": The Longing for a Masculine World in Nineteenth-Century Germany', *Gender & History* 15/1 (2003): 1–31.
26. Hagemann, '*Mannlicher Muth*', 143–148. See also Ann Taylor Allen, 'Religion and Gender in Modern German History: A Historiographical Perspective', in *Gendering Modern German History: Rewriting Historiography*, ed. Karen Hagemann and Jean H. Quataert (New York, 2007), 190–207.
27. See 'Reichenbach, den 22. April 1813', *Schlesische Provinzialblätter* (hereafter *SP*), no. 4 (April 1813): 389–390.
28. Ibid. 390.
29. See Hagemann, 'Occupation', 603–609.
30. 'Reichenbach, den 22. April 1813', 389–390.
31. Hagemann, '*Mannlicher Muth*', 222–242.
32. See Dirk Alexander Reder, *Frauenbewegung und Nation: Patriotische Frauenvereine in Deutschland im frühen 19. Jahrhundert (1813–1830)* (Cologne, 1998), 425–427.
33. 'Brief aus Düsseldorf vom 25. Januar 1814', *Deutsche Blätter* (hereafter *DB*) 2/85 (19 February 1814): 497–499.
34. Hagemann, '*Mannlicher Muth*', 143–148.
35. See Karen Hagemann, 'Female Patriots: Women, War and the Nation in the Period of the Prussian-German Anti-Napoleonic Wars', *Gender & History* 16/2 (2004): 397–424.
36. 'Sachsens Töchter an den Banner der freiwilligen Sachsen bei der Aushändigung einer Fahne (Aus Dresden, im Februar 1814)', *DB* 2/86 (21 February 1814): 505–508.
37. Ibid. 507.
38. Friedrich Ehrenberg, Der Charakter und die Bestimmung des Mannes (2nd edn, Elberfeld, 1822), 11–12.
39. See Karen Hagemann, 'A Valorous *Volk* Family: The Nation, the Military, and the Gender Order in Prussia in the Time of the Anti-Napoleonic Wars, 1806–15', in Blom, *Gendered Nations*, 179–205.
40. See Karen Hagemann, 'Gendered Images of the German Nation: The Romantic Painter Friedrich Kersting and the Patriotic-National Discourse during the Wars of Liberation', *Nation and Nationalism* 12/4 (2006): 653–679.
41. 'Sachsens Töchter', 507.
42. See Reder, *Frauenbewegung*, 425–427.
43. Walter Transfeldt and Karl Hermann Frhr. v. Brand, *Wort und Brauch im deutschen Heer. Geschichtliche und sprachkundliche Betrachtungen über Gebräuche, Begriffe*

und Bezeichnungen des deutschen Heeres in Vergangenheit und Gegenwart (6th edn Hamburg, 1967), 214–216.
44. 'Allgemeine Kabinettsorder. An den Staatsrat Graf zu Dohna-Wundlacken, Breslau, 8.4.1813', in *Geschichte der Königlich Preußischen Fahnen und Standarten seit dem Jahre 1807*, ed. Königl. Kriegsministerium, 2 vols (Berlin, 1889–90), vol. 2, 24–26.
45. 'Allgemeine Kabinettsorder. An das Militair-Gouvernement v. Schlesien, Bautzen, 11.5.1813', in ibid. vol. 2, 25–27.
46. Ibid. vol. 1, 15.
47. See, for example, 'Ehrendenkmal zu Grünberg', *SP*, no. 2, (February 1814): 163–165.
48. 'Armee-Befehl für die vier Armeekorps, Teplitz 1.10.1813', *Amtsblatt der Königlich kurmärkischen Regierung*, no. 45 (22 October 1813).
49. 'Allgemeine Kabinettsorder. An den Staats- und Kriegsminister v. Boyen, Paris 3. Juni 1814', in *Geschichte der Königlich Preußischen Fahnen*, vol. 2, 29–30; this Cabinet Order was also widely published in the press.
50. 'Glewitz, den 7. März 1816', *Schlesische Privilierte Zeitung* (hereafter *SPZ*), supplement to no. 38, 27 March 1816.
51. For example, 'Friedensfeier in Bremen am 26.6.1814', *Tageblatt der Geschichte*, no. 135, 8 July 1814.
52. For an example, see 'Bekanntmachung wegen der glorreichen Einnahme der Festungen Stettin, Torgau und Wittenberg, Berlin 18.1.1814, v. Departement für den Kultus und öffentlichen Unterricht im Ministerio des Innern, gez. v. Schuckmann', *Vossische Zeitung* (hereafter *VZ*), no. 8, 18 January 1814, no. 99, 14 August 1814.
53. See Karen Hagemann, 'The First Citizen of the State: Paternal Masculinity, Patriotism, and Citizenship in Early Nineteenth-Century Prussia', in Dudink, *Representing*, 67–88.
54. 'Berlin, den 5ten Juli', *VZ*, no. 80, 5 May 1814.
55. See Karen Hagemann, 'Reconstructing "Front" and "Home": Gendered Experiences and Memories of the German Wars against Napoleon—A Case Study', *War in History* 16/1 (2009): 25–50.
56. 'Berlin, vom 5. Juli', *SPZ*, no. 80, 9 July 1814.
57. Ibid.
58. 'Berlin, den 5ten Juli', *VZ*, no. 80.
59. 'Berlin, vom 5. Juli', *SPZ*, no. 80.
60. 'Berlin, den 5ten Juli', *VZ*, no. 80.
61. 'Berlin, vom 5. Juli', *Berlinische Nachrichten* (hereafter *BN*), no. 80, 5 July 1814.
62. 'Berlin, den 5ten Juli', *VZ*, no. 80.
63. See 'Feierlicher Einzug Sr. Maj. des Königs und der königlichen Garden zu Berlin am 7ten August I u. II', *Zeitung für die elegante Welt*, no. 163, 28 August 1814; and no. 164, 19 August 1814.
64. See, for example, 'Auszug aus einem Schreiben', *VZ*, supplement to no. 15, 3 January 1816.
65. See Hagemann, 'Gendered Images'.
66. See, for example, 'Der heimkehrenden Königsbergschen Landwehr und den sie begleitenden Waffengefährten', *BN*, no. 109, 10 September 1814.
67 'Hamburg, den 1ten Juli', *VZ*, no. 82, 9 July 1814. See also Chapter 11 by Katherine Aaslestad in this volume.
68. Agnes and Wilhelm Perthes, *Aus der Franzosenzeit in Hamburg. Erlebnisse* (Hamburg, 1910), 89–90; for more on the Perthes family, see Hagemann, 'Reconstructing'.

69. Perthes, *Aus der Franzosenzeit*, 45.
70. Ibid. 90; Matthias Claudius, 'Lied für die heimkehrenden Vaterlandsvertheidiger', *DB* 5/182 (10 September 1814): 126–27.
71. Ibid.
72. On postwar masculinities, see Hagemann, 'German Heroes'; and Karin Breuer, 'Competing Masculinities: Fraternities, Gender and Nationality in the German Confederation, 1815–30', *Gender & History* 20/2 (2008): 270–287.
73. See Hagemann, 'Female Patriots'.
74. See idem, 'The First Citizen'.
75. See idem, *'Mannlicher Muth'*, 105–158.
76. See Hettling and Nolte, *Bürgerliche Feste*, 8–36.
77. See Christopher Clark, 'The Wars of Liberation in Prussian Memory: Reflections on the Memorialization of War in Early Nineteenth-Century Germany', *The Journal of Modern History* 68/3 (1996): 550–576.

Part V
Demobilization, Commemoration and Memory

15
Gender, Loyalty and Virtue in a Colonial Context: The War of 1812 and Its Aftermath in Upper Canada

Cecilia Morgan

The spring of 1812 in the Upper Canadian village of Queenston, overlooking the Niagara River, was a pleasant, if busy, time for Augusta Jarvis McCormick. Writing to her father, William Jarvis, a Loyalist and member of the colonial government, McCormick opened her letter by begging his pardon 'for so long delaying to write you,' explaining that her household responsibilities had kept her from putting pen to paper. Perhaps a recent gift from him of some asparagus had prompted a twinge of daughterly guilt, as she made sure to thank him for the 'very fine... and very acceptable' vegetables. McCormick also sent other local news, such as the birth of her sister's son, a neighbour's affliction with gout and the dispatch of a cake from Queenston to her father's home in York, the colony's capital. McCormick looked forward to a peaceful summer, with her days shaped by domestic duties and delights: babies, asparagus, cakes and a landscape that 'looked like a flower garden'.[1]

Yet her letter also hinted that Queenston was not entirely insulated from the transatlantic world of war and colonial expansion of the early nineteenth century. Almost buried in a discussion of her brother Thomas's recovery from a leg injury was the news that 'the General arrived yesterday'. In this case 'the General' was the British Major-General Isaac Brock, civil and military commander of Upper Canada. Less than six months after McCormick wrote to her father, Brock would die, not far from McCormick's home, at the Battle of Queenston Heights. Moreover, McCormick's tranquil village and the Niagara area would see some of the fiercest and most destructive land battles of the War of 1812.

Officially created as a British colony in 1791, Upper Canada was originally populated primarily by refugees fleeing the American Revolution who would come to be known as United Empire Loyalists (UEL), a designation that evoked notions of steadfast devotion to Britain and substantiated claims to the free land grants promised to those refugees. Upper Canada was drawn into transatlantic conflicts because of its colonial status. By 1811, British North America, seen as an impediment to American political and economic expansion, had become the target of those American politicians who sought to exploit Britain's preoccupation with European conflicts. They also believed that invasion—particularly of Upper and Lower Canada—would secure the legacy of the American Revolution.[2] Upper Canadians were thus at the mercy of larger imperial struggles that were to have very tangible effects on their lives. Yet the war was experienced not just in terms of crops burnt, homes looted and loved ones maimed and killed. The conflict was equally—one might even argue more—significant for the legacy it bequeathed to colonial political discourse and culture. Participation in the War of 1812 became an important measure for defining who could—and who could not—claim patriotic virtue and loyalty to Britain.[3] Moreover, such claims were shaped by constructs of gender, race and ethnicity as well as of nation and empire, constructs that were expressed in patriotic discourse before, during and after the war.

While Upper Canada inherited much from the larger transatlantic context, the local context also influenced the tenor and direction of that language of loyalty. During the War of 1812 and in its aftermath, the defensive nature of the conflict helped to locate male military activities and images of courageous militia members as central to public definitions of patriotic duty and service, undertaken to defend homes, helpless wives and children and British liberty itself. Such images of manly courage exercised in the protection of feminine virtue may have had only a tenuous relationship to the lived experience of many colonists during the war. Nevertheless the gendered language of patriotism was a powerful legitimating force, used to underpin claims on the public and political life of the colony and, eventually, that of the nation and British Empire. In theory, all men were equally capable of loyalty and patriotic virtue and of demonstrating through words and deeds their allegiance to Upper Canada and Britain; in practice, however, race complicated matters. Upper Canadian black men discovered that proof of manly loyalty was not enough to eradicate the colonists' perceptions of them as racially inferior. Native men found that the war's end marked the start of an intensified process of marginalization and the consolidation of colonial rule. Simultaneously, some incorporated their military service into narratives of Native loyalty, preserving older constructs of aboriginal masculinity that valorized men's role as warriors and using these ideals to counter the pressures of an expanding imperial modernity. The long-term implications of patriotic discourse for women were similarly complicated. By the 1870s Native women were disfranchised by the federal state on the basis of gender and race, their contributions to the imperial tie forgotten or ignored by mainstream Canada. While white women also saw themselves officially excluded from the colonial body politic, by the late nineteenth century they insisted that narratives of the war must include their foremothers' participation.[4] In this chapter I analyse the complicated interplay of gender, race and ethnicity and of the local, the national and the imperial in Upper Canada during and after the War of 1812. The United States declared war on Great Britain in August 1812. Peace was concluded with the Treaty of Ghent, signed on 24 December 1814. According to the terms of the treaty, hostilities would cease on 18 February 1815, all conquered territory would be returned to the prewar claimant, and both the United States and Britain would recognize the prewar boundary between Canada and the United States.

The colonial context

When Augusta McCormick wrote of asparagus and Brock's arrival, the colony of Upper Canada was made up of around 75,000 people, including settlers of European extraction, the Six Nations and a small black minority, and stretched from the Ottawa River in the north and east to the St Clair River in the west and Lakes Erie and Ontario in the south.[5] The majority of Europeans had arrived since 1783 with the Loyalist influx from the former thirteen colonies, which also included the Six Nations, who created a community along the banks of the Grand River in the southern portion of the colony, on land that the colonial government had purchased from the resident Ojibwa. Among the new arrivals were also approximately 700 slaves and an unknown number of free blacks; the former group declined in number after Lieutenant-Governor Simcoe abolished the importation of slaves and legislated for the manumission of the children of colonial slaves after a period of indentured service.[6]

Agriculture dominated the colonial economy well into the mid-nineteenth century, while lumbering, milling, and small workshops also marked the landscape. Although the majority of colonists were farmers, a small elite, clustered primarily in Niagara, York, and Kingston, were involved in commercial enterprises and tended to occupy political offices and patronage positions. After the War of 1812, the arrival of another wave of British immigrants brought challenges to the elite's dominance of colonial politics. These challenges would develop into a more sustained and very vocal reform movement. By 1837 reformers in both Upper and Lower Canada were frustrated by internal political and economic conditions and a strained relationship to the imperial government that, for some, could be resolved only through armed rebellion. Although the colonial government crushed the Rebellion of 1837 with the help of the colonial militia and British troops, in its aftermath the two Canadas united, established political parties and achieved a substantial degree of self-government. Through these developments the War of 1812 was frequently invoked as a significant measure of past—and present—loyalty to Britain.

Virtuous manliness and colonial defence

While the colonial press was small in numbers prior to the war and would expand more significantly in the 1820s, in the years immediately preceding the outbreak of the War of 1812 it is possible to uncover a few declarations of patriotism and loyalty by Anglo-American men, particularly when new governors arrived in the colony.[7] In these statements loyalty and devotion to Britain were linked to the honest manliness of the authors. They claimed a relationship to the imperial government and, in so doing, helped to define the political realm as the domain of loyal male British subjects. Honest manliness might also flow from the imperial centre across the Atlantic, serving as a model for colonial subjects and thus contributing to the colony's virtue, prosperity and happiness.

In 1810 John Strachan, the Anglican rector of York, published his *Discourse on the Character of King George the Third*, a pamphlet that was written not only to commemorate the late monarch's birthday but also to warn fellow colonists of the dangers of republicanism—past and present—in the United States and in Revolutionary France (although at the time of Strachan's writing France was an empire). For Strachan, loyalty to Britain and her institutions (including, not surprisingly, the Church of England) would simultaneously manifest and promote the future development of public and private morality. Moreover, George's domestic role as a devoted father and loving, faithful husband was identified as the wellspring of his ability to govern nation and empire with wisdom and compassion.[8] His support and encouragement of the 'purest morals' in all aspects of society came from his 'deportment as an affectionate husband, and tender parent' who had sent out into the world his many offspring, 'the steady pillars of the constitution, and the pride of the British nation'.[9] Unlike the sad but instructive example of Louis XV of France, who had fallen under the sway of his mistress, George had not allowed his court to sink into 'licentiousness...[,] intrigues, and corruptions', nor had he succumbed to tyrannical behaviour brought about by a lower-class woman's wiles.[10] Instead, he had maintained his proper role as the patriarch of both home and nation, thus protecting Britain and, by extension, her loyal colonial subjects from the excesses and destruction of the French Revolution, most of which could be attributed to private immorality in a degenerate domestic sphere. Strachan had little to say about the role of upper-class women in setting good examples: Queen Charlotte's sexual chastity, affection for her husband and children and an all-encompassing, if somewhat vague, moral purity said all that was needed on the subject of women's role in creating nation and empire.[11] Women—especially those from the plebeian class—were more likely to seduce and corrupt. It was up to men, particularly in their capacity as husbands and fathers, to exercise beneficent patriarchal power to prevent such calamities.

While it is easy to see Strachan's *Discourse* as conveniently overlooking the less than exemplary behaviour of a number of George's many offspring and to point to the somewhat self-serving nature of the pamphlet, nevertheless the themes that Strachan set out—loyalty, patriotism and the defence of the colony by public-spirited men—became increasingly popular with the outbreak of the war.[12] Although the colonial press shrank in size and frequency of publication during the war, nevertheless military proclamations, general orders, special addresses, editorials and letters demonstrate how the British and colonial authorities constructed the conflict. Upper Canadian men were poised to battle American viciousness, a struggle that pitted particular configurations of nation and empire, race and gender against each other. Unlike the colonial militia, the republic's soldiers could not claim honest manliness in defence of home and family; rather, they were rapacious savages who came from a society based on the importation of slaves (a mark of a tyrannical and effeminate government), that had now thrown in its lot with the despotical and wanton Napoleon.[13] Set to invade and despoil Upper Canada, American troops and their supporters had 'set up the war-whoop' and would arrive intent on plunder and rape. These writers were quick to prophesy, in the words of the *Kingston Gazette*'s editor, the 'liberties that may be taken with the weaker and unprotected sex by the unlicensed Banditti that may compose this army. I present merely an outline, and leave it to the feelings of every husband and father to fill up the picture'.[14] Notions of class, rank and status shaped these authors' attitudes. It was 'common soldiers', not American officers, who were generally viewed as the most horrific threat.[15]

The key to repelling the brutish American forces, argued a number of colonists, was the Upper Canadian militia. Acting as husbands, fathers and sons, armed by their patriotic virtue, these men would meet such a threat and stare it down. And just as their numbers and military backgrounds needed to be bolstered by the greater mass and superior experience of the British regulars, the militia's virtue as men sprang from British values and institutions. Far from being passive, though, this virtue could and should be performed on the field of battle with vigour and enthusiasm. The prominent Kingston merchant Richard Cartwright urged his fellow colonists to display 'zeal and spirit' when countering American aggression, and he invoked the example of Admiral Nelson, adding that 'we feel as men ought to feel when their best interests are at stake, and are determined to act as British subjects'.[16] 'We have daily experienced that bold and manly policy is the safest and the wisest', 'A Loyalist' reminded the *Gazette*'s readers, and continued: 'Do you suppose we are a parcel of Quakers?'[17] John Cameron, the editor of the *York Gazette*, was pleased to report in July 1812 that people from all 'ranks' of the town's population had been praising its militia. A 'veteran commander' had stated within Cameron's hearing that 'the present Garrison were a set of active and well behaved young men, whose *conduct* does honour to their King, their country, and themselves...men who would ably distinguish themselves in preserving the Sacred rights of Religion, Property, and Liberty, which we now under the blessings of Providence enjoy'.[18] Other colonists and the British military officials were happy to agree. In an address issued from Niagara's Fort George on 1 November 1812, Major-General Sheaffe praised the militia's 'manly and cheerful spirit with which (they) had borne the privations which peculiar circumstances have imposed on them'.[19]

But the militia's 'bold' manliness might, when exposed to the exigencies of battle, become prey to the bestial forces that had undermined and degraded their opponents. How to prevent the qualities that could guarantee success in battle from becoming 'licentious wantonness' in its aftermath? On occasion the militia was more concerned with the state of their crops than with fighting, colonists' military participation was at times uncertain or reluctant, and the war itself was the result of a larger imperial conflict from which many (particularly those who had arrived in the 1790s from the thirteen American colonies to the south) might wish to stay aloof.[20] Something more was needed as a unifying symbol of manly self-sacrifice and decency under wartime duress: the Christian Soldier and his real-life embodiment, Major-General Isaac Brock. At services, in sermons and in addresses, both figures were heralded as a reminder to the militia to commit only those acts of violence that would bring 'equitable terms of accommodation', to steel themselves to face privation and fatigue, to go without domestic comforts and, if necessary, to die for country and empire and to do so in obscurity, without thought of praise or fame. 'Go forth then to the battle, my Brethren', exhorted Strachan in a sermon preached before the Legislative Council and Assembly, 'clothed in the Christian armour, our cause is just...acquit yourselves like men, perform your duty with vigour and alacrity, and the calamities which the enemy are preparing for us shall return upon their heads'.[21] If the Christian Soldier was too abstract a symbol, then Brock, a respected outsider who had not been part of the political squabbles that marked the prewar years, could be adduced as his flesh-and-blood incarnation. His death at Queenston Heights in October 1812 provided those who shaped patriotic discourse with an impeccable symbol of the courageous Christian soldier who sacrificed himself for his country and who epitomized a morality exercised both in the domestic realm and on the battlefield. Such tributes were expressed not only during the war but also afterwards: in poetry recited at school examinations, in the building of a Queenston monument, in memorial services that commemorated the battle and in the work of the historical societies and school textbook writers of what was by then the province of Ontario.[22]

But Christian soldiers and gallant militia were not the only combatants fighting for the colonial link to empire. The Crown's Native allies often were more critical to the colony's defence than the militia; at times British officers bluffed their way to victory by playing on American fears of 'Indian savagery', evoking memories of various Native-white conflicts that had occurred south of the Canadian border.[23] However, both the British and the colonists of Upper Canada were, at best, ambivalent about these allies. Their bravery could not be doubted; furthermore, they had 'sprung to the defence of their country' in 1776, thus establishing a history of loyalty to Crown and empire. While reluctant to go looking for trouble, Native fighters were also men and, as one Canadian writer observed, had 'equal rights with all other men to defend themselves and their property when invaded'.[24] Yet the boundary between displaying manly courage and degenerate brutality could shift quite quickly. Today's brave warrior could become tomorrow's archetype of a vicious and rapacious savage. Despite Brock's public declaration that 'the brave bands of natives which inhabit this colony were, like His Majesty's subjects, punished for their zeal and fidelity in the Revolutionary War', in private dispatches he urged one of his colonels to 'restrain the Indians...in their predatory excursions,' directions which he and others repeated over the course of the war.[25] Native warriors inhabited a different dimension: they were not disciplined troops but fierce fighters whose methods and performances were atavistic, enacting not well-organized strategies but rather a 'natural' and animalistic propensity to violence. Their battlefield appearance included earrings, body paint and tattoos, shaved heads, feathers and skimpy clothing.[26] The colonists' allies could not be trusted to observe wartime codes of honourable conduct and manly self-control; in that sense they were as much to be feared as the invading Americans.

Such public constructions of Native fighters did not take into consideration that the Iroquois, Ojibwa and Shawnee might have their own motivations for their alliance with the British; nor did they take into account the complex cultural and political codes and symbolism that shaped Native men's military practices.[27] In many ways the Native participants in the War of 1812 were treated much like women and children, assigned to the role of 'Other' and objectified in patriotic discourse. Not all 'Others' occupied the same discursive position, however. Women and children were to be pitied for their vulnerability and were therefore seen as being in need of protection and rescue from the invaders. Native men, while theoretically allied with empire, were allies in the context of a colonial society—one with many former American residents who feared and hated Native peoples, and with an imperial administration that did not entirely trust its Native allies. This 'Other' thus might evoke the desire to be defended from one's allies, thus strengthening the need for British troops and the militia to protect civilians on a number of fronts.

Upper Canadian women and patriotism

Although symbols of patriotic womanhood did not emerge to complement or rival Brock's image of the Christian soldier, women were not altogether absent from the wartime theatre of patriotism and loyalty. At an 1813 commemorative service, for example, the Patriotic Young Ladies of York presented the Third Regiment of the York Militia with a special banner that they had sewn. While Anne Powell, the Young Ladies' spokeswoman and a daughter of the colony's Chief Justice, cited the banner as proof of how strongly women shared 'in that generous patriotism which burns with so pure a flame through the Province', the rest of her speech and the ceremony itself positioned women as dependent on men and the banner as representative of women's emotional ties to men, not their own hard labour in defence of the colony.[28] This patriotic women's group may have drawn on the work of similar groups in Britain that, as Linda Colley has shown, made regimental flags and banners, organized clothing drives and sometimes delivered public speeches declaring their support for the nation.[29] Unlike their British counterparts, however, Upper Canadian women were often spouses, relatives or neighbours of the men whose military activities they supported; so the work they did was more readily perceived as private and domestic.[30] Furthermore, they undertook such activities where invasion was not just a threat but a reality, as the occupation of York and the burning of Niagara in 1813 demonstrated. These experiences heightened and reinforced patriarchal relations among the elite, making it more difficult for women to speak and act publicly as patriots unless they used the language of emotion, familial connection and physical vulnerability. Of course, they may have been privately sceptical about such lofty sentiments. During the invasion of York, when the Third Regiment's banner was returned to its creators for safe-keeping, Powell greeted its return by militia colonel Archibald McLean with 'bitter words of indignation and...[the] taunt that after all their protestations [of manly courage,] the men had sent the banner back for the women to protect'.[31]

The view of patriotism as a primarily manly domain and activity was complicated by the war's being fought, quite literally, on the colonists' doorsteps. The colonial government quartered the militia in the stables and barns of York, Kingston and Niagara residents, and claims filed after the war sought restitution not just for crops trampled and livestock taken but also for furniture ransacked and food provided—not always willingly—to soldiers.[32] The records of the Loyal and Patriotic Society, formed in York in December 1812 to offer charitable assistance to the militia and reward patriotic deeds, also testify to the impact of war on women colonists. Polly Spareback, for example, a widow with two children who farmed in the Niagara peninsula, petitioned unsuccessfully for compensation for the loss of her grain crop, destroyed by British troops and Native allies.[33]

In addition, the military itself was not a homosocial organization. In dispatches and letters, British military officials discussed the evacuation of women and children from British garrisons and calculated allowances for soldiers' wives and families.[34] And wives might not have been the only women at the garrison. In his 'General Orders', issued at Kingston on 14 July 1813, Adjutant-General Edward Baynes notified the 89th Regiment that Captain James Basden had been relieved of his command for allowing 'several instances of irregularity and misconduct'. Not least of these 'irregularities' was the fact that Basden, 'in violation of all regard to decency and decorum, encumbered the brigade of boats by bringing up under his protection a female of improper character'.[35]

Upper Canadian women were not, however, helpless victims of the vicissitudes of warfare. Although the sources are not as forthright about women's 'heroism' as they are about men's, it is still possible to catch glimpses of individual white women's patriotic actions. Sarah Willott took it upon herself to write to the British officer Major Sheaffe to inform him that Pennsylvania troops were planning to attack Fort Erie and that they might be in a weakened condition due to a lack of provisions.[36] Mrs Gessean helped to free her son, who had been taken prisoner by the American army and jailed in Lewiston, New York, a small village directly across the Niagara River from Queenston. She smuggled her father's parole to him, hidden in the butter that she sold to the American garrison, and he then used the parole to pass through the border guards and rejoin his regiment.[37] Near Lundy's Lane in Niagara, Mrs Defield witnessed a skirmish between American troops and the colonial and British forces under the command of Lieutenant-Colonel James Fitzgibbon. Seeing that Fitzgibbon was about to be stabbed with his own sword by an American rifleman, she dropped the child she was holding, wrenched the sword out of the assailant's grasp, took the weapon and retreated into her home (presumably with the child). A nearby neighbour, Mrs Kerby, helped by shouting a warning to the militia and British troops that the Americans were nearby.[38] Later in the century Queenston resident Laura Secord, who undertook a 20-mile walk to warn British forces of an impending American attack, would become a symbol of Upper Canadian patriotism and heroism.[39]

Although they went unmentioned in public commendations of Native bravery, Iroquois women were just as engaged in the war as white female colonists. Indeed, it is possible that their involvement was more extensive and direct. Clan matrons had a significant voice in deciding whether or not their society would engage in war in the first place. Iroquois women played important symbolic and material roles in praising and shaming acts of male courage and cowardice, and many accompanied male partners on campaigns.[40]

But none of these deeds, by either white or Native women, received the public attention given to the militia or to such figures as Major-General Brock. Despite the fact that William H. Merritt applauded the bravery and ingenuity of these women, the image of terrified and helpless women in need of manly protection was a far more common theme in patriotic discourse. And until Laura Secord's story and those of other pioneer and United

Empire Loyalist women were popularized in the late nineteenth century, this image generally predominated in postwar accounts.[41] In its work after the war's end the Loyal and Patriotic Society, for example, recognized only one woman for patriotism unaccompanied by male valour, awarding £15 to Mrs Rice of Niagara for having been 'a most active loyalist and a great sufferer by the enemy'.[42] Typically the Society insisted that women's appeals for financial assistance be established on the basis of a male relative's patriotic deeds and the subsequent loss of his support through disability or death, not on the basis of their own loyal service or poverty brought on by wartime depredations.

Men made up the largest number of applicants to the Society, except in 1816, when women outnumbered men by a ratio of eleven to one.[43] Yet the Society's explanations of its decisions demonstrated a clear preference for women as distressed victims whose primary relationship was to home and family, not to the public arena of patriotic and loyal behaviour which belonged to men. To be black and widowed placed a woman even closer to the margins; the anonymous 'negro woman' mentioned in the society's account books for 1815 received only 15 shillings, despite the fact that her husband had died while imprisoned by the Americans (the average disbursement received by white women, with or without husbands, was £10).[44]

A similar understanding of gender relations shaped the colonial government's land-granting policies after the war. It announced in 1816 that those who presented petitions based on their descent from United Empire Loyalists would need to provide proof of their parents' wartime loyalty. Moreover, sons of Loyalists who had been 'of age' during the war would need to document their own loyal and dutiful conduct. Daughters who married were required to supply similar assurances of their husbands' loyalty, and though unmarried daughters were entitled to receive land grants, little was said about their having to demonstrate patriotism.[45]

It is not very surprising that the war was cast in these terms, with the militia and British troops as the protagonist in its narrative and white colonial women, Native peoples and (to a much lesser extent) African-Canadians allowed brief appearances in which they played suitable supporting roles. In other conflicts, however—ones that for a number of colonists would have been within living memory—white colonial womanhood had been mobilized to support national causes. Patriotic American women had displayed their spinning for the republic and had boycotted British goods during the American Revolution.[46] Although Upper Canadian writings on patriotism and loyalty contained no comparable history of republican women's activities, perhaps that selective memory helped to ensure that images of femininity were generally limited to helplessness and besieged innocence, so that military manhood—and those men who were the bearers of its virtues—remained at the centre of patriotic discourse. On the other hand, given that colonial officials were uneasy about colonists' loyalty they might have celebrated white women's support of ties to Britain.

The multiple legacies of the War of 1812

While the War of 1812 lasted only three years, the colony felt its aftermath in multiple ways. Patriotic service to colony and empire figured in requests for official patronage and in political discourse during battles over reform in the 1820s and 1830s, as did assertions of United Empire Loyalist descent. However, as the relationship between the new Executive Council and the elected legislative assembly became increasingly polarized, the war's legacy was a mixed blessing for men who wished to prove their loyalty and political legitimacy. Reformers might frame their wartime actions as a type of service that had not been rewarded, arguing that the actions of the colonial government after the conflict had in fact betrayed the manly sacrifices of those young men who had offered themselves for Crown and colony.[47] They were not alone, though, in using wartime service in order to stake political positions. Both conservatives and reformers wished to claim the war and virtuous manhood as part of their political heritage in a context in which loyalty was subject to multiple contestation and affirmation by various colonial groups, conservative and reforming, Anglican and Methodist. Moreover, in disputes over the nature of the imperial connection, the dispensation of patronage and the structure of Upper Canadian government, reform discourse was faced with the obstacle of conservative assertions of valiant militia service in defence of home and family, colony and empire. No one, it seemed, had a monopoly on this particular embodiment of manliness and its performance. This was a problem for reformers, whose calls for changes to the colony's political structure and life were made in the language of eighteenth-century Commonwealthmen and civic humanism, and were highly critical of patronage and placemen (those who accepted patronage appointments).[48] But in using a language that also drew on the republican image of the armed citizen, poised to defend his country's interests, reformers overlapped with conservatives who also claimed wartime service as the leaders of the York and Kingston militias and continued in such roles in the 1820s and 1830s, turning out in those units in 1837 in support of the Crown. Thus military service and masculine virtue, as embodied in both Christian soldiers and republican citizens, occupied an uneasy position in reform discourse; other forms of masculine loyalty were founded to support their loyal opposition to the Executive Council.[49]

But if reformers found their military records a less valuable bargaining chip in postwar politics than they might have wished, other members of colonial society discovered that their demonstrations of loyal manliness were cancelled out by colonial society's racism. Freed slave and loyalist Richard Pierpoint's efforts to raise and lead a Coloured Corps during the war were unsuccessful, as the colonial authorities gave command of the Corps to a white officer under whom Pierpoint served. He and the rest of the Corps saw most of their service at the Niagara garrison and as labourers, although they fought in a few critical battles. After the war, Pierpoint and his fellow soldiers were not paid the six months' severance they had been promised, but instead were given land grants in an area reserved for fugitive slaves.[50] Without land by 1821, Pierpoint petitioned the colonial government for passage to Africa, his narrative one of transatlantic upheavals and transformations:

> Your Excellency's Petitioner is a Native of Bondon in Africa; that at the age of sixteen years he was made a prisoner and sold as a slave; that he was conveyed to America about the year 1769; and sold to a British officer; that he served his Majesty during the American Revolutionary War in the Corps called Butler's Rangers; and again during the late American War in a Corps of Color raised on the Niagara Frontier. That your Excellency's Petitioner is now old and without property; that he finds it difficult to return to his native country; he wishes it may be by affording him the means to proceed to England and from thence to a Settlement near the Gambia or Senegal Rivers, from whence he could return to Bondon.[51]

Pierpoint did not return to Bondon, nor did he see Africa again. His request was refused and instead he was granted one hundred acres of uncleared land along the Grand River in Garafraxa Township. He died there approximately sixteen years later, his wartime service recognized primarily through his own hard work of clearing and fencing five acres and building a house.[52]

Further south on the Grand River, the Six Nations also found their lives and relationships with white colonists reshaped. Historians have pointed to the disruption brought to both the Six Nations and the Ojibwa people in southern Upper Canada through the effects of the war. These included the disruption of relationships between the Iroquois on both sides of the British-American border through an influx of British settlers in the 1820s and 1830s (themselves often uprooted through postwar upheavals in Britain), whose presence meant pressure on Native peoples for their land and resources. The British Indian Department's position as a military agency came to an end as it developed a new life as a civilian institution, dedicated to the assimilation of Native people into white agricultural society. Greater numbers of missionaries were arriving, their presence the result of those 'democratic upheavals' both south of the border and across the Atlantic.[53] The year 1815 can thus be seen as a pivotal moment in which Upper Canadian Native peoples' experiences of nineteenth-century colonization began in earnest. As with colonial projects elsewhere around the globe, colonialism in Upper Canada was very much a gendered practice: Iroquois women, for example, would see an erosion of their political roles within Iroquois society.[54] Yet wartime service was also incorporated into Mohawk narratives, and performances of masculinity written and staged over the course of the nineteenth century were used to remind colonial authorities of the Mohawks' historic alliance with the Crown. Over time this alliance was deployed to bolster arguments for the Mohawks' independence from Indian agents' colonial scrutiny.[55] White colonists, Native men were quick to point out, held no historical monopoly on masculine courage.

And what of Augusta Jarvis McCormick with her asparagus and cakes, the Patriotic Young Ladies of York and their banner, and those lesser-known, predominantly white women who appeared before the Loyal and Patriotic Society seeking compensation for their ruined furniture and requisitioned food? White colonial women might put forward their service to the Crown in order to justify requests for government positions or pensions: such was the case in the series of petitions that Secord began to file in the 1820s, requesting support for her disabled husband, herself and their large family of (mostly) daughters.[56] But images of femininity and women's relationship to political affairs took a different, often nastier, turn after the war, as political debates employed images of effeminacy. The colony's reform faction levied charges of corruption at the governing elite, the 'Family Compact', tying these charges to notions of the family, domesticity and the private realm of dependence. These political debates frequently relied on ideals of 'honest' manliness that could not envision women's participation in the political realm.[57] Moreover, the achievement of responsible government also saw the direct and deliberate exclusion of women—white and black—from the Upper and Lower Canadian franchise in 1849.[58] By the 1870s, Native women had been disfranchised from positions of authority within their bands or tribes and—if they had chosen to exercise it and lose their legal status as 'Indians'—from the federal franchise.[59]

White colonial women such as Augusta Jarvis McCormick and Anne Powell, who belonged to the colony's elite or its growing middle class, found other grounds and means to participate in and influence colonial society. Evangelical religion, charitable and philanthropic societies, temperance groups, missionary enterprises and, by the 1850s, the province's small anti-slavery movement would provide important platforms for them. That they participated in these groups in a much more mediated fashion than their male counterparts should not prevent us from appreciating their involvement in the colony's social realm; equally, these platforms alert us to the significance of the ongoing and often intensified transatlantic and imperial movements in which these women crafted and enacted scripts of white colonial femininity and virtue.[60]

Later in the nineteenth century, as imperial relationships were reforged within the context of late Victorian and Edwardian English-Canadian nationalism, these women's granddaughters would begin to rewrite narratives of the war, recasting the white women of Upper Canada as heroic and virtuous actors whose struggles and sacrifices were integral to wartime patriotism and loyalty. Yet while these narratives challenged gendered conceptions of heroism and virtue, they continued to be shaped by the racially inflected notions of loyalty constructed during the war itself. Individual Native leaders such as the Shawnee chief Tecumseh might be applauded as a British ally; in the aggregate, though, Native men epitomized a primitive savagery that had no place in a modern, imperial nation.[61] And with a few exceptions, African-Canadians' wartime participation, along with their presence in Upper Canadian society in general, was rarely deemed worthy of much comment by these historians. Just as these relationships of power had structured the discourses and lived experiences of the War of 1812, they later framed and underpinned the memories of that war.

Notes

1. Niagara Historical Museum, Niagara-on-the-Lake, Ontario, Niagara Historical Collection, Vault Box 44, Augusta Jarvis McCormick to William Jarvis, 28 May 1812.
2. Carl Benn, *The Iroquois in the War of 1812* (Toronto, 1998), 27–28.
3. David Mills, *The Idea of Loyalty in Upper Canada, 1784–1850* (Montreal, 1988), 25–28; E. Jane Errington, *The Lion, the Eagle, and Upper Canada: A Developing Colonial Ideology* (Montreal, 1987), 89; J. K. Johnson, *Becoming Prominent: Regional Leadership in Upper Canada, 1791–1841* (Montreal, 1989), 76.
4. For a survey of the colony, see Gerald Craig, *Upper Canada: The Formative Years* (Toronto, 1963); also Edward S. Rogers and Donald B. Smith (eds), *Aboriginal Ontario: Historical Perspectives on the First Nations* (Toronto, 1994); Peter S. Schmalz, *The Ojibwa of Southern Ontario* (Toronto, 1991); Michael Power and Nancy Butler, *Slavery and Freedom in Niagara* (Niagara-on-the-Lake, 2000). For later developments pertaining to the Indian Act and Native women, see Jo-Anne Fisk, 'Political Status of Native Indian Women: Contradictory Implications of Canadian State Policy', in *In the Days of Our Grandmothers: A Reader in Aboriginal Women's History in Canada*, ed. Mary-Ellen Kelm and Lorna Townsend (Toronto, 2006), 336–366. For women's work in historical societies, see Beverley Boutilier and Alison Prentice (eds), *Creating Historical Memory: English-Canadian Women and the Work of History* (Vancouver, 1997); Cecilia Morgan, 'History, Nation, Empire: Gender and the Work of Southern Ontario Historical Societies, 1890–1920s', *Canadian Historical Review* 82 (2001): 491–528.
5. Because of problems with evidence, the population figure excludes the resident Ojibwa. The Six Nations, also known as the Haudenosaunee, consisted of those members of the Iroquois Confederacy who had chosen to ally with the British during the American Revolution. The majority settled on a tract of land on the banks of the Grand River. A smaller group of Mohawk formed a community, Tyendinaga, on the northeastern shore of Lake Ontario.
6. See Craig, *Upper Canada*; Rogers and Smith, *Aboriginal Ontario*; Schmalz, *The Ojibwa*; Power and Butler, *Slavery and Freedom*; Janice Potter-McKinnon, *While the Women Only Wept: Loyalist Refugee Women in Eastern Ontario* (Montreal, 1993).
7. 'Notice to Peter Hunter', *Canada Constellation*, 6 September 1799; 'Announcement of the Loyal and Patriotic Association', *Upper Canada Gazette*, 21 August 1794.

8. John Strachan, *Discourse on the Character of King George the Third Addressed to the Inhabitants of British America* (Montreal, 1810), 21–28, 37–38.
9. Ibid. 8, 10–11.
10. Ibid. 32–33.
11. Ibid. 10–11.
12. Historians of Upper Canada have mentioned Strachan's *Discourse*, but none have commented on its gendered nature. See, for example, Errington, *The Lion, the Eagle, and Upper Canada*, 27; Mills, *The Idea of Loyalty*, 19; and Robert Fraser, ' "Like Eden in Her Summer Dress": Gentry, Economy, and Society, Upper Canada, 1812–1840', Ph.D. diss. (University of Toronto, 1979), 115. On the *Discourse* as part of a larger trend in British royal propaganda glorifying George for his domestic simplicity, see Linda Colley, *Britons: Forging the Nation 1707–1837* (New Haven, 1992), 223.
13. 'Editorial', *Kingston Gazette* (hereafter *KG*), 28 January 1811, 28 February 1812, 28 July 1812. See also Isaac Brock, 'Proclamation', 22 July 1812, in *The Documentary History of the Campaign upon the Niagara Frontier*, ed. E. A. Cruikshank, 9 vols (Niagara Falls, 1896–1908), vol. 3, 135–138.
14. 'Editorial', *KG*, 28 January 1811, 28 February 1812.
15. The threat of internal enemies also captured government officials' imaginations. See 'Proclamation', Isaac Brock, *KG*, 18 September 1812; and the House of Assembly's 'Address', *KG*, 28 July 1812.
16. Richard Cartwright, 'Letter to the Editor', *KG*, 3 March 1812.
17. 'A Loyalist', *KG*, 18 February 1812. It is not clear whether or not *Loyalist* was being used to refer to United Empire Loyalist (UEL) ancestry or simply to the writer's support of Britain (possibly both).
18. John Cameron, 'Editorial', *York Gazette*, 4 July 1812.
19. General Sheaffe, 'Militia District Orders', 1 November 1812, in Cruikshank, *Documentary History*, vol. 4, 174.
20. George Sheppard, *Plunder, Profit, and Paroles: A Social History of the War of 1812 in Upper Canada* (Montreal, 1994); W. W. Weekes, 'Civil Authority and Martial Law in Upper Canada', in *The Defended Border: Upper Canada and the War of 1812*, ed. Morris Zaslow (Toronto, 1964), 193.
21. Archives of Ontario, Toronto (hereafter AO), Pamphlet 1812 #4, John Strachan, *Sermon Preached at York before the Legislative Council and House of Assembly*, 2 August 1812.
22. 'Life of Isaac Brock', *KG*, 7 November 1812; 'Patriotic Service', *KG*, 20 April 1813; 'Battle of Queenston Heights, a Description by an Onlooker', in Cruikshank, *Documentary History*, vol. 4, 114–116; Allen McDonnell, 'Poem Delivered at Annual Examination of Scholars, York District School', *Upper Canada Gazette* (hereafter *UCG*), 6 August 1812; 'Address Given at the Anniversary of the Battle of Queenston Heights', *UCG*, 21 October 1824; 'Public Meeting at Brock's Monument', *The Examiner*, 5 August 1840; 'General Brock', *British Colonist*, 24 July 1840. See also Keith Walden, 'Isaac Brock: Man and Myth, a Study of the Militia Myth of the War of 1812 in Upper Canada, 1812–1912', MA thesis (Queen's University, Kingston, 1971).
23. George F. G. Stanley, 'The Indians in the War of 1812', in *Sweet Promises: A Reader in Indian-White Relations in Canada*, ed. J. R. Miller (Toronto, 1991), 105–124; also Carl Benn, *The Iroquois in the War of 1812* (Toronto, 1998). For the attitudes of former American colonists toward Native peoples, see Sheppard, *Plunder*, 121–129.

24. 'Editorial', *KG*, 28 July 1812.
25. Brock, 'Proclamation', 22 July 1812, in Cruikshank, *Documentary History*, vol. 3, 135–138; also Brock to Colonel Proctor, 25 August 1812, ibid. vol. 3, 303.
26. Lieutenant-Colonel Harvey to Colonel Claus, 15 July 1813, in ibid. vol. 6, 236; Sir George Prevost to General Drummond, 17 February 1814, ibid. vol. 9, 188–189; Harvey to Colonel Matthew Elliott, 17 December 1813, ibid. vol. 9, 23. See also Matilda Edgar, *Ten Years of Upper Canada in Peace and War, 1805–1815; Being the Ridout Letters* (Toronto, 1908), 174; Dr William Dunlop, *Recollections of the War of 1812* (1846; repr. Toronto, 1908), 77–78.
27. In private correspondence British officers might admit that Native allies had their own reasons for fighting on the side of the Crown. See Stanley, 'The Indians in the War of 1812', 109–110; also Benn, *The Iroquois*, chs 2 and 3.
28. 'Dedication of the Banner', *KG*, 20 April 1813.
29. Colley, *Britons*, 261.
30. Such would be the case for elite women from families such as the Jarvises, Powells, Ridouts, Boultons and Cartwrights, whose husbands, fathers, brothers, sons, and other relatives were members of the militia. See Katherine McKenna, *A Life of Propriety: Anne Murray Powell and Her Family, 1755–1849* (Montreal, 1994), 144–145; Johnson, *Becoming Prominent*, 175, 180, 200–201, 221.
31. Mary Agnes Fitzgibbon, 'A Historic Banner', *Transactions of the Canadian Women's Historical Society of Toronto* 1 (February 1896): 20. Anne Powell was known for her forthright speech; see McKenna, *A Life of Propriety*, 206–229.
32. AO, Department of Finance, Upper Canada, *War of 1812 Losses Claims*, 1816.
33. AO, Loyal and Patriotic Society of Upper Canada, *The Report of the Loyal and Patriotic Society of Upper Canada* (Montreal, 1817), 104.
34. Drummond to Prevost, 16 July 1814, in Cruikshank, *Documentary History*, vol. 1, 60; Mrs Hannah Janoway to her sister-in-law, 14 September 1814, ibid. vol. 2, 230–231; William H. Merritt, 'Personal Note', 8 July 1813, ibid. vol. 6, 208–210. See also Brian Leigh Dunnigan, 'Military Life at Niagara, 1792–1796', in *The Capital Years: Niagara-on-the-Lake, 1792–1796*, ed. Richard Merritt et al. (Toronto, 1991), 67–102.
35. Adjutant-General E. Baynes, 'General Orders', 14 July 1813, in Cruikshank, *Documentary History*, vol. 6, 235–236.
36. Sheaffe to Prevost, n.d., ibid. vol. 4, 229.
37. Merritt, 'Personal Note', ibid. vol. 6, 99.
38. Ibid.
39. Cecilia Morgan, '"Of Slender Frame and Delicate Appearance": The Placing of Laura Secord in Narratives of Canadian Loyalist History', *Journal of the Canadian Historical Association* 5 (1994): 195–212.
40. Benn, *The Iroquois*, 11–13, 43, 56–59, 61, 88, 92, 159.
41. Morgan, '"Of Slender Frame"'.
42. AO, Loyal and Patriotic Society, *Report*, 201; the system of currency referred to here is that of Great Britain prior to decimalization in 1971. It was based on the pound (£), the shilling (s.) and the penny (d.). Twelve pennies equalled one shilling; twenty shillings equalled one pound.
43. Ibid. 76–203. It is difficult to explain the anomaly of 1816; possibly the Society's work had become better known in the colony. It does seem to have been much faster in disbursing its funds than was the government in settling war losses claims.
44. Ibid. 237.

45. 'Proclamation', *UCG*, 10 February 1816. Anne Powell received a grant as the daughter of a Loyalist; see McKenna, *A Life of Propriety*, 224.
46. Linda Kerber, *Women of the Republic: Intellect and Ideology in Revolutionary America* (Chapel Hill, 1980); Mary Beth Norton, *Liberty's Daughters: The Revolutionary Experience of American Women, 1750–1800* (Boston, 1980); Ruth H. Bloch, 'The Gendered Meanings of Virtue in Revolutionary America', *Signs* 13 (1987): 37–58; Paula Baker, 'The Domestication of Politics: Women and American Political Society, 1780–1920', *American Historical Review* 89 (1984): 620–647.
47. See Robert Gourlay, *Statistical Account of Upper Canada*, 2 vols (London, 1822), vol. 1, 571–572, 576, 579–580. A Scottish-born agrarian reformer, Gourlay was jailed and banished from the colony in 1819.
48. For a discussion of Commonwealthmen and civic humanism, see J. G. A. Pocock, *The Machiavellian Moment* (Princeton, 1975); idem, *Virtue, Commerce, and History: Essays on Political Thought and History* (Princeton, 1985); H. T. Dickinson, *Liberty and Property: Political Ideology in Eighteenth-Century Britain* (London, 1979); Caroline Robbins, *The Eighteenth-Century Commonwealthman* (Cambridge, 1961).
49. See Cecilia Morgan, '"When Bad Men Conspire, Good Men Must Unite!": Gender and Political Discourses in Upper Canada, 1820s–1830s', in *Gendered Pasts: Historical Essays in Femininity and Masculinity in Canada*, ed. Kathryn McPherson et al. (1999; repr. Toronto, 2003), 12–28.
50. Pierpoint's narrative is discussed in Power and Butler, *Slavery and Freedom*, 43–46. See also Robert L. Fraser, 'Richard Pierpoint', *Dictionary of Canadian Biography*, 16 vols (Toronto, 1966–), vol. 7, 697–698.
51. Reprinted in Power and Butler, *Slavery and Freedom*, 45.
52. Ibid. 45–46.
53. See Benn, *The Iroquois*, ch. 8; and Schmalz, *The Ojibwa*, chs 6 and 7.
54. I do not wish to suggest that this was a straightforward process, for a range of scholars have noted the uneven and contradictory ways in which colonialism played out among Native peoples. See, for example, the essays in Kelm and Townsend, *In the Days of Our Grandmothers*.
55. Such arguments were often made when representatives of the Crown visited British North America. Ian Radforth, 'Performance, Politics, and Representation: Aboriginal People and the 1860s Royal Tour of Canada', *Canadian Historical Review* 84 (2003): 1–32.
56. Morgan, '"Of Slender Frame"', 197–198.
57. Morgan, '"When Bad Men Conspire"', 22–24.
58. Women were not initially excluded from the franchise in most of the British North American colonies, although colonial officials assumed that women would not vote. From the 1790s until the 1840s some women voted on the basis of their status as property holders. From the 1830s onwards, however, women were explicitly disenfranchised by colonial assemblies; see John Garner, *The Franchise and Politics in British North America, 1755–1867* (Toronto, 1969), 155–158. Upper Canadian reformers called for 'responsible government' in the 1830s and 1840s, a term that historians generally understand to mean that the Executive Council would be accountable to the elected legislative assembly.
59. Native women in Canada could not vote as Indians in federal elections until 1960. In the Canadian context, the term 'band' was defined in the 1876 federal Indian Act as a body of Native people for whom the government had set aside land and funds; see Olive Dickason, *Canada's First Nations: A History of Founding Peoples from Earliest Times* (Toronto, 1993), 284.

60. Aspects of this complex topic are discussed in Jeffrey McNairn, *The Capacity To Judge: Public Opinion and Deliberative Democracy in Upper Canada, 1791–1854* (Toronto, 2002); Allan P. Stouffer, *The Light of Nature and the Law of God: Antislavery in Ontario, 1833–1877* (Montreal, 1992); and Cecilia Morgan, *Public Men and Virtuous Women: The Gendered Language of Religion and Politics in Upper Canada, 1791–1850* (Toronto, 1996).
61. Boutilier and Prentice, *Creating Historical Memory*; Morgan, 'History, Nation, Empire.'

16
Masculinity, Race and Citizenship: Soldiers' Memories of the American Revolution

Gregory T. Knouff

In the aftermath of the American Revolution, two divergent memories of the conflict developed among its North American veterans. Loyalist and Revolutionary soldiers created recollections that revealed distinctive concepts of political manhood emerging among them. Revolutionary veterans told stories in their nineteenth-century pension applications that emphasized their identity as politically empowered white men.[1] This image related to the steady post-Revolutionary progression towards universal white-male suffrage and the formation of an ideology that linked white-male status with citizenship in the United States. As eligibility for citizenship expanded, Revolutionary veterans created democratized recollections. Additionally, they remembered their military service in ways that emphasized their roles as white prosecutors of race war against Native Americans. Such memories paralleled popular notions of independent, democratic white-male citizenship in the early United States.[2]

In contrast, most Loyalists lost not only their voting rights in their North American communities but typically their property as well. Rather than gaining a sense of political empowerment, they rued their losses and sought recompense in Loyalist claims. In the process, they presented to British authorities an image of suffering, emasculated subjects. This portrayal was deliberately designed to aid propertied Loyalists in recovering their place as viable heads of household and enfranchised citizens. At the same time, however, Loyalists' representation of themselves as victims underscored their image as provincial dependants in an increasingly hierarchical empire. Thus their memories of the Revolution illustrated both their traditional commitment to North American colonial ideas of political manhood and their newly liminal status in the British Empire. Unlike those of the Revolutionaries, Loyalists' memories expressed emasculation and loss, not empowerment.[3]

This chapter will examine the memories of Pennsylvania veterans of the American Revolution, both Revolutionaries and Loyalists. Pennsylvania's unique experience in the Revolution made this state emblematic of the diverse democratic federal union in which white-male supremacy would become the political common ground. The Revolution ushered in a radically democratic state constitution that allowed formerly disenfranchised men, such as propertyless white soldiers, to exert political influence. While subsequent frameworks for both state and federal governments were less democratic than the Revolutionary one, they continued the expansion of voting rights among white men. As a province, Pennsylvania was populated by diverse groups of European colonists who, during the Revolution and beyond, called themselves 'white', a term that transformed western European ethnicity into a racial category. It also had frontier regions in which Europeans and independent Native American groups vied for control of land and where concepts of whiteness were articulated. Furthermore, Pennsylvania had a significant African-American population comprised of free men and women as well as slaves. As the white-male citizen was celebrated, the free black men of Pennsylvania saw their political standing erode.[4] Finally, Pennsylvania was home to numerous Loyalists. Like other states, it circumscribed Loyalists' political and civil rights, as well as confiscated their estates. Active Loyalists were typically forced into exile.[5] In short, Pennsylvania soldiers' memories offer a window onto the divergent concepts of United States and British colonial manhood shaped by the Revolution.

The Revolutionary idea of citizenship

Pennsylvania veterans' memories of their service emerged from the fundamental changes in concepts of citizenship during the Revolutionary War. The franchise was expanded and a series of laws passed which stipulated that militia service and oaths of allegiance to the Revolutionary state of Pennsylvania were required of white men only. Thus the nineteenth-century US shift away from property-holding as the essential qualification for suffrage and towards universal white-male suffrage was evident during the Revolution. The conflict enfranchised many poorer men who had never before been able to claim the chief right of citizenship in the British Empire. Colonial Pennsylvania law allowed only resident men over the age of twenty-one who owned fifty acres or had an estate worth £50 the right to vote. Non-naturalized residents, servants and male slaves were all denied the vote.[6] Estimates of voter eligibility among Pennsylvania taxpayers in the pre-Revolutionary period range from 50 to 75 per cent. With perhaps half of all male taxpayers denied enfranchisement, it is clear enough that full citizenship in Pennsylvania, as in the British Empire in general, was in no way synonymous with merely being male.[7]

Revolutionary soldiers from Pennsylvania participated in the struggle for political change and expanded voting rights. The state's rank-and-file militiamen became a powerful political constituency of the new government. They organized a 'Committee of Privates' that demanded a democratic militia structure and the franchise for all who were eligible for militia service. Militiamen also supported the passage of one of the most democratic constitutions that the English-speaking world had yet seen.[8] The Pennsylvania Constitution of 1776 provided for a unicameral legislature open to public scrutiny and an executive branch whose power was diffused among a Supreme Executive Council. Voting rights were granted to all 'freemen' who paid taxes and their sons over the age of twenty, regardless of taxpaying status. The militia's democratic structure was also stipulated in the constitution, making all 'freemen' and their sons liable for service and guaranteeing soldiers the 'right of choosing their Colonels and all commissioned officers under that rank'. The property-owning requirement for voting was thus repealed, and Pennsylvania was on its way to equating citizenship with maleness. In addition, the link between a man's liability for militia service and his right to the franchise was publicly recognized. 'Freemen' without significant property were now both citizens and eligible to be citizen soldiers. While this link was peculiar to militia service and not to the Continental Army, veterans' memories of the war would conflate military service in general with the expansion of democracy.[9]

The next major step in defining the prerequisites for citizenship in the state came in 1777. In the spring of that year the Pennsylvania legislature passed a new militia act that made 'every male white person...capable of bearing arms' eligible for the draft.[10] This was a continuation of the province's practice of making 'every male white person capable of bearing arms, between the ages of sixteen and fifty years' liable either for militia service or for payment of a fine if they did not join from early in the war (1775).[11] The 1777 act, however, was related to Revolutionary US identity, as it was passed after national independence. In June 1777 the state further politicized race by passing '[a]n Act obliging the male white inhabitants of this State to give assurances of allegiance to the same'.[12] This test oath act was designed to force all white men either to declare their allegiance to the Revolutionary government or to lose their rights (including the vote). Coupled with the militia act, it reinforced white maleness as a prerequisite for political subjectivity. Linking soldiering and citizenship with race and gender was not particular to Pennsylvania. Other states identified white maleness as a prerequisite for militia service, and there was a national connection between whiteness and liability to service in the Continental Army. The Articles of Confederation directed the Continental Congress to 'agree upon the number of land forces, and to make requisitions from each state for its quota, in proportion to the number of white inhabitants in such state'. The conflation of democracy with racial identity had major political and social consequences. While the Pennsylvania constitution granted voting rights to qualified African-American men, the test oath, which recognized the fundamental ability to declare allegiance to the state, did not apply to them. Thus, while the test act was in effect, taxpaying free black men occupied a liminal political position. Veterans could remember this period as one in which male political subjectivity moved beyond the criterion of property-holding and became contingent on race. The state's ethnically diverse European-American population, previously united by allegiance to the British crown, was in the post-Revolutionary period united as white Americans. The vanguard of the Revolutionary cause would be defined in culturally constructed terms as the white male.[13]

Obviously, there was no expansion of citizenship for Loyalist men. White men who refused to take the oath of allegiance forfeited their rights, being legally rendered 'incapable of holding any office in this State, serving on juries, suing for any debts, electing or being elected, buying, selling or transferring any lands, tenements or hereditaments.'[14] Significantly, the penalty entailed not just the loss of political and civil rights but the loss of economic agency as well. Loyalist property-holders were disenfranchised by the Revolutionaries and saw the basis of their independence threatened. In 1777, as the British army began its Philadelphia campaign, the Pennsylvania Council of Safety passed an emergency ordinance authorizing the confiscation without trial of personal property from anyone who joined or assisted the enemy. This measure was superseded by a confiscation law passed in March 1778 that authorized the seizure of entire estates belonging to 'traitors'. Anyone who did not appear in court to answer charges of treason could be declared guilty without a trial. Attainder for treason carried a death penalty and automatic loss of property, which would then be sold for public use. In addition to providing the Revolutionaries with funds, the confiscation of property was a symbolic emasculation of white men who had turned their back on the offer of inclusion in the new Revolutionary community.[15]

Revolutionary veterans' memories

This shift in concepts of male citizenship led to a tendency among Pennsylvania's Revolutionary veterans to construct a memory of their experiences that asserted a democratic, white-male identity. These men applied for federal pensions between about 1818 and 1838; precisely the time when ideas of universal white-male suffrage were beginning to exert a shaping influence on American politics. When old soldiers gave their pension depositions in open court, their narratives were objects of public interest that often promoted the process of democratization in a number of ways.[16] For example, some pensioners specifically recalled the participatory aspects of militia service, such as voting for officers. Henry Greninger's participation in the election of Adam Sheafer as his captain figured prominently in his pension deposition. Similarly, Robert Gray and James Alworth recollected more than 40 years after the Revolution how they elected their officers. Jacob Kreider recalled his own election by his fellow militiamen to the rank of ensign. Such narratives indicate that militia service had political dimensions beyond the defence of the community.[17]

Another way in which both former militiamen and Continental regulars expressed their own political agency as public men was by linking their service to historic events or heroic leaders. Connecting their service to the Declaration of Independence was common. In their depositions veterans consciously tried to portray themselves as autonomous political agents making momentous patriotic decisions that were evinced in their military service. For example, Griffith Smith stated that 'immediately after the Declaration of Independence', he joined the militia.[18] Jacob Stahle remembered his enlistment this way: 'I resided at Philadelphia in the year 1776 and on the 4th day of July that year, being the day of the Declaration of American Independence, I entered into the service of the United States by signing the association at Philadelphia.'[19] The proclivity to date service to the Fourth of July obviously evoked associations in the audience, which would certainly have recalled the reading of the Declaration as an important event in all Revolutionary communities and in Pennsylvania in particular, where it coincided with the rise of the radically democratic state government. As historian Pauline Maier has persuasively argued, the Declaration articulated the Revolutionary spirit, and its 'rediscovery' after the War of 1812 as a 'sacred' text of the founding of the United States allowed soldiers to meld their important memories of the document with popular notions of nineteenth-century patriotism. It also allowed them to assert themselves as politicized men in the new republic.[20]

Veterans also evoked the democratization that grew out of the Revolution in their discussions of wartime heroes and leaders. This association is perhaps most visible in Revolutionary veterans' numerous references to George Washington. Some enlisted men remembered closely interacting with the genteel Virginian, rendering him a man of the people. John Allen, a former private, described himself as 'acquainted' with Washington.[21] Some, like Valentine Shoufler, remembered being singled out by the commander to perform some special duty or assignment. Shoufler was 'ordered to Long Island by General Washington'.[22] Similarly, Nathaniel Burrows asserted that after a battle in which all his officers were killed, he took command of his company, which 'by especial request of General Washington attached itself to a [Continental] regiment'.[23] Burrows then went on to describe how he in particular was 'employed by General Washington on express and other enterprises deemed to be of importance to the service'.[24] Abraham Goss recalled that, as a young fifer in the Pennsylvania Line, he 'frequently played by the direction of Washington'.[25] Samuel Graff's attempt to democratize popular memory of Washington was perhaps the boldest. The militiaman and his comrades captured a British soldier during the Philadelphia campaign and refused to turn him over to their own officers. Instead, Graff asserted, they 'took him to General Washington at Whitemarsh, who treated them with brandy'.[26] Typically the commander-in-chief maintained the class distinctions of an eighteenth-century gentleman officer, keeping his enlisted men at a respectable social distance.[27]

What is striking in the veterans' recollections is their implied image of Washington as a populist military leader. Such accounts reveal at least two important factors about how soldiers remembered the Revolution, factors that reinforce each other. First, the attempt to create a general who was a friend to the privates demonstrates the ways in which some of the rank and file were changed by the war. Retrospectively seeing themselves as full citizens of the republic with a special stake in its creation, they could participate with their commander in the national narrative as well as in the fraternity of comrades-in-arms. Second, the individualist culture of the early nineteenth century contributed to a revised memory of Washington. Mason Weems's popular 1858 biography casts Washington as a humble, self-made man. In Weems's portrayal, Washington reflects the industrious, nineteenth-century middle-class ideal rather than an eighteenth-century planter.[28] In such a context, veterans could not help but remember their commander as a figure similar to Andrew Jackson, another former general who became US President (1829–37) at the time when the later pension depositions were being given. Jackson, too, was celebrated as a self-made man who led fellow common men during this period. In this case, subsequent cultural developments validated perceptions that in previous eras had been seen as radical. While considered revolutionary in the eighteenth century, the idea that a private could regard himself as a 'brother soldier' to his commanding officer became more acceptable in the nineteenth century. Veterans could freely express this view of their service without fear of suggesting social radicalism or disrespect, as it seemed consistent with contemporary American values.[29]

However, veterans' imagining themselves as white men in arms articulated the new American political subject. References to race and gender were particularly frequent in the pension depositions offered by frontier soldiers who fought Native Americans.[30] When widespread hostilities broke out in the northern trans-Allegheny West in 1777, many of the young men who went to war later remembered doing so with a notion that they were fighting *all* Indians, despite the fact that many groups were neutral and some, such as numerous Oneidas, Tuscaroras and Delawares, were actively allied with the Revolutionaries. Veterans stated their reasons for fighting as responses to undifferentiated Indian violence. In some cases, frontier soldiers justified their inability to recall Revolutionary heroes or the war against Britain by focusing their story on race war against 'the Indians'. Peter Keister, for example, noted in his pension application that 'such was the nature of [our] service that [I] cannot remember any prominent fact which entered into the history of the country'. He then went on to say that,

> it was an arduous service marked by individual murders and burnings [by] the Indians of our men. I recollect Michael Lamb, John Ebby, John Clinesmith[?], and Jacob Beekle were killed by the Indians. John Stomilch[?] and his wife were murdered on their farm. ... They were tomahawked and scalped[,] and the old man had seven stab [wounds].[31]

Similarly, John Dougherty recalled:

> The Indians were continually committing depredations against the whites. ... Some of my relations and acquaintances had been killed by the Indians and I thought it my duty at all times to assist in protecting those that remained. ... My service and readiness to fight the Indians was well known at that time.[32]

In addition to lumping all Native Americans together as a single entity, Dougherty described members of his own community as 'the whites'. This tendency was pervasive among the pension applicants, who habitually referred not to perceived Native American skin colour but to their own. John Foster recalled that Indians 'massacred the whites'.[33] Adam Wolfe was a guard 'between the Indians and whites during the holding of a treaty at Pittsburgh'.[34] Andrew Myers remembered that 'the Indians... [were] determined not to yield to the white people'.[35] David Freemoyer decried Indians' 'predatory incursions upon the whites'.[36]

Despite widespread usage of the word *red* to denote Indian skin colour in the early nineteenth century when pension depositions were given, these Revolutionary veterans did not employ the term.[37] They chose to emphasize their own identities as *white* men. It clearly indicated veterans' claim to membership in the dominant group of political subjects. Given the importance of racial criteria in the militia and test-oath acts during the Revolution, coupled with the postwar movement towards universal white-male suffrage, veterans connected their military service to then-prevailing concepts of US citizenship. Although racial ideology and the term *white* existed in the colonial period, Revolutionary veterans were actively attempting to meld the concept of whiteness with the new republic's national identity. They portrayed the Revolutionary cause as that of whites. Thus they themselves were helping to dismantle the traditional Anglo-American concept of the male political subject as defined through property ownership and therefore class. Not surprisingly, the majority of pension applicants were desperately poor and seeking modest stipends to enable a modicum of financial independence. They buttressed their claims by invoking not only the image of the suffering veteran but also that of the suffering fellow white-male citizen.[38]

Articulation of whiteness also provided former soldiers with a rationale for the blurring of cultural standards of male martial behaviour. Like Native American warriors, Revolutionary soldiers carried out guerrilla attacks on villages, destroyed crops, captured, or killed non-combatants and took scalps as war trophies. As a result, soldiers created a double standard in their memories. When recalling hit-and-run attacks by Native Americans on Revolutionary communities, veterans portrayed them as unprovoked and unjustified. William Elliott, for example, recalled how the Indians 'frequently came down upon the defenceless settlers and on one occasion killed nine out of one family'.[39] Yet Pennsylvania frontier soldiers recounted their own comparable actions with pride. George Roush candidly described how his unit ambushed an Indian hunting camp:

> We fired and killed three, one of which was a squaw, and then approached the camp.... Whilst we were examining their guns, an Indian boy, which we supposed to be of the age of fifteen or sixteen years, came near and halloed to us and said, "Unhee, what did you shoot at?" And a man by the name of Fulks answered in the Indian language and said, "A racoon." The Indian came across the creek, and when he came in shooting distance[,] one of our company shot him.[40]

George Reem stated that he participated in 'destroying the cornfields and burning the Indian villages'.[41] John McCasland, who described Indians in the Ohio country as 'troublesome', noted that on an expedition against Shawnee towns, his unit 'burnt their corn, which was gathered, and burnt as many as seven little towns, took five Indians (women and children) prisoners, and killed five or six warriors.'[42] The rationalization for this glaring hypocrisy was white racial identity. Soldiers were able to appropriate elements of Indian warrior masculinity without fear of being seen as 'savage', because race rather than culture was the definitive boundary between European-Americans and Native Americans. Thus, while warrior gender identities might intersect and blur, race could serve as the immutable characteristic. White men did not see themselves as 'savage' because they relied on the equation of whiteness with the American cause.[43]

This image of the white-male frontier warrior was consciously designed to strike a responsive chord among listeners in the early American republic. Many of those hearing the pension applications would concur with the veterans that the one thing which distinguished Americans from Europeans was adaptation to the American environment. The frontiersman who mixed Indian and European culture, especially methods of warfare, was a staple of popular literature and culture. While audiences in the courts might have desired stories of George Washington, they certainly recognized a truly American experience in the frontier war. Like the veterans, they would have been untroubled by the contradiction between lauding Revolutionary military actions while disdaining similar Indian acts. The Indianized white man was an archetype of a new national identity: biologically superior to Indians, culturally superior to Europeans.[44]

Collectively, the image of the democratic, white-male veteran as a maker of the new nation illustrated how the American Revolution and its aftermath forged a new definition of citizenship. While class conflict in the early US republic was pervasive, it was mitigated by the imagined fraternity of white men. Indeed, while many veterans may have been disappointed with the inequalities produced by the Revolution, they could at least see certain political gains for them coming at the expense of others.[45] Moreover, frontier veterans' narratives of race war against Indians offered a historical precedent and justification for racial imperialism in this period. The cultural issues inherent in debates over Indian removals could be dismissed by using the logic of white-male citizenship. Cherokees, Creeks and other Indian nations who had republican government, Christianity, farming, livestock, European gender roles and a written language could be simplistically described as racial Others and obstacles to US expansion. While few Native American men sought the benefits of US citizenship, African-American men, of course, did. For them, the new image of the white-male citizen was especially ominous. By implication, the statements made by veterans regarding national racial identity further bolstered the marginalization of African-American men. Building on the laws in the Revolutionary period that specified only white males were eligible for militia service and oaths of allegiance, the early republic developed popular practices as well as federal and state laws in which free black men were gradually but explicitly denied the rights of full citizenship. By the end of the 1830s, the decade during which the most descriptive pension applications were made, most states, including northern ones, denied the right to vote even to propertied African-American men. In 1837–8, Pennsylvania convened a new constitutional convention that revoked the rights of African-American men to vote.[46] Additionally, the federal government passed laws in the early nineteenth century that restricted naturalization and eligibility for national militia service to whites only.[47] The racial ideology expressed in veterans' memorial narratives promoted a notion of citizenship in which all men were entitled to participate in the political life of the new republic as long as they were white. In other words, the American Revolution laid the ground work for the transformation of the citizen from someone whose rights and privileges derived from his social class to a political subject whose identity and rights were entirely biologically defined.

The Loyalist memory of the revolution

For Loyalist veterans in Pennsylvania the memory of the American Revolution was radically different. Rather than recalling the fraternity of white-male soldiers fighting for a new nation, these veterans told stories of manhood lost. For a group of people who largely thought of themselves as imperial British subjects, the legacy of the American Revolution underscored their dependence and provincial inferiority. Many of these men left records of their memories in Loyalist claims made in the 1780s, several decades earlier than Revolutionary veterans' pension applications.[48] Additionally, the claimants did not include all Loyalist veterans but only those who were propertied men. Nonetheless, their recollections offer a useful comparison to those of the Revolutionaries, showing the variations in concepts of masculinity and citizenship shaped by the war and by social class. In order to be recompensed for their myriad losses, Pennsylvania Loyalists were forced to portray themselves as dependent, emasculated, provincial subjects. Such representations underscored the desire to return to their traditional status as property-holding subjects within a changing and increasingly hierarchical British empire.[49]

Not surprisingly, Loyalists recalled the Revolution in Pennsylvania as oppressive and emasculating, not democratic. By definition, any white male who could not or would not take the oath of allegiance to the Pennsylvania Revolutionary constitution was placed outside the new body politic. For those who refused to take the oath and held property and voting rights, the Revolution marked a tragic loss of the British citizen's traditional prerogatives. This was true of neutrals and even moderate Whigs who opposed the radical new regime, as well as active Loyalists. As the civic sphere was expanding for poor white Revolutionary soldiers, the so-called disaffected experienced its contraction. Loyalists such as James Sheppard recounted their heroic resistance and the attendant penalties. Sheppard noted that even before the formal test act was passed, refusal to swear loyalty to the rebel cause was dangerous. He recalled how 'the rebels wanted him to take the oath in the year 1775 and he refused to do it in consequence of which they tarred and feathered him'.[50] Others did not wait for the Revolutionaries to implicate them as traitors among the brotherhood of white men. Charles Holmes refused to take the oath and was 'apprehensive that he should be sent to prison[, so] he made his escape to New York'.[51] John Webster, a Philadelphia artisan, recalled the economic implications of his actions as the rebels denied him the prerogatives of a propertied patriarch. When he refused to take the oath, he was 'proscribed to certain limits, his shop shut up, prevented from doing his business, or to collect debts due to him, and in daily expectation of imprisonment'.[52] Joshua Thomas, a small farmer recalled the humiliation of not being able to practise his livelihood, noting: 'he was often required to sign associations, to take oaths, etc. but he never did any thing of the sort. For some time before he escaped he was obliged to live in the woods.'[53] Daniel Batwell recounted how 'the Americans came and took him out of his bed. They gave him the alternative of taking the oath of allegiance or of removing his family into the British lines, the latter of which he agreed to.' Thus, Batwell's whole family's standing in the community was eradicated overnight.[54]

Given that the purpose of Loyalist claims was reimbursement for documented material losses, a central theme of the depositions is the loss of property. Loyalists recalled these experiences with bitterness not only because of the economic deprivation but also because this dispossession threatened the very foundation of British citizenship. Abraham Pastorius lost his estate and thus the basis of his citizenship. He complained that the British government had never come close to addressing his losses, adding that he had 'never received a shilling' for his service during the war as a guide for British troops.[55] William Morehead, a farmer, testified that he was imprisoned, lost his estate to confiscation and was eventually forced to abandon his family in order to escape behind British lines.[56] When Loyalist Lawrence Fegan fled to safety, the Revolutionaries confiscated his estate and 'turned his wife and children into the streets in a most rigorous season'.[57] Edward Jones described a similar humiliation of 'his wife and children turned out of house and home in an enemy's country and nothing to support them' after Pennsylvania confiscated his estate while he served in the Bucks County Loyalist Volunteers.[58] Such imagery indicates the helplessness that Loyalists felt in being unable to protect their families. Indeed, Margaret Lister, the widow of Andrew McGlone, noted how her own and other Loyalist families were 'exposed to the rage and rapine of a villainous and incensed soldiery'. Here was the converse image of what the Revolutionaries remembered about their military service. Lister showed the Revolutionary soldiers as threats to, rather than guardians of, male independence.[59]

Other Loyalists echoed Lister's account and portrayed themselves as victims of Revolutionary tyranny. Isaac Gray joined the British army after 'suffering much from the tyranny of the rebels'.[60] William Rankin suggested that many loyal British subjects were 'obliged to submit to the tyranny of their rulers, the payment of heavy taxes, and ultimately to remain under a government truly oppressive and which they abhor[red]'.[61] According to David Jones, after 'His Majesty's troops evacuated Philadelphia, ... American tyranny and oppression soon followed, and all those who favoured the government of Great Britain were made the immediate objects of its effect'.[62] Loyalty to the British government was another recurring trope in these claims. While such declarations were a conventional feature of the depositions, they implicitly reaffirmed the principle of colonial subordination to the imperial metropole. Metropolitan supremacy was an issue that some Loyalists had challenged during the debate over parliamentary taxation in the 1760s and early 1770s.[63] To some extent, the Loyalist claims showed deponents carefully delineating their place in the empire as deserving British subjects and as colonists showing due deference to central government. Accordingly, Loyalists tended to portray themselves as both dutiful provincials and active proponents of British government in North America.

Jasper Harding was typical of those who stated that they served due to their 'attachment to British government'.[64] Similarly, George Sinclair recalled that he was 'employed in many secret and dangerous services for government'.[65] Significantly, they placed their own particular stories under the rubric of 'services for government', something that Revolutionary veterans almost never did. In contrast to Revolutionaries who asserted that they were serving the people and their own interests, Loyalists readily acknowledged the British monarch as the head of the imperial coalition fighting the colonial rebels and their allies. Moreover, while it made perfect sense for Loyalists to portray their service as selfless commitment to British government when seeking reimbursement for losses, their testimonies underscored the claimants' status as dependents. Cumulatively, these narratives created an image of British patriots who had lost everything and were now displaced provincials, utterly reliant on the beneficence of government. Again, the Loyalists constructed an emasculated image of themselves simply to protect their own interests.[66]

Such a view of the Revolution reflected Loyalists' attempt to articulate their place in the postwar British Empire, the composition of which had changed radically over the course of the eighteenth century. By the eve of the Revolution, constituent parts of the British Empire in North America included French Catholic Quebec and independent allies among the Indian nations, as well as colonies on the mainland and in the West Indies. The exigencies of war forced Britain to utilize every resource to defeat the rebels, including fighting with large numbers of Indian allies and tens of thousands of freed slaves.[67] With the loss of thirteen North American colonies by 1783, the importance of the multi-ethnic components of the empire grew. Native Americans and Canadians were bulwarks against US expansion. Freed slaves who settled in Sierra Leone represented the empire in Africa. Imperial power was centralized in parts of Asia with the India Act of 1784. Moreover, with the secession of the particularly obstreperous mainland colonies that demanded equal rights as British subjects, some of the most vocal opponents of a more centralized empire were gone. North American Loyalists were now widely dispersed refugees, who were more concerned with receiving compensation for losses than with claiming full equality as Britons in the colonies. As historian Linda Colley has shown, Britons came to define their nationalism, in part, in opposition to a subordinated, exotic empire in which non-Europeans were at the bottom of the hierarchy. The place of European-descended provincials was less clear. In this new imperial context, Loyalist claimants were careful to offer memories that represented them as colonial subjects whose steadfast allegiance and faithful service to the crown entitled them to compensation from the British government. Many were able to assert a common British political identity with the hearers of their claims, thus contradicting any suggestion that they were exotic Others within the empire. Simultaneously, their many references to 'service' underscored their acceptance of an inferior provincial status. This formulation mirrored their tenuous liminal position as subordinate but not fully marginalized members of the empire. They did not demand full equality as citizens of Britain, nor did they dare to claim their commanding officers as brothers in arms.[68]

Perhaps the most remarkable and most telling feature of the Loyalist depositions is what they do not say. There is an utter paucity of any Loyalist self reference to whiteness. As Loyalists fought in coalition with large numbers of Native American warriors and former slaves, it is unsurprising that they could make no easy equation between the cause of Great Britain and that of white men. Nonetheless, most Pennsylvania Loyalists probably shared the prevailing Anglo-American attitude that Native Americans and African-Americans were inferior to whites.[69] They rarely, if ever, mentioned the contribution of emancipated slaves or of independent Native Americans fighting the Revolutionaries on behalf of the imperial cause. Still, given the reality of this contribution and the empire's multi-ethnic nature, it also made no sense to suggest any simplistic formula of race war such as was offered by the Revolutionaries. Indeed, some Loyalists' military service was so closely tied to non-white allies of the crown that they had to speak to this issue. For example, John Depue noted his service in Butler's Rangers, a unit that fought in conjunction with Iroquois and other Native warriors, and his later service in the British North American Indian Department.[70] Matthew Elliot clearly addressed the larger imperial coalition when he characterized his service as being primarily 'to retain the Indians in their attachment to His Majesty.'[71] George Girty described Native American territory as a refuge from Revolutionary oppression when recounting how he broke out of prison and 'escaped through Indian country to Detroit,' where he enlisted in the Indian Department.[72] The stigma of Loyalism was great on the Pennsylvania frontier, as it led Revolutionaries to see their internal enemies, who were potentially willing to fight with Native Americans, as traitors to the brotherhood of white men. These recollections speak to racial identity only indirectly. Like the Revolutionaries, the Loyalists lump various Native Americans into one group—'the Indians'—even though they were well aware of cultural and other differences among them. In the depositions the narrators' own race is evoked without being directly stated. Thus in a hierarchical multi-ethnic British Empire, the claimants were able to benefit from the privileges of whiteness without explicitly asserting them. They had good reasons for employing this strategy of indirection. The emergence of Revolutionary Pennsylvania's white-male political subjectivity was a key source of their misfortune. The Revolutionary militia drafts and test oaths for white men typically led to the loss of citizenship rights and property for those who refused to submit to them. Moreover, claiming the privileges of a white male would serve no purpose in the traditional British-American context of a property-holding male franchise. Propertied Loyalists merely sought a return, even if only a partial one, of the privileges that they had lost. Their memories expressed conservatism in the face of a changing world and empire.[73]

Conclusion

The memories of Pennsylvania Revolutionary and Loyalist veterans of the American War for Independence highlight two divergent gendered formulations of civic identity in their memories. For Revolutionaries, the careful construction of their memorial narratives to highlight an image of soldiers as independent, democratic white men speaks to the movement towards universal white-male suffrage that emerged from the American Revolution. The US veteran and citizen portrayed himself as a capable, self-assured white male, fit to participate in his country's politics. The agency that former soldiers attributed to themselves and their relentless attempts to claim the privileges of whiteness undoubtedly derive from the fact that most rank-and-file Revolutionary soldiers were men without property who would have had no vote under the British system. Wartime laws that implied whiteness as a prerequisite for citizenship empowered them. Their memories reflect the Revolution's darker legacy of exclusion. Revolutionary narratives of frontier race war equated American national identity with white manhood. Also, the Revolutionaries' focus implied a physiological basis for citizenship and definitively excluded non-white men as well as all women.[74] In contrast, white-male Loyalist claimants did not create a new political subjectivity but clung instead to traditional British notions of propertied male citizenship. These claimants did, however, undergo a fundamental change in their views of themselves. Arguably, they were some of the worst losers of the American Revolution. Because they lost their status in provincial America, they were compelled to portray themselves as victims dependent on the crown to restore their rights as citizens. Previously independent heads of households petitioned for the paternalistic beneficence of British government to restore some measure of their manhood. These emasculated, displaced provincials struggled to regain their former status in the increasingly hierarchical and multi-ethnic British Empire. In so doing, they looked back to past models of political manhood rather than to radical new ideas such as those of the Revolutionaries that racialised citizenship.

Notes

1. The analysis in this chapter is adapted from my monograph, Gregory T. Knouff, *The Soldiers' Revolution: Pennsylvanians in Arms and the Forging of Early American Identity* (University Park, PA, 2004).
2. Gordon S. Wood, *The Radicalism of the American Revolution* (New York, 1991); Dana D. Nelson, *National Manhood: Capitalist Citizenship and the Imagined Fraternity of White Men* (Durham, NC, 1998).

3. Robert M Calhoon, *The Loyalist Perception and Other Essays* (Columbia, SC, 1989).
4. Terry Bouton, *Taming Democracy: The People, the Founders, and the Troubled Ending of the American Revolution* (New York, 2007); Wayne L. Bockelman and Owen S. Ireland, 'The Internal Revolution in Pennsylvania: An Ethnic-Religious Interpretation', *Pennsylvania History* 41 (1974): 125–156.
5. Anne M. Ousterhout, *A State Divided: Opposition in Pennsylvania to the American Revolution* (Westport, CT, 1987).
6. Robert J. Dinkin, *Voting in Provincial America: A Study of Elections in the Thirteen Colonies, 1689–1776* (Westport, CT, 1977), 29–38; John B. Frantz and William Pencak (eds), *Beyond Philadelphia: The American Revolution in the Pennsylvania Hinterland* (University Park, PA, 1998), xii and 70.
7. Dinkin, *Voting*, 44.
8. David Hawke, *In the Midst of a Revolution* (Philadelphia, 1960), 170–173, 184.
9. Gordon S. Wood, *The Creation of the American Republic, 1776–1787* (New York, 1972), 226–237. The voting and militia provisions are from the 1776 Pennsylvania Constitution, repr. in Theodore Thayer, *Pennsylvania Politics and the Growth of Democracy* (Harrisburg, PA, 1953), 215.
10. The 1777 militia law, as published in *Pennsylvania Gazette*, 26 March 1777.
11. Militia Association, as published in ibid. 6 December 1775.
12. Test Act, as published in *Pennsylvania Packet*, 20 May 1778.
13. On the liability of white males in Delaware for militia service, see, for example, *Pennsylvania Gazette*, 28 May 1777. Article IX, Articles of Confederation, repr. in Edmund S. Morgan, *Birth of the Republic, 1763–89* (3rd edn, Chicago, 1992), 168.
14. Provision from the Test Act, quoted in *Pennsylvania Gazette*, 4 June 1777.
15. Ousterhout, *A State Divided*, 171–173; Henry J. Young, 'Treason and Its Punishment in Revolutionary Pennsylvania', *Pennsylvania Magazine of History and Biography* 90 (1966): 287–313.
16. In 1818 an act of Congress provided half-pay pensions to all enlisted men in the Continental army for nine months and were in 'reduced circumstances.' A subsequent act required the appending of a personal property schedule to prove the applicants' indigence. The pension legislation of 1832 offered a stipend to anyone who had served six months in any military capacity, including the militia, regardless of financial need. For analysis of the provisions of the 1818 act, see John Resch, *Suffering Soldiers: Revolutionary War Veterans, Moral Sentiment, and the Political Culture of the Early Republic* (Amherst, 1999), 118. On the provisions for the federal Revolutionary War pension acts, see John C. Dann, *The Revolution Remembered: Eyewitness Accounts of the American Revolution* (Chicago, 1980), xv–xvii.
17. The United States National Archives and Records Administration, Washington, DC (hereafter NARA), Files S10764, W4446, S2208, and W10186 in Revolutionary War Pension Application Files, Collection M804, hereafter cited as RWPF.
18. NARA, RWPF, W3467.
19. Ibid. 3472.
20. Pauline Maier, *American Scripture: Making the Declaration of Independence* (New York, 1998), 3–96 and 155–208.
21. NARA, RWPF, S22622.
22. Ibid. S22506.
23. Ibid. S22151.
24. Ibid.
25. Ibid. S22799.

26. Ibid. W7566.
27. According to Marcus Cunliffe, Washington 'did not inspire enthusiastic affection among the rank and file' during the Revolution; see Cunliffe, *George Washington: Man and Monument* (New York, 1960), 108.
28. M. L. Weems, *The Life of George Washington* (Philadelphia, 1858). On the influence of Weems's portrayal of Washington in the early nineteenth-century as a 'self-made man' around the time of the pension depositions, see Steven Watts, *The Republic Reborn: War and the Making of Liberal America* (Baltimore, 1989), 144–145.
29. Alfred Young comes to similar conclusions regarding the democratized memory of the Massachusetts veteran George Robert Twelves Hewes, who recalled standing next to John Hancock at the Boston Tea Party; see Young, *The Shoemaker and the Tea Party: Memory and the American Revolution* (Boston, 1999), 44–45, 55–57.
30. Europeans and European-Americans had long articulated various formulations of racial identity and whiteness in relation to Native Americans in particular, as shown by Kathleen Brown in 'Native Americans and Early Modern Concepts of Race,' in *Empire and Others: British Encounters with Indigenous Peoples, 1600–1850*, ed. Martin Daunton and Rick Halpern (Philadelphia, 1999), 79–100. However, the Revolution was vital in tying white racial identity in relation to Native Americans to early concepts of United States national identity.
31. NARA, RWPF, R11329.
32. Ibid. S12779.
33. Ibid. S23637.
34. Ibid. S4731.
35. Ibid. W5155.
36. David Freemoyer, quoted in Dann, *The Revolution Remembered*, 304.
37. On the nineteenth-century conception of Native Americans as 'red', see Alden Vaughan, *Roots of American Racism: Essays on the Colonial Experience* (New York, 1995), 3–33.
38. On poor veterans portraying themselves in a pervasive sentimental image of a 'suffering soldier', see Resch, *Suffering Soldiers*, 64–92.
39. NARA, RWPF, S16378.
40. George Roush, quoted in Dann, *The Revolution Remembered*, 260–261.
41. NARA, RWPF, R8633.
42. John McCasland, quoted in Dann, *The Revolution Remembered*, 157.
43. For a fuller analysis of frontier military culture and the construction of white racial identity, see Knouff, *Soldiers' Revolution*, 155–193.
44. On the 'Indianized' Indian-hater, see Richard Slotkin, *Regeneration through Violence: The Mythology of the American Frontier, 1600–1860* (Middletown, CT, 1973); and Richard White, *Middle Ground: Indians, Empires, and Republics in the Great Lakes Region* (New York, 1991), 368–375. On Indianized Americanness as a statement of identity and opposition to Europe in general and Britain in particular, see Philip J. Deloria, *Playing Indian* (New Haven, 1998), 10–37.
45. Bouton, *Taming Democracy*, 257–265.
46. Gary B. Nash, *The Forgotten Fifth: African Americans in the Age of Revolution* (Cambridge, MA, 2006), 163.
47. On the denial of voting rights for black men by most American states and federal laws limiting naturalization to whites and militia enrolment to white men, see Joyce Appleby, *Inheriting the Revolution: The First Generation of Americans* (Cambridge, MA, 2000), 47. Appleby points out that only Vermont and New

Hampshire had '"colour-blind" constitutions' and that New York allowed only propertied black men the vote while all white men were enfranchised.
48. On the British acts of compensation to American Loyalists, see Wallace Brown, *The Good Americans: The Loyalists and the American Revolution* (New York, 1969), 181.
49. On Loyalists clinging to their traditional pre-Revolutionary view of colonial self-government even while in exile, see Neil MacKinnon, *This Unfriendly Soil: The Loyalist Experience in Nova Scotia, 1783–1791* (Montreal, 1986), 118–136. On the highly centralized nature of the British administration of post-Revolutionary North America, see Alan Taylor, 'The Late Loyalists: Northern Reflections of the Early American Republic', *Journal of the Early Republic* 27/1 (2007): 1–34.
50. Records of the American Loyalist Claims Commission, 1776–1831, The National Archive of the United Kingdom, Kew (hereafter TNA), Great Britain, Audit Office 12 (hereafter AO12), vol. 99, 49.
51. TNA, AO12 100/346.
52. Ibid. 38/158.
53. Ibid. 40/242.
54. Ibid. 42/308.
55. Ibid. 42/21–24.
56. Ibid. 38/14–16.
57. Ibid. 38/403–405.
58. Ibid. 40/222.
59. American Loyalist Claims Commission Papers, 1780–1835, TNA, Great Britain, Audit Office 13 (hereafter AO13), vol. 71, 156.
60. TNA, AO12/40/118–120.
61. Ibid. 205–206.
62. TNA, AO13/71/122.
63. Steven Sarson, *British America, 1500–1800: Creating Colonies, Imagining an Empire* (New York, 2005), 239–240.
64. TNA, AO13/96/367.
65. Ibid. 22/261.
66. On the typical Loyalist self-presentation as dependent victims, see Janice Potter-MacKinnon, *While the Women Only Wept: Loyalist Refugee Women in Eastern Ontario* (Montreal, 1993), 94–160.
67. Edward Countryman argues in 'Indians, the Colonial Order, and the Social Significance of the American Revolution' (*William and Mary Quarterly* 53 [1996]: 342–363) that the British viewed Indians as constituent parts of their hierarchical empire. On the thousands of slaves who sought to free themselves by taking advantage of British promises of emancipation in return for serving the British military, see Cassandra Pybus, *Epic Journeys of Freedom: Runaway Slaves of the American Revolution and Their Global Quest for Freedom* (Boston, 2006); and Simon Schama, *Rough Crossings: Britain, the Slaves, and the American Revolution* (New York, 2006).
68. Linda Colley, *Britons: Forging the Nation, 1707–1837* (New Haven, 1992). On the more hierarchical model of empire (epitomized in laws such as the India Act) that emerged as an immediate result of the American Revolution, see ibid. 143–145. See also Eliga H. Gould, *The Persistence of Empire: British Political Culture in the Age of the American Revolution* (Chapel Hill, 2000), 181–214; and C. A. Bayly, *Imperial Meridian: The British Empire and the World, 1780–1830* (Harlow, UK, 1989), 75–132.

69. On white Loyalist racial hostility to non-white Loyalists, see MacKinnon, *This Unfriendly Soil*, 49–50, 83; and Schama, *Rough Crossings*, 235–239.
70. TNA, AO12/40/376–377.
71. Ibid. 40/382–384.
72. Ibid. 40/407.
73. On the complex intersections of ideology, economic interests and imperial politics in Britons' changing views of 'indigenous peoples' throughout the British Empire during this period, see C. A. Bayly, 'The British and Indigenous Peoples: 1760–1860: Power, Perception, and Identity', in Daunton and Halpern, *Empire and Others*, 19–41.
74. For archival evidence that rank-and-file soldiers were disproportionately drawn from the lower and propertyless classes, see Charles Patrick Neimeyer, *America Goes to War: A Social History of the Continental Army* (New York, 1996), 8–26; and Steven Rosswurm, *Arms, Country, and Class: The Philadelphia Militia and the 'Lower Sort' During the American Revolution* (New Brunswick, NJ., 1987), 113–199.

17
'Drying Their Tears': Women's Petitions, National Reconciliation and Commemoration in Post-Independence Chile

Sarah C. Chambers

> Public gratitude for good deeds can never be more justly awarded than when the blood of heroes is sacrificed for the Liberty of the Nation. The widows and mothers of the victors of Chacabuco deserve the recognition of the Government, for in them lives on the memory of the brave who extinguished tyranny; but the State's lack of funds cannot provide a worthy compensation.[1]

In February of 1817, just as the winter snows were melting, Argentine and Chilean soldiers braved the high passes of the Andes and defeated the Spanish army at Chacabuco on the Chilean side. The dramatic nature of this campaign captured the imagination of contemporaries, as the government decree quoted in my epigraph shows, and it came to dominate commemorations of Chilean independence. But remembering and forgetting go hand in glove. Most subsequent narratives of independence reduced over a decade of civil war to this one battle and the complicated allegiances of participants to a dichotomy between active male heroes and their supportive yet passive wives and mothers. First, the official history favours a particular chronology that begins with Chileans' initial efforts at self-governance in 1810, continues with the interruption of those efforts by a Spanish 'reconquest' of Chile in 1813, and culminates with the Battle of Chacabuco in 1817.

Coevals, however, were not confident that Spanish power in Chile had been 'extinguished', despite the decree's optimistic pronouncement; on the contrary, patriot and royalist forces in southern Chile remained in a stand-off for several more years, during which the Spaniards almost recaptured Santiago twice. Second, although the decree and later commemorations highlight the victory over foreign tyranny, many Chileans (women as well as men) supported the Spanish crown; hence the conflict, especially in the south, was as much a civil war as one of national liberation. Finally, the passage quoted from the decree underscores the gendered nature of national memories of war: brave, masculine heroes shed their blood to win liberty, while the memory of their deeds would live on through their widows and mothers.[2] This essay argues that the official history recalling the glorious birth of the nation could not become hegemonic until the compensation alluded to in the decree's final line silenced the tearful pleas of women whose stories evoked more contested memories.

The understanding of historical memories of war and civil conflict has become crucial for Chile and other Latin American countries in the wake of military regimes responsible for widespread human rights abuses since the 1970s. Such memory struggles are highly gendered; in the case of Chile, women became emblematic both of those who portrayed the 1973 coup as necessary to save the nation from communism and of those who publicized the fate of the tortured, assassinated and disappeared.[3] Moreover, some scholars have argued that the feminization of the human rights 'victim' has made it difficult to renew the explicitly political activities interrupted by the coup.[4] Not surprisingly, historians have become interested in the construction of historical memory in earlier periods of Latin American history, but such studies primarily analyse the official process of commemorating male heroes.[5] The farther into the past we venture, without rich oral testimonies or truth commission reports, the more difficult it is to find recorded contestations of the dominant story, particularly in the voices of women.

Though radically oppositional narratives from the nineteenth century are lacking, this essay nonetheless draws out the ambivalences in women's petitions that initially prevented the Chilean government from controlling stories of male heroism for its own propaganda. Although the idealized role of the Chilean woman as loyal to her man and honouring his sacrifice for the nation quickly became hegemonic, the image of the mourning woman or female victim could be problematic for those trying to establish a new nation-state.[6] Chilean nationalists denounced royalist abuses of women, but had to respond to petitions from women who had suffered losses because of patriot actions as well. Moreover, the hero's widow or mother who had to keep repeating her story because she had not received compensation for the loss of a loved one and breadwinner, even if she simultaneously expressed her support for the cause of independence, kept alive painful rather than celebratory memories of war. Finally, the claims made by relatives of those who had been heroes during the war against Spain but later found themselves on the losing side of subsequent civil wars revived memories of partisan conflict in periods when the state wished to promote an image of national unity and reconciliation.[7]

A quick overview of the events reveals some of the complications elided by the official history of independence. After Napoleon invaded

Spain and captured King Ferdinand VII in 1808, certain factions of the American-born elite responded to the crisis by forming a local assembly in 1810 to replace the royal governor. However, differences based on kinship, region and ideology soon divided even those Chileans who favoured some degree of autonomy. These conflicts, especially between rivals Bernardo O'Higgins and José Miguel Carrera, aided the Spanish cause. In March of 1813, royal troops sent by the Viceroy of Peru landed in southern Chile, and by October they had regained control of Santiago; they rounded up suspected insurgents and sent them to a penal colony on the Juan Fernández Islands. Some revolutionaries were able to escape over the Andes to the independent provinces of La Plata (the future Argentina), but they carried with them their internal disputes. O'Higgins emerged victorious from his conflict with Carrera, recruited the support of Argentine General José de San Martin and managed to retake central Chile in 1817. Despite attempts to depict the Battle of Chacabuco as definitive, however, fighting continued in the south against the Spanish army until 1826 and against Chilean guerrillas who opposed the new national government into the 1830s. There the support for the Spanish crown among much of the region's population, including the majority of the Mapuche Indians south of the Biobío River, delayed a definitive patriot victory.[8] Although these conflicts would be relegated to a few lines or a footnote in later official histories, they were called a 'War to the Death' by contemporaries to whom the final outcome was still unknown. Finally, even as the patriots gained the upper hand over the royalists, rivalries among them for power continued to fuel partisan strife.

The prolonged and divisive nature of the Wars of Independence and their aftermath in Chile shaped gendered memories of its history. Patriot depictions of the proper role of women during the extended period of war emphasized passive loyalty to husbands and acceptance of their sacrifices for the nation; royalist wives, by contrast, were denounced not only for their personal relationships with Spaniards but also for their own obstinate loyalty to the king and support of his cause. In the wake of independence, however, the new government gradually came to identify royalist women as passive victims in an effort to promote national unity. Petitions from women for restitution of confiscated property and military pensions during this period kept alive memories of the wars as violent and tragic, yet they also invited the government to provide an appropriate ending to their stories through compensation. By showing mercy for the families of former enemies, successive regimes attempted reconciliation. Finally, by the 1840s, after an external war against Peru and Bolivia and at a time when surviving veterans of independence were beginning to die of old age, the Chilean government could more successfully shape commemorations to highlight masculine heroism rather than feminine suffering and national unity rather than civil conflict.

Wartime symbols of femininity: loyal patriot wives and perfidious royalists

During the period of the Spanish 'reconquest' from 1813 to 1817, the wives and daughters of the patriot prisoners exiled to the penal islands pleaded on their behalf with royal officials. Their petitions for mercy were certainly sincere and in some cases may have been spontaneous, but letters sent by Gaspar Marín from the penal colony to his wife, Luisa Recabarren, urged her to organize family members in a campaign of pressure on the royal government. In official histories, Recabarren came to epitomize patriotic Chilean womanhood.[9] But a fascinating set of lawsuits brought by quarrelling spouses reveals the ambiguous origins of the idealized Chilean woman during the war.

On 31 October 1814, Mercedes Fontecilla presented herself to the recently restored royal officials and requested the return of her dowry from Felipe Calderón on the grounds of adultery. She asked the authorities to take quick action to prevent his fleeing with her assets 'because he has been one of the most decided and public supporters of the revolutionary and insurgent party on account of which he feared the arrival of royal troops'.[10] The case followed the slow course of mutual recriminations and presentation of evidence typical in marital disputes; although Calderón mentioned politics a few times in three hundred manuscript pages, for the most part his lawyer attributed his wife's supposedly false accusations to 'the weakness characteristic of the ignorance of her sex'.[11] Two years after Fontecilla initiated proceedings, a judge sentenced Calderón to return her dowry and in January of 1817 (as San Martín and O'Higgins began their ascent over the Andes) the court ordered the parties to settle accounts.

The story of the turbulent marriage, including its relationship to the state of civil war and to depictions of ideal Chilean womanhood, was taken up six months later in a lawsuit filed this time by 'the citizen' Calderón in the courts of the restored republic. Claiming that ecclesiastical authorities had never approved a permanent separation, he requested custody of his daughter and the right to administer the joint marital property. Moreover, he attributed the marital conflict explicitly to a difference of political opinion, accusing Fontecilla of having reported his support for the insurgents to royal authorities who fined and ultimately arrested him. Appealing to the notion that women were inherently apolitical, her lawyer countered that the couple's dissension was rooted in his infidelity, 'not political opinions in which the [female] sex always cedes to the gentle influence of the husband'.[12] But these were not apolitical times, and Calderón's lawyer contrasted the behaviour of Fontecilla with that of other wives of incarcerated patriots:

> In Chile, whose women have been models of conjugal virtues, should we allow such a horrible example of immorality and cold cruelty to go

unpunished? [This woman was]... unmoved by the tears and the most heroic tribulations of the other wives who, throwing themselves at the feet of the tyrants, pleaded for mercy and proclaimed the innocence of their persecuted husbands.[13]

Although the prosecutor at one point recommended confining Fontecilla to a convent, in the end Calderón was awarded one third of her income. They continued to fight in court over payments, and in 1829 he was still calling her a *goda* ('Goth'), an insulting term for a royalist.[14]

While Calderón faced arrest by royalist authorities, conflicts among the patriot refugees in Argentina also reaffirmed the image of a loyal wife pleading for mercy on behalf of her husband as the icon of Chilean womanhood. The Carrera siblings included three brothers and a sister; all of them went into exile with the royalist restoration in 1813, but only the latter challenged gender expectations by doing so. Javiera Carrera placed her politics above her duties as wife and mother, leaving behind her husband and most of her children to follow her brothers for what turned out to be a period of ten years. Her sisters-in-law, by contrast, were complying with both Spanish laws and cultural norms by following their husbands into exile. By 1821 all three brothers had been executed by the allies of O'Higgins in Argentina, and the widow of the eldest, Mercedes Fontecilla (apparently no relation to Calderón's royalist wife of the same name), was granted a safe conduct to return to Chile with her children. 'For me the highest recommendation on her behalf is having been the wife of an enemy', wrote the official issuing the passport; 'A well governed sense of pride would be offended at extending hate beyond the grave'.[15] Seven years later the Carrera brothers were posthumously rehabilitated and their remains repatriated, and Fontecilla's children were finally granted the military pension 'that the sword of their father earned them', in the words of their guardian.[16] It was expected that wives would further the causes of their husbands; hence they had to be watched closely in wartime but could be treated with sympathy in periods of national reconciliation. Mercedes Fontecilla is generally remembered as a beautiful and self-sacrificing wife rather than a political activist. Javiera Carrera, by contrast, is identified along with her brothers as having played a key role in the independence movement, but for the same reason she is often painted as ambitious and domineering beyond what was considered proper for a woman.[17]

When they returned to Chile, the patriots denounced the abuse and murder of women and children by royalist guerrillas and their indigenous allies while justifying their own measures against the civilian population.[18] As control over the southern province of Concepción changed hands several times, for example, each army ordered massive population evacuations and the destruction of crops in an attempt to deprive their enemy of support.[19] Chilean officials issued a series of decrees prohibiting the provisioning of royalist troops and carrying correspondence across enemy lines, whether these missives were attempts to provide intelligence to the Spanish army or simply to contact loved ones displaced by the war. One officer prosecuting such a case, declared to his superior:

> [I]t is the experience in all the Revolution that the Enemy has sustained its Espionage, inflicting incalculable evils upon the Republic, by means of the women. Your Lordship is well aware of it and the pity and leniency with which they have been regarded has not had the proper result since they still persist in their obstinate opinions.[20]

Increasingly, the mostly female couriers were punished severely, with lashes, imprisonment or even execution.

Articles in the official patriot newspaper, the *Gazeta de Santiago de Chile*, satirized royalist women, who were depicted as being under the sway of fanatical priests: 'Those [women] who call themselves royalists because one of these [priests] supports them should prefer shortages and even misery to the shame of associating themselves by this hated term with the foolish, atrocious and petrified monuments to our ancient servitude'.[21] A group of unfortunate Trinitarian nuns in Concepción came in for particular ridicule. An article of 1817 denounced Spanish authorities for having convinced the gullible sisters that the insurgents would persecute Catholics and rape virgins; moreover the article accused the Spaniards of taking valuables from the convent on the pretext of paying for the nuns' passage by sea to Lima and then failing to fulfil their promise.[22] Two years later the nuns abandoned their cloisters rather than face an occupying patriot army and evacuated with royalist forces into Indian territory, 'watering with their tears every step they took'.[23] Their penurious pilgrimage was a public-relations nightmare for the patriots, as even local residents who supported independence felt sorry for the sisters.[24] In an effort to counteract public opinion, articles in the official *Gazeta* insisted that Chilean authorities had been very lenient toward the nuns during a prior occupation and asserted that whatever orders the Spanish commander may have issued, the sisters were free to choose whether to stay or go. 'Have they forgotten', inquired the editor, 'that their divine husband has declared that his kingdom is not of this world?'[25]

The patriots were ultimately, if not inevitably, victorious in the south. But the war had taken such a toll on the region that even those committed to independence grew disenchanted with the central government in Santiago. Liberals throughout the country, moreover, were unhappy with the conservative constitution drafted in 1822 and its apparent perpetuation of O'Higgins in power as Supreme Director. O'Higgins had earlier feared that the Carreras would return from Argentina to overthrow his government, but the challenge instead came from his trusted protégé, General Ramón

Freire, the governor of Concepción. Although Freire went on to defeat the last remnant of the Spanish army on the island of Chiloé in 1826, his opposition to O'Higgins reopened civil strife; the landowning elite resented the liberals' anticlericalism and their abolition of entailed estates. When the results of a close election in September of 1829 were disputed, conservatives took advantage of the controversy to launch a revolt with their own southern general, Joaquín Prieto. Freire attempted to defend the constituted government but was defeated at the Battle of Lircay in April of 1830 and exiled to Peru, as O'Higgins had been before him. During subsequent decades the new nation finally experienced relative political stability as Interior Minister Diego Portales constructed an authoritarian, if nominally republican, state.[26] Female activism during the civil wars of the 1820s decreased compared to the period of the independence movements, but the wives of the defeated liberals would later provide an opportunity for national reconciliation.

Recasting royalist wives as defenceless mothers

The exposés of fanatical royalist women, on the one hand, and the victimization of innocent Chilean ladies by the Spanish tyrants and their barbarous allies, on the other, were useful as wartime propaganda. But to keep alive the memories of Chileans who had opposed independence would make forging national unity problematic. Moreover, the new government officials not only had to contend with competing memories of war but also had to decide in the present how to resolve the petitions of women affected by the civil conflict. Although they had earlier denounced royalist women as wilful political actors on the wrong side, increasingly it was more expedient to depict them as weak women unable to resist the orders of Spanish commanders or their royalist husbands and fathers. O'Higgins, for example, had ordered the arrest of 'all the harmful *godas* and especially those who by marriage or other means are related to the enemy'.[27] But when such Chilean-born women and their children were abandoned by their émigré husbands, their primary identities could shift from being wives to mothers: mothers who had to repent, to be sure, but whose children might grow up to be useful and patriotic citizens of the new nation. Female petitioners, desperate for relief, were only too willing to participate in constructing an image of themselves as victims.

Anyone who fled patriot troops was assumed to support the enemy, and their belongings were subject to confiscation. As the properties and merchandise of émigrés were seized, their wives flooded Chilean officials with petitions to protect their dowries and provide sustenance for their children. As early as April of 1817, the attorney general of the new government, José Gregorio Argomedo, outlined the principles for responding to such requests. With memories of the reconquest still fresh and the war still proceeding in the south, he denounced the seizures and fines authorized by the royal governors, which had violated 'all morality, all social relations and all manner of justice toward the daughters, wives and family of the unfortunate persons assessed'.[28] Although he was not yet ready to forgive and forget, Argomedo advocated policies that he believed would demonstrate the greater justice and benevolence of the patriot cause. He interpreted the law as making women's dowry property subject to seizure but proposed providing families with support payments from the income generated by the confiscated property. 'What are we to do with Chilean women and children?' he asked, answering his own question by saying 'We must protect them'.[29]

In response to sorrowful petitions from women telling of their inability to feed their families, Argomedo offered both assistance and admonitions that they prove their allegiance to the nation by raising their children with love for their homeland. María de los Dolores Araos insisted that her husband was innocent, having left for Spain on commercial business before the decisive battle of Chacabuco, and lamented that the seizure of his assets reduced her 'to the unfortunate condition of being absolutely unable to provide bread for my poor, innocent children'.[30] Argomedo denounced her husband as 'ungrateful' but was willing to give Araos a temporary allowance from the government so long as she educated her children 'according to the principles of allegiance to our System'.[31] The familial language throughout these cases is striking. The petitioners were ordered to cease their obedience to Spanish husbands who were 'ungrateful to the land who had given them these women', and to transfer their love and allegiance to the republic, which would assume the role of father to their native-born children. Presumably, once past associations had been broken, the nation could forget its origins in civil war and begin to forge a unity based on a shared birthplace.

In the south, women were not simply married to émigrés; they, too, had accompanied the Spanish army into Mapuche territory, from where it continued to attack Chilean forces. As early as 1819, Freire, in his capacity as governor of Concepción, issued amnesty decrees for any who returned from royalist-held territories.[32] María Jesús Arregui failed to return within the amnesty period but in 1826 requested full restitution of her confiscated property. To support her case, she depicted her husband, a Spanish merchant, in terms more often associated with feminine than masculine qualities: 'His passive character and the hatred he professed for anything having to do with warfare meant that during that time he was committed only to domestic matters, without having the least involvement in any kind of political affairs.'[33] Needless to say, she continued, her own age, sex and widowhood after 1816 meant that she could never have actively supported the Spanish crown, even though she had fled Concepción when the patriot forces approached:

> But if one considers that this [evacuation] was universal, due to the Decree of Terror published by [the Spanish commander] Sánchez to that

effect, and because this city was left without any inhabitants and threatened with destruction by the barbarous Indians, one should not consider me guilty because of that one act, since I found myself in the situation of fearing my death if I did not follow all the others.[34]

Her request for restitution, along with several others, was approved. Indeed by the end of 1826, the provincial assembly of Concepción, noting that many of the confiscated farms were going untended and therefore deepening the region's postwar economic crisis, requested that Congress approve a general return of properties to their former owners.[35]

Comforting (and silencing) grieving widows

Royalist women had to be recast as gullible victims of Spanish husbands or officers rather than active supporters of the king in order to be incorporated into a new national identity. The wives of patriot soldiers had already played the proper role of the Chilean woman loyal to both her man and her nation and ready to sacrifice the former for the latter. But to fit into the emerging nationalist narrative, their mourning had to be converted quickly into support for the paternal state lest their tears put a damper on attempts to commemorate the glory rather than the horror of the war for independence. Widow María Mercedes Portus was careful not to criticize the government but did lament that petitioning for a pension 'revived her suffering by recalling [her husband's] death that so tormented her'.[36] The best way both to recognize male heroism and to comfort grieving family members was to compensate widows and orphans. Spain had established a military pension system, the *montepío*, in the eighteenth century to promote suitable marriages for high-ranking officers and reward their service by providing for their families.[37] The Chilean national state inherited the system at independence, but the denial of benefits to dependents of war veterans who did not meet the highly restrictive requirements of the Spanish regulations became a political embarrassment for the elected executive and legislative branches.

One way around such technicalities was for the president or the senate to grant exceptional pensions, either on a case-by-case basis or as O'Higgins did in decreeing modest payments to the families of all soldiers who died at the Battle of Chacabuco. Patriot officer José Cienfuegos died defending the southern frontier, allegedly lanced by Mapuche warriors after having been captured by royalist forces. His 'murder' became a symbol of the savage barbarity of the nation's enemies, and O'Higgins granted his widowed mother a generous monthly pension. It was an opportunity, declared Cienfuegos's commanding officer, Luis de la Cruz, 'to show the New World that the Government knows how to gather up and dry the tears shed on behalf of those sacrificed for the Fatherland'. When informed of her pension, Cruz later reported, this patriotic lady wept and praised the generosity of the government, even asserting that she and her daughters would take up arms if necessary. The story, which followed the official script perfectly, was then printed in the government *Gazeta* 'in order to be a source of encouragement for those parents who have sons in the army, and of envy for those who prohibit their sons from even participating in militia service on the pretext of needing them at home'.[38] Granting a special pension to another widow of an executed patriot provided an occasion to predict that masculine heroism would be passed down through the generations and help to forge unity in the national family:

> The blood of heroes is fertile: it produces those who will avenge the resentments left to them as an inheritance. The son of the unfortunate Moyano will seek, with ardour, satisfaction for the offence committed against his father! We are all one family: the cruelty of the Spaniards forges in us a common cause to resist them, exterminate them, and execrate them with eternal hatred.[39]

In this case, not only were mothers passive but also paternal blood, rather than maternal wombs, was credited with reproductive powers.

The granting of extraordinary pensions was fairly common during wartime due to the need to maintain morale among the troops and recruit new soldiers, but such ad hoc solutions could not address the problem in the longer term. The first legal challenge was brought by Juana de Dios Baeza, the daughter of a former Spanish officer whose mother had been awarded a military pension during the colonial period. She asserted that the new government, which had acquired Spanish assets in Chile, should likewise honour Spanish debts. Recalling the hardships of war, Baeza also emphasized her pitiful situation as a refugee compelled by patriot orders to abandon her home in Concepción during an evacuation to Santiago:

> The state of nakedness, hunger, and other accumulated misfortunes in which we arrived caused my mother to breathe her last, leaving me an abandoned orphan; and unable to find resources owing to my sex and lack of relatives in this strange land, my fate cannot get any worse, and only from the paternal goodness of Your Excellency do I hope to find relief from my misfortunes.[40]

In 1823 the senate committed the Chilean state to continue paying pensions granted by the previous Spanish government so long as the officer had not opposed independence.[41]

The favourable treatment granted to the families of former royal officers thus became an embarrassing contrast to the denial of benefits to the relatives of many veterans who had fought for independence. Shortly after

Baeza's successful lawsuit, a petition submitted by María del Rosario Gómez was denied. Gómez's husband, like Baeza's father, had been a career officer in the Spanish army since at least 1780, posted to the indigenous frontier of Valdivia where his father and father-in-law had also served. Unlike Baeza's father, Captain Gregorio Henríquez was still living at the outbreak of the wars for independence, and he switched sides to join the patriot cause. According to his widow, 'While, along with the founding Heroes of the Nation, he was cooperating in the defence of the Common Cause in the interior of the Republic, I endured in this Fort [Valdivia] for this principle the vexations and sufferings inflicted upon my family by the monstrous intentions of our oppressors'.[42] Nonetheless, the treasury ministers denied her claim on the grounds that her husband had wed her when he was merely a cadet, whereas the *montepío* regulations provided only for those who married at the rank of captain or higher.

About a year later, a different Gómez petitioned for a pension and was initially turned down because she, too, had married her husband when he was only a soldier, even though he later attained the rank of captain. Determined, she resubmitted her petition, and it was approved without further consultation by the executive.[43] When the treasury officials refused to authorize payment of the pension, the president issued a general decree on 20 February 1826 making dependants of any deceased officer, from the rank of second lieutenant upward, eligible for a pension as long as he had served for at least ten continuous years. The preamble pointed out that the strict limits of the pension code penalized precisely 'the most meritorious servants of the nation who, moved and animated by the echo of liberty and patriotic enthusiasm, had flown to take up arms' without considering the impact on the fortunes of their families.[44] The expansion of the pension system did not encompass all soldiers, but it certainly incorporated a class of men who would never have qualified under Spanish law. According to the data compiled by Sergio Vergara Quiroz, almost half of the 844 pensions granted between 1819 and 1884 went to families of officers who had died at a rank below captain, most of whom would have been ineligible prior to the 1826 decree.[45]

Throughout the 1820s, Freire promoted a vision of national unity symbolized by the state's merciful treatment of Chilean-born women and children, regardless of their conduct during the Wars of Independence. As governor of Concepción, he declared amnesties to encourage families who had accompanied royal troops into Mapuche territory to return to Chile, and he approved the return of properties to all Chileans who had not actually fought for the king's cause. As president, he advocated expanding the military pension system on behalf of families whose fathers, husbands and sons had sacrificed their lives in service to the nation. Just at the moment that the government might have begun rewriting the history of the war as one that united Chileans, however, civil war again broke out. Ironically, shortly after the pension decree was ratified by Congress in 1829, conservatives challenged the constitutionality of that liberal-controlled assembly. When Freire was defeated at the Battle of Lircay, his supporters were dishonourably discharged from the army and their wives lost their future eligibility for pensions.

By the end of the 1830s, a war against the Peru-Bolivia Confederation strengthened national sentiment within Chile, changing the political climate once again. In 1838, widows of officers who had fought under Freire began petitioning the government for extraordinary pensions, despite their husbands' discharge from the army. Carmen Mújica was one of the first, appealing to President Prieto as a widow with five children under the age of twelve. Her husband, Ramón Picarte, had joined the patriot army in 1810 as a sergeant and had risen to the rank of general-commander when he was cashiered in 1830. Prieto approved a pension in recognition of 'the gratitude that the Nation owes to the first and oldest defenders of its independence'.[46] Once the precedent had been set, it did not take long for other widows to follow suit. Within a month, Francisca Fuenzalida, widow of Manuel Urquizo, cited the Picarte case in her petition to the president. Noting that her earlier petition in 1836 had been rejected, she revived painful memories: 'since then submerged in sorrow and bitterness on account of my lack of resources...I resigned myself to waiting for another time that would be more fortunate for me'.[47] After granting a number of special pensions, the government issued a general decree in 1839 to restore the decommissioned officers to their employments and honours so long as they presented themselves before a deadline, had joined the army prior to 1826, and had not committed any crimes or treason after 1830.[48] Article 3 made the widow and orphans of any officer who met these qualifications but who had died in the interim eligible for the official pension system. As with the incorporation of royalist wives into the national family, the granting of pensions to the presumably innocent widows and children of former political rivals could be another step toward national reconciliation.[49]

Conclusion

The losers at the Battle of Lircay had been heroes during the wars for independence, and those who had not perished in the battle itself were beginning to die of old age by the 1840s. The successful conclusion of an external war in 1839 gave the party in power an opportunity to reconcile with their former internal opponents, who no longer posed a serious threat. Those who did not themselves survive to be reincorporated into the national family could be honoured posthumously with the pensions granted to their widows. By drying their tears, however belatedly, the government in effect silenced their stories of suffering and injustice. It is surely no coincidence that the 1840s also marked the beginning of a campaign to create official, patriotic commemorations of independence heroes that would elide their often complicated histories.[50]

When José Miguel Infante, one of the strongest proponents of federalism and liberalism in the 1820s, died in 1844, rumours swirled over whether or not this avowedly anti-clerical political thinker had accepted last rites. His family claimed that he had died as a faithful Catholic and declared at his funeral: 'Chileans, receive his remains: don José Miguel Infante belonged to the fatherland, not to his family'.[51] Within three years, congressional deputies did indeed claim him as one of their own, commissioning a portrait, statue and monument inscribed with the dedication: 'The Republic of Chile as a testimony to its veneration of and gratitude to the memory of the illustrious citizen don José Miguel Infante, one of the first and most forceful defenders of independence'.[52] Protestant Enrique Ross, an immigrant from the United States who had left civilian life in 1813 to defend the patriot cause, also died in 1844; his military record indicated that his name should be included among those inscribed on a 'Pyramid of Glory that should be erected to those worthy Citizens who died defending the Fatherland'.[53] Twenty years later, Congress increased the pension paid to his Chilean widow, Josefa Cevallos.[54]

The government also began rehabilitating O'Higgins and his various rivals. When O'Higgins died in Peru in 1842, a month after Congress had voted to pay him a lifetime salary, all government employees were ordered to dress in mourning for a week.[55] Two years later the government announced its intention to repatriate his remains and commissioned a public statue and a painting to be hung in the 'portrait gallery of the eminent men of the republic'.[56] It would take another quarter of a century, however, to bring these plans to fruition.[57] In the meantime, the widow of O'Higgins's mortal rival, José Miguel Carrera, had already been compensated during an earlier period of reconciliation. In 1864 the Chilean Congress again paid tribute to the family, awarding a special pension to the widow of José Miguel Carrera Jr., who had himself never joined the army, to commemorate the three Carrera brothers (no mention of their sister, Javiera) and their father, Ignacio.[58] Many years earlier, in 1845, the Congress had also overturned a supreme-court decision that had denied compensation to Freire for his service to the cause of national independence; seven years later it awarded a sum of 25,000 pesos to be divided between his widow and children.[59] When Freire died in 1851, the government ordered two weeks of mourning in tribute to his role 'in the most honourable deeds of our history and his having gloriously ended the War of Independence with the capture of Chiloé'.[60]

The process of restoring the reputations of the nation's controversial founding fathers was connected to the recognition of the claims of more modest heroes and their families. In the 1840s the government began to grant special pensions to surviving veterans to maintain them in their old age and, after their deaths, to support their widows. In 1847, for example,

Congress awarded Isidro de la Cruz 15 pesos a month 'in recognition of the good services he performed for the Republic during the period of the War of Independence'.[61] Pensions to independence veterans, presumably quite elderly ones, continued into the 1860s.[62] Fernando Baquedano had entered military service as a soldier in 1808; by the time of his death in 1862, he had served for more than fifty years. Congress granted his widow and children a supplemental payment in addition to the standard military pension.[63] Mothers, widows and children of deceased military officers had been incorporated into the pension system by 1829; as the generation of independence began to pass away, Congress also began to grant exceptional payments to sisters of heroes who had died during the decisive battles against Spain but not to women for their own actions on behalf of the nation.[64]

The 1840s, therefore, initiated a period during which the government completed the process of compensating the service of independence veterans and their dependants and began commemorating Chile's more famous founding fathers. Ensuring that the former were taken care of would ideally heal their memories of war as a time of suffering, loss and often injustice; at least, the government could close the books on their pitiful stories, confident that it had comforted them in their grief, however belatedly. Simultaneously, the posthumous honouring of more prominent heroes served to highlight their shared struggle against Spain and to de-emphasize their subsequent rivalries. O'Higgins and the Carreras, Infante, Freire and Portales may have fought bitterly while alive, but dead they would all hang together in the 'gallery of eminent men of the republic', and ultimately they would find a common resting place in the national cemetery. Even the wives and children of Spaniards who had resisted the birth of the nation had been reconfigured as victims so that they could be incorporated as fellow Americans into the new Chilean family. Ironically, it was harder to find a comfortable space in the official histories of war for women like Javiera Carrera who had actively participated in the pro-independence movements. They challenged the gendered division of labour in which men were the heroes to be commemorated while women stood on the sidelines, both to grieve their passing and to celebrate their sacrifices.

Acknowledgments

I thank Patrick McNamara, Judith Miller, Karen Hagemann, Jane Rendall and the anonymous readers for their suggestions on various drafts of this essay.

Notes

1. Decree of 1817, quoted here from Ricardo Anguita Acuña, *Leyes promulgadas en Chile desde 1810 hasta el 1.o de junio de 1912*, 4 vols (Santiago, 1912–13), vol. 1, 44. Unless otherwise noted, translations from Spanish to English are by the author.

2. For analyses of masculine 'heroism', see Stefan Dudink et al. (eds), *Masculinities in Politics and War: Gendering Modern History* (Manchester, 2004); Matthew Brown, *Adventuring through Spanish Colonies: Simón Bolívar, Foreign Mercenaries and the Birth of New Nations* (Liverpool, 2006).
3. Margaret Power, *Right-Wing Women in Chile: Feminine Power and the Struggle against Allende, 1964–1973* (University Park, PA, 2002); Steve J. Stern, *Remembering Pinochet's Chile: On the Eve of London 1998* (Durham, NC, 2004). For a comparative example, see Elizabeth Jelin and Susana G. Kaufman, 'Layers of Memories: Twenty Years After in Argentina', in *The Politics of War Memory and Commemoration*, ed. T. G. Ashplant et al. (London, 2000), 89–110.
4. Lessie Jo Frazier, 'Gendering the Space of Death: Memory, Democratization, and the Domestic', in *Gender, Sexuality, and Power in Latin America since Independence*, ed. William E. French and Katherine Elaine Bliss (Lanham, MD, 2007), 261–282.
5. Lyman L. Johnson (ed.), *Body Politics: Death, Dismemberment, and Memory in Latin America* (Albuquerque, 2004); Rebecca Earle, '*Sobre Héroes y Tumbas*: National Symbols in Nineteenth-Century Spanish America', *Hispanic American Historical Review* 85 (2005): 375–416; Carmen McEvoy (ed.), *Funerales republicanos en América del Sur: Tradición, ritual y nación, 1832–1896* (Santiago, 2006).
6. For additional examples, see Patrick J. McNamara, 'Saving Private Ramírez: The Patriarchal Voice of Republican Motherhood in Mexico', *Gender & History* 18 (2006): 35–49; LeeAnn Whites, *Gender Matters: Civil War, Reconstruction, and the Making of the New South* (New York, 2005), 87–91; Lessie Jo Frazier, '"Subverted Memories": Countermourning as Political Action in Chile', in *Acts of Memory: Cultural Recall in the Present*, ed. Mieke Bal et al. (Hanover, NH, 1999), 105–119; G. Kurt Piehler, 'The War Dead and the Gold Star: American Commemoration of the First World War', in *Commemorations: The Politics of National Identity*, ed. John R. Gillis (Princeton, 1994), 168–185; Nancy Huston, 'Tales of War and Tears of Women', *Women's Studies International Forum* 5 (1982): 271–282.
7. On the complications of producing official commemorations of civil wars, see T. G. Ashplant et al., 'The Politics of War Memory and Commemoration: Contexts, Structures and Dynamics', in idem, *The Politics of War Memories*, 3–85, 23–24; Kirk Savage, 'The Politics of Memory: Black Emancipation and the Civil War Monument', in Gillis, *Commemorations*, 137–149.
8. Sarah C. Chambers, 'Los mapuche: ¿los iconos de la americanidad o los seguidores salvajes del Rey?', paper given at the 52nd Congress of Americanists, Seville, Spain, 17–21 July 2006.
9. Vicente Grez, *Las mujeres de la independencia*, ed. Raúl Silva Castro (1878; repr. Santiago, 1966).
10. References which follow will be given to the Archivo Nacional Histórico de Chile, Santiago (hereafter AHNCh), followed by the document group consulted, and the volume (if bound) or *legajo* (bundle, hereafter 'leg.'), the number (when in a bound volume, hereafter num.) or *pieza* (part, when in a bundle, hereafter "pza."), title in Spanish, year, and the page or folio number, with the abbreviation fa. (single foja). AHNCh, Judiciales de Santiago–Civiles, leg. 374, pza. 1, 'Divorcio entre doña Mercedes Fontecilla y don Felipe Calderon' (1814), fa. 3.
11. Ibid. fa. 82^v; see also fa. 38.
12. ANHCh, Judiciales de Santiago–Civiles, leg. 192, pza. 1, 'Don Felipe Calderón contra su Mujer doña Mercedes Fontecilla sobre perjuicios', fa. 17^v and 18^v.
13. Ibid. fa. 31.

14. AHNCh, Judiciales de Santiago–Civiles, leg. 374, pza. 1, 'Divorcio entre doña Mercedes Fontecilla y don Felipe Calderon' (1814), fa. 328^v.
15. Quoted in Antonio Ondarza O., *Javiera Carrera: Heroína de la patria vieja* (Santiago, 1967), 110.
16. Petition of Francisco Ruiz Tagle in ANHCh, Ministerio de Guerra, vol. 150, Montepíos, 'Doña Mercedes Fuentecilla, viuda del Brigadier don José Miguel Carrera', (1828), fa. 248.
17. For depictions of these and other women of the independence era, see Benjamín Vicuña Mackenna, *Doña Javiera de Carrera: Rasgo biográfico leido en el Círculo de Amigos de las Letras*, Biblioteca de Autores Chilenos, vol. 23 (1862; repr. Santiago, 1904), 5–44; Grez, *Las mujeres de la Independencia*; Jerome R. Adams, *Notable Latin American Women* (Jefferson, NC, 1995), 123–132.
18. Memorandum dated 8 July 1817 from Ramón Arriagada in AHNCh, Ministerio de Guerra, vol. 23, Intendencia de Concepción (1817–34), fa. 192.
19. See, for example, Diego Barros Arana, *Historia jeneral de Chile,* 16 vols (Santiago, 1884–1902), vol. 11, 325.
20. Memorandum of the Sergeant Major on 16 August 1821 in ANHCh, Ministerio de Guerra, Sumarios y Procesos, vol. 123, num. 3, 'Proceso formado contra Josefa Garrido por infidencia i espionaje' (1821).
21. *Gazeta de Santiago de Chile* 7 (2 August 1817), reprinted in *Archivo de don Bernardo O'Higgins*, 36 vols (Santiago, 1946-[2005]), vol. 10 (1951), 62–63.
22. *Gazeta de Santiago de Chile* 24 (29 November 1817) in ibid. vol. 10, 222.
23. *Gazeta de Santiago de Chile* in ibid. vol. 12 (1953), 89.
24. Isaac Foster Coffin, *Journal of a Residence in Chili* (Boston, 1823), 132–133, 189–191.
25. *Gazeta de Santiago de Chile Extraordinaria* in *Archivo de don Bernardo O'Higgins*, vol. 12, 93.
26. For the events of this period, see Simon Collier, *Ideas and Politics of Chilean Independence, 1808–1833* (Cambridge, UK, 1967).
27. *Archivo de don Bernardo O'Higgins*, vol. 18 (1958), 156.
28. Report of José Gregorio Argomedo, 30 April 1817, in *Archivo de don Bernardo O'Higgins*, vol. 24 (1964), 45.
29. Ibid. vol. 24, 48.
30. ANHCh, Fondo Varios, vol. 237, num. 4470, 'Doña María de los Dolores Araos pide alimentos'.
31. Ibid.
32. ANHCh, Intendencia de Concepción, vol. 6, Oficios enviados (1818–1823).
33. ANHCh, Judiciales de Concepción–Civiles, leg. 28, pza. 3, 'Doña María Jesús Arregui sobre devolución de casa y sitio secuestrados', fa. 1.
34. Ibid.
35. Entry dated 19 December 1826 in ANHCh, Intendencia de Concepción, vol. 31, Correspondencia de la Municipalidad con los Colejios Electorales (1820–1828). Ultimately men as well as women were excused for fleeing in terror, though their petitions often presented themselves as in some way dependent owing to old age, disabilities or dependence upon a more powerful relative.
36. *Archivo de don Bernardo O'Higgins*, vol. 10, 13–14.
37. As a shorthand, the term 'military pension' will here relate to the pension received by widows and not to the pensions of retired military personnel. This section is based on 252 applications for pensions between 1819 and 1850 and seven civil lawsuits contesting rejected applications. See also Sergio Vergara Quiroz, *Historia social del ejército de Chile*, 2 vols (Santiago, 1993), vol. 1.

38. *Archivo de don Bernardo O'Higgins,* vol. 21 (Santiago, 1960), 124–127.
39. Ibid. vol. 10, 271.
40. ANHCh, Judiciales de Santiago-Civiles, vol. 105, pza. 3, 'Expediente seguido por doña Juana de Dios Baeza con su hermana doña María sobre derecho al Montepío de su Padre don José Baeza', fa. 8.
41. For the new law, see *Boletín de las ordenes y decretos del Gobierno*, lib.1, num. 18, Santiago, 8 de noviembre de 1823, 207–208; Anguita, *Leyes promulgadas en Chile*, vol. 1, 12.
42. ANHCh, Judiciales de Santiago–Civiles, leg. 435, pza. 5, 'María del Rosario Gómez solicita pensión de gracia por viudez de Gregorio Henríquez' (1824), fa. 15. See also ANHCh, Ministerio de Guerra, vol. 92, Montepíos, 'Doña Micaela Calderón, viuda del Capitán don Justo Polloni' (1823).
43. ANHCh, Ministerio de Guerra, vol. 150, Montepíos, 'Doña Josefa Gómez, viuda del Capitán don Justo Quinteros' (1826).
44. Anguita, *Leyes promulgadas en Chile*, vol. 1, 166.
45. Quiroz, *Historia*, vol. 1, 156.
46. ANHCh, Ministerio de Guerra, vol. 325, Montepíos, 'Doña Carmen Mújica viuda del Teniente Coronel don Ramón Picarte' (1843), fa. 1. Another widow indicated that she had tried to apply for a pension as early as 1831; ANHCh, Ministerio de Guerra, vol. 273, Montepíos, 'Doña Loreto Villagrán, viuda del ex-Capitán don Manuel José Gutierrez' (1838).
47. ANHCh, Ministerio de Guerra, vol. 309, Montepíos, 'Doña Francisca Fuenzalida, viuda del Coronel graduado don Manuel Urquizo' (1842), fa. 1. See also 'Hijos del Capitán don José Domingo Meneses' (1841), fa. 1, in the same volume.
48. José A. Varas, *Recopilación de leyes, decretos supremos i circulares concernientes al ejército, desde abril de 1839 a diciembre de 1858* (Santiago, 1860), 5–6.
49. For a study that highlights the importance of amnesties to Chilean political culture, though not their gendered nature, see Brian Loveman and Elizabeth Lira, *Las suaves cenizas del olvido: Vía chilena de reconciliación política, 1814–1932* (Santiago, 1999).
50. Of course factors other than gender also influenced this timing. Rebecca Earle discusses the shift from using symbols of the ancient indigenous cultures to the honouring of independence heroes; see Earle, '*Sobre Héroes y Tumbas*'. For the timing of the commemoration of independence in the United States, see Michael Kammen, *Mystic Chords of Memory: The Transformation of Tradition in American Culture* (New York, 1991).
51. Quoted in Ana María Stuven, 'Guerreros y sabios al Panteón Republicano: Los funerales de José Miguel Infante y Andrés Bello' in *Funerales republicanos*, ed. McEvoy, 31–56, 41.
52. Anguita, *Leyes promulgadas en Chile*, vol 1, 490.
53. ANHCh, Ministerio de Guerra, vol. 330, Montepíos, 'Doña Josefa Cevallos viuda del Sargento Mayor don Enrique Ross' (1844).
54. Anguita, *Leyes promulgadas en Chile,* vol 2, 164.
55. Varas, *Recopilación de leyes*, 61–62 and 65–66.
56. Ibid. 123–124.
57. Carmen McEvoy, 'El regreso del héroe: Bernardo O'Higgins y su contribución en la construcción del imaginario nacional chileno, 1868–1869', in *Funerales Republicanos*, 125–155.
58. Anguita, *Leyes promulgadas en Chile*, vol. 2, 168.
59. Varas, *Recopilación de leyes*, 149 ; Anguita, *Leyes promulgadas en Chile*, vol. 1, 599.

60. Varas, *Recopilación de leyes,* 297–298.
61. Anguita, *Leyes promulgadas en Chile,* vol. 1, 494.
62. Ibid. vol. 2, 94, 128, 132, 142, 162, and 200.
63. Ibid. vol. 2, 163; Quiroz, *Historia,* vol. 2, 21.
64. Anguita, *Leyes promulgadas en Chile,* vol. 1, 331 and 599–600, and vol. 2, 111, 143, 147.

Index

Aaslestad, Katherine B. 3, 23
Abolition of slavery 13–4, 18, 47–55
  in Britain (1833) 15, 45–6
  in France (1794/1848) 15, 17–8, 41–55, 58, 67, 72
  in the United States (1865) 45
Abolition of the slave-trade 5, 13–5, 41, 45–55
  in Britain (1807) 15, 41–55
  in Denmark (1792) 15
  in the Netherlands (1814) 15, 123
  in Portugal (1851) 15
  in Spain (1867) 15, 49
  in the United States (1807) 15, 41–55
Adams, Abigail 172
Africa 10, 12, 42, 44–6, 51, 53, 318
  Central 65, 80
  sub-Saharan 44
  West 43, 44, 49, 65
  West Central 44
Afro-American (*see* Canada and United States)
Age of Revolution/Age of Democratic Revolutions 41, 51, 55, 111, 188, 202, 206, 219
Age of Romanticism 266
Aikin, Lucy 266
Alexander I, Russian Tsar 11, 159, 162
Allen, John 329
Alonzo, Antonio 208
Alonzo, María 208
Alvarado, Ignacio 212
Álvarez, Antonio 214
America (*see* individual countries)
American Revolution (*see* United States)
American War of Independence (*see* war)
Amsinck, Wilhelmine 227, 237
Ancien régime 9, 17, 20, 24, 104, 117–18, 121–2, 148, 189, 192–6
André, John 249
Angola 43–4, 52
Anti-Napoleonic Wars (*see* war)
Anti-slavery (*see* abolition)

Araos del Pino, María de los Dolores 350
Arc, Joan of (d'Arc, Jeanne) 96
Arenciba, Juan Bautista 215
Argentina 345–8
Aristide, Jean-Bertrand 83
Army 3, 5, 6, 7–8, 15–16, 19, 94–5, 128–40, 173–4, 176–81, 284–300
  British (*see* Great Britain)
  Continental (*see* United States)
  French (*see* France)
  Prussian (*see* Prussia)
Arndt, Ernst Moritz 287
Arregui, María Jesús 350
Arrivas, Raymundo de 211
Asia 10, 45, 269
  migrants from 45
Assmann, Aleida 28
Atlantic 22, 30, 42–5, 48, 50, 52–3, 55, 71, 77, 310, 318
  North Atlantic 41, 49
Austria 1, 10, 11, 16, 118
  Habsburg Empire 9, 11
Authors (*see* print culture)
Avero, Ursula de 211
Azze, Josepha de 208

Baillie, Joanna 269, 274
Baland, Catherine 198
Baquedano, Fernando 356
Baquero, Josef 217–18
Bara, Joseph 102
Barbauld, Anna 27, 265–78
Barreau, Rose 102–3
Batavian Republic (*see* Netherlands)
Batwell, Daniel 334–5
Baxter, Eliza 270
Baym, Nina 171
Bayona, Agustina 214
Beauharnais, Hortense de 155
Beauvais, Martinette de 173–4
Behrendt, Stephen 267
Bell, David A. 7, 110
Beneke, Ferdinand 235

Beneke, Karoline 236
Bennett, Betty 271
Bentley, Elizabeth 271, 276–8
Berkin, Carol 173
Berlin (Prussian capital) 284, 294–6
Bermúdez, Ana 209
Bingham, George 140
Black, Jeremy 15
Blanning, Tim 93
Bolivia 345, 354
Bonaparte, Louis 119, 121–2
Bonaparte, Napoléon (*see* Napoleon I)
Boothby, Brooke 255
Bouchet, Blas du 211
Bouchet, Juan Manuel du 216
Bouillon, Rose 103
Bouquet, Geneviève 201
Bourdon, Léonard 103–4
Boyer, Marianne 195
Brazil 11, 12, 15, 42–3, 44, 48–52
Bremen 236–8
Brévilier, Angélique 194–5
Briffault, Anne-François 82
Britain (*see* Great Britain)
Brock, Isaac 307
Brockden Brown, Charles 173
Browne, Felicia (*see* Hemans, Felicia)
Bruce, Robert 273
Bull, John 127–8
Burke, Edmund 248, 251, 255–9
Burney, Fanny 255
Burns, Robert 272
Burrows, Nathaniel 329
Büsch, Margaretha Augusta 231
Byron, George Gordon Noel 260, 272

Cameron, John 311
Campe, Joachim Heinrich 232
Camp-followers (*see also* women in the army) 21, 100, 173, 179, 182, 251
  children 21, 176–8, 191, 197
  enfants de troupe 191, 200
Canada 9, 12, 177–8, 307–20
  English-Canadian nationalism 319
  Lower 9, 10, 13, 29, 308–9
  Loyal and Patriotic Society 314, 316, 319
  Native Americans in 313–20
  United Empire Loyalists 307, 316
  Upper Canadian militia 311–12
  Upper 9, 10, 13, 25–6, 27, 29, 30, 307–13, 318–19
  Upper Canadian women 313–17
  War of 1812 (*see* war)
Cancloro, Manuela 218
Canning, George 273–4
Cantón, Félix 217
Caravali, Joseph Antonio 217
Cardoza, Thomas 21
Caribbean 5, 10, 11–16, 18–19, 43, 46, 49, 52, 72, 206, 211
  British 48, 50
  French 58–68, 79
  Hispanic 206–7
  Spanish 44
Carques, Cristóval 214
Carques, Francisco Xavier 213
Carrera, Javiera 347, 356
Carrera, José Miguel 245, 355
Carter, Elizabeth 248–56, 259
Carter, Louise 248
Cartwright, Richard 311
Castellanos, Antonio 214
Castillo, Francisco del 214
Castillo, María Dolores 215
Castillo, Roque 215
Catholicism (*see* religion)
Cawfield, Mary 179
Cevallos, Josefa 355
Chambers, Sarah C. 19, 25, 29
Chandler, James 266
Charlotte, Queen, wife of George III 310
Chassé, David Hendrikus 112–24
Chickering, Roger 8
Children (*see also* camp-followers)
  illegitimate 63, 76, 78–9, 82
Chile 29, 343–56
  civil war in 343–4, 346, 350, 353
  Chilean liberals 348–9
  federalism 355
  montepío (military pension system) 351–3
  national reconciliation 347, 349, 354, 355
  Native Americans in 345, 350, 351, 353
  patriotism 345, 347–8
  post-Independence period of 343–5, 351–6

Chile – *continued*
  Spanish reconquest of (1813–17) 343–9
  Spanish royalists in 343, 345–8, 353
  veterans 345, 351–2, 355–6
  Wars of Independence, Chilean (*see* war)
  war widows/pension 345, 347–56
  womanhood, ideal of 344, 346
Chivalry 272, 277–9
Church (*see* religion)
Cienfuegos, José 351
Citizen 19, 22, 27, 83, 95, 111–12, 114, 157, 207, 229, 233, 253, 326, 333
  Bürger 23, 229, 232–3
  citizen-soldier 18, 23–4, 29, 58, 72, 94–5, 101, 105, 111–24, 127–8, 237, 299, 327
  citoyen actif 97
  citoyennes 60–8, 73, 82–3, 195
Citizenship 4, 22–3, 27, 29–30, 58–9, 66, 72–4, 83–106, 114, 228–9, 232–3, 326–38
  legal 229–30
  and masculinity 18, 27, 96, 214, 325, 327, 334
  and military service 7, 18, 74, 94–6, 327
  national 95
  political 23, 95
  and property 23–4, 229, 335, 338
  and suffrage 325–6, 328, 331, 338
Civil society 3, 19, 94, 95–6, 98–9, 227, 233, 298–300
  participation of women 6, 227–40
  relation to military 5, 7, 28, 100–12, 128, 132, 299–300
Civil war (*see* war)
Clark, Anna 252
Clarkson, Thomas 268
Class 3, 4, 6, 13, 19, 25, 128, 150, 229, 267, 270, 300, 310–1, 330–1, 333–4
  lower class/working-class 21, 153, 158, 177
  middle-class 26, 157–8, 161, 180, 188, 285, 291, 293, 319, 330–4
  upper class 137, 151–3, 158–9, 188
Claudius, Matthias 298
Claudius, Rebekka 232
Clément, Claude 62

Clode, Charles 130
Cobbold, Elizabeth 276–7
Code de Napoléon (*see* France)
Code Noir 61, 71, 73
Coffee 12, 50, 59–60, 71, 236
Cohen, Michèle 137
Coles, W. C. 133
Colley, Linda 18, 128, 130, 134, 314, 336
Collingwood, Luke 54
Colombia 12, 25
Colonies 12, 49
  British 9–10, 12–13, 24, 42, 309, 336
  Dutch 10, 122
  French 14, 18, 59, 60–7, 75, 78
  Portuguese 10, 11, 12
  Spanish 10, 12, 42–50
Columbia 27, 44–53
Columbus, Christopher 53
Colwill, Elizabeth 13–15, 64
Commemoration (*see* memory)
Congo (*see* Kongo)
Congress of Vienna (1814–15) 105
Conscription 6, 15–18, 83, 95, 105–6, 234
  mass 16, 127–8
  universal 7, 16–18, 136, 285–7
Continental system in Europe (1806–14) 234
Corbin, Margaret 175–6
Corday, Charlotte 232
Cosmopolitanism 26, 155, 162, 266
Cotilla, Tomas de 208
Cotton 12, 50–1
Cowper, William 268, 271
Crimean War (*see* war)
Cross-dressing women (*see* women)
Cuba 10, 12–13, 15, 20, 29, 48–51, 206–19
  coartación (*see also* freedom) 214–5
  criolla 216
  floridana 210–11, 218
  freed *morenos* 214
  freed *pardos* 214
  fuero military 213, 216
  home front 207–19
  jornalero 213
  militarized society 206–7
  militia 207–8, 212–19
  pension system 210–14

Cuba – *continued*
  Spanish military in 207, 212
  volunteers in the *pardo* and *moreno*
    battalions 212–17
  widows of soldiers 209–14, 218

Daendels, Herman Willem 112–24
Dauranne, Marie 195
David, Jacques-Louis 24
Davis, David Brion 50
Declaration of Independence (1776)
  (*see* United States)
Declaration of the Rights of Man and
  Citizen (1789) (*see* France)
Delgado, Juana 217
Demobilization (*see* war)
Denmark 15
Desan, Suzanne 83, 201,
Dessalines, Jean-Jacques 68
Diaspora
  African 80
  European (*see* Russia)
Díaz, María Antonia 215
Díaz, María Soledad 215
Dios Baeza, Juana de 352
Dios Castro Palomino, Juan de 217
Domestic sphere (*see* sphere)
Dubois, Laurent 14, 78, 79, 83
Dudink, Stefan 17, 23,
Dudley, Constantia 173–4
Dunn, John 182
Dutch Republic (*see* Netherlands)

Edgeworth, Maria 269, 275
Education 158, 228, 230–2
  female 231–2, 270
Ellet, Elizabeth 171
Elliot, Matthew 337
Eltis, David 12, 15
Emancipation
  of slaves (*see* slaves)
  of women (*see* women)
Empire 5, 7, 9–11, 49, 50
  British (*see* Great Britain)
  Dutch (*See* Netherlands)
  French (*see* France)
  Habsburg (*see* Austria)
  multi-ethnic 147, 337
  multi-national 22, 25, 49, 163
  Ottoman (*see* Ottoman Empire)

  Russian (*see* Russia)
  Spanish (*see* Spain)
England (*see* Great Britain)
Enlightenment 3, 7, 13, 111, 148, 151,
  158–9, 231–2, 285
Erskine, Thomas 256
Escovedo, José Ricardo 214
Escovedo, María Loreto 214
Espíritu Santo, María Josefa del 214
Etat Civil (*see* France)
Ethnicity/ethnic differences 4, 7, 17, 29,
  54, 162, 206, 308, 326, 328, 336–8
Europe 5, 6, 9–11, 16, 18, 20, 44, 47, 54,
  94, 147–9, 162, 227–8, 232, 285

Family 6, 14–15, 20–1, 68, 71–84,
  100–11, 161, 170, 172, 176–7,
  208–10, 231–2, 289–9, 311, 319,
  346, 355–6
  marriage (*see* marriage)
  as metaphor of the nation (*see* nation)
  nuclear 73, 78, 153
  and slavery (*see* slavery)
Favret, Mary 266
Fegan, Lawrence 335
Femininity 3, 18, 103–4, 153, 169–74,
  174, 188, 206, 237, 278, 289, 316–19,
  346–50
  attributes of 103–4, 131, 172–4, 181,
    257, 266, 289, 316, 346, 351
  female gender roles 183, 189, 192,
    198, 206, 308
  middle-class femininity 188, 319
  upper-class femininity 188
  womanhood 177, 313, 316, 346–7
Ferdinand VII, King of Spain 345
Fernández, Antonio 208
Festival culture 24, 284–300
  flag consecrations 284, 286, 290–3
  induction ceremonies 25, 284, 286–93
  homecoming festivities 28, 284, 286,
    295–300
  thanksgiving ceremonies 284–6,
    294–5, 300
Feudalism 47, 121
Fick, Carolyn 74, 76
Fish Silliman, Mary 182–3
Fitzgibbon, James 315
Flahaut de la Billarderie, Charles
  de 155–6

Fleming, George 179
Flores, Juan Joseph de 214
Flores, María Josepha de 214
Florida 9–10, 13, 15, 210–11, 214, 218
Förster, Stig 8
Folch, Vicente 208
Fontecilla, Mercedes 346–7
Forrest, Alan 17, 21
Fox, Charles James 54, 248, 256
France 1, 9–11, 15, 17–18, 20, 58–60, 62, 75–6, 93–4, 96, 104–5, 117, 122, 155, 157, 188–9, 232, 234, 247, 257–8, 286, 310
  Bourbon monarchy (1814–48) 10, 48, 199–202,
  Bourbon restoration 10, 199–202
  citizen-army 94–6, 105, 127
  Code de Napoléon 47, 201
  Consulate 20, 95
  Declaration of the Rights of Man and Citizen (1789) 18, 94
  Etat Civil 78–83
  French Empire 9, 71–2, 122, 189
  French nation/nationalism 7, 103, 105–6, 189
  French Republic 1, 58, 72–6, 93–8, 100–6, 149, 189, 194, 259
  French republicanism 96
  French Revolution (1789–99) 9, 14, 25, 49, 52, 93–105, 110, 162, 232, 248, 256
  Légion d'Honneur 99, 120
  levée en masse/volunteers 16, 20, 95–6, 127
  military 9, 16, 21, 79, 81, 100–2, 117–24, 131, 177, 188–92, 196
  monarchy 24, 41, 155, 191–2
  Napoleonic Empire (1804–15) 7, 9–10, 20, 155–7, 196–9, 201
  officers and soldiers 16, 96, 127
  Revolutionary Wars (*see* war)
  universal conscription 16, 95, 105, 285
  women in the French military (*see* women)
Francis II, last Holy Roman Emperor 11
Franco-Prussian War (*see* war)
Freeborn people of colour 14, 63–4
Freedom 14, 16, 58–68, 71–83, 130, 132, 158, 206, 212, 214–15, 218, 236–7, 259–60, 269, 277

coartación (*see also* Cuba) 214–15
  individual 16, 18, 64
Freedpeople/former slaves 58–9, 65–6, 73, 75, 78–82, 212, 336–7
  female 4, 14–15, 65, 73
  male 14–15, 18, 73
Freemasonry 158–9
Freemoyer, David 331
French Revolution (*see* France)
Friedrich Wilhelm III, King of Prussia 287, 292–4
Fuenzalida, Francisca 354

Gannett, Benjamin 174
García, Tomás 206, 208–9
Gardiner, James 138
Garrigus, John D. 63, 83
Gato, José Manuel 208
Gender (*see also* masculinity and femininity) 3–4, 8, 13, 23, 28, 41, 45–7, 60, 65, 78, 111, 127, 206, 229, 230, 266–7, 270, 274–8, 286, 288, 299–300, 308–9, 327, 330
  difference 3, 251, 286
  identity 4, 79, 101, 170, 174
  order 1, 20–2, 24, 150–1, 171, 181, 201, 291, 299–300, 308–9
  politics 4, 266, 278
  relations 3, 15, 140, 188, 217, 316
  roles 72, 171, 183, 192, 219, 240, 333
George III, King of Great Britain and Ireland 138
Germany 11, 119, 122, 147, 148–9, 153, 162, 227, 234, 286, 289, 290–6, 299
  German Confederation (1815–66) 11
  German nation/nationalism 11, 162, 238, 284, 288–9
  female national dress 295–6
  National Festival of the Germans 284
Girard, Jeanne 195
Girty, George 337
Gleim, Betty 237
Golitsyn, Aleksandr N. 159
Goodwin, Jennie 180
Goss, Abraham 329
Gouges, Olympe de 104
Gran Colombia (*see* Colombia)
Grant, Anne 266, 268–76
Grant De Pauw, Linda 173
Grattan, William 137

Gray, Christian 267
Gray, Isaac 335
Gray, Thomas 271
Great Britain 9, 10, 127–42, 207, 210, 269, 309, 232, 335, 337, 247–60, 265–79
  bluestockings 249, 251, 253–60
  British army as a homosocial institution 137–9, 314
  British Empire 265–78, 308, 325, 326, 334–8
  British gentleman 18, 130–2, 135, 137, 141
  British Indian Department 318, 337
  female authors 26, 250–60, 270–9
  Glorious Revolution (1688–89) 257
  home front 134–5, 247, 250
  independent country gentlemen 252–3, 260
  Ireland 94, 129, 136, 269
  masculinity 128–42
  military 14, 16, 18, 127–41, 183, 208, 282, 312, 314, 328
  militias 129
  monarchy 18, 128, 132, 268, 310
  nation/nationalism 26, 274, 277
  navy 49, 129, 250
  officers 130, 139
  patriotism, female 248–60
  poetry 26–7, 249–50, 270–9
  print culture (*see also* print culture) 267, 270, 278
  Scotland 269–73, 276
  Tories 260
  volunteer movement 25, 129, 272
  Whigs 170, 248, 258, 260, 273, 334, 360
Greece 96, 114
Greuze, Jean-Baptiste 97
Guadeloupe 10, 58–68, 78
Guest, Harriet 247, 249, 259
Guillén, Victoria 208
Gundersen, Joan 173
Gutiérrez, Andrés 212
Guyard, Laurent 97

Habermas, Jürgen 25, 267
Habsburg Empire (*see* Austria)
Hagemann, Karen 17, 25, 28, 136, 249

Haiti 10, 11, 14, 50, 67–8, 71–83
  Haitian Revolution (1791–1804) 1–2, 10, 46, 48, 59
  plantation system (*see* slavery)
Hamburg (German city republic) 23, 26, 227–41, 297
  French occupation of (1806–14) 228, 234, 237
  Hanseatic republicanism 229, 230, 232
  liberation of 227, 234–5, 239
  military 227–41, 233–5, 238–9, 297
  Patriotic Society 230, 231
  patriotism (*see also* patriotism) 227–41
  Women's Association at the Church of St. Katharine (*see also* patriotic women's associations) 238–40
Hanfft, Johann Joachim 235
Haskell, Thomas 53, 54
Hawkins, Laetitia Matilda 250
Hays, Mary Ludwig 175
Hazen, Moses 179
Hemans, Alfred 277
Hemans, Felicia 277
Hennings Reimarus, Sophie 231
Heroism 98, 127–8, 130, 133–4, 189, 315, 320
  female/heroines 21, 104, 174–6, 180–3, 188, 197–8, 238, 315
  male/heroes 30, 94, 102–3, 276–8, 284, 295–6, 329–30, 343–5, 351–3, 355–6
Herrera, María Luisa de 211, 216
Hesse 15, 94
Heuer, Jennifer 201
Hidalgo y Costilla, Miguel 17
Holland (*see* Netherlands)
Holmes, Charles 334
Holy Roman Empire of the German Nation (962–1806) 11, 227
Home front 8, 20–1, 169, 180–3, 206–19, 237, 247, 295
  civilians at the 8, 182
  women at the 20, 169–70, 180–3, 250, 295
Hommes de couleur 58
Honour 93–4, 98–101, 104, 135, 158, 176, 180, 206–9, 216, 218–19, 239
  code of 110, 120, 278, 338
  duelling 135
  military 18, 93, 98, 114, 130, 134–6, 156, 292–3, 295

Honour – *continued*
   national 133–41
   personal male 18, 134–41
   republican 94
Hopkin, David 21
Hughes, Michael 99
Hugues, Victor 59, 65
Human rights 344
Humanism 158, 162, 275, 317
Hunt, Lynn 53, 54

Identity 29, 42, 51–5, 72, 74, 94, 157, 160, 229, 277, 292, 327, 336
   civic 78, 228–9, 233
   gendered 101, 127, 129–31, 139–41, 172–4, 180, 328
   national 29–30, 105–6, 127, 139, 172, 331, 333, 338, 351
   racial 327, 332–3, 337
Immigrants
   European 12, 42, 47, 149, 161, 309
   German 161
Industrial Revolution 51
Infante y Rojas, José Miguel 355
Ireland (*see* Great Britain; British military; British officers)

Jackson, Alexander 138
Jackson, Andrew, American president 330
Jamaica 46, 54, 60, 208, 255
Jarvis McCormick, Augusta 307, 319
Jarvis, William 307
Java 119–23
Jefferson, Thomas 171, 180
Jeffrey, Francis 271, 274
Jennings Small, Martha 172
Johnson, Samuel 267
Johnson, Sherry 20
Johnstone, Elizabeth 182–3
Jolicoeur, Laurent 64–5
Jones, David 335
Jones, Edward 335
Jones, William 268
Jung-Stilling, Johann Heinrich 161–2

Keep, William Thornton 135
Keister, Peter 330
Kelly, Gary 256
Kennedy, Catriona 18, 26

Kerber, Linda 173
Kestnbaum, Meyer 95
Kimber, John 54
Kingston (Jamaican town) 309, 311, 314–5, 317
Kinship 54, 80, 83, 116, 213–14, 345
Kintelburger, Madeleine 197
Kleudgen, Philippine 238
Klopstock, Meta 232
Knouff, Gregory T. 17, 23, 29
Knox, Wright 132
Kongo, Kingdom of 80
Kopperman, Paul 173
Körner, Theodor 287–8
Koselleck, Reinhart 9

Labate, Petrona 209
Labothière, Geneviève 66
Labour (*see* work)
Lacour, Auguste 67
La Cruz, Fernando 218
La Cruz, Isidro de 256
Lamb, John 179
Lambert Myers, Susannah 178
Landis, John B. 176
Lane, Anna Maria 175
La Puente, Josepha Eligio de 211
Leclerc, Victor-Emmanuel 77
Le Couteulx de Canteleu, Charles Emmanuel 155–6
Lewald, Fanny 161
Lewis, Paul 173
Liberty, concept of 13, 24–5, 214, 229–33
Lickbarrow, Isabella 271, 177
Lister, Margaret 335
Literature (*see* print culture)
Llanes, Teresa 208
London (British capital) 27, 250, 253, 255, 268–72
Louis XV, King of France 155, 310
Louis XVI, King of France 117, 155
Louisiana 9, 10
Louverture, Toussaint 14–15, 59, 65, 68, 71, 75, 77
Lühring, Anna 237–8
Lumsden, Samuel 134
Lusty, John 182

Macaulay, Catharine 252
Machado, Juan 214

Macleod, Emma V. 26
Macpherson, James 269
Maier, Pauline 329
Major, Emma 249
Mancebo, Francisco 210
Mancebo, Isabel 210
Mann, Herman 174
Marín, Gaspar 346
Markus, David 161–3
Marriage 15, 20, 47, 64, 71–84, 105, 106, 115, 161, 171, 229, 349
  church and 71, 74–5, 78
  concubinage 21, 77, 217
  polygamy 21, 46, 77
  republican 74, 78, 80
  between slaves 47, 71, 78–9
  of soldiers 72–3, 178, 190, 351
Martin, Alexander M. 26
Martínez, Gregoria 214
Martinique 10, 49, 58, 60, 63, 66
Masculinity 3–4, 7, 15–19, 24–5, 93–106, 111–16, 121–2, 124, 128–42, 147, 154–7, 160, 172, 233, 253, 266–7, 278, 308, 319, 334
  manhood 105–6, 128, 135, 140, 155, 160, 163, 177, 316, 317, 325–6, 334, 338, 346–7
  manliness 97–8, 128, 130–2, 140, 310–13, 317, 319
  class-specific 128, 140, 334
  in commemoration 4, 28, 255, 284, 343–5
  genteel masculinity 138, 147
  fraternal 98
  hegemonic 137, 141, 198
  middle-class 130, 147–63, 291
  military 7, 93–106, 111–24, 127–42, 147, 169, 288, 308, 317, 332
  national 21, 30, 344
  officers 7, 111–24, 128–42
  polite 137–9
  political 17, 111, 147, 253, 267
  and religion 4, 151, 289
  soldiers 7, 96, 98–9, 102, 105, 111–24, 288–9, 332
Mayer, Holly A. 20, 21
McCarthy Brown, Karen 80
McCasland, John 332
McCormack, Matthew 131, 253
McGlone, Andrew 335

Mellor, Anne K. 251
Memory 4, 28–30, 316, 325–30, 333–8, 344
  cultural 28
  collective 4, 28, 161, 286, 300
Méricourt, Théroigne de 101
Mexico 10, 12, 26
Migration 13, 53–4
  forced (*see also* slave-trade) 13, 41–5
  transatlantic 41–5, 47, 53–4
  voluntary 13
Military (*see also* countries) 1, 4, 7, 15–20, 110–12, 128–40, 173–4, 176–81, 284–300
  and civil society (*see* civil society)
  conscription (*see* conscription)
  levée en masse (*see* France)
  military pensions (*see* individual countries)
  military service 4, 14, 66, 72, 74, 75, 83, 95, 98, 105–6, 127, 137, 178, 188, 209–12, 214, 291, 298, 308, 325–7, 331, 337
  officers (*see* individual countries)
  volunteers (*see* individual countries)
Miller, Judith 3
Mills, John 131
Milne, Christian 270, 278
Miralles, Juan de 211
Mitford, Mary Russell 270, 276–7
Moïse, Claude 77, 83
Monarchy (*see* individual countries)
Montagu, Elizabeth 251, 261–2
Montero, Manuel 215
Montero, María Gertrudis 215
Moor, Huldah 181
Moore, John 134, 274
Morehead, William 335
Morey, Elizabeth 181–2
Morgan, Cecilia 25, 27, 30
Morrison, Elizabeth 177
Moscow 148–63, 268, 271
Motherhood 61, 65, 171
Mott, Ezekiel 177
Mújica, Carmen 354
Mungrey, María Leonora 208
Myerley, Scott Hughes 132
Myers, Andrew 331
Myers, Anna 178, 181
Myers, John 178

Namier, Lewis 252
Napoleon I/Napoléon Bonaparte,
　　Emperor of France 1, 5, 10, 14, 16, 48,
　　67, 77, 119–24, 127, 139, 147, 153–7,
　　196, 198–201, 284, 288, 311, 344
Napoleonic Wars (*see* war)
Nation/nationalism 4–5, 6–7, 10–11, 17,
　　19, 22–30, 51, 97, 106, 134–6, 238,
　　270, 286, 308, 310–11, 336, 344
　image of the nation as a family 24–5,
　　68, 291
　gendered image of 18–19, 24, 127
　militarized/valorous 127, 147, 278, 291
　nation-in-arms 94–5, 105, 291, 299
　nation-state (*see* state)
　national culture 285
　national stereotypes 148, 154
Nationality 45, 147, 152, 161
Native Americans (*see also* Canada,
　　Chile and United States) 8, 13, 29,
　　325, 330–2, 336–7
Navarro, Diego José 217
Navarro, Jacinto 214
Nelson, Horatio 129
Netherlands/Holland 9, 15, 17, 43, 114,
　　118, 120–3, 149, 155, 250, 268
　Batavian Republic (1795–1806) 17, 23,
　　112, 114, 116–19, 121
　Dutch Republic (1581–1795) 9, 17,
　　113–16, 124, 258
　House of Orange 112
　Kingdom of the Netherlands
　　(since 1815) 9, 17, 123
　Légion Franche Étrangère 117–18
　military 110–24
　officers 17, 111–24
　Patriot movement 113–17, 123
　Patriot Revolution (1780–87) 113, 120
　Stadholder 112–18, 123
　Velvet Revolution 118
Newton, Isaac 268
Noailles, Alfred de 155
Norton, Mary Beth 173
Núñez Villavicencio, Ysolda 212
Nye, Robert 134

Ocean
　Atlantic (*see* Atlantic)
　currents 42–7
　Indian 48

Officers (*see* individual countries)
O'Higgins, Bernardo 345–51, 355–6
Oquendo, Gabriela Josefa 214
Ottoman Empire 1
Ozouf, Mona 93

Pacifism 278
Paine, Thomas 255–6
Paris (French capital) 24, 58,
　　138–9, 200
Patriot movement (*see* Netherlands)
Patriotism 6, 18, 21, 22–9, 96–7,
　　104, 172, 228–9, 233–41,
　　247–60, 266, 276–8, 284–99,
　　308, 310, 329
　civic 23, 228, 230–1
　communal 240
　female 24, 26, 181, 227–8, 315,
　　233–41, 248–60, 290–6
　imperial 25, 228
　independent 248, 252–60
　local 93, 228, 290
　male 116, 129
　martial 237, 240
　militarization of 235–7
　regional 228, 288–9, 294
　republican 93, 238, 240
Patriotic women's associations 26, 29,
　　238–40, 295, 299
Pauli, Magdalena 231
Paulin, Antoine 177
Paulin, Theotist 177–8
Pedroso, Eliseo 214
Peñaloza, Juan de 211
Peninsular War (*see* war)
Pennsylvania 13, 23, 29, 176, 326–38
　African-American population 326,
　　328, 333, 337
　and the American nation/
　　nationalism 29, 170–2, 327, 332–4
　concept of citizenship 325–8, 333–4
　Constitution of 1776 327
　Daughters of the American
　　Revolution 172
　Loyalists 325–6, 334–7
　Native Americans 330–7
　Pacifism (*see* pacifism)
　Revolutionaries 325–38
　suffrage 325, 326, 328, 331, 338
　Wars of Independence (*see* war)

Pereira, Henriette v. 288
Pérez, Agustín 208
Pérez, Gabriela 213
Perthes, Karoline 236–7
Perthes, Agnes 297
Peru 12, 345, 349, 354
Picarte, Ramón 354
Pierpoint, Richard 317–18
Pitt, William 248, 259
Plantation system (*see* slavery)
Pochelat, Catherine 101
Poel, Fredericke 232
Politics 7, 17, 24, 113–19, 150, 230, 247–8, 328
  political rights 18, 113, 128, 228, 253
  political rights and military service (*see* citizen-soldier)
  political rights of women 228, 231, 251, 347
  and war 3, 8, 19, 110–12, 120–1, 252–3
  women's exclusion from political rights 29, 68, 228, 319
Polverel, Etienne 65–6, 72, 74
Polygamy (*see* marriage)
Portugal 9–10, 15, 26, 42, 137–8, 268
Portus, María Mercedes 351
Postwar 6, 29, 159, 239–40, 293, 298–300, 317, 336
  culture 284
  demobilization (*see* war)
Prados, Manuel de 214
Price, Richard 256
Print culture 3, 25–7, 114, 267, 270, 278, 311
  authors 26, 114, 172, 176, 235, 265–79, 311–12
  authors, female 26, 251, 265–79
  literature market 26, 268, 270–5
  literature production 150
  literature reviews 138, 270–5
Private sphere (*see* sphere)
Prostitution (*see* women in the army)
Prussia 10–11, 16, 94, 136, 162, 227, 234–5, 240, 284–300
  Freikorps/volunteer units 287–8
  Landsturm/territorial reserve 287
  Landwehr/militia 287, 285
  military 16, 18, 25, 113, 116, 127, 284–300

monarchy (1701–1918) 9, 284–5
patriotic-national festival culture 25, 28, 284–300
patriotic women's associations (*see also* patriotic women's association) 240, 290–5, 299
patriotism 127, 136, 227–8, 235, 284–300
standing army 285, 292–3
town's citizen guard 289, 293, 294
Wars of Liberation (*see* wars)
Public sphere (*see* sphere)
Puerto Rico 10, 48

Quadruple Alliance (1815) 10
Quaker (*see* religion)
Quiñones, Joseph Antonio 216–7
Quintuple Alliances (1818) 11
Quiros, María 214

Race/racial differences 3, 4, 6, 12, 13, 23, 27, 54, 64, 72, 78–9, 173, 207, 308–9, 330–2
  mixed 61
  politicization of 23, 78–9, 327–8, 330
  race war 325, 330, 333, 337
  whiteness 24, 29, 54, 326–7, 331–2, 337, 338
Radet, Jean-Baptiste 62
Rankin, William 335
Rape (*see also* violence) 61, 63, 152, 182, 275, 311, 348
Recabarren, Luisa 346
Reconquista/reconquest (*see* Chile and Spain)
Reem, George 332
Reid, George 181
Reimarus, Elise 231–2
Religion 3, 4, 23, 68, 151, 159, 249, 265–6, 277, 289, 312, 319
  Catholic 23, 24, 74, 76, 80, 152, 290, 336
  gender and 151, 289
  Quaker 13, 27, 48, 277
  Pietism 159, 162
  Protestant 25, 149–52, 158, 160, 287, 290
  religious differences 13, 54
Rendall, Jane 26–7, 260
Reproduction 13, 21, 61, 74, 82–3, 352

Republic 20, 22–7
  Batavian (*see* Netherlands)
  Dutch (*see* Netherlands)
  French (*see* France)
  Jacobin (*see* France)
Republicanism 24, 65, 116, 229–32, 256, 310
  classical 23, 131, 133
  urban 113
Restoration 24, 41, 81, 113, 201, 269
  Bourbon (*see* France)
Revolution 1–2, 4, 6–7, 11, 41, 47–8, 50, 55
  American Revolution (*see* United States)
  French Revolution (*see* France)
  Glorious Revolution (*see* Great Britain)
  Haitian Revolution (*see* Haiti)
Revolutionary Wars (*see* wars)
Richardson, Charlotte Caroline 276
Rigaud, André 76
Rio de la Plata (*see* Argentina)
Robespierre, Maximilien 96, 100
Rodríguez del Junco, María Mercedes 208
Romand, Jacques-Louis 198
Rosario Gómez, María del 353
Rosario, María Dionisia 214
Rosario Molina, Doña María 206, 209
Rosenstrauch, Johannes Ambrosius 26, 147–63
Ross, Enrique 355
Rous, John 138
Rousseau, Jean-Jacques 228
Rudolphi, Caroline 232
Russia 9, 16, 26, 122, 147–63, 200, 227
  diaspora in 147–63
  Russian Empire 9–11, 147–8, 161
  immigrants to 147–50
  nobility of 147–8, 154
  patriotism 152
  peasantry of 148, 156
  War of 1812 (*see* war)

Sabatier, Catherine 200
Saint-Domingue 10, 12–3, 14, 48–50, 58–68, 71–84, 208–9, 211
  North Province 73, 77, 79
  post-emancipation regimes 59, 60, 67, 71–82
  South Province 74
  War of the Knives (1799) (*see* wars)
Sampson, Deborah 173–5
Sanabría, Josefa Joaquina 214
San Martin, José de 345
Sattelzeit der Moderne 9, 23
Sayn-Wittgenstein, Ludwig Adolf Peter zu 284, 294
Schiller, Friedrich 298
Scotland (*see* Great Britain)
Scott, Joan W. 3
Scott, Walter 269, 272–8
Selleck Silliman, Gold 182
Seward, Anna 247–59
Sexuality 60–5, 99, 100, 102–4, 153
  and slavery 60–2, 64
Shafer, Elizabeth 181–2
Shakespeare, William 268, 273, 274
Sheppard, James 334
Sherburne, Pomp 181
Sheridan, Richard Brinsley 256
Shoufler, Valentine 329
Showalter, Dennis 5
Shurtliff, Robert 174
Shy, John 15, 20
Sierra Leone 44, 52, 336
Sieveking, Amelie 240
Sieveking, Heinrich 235
Sieveking, Johanna Margaretha 232
Sieveking, Karl 235
Silva, María Margarita da 218
Slavery 5–6, 12–5, 41–55, 58–68, 71–83, 215, 219, 319
  coartación (*see* Cuba)
  and family 15, 63, 71–83
  plantation system 12, 41–52, 59–68, 75–8
  slave commodities 42, 44, 50
  slave labour 11, 41–9, 60, 65–8
  slave population 12–15, 46–7, 49–51, 60–1, 80
  slave ships 44, 48–55, 65, 215
Slaves 12–16, 42–55, 58–9, 80, 208, 213–5, 309, 311
  African 12, 13, 15, 44–7, 53
  criolla (*see* Cuba)
  emancipation of 10, 14–15, 48, 58–60, 63–8, 71–3, 75, 79–80
  female 4, 12, 46, 61–3, 79, 81, 215
  male 14, 16, 46, 61–3, 214, 326

Slave-trade 4, 5, 11–13, 41–55
  Atlantic 43, 45
  British 45, 50
  Dutch 48, 50
  French 48–50
  international 47
  North European
  Portuguese 12, 15, 42–50
  Spanish 15, 42–50
  transatlantic 13, 41–55
  US 12, 45–51
Smith, Adam 48
Smith, Charlotte 249, 270
Smith-Rosenberg, Carroll 137, 139
Soldiers 15–22, 29, 93–106, 110, 114–18, 121, 132, 134, 136, 139–49, 178–9, 190, 214, 237–40, 284–6, 290–2, 311–12, 317, 327–38
  citizen-soldier (see citizen)
  female soldiers (see women in the army)
  officers (see individual countries)
  pensions (see individual countries and women)
  wives (see women in the army)
  widows (see women in the army)
Soledad, Antonio 212
Sonthonax, Léger Félicité 59, 65, 72–3, 75, 85
Sorel, Albert 96
Southey, Robert 272
Spain 9–10, 13, 72, 74, 94, 119–22, 153, 198, 207, 210–12, 351
  Muslim domination of Spain (711–1492) 207
  reconquista/reconquest 207
  military 141, 343, 345, 349
  monarchy 10, 208, 210, 212, 343, 345, 350
  Spanish Empire 206–7
Spareback, Polly 314
Sphere
  domestic 46, 150, 181, 291, 310
  military 110–12, 132, 180–1
  private 170–1, 181
  public 25, 101, 170–1, 174, 189, 210, 228, 241, 267
  separate 3, 7, 169–71, 173, 183, 240, 291
State 6, 8, 11, 21, 22, 27, 110, 116, 267, 286, 299
  nation-state 11, 18, 110, 344

St Clair, William 271
St Cyr, Gouvion 200
Struve, Elisabeth von 238
Suffrage 22, 83, 326
  female 59
  male 23, 325, 326–8, 331, 338
  universal 23, 326–38
Sugar 12, 15, 42, 44–51, 59, 60–1, 68, 71
Sweden 94
Switzerland 94

Taggart, Flora 181
Thomas, Joshua 334
Tobacco 12, 50, 60, 190
Total war (see war)
Treaty
  of Amiens (1802) 138
  of Lunéville (1801) 1
  of Paris (1763) 49
  of Paris (1814) 294
  of Tilsit (1807) 285
  of Utrecht (1713) 49
  of Versailles (1918) 49
Transatlantic world 5, 9, 15, 17, 24, 307

United States of America 9–11, 23, 29, 45, 47–51, 173, 211, 309, 310, 325–38 (see also Pennsylvania)
  Afro-Americans 23, 29, 47, 326–8, 171, 307–8, 316, 333, 337
  American Revolution (1775–82) 9, 13, 20, 24, 25, 29, 41, 251, 325, 326, 333–4, 338
  British colonial army in America 9, 177, 328
  Continental army 15, 19, 169, 173–4, 176–81, 211, 327
  Declaration of Independence (1776) 171, 329
  memory of the American Revolution 29, 171–6, 183
  participation of women in the Continental army 173–80
  women's contribution to the American Revolution 25, 170–83
Urquizo, Manuel 354
Uruguay 133, 277

Vergara Quiroz, Sergio 353
Verier, Françoise 201
Viala, Agricol 102

Violence 6, 52, 64, 67, 82, 116–17, 121, 135, 147, 153, 256, 284, 312–14, 330
  against slaves 54, 79, 82
  against women (*see also* Rape) 153, 180, 217–18
Voltaire (François Marie Arouet) 65
Voß, Ernestine 232

Walker, Mack 149
Wallace, William 269, 273
War 1, 3–10, 13, 15–30, 48–9, 58, 71–4, 81, 82, 93, 110–12, 135
  Anti-Napoleonic Wars, German (1806–15) (*see also* German and Prussian Wars of Liberation) 238, 284, 288–9, 293–4, 299
  Chilean Wars of Independence (1810–26) 19, 29, 343–56
  Civil war 6, 10, 19, 72, 76
  Civil war, Chilean 343–4, 346, 349, 353
  Civil war, Dutch 112–13, 116, 120
  Civil war, English 253
  Civil war, French 76
  Crimean War (1853–56) 105
  Franco-Prussian War (1870–71) 96, 105
  memories of the British-American War of 1812–15 316–20
  memories of the Chilean Wars of Independence (1810–26) 343–5, 349–54
  Napoleonic Wars (1803–15) 3, 5, 10, 19–20, 26, 47, 67, 110–11, 127–9, 141, 147–9, 202, 227–8, 266, 272
  Peninsular War (1808–14) 128–38, 265, 268, 272–3, 277
  postwar demobilization 6, 27–9, 298–300
  Revolutionary Wars, French (1792–1802) 18, 117, 127–9, 141, 202, 228
  total war 7–8, 110–11
  War of 1812, Russian 10, 147–62
  War of 1812–15, British-American 10, 307–20, 329
  War of Independence, American (1775–83) 1, 9, 13, 15, 16, 18, 21, 94, 169–70, 183
  Wars of Independence, Spanish-American (1808–29) 3, 5, 10, 16, 25, 344
  Wars of Liberation, Prussian and German (1813–15) 25, 227–41, 284–304
  Wars of Revolution and Liberation, transatlantic (1775–1830) 1–5, 19, 22–4, 27–8, 47
  World war 8, 17, 20
  War of Knives 77
Warfare 5–9, 14, 19–21, 49, 120, 169, 332, 350
  modern 5, 111, 273, 278
Washington, George 5, 15, 211, 250, 329–30, 332
Washington, Martha 177
Waterloo 123–4, 130, 197–8, 199, 294
Webster, John 334
Weems, Mason 330
Wellesley, Arthur, Duke of Wellington 129, 273
West Indian Islands/West Indies 12, 336
Westphalen, Engel Christine 232, 237
Whiteness (*see* race)
Willett, Marinus 178
William I, King of the Netherlands 122–3
Williams, David 255
Williams, Eric 51
Williams, Helen Maria 255, 257, 270
Willott, Sarah 315
Wilson, Kathleen 251
Wolfe, Adam 331
Wollstonecraft, Mary 131, 274–5
Women 3–4, 6, 8, 12, 19–30, 42, 45–6, 59–62, 67–8, 71, 74, 79–83, 98–9, 115, 137–8, 140–1, 153–4, 169–83, 188–202, 206–19, 227–40, 248–54, 260, 266–79, 290–9, 310, 313–9, 343–56
  associations of (*see also* patriotic women's associations) 26–7, 29, 231, 238–40, 290, 295, 299
  black 12–13, 14–15, 46, 61–2, 73, 207
  enslaved (*see* female slaves)
  freed 14–15, 61, 64, 67, 207, 216
  historical agency of 170–3, 189
  and patriotism 24, 26, 236–40, 248–60, 266–8, 276–8, 290–300
  white 13, 61–3, 73, 213–14, 219, 308, 315–17, 319
  women's work (*see* female work)

Women – *continued*
  working 46, 60–1, 66, 173–9, 238
  writing (*see* authors)
Women in the army 19–22, 100–4, 138, 169–76, 188–202
  camp-followers 21, 100–6, 169, 173–82, 189–202, 251
  cross-dressing 6, 21, 101, 104, 173–5
  female soldiers 6, 21, 101–14, 173–6, 189–99
  female participation in war 170–3, 195–9, 227
  pensions of soldiers'/officers' widows 29, 176, 181, 195–6, 198, 199, 210–11, 214, 351–2, 355–6
  pensions of soldiers'/officers' wives 29, 179, 198, 210–11, 214
  prostitution in the army 100–1, 180, 190–3
  wives of soldiers/officers 20, 100–1, 103, 176–7, 180, 191, 194, 206, 208–9, 314, 346–9, 351, 354

widows of soldiers/officers 29, 178, 181, 200, 206, 209–18, 229, 239, 285, 351–4, 356
Woodberry, George 136–7
Wordsworth, William 268, 270
Work/labour 9, 12–15, 46, 59–6, 72–83, 158, 161, 181–2, 230, 232–3, 240
  agricultural 14, 42–7, 60–1, 73–4, 79, 81
  domestic 12–13, 61, 182, 197
  female 13, 65–6, 68, 73–4, 82, 172, 182, 188, 192, 200–2, 238, 249, 291
  labour force 15, 42, 44, 46, 51, 73, 182
  slave labour (*see* slaves)

York (town in Upper Canada) 307, 309, 314, 317
Young, Alfred F. 173

Zong trial 54

Printed and bound by
CPI Group (UK) Ltd, Croydon, CR0 4YY